THE BUSINESS STUDENT'S GUIDE TO STUDY AND EMPLOYABILITY

SAGE was founded in 1965 by Sara Miller McCune to support the dissemination of usable knowledge by publishing innovative and high-quality research and teaching content. Today, we publish over 900 journals, including those of more than 400 learned societies, more than 800 new books per year, and a growing range of library products including archives, data, case studies, reports, and video. SAGE remains majority-owned by our founder, and after Sara's lifetime will become owned by a charitable trust that secures our continued independence.

Los Angeles | London | New Delhi | Singapore | Washington DC | Melbourne

THE BUSINESS STUDENT'S GUIDE TO STUDY AND EMPLOYABILITY

PETER MORGAN

Los Angeles | London | New Delhi
Singapore | Washington DC | Melbourne

Los Angeles | London | New Delhi
Singapore | Washington DC | Melbourne

SAGE Publications Ltd
1 Oliver's Yard
55 City Road
London EC1Y 1SP

SAGE Publications Inc.
2455 Teller Road
Thousand Oaks, California 91320

SAGE Publications India Pvt Ltd
B 1/I 1 Mohan Cooperative Industrial Area
Mathura Road
New Delhi 110 044

SAGE Publications Asia-Pacific Pte Ltd
3 Church Street
#10-04 Samsung Hub
Singapore 049483

Editor: Kirsty Smy
Development editor: Sarah Turpie
Assistant editor: Lyndsay Aitken
Production editor: Nicola Marshall
Copyeditor: Neville Hankins
Indexer: Gary Kirby
Marketing manager: Alison Borg
Cover design: Shaun Mercier
Typeset by: C&M Digitals (P) Ltd, Chennai, India
Printed in Great Britain by CPI Group (UK) Ltd,
Croydon, CR0 4YY

Library of Congress Control Number: 2016942047

British Library Cataloguing in Publication data

A catalogue record for this book is available from
the British Library

ISBN 978-1-4462-7412-5
ISBN 978-1-4462-7413-2 (pbk)

At SAGE we take sustainability seriously. Most of our products are printed in the UK using FSC papers and boards.
When we print overseas we ensure sustainable papers are used as measured by the PREPS grading system.
We undertake an annual audit to monitor our sustainability.

CONTENTS

About the Author   vii
Acknowledgements   viii
Publisher's Acknowledgements   ix
Guided Tour of Your Book   xi
Companion Website   xiii

Introduction   1

PART I   LIFE AT UNIVERSITY   **3**

1   Studying at University   5

2   Personal Development and Learning   18

PART II   LEARNING HOW TO STUDY   **47**

3   Time Management   49

4   Critical Thinking   68

5   Teaching Methods at University   93

PART III   UNIVERSITY ASSESSMENT   **115**

6   General Principles of Assessment at University   117

7   Writing Assignments and Dissertations   134

8   Examinations at University   156

PART IV   EMPLOYABILITY SKILLS   **177**

9   Presentation Skills   179

10   Team-working   201

11   Leading Others   219

12   Communicating Effectively   242

13 Developing Cross-cultural Awareness   271

14 Problem Solving and Creativity   296

PART V UNDERSTANDING EMPLOYEE SELECTION   **323**

15 Understanding Employee Selection   327

16 CVs and Application Forms   338

17 Selection Interviews   366

18 Psychometric Tests and Assessment Centres   391

19 Alternative Options after Graduation   414

20 Conclusion: Skills and Employability   435

References   444
Index   447

ABOUT THE AUTHOR

Dr Peter Morgan is currently Associate Dean for Degree Programmes at the Nottingham University Business School in China. He qualified as a teacher of English as a Foreign Language in 1992, and began his academic career in 1996, first graduating with a PhD in Occupational Psychology from – and subsequently working at – the University of Bradford School of Management. He led the development of the School's learning and teaching strategy as Learning and Teaching Coordinator, had responsibility for the development of academic staff as Faculty Development Coordinator and was on interviewing panels for administrative, academic and senior institutional appointments as a member of the senate.

He moved to China in September 2012, taking up the role of Associate Dean at the Business School in June 2013, and became the Director of Teaching for the Faculty of Social Sciences in October 2013. In these roles, he has had oversight of quality assurance and pedagogy, organised and led the teaching and learning conferences for the School's campus in China (the University of Nottingham Ningbo China – UNNC) and has been a member of the PGC HE management board.

As a passionate believer in the student experience and the importance of personal development, Dr Morgan has been developing and delivering skills development modules for undergraduate, postgraduate (including MBA) and doctoral students since beginning his academic career. He has delivered interactive and engaging workshops on study skills, personal transferable skills and employer selection methods to students in the UK, Singapore, India, China, the Netherlands, Malaysia and Israel; trained academic staff in Poland, China, India and Singapore on issues of educational pedagogy; presented at the Academy of Management and provided workshop sessions organised through the Higher Education Academy; and received institutional awards for his teaching work at both the University of Bradford and The University of Nottingham.

ACKNOWLEDGEMENTS

Writing a text like this has not been easy. It has taken a long time and, in the middle of a very busy role in China, has taken determination. That has needed a great deal of patience from the publishers and a great deal of encouragement from a number of others.

So, my sincere thanks go to my many colleagues, friends, critics and publishers who have helped with this book in so many ways. To my colleagues who have taught and worked with me in the UK and helped to develop and steer my teaching in this area in order to support several thousand students, I am deeply appreciative. I am particularly grateful to my father, who has given me more support and resources than I could have expected to help me get this far in life – and with this book. I am also grateful to my family and friends who have not seen me for some time.

I would also like to thank those colleagues and friends who have contributed so freely to the final chapter of this text, giving insights and learning developed over the course of their careers to date. On behalf of those who will read and benefit from what they have written, many thanks indeed.

I would also like to thank those who have contributed to the content through their comments or their editorial input. My thanks go to the anonymous reviewers who have been extremely encouraging and helpful – without their input, this text would not have been what it is. Most of all, I would like to thank all those at SAGE with whom I have worked, and who have encouraged me with this book over the many months that it has taken to get this far: to Kirsty Smy, Sarah Turpie and all the editorial and production teams who had faith in me at the start, provided encouragement even when little was arriving in their inbox, and who have guided the production of this text so smoothly.

And finally … to all my students over the years, my deepest and sincere thanks for engaging with me and helping me to improve what I do. Without you, there would be no book. Thanks, indeed.

PUBLISHER'S ACKNOWLEDGEMENTS

The publisher's would like to extend their warmest thanks to the following individuals for their invaluable feedback on the proposal and the draft material for this book.

LECTURER REVIEWERS

Aarti Vyas-Brannick, Manchester Metropolitan University

Anni Hollings, Staffordshire University

Aron Truss, University of Portsmouth

Edward Thompson, De Montfort University

Geetha Karunanayake, University of Hull

Izabela Robinson, University of Northampton

Jela Webb, University of Brighton

Kathy Daniels, Aston University

Keith Pond, Loughborough University

Maria McCabe, University of Leeds

Moira Hughes, Edinburgh Napier University

Peter Naudé, University of Manchester

Silvia Szilagyiova, York St. John University

Stephen Robinson, University of Kent

Sunrita Dhar- Bhattacharjee, Anglia Ruskin University

Tracy McAteer, Oxford Brookes University

STUDENT REVIEWERS

Ben Summerton, De Montfort University

Carrie Stevens, De Montfort University

Chen Dong, University of Leeds

Daniel Pallas, Aston University

Emma Wilson, Aston University

Hannah Derry, Aston University

Karen Stringer, Aston University

Michaela Maginnis, De Montfort University

Moondy Zheng, University of Leeds

Saif Javed, Aston University

Weiwei Lin, University of Leeds

Every effort has been made to trace the copyright holders and we apologise in advance for any unintentional omissions. We would be pleased to insert the appropriate acknowledgement in any subsequent edition of this publication.

GUIDED TOUR
OF YOUR BOOK

SKILLS SELF-ASSESSMENT TABLES

Skills Self-assessment tables list tasks that help you to evaluate your own skills, attitudes and behaviours, before studying each topic. Answers or guidance can be found on the companion website for the book.

KEY LEARNING POINT

A useful stop-point to help make sure you have understood the key concepts and issues.

'BUT I HAVE A QUESTION ...'

Offers common FAQs and helpful advice on the topic you are studying.

FOR YOU TO DO

Short exercises to help you to apply the learning that has been given elsewhere in the chapter.

REFLECTION POINT

Encourage you to pause from your reading and think further about key topics that have been presented.

BOXES

Offer key points of interest or examples of real-life situations to help explain the content of the chapter or relate to pieces of research to real-life experiences.

DEFINITIONS

Give informative definitions on key concepts.

FINAL REFLECTIONS

These brief exercises at the end of each chapter provide an opportunity for you to review and note down what you have learnt throughout the chapter.

INTERVIEW QUESTIONS

In Parts I–IV, each chapter concludes with a list of possible interview questions that an employer might ask around the topic. Discussion of these questions is provided on the companion website (Chapter 17).

ADDITIONAL RESOURCES

Each chapter ends with a list of key additional resources to help you broaden your understanding of the topic.

Web Icons

Indicate when you will find exciting and relevant additional content on the companion website at https://study.sagepub.com/morgan

COMPANION WEBSITE

For students

A wealth of interactive and informative online content designed to help you go further in your studies and achieve success in your journey from student to graduate can be found on the book's companion website. Visit https://study.sagepub.com/morgan to find:

- Interactive tests (complete with answers and guidance to the skills assessment tests)
- Practical tasks
- Templates for you to download and use
- Additional further reading from the author on key topics

For lecturers

A selection of tried and tested teaching resources have been honed and developed to accompany this text and support your course. Visit https://study.sagepub.com/morgan and use your instructor login to access:

- Editable and adaptable powerpoint slides to integrate into your teaching
- A tutor's manual providing ideas and inspiration for seminars and tutorials, and guidance on how you might use the features in the book in your own teaching

When you see the 🌐 this means go to the companion website https://study.sagepub.com/morgan to do a quiz, complete a task, read further or download a template.

INTRODUCTION

Welcome to this book … and the start of your time at university. This text has been written to help you move from pre-university studies to completing those studies successfully *and* then to move into employment by performing well in employer selection events. There is no other text which does this at this level of detail.

MY OWN BACKGROUND

I would like to tell you something about myself – it might help you to learn more about how I have recognised and learnt the things written in this book. I studied at a university some 300 miles (480 km) away from my home: I moved from a seaside resort to a very diverse inner city to join about 170 other students on a four-year management course. I had particular reasons for choosing the university and the course – it was the only course at a university (we had academic universities and the more applied 'polytechnics' in the UK at that time) I could do that gave me a year in industry. I was aiming for a career in human resources management, and chose a course that gave me a sufficient mix of HR and psychology to enable me to enter that career.

Despite my understanding of employee selection issues, I graduated without a job, an experience I would never want to repeat, nor would I want anyone else to do so. I had a place on a PhD programme, but no funding, so I trained for a month as a teacher of English as a Foreign Language, became a teacher in a local language school and eventually received the funding I had sought to begin a PhD a year after graduating.

After I had completed my PhD, I started using the interactive teaching techniques I had picked up while teaching English to deliver skills workshops to undergraduate students for two hours once a week – first interpersonal employability skills, and then study skills support as the need became apparent. Some of that teaching involved asking students to develop ideas to raise money for well-known charities, while other ideas included bringing in managers from a local business to mentor or assess student presentations.

I moved from the UK to work in China in 2012 and became Associate Dean at Nottingham University Business School (and Faculty Director of Teaching for the Faculty of the Social Sciences) the following summer.

All this has not been particularly planned, I have to confess. While most of my family are or were teachers in some form or another, it was not my intention to follow them, although that is what happened. As I have moved through my 20+ years in academia, I have picked up some ideas about what university education is really about and how it works – and many of those are written here for you.

The world has changed a great deal since I studied at university. That was a time before mobile phones and when the Internet and email did not exist (which makes me sound very old!), when plagiarism was not a concern, when a BlackBerry was a fruit from the garden, and when we picked up how to do citations through some magic process of mimicking what we saw when we read journal articles.

Student numbers were much lower then and we could access our lecturers far easier than seems to happen in some places nowadays. Some of the luxuries I grew up with at university are not quite so apparent now, yet studying at university is one of the most fantastic and challenging experiences any individual can have. This book is intended to support your experience, so please use it wisely and get any additional advice from your lecturers.

PART I
LIFE AT UNIVERSITY

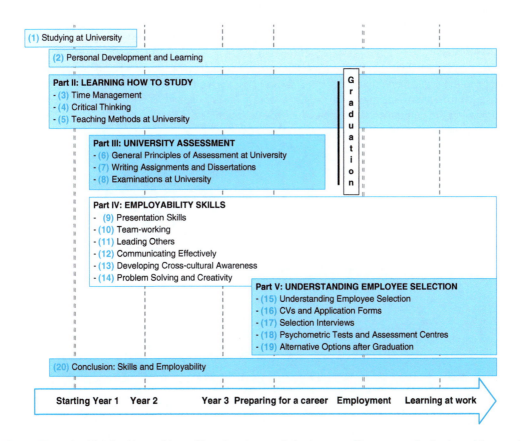

Figure 0.1 An illustration of how the chapters relate to your time as a student and beyond

This text is intended to take you – as a student – from your first weeks as a university student (or returning student, if you are studying a postgraduate course), through your university years and into employment. As such, it is fairly unique. In fact, if I had included everything I wanted to write, this book would have been a lot larger than it already is, so there is a lot of information on the companion website.

There is a very clear reason why the two chapters in this part appear before other chapters. The first chapter is intended to provide a supplement to any induction you might be given at university and to help provide some explanation of what universities do and how they do it: having that understanding means that this text can be more useful to you. However, before we can demonstrate the importance of this first section in its entirety, it is helpful to outline briefly the content of Parts II, III and IV. As shown in Figure 0.1, this text is broken down into parts, broadly following the various stages of your university studies. For undergraduate students, this will last for three or four years, and for most UK postgraduate courses, it will last between one year and 18 months. Part II is about learning at university and includes chapters on time management, the teaching methods used at university, and the nature and importance of critical thinking. Part III covers issues of assessment at university. The chapters here can never cover every method of assessment used, but this part gives some broad principles and then applies them to written coursework assessment and examinations.

Part IV provides something of an overlap between the skills that you will develop during your time at university as a student and those you will almost certainly use in the workplace. University is supposed to be a period in your life that will prepare you for what some people call 'the real world', where what you do will have a very real impact on others' lives; that preparation is often more about the skills you develop than the knowledge you gain.

To really benefit from Parts II to IV, it is really helpful to have an understanding of how skill development and personal learning takes place, and to feel comfortable in this new world of 'university'. To that end, the first part of the text covers two areas: a brief initial chapter outlining something about life at university, which is intended to help you make sense of the new world of 'university' in which you now find yourself, and the second which discusses the processes of personal development. This is a text about personal development and the acquisition of personal transferable skills, and so the content of this second chapter gives a foundation to your development of the skills covered in Parts II, III, and IV, skills which will then be crucial in your moving through the employee selection processes outlined in Part V.

STUDYING AT UNIVERSITY

CHAPTER STRUCTURE

| What is University All About? | Understanding the Non-academic Side of University Life | University Culture | University Processes | Student Culture | Differences between University and Your Previous Education | Employability |

Figure 1.1

When you see the 🌐 this means go to the companion website https://study.sagepub.com/morgan to do a quiz, complete a task, read further or download a template.

━━ AIMS OF THE CHAPTER ━━━━━━━━━━━━━━

By the end of this chapter, you should be able to:

- Describe what it is that universities do, and start some thinking about how they do it.
- Understand how university may differ from previous learning environments you might have come across.
- Understand why university differences between university and other forms of education exist.
- Find your way around the university bureaucracy and systems so that your time at university will be enjoyable, rather than stressful.

INTRODUCTION

This chapter is an introduction to what might seem like a large book. The chapter is intended to act as a sort of 'knowledgeable friend' to guide you through the world of study (as either a postgraduate or an undergraduate student).

The chapter provides a welcome to university and sets out to clarify what universities are about and how they do what they do. So, let's have a look at how this chapter and those which follow can help you to develop yourself.

Before we go too far, it is important to say that different universities will do things differently: terminology might vary, the methods and facilities used to support students will vary, and the course structures and regulations will also vary.

We will begin by giving you a chance to develop your own expectations regarding university life. We will also provide a welcome to university life and help you to answer questions such as 'What is university all about? and 'How can I access any help I might need while at university?' The chapter will then give some ideas as to why the non-academic side of life at university can be as important as the academic side, before providing some analysis of university culture, university processes and student culture. The chapter will conclude by giving you the chance to consider and recognise some differences between your previous education and education at university.

Let's start by finding out how much you know.

SKILLS SELF-ASSESSMENT

How much do you know about university? Please indicate whether you think that the following statements are true or false.

Item	True?	False?
1. University is just about attending lectures, getting to tutorials and passing your modules		
2. I am excited about starting university		
3. I do not think my university experience is going to be very different from my previous school or college experience		
4. Personal development is something which I do not really need to think about very much		
5. I do not really have much of an idea what I will do after I finish university		
6. I want to do as much paid work as I can during university		
7. Lectures are where all my learning will take place		
8. I am committed to getting the best grades I can; I do not want 'just to pass'		

(Continued)

(Continued)

Item	True?	False?
9. I expect that most of my assessment will be by examination at the end of the module		
10. If I can, I would prefer to live outside of the university and study as much as I can		
11. Universities exist solely to teach students		
12. I do not really need to think about getting a job or start a career yet, I need to focus on my studies		
13. My parents are really interested in my university studies, so I am likely to talk to them about my progress		
14. My learning will depend on my own effort and the work I put in		
15. I think I am going to find it easy to manage my budget		
16. I know how to use the Internet well and am comfortable with using it for my learning		
17. Study skills are simply skills which teach me how to study; when I finish university, I will have no need for such skills		
18. I intend to use my time at university to have as much fun as possible		
19. I will always ask my lecturers if I have some questions about university		
20. Lecturers will always be available for me when I want		
21. My university will always understand that I need to pay for university by working, rather than attend classes – if there is ever a clash		
22. If I have domestic duties (e.g. looking after children), then I will need to give these up in order to develop myself		
23. Every employer will be looking for the same skills from the university graduates they take on		

An interactive version of this test, along with answers, comments and thoughts about these questions can be found on the companion website for this book at https://study.sagepub.com/morgan. So, let's begin to look at your life as a university student. This may be as a mature student, an undergraduate or postgraduate student, an international or domestic student, and so on; students come to study for a variety of reasons and a variety of circumstances.

INTERACTIVE
TEST

WHAT IS UNIVERSITY ALL ABOUT?

To be honest, there are few situations in life (outside of education, professional conferences or religious services) where you are expected to sit and listen in relative silence to one person speaking to a large group for such a long time. It is through those situations that are a bit new to us that we start to ask 'Why am I here?' and 'What is it all about?' So, what *is* university all about?

The Purposes of Universities

Universities are changing – in nature and in purpose. Traditionally, they have had three roles in society:

- To disseminate knowledge.
- To create knowledge through research.
- To enhance the skills of those who come to come to study.

Of course, these activities will vary from university to university, as will the extent to which they are seen as a priority for the university. The implications of this are that universities – and their staff – are continually engaged in two key activities: firstly, in helping you to learn and develop your ability to think about what you read; and secondly, in developing an area of knowledge through research.

As such, there are a range of organisations and individuals who have a stake in what your university does and how well it does it. The government has been a major stakeholder and it gives permission to universities to award degrees; it also has the right to withdraw that permission. It has been a major funder of universities, both in terms of the research and investigative work that is done, and in terms of the teaching quality and overall student experience offered at each institution. In this regard, the national Quality Assurance Agency works with student unions and universities to ensure that the student experience is a valuable one for all students.

Other stakeholders in the educational process include:

- **Employers:** Employers have a huge interest in what happens in universities, both for the purposes of collaboration with university researchers and from the perspective of being future employers of the graduates.
- **Parents:** Parents usually have a huge stake in what is done at university, especially if they are funding your studies. If your parents want to know whether you passed a course (or information on any other aspect of your data held by your university), they have to have your *explicit* permission.
- **The Students' Union:** The SU is one way to ensure that your voice gets heard. It acts as a representative body for all students on campus and organises much of the social life for students. (See 'Student Culture' section below.)

FURTHER READING

Further reading about stake-holders in the university process are provided on the companion website at https://study.sagepub.com/morgan.

What is 'the university experience'? The next few years of living and studying at university will give you a range of experiences. Some of these will arise from your degree course (or 'academic') experiences. Others will be social. Some parts of this experience will be compulsory for you, and some parts will be entirely optional. Your choice has been to take up a university place with all the enjoyment (and challenges) that being a university student involves. It can be a scary experience, but the variety of opportunities is generally unrivalled in life and, for many, the impact of making mistakes is much smaller than it would be after graduation.

The academic staff – your tutors, lecturers, professors and associated administrative staff based in the various departments of the university – have responsibility for managing your academic experience. That means they have responsibility for ensuring that you are being given a teaching, learning and assessment experience which encourages and facilitates your learning and personal development. One of the key things you need to be aware of is the following: *Everything else* – the content of lectures, the ways that you are taught and assessed, the organisation of social activities, living independently – *arises from this key goal*. That is why this text focuses so extensively on your personal development.

KEY LEARNING POINT

University is about preparing you for the start of your career and the rest of your life – extending your knowledge, your skills and your view of 'how the world works'.

There are other reasons as to why studying at university is a good idea. Some argue that university is artificial, that it is not 'real life'. Some suggest that you can learn better from being in a work environment or even that you can study all the videos and materials available online or use your Kindle or another e-reader and learn that way. There are certainly courses and programmes available online from universities where you have the option of reading through academic materials and using/watching online resources (grouped together around certain topics), and then undertaking some assessment on a voluntary basis with the payment of a fee. These are called 'MOOCs' (Massive Open Online Courses).

The question then arises, 'Why study at university?' To answer this, we need to look at some principles that are widely accepted as important as part of any good and credible academic experience:

1. Face-to-face contact time is crucial in developing your ability to think through issues.
2. Feedback on your ideas and opinions is vital in ensuring that you are developing a correct understanding of the course material.
3. Interacting with others develops your ability to defend and debate your ideas.
4. Accessing resources outside of the classroom extends your awareness of the way that different researchers deal with different ideas.

It is around these four 'pillars' (and sometimes others, depending on the nature and subject of a university course) that nearly all university education is constructed, including most good online courses. To return to the question 'Why study at university?', or rather 'Why not learn in a different environment?', the answer is fairly straightforward: actually, it is *only* university that offers these four aspects for your learning (see Chapter 4, 'Critical Thinking').

'BUT I HAVE A QUESTION ...'

... What do I need to do to graduate?

The answer is in some ways simple and in other ways more complex. Basically, in most UK universities, you need to pass your subjects. Each module you pass will give you some credits - think of this like a currency. You have to obtain enough credits to pass the degree (360 'credits', over three years in the UK system). If you fail a subject, then you might not get the credits you need.

Some modules might be 10 credits, some might be 15 or 30, or even 60. The higher the number of credits given for a module or subject, the higher the number of hours you will probably have to put into the subject. The number of credits is usually related to the amount of work involved in attending classes, doing the independent studying (reading etc.) and preparing for and undertaking the assessment.

This does not sound too complex until you realise that universities can have very different rules about giving you credits when you do not do well. Some universities, for example, will give you a pass if (let's say) you are taking 60 credits and you pass at least 40 of them with an average of more than 50%. In other universities or degree programmes, you will not be able to continue to your second year without passing all of your courses, and so on.

In most cases, undergraduate students will graduate with a first-class honours degree (usually above 70% average in the UK), an upper second-class or 2:1 (60-70% average), a lower second class or 2:2 (usually 50-60%) or what is known as a 'pass' or third-class degree (40-50%). For Master's degrees (which will usually include a dissertation), a 'Distinction' is given for work with an average above 70%, a 'Merit' for 60-70% and a 'Pass' for work with an average of 50-60%, though institutions will vary on how they give these awards.

This should give you an idea of the purposes of this large organisation in which you have just registered, particularly in relation to learning. Of course, as mentioned earlier, there are other stakeholders and other roles that universities fulfil. Those benefits – relating to research, training and consultancy – for businesses, public and charity sector organisations (locally and nationally), and for other individuals and groups, are very important but are less relevant for us here. At the start of your time at university, it is helpful to look at *how* universities do what they claim to do, so you might want to take a careful look at Chapter 5, 'Teaching Methods at University'.

Remember that, in terms of your experience, universities seek to prepare you for the start of your career and the rest of your life – extending your knowledge, your skills and your view of 'how the world works'.

REFLECTION POINT

Take some time to think about the following questions and write down some answers.
List three reasons why you have come to university:

1.

2.

3.

What excites you about being at university? What scares you? You can keep these answers as personal as you wish.

UNDERSTANDING THE NON-ACADEMIC SIDE OF UNIVERSITY LIFE

Universities are about far more than just studying: they provide a process of education, but also structures to support you through and after that educational experience. When you arrived at university, you were probably given lots of information about many different activities provided by the university. The information may have been too much or insufficient, but it is up to you to review and understand (or ask about) what you are being given. This becomes more confusing if English is not your first language.

Being an International Student

If you are an international student, then your induction will have included a visit to register with the local police. Induction for international students tends to involve a lot of activities aimed at helping you to get to know the local culture and the area. This might involve daytrips out or visits to local homes, or just sessions where you can try your hand at local cooking or enjoying local specialities. There may be a local café run especially for international students and aimed at encouraging your confidence in speaking the native language more, or a language corner where you can share your own language with other students from other countries. If these sorts of activities are not available, then see if you can work with some native-speaking students to set something up. Regardless, it might be good to consider something about UK culture and life in a foreign culture. Box 1.1 below is based on an interview with a UK lecturer living and working in China.

BOX 1.1

LIVING AND STUDYING IN THE UK: A PERSONAL VIEW OF INTERNATIONAL STUDENTS

What is it like living and studying overseas? Well, according to one UK lecturer living in another country, it is not necessarily easy. Here are his thoughts.

'Living in another country is not easy: I have spent some months living and working at a UK university in China but I think I have it much easier than all of the students who come to the UK. We teach and speak English on campus and can often find some help when I need to. But even then, I spent most of my first day as a resident of China in my bedroom, feeling unsure of what was outside and being nervous about what I might expect. I had no money, no phone and no friends there. Thankfully, I did have a good boss who came out to meet me and show me around.

'Living here, though, there are some things I simply cannot do in the way that local Chinese people can. I can get a taxi, but I can't always describe exactly where I want to go. I can get a bus ticket at the bus station, but if I need to take a particular train or bus, I have to ask a friend. If I am in a shop, I can find what I think I need, but I sometimes get it wrong because I can't read the labels. I can't hold any kind of conversation, other than to ask the taxi driver if he likes English people and American people, though, and my ability to cook Chinese food has led to my being ill on some occasions.

'But if I think about studying or working in a second language – or producing a piece of work that is as good as a local student – then I start to have a lot of admiration for the students who come to the UK. Their English is going to be a lot better than my Chinese but it is still incredible. And I have seen Chinese presenters be a lot more confident than some of the UK students.

'And finally, I think about the living and cultural issues, which might be a bit similar to mine in some ways. How does a Chinese student feel when things go wrong? Many of them don't want to worry their parents,

(Continued)

(Continued)

feel desperately homesick sometimes and struggle to find the language to disagree with the UK students who feel so much more confident and able to argue their case. You can have all the vocabulary you want, but it is knowing how to use it is that really counts.'

Questions:

1. If you are an international student from another country, does this lecturer's view surprise or encourage you?
2. If you are from the UK, is there anything here which you had not thought about before? How do you react to these thoughts?

The issue of language is worthy of comment. You have probably entered university with a suitable English language qualification such as IELTS, and this will help to a certain extent, but there is always a need to improve on your listening, speaking, reading, writing or grammar, so then the question is about how to improve. There is a very human issue here of applying what seems to be one of the best solutions: *spending time with English/native language speakers.*

There is a common issue which affects many international students (and actually anyone wishing to develop a skill): that is, the best way to learn and develop English language skills is to do what is mentioned above – spend time with people who speak the language. But that very thing brings with it a number of anxieties and fears: 'How will I cope if they use language I don't understand?', 'What if they think I am being rude?' or 'What if they have an accent and I can't make out the words they are using?' These fears are usually not real, and most people and students will be happy to help. If you are an international student, making English-speaking friends is the best thing you can possibly do to improve your English, and it might just help you get to know a little more about your new country.

Being an international student is perhaps one of the most challenging things that you – if you are an international student – will do. It is a huge challenge on so many levels – emotionally, practically, educationally and physically. However, although being an international student in an unfamiliar country can be challenging, it can also be an immensely rewarding experience, and something that many UK students might not have done.

Sources of Practical Student Support

More on this section can be found online, but, for a brief introduction, you might want to find out about the following:

(a) **Student Representative Committees:** Every university in the UK will need to ensure that there is a good amount of student input to ensure that your experience – the 'student experience' – is a good one. (This does not necessarily mean it is an easy one.) The role of a student representative is key to this: becoming a student representative can send a signal to potential employers that you are willing to take responsibility and lead others, and, in terms of your future career, it is a good thing to do.
(b) **Student Support Services:** There should be various sources of support available for you on campus, electronically and/or at the end of a telephone. These will include counselling, disabilities, academic study assistance, a student buddy system, the library, IT support and the SU.

(c) **Personal Tutors:** The personal tutor is an academic member of staff who has particular responsibility for a number of students and can advise and assist them through their university studies. They will not have all the answers but will be able to direct you to relevant sources of support. It is important to get to you know your personal tutor: they will probably write a reference for you when you complete your degree. In particular, they will be able to speak up for you or to help you when things do not go according to plan. (Visit the book's companion website at https://study.sagepub.com/morgan to find additional information on extenuating and mitigating circumstances.)

FURTHER
READING

(d) **Careers Services:** Everything you do in your studies from the time you apply for your university course has implications for your future career. The careers services are there to help you make your own decisions, and not to tell you what you should do (nor can they usually give you a job!). It is worthwhile to use the careers services as soon as possible.

(e) **International Office:** The purpose of a university's International Office can vary, but they usually provide support for living in the UK, organising sightseeing trips and providing advice on visas.

If you are a postgraduate student, then you may be familiar with some of these issues, but bear in mind that different universities work in different ways and your previous experience may not reflect the reality of your current university. The advice you would seek from the careers services may also be somewhat different.

UNIVERSITY CULTURE

If the above systems are there for your support, and how you interact with them can have some impact on whether you obtain all that you hope for, then understanding the way that the university operates can help you interact with them better. An understanding of university culture will help you understand how to do this. If the services and systems (personal tutoring, careers, etc.) are the visible signs of 'what' the organisation does, then the culture will reflect 'how' those things are done.

WHAT IS 'CULTURE'?

Culture is famously defined as: 'The way we do things around here.' It is used to describe how 'friendly', 'supportive', 'bureaucratic', and so on, any organisation is.

Language is a key aspect of the culture for any organisation, including universities. By using particular words, universities tend to signal to the rest of society that they have a different purpose, go about things in a different way and have a different culture. For those reasons, universities tend to use language that is very different from that in most organisations. Some of this language can make you feel uncomfortable and uncertain, but in many cases you will be familiar with what things really mean in practice. It may be useful to consider making a list of the words you hear and read, but which are new to you. See the 'For You to Do' section below.

───── FOR YOU TO DO ─────

Over the next three weeks, watch out for any words that you have not come across before and try to guess what you think they mean. Different cultures will have different languages. If you are an overseas student,

(Continued)

(Continued)

this list may be large, but even if you have studied at a university before, there will be some words that could be new or, importantly, words that get used in a different way.

Write them down and guess what you think they mean.

Once again, a cautionary note for postgraduate students is in order: the language used by one institution may be similar to those used at your previous university, but it is wise not to make that assumption and to check your understanding.

UNIVERSITY PROCESSES

Universities are very diverse in their nature. They can be small or large, new or old, rich or poor, have great diversity in their student population or focus on one particular type of student. They can be very focused and specialise in a small number of areas or be very broad in the subjects they teach, and they can do a lot of research or focus mainly on teaching. You have probably chosen to study at your university because of three or four factors – the grades required, whether there was a course you were interested in, the cost (course fees and maybe living expenses) and whether your friends were going there – rather than the culture of the university.

However, one thing that UK universities do share is a need to comply with a number of UK government requirements, and this includes providing information, ensuring that degrees of similar subjects cover similar subjects, ensuring that a degree develops your thinking and skills, and ensuring that decisions about qualifications are similar to those made at other universities. There is actually a lot of monitoring that goes on within your university to ensure that there is innovation and improvement where needed. The good news for you is that there is also a need to involve students in nearly everything the university does.

All of this means that there is a lot of compliance with government requirements, which can make the organisation seem very bureaucratic with its large number of committees and administrative processes – and also seem apparently very slow to deal with issues sometimes, or even unhelpful on rare occasions.

Your Voice at the University

All of this can make a university seem like a large, impersonal organisation that operates in an unhelpful way by implementing rules about what it can and cannot do for you as an individual student; this can appear very disappointing. There is, however, another side to all this bureaucracy: that you – as an individual student – will have some input into what universities do and how they do it, and that universities need to demonstrate that they are changing to take account of your views as a student. For example, you will almost certainly be asked to complete questionnaires regularly on how effectively the different subjects and modules are taught. Universities are accountable for how they use this information and what they do with it.

 KEY LEARNING POINT

No two universities will do exactly the same thing in exactly the same way, but they will likely achieve the same kinds of outcomes to fulfil the needs of diverse stakeholders.

STUDENT CULTURE

Of course, from a student's perspective university can be a very rewarding and enjoyable experience. The lectures can be entertaining and enjoyable, the learning should be interesting, and the social side can be fun in the short term (while you are at university) and useful in the longer term (as you meet other people who will become friends for life).

The various forms of entertainment you might experience at university may or may not be attractive and some students will prefer to study hard rather than socialise. It is a personal choice, of course, though social activities are a great way to develop your interpersonal skills and it is by studying that you will develop your thinking skills and make the most of the complex life at university which will develop your planning and organisational skills. It is often said that the years at university are the best years of your life: you can make it what *you* would like it to be. Being part of a university community – whether postgraduate or undergraduate, domestic or international student – is preparation for the rest of life in a much larger community.

UNIVERSITY EDUCATION AND YOUR PREVIOUS EDUCATION

If we have already experienced university, then we may think we know what to expect. Of course, the reality (as this chapter has tried to note) is that every university will do things in a slightly different ways so the issue is then learning to make sense of why those differences exist and how to adjust to them (see Chapter 5 for more details on teaching methods at university and Chapter 6 for information on assessment of academic work at university).

—— REFLECTION POINT ——

Take some time to think about the following questions and write down some answers.

How do you think university is similar to – and different from – the experiences you might have had in your earlier education?

What do you think are going to be some of the challenges you might face in coping with university life in general over the next three weeks?

What do you think you need to do in order to make the most of your life at university?

THE START OF THE REST OF YOUR LIFE: EMPLOYABILITY

This chapter has outlined a range of experiences and issues faced by universities and has tried to enable you to make sense of what you have entered into. There is, however, a very important aspect of what universities do through their degree programmes, and this is to enhance you as an individual by developing your interpersonal skills, your ability to think critically and analytically, and your knowledge so that you can leave university and contribute to society.

In a well-known text, Steven Covey (1989) noted that one of the 'habits' effective people possess is that of beginning 'with the end in mind'. The last part of this text is about life towards the end of your studies and being able to start the career that you want. The introduction to that part (which you might like to read now) states the following:

Your academic success in your degree is going to be a very significant factor in your being able to get the future you want, but it is not the only factor. To an employer, a student who has a first-class degree in Philosophy but no leadership or work experience or no involvement in social activities is more likely to be overlooked for a graduate role than one who has a lesser degree (e.g. 2:1 or 2:2, more rarely a 3rd class), but leadership experience in a student society and some work experience. It is about balance, and employers are looking for competent and able individuals who are critical thinkers, analytical and able to use their communication and interpersonal skills to work well with others. This means that your working career starts on day 1 of your university studies – and your choices made during the start of your time at university *can have* a significant impact on your employability at the end of it.

In effect, the rest of your life *after* your university studies begins during your early days *at* university. Make decisions not to get involved in student clubs and societies, or make a choice to spend nearly all your time socialising or at your part-time job, and you may find that there are consequences to those choices some significant time later.

CONCLUSION

This chapter set out to ensure that you would be able to achieve the following:

- Describe what it is that universities do, and start thinking about how they do it.
- Understand how university may differ from previous learning environments you might have come across.
- Understand why university differences between university and other forms of education exist.
- Find your way around the university bureaucracy and systems so that your time at university will be enjoyable, rather than stressful.

It is important to note that every university will have its own way of doing things and two different universities will give you different experiences: that is, terminology and processes will probably vary somewhat from the ideas set out above, but all universities will seek to give you an experience that will be memorable and which will have a significant impact on your life for many years to come.

It is probably a good idea to get more details on the final bullet point by reading Chapters 6 to 10, which will give you more of an introduction to university life and an understanding of the ways that learning at university takes place, and discusses assessment, respectively.

This chapter has looked at the various processes which make universities run as they do and the activities that you may have been involved in at the beginning of your time as a university student. It has also tried to give some indication of how you might be able to manage your first days as a university student. It is for you to determine how you will make the most of them.

 INTERVIEW QUESTIONS

This text – as indicated above – has several aims, but one of the most important is to prepare you to enter what is usually referred to as 'the workplace'. This is done in a number of ways: helping you to pass your

(Continued)

(Continued)

studies (Part I), developing your thinking and interpersonal skills (Parts II–IV) and guiding you through the selection process (Part V). However, as many management writers point out, having a goal to achieve and thinking about that goal at the very start are vital in order to plan effectively.

With that in mind, each chapter will contain two or three interview questions for you to think about. These are questions which might be used when you have a graduate selection interview after university, but it is worth thinking about them at the start of your university studies so that you know what you need to achieve as you move through life at university.

Think about the following questions. What might your answers be?

1. Why did you choose the university and the course you have been studying?
2. How successful have you been at achieving the goals you set out to achieve by studying at university?

Chapter 17 gives a lot more information on selection interviews and the online content gives some guidance on these questions.

ADDITIONAL RESOURCES

Want to learn more? Visit https://study.sagepub.com/morgan to gain access to a wide range of online resources, including interactive tests, tasks, further reading and downloads.

Website Resources

Student Minds website: www.studentminds.org.uk/starting-university.html

Studential.com website: www.studential.com/info/freshguide.htm

The Independent – national newspaper website, providing some reassurance to those who might be nervous: www.independent.co.uk/student/student-life/health/starting-university-anxiety-902439.html

Top Universities website: www.topuniversities.com/student-info/health-and-support/starting-university-what-expect

Textbook Resources

Courtney, M. and Du, X. (2014) *Study Skills for Chinese Student,* 'Introduction: Living and Studying in the UK'. London: Sage (offers essential information to Chinese students coming to the UK to study).
Davey, G. (2008) *The International Student's Survival Guide.* London: Sage (particularly chapter 7).
Lewis, M. and Reinders, H. (2003) *Study Skills for Speakers of English as a Second Language:* Basingstoke Palgrave Macmillan (particularly chapters 9 and 11).
McIlroy, D. (2003) *Studying @ University.* London: Sage (particularly chapter 1).
McMillan, K. and Weyers, J. (2012) *The Study Skills Book* (3rd edition). Harlow: Pearson (particularly chapters 3, 5, 10 and 11).
Smale, B. and Fowlie, J. (2009) *How to Succeed at University: An Essential Guide to Academic Skills, Personal Development & Employability.* London: Sage (particularly chapter 1).

PERSONAL DEVELOPMENT AND LEARNING

CHAPTER STRUCTURE

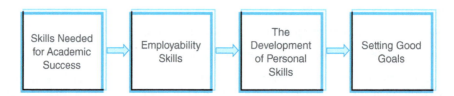

Figure 2.1

When you see the 🌐 this means go to the companion website https://study.sagepub.com/morgan to do a quiz, complete a task, read further or download a template.

═══ AIMS OF THE CHAPTER ═══

By the end of this chapter, you should be able to:

- Discuss how academic and interpersonal skills are developed during a degree.
- Analyse some of your own strengths and weaknesses as they relate to your immediate, medium-term and longer-term development needs.
- Develop some ideas for working on your weaknesses and enhancing your strengths.

INTRODUCTION

The contents of this chapter provide a foundation for Parts I – enhancing your study skill – and II – enhancing your employability skills. Learning a skill can sometimes take a matter of hours or sometimes take years – it depends entirely on a range of factors such as how quickly you learn, how you learn, what opportunities you have to practise those skills and the availability of any objective feedback. Failing to develop the skills you need quickly enough will have consequences. In the world of management, those who fail to develop the skills they need find that their promotional prospects become less and less, and, at university, failing to develop the appropriate skills means performing below potential and possibly failing modules. So, it is vital to develop your skills.

In this chapter, we will spend a little time examining the skills needed for successful study at university as well as those sought by employers (commonly but perhaps incorrectly called 'employability skills'), especially in terms of the development of independent and confident thinkers who can lead and manage others after their graduation. We will provide you with a way of evaluating yourself against those skills and give you some guidance on how you might go about developing all of your skills while at university. Of course, failing to develop your study skills has consequences for your academic success and failing to develop the skills required for 'the workplace' has consequences for your career.

We will begin this chapter by giving you the chance to analyse your own thinking about yourself, and your views about academic and career success, before spending some time looking at the kinds of skills that will be important for your life in both areas. We will then look at how skill development works, and give you some ideas from research and theory. Finally, the chapter will suggest some ways and give you some tools which you could use to develop those skills that you think will be necessary for your future success.

SKILLS SELF-ASSESSMENT

Complete the questionnaire below to see how well you think you know the items covered in this chapter. Give each item a score between 0 and 5, where 0 is 'not at all like me' and 5 is 'very much like me'. Answer each item quickly, but take a little time to think about why you give the answers that you do. This thinking may reveal something about yourself (and perhaps the way you relate to others) that you had not thought about before.

Item	Statement	Score
1.	I am confident that I understand what university education is all about	
2.	I know what makes the difference between good work at school and good work at university	
3.	I think the skills I have developed during my earlier education will be important to me at university	
4.	I am confident that I will do well in my university career	
5.	I have high expectations of myself and of the grades I will eventually obtain	

(Continued)

(Continued)

Item	Statement	Score
6.	I have a good understanding of how the skills I develop at university will relate to those I will need for my future career	
7.	I am clear about what my future career will be	
8.	I want to achieve the very best I can for me, my family and those I will work with	
9.	I have the capacity to lead others and enjoy leadership roles	
10.	I am competitive and will do nearly anything to ensure that I win	
11.	I think competition among students is a good thing, so I will use this to motivate myself	
12.	My motivation comes from seeing others benefit from the advice I give them	
13.	I enjoy achieving something good when working with others	
14.	I prefer to do academic work on my own	
15.	At university, I will try to focus only on my studies rather than on student clubs and societies	
16.	There is nothing more important than academic grades to get a good career	
17.	All the skills I will need for a good career will be developed through the activities I do during my studies	
18.	I am good at developing my skills and can now do things that I could not do before	
19.	I am very clear in my mind about the skills I will develop during my degree	
20.	I know how to develop my skills	
21.	I think it is easy for me to be aware of my own strengths and weaknesses	
22.	I think I know myself better than other people know me	
23.	My parents can tell me what my skills are and can help me find a career	
24.	I find it very easy to change who I am	
25.	I think university is about developing knowledge, rather than skills	

INTERACTIVE
TEST

An interactive version of this test along with comments and thoughts about these questions can be found on the companion website for this book at https://study.sagepub.com/morgan. However, there are no right or wrong answers for most of the questions above; they are really about how we see ourselves – a common theme through this chapter and others. Nevertheless, certain issues suggested above may help or hinder you when working through your life at university.

In some cases, the development of your skills will be a conscious choice: you choose to develop your skills and take action to do so (or choose not do so), but in many situations at university, you will find yourself developing your skills unconsciously.

===== 'BUT I HAVE A QUESTION …' =====

… Why put effort into developing my skills, if they will develop 'naturally'?

We said earlier that failing to develop your skills quickly enough has consequences, and that one of the issues that can affect *how quickly* you develop your skills is *how much effort you put into doing so*. There is an impact on the development of academic skills if the development of the relevant skills is not fast enough (i.e. you will not do as well as you could do in your studies) and an impact on the development of your 'employability skills' if other students from other universities have put effort into developing their skills (or have them at a higher level already) and you have not done so; they will then be more successful at their employer interviews than you.

During your degree, you will grow and develop these skills anyway, as you mature as an individual. The more effort you put into your own development, however, the faster you will grow and develop these skills.

We will look at the processes involved in skill development in more detail later in the chapter, but, for now, it is important to realise that developing skills is never an easy thing to do and can often be challenging. If you are an athlete or if you enjoy undertaking a challenge, then there is nothing new to add that will motivate you, but if you are not used to 'being stretched', then it can be a difficult and perhaps painful experience. The long-term benefit will be immense if the short-term challenges can be seen in a positive light – that is, *challenges to be overcome, rather than avoided*.

We will cover the following topics together:

- Skills needed for academic success.
- Skills needed for success in starting a career.
- Understanding how skill development 'works'.
- Making the most of opportunities for skill development.
- Tools for assisting personal skill development.

SKILLS NEEDED FOR ACADEMIC SUCCESS

We start by looking at the skills required for academic success. Each university programme will develop specific skills through the exercises you undertake during your course.

===== FOR YOU TO DO =====

Have a look at the websites for your university, your department, your course/degree programme and a couple of your modules. You might also want to look at the website for your university careers service. What skills do your modules, your course, your department and your university develop during your studies?

You may have to search a little and take some time, but the information about these skills will be available somewhere on your university website.

TIP: You might like to search on 'Programme specifications' or 'Module specifications' or something similar.

As the first chapter identified, university life delivers to students both a social and an educational experience, and provides an education in the ways listed there. In the process, it tries to enable you to develop appropriate skills. As noted earlier, this part of the text is about developing those skills which will enable you to study well (see Table 2.1), but you cannot expect that all the skills you need for successful study will simply be developed through university without any effort from yourself, as if by magic. This is why the first part of this book looks at what are traditionally called 'study skills' … The list in Table 2.1 is not complete and there will be some variation in how important some of these are compared with others, but we will look at most of those listed here.

Table 2.1 Subjects typically classified under the heading of 'study skills' and usually important for enabling you to study well

• Time management • Critical thinking • Essay writing • Research and library skills • Quantitative skills	• Analytical skills • Report writing • Group working • Reading skills • Self-awareness	• Being able to work independently • Resourcefulness • Communication skills • Presentation skills • IT skills

The chapters that follow will provide a great deal more detail on good practice in most of these skills, but before we get to those chapters, it would be good for you to try to define briefly what each one is and why it is important.

 ━━━ FOR YOU TO DO ━━━━━━━━━━━━━━━━━━━━━━━━

Work with a partner to complete this exercise, which should take a maximum of 15 minutes to do.

1. Each of you take three skills from each of the columns. Try to take different skills if you can.
2. On your own, try to identify: (a) what you think each one means in practice; and (b) the implications of not being good at this skill.
3. Compare your answers with those of your partner. Do they match?
4. With your partner try to rank all the skills listed in terms of their importance to your studies.

How easy was it to define and then rank the skills?

Most 'study skills' textbooks will cover some or all of these skills – this text is by no means the only resource you could use to develop your understanding and abilities.

In developing an accurate view of our abilities, we need to gather evidence. Our brain is very good at telling us we are good at things that we are, in reality, not very good at. Look at the next 'For You to Do' section below, remembering that the more evidence you gather, the more accurate your response will be. (We look at this further when we discuss critical thinking in Chapter 4.)

━━━━━ FOR YOU TO DO ━━━━━

TEMPLATE

The skills listed below are those frequently seen as being important in a managerial role. Have a look through these skills and answer the *two* questions listed for each skill. You can download this template grid on the companion website for this book at https://study.sagepub.com/morgan.

1. According to your own definition of each of these skills, how good do you think you are at this skill?
2. What evidence do you have/can you find to prove how good you are?

This will enable us to start looking at what you are good at and where we need to refine what we do or how we behave.

Skill	How good do you think you are at this skill?	What evidence do you have?
Critical thinking/cognitive skills		
Problem solving		
Decision making		
Oral communication		
Written communication		
Numeracy		
Communication IT skills		
Self-management		
Team-working		
Listening skills		
Influencing others		
Research skills		
Self-reflection		
Business acumen/awareness		
Proactive attitude		
Leadership		

EMPLOYABILITY SKILLS

Imagine that at 2.30 p.m. tomorrow, you have an appointment for an interview with the regional manager for an international UK-based organisation. The manager will want to find out about what motivates you, what skills you have and whether you will be the sort of person the organisation will want as a future manager.

OK, the idea of imagining someone sitting in front of you asking some questions might be somewhat scary right now, or maybe not (let's assume it *is*, for the moment). In a few years' time, employers (if you choose to seek a job rather than take other options) will generally want to know that you *can and will* do two things:

1. Perform well in the role that they have given you. This means many different things in different organisations, but it certainly means adding 'value' to the organisation.
2. Learn, grow and develop yourself. Technology and knowledge are increasing all the time and the way businesses used to find success does not necessarily bring success today. The same is true for the individuals within that business.

  FOR YOU TO DO

In looking at the skills listed on p. 23, are there any there that are more important for you to develop than others?

1. Why is this the case?
2. Are there any skills that are missing?

Employers typically look for individuals who have a number of qualities. Employees should have the appropriate personal transferable skills, motivation, specific skills and abilities required for a particular role (if there are any) and personality (e.g. attitude towards risk, conscientiousness, willingness to learn) in order to do well. These qualities will be different from organisation to organisation, but there are some characteristics that are seen as important, whatever the organisation.

PERSONAL TRANSFERABLE SKILLS

Behaviours that can occur and can be developed in a variety of different situations in order to perform well. Examples include time management, critical thinking and communication skills.

Graduate employers usually look for motivated self-starters: confident individuals who are independent, who can lead and work with others, and who can add value to their business (and, as I have indicated above, there are few better places to demonstrate how much of a self-starter you are by taking the initiative and getting involved in university life). In more detail, the following skills typically get listed (this list is from the Quality Assurance Agency (2007) mentioned earlier):

*   Cognitive skills of critical thinking, analysis and synthesis.
*   Effective problem solving and decision making using appropriate quantitative and qualitative skills.
*   Effective communication, oral and in writing, using a range of media.
*   Numeracy and quantitative skills.
*   Effective use of communication and IT.
*   Effective self-management.
*   Effective performance, within a team environment (including leadership).
*   Interpersonal skills of effective listening, negotiating, persuasion and presentation.
*   Ability to conduct research into business and management issues.
*   Self-reflection and criticality.

This list (and other similar lists) gives government guidance to universities on what you – as students – should be able to do by the end of your course. Other lists come from research with employers carried out by careers advisory services and HR professionals across the UK and include:

- Oral communication (most sought after).
- Team-work.
- Listening.
- Written communication.
- Problem solving (least sought after).

(Mullen, 1997)

- General business acumen.
- Application of number.
- Commitment.
- Problem-solving skills.
- Flexibility.

(Prospects, 2011)

And finally, from the CBI (Confederation of British Industry, which represents employers to government in particular and society generally):

- Self-management.
- Team-working.
- Business/customer awareness.
- Problem solving.
- Communication and literacy (i.e. listening/questioning and written communication).
- Application of number.
- Application of IT.
- Can-do approach/positive attitude.
- An entrepreneurial/proactive personality.

(Confederation of British Industry/Universities UK, 2009)

Of course, these different pieces of research overlap significantly (which gives added credibility to their findings), but it is worth noting that they are lists of skills, not knowledge. The information you gather from lectures and seminars (i.e. your 'learning') will need to be there as well, which is why many employers seek individuals who reach a particular degree grade. However, without many or all of the skills listed above, you might find it tough competing in the job market in the months and years to come.

═══════════════ FOR YOU TO DO ═══════════════

This exercise follows on from the similar feature above. Work with a partner to complete this exercise, which should take a maximum of 20 minutes to do.

(Continued)

(Continued)

1. Each of you take three skills from each of the four lists above. Try to take different skills from each list if you can.
2. On your own, try to define: (a) what you think each means in practice; and (b) the implications of not being good at this skill.
3. Compare your answers with those of your partner. Do they match?
4. With your partner try to rank all the skills listed in terms of their importance to your career and working life.
5. Compare the content of the skills you took under (1) with those listed on page 23.

How many skills do you think are sought by employers and developed during your time at university?

If you examine the skills sought by employers and those developed at university, there will be some overlap. Of course, if there was no overlap, then either university would add nothing to the lives of students other than knowledge, or employers' expectations would be unrealistically high or low. But that is why referring to these skills as *either* study skills *or* employability skills is not always appropriate. It is the ends to which such skills are put that sometimes makes the apparent difference, not the skills themselves.

 ━━━ KEY LEARNING POINT ━━━━━━━━━━━

There is significant overlap between what we might refer to as 'study skills' and 'employability skills'. It is this overlap that enables universities to be sure that they are developing skills which will enable you to do well in future employment.

The implications of this overlap are seen in a clear way in Chapter 17, where we review the 'interview questions' from across the chapters. Part IV of this text covers a number of heavily sought-after 'employability skills', including:

*   Presentation skills (Chapter 9).
*   Team-working (Chapter 10).
*   Leading others (Chapter 11).
*   Communicating effectively (Chapter 12).
*   Developing cross-cultural awareness (Chapter 13).
*   Problem solving and creativity (Chapter 14).

We have examined the nature of the skills we are covering in this text, and if you have done the exercises above, you will have developed a definition of what you think these skills mean. We will present more academic and employer-focused definitions as we move through the book, so do not be too concerned about whether those definitions are correct just yet. What we are now going to do in the remainder of this chapter is to explore how you can develop such skills, both by understanding the skill development process itself and by understanding what opportunities you might have to develop these skills.

THE DEVELOPMENT OF PERSONAL SKILLS

There are several steps required for the development any skill. We will look at each step in turn and try to make this process as clear as possible.

Step 1: Decide What You Need to Develop

Imagine the following dialogue between a student Cindy, an international student studying in the UK, and her tutor.

Tutor: Hi Cindy, Hope you're OK. Which skill would you like to improve?

Cindy: Hello. I think I'd like to improve my presentation skills.

Tutor: OK, good. So, why do you want to improve you're your presentations skills, rather than, for example, your team-working skills?

Cindy: Well, maybe I should improve those as well. What do you think?

Tutor: Well, it is for you to decide perhaps – or maybe there are certain skills that your course director or dean need you to demonstrate. But presentation skills are often something that students do choose to work on. Yes. Are your presentation skills not very good?

Cindy: Hmmm, I don't feel very confident or able to do good presentations – they were something we never had to do when I have studied before.

Tutor: What do other people think about your presentation skills?

Cindy: You mean I should ask them? [Embarrassed smile.] Hmmm, I don't know. I have never asked my classmates what they think.

Tutor: Well, you could think of them as friends rather than classmates and maybe that might make it easier to ask them.

Cindy: OK, I will do that …

Tutor: Good. Do that and then let's discuss further when we know whether there is really a need to develop this set of skills.

Cindy: OK. Thank you for your time. And I will arrange the appointment soon.

So, in the example above, Cindy was starting to decide what she was good and bad at. This is one of the reasons why we did the second exercise earlier in this chapter. To decide what we need to develop is always a personal decision, and in some ways it needs to be. Having someone else tell us what we need to develop does not usually inspire us to go away with much enthusiasm for doing so. In business life, however, we often have to think about 'core skills', which are those essential for the continuation of the culture and processes of the organisation, and peripheral skills, which could be either those essential for certain roles or, more

TWO FORMS OF PDP

Personal development plans: Plans intended to develop those skills that are seen as peripheral or unnecessary for working life. This may include photography, sporting skills, language skills, cooking, etc.

Professional development plans: Plans intended to develop those skills that are seen as important for working life, particularly within an organisation. This may include IT skills, interpersonal skills, project management skills, etc. This list often reflects the skills listed by the CBI and others presented elsewhere in this chapter.

likely, those that are helpful but not essential. In some ways, this distinction also reflects the difference between what are both called PDPs – 'personal development plans' and 'professional development plans' (see the definition here).

Planning for anything is often about finding a gap between where you are and where you want or need to be. Personal development is no different. So, whether we are looking at skills which will assist us in our studies or those which will help us in our career (or both), the question is: 'In thinking about the important skills I need to develop, what skill do I need to develop the most? Where is the gap largest?'

That is easier said than done, but there are ways to do this. Some of what is written here overlaps with some of what we will examine when it comes to research skills.

Key to identifying this gap is *information*. The more information we gather from various sources on many occasions, the more we can be sure that such information is accurate and useful to us.

Subjective Information

So, we could ask a number of different kinds of people one of two questions: 'What do you think I am good (and bad) at?' or 'How good do you think I am at X …?' The follow-up question should always be 'Why do you think that?' As we will see in Chapter 17, employers will frequently use these questions when carrying out a job interview.

 FOR YOU TO DO

Look at the list of people below who can provide information about your skills. Who do you think can provide the most accurate information for you?

- Your mother
- Your father
- Your brothers and sisters, and other family members
- Your best friend
- Other students on your course
- A student
- Others …?

- A past employer
- A past schoolteacher
- A current employer
- Other students in a student society or in your dormitory
- Your personal tutor
- Other university tutors
- A university careers adviser

Figure 2.2 Identifying the gap between your current skills and your desired skill level

So, how about asking some of these people for their views?

There is one (or maybe two, depending on how you see it) more group of people missing from this list, namely *friends* (and boy- or girlfriends). If you are going to obtain accurate information, then it needs to be impartial (or objective) and the closer you are to someone emotionally (either positively or negatively), the less accurate that information is likely to be. This might also apply to parents, so it is up to you to make a judgement.

The Johari Window

There is a problem here: sometimes, we hide what we do not like about ourselves – and, sometimes, people do not tell us what we are really like because they do not want to offend us. These ideas led Joseph Luft and Harry Ingham to develop what became known as the Johari Window (Luft and Ingham, 1955). The model is outlined in Figure 2.3 and uses and categorises information according to what we know about ourselves and what other people know about us.

Panel 1:

What We Know about Ourselves and What Others Know about Us: The 'Arena'

When someone goes to fight in a boxing match or compete on a tennis court, everything that they do is public – their anxieties, their abilities and how they react when things are going well or badly.

The same is true when we talk about our day-to-day skills as well: people can see what we struggle with and what we excel at, hence the name of this conceptual place.

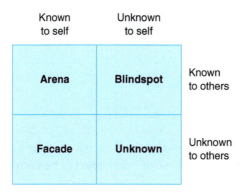

Figure 2.3   The Johari Window

Panel 2:

What We Know about Ourselves but What Others Do Not Know about Us: The 'Facade' or 'Mask'

There are certain times and occasions – or certain activities – that can make us behave in ways that we might consider embarrassing or wrong, and there are times when we do things we probably should not. In both contexts, we keep such behaviour hidden from others we know. For example, people at work

(Continued)

(Continued)

might see us quite differently from our family and friends, so we typically keep some parts of who we are hidden, or masked.

These activities would come into the box labelled 'Facade'.

Panel 3:

What We Do Not Know about Ourselves but What Others Believe about Us: The 'Blindspot'

In terms of vision, everyone has a blindspot: an area of vision that is momentarily obscured. If you drive, you might have a number of mirrors to enable you to see around the car, but there are places which may be missed and you will need to move your head to see. In both situations, we talk about the 'blindspot'.

In terms of personal development, the blindspot consists of those skills which you have but are not aware you have them, or those skills you think you have, but have never been told that you were poor at them.

Panel 4:

What We Do Not Know about Ourselves and What Others Do Not Know about Us: The 'Unknown'

If you have never been skiing, ice-skating or jumped out of an aircraft to go skydiving, then you will not know whether you are any good at it – and the same applies to any skill we might need to demonstrate. In addition, no one else will know whether you are any good at it either, and in such situations we would say that we are operating in 'the unknown', or – to put it more simply – we are exploring our skills.

When we are children, we do this all the time. Can I climb? Walk? Count from 1 to 100, and so on. But as adults, we start to slow down our development and often concentrate on things that we are good at. There is really nothing wrong with this, as long as we have all the skills we need to do everything we need to do both now and in the future; however, life rarely stays the same. We change jobs, change our plans, get married, start to use technologies we have never used before, become parents, and so on, and thus there will nearly always be something we need to develop.

 ━━━━━ 'BUT I HAVE A QUESTION ...' ━━━━━

... I've heard some people say that we should focus on our strengths and develop those rather than work on our weaknesses. After all, we're never going to be perfect are we?

There is probably no right or wrong answer to this – there are different views and there are different ways of approaching the issue of personal competence. It is often the case that people can be very successful in their careers but then only get so far because of a lack of certain important skills that are needed for more senior positions.

Working on your weaknesses is important to enable you to become a balanced individual. Over time, and as your life takes you in various directions, you might realise that certain skills are more important than others, but imagine for a moment your life now – as a university student.

Let's say that you are really great at essay writing. That is great, as long as the assessments you have to do are essays. As soon as they become calculations or presentations, you have a problem. Right?

The same is true in work: you can be great at some things, but as soon as something changes in your work, your lack of skills in some areas can become a real issue.

Since life changes, we need to learn in new ways and develop new skills. The exercise in the next 'For You to Do' section details some of the changes that your lecturers and tutors might have faced since they studied at university.

FOR YOU TO DO

Life begins at 40 …

If you are starting university, there is a range of items that you will be familiar with now which were not available to those who studied in the 1970s or 1980s:

- Smartphones
- Small mobile phones
- iPads and iPods
- Notebook computers

- Internet, Wi-Fi and 3G/4G
- Email
- Online learning
- Video conferencing

Questions:

1. Is there anything there that surprises you?
2. How well would you cope if your life in the next 20 years changed in the same way (or even faster)?

Gathering information can be problematic, of course. It is fine in theory to say that we can ask others to tell us what they think, but some may be very general in the feedback they give or some may not wish to give it at all. There may be particular cultural or gender issues with certain groups, and while stereotyping is very dangerous sometimes, Box 2.1 shows how some issues from Chinese culture can make gathering information from peers about skill levels (or any aspect of performance) sometimes problematic.

BOX 2.1

MIANZI OR 'FACE'

In Chinese culture, it is typically considered good fortune to 'bless' other people by paying them a compliment. It builds relationships, honours them and shows respect. Traditionally, arrogance and pride are attributes that are not usually welcomed. Such actions – often verbal – are seen as 'giving face' to the other person.

On the other hand, embarrassing someone and being blunt or direct to a Chinese person about a lack of skill is often seen as making someone 'lose face', and this can be seen as humiliating. It can sometimes apply to both parties when 'unhappy news' is delivered, with the giver of the information embarrassed that they have to give it, and the receiver embarrassed because of its content. So, communication between peers about each other's skill levels can be indirect or even untrue in order to preserve the *mianzi* of both the person giving the feedback and the person receiving it.

Although this can be true, no cultural stereotypes will be true of everyone from any one cultural group at all times.

KEY LEARNING POINT

Gathering as much information as possible from others is crucial for understanding how good we are at certain skills. The information needs to be accurate and so the more we gather, the more accurate our skills assessment becomes.

Gathering Objective Information

Objective information is often seen as being more definite and factual: for example, if you sell three pairs of shoes in a shop, then you sell three pairs of shoes and there really is not much debate about it. In reality, badly collected objective information can be more unhelpful than subjective information: for example, perhaps you sell three pairs of shoes but make a financial loss on each one.

The question is, 'What kind of objective information can you gather about your skills?' In reality, the answer is not easy to find. It is true to say that if you are good at something, you will achieve more success, but measuring that success factually is not easy. After all, it is perfectly possible to sell more shoes, for example, but maybe you have to press customers to buy them and actually do the business more harm than good.

REFLECTION POINT

Take some time to think about the following questions and write down some answers.

If someone were to ask you right now what your two strengths and two weaknesses were, what would you say? Why would you choose those?

STRENGTHS

1.   2.

WEAKNESSES

1.   2.

Step 2: How to Develop these Skills

Identifying strategies to develop these skills requires an understanding of how the process of skill development works. We will look briefly at two models of learning and skill development here, and examine the role of additional resources – including people – in our development. The first is known commonly as 'Kolb's Learning Cycle' (Kolb, 1984) and details some ideas about how we learn through an ongoing cycle of activities. The second is entitled 'The Four Stages of Learning a New Skill' (Robinson, 1974) and could be applied to both motor and cognitive skills.

Model 1: Kolb's Experiential Learning Cycle

David Kolb's experiential model of learning (Kolb, 1984) has been cited frequently in the literature on learning and development, and has been used as the basis for developing training and development programmes for some time. At its heart, it is experiential (i.e. it is based on individuals having and thinking about their experiences), rather than simply absorbing and trying to apply theory. The basic principle of the model is that, in learning a new skill, we go through four activities in a cycle (see Figure 2.4). We can best illustrate this by means of an example, so let's assume that you want to improve your examination skills (though the same ideas could be applied to any skill).

Before we go any further, however, it is important to say that we could start our skill development at any place on the cycle and that 'stage 1' is numbered that way just because it makes understanding the theory easier, but most applications of the model work in the way described below.

Stage 1: Experience

Imagine for a moment that one of your modules requires you to take an examination. So, you do what you think you need to do in order to pass or to do well: the reading, organising your notes, searching on the Internet, and so on. After a while you receive your examination timetable and take the exam. The task or activity is completed and your work is sent for marking by the tutor.

Stage 2: Reflection

Reflection was mentioned earlier in Chapter 1. It was defined as the process of considering what we do and how we do it, with a view to seeing if there is a way to improve. With the essay-writing example earlier on, we submitted the piece of work and are now taking a bit of time to reflect on how well we have done.

After the exam, you might have spent time discussing your ideas with other students – what theories you included, what you thought was relevant, what examples you gave and so on – and comparing your own answers, or maybe you simply go back to your notes and compare your answers with the information you tried to revise. When you do either of these things, you are reflecting on your performance. Or, to put it another way, you are evaluating how well you think you have done.

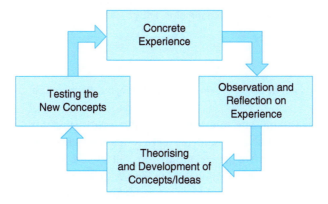

Figure 2.4   Kolb's Learning Cylce (1984)

KOLB, DAVID A., EXPERIENTIAL LEARNING: EXPERIENCE AS THE SOURCE OF LEARNING AND DEVELOPMENT 2ND ED., © 2015. Reprinted by permission of Pearson Education, Inc., New York, New York.

Some time later, you get the marks. Sadly, you have not done as well as you wanted to do; let's assume that this has come as a bit of a shock. Again, you think about what you could have done better, why you did so poorly and, importantly, develop your own thinking about where you need to improve. Again, you are reflecting.

To get the most out of any opportunity to demonstrate and improve on a particular skill, reflection involves thinking about a number of key questions (see Box 2.2 below), including some or all of the following:

- Did you notice ...?
- Why did that happen?
- Does that happen in life?
- Why does that happen?
- How can you use that?

Such questions enable individuals to do reflection on their own or with a tutor or coach in some way.

BOX 2.2

REFLECTION ON SPECIFIC INCIDENTS

Gallagher (2010) notes that it is generally good to reflect on specific events, and ask some or all of the following questions:

- What was the critical incident?
- What happened?
- What were my initial thoughts?
- What were my initial feelings?
- What skills/behaviours did I use?
- How well did I deal with the situation?
- How confident am I that my behaviours were appropriate?
- What have I learnt?
- What will I do differently next time?

Think about a time when something you did turned out not as you planned. Thinking about the questions above, was there anything you would have done differently?

Your lecturers and tutors might add more questions to these, but they go right to the heart of any *reflective* activity.

Of course, reflection without any information to guide you is simply 'thinking', and the biggest mistake after an examination that many students make is that they reflect *without* gathering extra information from their tutors, who will know more. You will almost certainly get feedback on your coursework but less often on an examination, and to ignore the chance to get feedback on your examination answers is not clever. It might not be comfortable to speak to the tutor who has given you a mark you do not feel you deserve, but it is vital, otherwise how will you know what to change if you never get that information from the individuals who will be marking your work?

============ **KEY LEARNING POINT** ============

In reflecting on the marks you get for your examinations, it is vital to get feedback from your lecturers. Not doing so means that you are relying on guesswork.

Stage 3: Theorising

The present situation is that you have taken your examination, you have reflected on what you could have done differently, and you now start to become somewhat more analytical and think about why you did what we did, or why it was successful. In other words, you and others will start to develop a 'theory' of what happened and why.

This stage should also involve some theory or input from experts and other tutors to help understand how you should have written the examination answers. In our example, you might have found out that you needed to manage time better, structure the answers in a different way or include more references.

These questions – and variations of them – are commonly used at universities to enhance learning, especially for modules that relate to personal or career planning in some way.

Stage 4: Planning

If you have gone through the three stages listed above, then there is just one major question left unanswered, as follows.

What am I going to do differently next time?

Since your last examination, nearly a whole semester has passed by and you are about to sit some more examinations. This time, you want to do better, so you go back to your reflections, think about the changes you need to make in what you did and how you did it, and actually implement those changes. This time, you know what you need to do and you are ready to achieve better results, which is exactly what you want.

Your university lecturers should also be able and willing to give you feedback on why you did so well (or not so well) as you did – either in oral or written form – and may well publish a report or equivalent document on the Internet for you to look at. If you do not get any response to a request for feedback, then be persistent: it is your degree which might be at stake.

Answering this final question – and importantly implementing your own thoughts – should enable you to do better in the next examination.

Thus, we complete the learning cycle (Figure 2.5). Or rather we have been through the cycle once.

If we are going to become very good at a particular skill, then we need to go through this cycle a number of times: you do not learn how to ride a bicycle or a horse or motorbike by riding, falling off and then simply thinking about what to do differently – you have to get back on and try again. The same applies to learning to drive, swimming, giving a presentation, communicating with others in a group, persuading team members or customers of something, learning to email your tutors, carrying out a selection interview, and so on.

It is the application of theory that makes it useful, so have a look at the exercise in the next 'For You to Do' section, which asks you to apply the learning styles to the development of writing skills (though it could apply to any skill).

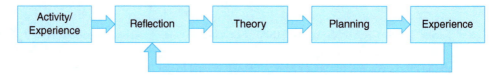

Figure 2.5   Repeating Kolb's Experiential Learning Cycle (1984)

Think through the information above regarding Kolb's (1984) ideas. Check your understanding of how each component of the learning cycle might work by applying the model to the development of your writing skills.

Stage of the learning cycle	In order to develop my writing skills at this stage of the learning cycle, I should ...
Concrete experience	
Observation and reflection	
Developing ideas and theory	
Testing new concepts	

There are no right and wrong answers for this exercise, but thinking through the 'For You to Do' exercise above will give you an understanding of how well you understand how Kolb's Learning Cycle works. We tend to think that experience on its own is sufficient to become 'perfect', though in reality we usually need more than just practice, as Box 2.3 illustrates.

BOX 2.3

A COMMON SAYING ... AND A RECIPE FOR IMPROVEMENT

There is a saying that most people seem to accept as common sense, and most people believe, and you will have probably have heard it, too:

'Practice makes perfect.'

Think about this. Maybe you can drive: does doing more driving make you better? Or maybe you can give presentations: does giving more presentations make you better at them?

Possibly; but for most people, practice – on its own – does not make someone better or perfect at something. Just doing something does not make you better at it. For many people, simple practice makes bad practice become a bad habit, and good practice become a good habit. Practice needs other things if it is to lead to any improvement.

The first thing to add to this mixture is *feedback*. If we think about the driving example, we can get feedback from passengers (if they are scared after being in the car with you, then something is probably wrong), other drivers (even if they are sometimes not polite), from the police, perhaps, from reflection on our own driving and as a result of any accidents that we might be unlucky to have. All of this is feedback.

(Continued)

(Continued)

The second item to add is *motivation to change*. If we do not care about how many speeding fines we have, or whether people want to be our passengers, then we are unlikely actually do anything about the feedback we get. The same is true for any of the skills we have – and for those we seek to improve on.

Questions:

1. In thinking about the skills you want to improve on, what sources of feedback could you use to see how much improvement you have made?
2. What is your motivation for changing and improving these skills? Is it strong enough to keep you focused until you are good enough at them?

Model 2: The Four Stages of Learning a New Skill

A very different model of learning was developed in the late 1960s and early 1970s. The exact origin of the model is not known, but a claim of authorship was noted in 1974 (Robinson, 1974). The model consists of four relatively simple stages in becoming skilled, and we will use presentation skills as an example to illustrate how the model works.

Unconscious Incompetence: We have no idea whether we can or cannot do something. It is simply a question we have never thought about or received any feedback on. For example, 'I have never done a presentation and I have no idea whether I am good or not. I think I might be, but …'

Conscious Incompetence: We are aware that we are not as good as we could be and have a desire to get better at this skill. For example, '*I have done* a presentation and the audience seemed confused because I did not explain myself well and some people could not hear me. I now know that I am not as good as I want to be.'

Conscious Competence: We have developed our skills and now know that we are good. We still have to try out certain things because they do not come naturally, but we are performing at a level where others can see that we can demonstrate this skill well. In relation to the example we are using here, 'I have regularly received feedback that my audience enjoys my presentations and find them informative. I have to try to appear confident because I still have lots of nerves and I work hard to hide them, but my presentations go down well.'

Unconscious Competence: The classic goal of any skill development activity or strategy is this one, where individuals are skilled without needing to put any effort into what they do. Everything seems to be done – and is done – naturally or effortlessly. The final stage in our example would be where: 'I feel good about what I do and can give a good and entertaining presentation without really thinking about it. My nerves don't affect me, and my confidence is there. In fact, I really don't need to think very much about what I am doing.'

Once again (as with Kolb's Learning Cycle above), there are obvious applications to nearly all the skills we are considering in this text and a range of others we are not looking at here.

━━━━━━ KEY LEARNING POINT ━━━━━━

All good personal development activities – based on the theories identified above – require some formal input and some forms of practice. In that sense, practice + feedback + motivation can help to 'make perfect' (see Box 2.3), but without practice, there will be very little skill development.

SETTING GOOD GOALS

Knowing how to plan is essential to a busy work life, and the same is no less true for life as a student. The very beginning of the chapter noted that 'managing' time is something we cannot do, but learning how to plan gives us a significantly greater sense of control over what we do.

If we can learn to plan during our time as students, then we will achieve three things very easily: (1) we will be able to do much better in our coursework; (2) we will have finished our coursework before others and will be able to relax more; and (3) we will be able to demonstrate good 'time management' and planning skills to future employers. Of course, we cannot plan what to do unless we know what is important, and that is where goal setting comes in.

In his influential book *The 7 Habits of Highly Effective People*, Covey (1989) outlines two 'habits' that have some place in this chapter: firstly, 'Begin with the End in Mind'; and secondly, 'First things first'. The first relates to setting goals and the second to effective planning and prioritisation. It is worth reading and thinking about what Covey has to say on the subject, but for us, looking at studying, we need to get down to basics with some fundamental questions.

 ═══════ FOR YOU TO DO ═══════

Have a look at the following questions. How easy are they for you to answer?

1. When you woke up this morning, how clear were you on what you wanted to achieve?
2. What do you want to achieve/complete/have done in the next three hours?
3. Was reading this chapter of the book something you intended to do today, or are you surprised you are doing this?
4. Why are you reading this chapter?

It may be that you woke up this morning, lay in bed for a while, thought you needed to get up (though not necessarily sure why), fed the cat or dog (or children) and then picked up the first thing to hand, which happened to be this book. (You might have had a shower somewhere in between, but we will let that go for the moment!)

Let's look at the second question above: do you know what you want to have completed in the next three hours? If we can answer this question clearly, then it means we have set a goal: 'Within the next three hours, I will have completed X, finished Y and discussed the topic with Z ....' We will look at what makes a good goal in a little while, but it is important to understand *why* we need goals in the first place. Some goals can relate to careers, and some will relate to the much more mundane activities involved in daily life (see Figure 2.6).

Of course, the longer-term goals can change a great deal, and we need to ensure we are not totally inflexible in what we seek, but as we look towards shorter term goals, we need to ensure that they are SMART.

The Nature of Good Goals: SMART Goal Setting

Good goals, as nearly any management website or textbook on the subject will tell you, should be SMART, although the meaning of each letter varies depending on who you read. This acronym is usually defined thus:

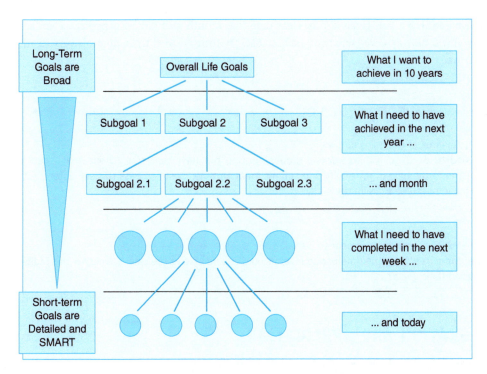

Figure 2.6 Relationship between career achievement and shorter-term goals

Specific: What exactly do you want to have completed?

Measurable: How will you know whether you have completed it or not?

Achievable: Are you likely to be able to achieve this goal/complete this work ...?

Realistic: ... in the timescale you have allocated? Or **Resourced:** Do you have sufficient resources available to you?

Time-based: By when do you want to have completed this? The shorter the timescale, the more precise you should be.

So, taking the three-hour example, we could write that the goal is SMART in the following ways:

Specific: It says, 'I will have completed X.' X could be 'read two chapters' or 'complete Exercise 2 which was set as homework'. Both are specific.

If we wrote, 'I will have done some of the reading from one of my textbooks,' then the example is not specific. How much reading? From which textbook?

Can you see the difference?

Measurable: It says, 'I will have completed X.' It is much better to have a goal which can be measured, because then you (and other people) know whether you have completed it. The key question here is 'How will you know whether you have achieved the goal or not?' If your goal is 'to graduate with the best degree you can', then that is a great broad intention, but it is not measurable. How will you know whether you have achieved it or not?

Achievable and **R**ealistic relate to the likelihood of your achieving the measure you set out, bearing in mind the resources at your disposal. This includes time, but also includes people, facilities, other commitments that you might have made, data and information, and so on.

Time-based: Have you given a very clear date (i.e. month and day, and perhaps even a time) by which you will have achieved what you have stated? 'Within the next three hours' is very clear; 'Within the next week' is not.

 ━━ FOR YOU TO DO ━━━━━━━━━━━━━━━━━━━━━━━━

Have a quick look at the goals below:

'I intend to be a good hard-working student during the next semester. I hope that I can write my assignments to the best of my ability and submit them on time. I want to pass this semester of study with only a couple of retake examinations.'

Questions:

1. How SMART do the goals appear to be?
2. If you came back after the time period given, would you be able to see clearly whether this individual had achieved their goals?

INTEGRATION AND APPLICATION

If we look at the information above, we end up with two stages:

1. Evaluation of our strengths and weaknesses.
2. Development of a plan to develop our weaknesses.

There are some weaknesses that we will struggle to develop – I am not really able to play a musical instrument, for example – but there are weaknesses that we can improve on, and where we might have some potential, so the second stage becomes really important.

Assuming for a moment that we have identified that we wish to develop our presentation skills (and in particular our ability to present in a confident manner (see Chapter 9 for more details on oral presentation skills) and also to work on our team-working skills, our personal development plan might look something like that in Table 2.2.

This example gives a clear indication of what this individual will do, how they will evaluate what they will do, how good they intend to be, and whether the goal is met. In real life, they would then go on and give additional comments to indicate what they intend to do or to work on next. They are very clear on exactly when they will take these actions and the goal is very clear.

Some skills are not easy to develop (e.g. presentation skills, critical thinking skills), so consider the ideas in Table 2.3.

CONCLUSION

By now, you should be able to:

- Discuss how academic and interpersonal skills are developed during a degree.
- Analyse some of your own strengths and weaknesses as they relate to your immediate, medium-term and longer-term development needs.
- Develop some ideas for working on your weaknesses and enhancing your strengths.

Table 2.2 Example of a personal development plan

Skill/behaviour	Action needed	Resources needed (incl. people)	Date(s) for action	Date for review (i.e. next opportunity to practise and demonstrate skill)	Aspirational goal (SMART)	Met?
Giving regular eye contact in presentations	Looking and rehearsing presentation in mirror and in front of friends Gather feedback from friends	Friends Books on presentation skills Online resources Computer	Rehearsing every Friday afternoon Reading of presentation every Thursday	Complete presentation in front of friends every Saturday morning: 18th, 25th, 2nd	I want to be hitting 5/5 for eye contact each time I do the practice presentation. I'll use the evaluation form to collect evaluations from friends	
Develop encouraging attitude towards others in coursework group	Refrain from being overly critical Ask for evaluation from others in the group Read up on having a positive approach towards group members	Friends to evaluate my progress Books on team-working skills Online resources	Group meeting on Thursday and Saturday to do accounting coursework	Discuss feedback from friends immediately after the group meeting on Thursday and Saturday for the next two weeks	I want to collect evidence of statements from my friends showing that I have encouraged others in the group. I want to have at least five such statements each meeting	

Table 2.3 Ideas for skill development

Skill	Ideas for development
Time management (see Chapter 3)	Identify how much better life would be if you were able to control what you do Write down daily goals somewhere where you can see them Reflect on why you might find this skill difficult. Is it prioritising? Is it planning? Is it about identifying personal goals? If you have a smartphone, then set reminders on your phone indicating what you have to do and when Buy and use an alarm clock, and set it for a time in line with the tasks you have to get done that day Review your use of time as regularly as possible and see how much improvement you are making
Critical thinking (see Chapter 4)	Have a look through the content in Chapter 4 to identify what is meant by each skill Arrange to discuss an issue with a friend: give them the chance to say whether they agree or disagree with a particular point of view and then take the opposite viewpoint - the role of 'devil's advocate' - in order to develop your abilities to think quickly of counter-arguments Identify where what is written in the example essay in Chapter 4 is different (more analytical) than what you might naturally write When the results from another essay are available, find someone who has a better mark than you and ask to see their assignment to see what they did differently As you read, take notes about what you are reading, but make sure you: (1) think carefully about what you are reading - ask questions about why an author is writing what they are writing (does it make sense?); and (2) write down your thoughts, so that you can think about them later and use them in your writing Discuss what you have been reading with a friend: Do they think it makes sense? Is there anything they notice about what you have been reading that you have missed? Join a debating club, to develop your abilities to identify and give the strongest arguments Listen to debates and interviews on the media: as you listen, critique the arguments you hear. Was any evidence presented? Was the point of view accurate?
Developing your writing skills - both timed examination essays and coursework (see Chapters 6, 7 and 8)	Try to write an essay plan about a particular question and get some feedback on it from a tutor or adviser Write an essay under timed conditions and review your work, preferably with a lecturer: Did you finish it in time? Was it sufficiently well structured? How analytical was it? (Do you understand what 'analytical' means?) Did it include everything that it should have included? Was the evidence there to support your argument? When the results from another essay are available, find someone who has a better mark than you and ask to see their assignment to see what they did differently. Review Chapters 6 and 7 to identify whether there is something you have missed in your written work

(Continued)

Table 2.3 (Continued)

Skill	Ideas for development
Presentation skills (see Chapter 9)	(Identify which aspect(s) of giving presentations you struggle with, since different areas may require very different actions)
	Preparation: If you never give yourself sufficient time to prepare (which could also mean that you are more of a perfectionist than you need to be), then set yourself specific goals for preparation. By when will you have visual aids ready? By when will you have rehearsed? By when will you have found out about the presentation facilities?
	Develop a presentation preparation checklist (based on Chapter 9), and use it
	Delivery: Practise and rehearse, preferably in front of others who can give you some feedback, but in front of a mirror if needed. Undertake some structured reflection/evaluation – be systematic in your self-evaluation/ask others to give you feedback on the same criteria each time. Get feedback on your para-linguistic and non-verbal behaviour (see Chapter 12) as well as your content
	Watch how others present (e.g. on TV, at videos of TED, at your lectures)
	Join a TEDx or University Toastmasters Club – to practise giving presentations and getting/giving feedback
	Evaluate what your lecturers do that is good and bad, in terms of presenting and engaging their audience
	Join and practise speaking at a debating club, to develop your ability to speak confidently
Team-working skills (Chapter 10), Leading others (Chapter 11), Communication skills (Chapter 12)	(Identify which aspect(s) of communicating and working with others/leading that you struggle with, since different areas may require very different actions; working in a team requires a great number of different skills)
	The specific actions which will be helpful will depend on the skills area requiring development, but there is little substitute for gathering real feedback from other team members and then working together to improve on whatever specific areas require development
	Watch others working in teams on TV: What do they do wrong? What should they do differently?
	Work with others to organise a charity event (or some other event that you are not required to do as part of your course, i.e. do it for fun). Removing the pressure means that you can enjoy it and relax a little more, and then let your real abilities and personality show
	Imagine yourself in different kinds of relationships with your current team members than those you have now (which could be unhelpful, very constructive, destructive, aggressive, etc.): What would need to happen in order for you to change your behaviour? View any issues from the others' perspective: Could they be seeing the problem in a very different way from you? What would need to happen for *them* to change *their* behaviour?
	Read some material on what it means to work well as a team – share it with others in an uncritical, objective manner. Is there anything the team can learn?
	Take some time to review how the team is working? Listen well and gather accurate feedback with specific evidence
	Write down and review some sentences that you speak: Was there any other way that they could have been interpreted? Ask a friend to help you answer this question
Developing cross-cultural awareness (Chapter 13) and Problem solving and creativity (Chapter 14)	Both these chapters include specific ideas for developing your skills

This chapter has aimed to give you an idea of how personal development and learning works in practice, at least as far as skill development is concerned. Some of the more detailed aspects of planning for personal development (especially in terms of how you might use opportunities to develop your skills) is given in the online content.

Each of the chapters which follow will relate to the development of your skills in some way or another. Some will only relate to your short-term situation – as a student. Others will be important for you in the short term and in the longer term – to help you become successful in a career after employment. Depending on the role you take after employment, there may also be knowledge gaps which employers will often help you to fill through professional qualifications (ACA, ACCA, SAP, PRINCE2, etc.). The key issue here is that nearly all the skills that you will use and develop during your degree will be important for personal success in the workplace as well, as shown in Figure 2.7.

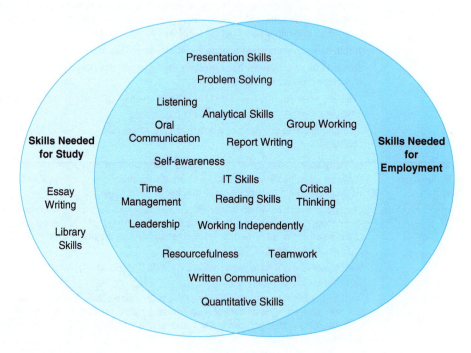

Figure 2.7   Overlap of 'study skills' and 'employability skills'

FINAL REFLECTIONS

Based on the content of this chapter, what do you now know about personal learning that you did not know before?

What key learning point had the most impact? Why?

Do your answers to either of the above questions have the potential to change your attitude to studies at university? If so, why?

(Continued)

(Continued)

Have a look at Donald Clark's webpage on learning and learning styles: www.nwlink.com/~donclark/hrd/styles.html. What does this teach you about the way you prefer to learn and the theory covered above?

━━━━ INTERVIEW QUESTIONS ━━━━

Think about the following questions, which might be asked at a job interview. What might your answers be?

1. How have you changed or tried to develop yourself while at university?
2. What were the most useful and least useful parts of your studies at university?
3. What are your personal strengths and weaknesses in relation to this role?

Chapter 17 gives a lot more information on selection interviews and the online content gives some guidance on these questions.

ADDITIONAL RESOURCES

Want to learn more? Visit https://study.sagepub.com/morgan to gain access to a wide range of online resources, including interactive tests, tasks, further reading and downloads.

Website Resources

University of Bath: www.bath.ac.uk/learningandteaching/enhance-learning-experiences/personal-development-planning.html

University of Bristol: www.bristol.ac.uk/arts/skills/self-evaluation/pdp/

University of Manchester Personal Development Planning: www.humanities.manchester.ac.uk/studyskills/progress/career_planning/PDP.html

Westminster Kingsway College: vle.westking.ac.uk/course/view.php?id=4569

Textbook Resources

Gallagher, K. (2010) *Skills Development for Business and Management Students*. Oxford: Oxford University Press (particularly chapters 1 and 2).

Horn, R. (2012) *The Business Skills Handbook*. London: CIPD (particularly chapter 3).

McMillan, K. and Weyers, J. (2012) *The Study Skills Book* (3rd edition). Harlow: Pearson (particularly chapter 7).

Robbins, S. P. and Hunsaker, P. L. (2003) *Training in Interpersonal Skills*. Upper Saddle River, NJ: Pearson (particularly chapter 2).

Routledge, C. and Carmichael, J. (2007) *Personal Development and Management Skills*. London: CIPD (particularly chapters 2 and 6).

Smale, B. and Fowlie, J. (2009) *How to Succeed at University: An Essential Guide to Academic Skills, Personal Development & Employability*. London: Sage (particularly chapter 2).

Trilling, B. and Fadel, C. (2009) *21st Century Skills: Learning for Life in Our Time*. San Francisco, CA: Jossey-Bass.

PART II
LEARNING HOW TO STUDY

We have presented above an outline of the text, so you should have a rough idea of the content of the next three parts. The first of these looks at your immediate short-term needs – that is, how to study successfully in order to achieve the best grades you can.

In order to make the most of the opportunities for learning that universities give us, a number of skills are needed and so these form the basis of the next few chapters. Chapter 3 examines what is seen by some to be the most important skill to possess whilst being a student – that of Time Management. Chapter 4 provides some insight into what academics call Critical Thinking. We have already said something about the teaching and learning methods used at universities, but we will discuss those in more detail in Chapter 5.

Each chapter will outline why a skill is important and the potential consequences of demonstrating a particular skill – or understanding a particular aspect of university study – poorly.

TIME MANAGEMENT

CHAPTER STRUCTURE

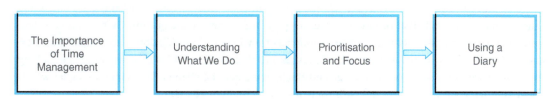

| The Importance of Time Management | → | Understanding What We Do | → | Prioritisation and Focus | → | Using a Diary |

Figure 3.1

When you see the 🌐 this means go to the companion website https://study.sagepub.com/morgan to do a quiz, complete a task, read further or download a template.

AIMS OF THE CHAPTER

By the end of this chapter, you should be able to:

- Assess your time management skills.
- Understand the expectations universities have of the time you spend studying.
- Waste less time and use more of your time productively.

INTRODUCTION

In reality, there is probably no such thing as 'time management'. It is not really something that can be managed or controlled – time is there regardless of what we do, and it ticks away regardless of whether we think we can really 'manage' it or not. We cannot add to it or take away from it – it is a finite resource. What we are really talking about here is *our ability to use our time effectively*.

As we noted in Chapter 2, there is a variety of skills needed for making the most of the academic opportunities you have been given by university study, but this skill is probably the most fundamental – which is why we are looking at this before anything else.

Being a student involves undertaking various tasks: from reading to attending lectures, thinking about subject matter, taking exams, and so on. Successful completion of those tasks requires time – usually a considerable amount of time. Of course, failing to manage our time well could mean that we really do not perform well. We give ourselves insufficient time to read (if we do any at all), do not do any of the seminar exercises, miss a load of lectures and then find that we are really stressed at assignment or examination time because we suddenly realise that we do not know half of what we probably should know (and are perhaps confused about a load of the lecture slides). The worst situation is where 'we are forced' to go without sleep simply to catch up on work we should have done earlier or the day before an important exam – or, worse, we download something from the Internet and submit that because we have not given ourselves enough time. In other words, failing to manage time well will mean that you end up behaving in all sorts of ways that you suspect are wrong – or you continue to do what you have always done, and maybe just about pass your degree.

We will begin the chapter by giving you the opportunity to analyse your skills, and then take some time to examine the role that others' expectations play in the way we use our time. We will then spend some time looking at goal setting – a major influencer on what we do in relation to time management – and apply this to how individuals set goals in relation to their careers. We will spend some time looking at the impact of motivation on time usage and finally conclude the chapter with some principles which could improve your use of time, and with some tools which might be helpful.

SKILLS SELF-ASSESSMENT

It is helpful to note down your reflections on your own abilities (reflection, remember, should be honest and open). It is private, so there is no need to deceive anyone or make yourself out to be better than you really are.

Read carefully each of the following descriptions and say how typical you think each statement is of your behaviour or attitude by giving it a score between 0 and 5, where 0 is 'not at all like me' and 5 is 'very much like me'.

Item number	Item	Score
1.	I get my things ready for the next day's study or work the night before	
2.	I get stressed if I am late	
3.	I rarely plan anything and would prefer just to deal with whatever comes along at the time	

(Continued)

(Continued)

Item number	Item	Score
4.	I get annoyed when I have to wait for others to come to pre-arranged meetings	
5.	I find doing many things at the same time very easy	
6.	I think I need someone else to help organise my life: I always forget what I should be doing or who I should be meeting	
7.	I have been known to lose my keys or my bags quite regularly	
8.	I have and use a diary	
9.	I find waiting for others or waiting for events to start really frustrating: why should I waste time waiting?	
10.	I often plan ahead and think through carefully every possible outcome	
11.	I know what I am doing tomorrow	
12.	I find there is nothing wrong with the excitement of doing everything at the last minute	
13.	If I find something hard, I will try and overcome the difficulties myself rather than ask for help	
14.	I 'live for the moment': tomorrow is another day which will take care of itself	
15.	I am not good at motivating myself over a long time for long projects	
16.	I need others to help me know where I should be and when	
17.	I find it easy to say 'no' to people who invite me for a meal when I have something more important to do	
18.	I probably spend too much time watching TV, playing computer games or chatting to friends online	
19.	I am used to using electronic 'tools' (iPhone, Galaxy Tab, PC, etc.) to organise my life	
20.	I keep a record of things I need to do each day, and tick them off as they get completed	
21.	I believe that only the very best work will do: I need to be proud of what I have done	
22.	I find it easy to begin assignments and essays	
23.	I have all my lecture notes in a pile on my desk or on the floor (or similar)	
24.	I am clear about my goals for this year of study	
25.	I think that studying does not usually take that much time: I have got just a few hours of lectures and tutorials each week	
26.	I have never had two appointments clashing at the same time	

An interactive version of this test along with answers, comments and thoughts about these questions can be found on the companion website for this book at https://study.sagepub.com/morgan.

INTERACTIVE TEST

THE IMPORTANCE OF TIME MANAGEMENT

It is not just for your studies that time management is important. In the workplace, arrive late at an important sales meeting without letting anyone know and you will lose the sale, or miss a deadline for your work and you will probably either miss a scheduled committee meeting or cause others real issues with their work. The implication is that you will be seen as unreliable, a perception that is hard to shake off. It is possible that people will not want to work with you and you might struggle to lead by example (which sometimes means that you will not get the leadership roles you might want in the future).

Being good at time management is vital, crucial, important, and so on, in lots of different ways. For a student, research has shown that 'being good' is more than important (Britton and Tesser, 1991). In fact, research such as that by George et al. (2008) shows a correlation between a student's ability to manage time and their academic success – and in some cases is the most significant predictor. The important questions here are: What does 'being good' mean? How do we measure our skills in this?

 ━━━ KEY LEARNING POINT ━━━━━━━━━━━━━━━━━━━

Learning to manage your ability to use time well will not automatically give you success as a student, but failing to do so well will make passing your courses difficult, if not impossible, to achieve.

DEFINING 'GOOD' TIME MANAGEMENT

Being 'good' can mean a number of things, and our personal values will have some part to play in deciding which definition suits us best. Have a look at those below and see which you like the best:

- Working for as long as possible, every day.
- Ensuring that you have enough time for leisure as well as study.
- Being able to do everything you need to do.
- Working in a way which gives an adrenalin rush, by doing things at the last minute.
- Being able to boast to others about how far in advance you have completed your work.
- A combination of the above.

Whichever definition you prefer, your reaction to some of the others might be one of surprise – how could anyone live their life that way?! But we need to think carefully about the definition we choose. The way we view 'good' time management is going to have a clear impact on what we do, and this will have a definite impact on how others perceive and work with us. Perhaps we can define 'good' time management in this way, as shown here.

 GOOD TIME MANAGEMENT

Good time management is the ability to control our use of time to such an extent that we are able to plan and manage what we do without undue stress or tension.

What we can be sure of is that there are few models in the literature about how to manage our time. There are a large number of good ideas and practices, and one or two frameworks, but little which actually provides an overarching framework on why we go about managing time in the way we do, and that is the reason why the content below may seem a little unstructured.

Either directly or indirectly, everything you do in your studies – and later in your professional and managerial life – will depend to some extent on how good you are at managing your time. Even the way you interact with others will depend on how frustrated and impatient you are, so it is important to get this right, *now*.

UNDERSTANDING WHAT WE DO

There are two possible ways to bring some order into our lives: either to control our lives, or to control what places demands on our lives. As we have already noted, controlling time is not really possible – it continues to move regardless of what we might like – so the only other possibility is that we control our lives. To do this requires that we know what our lives really consist of – and this requires that we develop some kind of job description.

'BUT I HAVE A QUESTION ...'

... I know what is expected of me. I need to attend my lectures, go to meetings with my tutors and prepare for the seminars by doing the work that is set.
If I do that – and revise well – I should pass my courses. Right?

There are a number of other variables and issues to look at as well. What we have listed here is part of what we might call a 'Student's Job Description', a list of what being a student really means, and it is good to do that. But there is more to it, and that is what the rest of this text is about.

FOR YOU TO DO

Before looking at Box 3.1, try the following.
  Make a list of everything you think you will need to do in order to study successfully. In other words, write a kind of job description.

If we look at the job description of a university student, we find a range of activities which need to be undertaken.

BOX 3.1

TYPICAL JOB DESCRIPTION OF A UNIVERSITY STUDENT

- Print out PowerPoint slides and attend and make notes of your lectures
- Attend and contribute to seminars and tutorials
- Complete relevant 'homework'
- Download course notes put online by your tutors
- Contribute to online discussions
- Compare the lecture content with other reading on the same subject/topics

(Continued)

(Continued)

- Complete and make notes on the essential reading
- Meet other students to discuss group work
- Find and make notes on journal and book reading from the library
- Complete required coursework
- Revise for examinations
- Communicate and meet with your tutor(s) as required
- Organise your notes so that they are easy to find and use

These may be similar to the words you listed for the exercise above. Therefore, the two challenging questions are, firstly, how many of these things have you been doing regularly since you started your studies? And, secondly, how much time have you been spending on each of them?

 ━━━ FOR YOU TO DO ━━━━━━━━━━

Using the list you developed for the first exercise above, write down the following *for each activity*:

1. How much time do you think *you are spending* on these activities?
2. How much time do you think *you should be spending* on these activities?

Personality does have a part to play here. If you are a person who is fairly optimistic and happy-go-lucky, your figures for the above are likely to be close and you can consider yourself 'totally sorted' as a human being; if you are more pessimistic, you are likely to see the differences and suffer from a huge explosion of guilt. Neither are perhaps reflective of reality, so let's have something of a reality check.

The importance of keeping a record of how you are using your time cannot be understated: it is one thing to have the idea that you cannot control time, but it is another thing entirely to be unaware of how you are spending your time – which is why the next exercise is so important.

 ━━━ FOR YOU TO DO ━━━━━━━━━━

What do you spend *your* time on?

TEMPLATE

Using the Time Management Log supplied on the companion website at https://study.sagepub.com/morgan use the next seven days to list everything that you do. You can be as detailed or as general as you wish, but remember that you should be trying to answer question 1 from the second exercise above, so make it as detailed as you need to.

Here is some broad guidance. It tends to shock the students I have taught.

You will be studying a number of modules and, as stated in Chapter 1, each one is allocated a number of 'credits' usually depending on how heavy the workload is for the module. Generally speaking, across a number of universities 10 credits would be roughly equal to 100 hours of study (15 credits equal to around 150 hours and so on). Semesters tend to be around 12–14 weeks in length, and each year of your degree will have approximately 120 credits allocated to it, so that means the calculation works out as follows:

1. Each year = 120 credits = 1200 hours of studying
2. Each year = 28 weeks of teaching and examinations
3. 1200 hours over 28 weeks = **42.8 hours a week**

What is that in percentage terms? If a week has 168 hours (7 × 24), then if we are studying we should be spending around 25% of our time on our studies. That is, 25% of *all* our time, including sleeping, eating, relaxing and travelling.

This is similar to the figures that others have come up with. For example, in asking students how they spend their time, Payne and Whittaker (2006) suggested that students spent 27% of their time on study-related activities. (Sleep was calculated at around 33% of students' time.)

This calculation is slightly flawed, however. For example, it assumes that you do no studying at all during the Christmas or Easter vacations (if each is two weeks long, then the figure goes down to 37.5 hours a week) and the notional figure of 100 hours per 10 credits will vary significantly from individual to individual, and from module to module, so the real figure may be less than the 42.8 hours a week given above. What it does mean, however, is that you should be spending something around this figure on your studies each week. If you do not, you might need to think seriously about increasing the amount of time you give to your studies.

Looking at your time log, is that figure of 42 hours a week (roughly 25% of your time) anywhere near the amount of time you spend studying? Or rather, *is the amount of time you spend studying anywhere near 42 hours?*

KEY LEARNING POINT

Understanding how you use your time is critical to knowing how much your behaviour needs to change.

'BUT I HAVE A QUESTION ...'

... I have 12 hours of lectures and tutorials each week and I can do the reading, etc. in another 4 hours or so. I think I am learning and I have a fairly clear understanding of the lecture material once I have read the book as well, so is there something else I should be doing?

Not necessarily, and some people work faster and harder than others. I know that some international students, for example, struggle a lot with the reading and it takes them much, much longer than it would take a native English speaker. But think about how many notes you take when you are doing the reading.

It is a good idea to take notes, otherwise you will forget what you have read. It also reinforces or strengthens the learning as well. Spending time thinking about what you read is a great habit to get into.

KEY LEARNING POINT

Understanding what is expected of you will give you some way of knowing how far away from those expectations you are, and how much you might need to change.

REFLECTION POINT

Take some time to think about the following questions and write down some answers.

When you think about it, how well do you manage your time? Does it match the expectations that others might have?

How do you think your 'job' as a student compares with the 'job description' listed earlier in the chapter? Is there anything missing?

TIP: Maybe find a student from another year and go through this list with them.

If any of the above points have surprised or alarmed you, you might need to do something about improving the way you use your time. One way to improve yourself (as we suggested in Chapter 2) in relation to *any* skill is to evaluate yourself and your progress against some goals. This requires a good understanding of how goal setting should be undertaken.

REFLECTION POINT

Take some time to think about the following questions and write down some answers.

How often do you set goals for your own activities? Or do you just do things because they 'come along'?

If you do not really set goals, why is that?

If you do set goals, do you achieve them? Would you advise someone else to set some goals for themselves?

PRIORITISATION AND FOCUS

The more focused we are in our career goals, the more likely we will be to achieve them simply because we will have directed our efforts towards those things in particular (and because being focused is seen as a strength by most graduate recruiters). However, one of the challenges is in understanding what is meant by being focused (see Box 3.2 below).

BOX 3.2

FOCUS

When we talk about people being 'focused', we mean that they are very clear about what they want and *the goals they want to achieve*. They probably have some good reasons for wanting to achieve those goals and some good ideas about how to achieve them (strategies).

(Continued)

(Continued)

These strategies probably include some activities people *do not* want to undertake as much as the ones they do.

How focused do you think you are? Do you need to have a little more focus in terms of your career goals?

By definition, 'focus' requires that some activities are not undertaken as much as others which are. This brings into play the second of the three time management activities we are looking at here, namely 'prioritisation'.

The argument is that focus is important: Li Na or Roger Federer must have had a strong sense of focus (some call it determination, others persistence) in order to become great tennis players. The same is true for some of the world's most successful business entrepreneurs. It takes focus, determination and a huge amount of persistence to achieve tough goals.

We will talk about priorities and prioritisation shortly. You might decide that you do not wish to be a top-ranked business person or a high-profile individual, and that is fine; it means of course that your priorities will be different. Focus is important for the achievement of tough goals, and it carries some risk. Keeping focused on a particular goal when technology and circumstances around you are changing rapidly and making the achievement of that goal impossible is not clever, and some people cannot see the changes in the external environment because they are *too focused*.

KEY LEARNING POINT

We establish personal career goals – or maybe goals related to our daily lives or over the next year – and we identify what we want to achieve.

PRIORITISATION

Determining our goals, however, is only part of the process. These goals may become more and less important to us as time goes by, so it becomes important to prioritise those things which are important against those which are not. Our priorities can relate as much to our careers as to what we choose to do on a Saturday afternoon.

PRIORITISATION

Prioritisation is the act of deciding which activities to undertake or which goals to aim for at the expense of less important goals and activities.

The issue of prioritisation is as important here as it is for our longer term career goals. In order to complete an essay due next week, for example, we might decide that it is more important to read an extra book chapter than it is to enjoy a meal out with friends. Whenever we use the words 'more important', we are prioritising, whether we realise it or not.

FOR YOU TO DO

Prioritisation

Look at the activities listed below. Some of them are taken from the 'student job description' and others are taken from anecdotes of typical student life.

(Continued)

(Continued)

For the next seven days, decide: (1) which of these are important priorities for you; (2) which you need to leave alone; and (3) which are not priorities but you would like to undertake if you had the time. Label each activity appropriately:

1. Print out the PowerPoint slides for the next lecture.
2. Go to your tutorials.
3. Enjoy a meal out with friends.
4. Go to the local supermarket for food shopping.
5. Complete relevant 'homework'.
6. Go to the bank.
7. Complete the essential reading.
8. Meet with other students to discuss group work.
9. Play some computer games.
10. Go to a meeting of a student club or society.
11. Meet a careers adviser.
12. Make notes on journal and book reading from the library.
13. Complete required coursework.
14. Do your laundry.
15. Revise for examinations.
16. Get a haircut.
17. Play a sport for an hour or two.
18. Download course notes put online by your tutors.
19. Contribute to online discussions.
20. Watch soap operas on TV.
21. Go for a drink in the student bar.
22. Spend time in the library.
23. Compare the lecture content with other reading on the same subject/topics.
24. Communicate and meet with your tutor.
25. Go shopping for clothes.
26. Chat to friends on social media.
27. Organise your notes so that they are easy to find and use.

Now make a list of the things you need to do today, and prioritise them according to their importance and how complex the task is (how long it will take to do, how many others it will involve, how many extra resources you will need, and so on).

TIP: If an activity involves another person (e.g. tutor) or limited resources (e.g. library book), you might need to arrange this before actually having the discussion or obtaining the resources.

The two issues we have discussed above – goal setting and prioritisation – go together. We cannot determine what is important to us without understanding our goals. If we could not define our goals, we would need to decide what we need to do based on other reasons:

- Others (and typically those who are influential in our lives, including managers and parents, sometimes) want us to do these things.
- We want to do these things because we enjoy doing them.
- We do not have anything more important to do.

- There is a crisis and we need to solve it.
- We are bored and we just waste time.

━━━━━━━━━━━━━━ KEY LEARNING POINT ━━━━━━━━━━━━

In identifying our own actions and goals, we need to set priorities. These may change over time as our goals change.

The Time Management Matrix

Developing your time management skills now – as a student – will be invaluable to you in your studies in a number of ways, as we have already seen. As has already been mentioned, being able to demonstrate this skill in the workplace will enhance your standing and personal reputation. Managers and other workers will see you as reliable, and there is nothing worse than an unreliable employee. Therefore, if you replace the word 'coursework' with the words 'business report' or something similar, you can see why good planning is essential in work as well.

In reality, however, both students and managers struggle with planning and time management. In 1989, Stephen Covey developed the 'Time Management Matrix' (Figure 3.2), a tool which illustrated how individuals tended to go about managing their time, using two broad categories – importance and urgency – as a way to differentiate between tasks.

The use of the ideas here has a lot to do with the issue of prioritisation, but brings into focus certain other ideas we mentioned above as well. The two dimensions of urgency and importance are described by Covey as follows:

Urgency: '*Urgent* means it requires immediate attention. It's "Now!" Urgent things act on us.' (1989: 150)

Importance: '*Importance* ... has to do with results. If something is important, it contributes to your mission, your values, your high priority goals.' (1989: 151)

	Urgency	
	High	**Low**
High **Importance**	**1** Crises	**3** Planning
Low	**2** Unscheduled Interruptions	**4** Escapes and Routines

Figure 3.2 Time Management Matrix (Covey, 1989)

The broad idea here is that managers tend to spend their time doing things which fit into one of the four categories listed above:

Crises: Individuals who constantly live their lives dealing with the urgent and important things. The word 'constantly' is deliberate here, since if you are fighting a crisis, you can be fairly sure that you will not have much – if any – time to do the long-term planning that can help to settle things down. Life constantly seems 'on edge' and while the occasional thrill can excite some people, dealing with crises on a constant basis over the long term is not the same as an occasional thrill.

Unscheduled Interruptions: The nature of such interruptions might vary, but if you are paying attention to urgent and not important things then, by definition, it is the urgent things that will get done and the important things will not (perhaps until a crisis occurs).

In terms of an application to student life, some students love interruptions, and it is the interruptions that add variety to a dull life as a student, where 'boring' activities just seem to continue for ever and ever, without any apparent end in sight. However much you might *want* them, though, a continuous stream of friends calling by and distracting you when you have an essay due the next day is probably the last thing you *need*. On a slightly different scale, text messages, social media chats and other similar apps on your phone or iPad can act in a similar way.

Escapes and Routines: Ironically (or maybe not), there is a point of view which says that managers who spend their time fighting crises tend also to be the ones who use 'escapes' more than others. 'Escapes' are those unimportant and non-urgent activities that managers and individuals undertake, such as having a cigarette, sitting in a park, 'vegetating' or watching something unrelated to work (or study) on TV – and they *can* be very big drains on time, even if they do not need to be. Escape activities are those which typically use up very little energy and are not seen in the same way as purposeful leisure activities such as playing sport or hiking to a countryside beauty spot.

The question therefore is: 'Why might those who have crises tend to seek escapes?' Put simply, constant 'firefighting' tends to take energy; it is tiring. Thus, the time spent on 'escape' activities tends to be longer, more noticeable and more relaxing than it might be for other individuals. The problem is that 'escape' activities are not always relaxing, as Box 3.3 demonstrates.

BOX 3.3

ARE HOLIDAYS A TYPE OF 'ESCAPE'?

For many busy managers, finding time to take a holiday can be seen as difficult – and if managers have a family, then the issue can become even more difficult sometimes. For university lecturers, a significant amount of scheduled university vacation time is spent doing research, supervising dissertations or marking assessed work. As a result, finding time to take a holiday is difficult.

In addition, taking a holiday can require a significant amount of coordination. A holiday is usually taken somewhere away from home, so there is at least travel and accommodation to sort out. For other places, there would be currency, visas, flights, what to do/see, suitable diets, and so on. For families, there is a need to arrange specific types of travel and activities for children. Some people love this kind of activity, but agreeing a holiday plan with other people can be challenging for others.

When people get to their destination, there might be a number of things which mean that the holiday is not quite as intended. The weather might be bad, the hotel environment might be smelly or noisy, the

(Continued)

(Continued)

activities may not be as planned – and if you are a pessimist, you would never even think of going on holiday because you can see all the things that can go wrong.

So, the question is: 'Are holidays relaxing and really a kind of escape?'

Planning: The final one of the four quadrants in the model proposed by Covey is that of planning and scheduling. Unlike the previous three quadrants – which reflect *types of activities* – planning and scheduling are activities in themselves. Managers would consider their goals for the day or week, identify the activities they need to do (i.e. develop a 'to do' list) and prioritise in the way we have seen above. The benefits are that there are few crises since things have been planned for and do not surprise anyone and that the relaxation does not need to be found through unintentional escapes: since life is calmer, there is less time wastage.

Covey makes the astute observation that, in reality, few managers really spend their time planning and scheduling, and most time is spent dealing with interruptions or crises. Of course, how many interruptions there are will depend on various factors such as whether the manager has a personal assistant or not and the nature of potential interruptions, and whether there are any crises will depend on the way a manager delegates (if at all), how well any delegation is monitored and the extent to which the nature of the work – and workload – is predictable.

Considering the first sentence above – that little time is spent planning and scheduling, while most time is spent dealing with interruptions or crises – the question that should be there for you is: 'Why is this the case?' We usually have a view of managerial life where managers are intelligent individuals who work in well-resourced offices and have people who behave professionally and get their work done in a calm and logical manner. So, why do they not sit down and plan, if it is such a good idea?

The answer is simple: managerial life is rarely as described above. It can be, but that is not the normal situation. Managers are not always calm, rational human beings who work together in a cooperative manner in well-resourced workplaces, so not everyone will have time to sit down and plan what they will do on any given day or week. Even if they do, they will not always think about doing so, and there are some who would prefer to escape from a crisis than calmly consider and plan how to avoid the next one (i.e. they do not like to plan). Do they need to work on their time management skills? Yes – and probably other skills as well.

To come back to 'important' and 'urgent' for a moment, what Covey is recommending is that we start to rebalance things so that we spend time looking and planning for the 'important' activities: if they are well planned, then they should never become 'urgent'.

REFLECTION POINT

1. Consider what you might typically do on a day-to-day basis. How much time would you typically spend in each of the four quadrants Covey identified?
2. What is preventing you from spending time planning and scheduling your week or day more than you currently do?
3. What could you do to overcome the issue(s) identified in answer to question 2?
4. Think about the tasks you need to do over the next three days. Prioritise them according to their importance. What do you see as being important or urgent?

The above exercise should have helped you to identify and prioritise what you need to do to become more effective at time management. Box 3.4 seeks to address the extent to which over-planning can also cause problems.

BOX 3.4

DANGEROUS FOR YOUR HEALTH: TOO MUCH FOCUS, PRIORITISATION AND PLANNING

Asia is enjoying – or suffering from (whichever way you see it) – a housing boom. Housing developments and apartment blocks are appearing everywhere. In Hong Kong and China, it is common to see scaffolding made from bamboo rather than steel. Why? Hong Kong, China and the South China Sea generally suffer from typhoons and when the wind becomes dangerous, the last thing you want is something that is likely to be hit by the wind and collapse because it is too inflexible. (Bamboo is also significantly cheaper and that may also play a part, admittedly.)

The point being made here is that setting goals, establishing priorities and planning 'with the end in mind' can mean that we are so inflexible that when something unexpected comes along it causes a problem, we are not well equipped to handle it, and we end up missing all our deadlines. Here is a simple example.

A colleague of mine can get to his workplace in seven minutes by car from his driveway to the car park. How long in advance should he leave his home?

If he leaves seven minutes early, he can probably guarantee that he will be late. Why?

There is one simple word there that we need to examine, and another one which is missing. The first word is 'can'. Being able to do something is no guarantee that he 'will' do so. The missing word is 'usually': there can be all sorts of obstacles or problems (e.g. car accidents, traffic lights, heavy rush hour traffic, diversions and road closures, slow-moving cars and buses) which affect his journey on any one particular day.

That is why any plan we make *must* include some contingency time and be sufficiently flexible that we have the time to adapt what we do if we need to. We will look at this further when we come to examine the use of a diary.

USING A DIARY

One tool we can analyse is a diary. Students often have interesting responses to three questions: firstly, whether they have a diary; most say 'no'. Then I ask whether they use a smartphone; most say 'yes'. If you have a smartphone then (by default) you have a diary app on it, but even if you do not, there will be a diary within Microsoft Outlook and on appropriate websites. The third question is then whether they use it; most do not. Therefore, key to this is learning how a diary can assist here. To be fair, trying to manage your time without using a diary is like trying to cut grass with a butter knife – it is difficult, if not impossible.

 KEY LEARNING POINT

As a student, your goal should be to do as well as you can in your studies – this is your priority and should come before other activities.

However, you may be someone with a child, or a part-time employee or with other responsibilities. Your challenge is to decide which of the activities/roles you have are your own personal priorities in the long and short term.

Keeping a diary is remarkably simple – and powerful. There are two issues here: identifying what we have to do; and prioritising them. It works like this. First of all, make a note of the tasks you need to do (e.g. attending lectures, do your reading) and, second, put into your diary the activities you have to do and have no control over (e.g. your lectures or seminar schedules; if you are going to do well in your studies, these two should be non-negotiable). These two steps mean that you have now blocked out the time taken for class. Next, follow the same idea but for activities over which you have more control (e.g. your reading, group discussions, preparing for seminars) and keep on doing this as you identify activities which become less important to your degree.

Three principles are important here: (1) being clear about how much time projects and activities will take; (2) ensuring that there is flexibility in your schedule; and (3) ensuring that you use your plan and stick to it. If you do not know how long the activities will take, you will find them overrunning or taking less time.

If the things you need to do are based around attending lectures and seminars, having group meetings for coursework, completing assignments, and doing appropriate textbook and journal reading, then your diary may look something like the diagrams in Figure 3.3.

When we have entered the things we have to do and the things we want to do, we need to build in some contingency time – there will always be a need for some flexibility.

Abbreviations: Mod, Module; Assign, Assignment; Meetg, Meeting; PT, Part-time; Readg, Reading.

Figure 3.3 Development of a weekly diary

We mentioned that a diary can be a powerful tool. So, why? It helps us to understand what we are doing from day to day, and hour to hour, and if we schedule things well and build in some flexibility, then we will find we meet our deadlines and have a more relaxed life. We will feel more in control of our lives. It is also powerful because it can help us to know when and where there is space for more unusual activities (such as visiting the bank or the dentist).

'BUT I HAVE A QUESTION ...'

... You say that a diary 'can be a powerful tool', but why not say 'it is a powerful tool'?

Because it is about whether and how we use it. It is no good developing a really useful diary and then never using it. Managers use a diary all the time for both short- and long-term activities, but it takes practice and discipline to get used to doing so.

Of course, procrastination can be a huge issue, regardless of how much information is put into a diary. If you put off doing an essay until it becomes essential, then a diary will be of no use and you will find that you are joining between 30% and 60% of undergraduate university students (Rabin et al., 2011) who are able just to hit deadlines and who manage just to avoid printer queues and traffic jams.

We talked earlier about being able to control time. We cannot, but it is much better to be able to manage ourselves than to be controlled by time.

REFLECTION POINT

Take some time to think about the following questions and write down some answers.

Of the ideas listed above, which three ideas could you implement?

1.

2.

3.

Do you ever use a diary (on your phone, a written diary or on your computer)? How do you use it? Does it help you to manage your time?

How will you change the way you manage your time?

ADDITIONAL TIME MANAGEMENT TECHNIQUES

FURTHER
READING
AND
TEMPLATES

To give a comprehensive overview in a short chapter like this is really hard, simply because there are so many issues which could be covered. You can find additional online content on the companion website at https://study.sagepub.com/morgan, providing a great deal more information and ideas relating to motivation and tips for managing your time. There are tips, templates and further online content regarding:

- Planning.
- Setting career goals.

- Goal setting in daily life.
- Gantt charts.
- Motivation and time management.
- Procrastination.
- Additional and practical tips for managing your time (including multitasking, using waiting time usefully, etc.).

Above all, however, keeping a diary and keeping track of how you use time are really at the heart of improvement in your time management skills.

INTEGRATION AND APPLICATION

Learning how to use time most effectively is a skill that takes some time, but we have now looked at some areas we can think about:

Step 1: Analyse how you use your time. There is a time log available online which you can download and use to analyse how much time you spend on different items. If you keep a diary, then analysing how you use your time should probably be fairly straightforward, but if not, then it might be a good idea to think about the last 24 hours.

Step 2: Identify your current priorities. What is important and urgent to you at the present time?

Step 3: Looking at the results of steps 1 and 2, determine whether your time is really being used according to the priorities you currently have. If not, what needs to change?

Step 4: Set yourself some SMART objectives relating to time management to ensure that you have a benchmark against which you can measure your success.

Step 5: Repeat steps 1 to 4 on a regular basis to ensure that you are doing what you need to do.

There are a number of ways we can improve our 'time management' abilities:

- Identify how much better life would be if you were able to control what you do.
- Write down daily goals somewhere where you can see them.
- Reflect on why you might find this skill difficult. Is it prioritising? Is it planning? Is it about identifying personal goals?
- Set reminders on your phone indicating what you have to do and when.
- Buy and use an alarm clock, and set it for a time in line with the tasks you have to get done that day.
- Review your use of time as regularly as possible and see how much improvement you are making.

CONCLUSION

By now, you should have a better idea of how to:

- Assess your time management skills.
- Understand the expectations universities have of the time you spend studying.
- Waste less time and use your time more productively.

There is a great deal more that could be written on this topic. We have only just scratched the surface here, even though it is quite a long chapter. We could talk so much more about the psychology of how personality affects how we engage with tasks in ways that may or may not help us to manage time, and we could talk more about other tools and how to deal with some of the key time wasters. Typing 'managing time' into the UK Amazon site yields more than 660 results, and a similar Google search yields more than 750,000 websites, so there is a wealth of advice and expertise available – some of it useful, some undoubtedly less so. But it is one of the most important skills, both for your studies and for your future life. As mentioned at the start of this chapter, be clear with yourself: be determined *not* to leave assignments to the last minute and to plan carefully within examinations.

FINAL REFLECTIONS

Based on the content of this chapter, what do you now know about time management that you did not know before?

What key learning point had the most impact? Why?

Do your answers to either of the above questions have the potential to change your attitude to studies at university? If so, why?

What will you now do differently? (Write this down and put it somewhere where you can see it regularly.)

Give yourself *two weeks* and complete the skills assessment exercise on pages 50–51. Has your score improved? What else do you need to work on?

 INTERVIEW QUESTIONS

Think about the following questions: what might your answers be?

1. Give an example of a time when you had to balance conflicting priorities. How did you do so? How successful were you?
2. How have you gone about establishing goals and objectives?

Chapter 17 gives a lot more information on selection interviews and the online content gives some guidance on these questions.

ADDITIONAL RESOURCES

 Want to learn more? Visit https://study.sagepub.com/morgan to gain access to a wide range of online resources, including interactive tests, tasks, further reading and downloads.

Website Resources

Kent University: www.kent.ac.uk/careers/sk/time.htm

Learn Higher Centre of Excellence in Teaching and Learning, based on research carried out at the University of Reading in 2005–10, has a good number of additional resources: www.learnhigher.ac.uk/learning-at-university/time-management/

(Continued)

(Continued)

Mindtools Website – The MindTools website has lots of practical tools and resources for time management for you to download and use: www.mindtools.com/pages/main/newMN_HTE.htm

Open University: www2.open.ac.uk/students/skillsforstudy/time-management-skills.php

Skillsyouneed website: www.skillsyouneed.com/learn/study-time.html

Tissington, P. and Orthodoxou, C. – *Study Skills for Business and Management website*: https://uk.sagepub. com/en-gb/eur/study-skills-for-business-and-management/book240110#contents (there are two chapters in this book that could be relevant further reading – 'Planning and Goal Setting' and 'Making Time Work').

University of the West of England (UWE): www1.uwe.ac.uk/students/studysupport/studyskills/timemanagement/timemanagementtutorial.aspx

Textbook Resources

Clayton, M. (2011) *Brilliant Time Management*. Harlow: Prentice-Hall.
Fry, R. (2012) *How to Study* (7th edition). Boston, MA: Cengage.
Gallagher, K. (2010) *Skills Development for Business and Management Students*. Oxford: Oxford University Press. (particularly chapter 4).
Horn, R. (2012) *The Business Skills Handbook*. London: CIPD (particularly chapter 1).
Pettinger, R. and Firth, R. (2001) *Mastering Management Skills*. Basingstoke: Palgrave (particularly chapter 7).
Turner, J. (2002) *How to Study: A Short Introduction*. London: Sage (particularly chapter 3).

4

CRITICAL THINKING

CHAPTER STRUCTURE

Demonstrating Critical Thinking → Providing Credible Evidence → Evaluating the Quality of Evidence → Theoretical Frameworks for Critical Thinking

Figure 4.1

When you see the 🌐 this means go to companion website https://study.sagepub.com/morgan to do a quiz, complete a task, read further or download a template.

━ AIMS OF THE CHAPTER ━

By the end of this chapter, you should be able to:

- Know what lecturers mean when they talk about 'critical thinking'.
- Understand what constitutes a strong and a weak argument.
- Evaluate the arguments that others present to you.
- Evaluate the sources of evidence used to support arguments that you see and hear.

INTRODUCTION

Chapter 1 mentioned that one of the great benefits of having the experience of studying at a university – rather than learning from websites or from textbooks alone – was that university helps you to learn how 'to think'. You may well hear your lecturers talking about the need for 'more critical thinking' in your assignments or in the examination or presentations, and so on, but what does it really mean? And how do you really show that you are 'thinking critically'?

This chapter is going to look at these questions, and others, so that you can develop what is arguably the most important set of skills for your life and career – both at university and beyond. You may already be used to thinking critically but do not know it, or you might be wondering how lecturers and tutors give higher marks for students' academic work. Whichever view you have of the skill, we will be examining what makes the differences which lead to work graded at 50% becoming work that is graded at closer to 70%. It is the main reason why employers value university-educated employees over most of those who have not been through that kind of a system. Developing critical thinking abilities is at the heart of what university education is about – which is why those who think critically are able to get the higher marks.

We will start by trying to define what we mean, but, as we do so, we will get into a discussion about what your lecturers and professors (and, in due course, employers when you graduate) will be looking for in your work and how we develop these skills.

We begin the chapter by providing some details of an influential model of skill demonstration which will likely be used by your lecturers in assessing your work and providing some application of this model to the work you would be likely to do, based around an essay on a fairly standard topic in many business studies degrees. We then look at logic, the qualities of a strong argument and provide some thoughts on how the sources of information can influence the academic credibility of your work. Some ideas on how you might develop these skills were given in Chapter 2.

UNDERSTANDING AND DEFINING CRITICAL THINKING

Perhaps the most obvious answer to 'What is critical thinking?' is to say that it is a form of thinking which is 'critical', where 'critical' is usually taken to mean something that is negative and painful to receive, rather than something that is helpful and that many people would not have spotted or thought about. In reality, 'critical thinking' means both, but it is far

CRITICAL THINKING

Critical thinking is the development and use of information beyond memory and repetition.

more than that. A much better name, perhaps, would be 'insightful thinking', though even lecturers have difficulty defining some of these things. A broad definition is given here.

Your lecturers will know that someone is demonstrating critical thinking when they: (1) can identify gaps, errors, assumptions and weaknesses in others' work; (2) can provide a strong argument for a particular view and taking a particular course of action; and (3) provide a clear and sometimes detailed interpretation of situations and events.

The content of this chapter is designed around these skills, and in a moment we will examine different levels of thinking and the grades associated with work which represents these differing levels. Firstly, however, it is useful to examine how good we might be at what your tutors and lecturers call critical thinking – and we will do this in a slightly different way from the skills assessments in other chapters.

SKILLS SELF-ASSESSMENT

There are various ways of considering your critical thinking abilities. The first way is to consider a piece of information and then answer some questions on it, but an easier method is to look at how often you do certain things with the information you have. Let's do each in turn.

Assessing your thinking

For the former, think about the following three sentences which examine issues of logic and how well we can identify our assumptions, two elements of critical thinking:

'I went on holiday to another country. I generally don't like holidays by the beach. This was a good holiday, though.'

So, now consider the following statements. Which of these statements are:

DT = *Definitely true, based on the information provided?*

PT = *Probably true, based on the information provided?*

UK = *Unknown – the information given does not tell you?*

UT = *Probably untrue, based on the information provided?*

DU = *Definitely untrue, based on the information provided?*

Statements:

1. This was a holiday by the beach.
2. I enjoyed this holiday.
3. I travelled on an airliner.
4. I don't like beach holidays because my skin gets burnt.
5. I needed my passport to get to my holiday.
6. I travelled with my family.
7. I really enjoy holidays away from the beach.
8. I regularly travel to other countries.
9. I needed to change money when I went on holiday.
10. I did not expect this to be a good holiday.

INTERACTIVE TEST

An interactive version of this test along with the answers are given on the companion website at https://study.sagepub.com/morgan, but it is important to think about what we read, hear and see in relation to the assumptions that we make and the extent to which information is as it first appears.

There is one other thing to say about the exercise above, which you may have noticed (or rather which you *should* have noticed) and it is a question: 'What is the difference between definitely and probably?' What one person thinks as 'definite' could be seen as 'probable', depending on how many alternative explanations individuals can identify and how likely these may be. If you did not ask yourself this question, then maybe you need to develop your thinking skills a little further. There is no shame in this; it is something we all need to do.

Assessing Your Behaviour

We can also examine how good we are at critical thinking (or any skill for that matter) by how likely we are to do certain things. So, have a look at the items in the exercise below and identify the extent to which you agree or disagree with the statements listed:

─────── FOR YOU TO DO ───────

TEMPLATE

Look at the statements given below and, for each one, determine whether you agree or disagree with any of the behaviours given below in terms of your typical behaviour. You can find a template of this task to download and use on the companion website at https://study.sagepub.com/morgan.

	Item	Strongly agree (SA)	Agree (A)	Neutral/ not sure (N)	Disagree (D)	Strongly disagree (SD)
1.	I think about whether the lecturer's comments and ideas match my experience					
2.	I consider whether information from others around me is true					
3.	I listen to gossip and generally believe what others tell me					
4.	Whenever I read something I find myself questioning whether it is true					
5.	I find it easy to identify weaknesses in others' arguments					
6.	In discussions with others, I identify issues that no one else has thought about					
7.	When I listen to a lecture, I try to find examples which support or contradict what the lecturer is saying					
8.	If I am reading from a book, I tend to make notes which just summarise what is in the chapter					
9.	I rarely think about 'why' something works as it does					

(Continued)

(Continued)

	Item	Strongly agree (SA)	Agree (A)	Neutral/ not sure (N)	Disagree (D)	Strongly disagree (SD)
10.	I am used to questioning information that others give me					
11.	I make sure that everything I say to other people is backed up by factual evidence					
12.	I generally believe that all information is unreliable					
13.	One or two examples are enough to prove my point					
14.	I believe that if something is said often enough by lots of people, then it is probably true					
15.	My own experience tells me more about the world than textbooks or other' experiences					
16.	When others give me new information, I try to relate it to information I have obtained from other sources on the same issue					
17.	If I am studying a topic for an exam, then I probably won't think about anything except that topic					
18.	If I read the research of two authors who come to different conclusions about the same issue, then one of them has to be wrong					
19.	I can know how good I am at a particular skill by asking my one closest friend					
20.	I know that everything my lecturer tells me is true					

Now, transfer your scores into the scoring key below. Some of the ideas and beliefs/assumptions listed in the exercise above are examples of what we might call critical thinking and others are an example of a lack of critical thinking.

Set A	Please tick if you answered SA or A	Set B	Please tick if you answered SA or A
1.		3.	
2.		8.	
4.		9.	
5.		13.	
6.		14.	
7.		15.	
10.		17.	
11.		18.	
12.		19.	
16.		20.	
TOTAL		TOTAL	

By counting the number of answers in each set, your personal score is: Set A minus Set B. The further away your score is from 0, then the more room for improvement there will be. However, we can all improve our ability to think critically.

DEMONSTRATING CRITICAL THINKING

We will start by looking at the ways in which we need to gather, analyse and use information in order to make sure that any decisions we take or want others to take are actions that will be successful. To do so, we and others need to be persuaded of our arguments – which means they need to be strong. Some of this can stretch our thinking abilities, so beware.

A Strong Argument

What do we mean by 'weak' and 'strong' arguments? The answer has three components:

- The extent to which evidence supporting the argument is provided.
- The quality of that evidence.
- The ease with which contradictory evidence can be provided.

An argument is strong when it is difficult to find any weakness in the comment being given. To take a very simple example, we might suggest that 'Tall people are more intelligent than short people,' and we might support this idea by giving examples of a few tall people who are indeed very intelligent, but it would not be difficult to find many tall people who are not intelligent or to find short people who are intelligent.

Being able to evaluate the strength of an argument (or theory or piece of research) is crucial to academic essays and assignments. For example, let's assume that someone has been set an essay for a module on 'quantitative methods' (i.e. statistics) and is deciding which investigative method to use to find out what people really like to eat at home on a Monday evening.

Let's imagine that we have been asked to address the following research question: 'What do people eat at home on a Monday evening?'

An individual addressing this question needs to be very clear on why they are choosing a particular method to find the answer. If they are not clear or if they have a weak reason for choosing the research method to find the answer, then their essay will likely get a poor mark. In our example, the individual undertaking the research might have decided to interview people and so will need to give a number of reasons (see the next exercise below) as to why they are doing interviews.

 ━━━━━━ FOR YOU TO DO ━━━━━━━━━━━━

Interviews for Food Research

In writing up the work, a student gives the following reasons for using interviews. Which reasons are strong and which are weak? Which are valid (true) and not valid (false)? Rate each of them on a scale of 0 to 10, where 0 is a 'very weak argument' and 10 a 'very strong argument'. You might like to compare your answers with those of other students.

1. Asking questions is easy.
2. There are very few other ways of doing this research accurately.
3. Any other way will cost too much.
4. I can't send out any questionnaires; I don't have enough time.
5. Going through rubbish bags on a Monday night is disgusting and dirty.
6. Going to watch what other people eat so that I can write it down is silly.
7. By conducting interviews, I can get lots of information quickly.
8. I can triangulate the results of the interviews with other data later, but I need to start somewhere.
9. Interviews are quick to do, so I shall do them.
10. I enjoy talking to people.
11. Interviews gather information that is more accurate than questionnaires.
12. Everyone likes to talk, so I can just ask people and get lots of information quickly.

An interactive version of this test along with the answers are on the companion website at https://study.sagepub.com/morgan.

INTERACTIVE
TEST

The more you know about the topic, the easier it will be for you to evaluate the arguments being used. For example, if you are unclear what an interview is, then you will struggle to identify whether some of the above ideas (e.g. 'Asking questions is easy') are true or false. Similarly, you will not be able to identify contradictory evidence unless you understand what evidence you are looking for.

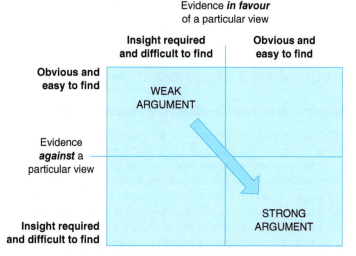

Figure 4.2   Understanding the nature of strong and weak arguments

Figure 4.2 provides a summary of how supporting evidence and contradictory evidence interact with each other to suggest whether an argument is strong or weak. If evidence contradicting a particular point of view (or 'argument' or 'hypothesis') is easy to find or does not require a lot of thinking, then the argument is seen as a weak one. Alternatively, if there is no evidence to contradict the argument being made (and the evidence has been gathered in a valid way), then the argument is seen as being strong. This is why giving examples and presenting evidence become crucial when writing your academic work. Politicians, however, often take advantage of a lack of critical thinking to make relevant points to the media, as shown in Box 4.1 below.

━━━━━━━━━━ BOX 4.1 ━━━━━━━━━━

COMMUNICATION, THE MEDIA AND POLITICIANS

In the UK, it is very common for journalists to question politicians on behalf of the general public. They do so because the public rarely get the kind of access to political leaders that doing so requires. One of the reasons why they do so is to challenge the arguments given by politicians. Government departments (and their civil servants) are very good at producing succinct reports into important issues which would logically lead the reader towards a particular point of view.

Those same reports can also be written in a way to make the reader believe that there is no contradictory evidence to the view being given. It is either discounted on the grounds that the evidence was not sufficiently strong or simply ignored altogether. The same is true with the use of anecdote (a specific example, and thus a form of evidence, though typically seen as very weak) which can be overplayed in order to 'get emotional buy-in' for a particular point of view, especially when people might already believe that same point of view themselves.

No one can argue with a specific example (other than to say that it was misinterpreted), but for every specific example there may be 200 other examples which show the exact opposite. So, politicians might ignore the 200 and focus on the 1 which supports the view they wish to discuss.

Question:

Do you agree with what is written here? Why, or why not? What evidence have I presented?

Ensuring that you develop strong arguments for the points you raise in your coursework and in your examinations is crucial.

 'BUT I HAVE A QUESTION ...'

... So is this an important skill to develop – identifying and evaluating arguments?

These are probably the most important skills you will develop. For assignments, this will enable you to get the higher level marks and demonstrate your ability to evaluate and analyse.

Employment in a management role works like this. When you get into work, you will need to be a member of a team, taking part in team discussions, leading others sometimes perhaps, deciding on ways to solve particular problems. If you are unable to evaluate the arguments that others come up with, then you could easily be misled or, worse, be encouraged to do something that is morally wrong or even illegal.

Even if we think we know what is right and wrong, working life can make things more complex.

Imagine that you are very open and honest, and prefer to play by the rules.

Someone comes up to you and says, 'I've found a way of motivating the staff: we can give our team an extra day off,' and you say, 'But HR says that we can't do that: it would open the floodgates to others wanting the same thing and would go against the contract we have with them.' Then the person says, 'But nobody would find out and it would create a really good atmosphere. Besides, you know how people feel about HR: you could blame HR for being inflexible and it would reduce their popularity even further.'

What would you do? Would you argue with the person on the grounds that it is wrong (in which case they would accuse you of being inflexible and say that you were not very popular), or would you accept their argument and gain popularity with your own team? The answer would depend on whether we think their arguments are strong or weak

Of course, management is not about being popular – it is about doing the right thing at the right time in the right way. So, we could say that their argument is a weak one.

If so, then we can dismiss them and make our own decisions, but unless we take time to think about the arguments and gather the evidence, then we might simply accept what others tell us. A great deal of management and achieving results is about developing your thinking.

This brings us back to the three areas noted above: (1) the provision of evidence which supports the argument; (2) the quality of that evidence; and (3) the provision of evidence contradicting the argument. An argument that has no evidence to support or contradict it simply becomes little more than gossip, so we need to ensure that we use some credible sources of information on which to base our arguments. This issue became significant during one UK episode of *The Apprentice* – see Box 4.2 below.

BOX 4.2

THE APPRENTICE: CALENDARS AND CATS

During an episode of *The Apprentice* screened on BBC TV in 2007, two teams had to raise money for a children's hospital (Great Ormond Street Hospital in London) by designing and selling calendars, so the question arose as to the nature of any photographs used in the calendar.

One team, 'Velocity', carried out research into what helped to sell calendars, discovering that the most popular calendars contained pictures of pets, so many of the team decided to use pictures of cats and dogs,

(Continued)

(Continued)

with the argument: 'People won't be buying this because it goes to Great Ormond Street: they'll be buying it because it's got pictures of kittens in there.'

One member vigorously disagreed, however, saying, 'To my mind, we should have some feel in there about what Great Ormond Street says, yeah? You know, I was thinking about getting in contact with some of the kids who have survived from there and we should sell some stories!'

Which argument was the stronger? How would you evaluate the arguments?

In the end, Velocity lost the task. One of the individuals that they were trying to persuade to buy their calendars noted, 'I don't really understand why it is a children's charity and a bunch of cats. I don't really understand how one is representing the other.'

The team that sold the most calendars used pictures of children in their calendar.

PROVIDING CREDIBLE EVIDENCE

Arguably, the most important aspect of providing credible evidence is determining the credibility of the sources that have been used. Using sources of information that have little credibility is going to weaken your own argument.

The next question arising from this is 'What makes a source of information credible from an academic viewpoint?' This question is central to what we mean by 'critical thinking'.

CREDIBILITY

'Credibility' refers to how believable a source of information (or the person delivering that information) appears to be, based on how easy it is to identify opposing arguments.

FOR YOU TO DO

Look at the various sources of information listed below. Rank them in terms of their credibility. Which ones are the most credible and which are the least credible?

- Wikipedia
- Textbooks
- Study guides (i.e. short booklets about the essentials you need to know, typically brief and with bullet points)
- Discussions with tutors
- Journal articles
- TV – 'factual'/documentary/news
- Rumours and opinions

- Lectures
- Discussions with other students
- Common sense
- Popular magazines
- Discussions with business leaders
- Blogs
- TV – 'popular' programmes
- Comments on Facebook, Weibo, etc.

In answering this question, you should be led to the question 'What defines credibility?' Put simply, there is a variety of ideas which constitute credibility. Figure 4.3 gives some ideas.

Of course, identifying what is a 'fact' and what is an 'opinion' is not straightforward: facts – even if numerical – can be misinterpreted or attempts can be made to discredit statistics. People can give their own interpretation of facts based on personal desires, as Box 4.3 suggests.

Qualities of Good sources

- Authenticity
- Validity
- Currently revelent
- Reliable
- Samples
- Few generalisations
- Facts, but not opinions

Figure 4.3 Qualities of good sources of information

━━━━━━━━━ ▪ BOX 4.3 ▪ ━━━━━━━━━

RUMOUR, FACT AND SPECULATION

Any group of people acting together is likely to have among their number those who operate by gossip. A nation will have a set of media which may or may not be controlled for the purposes of particular individuals; an organisation will likely have those who operate politically and who may invent stories of what others have done for their own purposes; a manager may need to manage those who dislike their approaches to solving business problems and who may try to sabotage any actions being taken through rumour and speculation.

If your university studies are intended to teach you to think critically, how might you – as a manager – deal with such a rumour if you hear it?

If the gossip is important to you or the organisation or to someone you have to manage, then the correct thing to do would probably be to gather factual evidence. To accept something as true just because someone with good interpersonal skills or a national newspaper says that it is true is to turn off your ability to think critically. If the gossip is not important to you or there is no evidence for what is being said, then it can be ignored or put to the back of the mind.

The same, though, goes for the quality of evidence that you gather. If the evidence is from the same source as gave rise to a rumour in the first place, then that is clearly going to be biased in favour of the gossip that the source has given to you. Gathering information from a variety of sources is vital: this is called 'triangulation'. Regardless, separating fact from rumour can be hard and take time.

Of course, good management means that you do not just think critically, you also need to develop plans to manage activity so as to motivate others and bring them on board with what it is that you wish to do – or to modify such plans accordingly.

Listening to rumour can be useful, but it can be disastrous if not thought through critically.

━━

FURTHER READING

The ranking from most credible to least credible should probably look something like Table 4.1. More detail on why the ranking is given in this way and how to ensure our argument is of 'good' quality is provided on the companion website at https://study.sagepub.com/morgan.

As a future manager, you will be expected to make a judgement about what is credible and what is not, which takes us back to Box 4.3 listing sources of information and determining how credible each is. Some thoughts are given on the companion website, but even with the most credible sources and detailed statistics, there is always room for a little uncertainty. So, in the face of all of this, how can you be 100% sure that the sources you are using are definitive and factually correct? The simple answer is that you cannot.

Table 4.1 Ranking of credible sources

• Journal articles • Textbooks • Lectures • Discussions with tutors • Discussions with business leaders • TV – 'factual'/documentary/news • Study guides (i.e. short booklets about the essentials you need to know, typically brief and with bullet points)	• Discussions with other students • Wikipedia • Common sense • Popular magazines • TV – 'popular' programmes • Blogs • Comments on Facebook, Weibo, etc. • Rumours and opinions

'BUT I HAVE A QUESTION…'

… You said that we cannot be 100% sure?

If you thought that you had come to university to learn facts and to learn how to do what we wish to do, then that is true to some extent, but developing our thinking skills is really important.

The statistics in published articles mean that we can be pretty certain that ideas and theories established through statistical analyses are as true and complete as they can be, but the statistics are based on the probability of things being true, and if this probability is high enough and proved often enough, then the interpretation is that something is true (or, to speak literally, it is highly probable that the interpretation is true).

So there is no certainty that something is absolutely true, just very high probabilities.

This idea might be alarming, since you might have come to university wanting to learn some definite knowledge. In all areas of academic life (which includes subjects such as economics, politics, business studies and psychology), theories and ideas are constantly being evaluated and re-evaluated, which is why undertaking research in the social sciences is both exciting and challenging.

However, working on academic assignments and essays is all about ensuring that the quality of evidence is good. In practice, this means that as long as the information is gathered well, analysed well and reported accurately, the information should be credible, and the *more sources of information that say the same thing, the more something is going to be seen as 'true' and 'fact'*.

KEY LEARNING POINT

Gathering accurate information from a number of sources is key to building up a body of evidence which suggests that some idea or theory is 'true'.

EVALUATING THE QUALITY OF EVIDENCE

Once evidence is provided (and the more evidence there is, the better), the task is then to ensure that your essay uses the strongest evidence and logic that it can to persuade others that your point of view is correct. The issue of having the 'strongest evidence' is particularly important where objective truth and reality can be difficult to find, as discussed in Box 4.4 on the next page.

━━━━━━━━━━━━━━ **BOX 4.4** ━━━━━━━━━━━━━━

BEYOND CORRECT AND INCORRECT

You are going to be studying a number of different subjects and modules within your degree. These modules will require different skills, and some may emphasise concepts or ideas (e.g. economics, psychology, accounting) while others will want to make sure that you can apply particular methods (accounting, operations management, statistics) to various situations.

But many of your modules will be looking for you to justify the actions you have taken and to give a reason why you have done things the way you have done them. It is this justification that enables your lecturers to see how you are developing and using your critical thinking skills.

The implication of this is that your mark is going to have a lot more to do with whether you can provide good evidence to justify your viewpoint than with whether you give the lecturer what you think might be the correct answer.

This is particularly hard for some students who come to the UK from certain overseas educational backgrounds. In some countries, students can receive marks easily for giving back to the lecturer the information that the lecturer has given them (i.e. knowledge) without a great deal of that information being processed or thought about.

It can be a shock when a piece of coursework comes back with a mark of 50% when the student has given everything back to the lecturer that was provided in the lectures and expected to receive a mark of 70%. In the lecturer's mind, the assignment may not have given sufficient evidence to support the arguments being made or may not have added any value to the lecturer's material by doing any outside reading. Academic work is about demonstrating your own thinking and argument, it is not just about being 'correct' or 'incorrect'.

───

 ━━━━━ **KEY LEARNING POINT** ━━━━━━━━━━━

Identifying assumptions and strengths/weaknesses in arguments from others and yourself is important in ensuring that those arguments are credible and based on good evidence.

───

 ━━━━━ **REFLECTION POINT** ━━━━━━━━━━━━

Take some time to think about the following questions and write down some answers.

Which sources of information (including friends) do you use each day? How accurate is that information likely to be? Are there any reasons why you think the information may not be accurate or necessarily true?

Think about the last interview you watched (online or on TV). Do you think the interviewee was telling the truth? Why or why not?

How might the information in this chapter help you when you are writing essays or submitting coursework?

───

THEORETICAL FRAMEWORKS FOR CRITICAL THINKING

Most – if not all – of your lecturers will have been trained to think critically (or insightfully). Some of that training will have occurred during their own university education, either as part of their PhD training or before, and some will have developed the skills needed as part of writing their own research papers for academic journals. We will look at the development of these skills, but however your lecturers have developed these skills, they will be expecting you to demonstrate the skills as well – and will be marking your work against them.

Understanding Bloom's Taxonomy

Perhaps the most often cited work on critical thinking was developed by Benjamin Bloom and colleagues, and is known by lecturers as 'Bloom's taxonomy' (Bloom et al., 1956). It is seen as a hierarchical set of skills by which work is typically assessed. The hierarchical view is given in Figure 4.4.

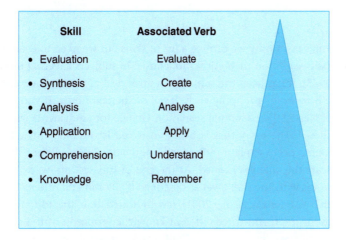

Figure 4.4   Bloom's taxonomy of academic skills

The essential thinking here is that students who demonstrate the skills at the lower end of the hierarchy will tend to do poorly in their assignments.

For example, reproducing knowledge does not require a high level of skill or any understanding of what is being presented, it simply requires a good memory.

On the other hand, and at the other end of the scale, it is impossible to evaluate ideas unless you can understand them.

There is some appreciation of the value of the model, though some discussion as to whether analysis, synthesis and evaluation are quite as hierarchical as has been suggested (Anderson et al., 2001). This latter point will be explored below (see page 82), but the pyramid given in Figure 4.4 implies that fewer students will be receiving marks at the higher end of the hierarchy and, broadly speaking, this does reflect the smaller number of students which typically graduate with a first-class honours.

'BUT I HAVE A QUESTION ...'

... Does that mean that if we demonstrate the higher levels of skill, then we will do well in our work? Or is length of work important as well?

Actually, length is no guarantee of any academic success. Your tutors may have marked essays that are one page long and have passed – admittedly only a slight pass – but perhaps also marked essays six sides long and which basically said the same thing over and over again, and received a fail mark. Having said that, an essay which is too short will usually contain insufficient detail and comment to do well. So, while length is not directly assessed, it does play a part.

The language we use plays a part and we have to get the content right, of course. But critical thinking skills are more important than content. In fact, if you reproduce in your essay all the relevant content from your lecture *and* your reading, then perhaps the maximum you can expect will be around the 50% mark in many places. It is evidence of the critical thinking which then lifts that 50% to a higher mark – and the amount and depth/level of that thinking which takes it beyond 60%. Those skills are detailed in Bloom's work, which is applied below.

When we look at Bloom's taxonomy we can see a list of skills but we need to examine each one. To do so, we will look at a fairly common theoretical model used in subjects covering motivation – Maslow's Hierarchy of Needs (1943). It has been the subject of a great deal of critique over the years, but we can use it to demonstrate how we might apply each 'level' of the taxonomy. If you are not familiar with Maslow's Hierarchy of Needs, then a simple search on Google (or equivalent) will take you to a basic introduction of the model. The essay that is being answered is the following: 'To what extent does Maslow's theory of human needs explain individuals' motivation?' We will not show the whole essay, just a portion to indicate the changes needed. At the end of this section, we will try to see if we can match the question words with the skill level as described by Bloom and others.

More recent research (Anderson et al., 2001) has indicated that the top three levels – Analysis, Synthesis and Evaluation – represent three different knowledge concepts at the same level rather than three different levels. Therefore, it might be helpful to note that the ways that your tutors use these abilities might vary in terms of the marks that you receive.

NOTE

A word of caution about the essay below. Portions of the essay have been written with just one purpose in mind: to give you, as a student, an illustration of what the different skills look like when written in an essay.

The information contained in the essay is partially made up – that is, in parts, the content is not true or accurate.

Due to this inaccurate content, do *not* reproduce any of what is written below in any essay you write.

Level 1: Knowledge

The first level of Bloom's taxonomy is demonstrated by reproducing knowledge. There are some cultures and environments where the reproduction of knowledge is what defines educational success (and which might include certain results for pre-university exams), but that is not what will help you get good marks at university. The reproduction of knowledge simply takes a good memory – you do not even have to understand what you are talking about in an essay to show 'knowledge'.

So, in Box 4.5 is a portion of an essay which shows just basic knowledge.

=== BOX 4.5 ===

MASLOW'S THEORY OF NEEDS – KNOWLEDGE

'To what extent does Maslow's theory of human needs explain individuals' motivation?'

Maslow (1943) developed a theory about human motivation following research done in the United States. His theory – known as the Hierarchy of Needs – gives a number of hierarchical levels to explain motivation. This essay will outline those needs and will show how his model helps to explain why people want to do what they want to do.

Firstly, there are physiological needs, for example food and drink and physical health. Secondly, there is safety and security, but Maslow said we are only motivated to fulfil all our safety needs when we have fulfilled our physiological ones. Thirdly, there is a sense of belonging with other people. Fourthly, we have esteem needs and then, finally, we are motivated to achieve our self-actualisation needs.

Typically, lecturers at university level will rarely expect you solely to demonstrate your ability to remember or reproduce knowledge; the exceptions might be some or all of your first-year modules. Questions at this level tend to be in the form 'Who did this?' or 'List the main factors ...' Often, demonstrating solely the recall of knowledge might enable a student to receive a maximum mark in the mid-40s to low 50s when it comes to grades, but nothing much more than that.

Level 2: Understanding/Comprehension

The second hierarchical level relates to an ability to explain something to another person, in other words to understand the ideas. There is a fairly clear hierarchical link here with level 1: it is impossible to explain something unless you know what you are explaining.

The relevant portion of the Maslow essay might go something as shown in Box 4.6. The additional content showing understanding has been put into bold text.

=== BOX 4.6 ===

MASLOW'S THEORY OF NEEDS – UNDERSTANDING

'To what extent does Maslow's theory of human needs explain individuals' motivation?'

Maslow (1943) developed a theory about human motivation following research done in the United States. His theory – known as the Hierarchy of Needs – gives a number of hierarchical levels to explain motivation. This essay will outline those needs and will show how his model helps to explain why people want to do what they want to do.

(Continued)

(Continued)

Maslow's theory – called the Hierarchy of Needs – sets out a number of levels around which motivation takes place. The basic concept that Maslow had was to indicate that in order to reach the next level of motivation, the previous level would need to be satisfied.

The first level relates to physiological needs. These are needs of food and drink and physical health **as well as sex and sleep. They are put at the bottom of the hierarchy because everyone will want to have these needs met**. The second level relates to safety and security – **which means we are secure in our situation,** but we are only motivated to fulfil all our safety needs when we have fulfilled our physiological ones.

There is some explanation here, and the student has clearly understood something of what they have been taught. Questions at this level will ask students to explain an idea or summarise a theory. Again, marks will not necessarily be particularly high at university simply for understanding the ideas, nor will these questions usually be used on their own for courses much beyond first-year degree studies, but marks will typically be higher than for students who merely reproduce what they have been given.

Level 3: Application

If you know what you are writing about and are sure that you have understood the main ideas, then the next stop is to do what your lecturers will do during classes. That is, providing and using examples to show that not only do you have a solid understanding of the concepts and ideas covered, but also you can provide examples of their working. Box 4.7 takes us back to the Maslow essay. Again, additional content demonstrating 'Application' has been emboldened.

■■■■ BOX 4.7 ■■■■

MASLOW'S THEORY OF NEEDS – APPLICATION

'To what extent does Maslow's theory of human needs explain individuals' motivation?'

Maslow (1943) developed a theory about human motivation following research done in the United States. His theory – known as the Hierarchy of Needs – gives a number of hierarchical levels to explain motivation. This essay will outline those needs and will show how his model helps to explain why people want to do what they want to do.

Maslow's theory – called the Hierarchy of Needs – sets out a number of levels around which motivation takes place. The basic concept that Maslow had was to indicate that in order to reach the next level of motivation, the previous level would need to be satisfied. **Some examples are given below.**

The first level relates to physiological needs. These are needs of food and drink and physical health as well as sex and sleep, **so, for example, when someone is struggling to find food, they will look hard for it.** The second level relates to safety and security – which means we are secure in our situation, but we are only motivated to fulfil all our safety needs when we have fulfilled our physiological ones, **so, for example, someone will search for a safe place to live, once they are sure they have enough food to eat. Workers at Foxconn are strongly motivated by this, according to Purcell (2001).**

You can see that most of the additional content here relates to examples, which is essentially what we mean by application: you demonstrate your ability to apply your understanding (i.e. knowledge + understanding) by providing examples of how the ideas work in practice.

It is worth noting that the Maslow essay is getting longer as we put more information into it, but the information we have added has not mentioned any new theories, it has simply applied Maslow's ideas to workplace practice. If we kept the length the same and just added more theories, then the depth would suffer and each extra sentences would give us diminishing returns.

The marks given to an essay demonstrating 'Application' in many institutions may reach the mid 60s and questions expecting the demonstrating of 'application skills' would often be found for questions across all three or four years of a degree.

Level 4: Analysis

As indicated earlier (see page 82) in relation to 'Analysis' and the remaining two 'higher level skills', there is some debate as to whether they are seen as hierarchical or equal (in terms of cognitive or thinking skills). In any event, we are talking about three different kinds of skills anyway. Analysis asks the question 'Why do things happen as they do?'

 **'BUT I HAVE A QUESTION ...'**

... You mean that analysis is all about asking 'why'? For example, why do leaders sometimes have success and at other times, don't?

Yes, that's exactly what I mean. Asking why means that we have to have a pretty decent understanding of how the ideas work; then the next question is why they work like that. You can't ask why until you know the how.

If we start to ask questions about 'why' things work the way they do (and children can sometimes be very good at asking those kinds of questions!), then we can start to consider what might happen if we change things and see if we can do things a little more creatively. This goes beyond 'Analysis' and starts getting us into skills of synthesis. Box 4.8 gives a portion of the essay on Maslow's Theory of Motivation.

BOX 4.8

MASLOW'S THEORY OF NEEDS - ANALYSIS

'To what extent does Maslow's theory of human needs explain individuals' motivation?'

Maslow (1943) developed a theory about human motivation following research done in the United States. His theory - known as the Hierarchy of Needs - gives a number of hierarchical levels to explain motivation. This essay will outline those needs and will show how his model helps to explain why people want to do what they want to do.

Maslow's theory - called the Hierarchy of Needs - sets out a number of levels around which motivation takes place. The basic concept that Maslow had was to indicate that in order to reach the next level of motivation, the previous level would need to be satisfied. Some examples are given below.

The first level relates to physiological needs. These are needs of food and drink and physical health as well as sex and sleep, so, for example, when someone is struggling to find food, they will look hard for it. **This level was seen by Maslow as the most basic because without such biological needs being fulfilled, there would be no individual to motivate anyway (Johnson, 2003).** The second level relates to safety and security - which means we are secure in our situation, but we are only motivated to fulfil all our safety needs when we have

(Continued)

(Continued)

fulfilled our physiological ones, so, for example, someone will search for a safe place to live, once they are sure they have enough food to eat. Workers at Foxconn are strongly motivated by this, according to Purcell (2001). **This is because a feeling of contentment and personal security is seen by most employees at work as being less important than the search for food, or need for sleep or drink etc. (McKenna, 2002).**

[The remainder of the essay would be changed in a similar way.]

The emboldened sections of the text above represent answers to the question 'Why is this important?' or 'Why does something work in this way?' and that is at the core of this skill we call 'Analysis'.

I hope that you can see the differences in this essay as we start to show higher levels of thinking about the ideas, rather than simply reproducing them. Work demonstrating such skills could receive marks in the low to high 60s, depending on whether the relevant content was there, whether the citations were accurately done and whether the structure was clear and made sense.

Level 5: Synthesis/Create

We will keep the idea of a hierarchy – and the 1956 hierarchy of skill – for the moment as we examine the penultimate skill, namely that of synthesis. The verb attached to this skill is called 'create', so it may seem a little strange to have the verb 'create' and a skill which is not called 'creativity'. Hopefully you will understand why as I explain what I mean here.

'Synthesis' is the ability to understand how one topic that is studied in a module fits into a much larger picture and, by doing so, you demonstrate that you understand not only how this one topic works and why it works as it does, but also how it influences and is influenced by other issues. From an HRM or organisational behaviour viewpoint, we might look at human behaviour and motivation but then seek to understand how these issues are affected by organisational culture and structure as well as by other factors which might have been studied throughout the course.

The reason why 'create' is there as the associated verb is that once we can see relationships between ideas and why things happen as they do, then we can see what happens when such relationships between business practices, for example, change; it is through this kind of analysis that we can then start to be much more creative. There are many ways of representing such relationships when you are preparing for assignments or trying to solve organisational issues, the most obvious (for note-taking purposes) being the mind-map, where central themes are separated out into smaller and smaller ideas. In management development, however, some trainers use practical tools such as Lego® to enable participants to represent physically how their organisation is structured and functions (see Chapter 14, on Creativity and Problem Solving).

Let's add some synthesis to our essay on Maslow (Box 4.9).

===== BOX 4.9 =====

MASLOW'S THEORY OF NEEDS – SYNTHESIS

'To what extent does Maslow's theory of human needs explain individuals' motivation?'

Maslow (1943) developed a theory about human motivation following research done in the United States. His theory – known as the Hierarchy of Needs – gives a number of hierarchical levels to explain motivation.

(Continued)

(Continued)

This essay will outline those needs and will show how his model helps to explain why people want to do what they want to do.

Maslow's theory – called the Hierarchy of Needs – sets out a number of levels around which motivation takes place. The basic concept that Maslow had was to indicate that in order to reach the next level of motivation, the previous level would need to be satisfied. Some examples are given below.

The first level relates to physiological needs. These are needs of food and drink and physical health as well as sex and sleep, so, for example, when someone is struggling to find food, they will look hard for it. This level was seen by Maslow as the most basic because without such biological needs being fulfilled, there would be no individual to motivate anyway (Johnson, 2003). **It could be possible that certain physiological needs may be more important at different times as some individuals seem to need less sleep than others, of course, and some may wish to abstain from fulfilling certain physiological needs from time to time (e.g. Ramadan).**

The second level relates to safety and security – which means we are secure in our situation, but, according to Maslow, we are only motivated to fulfil all our safety needs when we have fulfilled our physiological ones, so, for example, someone will search for a safe place to live, once they are sure they have enough food to eat. Workers at Foxconn are strongly motivated by this, according to Purcell (2001). This is because a feeling of contentment and personal security is seen by most employees at work as being less important than the search for food, or need for sleep or drink etc. (McKenna, 2002). **The importance or nature of this need may vary in the same way that physiological needs may vary: job security may be seen as irrelevant to someone whose need for a place to stay is as much of an issue. It is also possible that individuals may feel content in certain aspects of their lives (e.g. at home) but insecure in other situations (e.g. at work): in such a situation, the individual might seek another job, perhaps, but this issue also applies to the third need – that of belonging.**

The value of such ideas is enhanced by recognising that Herzberg's (1959) findings include some similar ideas. The fact that safety is included in Herzberg's model – and even the naming by Herzberg of such ideas as 'hygiene' factors – goes some way to showing that such factors do indeed have an impact on motivation. It is possible to then argue that organisational cultures which seem to place less emphasis on safety might be seen as struggling to motivate their employees.

[The remainder of the essay would be changed in a similar way.]

You can see here how the ideas have been developed and how additional concepts have now been brought into the debate. There is an additional theory (Herzberg) that has been introduced to the reader and has been compared with Maslow's ideas. The question did not ask about this additional theory, but the student writing the answer has gone beyond the ideas of Maslow and has shown how additional theories have relevance.

The second thing that has happened is that additional concepts have been introduced, namely organisational culture and personality theory. The student has shown how these issues also have relevance here and, by doing this, has demonstrated that they have not only a good understanding of the question, but also an ability to understand how additional topics studied throughout the course are also relevant.

This does not mean that a student can talk at length about these additional topics, though. One mistake that students make at examination time is to write about a topic that is only slightly relevant, perhaps because they have studied that particular topic.

If a student demonstrated the ability to synthesise information and wrote well (with good structure, appropriate evidence, good academic style and examples), then marks could well extend into the 70s.

Level 6: Evaluation

In an academic context, 'to evaluate' means 'to identify whether arguments, facts and information are true, untrue or unclear', and this is seen as one of the most important – if not the most important – skill to demonstrate.

Whether or not this item is equal in standing to those of synthesis and analysis, the original hierarchy had this at the top and it was thus seen as the most worthwhile skill to demonstrate. It is at this level that we demonstrate the ability to comment on the research work that others have done, and identify areas of argument that others might have missed. To do so takes an insightful mind which has a deep understanding of the issues and has spent a little time thinking about what the research evidence really says. That is why students who demonstrate this skill are seen as 'first-class' students. But, in some ways, the task is clear: to know and identify why certain research says one thing and similar pieces of research carried out in other situations come to different conclusions. The realisation of this, however, is not so easy.

Let's go back to the Maslow essay one last time to see what this looks like in practice (Box 4.10). As we have added information in order to demonstrate the skills we are focusing on, the essay has become longer. This may therefore take a little time, but you can see what we have added.

━━━━━━━━━━━━━ ■ BOX 4.10 ■ ━━━━━━━━━━━━━

MASLOW'S THEORY OF NEEDS – EVALUATION

'To what extent does Maslow's theory of human needs explain individuals' motivation?'

Maslow (1943) developed a theory about human motivation following research done in the United States. His theory – known as the Hierarchy of Needs – gives a number of hierarchical levels to explain motivation. This essay will outline those needs and will show how his model helps to explain why people want to do what they want to do.

Maslow's theory – called the Hierarchy of Needs – sets out a number of levels around which motivation takes place. The basic concept that Maslow had was to indicate that in order to reach the next level of motivation, the previous level would need to be satisfied. Some examples are given below.

The first level relates to physiological needs. These are needs of food and drink and physical health as well as sex and sleep, so, for example, when someone is struggling to find food, they will look hard for it. This level was seen by Maslow as the most basic because without such biological needs being fulfilled, there would be no individual to motivate anyway (Johnson, 2003). It could be possible that certain physiological needs may be more important at different times as some individuals seem to be able to need less sleep than others, of course, and some may wish to abstain from fulfilling certain physiological needs from time to time (e.g. Ramadan).

The second level relates to safety and security – which means we are secure in our situation, but, according to Maslow, we are only motivated to fulfil all our safety needs when we have fulfilled our physiological ones, so, for example, someone will search for a safe place to live, once they are sure they have enough food to eat. Workers at Foxconn are strongly motivated by this, according to Purcell (2001). This is because a feeling of contentment and personal security is seen by most employees at work as being less important than the search for food, or need for sleep or drink etc. (McKenna, 2002). The importance or nature of this need may vary in the same way that physiological needs may vary: job security may be seen as irrelevant to someone whose need for a place to stay is as much of an issue. It is also possible that individuals may feel content in certain aspects of their lives (e.g. at home) but insecure in other situations (e.g. at work): in such a situation, the individual might seek another job, perhaps, but this issue also applies to the third need – that of belonging.

The value of such ideas is enhanced by recognising that Herzberg's (1959) findings include some similar ideas. Of course, there has been criticism of Herzberg's model in the same way that there has been criticism

(Continued)

(Continued)

of Maslow's ideas, but the fact that safety - and even the naming by Herzberg of such ideas as 'hygiene' factors - goes some way to showing that such factors do indeed have an impact on motivation. It is possible to then argue that organisational cultures which seem to place less emphasis on safety might be seen as struggling to motivate their employees.

Of course, cross-cultural research into collectivism (Hofstede, 1979) casts some doubt over the extent to which Maslow's findings regarding the first two layers of the hierarchy can be seen as valid. There are some concerns about the extent to which his research was separated from the time and place where the research has been done. Such research suggests, for example, that in certain collectivist societies, the needs of the country might come before the needs of any one particular individual (Thompson, 2008). Certain professions (e.g. army, fire) clearly ask individuals to put themselves into potentially dangerous situations, so whilst Maslow's ideas seem to have some relevance in certain places, there are times and situations where other factors seem to be at work.

[The remainder of the essay would be changed in a similar way.]

We can see here that the additional text presents some insightful and detailed comments which assist us to evaluate whether Maslow's ideas have some validity. Evaluation is – as is noted above – a complex and high-level skill, requiring a detailed understanding of the literature on a particular subject. That is why those demonstrating this skill get the highest marks, and deservedly so.

KEY LEARNING POINT

The quality of your assignments will be based upon the extent to which you show you have a competent and solid grasp of the content, and the extent to which you demonstrate the academic skills associated with critical thinking.

REFLECTION POINT

Take some time to think about the following questions and write down some answers.

How does the writing here in the essays on Maslow differ from the kinds of work you have been used to writing? Think of three or four differences, if possible, but try not to think of physical qualities such as length.

1.

2.

3.

Which of the six levels given above typically represent the kind of work you might usually produce? Do you think it will be easy for you to demonstrate all the skills here, including level 6? What do you need to do in order to include evaluative material in your essays and work?

INTEGRATION AND APPLICATION

As suggested at the start of this chapter, being able to think critically is essential in ensuring that you can do well in your degree, but also in your career and life. The above sections have given you some idea of what critical thinking is and some exercises to start assessing and developing those skills.

The real development of these skills, though, comes through practice and debate. So, below are some ideas that you might like to think about using to develop these skills:

- Join a debating society (or begin one if there is not one at your department or university). You will be forced to think through and evaluate your arguments and ideas in order to win the debates.
- Watch or listen to the news and try to evaluate whether the views of the journalists or those they are interviewing (e.g. politicians, organisational leaders) actually reflect reality. Is there any evidence they are missing, any assumptions they are making or any information they are misinterpreting?
- When you meet with classmates for a group assignment, think about the comments they are making in order to complete the group assignment. Are they correct in their assumptions about what the tutor is looking for? Do they have evidence to support the arguments and ideas that they give?
- Take some articles from different newspapers about a recent national news issue and discuss it with some other students. Take some time to check whether the evidence is good or whether there are other explanations for what has been reported. Do the articles agree? If not, how do they disagree? And why might they disagree?
- Ask a tutor if you can have 30 minutes of their time to discuss something you have covered in their module. See if you can have a good discussion about that subject and prepare by reading two or three relevant journal articles on the subject first. Does your tutor have the same views as those of the authors whose work you have read on the subject?
- Take one popular topic that you hear others talking about (or read others' comments on Facebook or another social networking source). What do you think about that topic? Is your thinking based upon any evidence or just an uninformed opinion?
- If you can, get involved in a law society on campus (if your university has a law course). The society might hold debates which you could listen to or join. Debates are important for developing thinking and testing out arguments.
- Arrange to discuss an issue with friends. Give them the chance to say whether they agree or disagree with a particular point of view and then take the opposite viewpoint – the role of 'devil's advocate' – in order to develop your abilities to think quickly of counter-arguments.
- Identify where what is written in the example essay in this chapter is different (more analytical) than what you might naturally write.
- When the results from another essay are available, find someone who has a better mark than you and ask to see their assignment to see what they did differently.
- As you read, take notes about what you are reading, but make sure you: (1) think carefully about what you are reading, by asking questions about why an author is writing what they are writing and whether it make sense; and (2) write down your thoughts so that you can think about them later and use them in your writing.
- Discuss what you have been reading with friends. Do they think it makes sense? Is there anything they notice about what you have been reading that you have missed?

This is one of the most important sets of skills that you can develop, which is why it is given so much importance in terms of your degree.

CONCLUSION

By now, you should be able to:

- Know what lecturers mean when they talk about 'critical thinking'.
- Understand what constitutes a strong and a weak argument.
- Evaluate the arguments that others present to you.
- Evaluate the sources of evidence used to support arguments that you see and hear.

This chapter has given you some illustrations of what critical thinking means in practice and has explained why this is important in both your studies and your career. It has looked at the skills identified as important by Bloom, moving from a relatively unskilled position of being able to recall and describe information to skills involving the synthesis and evaluation of information.

It has also examined the qualities of credible evidence and the need to ensure that, in academic work, good-quality evidence is provided to support the arguments being made. We have looked at what is meant by good-quality evidence and how evidence can be challenged according to the logic and assumptions being made. Finally, the chapter has identified some actions which can be taken in order to develop this set of skills.

FINAL REFLECTIONS

Based on the content of this chapter, what do you now know about critical thinking that you did not know before?

What key learning point had the most impact? Why?

Do your answers to either of the above questions have the potential to change your attitude to studies at university? If so, why?

What will you now do differently? (Write this down and put it where you can see it regularly.)

Give yourself *two weeks* and complete the skills assessment exercises on pages 70–73. Have your scores improved? What else do you need to work on?

━━━━━━━━━━ INTERVIEW QUESTIONS ━━━━━━━

Because of the nature of critical thinking, the ability to think carefully and quickly can be determined by any question. For example, if we take the answer to one of the questions in Chapter 1, 'Why did you choose the university and course that you have been studying on?', we can imagine that the clarity of thought, the use of information and the ability to evaluate information quickly all combine to produce a reasonable answer. However, if an employer did think that additional questions were needed, they might develop the questions below.

(Continued)

(Continued)

What might your answers be?

1. Imagine that you are in charge of a government department. The employees in that department want you to achieve one thing, the public want you to achieve something else, and you personally believe that the right thing to do is one that neither group have thought about. What would you do?
2. What do you think are the most challenging problems facing society today? Do you think there are any ways to solve them?*

(* Or an interviewer could ask a very similar question, based around one specific problem, i.e. 'Thinking about [a current affairs issue], how would you go about proposing a solution?')

Chapter 17 gives a lot more information on selection interviews, though employers would be more interested in how you deal with these questions and give your answer than with the actual answer you give.

ADDITIONAL RESOURCES

Want to learn more? Visit https://study.sagepub.com/morgan to gain access to a wide range of online resources, including interactive tests, tasks, further reading and downloads.

Website Resources

How to Study website: www.how-to-study.com/study-skills-articles/critical-thinking.asp

University of Bolton website: www.bolton.ac.uk/bissto/Study-Skills/Critical-Thinking.aspx

University of Sheffield website: www.sheffield.ac.uk/ssid/301/tash/everyday/core/thinking

University of Worcester website: www.worcester.ac.uk/studyskills/645.htm

Textbook Resources

Bailey, S. (2011) *Academic Writing for International Students of Business*. Abingdon: Routledge (particularly part 1.2).
Fisher, A. (2011) *Critical Thinking: An Introduction* (2nd edition). Cambridge: Cambridge University Press.
Horn, R. (2012) *The Business Skills Handbook* London: CIPD (particularly chapters 10 and 11).
Kaye, S. M. (2012) *Critical Thinking*. Oxford: Oneworld.
Metcalfe, M. (2006) *Reading Critically at University*. London: Sage.

5

TEACHING METHODS AT UNIVERSITY

CHAPTER STRUCTURE

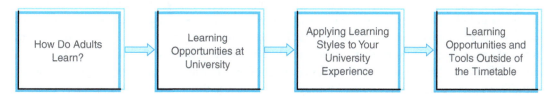

| How Do Adults Learn? | Learning Opportunities at University | Applying Learning Styles to Your University Experience | Learning Opportunities and Tools Outside of the Timetable |

Figure 5.1

When you see the 🌐 this means go to the companion website https://study.sagepub.com/morgan to do a quiz, complete a task, read further or download a template.

━ AIMS OF THE CHAPTER ━

By the end of this chapter, you should be able to:

- Describe the ways in which your lecturers and professors will help and expect you to learn at university.
- Understand what is meant by 'independent learning'.
- Use time outside of the classroom to study effectively.

INTRODUCTION

The methods used to help you learn at your university may be different to those you have come across before. If they are, then that has implications for what you do and the extent to which you will succeed in your studies. Chapter 3 on time management showed you that there are various activities which can occupy your time, but the question is always how to balance social activities with your academic responsibilities. This text will try to help you with that through this chapter. It will also try to help you 'see into the mind' of your lecturers, so that you can understandwhat their expectations might be and examine what is meant by 'independent study'. The chapter is not going to cover every possible opportunity for learning used in every university – and cannot do so – but it will cover the main methods of facilitating your learning used in the social sciences.

It is important to note that this chapter (on learning) and those in Part III (on assessment) are linked: the feedback you get from the assessment of one module or piece of work should get you to think about what you did well and not so well – and every occasion for assessing your thinking is an occasion for developing your work. This applies to everything we might do in class, from giving a presentation to making a verbal contribution during a class discussion, so it is difficult to separate opportunities for learning from those for assessment.. The link between receiving feedback and learning may not always be clear to you as a student completing a number of what often appear to be separate modules, but it will be there in the mind of your lecturers and they will expect you to develop your skills based upon the feedback from assessed work.

There is just one additional comment to make about terminology before we get into the chapter properly (every introduction should define the terms used before moving on to the main body): 'teaching' is about 'information transfer' together with a touch of inspiration. It is usually passive from your perspective, as a student, and is something that is *done to you*. 'Learning', covered in Chapter 2, is the result of your engagement with that information. Some academics would rather call themselves 'facilitators of learning' rather than 'teachers'. This emphasises their role as someone who 'helps you to learn' rather than just teaches. That can occur through their feedback, through giving you things to read and through asking you questions.

Chapter 1 gave you some information about the ways that university operates and how the language and culture might vary from experiences you have had before. This chapter adds to that introduction by giving you background on how the learning works, and needs to be read alongside Chapter 2 on learning and self-development. If you have never studied at university before, this chapter explains how university can help you to learn, but if you have studied at a UK university before, then this chapter will help you to deepen your learning.

The chapter will begin by giving you an opportunity to consider your own understanding of how learning at university works, before providing and applying three models of adult learning which impact on practices at university and affect how activities are scheduled and timetabled. The chapter will then examine how learning can occur through more informal, unscheduled activities and will specifically look at study groups as a means for enhancing learning. The final exercise in the chapter will ask you to consider how you might apply the ideas covered in it to your own learning.

 TEACHING

Teaching is what a lecturer or teacher or professor *does to you* as a student or learner by giving you information. A lecturer teaches. A lecture is one situation where that information is given to you.

We will spend some time looking at the ways in which universities provide opportunities for you to learn and give some suggestions on how best to use those opportunities. We will use the words 'learning opportunity' to refer to any activity or event that can be used for learning – a list which is nearly infinite, of course.

SKILLS SELF-ASSESSMENT

Since this chapter is largely about learning at university, the self-assessment exercise here is more about your *knowledge* (what you *know*, rather than what you can *do*).

Have a look at the various learning opportunities listed below. Which of these have you experienced before?

- Lectures
- Seminars or tutorials
- Written coursework assignments
- Reading academic journals
- Receiving feedback on your work
- Discussing your learning with other students
- Doing some practical research
- Thinking through a case study

- Completing a group project
- Developing a presentation
- Being asked to reflect on your own experiences of a topic in a module
- Reading a chapter of a textbook
- Completing questionnaires about yourself
- Using a course or textbook website
- Asking a lecturer for help

Now rank each one in terms of their importance to your learning, with 1 being what you think is the most important and 10 the least important.

Comments and thoughts about these questions can be found on the companion website for this book at https://study.sagepub.com/morgan. The exercise above does not necessarily have any right or wrong answers, but should start to get you thinking about the many activities which can help your learning whilst at university. It is really an exercise developed just to get you to identify those learning opportunities used at university that you may have experienced previously. There is no such thing as a complete list: anything which stimulates your thinking – especially your reflection – can help you to learn. However, let's look at some of the most common aspects of learning at university, and how you can use and engage with each of them in ways that will really help your learning. We will start by looking at how adults tend to learn, then give some insight regarding the various activities you will probably undertake as a student, and then try to apply those to the learning styles covered immediately below.

TASK

HOW DO ADULTS LEARN?

We covered issues of skill development in Chapter 2 and Bloom's ideas about critical thinking in Chapter 4, but as we saw in the latter chapter learning has many different components and levels. We start this chapter by examining how individuals at university learn, and we do that in different ways. We will look at three models, beginning with one developed by Peter Honey and Alan Mumford, based on Kolb's learning cycle (see Chapter 2 for more details), a second one looking at how we take in information, and a third based on research into study behaviour.

It is worth noting that there are differences between the ways that adults learn and children at school learn, and if you are on a postgraduate course, then those differences should be very evident. The first refers to a teacher-led process called 'pedagogy', where the teacher is seen as 'the expert' and the learner is there to take in information and subsequently use it. The second is a process which expects more engagement on the part of the learner and is called 'andragogy', where the prior experience and thinking of the adult is used to refine, evaluate and analyse information given to them by a 'facilitator of learning'. Both models referred to below relate to the second of these processes.

Honey and Mumford's Learning Styles

Honey and Mumford (1992) identified that different people have innate learning preferences, and their model of learning styles relates closely to each of the four stages noted in Chapter 2 in relation to Kolb's thinking, though with slightly different labels (see Figure 5.2).

Research conducted by Honey and Mumford suggests that some people are better at learning from experience (Activists), others better from learning by reflection (Reflectors), others by developing their own ideas about how the world works and preferring theoretical input (Theorists), and finally some individuals prefer to take information, plan for the future and ask 'what if?' (Pragmatists). The authors argue, though, that few individuals are definitely one or another and that in reality we learn in a variety of ways depending on the learning opportunities we are offered.

The 'typical' characteristics possessed by each of the four learner 'types' – *preferences* is a much better word – are as follows, though because we possess a main preference, our overall engagement in learning is dependent upon a mixture of the four preferences (as well as the way that any tutor tries to engage you):

Activists will tend to thrive on the immediate. They will be reluctant to spend a great deal of time thinking about what they do and will rarely take time to think through how well they did and why.

Reflectors will tend to be cautious and careful in what they do. They will collect a great deal of information before arriving at any decisions or making judgements, and in a group discussion they will prefer to listen to others' contributions before making their own views known.

Theorists will tend to be highly logical and systematic in what they do. There will be evidence of a perfectionist attitude and they like to use information to build logical models of the world around them that they will defend rigorously when challenged.

Pragmatists will tend to be as energetic as activists, but will prefer to test already-formulated ideas. Their keyword might be experimentation, and, typically, pragmatists will jump at the chance to try out ideas in the real world.

Figure 5.2   Learning styles as developed by Honey and Mumford (1992)

VA(R)K Learning Styles

This model of learning styles was developed in the early 1990s by Fleming and Mills (1992). The basic idea is that the way we take in information can differ from individual to individual, with some learning through hearing (Auditory), others through what they see (Visual, Verbal), some through reading (Reading/Writing) and others through actively touching and experiencing or using information (Kinaesthetic).

Fleming and Baume (2006) argue that it is not strictly a learning styles questionnaire but more a communications questionnaire which should be used for learning rather than solely recreation. The model itself has more to do with whether you, as a student, can engage with the way you are taught and whether you learn most from your lectures and tutorials than through the development of personal skills, but common sense might suggest that trying to learn skills without any input (whether auditory, visual, read/write or kinaesthetic) is unlikely to succeed.

BOX 5.1

'RIGHT-BRAINED' AND 'LEFT-BRAINED'

Until recently, it was a common belief that our educational achievements and processing of information depended strongly on whether we were 'right-brained' or 'left-brained'. The idea became a popular and simple way to understand why some people had more of an artistic side than others, and why some seemed to be more analytical than others. It was suggested that right-brained individuals would be better able to show creativity and lateral thinking, while those who were left-brained were seen as more analytical.

The ideas translated into behaviours such as note taking: those who were left-brained would be more likely to write their notes as bullet points and remember mnemonics, while those who were right-brained might use colour and draw mind-maps.

However, research by Nielsen and colleagues at the University of Utah (Nielsen et al., 2013), cited by the American Psychological Association and published in the freely accessible journal PLoS One (plosone.org), seems to cast significant doubt over this model. It appears that the brain is a much more complex than simply dividing it by hemisphere. 'It's absolutely true that some brain functions occur in one or the other side of the brain,' Anderson – one of the authors of the paper – reports. 'Language tends to be on the left, attention more on the right. But people don't tend to have a stronger left- or right-sided brain network' (www.apa.org, 2013).

On a more philosophical basis, the idea does find a willing audience, with those who are seeking a simple way of understanding how the world operates, regardless of what research actually indicates about the complexity of reality.

Which would you – as a student or as a future manager – prefer to use: a simple model that may not actually be proven through research, or a more complex model that is difficult to apply but bears a stronger reflection of reality?

Deep and Surface Learning

While some have examined learning styles (which deal with the psychological factors affecting our preferences for learning, in the same way that our psychology often affects how emotional we are as human beings), others have taken an approach which looks much more widely at the impact that both our psychology and sociological factors have on how students engage with their learning in academic settings. The latter has led to the powerful concept of an 'approach to learning'.

In the mid-1970s, Marton and Säljö (1976) identified two major approaches that individuals took to their learning. Rather than being a purely psychological analysis, this model suggested that there were two broad approaches that students at university were taking to their studies – either a surface approach or a deep approach. A surface approach might describe a set of behaviours and attitudes where an individual would not necessarily be interested in what they are learning, would focus on memorisation and would principally do what was needed to pass a course and little more. A deep approach, on the other hand, would show itself through a student who was doing extra reading, really seeking to understand what they were being asked to learn and would think critically about the information they were taking in. Their motivation will be much stronger than that of the surface learner and they will usually learn for the enjoyment of learning. In terms of the amount of time spent on studies, therefore, a student adopting a surface approach would probably get the work done as quickly as possible, while the student adopting a deep approach would spend a great deal of time – and perhaps more than was expected – examining the research on a particular topic.

The outcomes of these two approaches are quite different, and you might wish to review the Maslow essay given in Chapter 4 to see these differences clearly. The student adopting a surface approach is likely to produce an essay that is 'OK', contains the basic information, but does not show a detailed grasp of the reading or an understanding of how additional factors may influence how successful individuals are in business (for example). If you examine the information regarding Bloom's taxonomy given in Chapter 4, you will see that such an essay probably demonstrates the main facts (knowledge), some understanding of the main concepts (understanding) and perhaps some examples (application).

The student adopting a deep approach to learning is likely to produce something which shows a great deal more thinking, as you might expect. The amount of reading that has been undertaken will be greater, the understanding will be significantly deeper and, as the reading has been done, the student will have taken time to develop questions in their mind about what they are reading. When it comes to assessment, this will enable the student to demonstrate much more analysis (why things are happening), to evaluate what they are reading (Bloom's 'evaluation' level – after all, how can you demonstrate evaluation if you are not actually doing any reading?) and to understand how this theory fits into a wider picture (synthesis). As a result, the marks are typically higher.

There is a third approach that some educational researchers have referred to: the 'strategic approach'. Here the behaviour is similar to that of the deep learner, but the motivational drivers are different. The strategic learner will study hard, do a significant amount of reading over and above expectations, and seem interested in the subject, but the motivation here is to do well in assessment rather than learning simply because learning is a great thing to do. Their focus is solely on doing well in assessment and so, for examinations, strategic learners will spend a great deal of time question spotting and preparing for a limited number of topics. Similarly, in assignments, a strategic learner will concentrate on the particular topic at hand and demonstrate the higher levels of Bloom's taxonomy in their work. Their understanding and thinking around the entire subject will likely be limited, but they may none the less do well if their focus is the right one. (The risk in an examination may be that it will not be, of course.)

Many of your lecturers will think that a surface approach to learning is less helpful than deep learning, and the question often asked, therefore, is: 'Are you a surface learner or a deep learner?' The reality is a little more complex than that, however. Some individuals will be either one or the other for all their subjects and all their years of study, but rarely will the lecturing style of your lecturers (or assessment approach of your modules) have no impact on your motivation. In addition, there are some rare occasions where a surface approach can be useful (e.g. when there is a lot to read and some of that reading may be less useful than other parts) but, in general, a deeper approach does tend to lead to higher marks as laid out in earlier chapters.

LEARNING OPPORTUNITIES AT UNIVERSITY
How Does the University Help You to Learn?

There are, of course, several answers to this question. You have probably had the first lecture and some kind of student induction. You will almost certainly have had a student handbook and you might have been given some work to do before you arrived at university, but what are the other ways that universities facilitate your learning and development? We will provide a very brief outline here which covers some of the teaching and learning methods used, and then discuss how best to engage with those opportunities, but we will start with a very brief overview of two key concepts.

Teaching and learning tools

There is a variety of mechanisms by which you will be gaining knowledge at university. Some of them are inductive and some are deductive (information on this can be found online on the companion website, but, basically, deductive learning usually occurs when you learn from what someone has told you, and inductive learning takes place when you discover something for yourself by making conclusions based on what you see). These include some or all of those listed in Table 5.1 (and more).

Table 5.1 Teaching and learning opportunities commonly given at university

Opportunity	Typical description	Potential relationship to your learning and development
Lectures (deductive)	One-way presentations around an hour in length. Could include examples of how ideas have been used, theoretical models, concepts which are important for the course	Good for introducing you to relevant knowledge
Seminars (partially deductive, partially inductive)	Small to medium-sized groups (maybe 20-30 students) discussing the application of course material with a tutor for around an hour. Usually includes discussion, interaction, maybe student presentations and requires some reading and preparation on the part of the student	Good for ensuring your understanding of key ideas. Checks your ability to apply theories introduced elsewhere. Develops your communication/discussion skills
Tutorials (partially deductive, partially inductive)	Very small group (maybe 1-6 students) opportunity to discuss specific learning and research with others and a tutor, through examining personal reading and thinking. Has more widely been used at universities as a means of supporting students pastorally	Develops ability to debate and defend your ideas. Develops your own thinking. Forces students to read and engage with relevant theories/literature. Where used pastorally, ensures that skill development and career planning are taking place
Independent reading and research (largely deductive, partially inductive; depends on what you are reading)	Lists of relevant reading - books, journal articles, online resources, handouts, etc. - are produced at the start of modules and some reading materials may be posted online. Generally, students not doing any reading would be in danger of not knowing enough to pass the course assessment	Develops time management skills. Develops understanding of a broader knowledge base than given in a lecture. Enables the development of thinking skills

(Continued)

Table 5.1 (Continued)

Opportunity	Typical description	Potential relationship to your learning and development
Virtual learning environment (largely deductive, unless using blogs)	A collection of materials, announcements, often some interactive resources and other tools to enhance your learning. The idea is that you regularly (weekly as a minimum) review what is there and engage in the learning opportunities given to you	Develops time management skills. Develops understanding of a broader knowledge base than given in a lecture. Enables the development of thinking skills

This is a very brief list and is not – by any means – an exhaustive one. Different lecturers and different universities will have different practices and activities to enhance your learning, but it gives a general overview at the start of your university experience. We will also cover two further 'learning opportunities': namely, the meaning and role of 'feedback' and the role of 'study groups'. It is important, therefore, to know how to use these opportunities.

Benefitting from University-Provided Learning Opportunities

We will start with the most common situation, that of the lecture.

Lectures

Let's assume you have been through induction and are 'enjoying' your first week of lectures. Have a look at the next exercise below. Do any of these ideas relate to actions you have been taking before your lectures?

 ━━━━ FOR YOU TO DO ━━━━━━━━━━━

Preparing for a lecture

Which of the following actions do you usually take before attending a lecture?

- Read the relevant chapter from the textbook
- Download and/or print out the lecture slides
- Look through any lecture slides
- Ensure that you know how the lecture topic fits into other topics that you have studied
- Discuss any lecture slides with other students
- Look for some additional reading on the same subject
- Check that you understand the meanings of any technical terms
- Check that you have some way to take notes of what was said

If you have never been to a lecture before, then be aware that people react very differently to being asked to sit still for an hour or longer and listen to someone talk about a subject related to your area of study. But if you are reading this, you should be thinking: 'We haven't yet defined what we're talking about.'

(A good point. We will come to the importance of providing definitions later on when we talk about assessment and assignments.) Defining any experience with clarity and in detail is actually not easy, principally because everyone's experience will probably be slightly different and lecturers may have very different styles and deliver their material in different ways, so we are forced to be quite general.

This does not mean that a lecture will be just one way, or that a lecturer will not engage in some kind of discussion during the class, or ask you some questions to consider. Lecturers will display information on a screen (I know this is getting quite basic, but stay with me here) and may use videos, quizzes and other media to enable you to remember and understand the information they present in an active way. Some lecturers may use multiple choice answer pads (commonly known as 'clickers') to enable you to answer questions during the lecture.

Some people enjoy them, others find them boring, and there will likely be a lot of variation between the styles of different lecturers. But whatever your own reaction to them, it is certainly true that attending a lecture is unlike many other situations outside of academic life (the exception might be attending church or a formal speech, possibly).

WHAT IS A 'LECTURE'?

A lecture is a class where a tutor will give information regarding an academic subject. Often this will be a one-way delivery of information, lasting about an hour.

The best lecturers will be those who really try to engage with you, to inspire and excite you, and this makes attending the lecture an enjoyable experience. Of course, some lecturers are better at it than others (we are not all good at everything) but, hopefully, most of those you have to listen to will have been lecturing for some time and will have some good examples and stories to tell.

We have already said that the lecturing styles of different lecturers can be very different. Sometimes this is dependent on the lecturer's personality and sometimes it is dependent on the size of the class. It is a lot easier to have a discussion and learn from other students in a smaller class, but the purposes of a lecture are often a little different from those in a small class. At a minimum, a lecture is intended *to give you information*, and only a lecture can engage, excite and motivate you in your studies, and get you thinking about the subjects you are studying. A lecture will probably also help you to set some boundaries to the limits of your reading and enable you to get a quick overview of the subject matter.

'BUT I HAVE A QUESTION ...'

... Does attendance at lectures really matter?

Yes. Attendance is the easy part, even though some students do not consider it necessary to attend lectures (and they are wrong about that). It is fine to turn up to a lecture, but engaging with a lecture and its content is the important part. Most universities will have rules about attendance, and these can particularly impact on students from overseas, who will have requirements about attendance given to them as part of their UK study visa.

You can get notes from your friends, of course, but then you are relying on the quality of those notes, how easy they are to read or understand, and you could miss out on the emphasis given by the lecturer to certain issues and words.

But the key point is that you 'engage with' information provided by your lecturers. 'Engage with' means to consider carefully the information, to think about something, to get involved with something. If you engage with lecture content, for example, you will be considering it, reading around it, deciding whether you agree with it, looking for evidence that confirms or denies what your lecturer was telling you.

(Continued)

(Continued)

Does that mean you have the right to disagree with your lecturers? Yes, of course – but politely. Start a debate with your lecturer and discuss the evidence. That is what active learning is all about. It makes learning much more interesting and gives you a much wider viewpoint than just the view of your lecturer.

We looked at this in Chapter 4, so get used to evaluating what your lecturers are telling you: apply the information, analyse it, compare it with other issues you have covered on a course. That is what university studies are all about. It is a bit like the difference between taking some nice food and quickly swallowing it, and taking the same food, chewing it, enjoying its flavour and then swallowing it. The second is far more rewarding and better reflects what you should be doing with the content of your lectures.

The information in this 'But I Have a Question ...' section above gives you some good indication of how most UK lecturers think and what they expect you to do. In addition, it makes learning at university far more interesting than simply attending lectures and spending all your time listening to what your lecturers will be saying. As noted above, you need to engage with your lectures, not just listen to them.

So how should you do this? This is an important question. There are the obvious issues, for example take a printout of lecture slides with you or a copy on your laptop or tablet; make sure you make some notes you can read some weeks after the lecture has finished; do not talk unless the lecturer asks you to do so and do not look at Facebook or other websites when the lecture is taking place; and turn off your phone. There are, however, some slightly less obvious and more subtle issues to consider. Table 5.2 lists some of these additional issues.

Table 5.2 Getting the maximum benefit from your lectures

1. Make sure you do the appropriate reading both before and after the lecture. This will help to ensure you understand any technical terms used during the lecture
2. Do not write down everything that your lecturer says – most of the key points will be on a PowerPoint or similar. Do write down examples or ideas that are not written on the slides
3. Find a way of abbreviating frequently used words (in business studies, these might be words like 'organisation' or 'consumer demand')
4. Review the slides from the previous week before going into the next lecture. Some subjects (especially mathematical ones or languages) are cumulative, i.e. if you did not understand the earlier week, you will find it even more difficult to understand the next week
5. Contact the tutor as soon as possible if there was something you did not understand
6. Use what was covered in the lecture as a framework for additional reading

It may sound somewhat surprising, but a lecturer cannot give you all the information you need about a particular topic. An hour or even two are insufficient for most lecturers to tell you everything that you should know. There may be a seminar for every lecture, but the purpose of the seminar is not to cover additional content, it is – as we will see – to give you and your tutor the chance to check your understanding and application of what has been studied, not to cover new material.

So, how can you ensure that you do get all the information you need? The answer is simple: by doing the reading prescribed for you. The online material covers reading in much more depth, but the impact of that reading will depend on the quality of your note taking during the lecture and then the time you take to consider and evaluate what the lecturer was telling you.

Of course, it is not just in lectures that you need to be good at taking notes. Different people work in different ways. Notes should also be taken from any reading you do, from group discussions or meetings you have, from seminars and from discussions with course tutors. Any situation where learning can occur is a situation where notes may need to be taken.

══════════ KEY LEARNING POINT ══════════

It is helpful to understand how important note taking is during lectures. Without taking notes, we will miss a great deal of what is said during the lecture.

Seminars and tutorials

While seminars and tutorials are listed separately above, the reality is that, in many universities, these two words are used interchangeably. Originally (when there were few universities and few university students), tutorials were occasions for a tutor (professor or lecturer) and maybe no more than six students to meet to discuss a topic or a piece of research, or to review a piece of work that one or more of the students had done. As such, tutorials are fantastic opportunities to receive almost personal coaching in how to think and how to conduct research.

These small tutorials do take place in some environments where there are few students, but many universities do not have the small numbers of students required to run such tutorials, and departments offer their students seminars alongside the subject-based lectures.

If the lecture is the place where you learn information (perhaps for the first time, if you have not done the reading ahead of the lecture), then the seminar is the place where you (and your lecturers) can check whether you understand well the ideas presented and can *apply that learning* to examples. Typically, a seminar will run with between 20 and 30 students and so should be a lot more interactive than a much larger lecture. It will be expected that you have done the reading and any exercises you have been set, and you may well be asked to show your work or give a presentation about your work or something which relates to the topic of previous lectures.

Benefitting from a seminar

There are some important guidelines about how seminars work, but the keyword here is 'interactive', and there are two issues:

1. If you contribute nothing to the seminar, then neither you nor your lecturer will be able to see whether you really understand what was taught. You might think that is fine, but imagine going into an examination not really sure of your own understanding.
2. You might feel sure of your own understanding, but you could just be incorrect or wrong.

Seminars are intended to be interactive so that you have a chance to get feedback on your thinking, that is you can receive some evaluation on whether your ideas are correct. Do not be frightened, then, of contributing your ideas, even if culturally that may seem strange (see Box 5.2 on the next page), you need to check that your understanding is correct. Saying nothing may leave you with the impression that you *do understand* something when actually your understanding is incorrect, and in an exam this can be disastrous.

■■■■■■■■ **BOX 5.2** ■■■■■■■■

CULTURE AND INTERACTION

When discussing culture, it is very dangerous to stereotype, since there will always be an exception to the rule, but classrooms in some countries are often very one-way experiences – even at school. Middle and high school students in China are usually expected to stand up and give an answer to a question only when the teacher asks that particular student. The classroom can be seen as formal and not necessarily a place where pupils are expected to have a great deal of fun.

The culture often enforces this. Chinese – and other 'Confucian Heritage' – cultures are frequently hierarchical, with a strong degree of what some call 'power-distance'. In the past this meant that the teacher is at the top of the hierarchy and cannot be questioned, so relations between schoolchildren and their teachers are not as friendly as those in other cultures.

When Chinese students enter university in China, there is often little change and those previous experiences impact on students' behaviour in the university. Class monitors may take the register on behalf of the lecturer (even in lectures) and students are sometimes nervous about contributing their own ideas. This is made worse – in an English-speaking environment – by the fact that Chinese students are required to speak or present in a second language. Many UK students could not even get close to this!

This can be difficult for some Chinese students who might have the ability to write, speak, listen and/or read English but not the confidence to use it, and who might also not be sure of how to interact with a tutor in a non-Chinese setting, so there are issues of both culture and language which affect some international students.

Some universities – such as Nottingham University in China – assess the contributions that students make in their classrooms and use that as part of students' course marks. This, it is said, encourages preparation before class and enables classrooms to be more interactive.

Participating and interacting in a classroom is not easy, but is vital if everyone is going to get some feedback on their ideas, to ensure that their learning is progressing well. Interaction, of course, also makes sure that students can learn from each other. See Chapter 13 for more information on cultural differences.

To benefit from seminars, there are some other important issues to consider:

- You must *do your reading and exercises* before coming to the seminar. Some lecturers will not allow those who have not prepared to attend and, in some cases, a lack of preparation may have an impact on whether you are allowed to take the examination.
- *Make notes* during the seminar in the same way that you would do during a lecture. This time, however, you might make notes on what other students say as well as the comments made by the tutor.
- Recognise that you have as much right to *speak* and say something during a tutorial as any other student. Making that first contribution is vital for your learning in other modules and courses.

Independent Reading

The importance of doing the required reading – and other reading if you have time – has already been mentioned several times, particularly in relation to deep learning. There is more information on reading on the companion website for this text. Reading can be of various sources but the most common ones are textbooks, academic research journals and credible information online.

Many students seem to struggle to read a textbook, and there may be some reasons for this. Have a look at two of your recommended textbooks (they do not have to be ones you own; they can be from the library) and complete the exercise below.

═══════════ FOR YOU TO DO ═══════════

PART A

Look at two of your textbooks, one that you think you enjoy reading and one that you have not yet used. Try to answer the following questions:

1. What makes the difference between the textbook you have read (or think you would like to read if you have not already done so) and the one you have not yet read? Is it an issue of time management, or preference for one type of textbook over another, or some other reason?
2. What kinds of books have you been used to reading before you came to university?
3. Do you usually try to read the whole chapter in one go, or break it down into small sections?
4. Which is more important to you when you look at a textbook: its appearance, length, content or something else?
5. If you are not motivated to read a book, do you give up quickly or show your determination by finishing the chapter or a section?
6. How long does it take you to finish a chapter in the book you have read before? How long do you think it would take you to finish a chapter in the book from which you have not read before?

PART B

Think about the following statements. For you, are they true or false?

1. I like reading books.
2. I prefer books that have some colour and/or some pictures.
3. If a textbook contains some exercises, then I will always do the exercises.
4. I can read around 10 pages of an academic textbook at a time, before I start to lose concentration.
5. I prefer to use e-books (on the Kindle or iPad) rather than physical copies of textbooks.
6. I'd rather talk to a classmate about the content of a chapter than read it myself.
7. Most textbooks are boring.
8. I get frustrated by some of the books I have bought: the lecturers seem hardly to use them.
9. I have decided to use the library rather than buy the books.
10. When I am reading, I usually write in my books.

Active Reading

Regardless of our previous experience with reading textbooks or our motivation or interest in doing so, reading is a vital component of study life at university, so much so that students used to say that they were 'reading for a degree in … [Business Studies, for example]'. But the value is not in reading alone, since what we read can easily be forgotten in the same way that what we hear can easily be forgotten as well.

The value in reading is gained when we think about what we have read, so we need to learn to 'read actively'.

ACTIVE READING

Active reading describes a process where we are actively engaged in our reading, usually by thinking about what we read.

Active reading can be done by:

- Trying to *evaluate* what we read. Do I agree with it? What evidence is presented, and is it convincing? Does it make logical sense? Does this match what other people have said? Why does the reader say this?
- *Applying* what we read. Does this seem to explain what I have seen? Does this work in my situation?
- *Synthesising* what we read. How does this reading relate to other ideas I have covered in the course?
- Checking our *understanding* of what we read. Can I think of examples of what the book is talking about?

Our thinking can easily be forgotten, so it is a good idea to write notes in the margin or on the pages somehow, and e-books often come with similar capabilities, but key to this is the idea that we use our reading in the same way that we would use any other source of information, such as lectures, seminars, information online, discussions with other students, and so on.

 ——— KEY LEARNING POINT ━━━━━━━━━━

Engaging actively with your course reading is as important for your learning as attending lectures. It helps you to do well, and the benefits are greater than simply reading the book's content.

Keeping a record of what you read

When you come to write up what you have read, you will need to compile a bibliography. To do so, you *must* keep a record of what you read and how it could be useful. In times gone past, students and researchers tended to do this through a card filing system, but computer software has developed since then and one of the best tools available now is called 'EndNote'.

Expressed simply, the details of any journal articles you find online (via a library database such as Emerald or ProQuest Direct) can be imported directly into EndNote so you then have a reference which EndNote can use to compile a bibliography. This makes the process of keeping a record of what you have read extremely easy.

You can also use EndNote to keep notes of that reading, so you can make notes about any article you read – content, research methods, conclusions, etc. – within EndNote. If you do not have access to EndNote, then a database tool or Microsoft Excel can be used for similar purposes, but keeping an accurate record is vital if your bibliography is going to be complete and accurate. There is more on referencing and giving citations on pages 126–30 in Chapter 6 on assessment.

APPLYING LEARNING STYLES TO YOUR UNIVERSITY EXPERIENCE

If we take the ideas identified above and apply them to the learning opportunities given through the typical university experience, then we will find that people with different and varied learning preferences find different activities *more or less* interesting (see Figure 5.3). This does not mean, of course, that we do not or cannot learn from the other activities given in Figure 5.3.

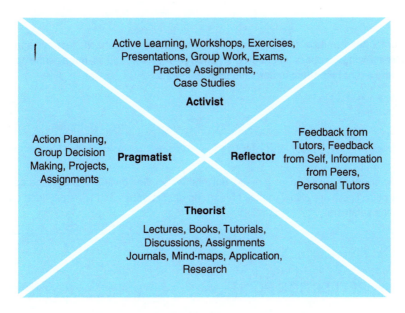

Figure 5.3 An application of learning styles to learn at university

The challenge, therefore, is to learn how to develop the different learning styles and use each learning opportunity as well as you can.

━━━━━━━━━━ **'BUT I HAVE A QUESTION ...'** ━━━━━━━━━━

... If my learning style is 'Activist', but my university uses only one-way lectures and tutorials, does that mean that I am not going to learn very much?

No, not at all. What it means is that you might find other activities more engaging, so there are three questions for you:

1. How could you 'interact' with non-interactive lectures?
2. How could you supplement the lectures and tutorials with other ways of learning which are more 'activist oriented'?
3. How could you encourage the lecturer to be more interactive?

The answer to the first is not that different from what you might be doing when you read (i.e. thinking about what you are reading and making notes), so when you are in your lectures (probably with the lecture slides in front of you), take a bit of time to think about what is being presented. Do you agree with what is being said? Are there any problems with it? In other words, engage in some critical thinking as you listen to what is being said – in the same way that you do when you are reading. Write down perhaps the questions that occur to you as you listen.

The answer to the second question is to look at all the various ideas mentioned in Figure 5.3 and use them to supplement what you experienced in the lecture. This may mean forming a group to discuss what you have learnt, or finding a friend to debate the content, or, if you have a job, talking to a manager to find out if they have a different point of view. The lecture is not the only way to learn and, as we saw in Chapter 3, a great deal of your time should be spent studying independently.

(Continued)

(Continued)

Finally, lecturers need to have feedback. This is not an excuse to go to the lecturer and be aggressive towards them (see 'Giving Feedback' in Chapter 12) and you should not do so, but *a gentle comment* to your lecturer after class might help them understand your reactions.

KEY LEARNING POINT

Adults learn in a variety of ways and, as a result, universities provide a variety of learning opportunities for you in the classroom. There are also varieties of learning opportunities and tools provided outside of time-tabled lectures and seminars.

REFLECTION POINT

Take some time to think about the following questions and write down some answers.

Do you enjoy reading, or do you find it hard to motivate yourself to read? If it is hard for you, what can you do to make it more interesting?

Which of these makes you think the most: listening to a lecture, doing a group exercise in a seminar, or reading the chapter of a book? Why?

Which are you supposed to spend more time on at university: reading the materials given to you, or attending your classes? Why do you think this is the case? Give two or three reasons which come to mind:

1.

2.

3.

LEARNING OPPORTUNITIES AND TOOLS OUTSIDE OF THE TIMETABLE

The following are learning opportunities provided by universities, but which are not going to feature in your scheduled timetable, or even in your time for independent study. However, since the majority of your study time is going to be doing reading and studying outside of the classroom, they are vitally important.

Using and Understanding Feedback

It might seem strange to be discussing feedback when we have not yet discussed assessment, and we will look at some aspects of feedback when we look at assessment in Chapter 6, but we first need to be very clear in our definitions and understanding of what we mean by 'feedback'. Have a look at the next exercise below.

━━━━ FOR YOU TO DO ━━━━

Look at the views given below and decide for yourself whether they are **True** or **False**.

1. I get feedback on my ideas every time I give my views in a seminar.
2. Feedback is not nice to receive, and it makes me nervous.
3. Other students can give me feedback in group discussions.
4. Feedback is something I would prefer to hear than to see written down.
5. Feedback is something I only get for my assignments.
6. I enjoy getting feedback; it helps me know where to improve next time.
7. Feedback is useful in my learning.
8. The mark is the only thing that counts; the feedback is not important.
9. I find my feedback is very impersonal.
10. I am sure my feedback will come very quickly after I submit my assignment.

This exercise gives 10 ideas on feedback, but it is helpful to understand what feedback really is.

Feedback can be written or verbal, or a facial expression, but it gives you information on what you have done well or what you need to change. There is one thing to be aware of, however: when it comes to assessment feedback, *'feedback' is far more than just your grade*. Your grade will tell you broadly how well you did, but the feedback is the detailed information that tells you what you did well and what you should think about improving. It is very common to want the grade or mark and not really bother about anything else – and bearing in mind that this is how your lecturers will evaluate your degree, it is understandable. However, the mark is only a very small part of the complete story. As a lecturer, I would never re-mark work (regardless of what my students might ask me to do), but I am generally happy to discuss the feedback and explain it if it does not make sense. The feedback in the mind of many of your lecturers will be more important than the mark.

Feedback given on class contributions or on any work that does not count towards a course grade is vital to learning. Not giving or seeking such feedback will very likely lead to your receiving poorer grades than you otherwise would have received.

If you type 'Coursework Feedback' into the UK's Google site, you will be given links to nearly every university in the UK. It is recognised as essential and important for learning, but the mistake that many students make is in thinking that the mark is more important. Whether you think it is or not depends on the impact of that mark, of course. Feedback is arguably the least used, worst understood and poorly noted aspect of learning at university, regardless of its impact. In some cases, feedback is rarely collected, but when it is, the mark is often seen as more important.

It is through feedback that you can learn what you did well and what you did less well. If you want to do better, this information is vital. How can you do better when you are not sure where you went wrong before? This becomes particularly relevant when examined in conjunction with other aspects of the learning process.

Feedback is an emotive subject, three reasons being as follows:

FEEDBACK

Feedback is any comment or information given to an individual which provides them with some idea of the value of their work.

1. Feedback is often the area where universities score lowest on the National Student Survey.
2. Feedback is something that students seem to demand more speedily, but it is not always understood, read or acted upon (Orsmond et al., 2002; Gibbs and Simpson, 2004).
3. Providing feedback is one of the main areas that generates concern for lecturers in terms of the time that it takes to provide. The lack of use of the feedback by some students does not encourage lecturers to give more time to this task.

The feedback is there for you to use, to enable you to know why you received the mark you did and to help you improve your future work. Your lecturers will expect you to collect it and use it appropriately.

It is also important to note, however, that feedback is far more than simply the written feedback that you might receive on your coursework. Feedback also includes the following:

- Comments given to you and others in seminars in response to something you say.
- Something that is emailed to you in respect of work that you have done or a comment that you have made.
- A comment from a classmate responding to something you have said.
- Something said in a one-to-one discussion between you and a member of academic staff.
- A surprised look from another student in response to something you have said.

To go back to the definition given above, feedback is *any* comment or information given to you by anyone at any time in any place relating to anything that you have done (or not done) or something that you have said, and which evaluates those comments you have made or the work you done. As you can probably deduce from the ideas above, feedback is *not* just about coursework.

The best feedback in relation to your academic work probably comes from a lecturer or tutor who has some years of experience, but other students and colleagues at work, friends or family members may all be able to give you some kind of feedback on areas that they understand well.

Virtual Learning Environment

Some of your lecturers will have completed their university studies before email and the Internet existed, but the Internet is now as important a source of learning as the lectures, if not more so. It is highly likely that the Internet will have formed a big part of your learning at school and you will have used it to demonstrate your ability to gather information. At university, the Internet is also used to give you information and provide you with support for your learning via a VLE (Virtual Learning Environment). This might be Moodle™, or Blackboard™ or another online platform.

VIRTUAL LEARNING
ENVIRONMENT

A virtual learning environment is an online portal for providing materials, information and interaction for students for their studies.

The VLE may or may not be used for a variety of purposes, and you may or may not have come across one before. The UK's Open University uses its own OpenLearn platform, a tool which it has now made available to other universities.

Universities typically put a variety of information online and you will be expected to look at these very regularly, probably *at least once a week for each module*. The elements listed in Table 5.3 will probably appear for each module each week, though universities and university departments will vary in what they will make available to you online.

Table 5.3 Content typically posted via a VLE

• Contact details for all module teachers • Copy of the module handbook • Class timetable • Details of coursework assignments including submission dates • Marking criteria for assignments	• Relevant lecture slides/notes/materials used in the classroom • Previous examination papers • Feedback on at least the last examination/coursework performance • Reading/resource list

Some additional elements might also be apparent from module to module. You might also find multiple choice questions there, blogs, assignment submission processes and a variety of other tools to support your learning and build the relationships between you and your lecturers.

Massive Open Online Courses

More recently, there has been a move in university education across the world to establish Massive Open Online Courses (MOOCs). MOOCs are open access courses, where anyone in the world can enrol in an online module from a large number of universities, usually without needing to pay any kind of fee. The UK's Open University has a long history of providing online courses (preceded by postal materials and late-night televised lectures in the 1960s) and has developed a platform for its own MOOCs, as Box 5.3 notes. MOOC modules are fully online and are taken by hundreds, or in some cases thousands, of students around the world at any one time. There are no direct face-to-face interactions between lecturers and students, but the materials posted can give students an opportunity to find out more about specific topics of interest to them. As a resource for learning, they can be fantastic: you can see resources and lecturers from some of the most important people in the world in a particular discipline, and get to see a view of a particular topic presented by someone other than your lecturer.

═══════ **BOX 5.3** ═══════

MOOCS AND LEARNING

A fairly recent edition of the online journal 'Information Age' (Information-age.com, December 2012) noted that the Open University had launched a company called 'FutureLearn' which had developed a learning platform for other institutions to use. A number of other universities had already signed up to use the platform to support their own MOOCs, some of which are themselves developed across universities, and some further developed across continents.

Whether this proves to be the way that most universities choose to go remains to be seen. While MOOCs are a new concept, most of them do not provide any free assessment or free tutoring, but the resources are usually provided free of charge and are available for anyone to access, whether they wish to get a degree from a particular university providing those resources or not. Payment is usually only needed when an individual decides to undertake some assessment.

As noted in the magazine article:

The Open University (OU) is the most advanced provider of online learning materials in the UK, as its courses are all based on distance learning. The OU's OpenLearn platform, launched in 2006, contains

(Continued)

(Continued)

around 11,000 hours of learning materials in over 600 study units, and attracts an average 400,000 unique users per month. (www.information-age.com)

The amount of expertise at the OU in providing online education is immense and well known.

Education online is not only becoming big business, but potentially going to transform how learning takes place and how degrees are given. It may be possible to get credits for one module at one institution that can be used as the basis for part of a degree at another university. We are not there yet, but it is likely that this will come sooner or later.

Would you ever think of additionally enrolling in a MOOC? What might put you off, or encourage you?

FURTHER READING

Visit the companion website for this book at https://study.sagepub.com/morgan for more information, tips and guidance on active reading, note taking in lectures, the use of cases and study groups which may be useful for your learning.

KEY LEARNING POINT

Learning opportunities can occur inside and outside of the formal timetable, but taking advantage of them all is important.

INTEGRATION AND APPLICATION

Your learning will be made up of a variety of situations. How you use them is going to be crucial to their effectiveness in assisting you to learn to think. There are some questions which might help you to bring the various opportunities together:

1. Which of the 'learning opportunities' will be easiest for you to undertake? Why?
2. Thinking about the descriptions of learning styles given above, which learning style appears to match your preference best? How might it affect your motivation to be involved in other opportunities for learning?
3. Which of the learning opportunities will be the most difficult for you to undertake? Why? Is it because of motivation or your own self-confidence, or both, or something else?
4. If you consider that lecturers cannot cover all that they need to cover in the depth they expect from you in your work, then there is a need to do the reading. So, what will you do to ensure that you undertake the reading you need to do for your subjects?
5. How can the Internet help or hinder your learning?
6. Would a study group work for you? Why, or why not?
7. How can you seek and receive feedback on your thinking? What can you do to get feedback to see whether you really understand the subjects you are studying?
8. What do you need to happen or to do in order for your motivation to use these 'learning opportunities' to increase?

Thinking about the answers to these questions at the start of your university career will give you some helpful ideas on how you might use them and other opportunities most effectively.

CONCLUSION

By the end of this chapter, you should be able to:

- Describe the ways that your lecturers and professors will help and expect you to learn at university.
- Understand what is meant by 'independent learning'.
- Use time outside of the classroom to study effectively.

This chapter has been about helping you to cope with the 'learning opportunities' provided by your university. Studying at University requires the use of different study skills from those typically developed at schools and colleges (see Chapters 3, 4 and the next chapter, Chapter 6, for more information).

The introduction to this chapter mentioned one issue that is very important to recognise as we finish this chapter: that although students often make a distinction between learning (the process) and assessment (the outcomes and evaluation of that process), the two are very closely linked. The feedback you get from the assessment of one module or piece of work should get you to think about what you did well and not so well. That thinking (or reflection) should then lead on to what you do for your next piece of work, so learning (the subject of this chapter) cannot be easily separated out from assessment (the subject of the next). The next chapter contains more details about the ways in which your lecturers will be assessing your work.

Understanding how these opportunities work together to enable you to be an independent learner is vital. University requires you to find and use the opportunities given to you, it does not give you everything you need on a plate. At school, you might have been able to take in information given to you, remember it and give it back to your teacher – and pass your subject. At university, you will do poorly if you do only this, so the understanding you develop of how university works and what your tutors are looking for will be key to doing well and ensuring that the money and time invested in your studies are well spent.

Learning should not be a finite process: learning – as we looked at in Chapter 2 – takes place in a large number of situations and over most of our life. Feedback from what we do is vital for our learning, but to receive feedback we need to do something, so the next chapter will look at the assessment methods used at university.

FINAL REFLECTIONS

Based on the content of this chapter, what do you now know about learning at university that you did not know before?

What key learning point had the most impact? Why?

Do your answers to either of the above questions have the potential to change your attitude to studies at university? If so, why?

What will you now do differently? (Write this down and put it somewhere where you can see it regularly.)

INTERVIEW QUESTIONS

It is unlikely that you will be asked any direct questions about teaching methods in a selection interview – no one is going to ask how many hours you spent in lectures and tutorials, unless they think you might have missed most of them – but they might ask you questions to find out about your ability to think critically or adapt to new situations.

Consider the following questions: what might your answers be?

1. Thinking about your learning at university, which parts of your course (lectures, tutorials, presentations, assignments, etc.) taught you the most?
2. How easy did you find it to adjust to studies at university after school or college?

Chapter 17 contains a lot more information on selection interviews and the online content also gives some guidance on these questions.

ADDITIONAL RESOURCES

Want to learn more? Visit https://study.sagepub.com/morgan to gain access to a wide range of online resources, including interactive tests, tasks, further reading and downloads.

Textbook Resources

Davey, G. (2008) *The International Student's Survival Guide*. London: Sage (particularly chapter 8).
Lewis, M. and Reinders, H. (2003) *Study Skills for Speakers of English as a Second Language*. Basingstoke Palgrave Macmillan (particularly chapters 4 and 5).
McIlroy, D. (2003) *Studying @ University*. London: Sage (particularly chapter 2).
McMillan, K. and Weyers, J. (2012) *The Study Skills Book* (3rd edition). Harlow: Pearson (particularly chapters 4 and 5).

PART III
UNIVERSITY ASSESSMENT

As we have seen, learning at university occurs differently from education that you might have had elsewhere. Lectures, tutorials, discussion and critical thinking are all part of the learning process at university because (1) you are an adult and (2) the number of universities is smaller than that of schools and colleges, so you tend to be taught in larger groups. We have also seen that you are expected to study for around 100 hours for each 10-credit block you study (or 150 for 15 credits, etc.), time which includes all those activities covered above, but which should also include time given for assessment.

Assessment is part of the learning process in two ways. Firstly, it provides evidence of what you are able to do and, secondly, in many cases it provides the motivation to learn. It would be wonderful to think that everyone learnt because they really enjoyed it and wanted to learn – and, thankfully, that is true of many – but this is not true for all, so the assessment does provide a push in many cases.

Therefore, the three chapters which follow will cover the aspects of assessment commonly used at university. Chapter 6 will give some general guidance on the principles for assessment and relates closely to some ideas on critical thinking noted in Chapter 4. Chapter 7 will look at essays and dissertations. Chapter 8 will cover issues related to assessment by examinations and will provide some ideas to assist your revision.

Two other chapters may be of relevance here as well, but are included in Part IV (Employability Skills): Chapter 9 (Presentation Skills) and Chapter 10 (Team-working). Both are highly relevant for both employability and assessment at university. This should not be a surprise, since your studies are intended to prepare you for employment, of course.

There is a disappointing issue connected with academic assessment. Assessment often ends up driving students' learning, though it should not. In reality, you will find that learning can become really exciting and interesting if you learn in order to discover things for yourself, rather than focusing on questions which might come up in an examination or on research for a single question in a presentation or assignment. Assessment has to be there for the reasons given above, but your tutors will hope that you will put your efforts into learning anyway, *as if there was no assessment*.

GENERAL PRINCIPLES OF ASSESSMENT AT UNIVERSITY

CHAPTER STRUCTURE

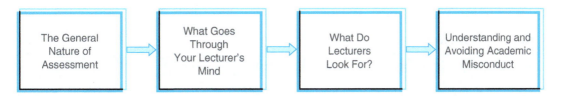

| The General Nature of Assessment | → | What Goes Through Your Lecturer's Mind | → | What Do Lecturers Look For? | → | Understanding and Avoiding Academic Misconduct |

Figure 6.1

When you see the 🌐 this means go to the companion website https://study.sagepub.com/morgan to do a quiz, complete a task, read further or download a template.

━ AIMS OF THE CHAPTER ━

By the end of this chapter, you should be able to:

- Understand some of the assessment methods and criteria used by academics in universities.
- Get a broad insight into what to do – and what not to do – in order to do well in your studies on a variety of forms of assessment.
- Ensure that you avoid any allegations of academic misconduct (commonly known as 'plagiarism') in your work.
- Develop your thinking regarding the criteria for 'good' assessed work.

INTRODUCTION

We will begin by giving you the opportunity to identify how much you know about assessment at university and then discuss the nature of what academics call formative and summative assessment. The chapter will analyse the requirements that lecturers will have for different forms of assessment, examine some of the key issues when completing group-based assessment, and present some detailed thinking about what is called 'academic misconduct' (or more commonly called 'cheating') in assessment, along with some ideas on how to avoid this and how to ensure that citations, quotations and bibliographies can assist.

Whatever forms of assessment are used on your courses, they should all help to assess the criteria referred to in Chapter 4 on critical thinking. Of course, some methods of assessment will seem more amenable to you than others: some people prefer examinations to coursework, others prefer group work to individual work, and so on. But whichever form(s) of assessment are used, most will seem stressful and challenging in some way.

SKILLS SELF-ASSESSMENT

Complete the brief questionnaire below to see how much you know about assessment at university. Give each item a score between 1 and 5, where 1 is 'I strongly disagree' and 5 is 'I strongly agree'. Answer each item quickly. There are right and wrong answers to *some of these items*, so be sure to compare your answers with those on the companion website.

Item	Statement	Score
1.	I know how my modules are going to be assessed	
2.	Assessment at my university is going to be stressful	
3.	If I remember what my lecturers have told me in lectures, then I should be OK when I have to do exams	
4.	The more content I put into an examination essay, the higher the mark I will receive	
5.	Multiple choice questions are easy, compared with essay answers	
6.	I can use ideas from anyone else (including other students) in my work	
7.	I understand very clearly what is meant by a bibliography	
8.	I can use quotations from other people in my work	
9.	I have must use at least 20 citations in my coursework	
10.	If I do well in one year of study, then I should do well in every year of study because the standards don't change	
11.	If I do well in one module, then I should do well in every module because the standards don't change	
12.	Essays and presentations are harder to do than examinations	

(Continued)

(Continued)

Item	Statement	Score
13.	In an examination, I won't have to refer to theory	
14.	I must have a good memory if I am going to do well in my modules	
15.	I would never cheat in an assignment	
16.	Plagiarism is something which only affects coursework assignments	
17.	I'm not allowed to put others' words into my assignments or examinations	
18.	I will only get one form of assessment in each of my modules	
19.	I expect that students who put less effort into their coursework will receive a lower mark	
20.	The amount of effort I put into a piece of work will relate directly to the mark I receive	

There will be some slight variation across universities, but on most things the regulations and practice will be very similar, so remember to check your answers against those available on the companion website via the interactive version of this test at https://study.sagepub.com/morgan.

INTERACTIVE
TEST

THE GENERAL NATURE OF ASSESSMENT

There are two forms of assessment: formative and summative. There is some difference in how these two terms are used across different international systems, but, broadly speaking, in the UK formative assessment refers to any form of work that you give to your lecturer that does not count towards your degree, while summative assessment refers to any work that you do that does count towards your degree.

Formative assessment is an input into the learning process and takes place whenever you accept the comments that a lecturer gives you in class, in a one-to-one discussion or in an email. It is spontaneous, rarely written down' and involves your getting feedback in any way, prior to submitting work which is part of a module assessment. As such it is invaluable, and formative feedback on your work and ideas is one of the most powerful sources of information for your learning that you will find during your time as a student.

Summative assessment is an outcome of the learning process. In other words, submitting a piece of work for a mark or a grade is intended – from your perspective as a student – to show your lecturers what you have learned and what you are able to do with what you have learned. From the lecturer's perspective, such work is required from you in order for them to ensure that you have achieved the 'outcomes' of the module (i.e. that you have learned what they intended you to learn through all the learning opportunities covered in Chapter 5) or at least to assess the extent to which you have done so.

This last comment introduces a key component into our discussion: namely, 'learning outcomes'. We will discuss these in more detail below because they are important and drive a great deal of the debate around the criteria used for assessment. However, it is important to understand how assessment generally

FORMATIVE AND SUMMATIVE ASSESSMENT OF LEARNING

Formative assessment of learning: This takes place when you receive some comment on your thinking or on some work that you submit that contributes solely to your own personal learning.

Summative assessment of learning: This occurs when you submit work as part of the requirements for your modules and degree programme.

and summative assessment in particular are viewed from a lecturer's perspective before we look at assessment in too much detail.

Most of the comments given in the remainder of this chapter deal with summative assessment; formative assessment was really covered in the previous chapter. (See pages 108–110 on feedback as a source of learning.)

WHAT GOES THROUGH YOUR LECTURER'S MIND WHEN THEY ARE ASSESSING YOUR WORK?

The reality is almost certainly that very few people like being assessed. It implies judgement, criticism perhaps and evaluation of some kind. Maybe we do not always realise it, but often we can think of our work as an extension of who we are, and believe that the effort we put in should relate to what we get back out. Therefore, when someone assesses our work, we might think that they are evaluating us, as a person sometimes. That view may or may not reflect our own thinking, but it is not what goes through the mind of a lecturer or professor when they assess your work. They will be assessing the piece of work. They will not be making a judgement about who you are, but just about that piece of work.

When a lecturer assesses your work, there will be a number of things going through their mind. They will be looking for examples of your thinking, seeking certain content and components and ideas that will make your thinking clear, and comparing that with the way that they operationalise the critical thinking skills covered in Chapter 4. Depending on how many students are in your class, they may or may not have a great deal of time to give you feedback; and depending on whether they know who it is that has written the assignment, the feedback might be tailored to you or not.

Lecturers love to mark good work. Lecturers are also human beings who sometimes get emotional about what they read. If they know the student who has written a poor piece of work and believe that they can do so much better, then it is as disappointing for the lecturer to read and assess that piece of work as it is for them to read a fantastic piece of work from a student whose classroom contributions have been few or poor. One of the best compliments that you can get from a lecturer is, 'Oh, I hadn't thought about that!', so your task is to show that you understand the content you need to understand and can think about it with insight, critical thinking and clarity.

 ━━━ 'BUT I HAVE A QUESTION ...' ━━━━━━━━━━━━━

... If coursework or exams are not anonymous and the lecturer has developed a biased view against you, does that mean it will be hard to get a good mark?

Anonymous marking has been brought in by most universities in the UK and it is there to guard against the kind of issue raised here. Few lecturers will be as biased as some students might think, but in any event there are some checks and balances in the UK educational system which mean that the marking process is very carefully monitored to prevent issues of bias arising.

The standard of marking for academic work submitted for assessment (e.g. exams, coursework) will be checked by an external examiner to make sure the marking is fair. This is done to ensure that the marking is not biased and that good work gets the marks it deserves. The external examiner will be a lecturer or professor from another university and will have no idea who you are and what you have said in class or to your lecturer. They can only check that the standard of marking is reasonable and similar to other universities. But, as I say, many universities have anonymous marking now and such issues do not arise that often anyway.

The key point to remember is that at the front of a lecturer's mind when they are marking work is the question: 'Does this demonstrate the content and depth of argument and thinking that I am seeking in this work?' If both content and depth are there, then there is little reason why a particular piece of work cannot receive a high mark.

────────── KEY LEARNING POINT ──────────

The best source of information about what your lecturers are looking for are the lecturers themselves. They are the best placed individuals to explain how they will expect you to demonstrate what they are looking for.

WHAT DO LECTURERS LOOK FOR IN ASSESSED WORK?

Developing an understanding of what your lecturers look for is one of the most important things you will do as a student. Ultimately, there is absolutely nothing better than asking your lecturer directly and getting some detail from them, but your tutor will almost certainly have made some information about this available to you already, so please check it before asking your tutor. Busy academics can get quite frustrated by requests to provide information that they have already provided in some other way. It is helpful to give some general guidelines, firstly relating to quantitative subjects and, secondly, relating to more discursive subjects such as marketing or HRM.

Quantitative or numerical subjects will traditionally be assessed on the basis of calculations, but it is rarely the case that the right answer will get all the marks. More usually, the marks will be given on the basis of both the answer and the working out. Put simply, this is because lecturers will not simply want to know your conclusion, but rather how you got there. In some ways, this is actually little different to the expectations of those who teach more discursive and 'essay-based' subjects, where the quality of the discussion is as important as the conclusion. Figure 6.2 shows how this works.

In the figure, there are two axes: 'Content' and 'Argument'. Content is self-explanatory, but when lecturers refer to argument, they are referring to the way in which content has been examined using

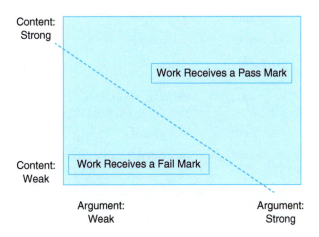

Figure 6.2 What do your lecturers look for in assessed work?

your critical thinking skills – and we covered that in some detail in Chapter 4. Including a lot of content without any signs of thinking about that content is no different to simply giving back to the lecturer everything they have told you, or you may include content that is irrelevant, which does not really help either. Similarly, giving a strong argument about only one part of the content that a tutor will expect you to cover is also insufficient, so there needs to be both.

Lecturers will usually be looking for both in your assessed work, whatever the nature of the assessment, and this does make some sense if you go back and think about the purpose of universities and the reasons for attending university which we covered in Chapter 1: that is, to teach you to think.

The dashed line across the diagram indicates a theoretical 'pass-mark line': too far below this line and you may be in danger of failing your module; the further you are above the line, the more chance you have of passing.

There are two important issues here, though:

1. The line might be steep for some pieces of work and gently sloping for other pieces of work, (which is why talking to the lecturer themselves is going to be extremely useful).
2. The line might shift left or right depending on which year of study the module is designed for. The expectations of students on a module in the first year will usually be different (usually easier) when compared with those in the final year, and producing work of identical quality in both years of study will sometimes result in the mark in the final year being lower.

The two axes tend to represent the way that many lecturers will assess work, especially work of a discursive nature.

Whatever the nature of the work, there is considerable overlap between the criteria used for assessing essays and those used for other forms of assessment (e.g. presentations and examinations). We will cover some of these issues in Chapters 8, 9 and 10 for the assessment methods noted below, but the commonalities and differences are given here in Table 6.1.

Table 6.1 Overlap and differences in expectations for different methods of assessment

Criterion	Essays	Presentations	Examination assessment
Demonstration of critical thinking skills	Yes, needed	Yes, needed	Yes, needed
Relevance	Yes, needed	Yes, needed	Yes, needed
Use of examples	Yes, needed	Yes, needed	Yes, needed
Support provided by citations and theory	Yes, needed	Yes, needed	If possible, yes
Grammar and spelling	Yes, needed	On slides, definitely. In oral delivery, yes, needed	Yes, though not the most important criterion
Structure	Yes, needed	Yes, needed	Yes, needed
Taking account of the audience	Yes, needed	Yes, definitely!	Yes, though while this is not the most important criterion, doing so may waste time on more important issues to be covered
Academic style	Yes, needed	Yes, to some extent	Yes, to some extent

(Continued)

Table 6.1 (Continued)

Criterion	Essays	Presentations	Examination assessment
Good memory needed	Not really needed	Yes, needed for coherent delivery	Yes, needed
Oral delivery skills	Not really needed	Yes, definitely!	Not needed at all
Need to deliver work in response to unseen questions	Not really needed	Not usually	Yes, needed
Need to avoid plagiarism	Yes, needed	Yes, needed	Yes, though not really an issue in most unseen examinations

This overlap, of course, is not unexpected: if universities are expected to produce critical thinkers who learn independently, then all assessment methods should go some way to producing and assessing those qualities.

KEY LEARNING POINT

The presentation of relevant content and the demonstration of critical thinking in academic work are crucial to performing well in academic assessment.

REFLECTION POINT

Take some time to think about the following questions and write down some answers.

What evidence will your lecturer look for in your work to determine how deeply you are thinking about the subject?

A mark is never going to be necessarily about the number of references to research you provide, but why is it better to have read a good number of journal articles and research papers?

UNDERSTANDING AND AVOIDING ACADEMIC MISCONDUCT

Attempting to demonstrate the criteria for assessment is vitally important in developing written work – you will not be able get marks without doing so. But there is an issue which becomes more important at university than it might be in other settings, namely 'academic misconduct'. We need to explain more about this here since it has relevance to both written and oral forms of assessment.

Read the information below carefully and in conjunction with other materials you have been given by your own university.

Academic Misconduct and Plagiarism

We need to start with a clear and simple definition, something that is not as easy as it sounds, but we will try.

 PLAGIARISM

Plagiarism is the use of other people's work and ideas without any kind of acknowledgement that you have done so.

If you have committed plagiarism, then you have pretended that other people's work is your own, which is why this is considered so serious.

Plagiarism is not an easy offence to explain technically, but the information in the definition here goes a long way towards explaining what it is and why it is a problem. This can be confusing, especially when it does not seem to be an issue at school. But it is an offence because you are misleading the reader into believing that the content of your essay is yours when it is not, so you receive marks for ideas and work that are not your own. Disciplinary offences like this are usually kept on a student's official record.

 'BUT I HAVE A QUESTION …'

… Why is reproducing material from the Web OK at school but not OK at university?

Universities do not stop you from using and gathering information – in fact, you must be good at this and in professional life too. Universities expect you to gather a great deal of information – from journals and your reading as well as from websites generally – but the issue here is that you have to tell the university or lecturer that you are using information gathered from another source, and to do so at the place in the assignment or work where you are using that information.

Universities will also have slightly different definitions of what constitutes plagiarism, but that is why the definition is given above and why examples are given below. All universities will require you to indicate where you are using information from someone else.

Plagiarism can take a number of forms. The list in Box 6.1 is not complete but it does contain the most common forms.

BOX 6.1

FORMS OF PLAGIARISM

- Copying and pasting any information from the Web without acknowledging that you have done so
- Getting someone else to write your work (with or without payment) without acknowledging their input
- Working together with another student and submitting nearly identical work
- Failing to use quotation marks when you are quoting from someone else's work
- Copying someone else's assignment from a computer and submitting it as your own
- Downloading an assignment already available online

Put simply, **you cannot do any of the above, or anything else which falls under the definition of plagiarism**. Universities typically have powers to ask students to leave their courses, to retake modules, to pay fines, to move to a lower qualification, and so on. Finally, committing plagiarism will not increase the respect your lecturers have of you, as the comments in Box 6.2 show.

BOX 6.2

A PERSONAL VIEW FROM A LECTURER

The following is a personal view, written by an associate dean at a business school in a UK university. It is emotional, and gives an insight into how senior staff react when they find plagiarised work:

> I get upset and angry when I see students blatantly committing plagiarism. To try to gain marks through what is effectively deception is unfair on other students, is wrong and makes me extremely irritated. And then there is also the idea that they think that we are not intelligent enough as lecturers to be able to spot it ...! How stupid do they think we are?
>
> I have come across everything from an MSc student thinking he can translate a dissertation in Chinese into English and think he can get away with it to another MSc student who simply copied and pasted their entire dissertation from the web – including the methodology, sample size and findings: they lost their chance to graduate with a Masters. I've also come across a student who copied his roommate's assignment, another who downloaded an earlier version of a similar assignment and changed all but two words and a student who actually plagiarised a piece of work that was about plagiarism! (An anonymous Associate Dean for Teaching and Learning)

Most academics react in similar ways and are very frustrated by students who attempt to cheat.

The question is often asked, 'Why do students commit plagiarism?' There is no acceptable reason for doing so. It would be a shame if you were to put all that money you have invested in your higher education at risk. There is further online content on this topic on the companion website at https://study.sagepub.com/morgan.

FURTHER
READING

Your university will have a plagiarism policy. Search on your university website under 'Academic Misconduct' to see what the policy is on the issue.

FOR YOU TO DO

Search on your university website under 'Academic Misconduct' (which you will probably find in a document called the 'Quality Handbook' or something similar) and then answer the following questions:

1. What definition does your university use for the terms 'plagiarism' and/or 'academic misconduct'?
2. Does it give any examples of 'academic misconduct'? If so, do any of those surprise you?
3. From what you can read there, do you believe that your university sees plagiarism as a less important offence than cheating in an examination?

Avoiding Committing Plagiarism

As indicated above, plagiarism is an offence that most universities take very seriously, but there are some simple steps that we can take to ensure that you do not commit this offence. To find out what these are, we need to revisit the definition given above: 'Plagiarism is the use of other people's work and ideas without any kind of acknowledgement that you have done so.'

It is important to note the following:

- The definition does not say that you cannot use others' work or ideas as part of your assignment.
- The definition does not say that you cannot source your information from the Internet.
- The definition does not say that you have to use your own ideas.

However:

- The definition does say that where you use others' work and ideas, you *must* state that they are other people's work and ideas.

 ━━━━━ 'BUT I HAVE A QUESTION ...' ━━━━━━━━━━━━━━

... Does that mean that I can completely fill my assignment with other people's work as long as I say that the ideas are from their work?

The question here covers the situation where a student finds a really good article or book which answers the question well and then submits the article as their answer, acknowledging it as someone else's work.

Put simply, if you want to get a mark which receives a 0 mark, then go ahead.

There are two issues here. Firstly, a student could do so and would not be committing plagiarism. But if all a student does is submit a piece of work that they state throughout the work that it is from another source, and there is nothing from them in the assignment, then they would get no marks.

This would be because they have added nothing to the work that someone else has done. It is not possible simply to copy and paste or quote from other people throughout your whole assignment and get a good mark because there is basically none of your work or ideas or thinking in the assignment. This is called 'poor academic practice'.

The issue, therefore, is *how we show that we are using someone else's ideas*. Some lecturers can be very keen that you do this correctly – and you should.

Citations and Quotations

Expressing others' ideas and work in assignments and essays is normally done in one of two ways:

- Other people's *ideas*, usually expressed in the form of what is known as a 'citation'.
- Other people's words, usually expressed in the form of a quotation, with a citation.

We will look at each in turn.

Giving citations

Citations are used throughout journal articles and most texts will give them as well, indicating that the ideas do not come from the author, but from someone else's work.

There are a number of different styles for citations. The most common in business journals is what is known as 'the Harvard style' of referencing (although, in reality, this, too, has a number of forms). However, it is not the only style used in academic writing and you *must* check what expectations your lecturers have in terms of the referencing styles they want you to use.

CITATION

A 'citation' is a short note in a piece of text – usually the author and date – indicating that an idea or material comes from someone else.

━━━━━━━━━━ **KEY LEARNING POINT** ━━━━━━━━━━

You *must* use the citation style requested by your lecturer. You need to check which style is required.

The following citations are taken from the fictional article on student learning (see 'For You to Do' exercise on page 147): (Watson, 2003), (Watson, 2003; Paulson, 2012), (e.g. Scott, 2004) and Blade (2002). By looking at these, you should be able to deduce the following:

- When you use another person's ideas but do not use their name in your essay yourself, then both surname and year of publication of their idea of theory should be put in brackets separated by a comma: (Watson, 2003). *(Surname, year)*
- When you use someone's name in the main text along with their idea or theory, then you simply put the date of the publication of their idea or their research in brackets after their name: Blade (2002) or Price (2003). *Surname (year of publication)*
- When you refer to ideas or theories that have been developed by a number of individuals, then you give the ideas or theories and then put the names and dates of each author in turn, separating each with a semicolon: (Watson, 2003; Paulson, 2012). *(Surname, year; Surname, year)*

In certain instances in your reading, you may find mention of something with the words 'et al.', for example: (Smith et al., 2004). There is variation in practice from publisher to publisher, but this type of citation refers to an instance where there are several authors and sometimes, where the full list of authors has already been cited in the text. Second and subsequent mentions of the same piece of work usually just list the first author and then use 'et al.' to indicate 'and others'.

━━━━━━━━━━ **KEY LEARNING POINT** ━━━━━━━━━━

Any information that we have obtained from someone or somewhere else (e.g. websites) needs to be indicated with a citation.

Using Quotations

Different lecturers will have different attitudes as to whether a quotation in an essay is acceptable, but if there is no way to summarise what an author is trying to say than to quote them precisely, then doing so is often acceptable. However:

1. Keep your quotations short: one sentence is usually seen as the maximum acceptable length.
2. Use them sparingly: this is supposed to be your piece of work, not a collection of quotations.
3. Cite them correctly.

On the third issue, the correct way to provide a citation *for a quotation* under the Harvard system usually takes one of two forms:

- Where the name is given in the text before the quotation:

  ○ Give the quotation in quotation marks (" and ") so that your lecturer can clearly see where the quotation begins and ends.
  ○ Then give the citation in brackets at the end of the quotation. The citation should be: (year; page from which the quotation is taken).
  ○ For example: As stated by Scott (2004), "These basic issues are key to doing well in academic work" (2004; p. 112).

- Where the name is *not* given in the text before the quotation:

  ○ Give the quotation in quotation marks (" and ") so that your lecturer can clearly see where the quotation begins and ends.
  ○ Then give the citation in brackets at the end of the quotation. The citation should be: (surname, year; page from which the quotation is taken).
  ○ For example: As one researcher has stated, "These basic issues are key to doing well in academic work" (Scott, 2004; p. 112).

Any writing without quotation marks will be assessed as if it was your own writing and/or your ideas. Therefore, if you are using quotations, then be clear to show that they are quotations. If you do not use quotation marks and are copying from someone else's work, then you are likely to be accused of plagiarism.

There are few better ways of learning this than by following the style used in the best research journals in your discipline, and few better ways of learning what that is than by reading the journal articles and copying their style.

Bibliographies

We have covered how you refer within the text to a piece of research that someone else has completed, and how you show when you are quoting, but there are two other items you need to think about as well. Imagine that I am reading a journal article, a student's essay or a textbook and I find reference to something that I would like to follow up and read for myself. How can I find that article? The answer is to look in the bibliography to find details of the piece of work – and every piece of work which references information obtained from another source should have one (including presentations, reflective writing, case studies, etc.).

Your bibliography should include all the sources in alphabetical (and then date) order, according to the surname of the first author in a piece of work.

 REFERENCE LIST AND BIBLIOGRAPHY

A reference list is the list of sources cited in the document.

A bibliography is a list of all the sources used in developing a piece of work, regardless of whether they were cited in the text or not.

Compiling a bibliography manually takes some considerable time, which is why we have referred to EndNote elsewhere in this chapter, but it is a hierarchical task and once you understand the order in which the details of your sources are put, it becomes relatively straightforward.

The information below uses one of the most accepted Harvard referencing styles: the one used by the American Psychological Association (APA) and adopted widely across the academic community within the Social Sciences. EndNote software can automatically format references to this style, but information on the specifics of the APA reference style can be found widely online (e.g. https://owl. english.purdue.edu, 2016). It is a good idea, though, to check with your lecturers as to whether this is the style that they wish to see. Some academic subjects (e.g. law and physical/natural sciences) take a different approach.

Formatting Each Reference

As mentioned above, EndNote can format and compile a bibliography automatically, but if you wish to do it manually, then the conventions are given below (the articles are real, so see if you can find them from the information given below).

FURTHER
READING

There is further online content on the companion website at https://study.sagepub.com/morgan, which includes information about citing webpages, but here we need to pause and think for a moment. In Chapter 4, we noted that websites (including Wikipedia) are perhaps one of the least credible sources of information, so they must not be your main source of information in writing and compiling essays.

Journal articles

Format: Surname, Initial. (year). Title of Article, *Title of Journal*, *Volume* (issue number): pages.
  For example:

Liang, N. and Lin, S. (2008). 'Erroneous Learning from the West? A Narrative Analysis of Chinese MBA Cases Published in 1992, 1999 and 2003', *Management International Review*, *5* (5): 603–636.
Liang, N. and Wang, J. (2004). 'Implicit Mental Models in Teaching Cases: An Empirical Study of Popular MBA Cases in the United States and China', *Academy of Management Learning and Education*, *3* (4): 397–413.

Books

Format: Surname, Initial (year) *Title of Book*. Location (city) of publication: Publisher.
  For example:

Arnold, J., Silvester, J., Patterson, F., Robertson, I., Cooper, C. and Burnes, B. (2005) *Work Psychology: Understanding Human Behaviour in the Workplace*. Harlow: FT/Prentice Hall International.

Chapters in books

Format: Surname, Initial (year) 'Title of chapter'. 'In' surname of book author, initial of book author ('Ed.'), *Title of Book*, page numbers. Location of publication: name of publisher.
  For example:

Greenberg, J. and Folger, R. (1983) 'Procedural justice, participation, and the fair process effect in groups and organizations'. In Paulus, P. (Ed.), *Basic Group Process* (pp. 235–256). New York: Springer-Verlag.

'BUT I HAVE A QUESTION ...'

... I need to ensure that every single thing is done in such correct detail. I have better things to do with my time, surely?

This is an understandable point of view, which is why there is the suggestion of using EndNote, but have a look at every article in one particular journal and you will find that they all have the same style.

The reason for referencing everything so thoroughly is so that readers can be very clear about where and how to find the items being referred to. If you imagine that one article includes several different types of source (e.g. a website, other journal articles, book chapters, books, and so on), then you would be unclear exactly how to find a particular source if one bibliography was not consistent.

It is frustrating, so that is why the suggestion is made about using EndNote. Take a journal – any journal – and look at the very back of it. There, the journal will be very clear about the style of referencing it expects from anyone expecting to publish research in it.

Your lecturers will expect the same precision from you that they have to show themselves, regardless of whether you will go into an academic career. In any event, academics will have certain expectations from you as someone submitting academic work, and getting your bibliography correct is little different from ensuring you use a reasonable academic style or structure your work appropriately or fulfil any other requirement of your lecturers. It is simply another aspect of writing work at university.

To get access to EndNote, the best thing to do is probably to ask your librarian. They may or may not have the answer directly, but they should almost certainly know who to ask.

KEY LEARNING POINT

Allegations of plagiarism can be avoided by making it clear where others' work and ideas are used by correctly citing them in your essay.

Chapter 7 includes information on how to make it clear when a comment is a personal view. This is often something that students are nervous about doing simply because they are concerned that they will be assumed to be plagiarising. The reality is very different. A student's evaluation of an argument or a piece of research based on the evidence *is exactly what lecturers look for*, so knowing how to do this well is crucial to getting a good mark.

ACADEMIC MISCONDUCT IN OTHER FORMS OF ASSESSMENT

While plagiarism is unacceptable in all work, including presentations, essays and dissertations, other forms of academic misconduct exist in group-based assignments and in examinations. Table 6.2 lists some of the dangerous activities which will be considered academic misconduct in most universities.

Table 6.2   Other forms of academic misconduct

Behaviour	Is this plagiarism?
Sharing your individual assignment with another student who then copies it and submits it as their own. This results in two, almost identical assignments being submitted	This *is* seen as plagiarism and may result in both students being investigated for academic misconduct. It is widely understood that students will discuss and share ideas when they are preparing their work, but the assignments must be different. If you use another student's ideas in the work that you submit, then you should acknowledge that
Purchasing an assignment online	This is *fraudulent* and will be picked up by the lecturers either through software available to them, or through a discussion with the you as a student. It will be penalised heavily
Copying an assignment that is available online, or from another university	As with the above, this is not permitted and is easy to track. Assignments translated from foreign languages are also fairly easy to find
Reading a page from the Internet or using a slide from one of your lectures in a different module during an oral presentation	Most lecturers will be able to pick this up fairly easily. The lecturer will be able to find this themselves without too much trouble
Taking unauthorised material into an examination	**Beware:** The issue is not the *use* of any authorised material, it is the *possession* of such material when you are clearly not permitted to have it. That includes written material, mobile phones and other Internet-enabled devices This also applies to notes that should not have been taken into the examination; whether they are used or are relevant is not important. It is the **possession of such notes** that is the offence
Copying material from the Internet, referencing it appropriately, but not adding any personal comment	This is *not* actually an academic offence, but if there is no work written by the student, then the work will get a zero mark. You cannot get marks by producing no work

REFLECTION POINT

Take some time to think about the following questions and write down some answers.

How different are issues of plagiarism at university from guidance that you might have had at school or college?

What are the disciplinary processes that your university operates for dealing with instances of plagiarism?

Why do you think plagiarism is taken so seriously?

INTEGRATION AND APPLICATION

Ensuring that you have a good understanding of what you need to do to perform well in your modules is essential to actually translating that understanding into action. This chapter has been about understanding the broad principles underlying academic assessment, so before you start any assessment, it would be worthwhile to answer the following questions:

1. Do I feel confident about what I am being taught? Are there any areas about which I am not clear? Am I seeking clarification of them?
2. Have I done the necessary work to find the relevant examples and research to support the arguments I want to make?
3. Have I taken time to evaluate the strength of those arguments that I want to make in the assignment? Is there evidence to support those points of view?
4. Are there any topics I need to include but have not looked into yet? Are there any arguments I need to make, but where I do not have the appropriate research evidence or examples?
5. Have I cited correctly all the quotations I have used? Have I included page numbers where I needed to within the essay itself? Is everything I have cited included in my bibliography? Is there *anything that I have read and used in my essay* that I have not cited in the essay or included in the bibliography?
6. Do I know how to use EndNote correctly in order to keep a good record of my reading and to produce a bibliography in the appropriate style?

Assuming that you understand and follow the guidance in this and subsequent chapters, you should be ready to produce a good piece of academic work.

CONCLUSION

By now, you should be able to:

- Understand some of the assessment methods and criteria used by academics in universities.
- Get a broad insight into what to do – and what not to do – in order to do well in your studies on a variety of forms of assessment.
- Ensure that you avoid any allegations of academic misconduct (commonly known as plagiarism) in your work.
- Develop your thinking regarding the criteria for 'good' assessed work.

This chapter has covered some of the general principles relating to all forms of assessment. We have looked at the criteria for assessment in academic assessed work and the balance between content and critical thinking skills. Clearly, issues of plagiarism will be more relevant in written essays and dissertations, and issues of cheating will become important during an examination.

More details on specific forms of assessment are given in Chapter 7 on written coursework-based assessment, in Chapter 8 on examinations and revision, and in Chapter 9 on presentation skills.

FINAL REFLECTIONS

Based on the content of this chapter, what do you now know about learning at university that you did not know before?

What key learning point had the most impact? Why?

Do your answers to either of the above questions have the potential to change your attitude to studies at university? If so, why?

What will you now do differently? (Write this down and put it somewhere where you can see it regularly.)

INTERVIEW QUESTIONS

In Chapter 5, it was suggested that there would be few interview questions regarding university studies specifically, but that interviewers might ask questions about the topic to find out about your ability to make decisions or think critically – or to find out more about the way you behave or react to certain situations. The same is true for issues around assessment.

Think about the following questions. What might your answers be?

1. What was the most stressful experience you have had?
2. Can you give an example of a time when you used feedback to improve your performance?

Chapter 17 contains a lot more information on selection interviews and the online content gives some guidance on these questions.

ADDITIONAL RESOURCES

Want to learn more? Visit https://study.sagepub.com/morgan to gain access to a wide range of online resources, including interactive tests, tasks, further reading and downloads.

Website Resources

Aston University website: www.aston.ac.uk/current-students/academic-support/ldc/get-ahead/podcasts/assessment-at-university/

University of Manchester website: www.humanities.manchester.ac.uk/studyskills/assessment_evaluation/index.html

University of Reading website: www.reading.ac.uk/engageinassessment/peer-and-self-assessment/self-assessment/eia-self-assessment.aspx

Textbook Resources

Bailey, S. (2011) *Academic Writing for International Students of Business*. Abingdon: Routledge (particularly part 1.8).

Courtney, M. and Du, X. (2014) *Study Skills for Chinese Students*. London: Sage (see 'Chapter 4: Assignments, Assessment and Feedback').

McMillan, K. and Weyers, J. (2012) *The Study Skills Book* (3rd edition). Harlow: Pearson (particularly chapters 32, 36 and 45).

7 WRITING ASSIGNMENTS AND DISSERTATIONS

CHAPTER STRUCTURE

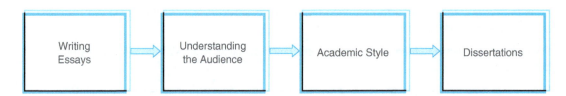

Figure 7.1

When you see the 🌐 this means go to the companion website https://study.sagepub.com/morgan to do a quiz, complete a task, read further or download a template.

═══ AIMS OF THE CHAPTER ═══

By the end of this chapter, you should be able to:

- Develop your own academic style for writing essays and assignments.
- Understand what your tutor means by the questions they set.
- Evaluate how good your English grammar and spelling are.
- Understand clearly how a tutor approaches the assessment for a piece of written work.
- Express the difference between an essay receiving a pass and one receiving a high mark.

INTRODUCTION

Writing an assessed piece of work is arguably one of the most stressful things a student has to do. It is more difficult when trying to complete those pieces under timed conditions without anything to assist you (as is the case of examinations covered in the next chapter), but writing assessed assignments can be stressful in a number of other ways, sometimes because of confusion over what is being sought and sometimes because the demands of the task seem excessive. This chapter seeks to remove some of the mystery and give you some helpful tips in terms of completing some of the written assignments you need to do.

We begin the chapter by giving you the opportunity to see how much you know and to develop your own thinking about your own abilities in terms of written assessment. We will then examine two significant forms of assessment: written essays and dissertations. In addition to content on critical thinking (see Chapter 4) and the general principles of assessment (see Chapter 6), we will spend some time looking at the specific thinking and criteria used when lecturers assess written essays and the need to find your own academic style. There is also a great deal more on the companion website at https://study.sagepub.com/morgan, including information on writing for case study assessment and writing reflectively.

FURTHER
READING

As will be clear at the end of this part and in other chapters, there is a great deal of overlap between the criteria for assessment of essay-based assignments and those for examinations, oral presentations and some other forms of assessment. Therefore, the content of this chapter also has relevance to Chapter 9 in the next part of this book.

SKILLS SELF-ASSESSMENT

Read carefully each of the following descriptions and say how typical you think each statement is of your behaviour or attitude towards written assessment by giving it a score between 1 and 5, where 1 is 'I strongly disagree' and 5 is 'I strongly agree.'

Item	Statement	Score
1.	I prefer writing assignments to presentations or taking exams	
2.	I am used to getting high marks for my written assignments	
3.	I do not need much time to plan my written work; I can develop a structure as I go along	
4.	The most difficult assignment question (i.e. the one for which I am likely to get the highest mark) is probably one which asks me to describe something	
5.	If an assignment question asks me to analyse something, then it is probably the same as asking me to evaluate something	
6.	It is easy to structure essays	
7.	The conclusion to my essays will probably have nearly the same wording as the introduction	

(Continued)

(Continued)

Item	Statement	Score
8.	I do not really pay much attention to my spelling and grammar: it is the content that really counts	
9.	If my essay seems too short, I might get penalised for not writing enough	
10.	When I am writing an essay, I am very clear about who my audience is	
11.	I find it easy to express my own thinking when I am writing an assignment	
12.	I am very clear on what makes the difference between pieces of work receiving high and low marks	
13.	I know what a case study is	
14.	I enjoy writing assignments based around case studies	
15.	I think that case studies typically have a clear solution	
16.	I know how to write a good dissertation	
17.	I understand research methodology and can argue for a particular methodology when writing a dissertation	
18.	When I am writing a dissertation, the supervisor is there to help me express myself clearly, and with good spelling and grammar	
19.	Reflective writing means that I simply write down my thoughts	
20.	I really enjoy reflective writing	

The ideas given in the questions above are detailed in the content below.

Some assignments need to be written as pieces of coursework done in groups. When it comes to the assessment of group work, the criteria for assessment are the same as those for individual pieces of work, even if the work has to be longer (which may not always be the case). We will look at group working throughout this chapter, as appropriate, but all the questionnaires and interactive exercises could be done both by an individual and as a basis for group discussion.

WRITING ESSAYS

The methods used to assess students have progressed a great deal over the past 30 years in the UK. Most assessment used to be by examination and then there was a move towards essays, which remains the case in some institutions. However, more recently, assignments have become more personal and practical. For this section, however, we will be dealing with a traditional essay, where you will be expected to examine the theories that you have been taught and to show your critical thinking skills by analysing, applying or evaluating the theories in some way.

 ESSAY

An essay is a piece of writing that applies your critical thinking skills to an area of theory relevant to the course in response to a question set by your lecturer.

It is important to note that everything that relates to essays will also relate to a number of other forms of assessment, including those examinations where you are required to write an essay in order to answer a question, presentations and dissertations. More of a comparison is given in Chapter 6, see Table 6.1.

The Mechanics of Writing Essays

Before we go too far into the discussion of what your tutors look for, it is helpful to provide some guidance on the mechanics of essay writing (i.e. how to go about writing an essay), from a practical point of view. Different people have very different strategies for this, and there is no one definite right way, but there are a number of ideas that people find useful, However, there is one thing to say here: writing your essay the day before the deadline is not going to give you the time you need if you suddenly find you need to talk to the lecturer or recognise that you do not really understand the question. Give yourself time to do this properly!

1. **Do some reading around the subject and make some notes.** For the moment, we will assume that you have done some reading and made some notes. An essay which shows no signs of reading will have lots of signs of personal opinion and 'common sense'; those kinds of essays tend to do very poorly when it comes to academic assessment.
2. Practically, **prepare yourself and your writing area.** You are preparing to write a draft, so you do not need to get too stressed about doing this; however, you do need to have all the relevant information available to you as you write.
3. **Consider the question carefully.** Try to rewrite the question in your own words two or three times. Try to understand what the question is really asking. If you need to, check your understanding of the question with the lecturer. There is no penalty for asking questions, but answering the question in the wrong way or answering the wrong question carries a large penalty indeed.

There are a number of verbs used regularly in questions for assessment and it is probably helpful to examine what these verbs mean in terms of the requirements of the essay. Have a look at the content in Table 7.1, which gives the verbs for essays requiring you to discuss different points of views and those which require you to present an argument.

Table 7.1 Expectations for different kinds of essay questions (from Marshall and Rowland, 1998)

Look at the verbs used below and the explanations of what the tutor expects from you. Some - like compare and contrast - regularly appear together in essay questions.

Verb	Expectation
QUESTIONS WHICH ASK YOU TO EXPOSE DIFFERENT POINTS OF VIEW	
Compare	Look for and explain similarities between differing points of view
Contrast	Look for and explain differences between differing points of view
Define	Set down the precise meaning of the word or phrase. Show that the distinctions implied in the definition are necessary
Describe	Give a detailed or graphic account of

(Continued)

Table 7.1   (Continued)

Enumerate	List or specify and describe
Examine	Present in depth and investigate the implications
Explain	Make plain, interpret and account for in detail
Illustrate	Explain and make clear by the use of concrete examples, or by the use of a figure or diagram
Outline	Give the main features or principles of a subject, omitting minor details and emphasising structure and relationship
Relate	Narrate/show how things are connected to each other, and to what extent they are alike or affect each other
State	Specify fully and clearly
Summarise	Give a concise account of the chief points or substance of a matter, omitting details and examples
Trace	Identify and describe the development or history of a topic from some point in time

QUESTIONS WHICH ASK YOU TO PRESENT AN ARGUMENT

Analyse	Show the essence of something by breaking it down into its component parts and examining each part in detail
Argue	Present the case for and against a particular point of view
Criticise	Give your judgement about the merit of theories or opinions about the truth of facts and back your judgement by a discussion of the evidence
Discuss	Investigate or examine by argument, sift and debate, giving reasons for and against
Evaluate	Make an appraisal of the worth of something, in the light of its apparent truth or utility; include your personal opinion
Interpret	Bring out the meaning of, and make clear and explicit, usually also giving your own opinion
Justify	Show adequate grounds for decisions or conclusions
Prove	Demonstrate truth of falsehood by presenting evidence
Review	Make a survey of, examining the subject critically

A guide to learning independently by Marshall, Lorraine A.; Rowland, Frances Reproduced with permission of Open University Press in the format 'Republish in a book' via Copyright Clearance Center.

4. **Draw up a rough structure of what you might cover in the essay.** You will then need to confirm the order of what you cover and ensure that there is some logical flow to what you are writing, but having a structure often makes it easier to begin the essay – and starting the essay can be the biggest struggle sometimes.

5. **Make a note of the references and the content you will use for each section.** Start making notes of what pieces of reading you have done will feature in which section of your essay. You might wish to copy some of your notes into the relevant sections or paragraphs, but *do not* insert direct quotations unless you are sure you will use them in your final essay. (We examined the reasons for this in the section on avoiding plagiarism in Chapter 6.)

6. **Start writing.** This is often seen as the toughest part of essay writing, due to the benefits that come with procrastination and the emotional thrill (ignoring, however, the likelihood of submitting a poor – or even plagiarised – piece of work!) of doing the essay at the last minute! Many people start with the introduction, which is a good thing if you have a good idea of your

final structure, but if the structure should change, then starting with the introduction might not be the right thing to do (unless you have a reminder to change the introduction as well). If you are clear on the structure of your work, then writing the introduction can focus your mind and make the essay structure clearer to you.

There is no need to start with the introduction or even to write the paragraphs in the order in which they appear in the essay, though some people find it easier to do so. If you decide not to do this, then you will need to revisit the essay and add phrases to link the parts of the essay together and enable the reader to see clearly how you have reached your conclusions.

7. **Review what you have written.** Ask yourself whether the structure makes sense for any argument you are presenting (see pages 143–4), whether the evidence you have is strong enough and whether your point of view comes through clearly in the conclusion (see Chapter 4 on critical thinking). Have a look at the next section below. Does your essay fulfil those criteria? You should also check any alternative or additional criteria that your lecturer has posted online or given you in some other way. **If not, then go back and rewrite the relevant sections.**

Above all, make sure that you cannot be accused of plagiarism by what you write and how you have presented the information.

8. **Check the formatting and bibliography** to ensure that all is as it should be. This generally takes a bit of time, so make sure you plan for it. In a long assignment, make sure that sections are numbered correctly.

All the above take time, so careful planning is needed. Go back to Chapter 3 on time management, particularly in terms of using a diary, and review what is written there, if you need to.

What Does a Tutor Look for in an Academic Essay?

Part of this is answered in Chapter 6, but there are some issues that go beyond simple critical thinking and content. Essays are just one form of assessment used in qualitative or discursive subjects, but in many universities they are arguably the most common.

A lecturer will expect you to provide an essay that is:

- **Insightful** and demonstrates your critical thinking skills (see Chapter 4).
- **Relevant** to the question(s) which has been set.
- **Supported by examples** to illustrate the ideas outlined in the essay and strengthen the arguments.
- **Supported by citations and theory** to give those ideas credibility (see Chapter 6).
- Using **good grammar and spelling**, so that it looks as if an effort has been taken over the piece of work.
- **Structured well**, so as to have a beginning, middle and an end.
- **Mindful of the audience**, in terms of what it says and the knowledge it expects the audience to possess.
- **Written in appropriate academic style** in order to give you the chance to show your own thinking and give a summary of others' research.

This is a fairly long list. We will take a bit of time to look at each point in turn, but before we do so, look at the exercise immediately below.

FOR YOU TO DO

Into the mind of the assessor

When trying to develop an understanding of what lecturers are looking for in coursework, it is really helpful to look at the work of others and try to examine what mark might have been given and why. (In a second exercise relating to this question in the online content, we will see how two students answered the following question and attempt to assess them for ourselves, but, in the meantime, you might like to have a go at putting some thoughts down on paper and thinking about how you might assess the answer. What would you expect to see from an answer to this question? It appeared in a study skills module at a UK university.)

What makes the difference between an essay receiving a fail and one receiving a mark of 75%?

1. How would you answer this question? What would you include?
2. How you would structure your answer?
3. What sources might you need to refer to for information?

TASK AND
TEMPLATES

The companion website https://study.sagepub.com/morgan contains the two essays which answered the examination question above. These were real-life essays completed under examination conditions, and many of the thoughts that you might have written down were probably the same as those from the tutor reading and marking the essays. Now we need to examine what the tutor might have written and see if our comments agree, but before we do so we need to understand what makes for good practice in each of the criteria we have adopted. Where useful, some additional information is given for each of the criteria listed below.

When looking to mark essays, the following are important in the minds of tutors:

(a) **Extensive content and insight/critical thinking:** These were addressed in the previous chapter. Just be aware that if you simply repeat everything that was given to you in the lectures, then you will probably get a low mark that might pass, but nothing more. You will need to show the thinking you have done around your reading in order to do well.

(b) **Relevance:** Any academic work has to answer the question that is being asked. In larger pieces of work, the tutor may not understand or follow the argument you are making, so it is a good idea to ensure regularly that you give the reasons for writing what you are writing – in other words, show that what you are writing is relevant.

(c) **Use of examples:** Examples help the reader (your tutor) understand what is being discussed and shows that you understand the ideas your lecturers will have discussed. It is very tempting simply to recall the examples that they used during their lectures, but it is much better to try to find your own – as long as they are accurate.

(d) **Support provided by citations and theory:** A citation is a reference to some reading you have done, and usually a piece of research that someone has done to develop a theory. It usually appears in this kind of form: (Morgan, 2014). Providing a citation (see pages 126–7) enables the reader to have confidence that what you are suggesting in your essay is supported by research (i.e. there is some evidence for what you are saying in your work). As we saw in Chapter 4, presenting evidence for your view is vital if you are to do well in your work.

(e) **Grammar and spelling:** You might think that any work developed on the computer should have good grammar and spelling – after all, the widely used Microsoft Office software has spell-checking and grammar-checking tools. These tools are not always used well and work can be submitted using incorrect words (such as there and their, or pair and pear) which appear fine but which are not correct.

There is no real substitute for being able to spell well and students expecting to work in the UK should have good grammar and spelling. It is the expectations of employers that make these two areas important for assessment. However, it is not always the case that lecturers will provide feedback on your spelling and grammar. Some take the view that their role is to comment on your thinking, not your English. Of course, if they cannot understand your essay because of bad English, then you will not receive any marks for your critical thinking either.

━━━ FOR YOU TO DO ━━━

How good is your English?

The following exercise is a quick check on how good your English grammar and spelling are. This book is not aimed at improving your English, but if you score badly, then you might like to seek some support from your university.

The first test was developed from mistakes that were noticed regularly in academic essays.

Circle the correct word in each of the 12 statements below:

1. They took *there/their/they're* dog with them on the walk.
2. In order to improve *morale/moral*, the company decided to increase pay.
3. The most *relevant/relative* ideas were those which helped solve the problem.
4. 'It is *defiantly/definitely/definately* the correct answer!', he shouted.
5. He was unsure *whether/weather* to choose the black or brown shoes.
6. 'Of course, the main question is *which/witch* road to choose.'
7. 'Let's start at the *begging/beginning*, shall we?'
8. The biggest *affect/effect* he had was to cause the company to close down.
9. *You're/your* clearly the tallest person here.
10. I didn't want to take his *advice/advise*.
11. It was common *practice/practise* to plagiarise work.
12. Three weeks ago, he *choose/chose* to finish his employment.

Choose the correct spelling in each of the 18 statements below:

1. accommodation, accomodation, acommodation
2. conscus, conscious, conscous
3. embaras, embarrass, emmbaras
4. immediatly, immediately, imediately
5. ocasion, occasion, occassion
6. preferred, prefered, prefferd
7. personel, personnel, personnal
8. separat, separete, separate
9. necesary, nesessary, necessary

(Continued)

(Continued)

10. devided, divided, dividid
11. benefited, benefitted, bennefited
12. disappeared, disapeared, disapperd
13. ocured, occurred, occured
14. comitted, committed, comited
15. garantee, guarantee, guarante
16. laison, liason, liaison
17. questionare, questionnaire, questionaire
18. posess, posses, possess

Indicate which of the following sentences use the apostrophe (') correctly:

1. The students' had always liked the lecturer.
2. The students had always liked the lecturer's.
3. Sometimes the lecturer's liked the students.
4. The lecturer's books were on the shelf.
5. The students usually kept their books' on the floor.
6. The parents were worried about their children's studies.
7. The students and lecturers always got on well with each other.
8. It was nice of the lecturers to care about their student's.
9. It was nice of the lecturer's to care about their students.
10. It was nice of the lecturers' to care about their students'.

An interactive version of this task, along with answers are on the companion website at https://study.sagepub.com/morgan. Be aware that there are some differences between US and UK English spellings.

INTERACTIVE
TEST

(f) **Structure:** Other than the critical thinking and content areas for assessment detailed in Chapter 6, this is one of the most important criteria for assessing the work. Giving your essay a clear structure enables a reader to follow your line of thought really clearly, and it ensures that your work has a clear 'beginning', a solid 'middle' and an 'end' which gives some clear thought as to the answer to the question asked. It makes sense to spend some time looking at these three elements of essay structure to ensure that you have a clear understanding of what you mean.

The Introduction

An introduction to an essay should set out the aim of the piece of work and the main issues that will be discussed, and do the following:

- Get the reader's interest.
- Indicate the central idea running through the work.
- Give the reader a brief understanding of why the issue is important.
- Explain any information that is needed before the main body of the essay begins.

If you look at the introductions to each of the chapters here, you will find that each one clearly sets out what will be discussed and in what order. Setting out this information clearly enables the reader to feel confident that they can follow the content of the chapter and know where the chapter will 'take them'.

A good introduction will usually have these kinds of phrases:

- 'This chapter aims to …'
- 'This essay will begin by discussing …'
- 'It will also discuss …'
- 'This topic is important because …'
- 'Finally, the essay will show that …'

If your reader does not really understand what your essay is about and is going to cover by the end of the introduction, then it is probably not doing a good job and needs rewriting.

FOR YOU TO DO

PART A

If you have written an essay or started a draft essay, then try the following. Take a look at one of your essays. What do you think of the introduction? Does your essay have an introduction? Does it do what an introduction should really do?

PART B

Have a look at the final essay on Maslow (Box 4.10, pages 88-9). Does it have a good introduction? If you were giving feedback on this work, what would you say about it? How would you rewrite it?

The Middle

The middle of the essay provides the main arguments, gives the evidence and enables the reader to feel confident that you – as the writer – understand what you are talking about. If the introduction (and conclusion) are written well, then this part of the essay is where you will demonstrate your critical thinking, show the tutor the reading you have done that you believe to be relevant, and present evidence which helps to answer the question.

Many essay questions from your tutors will require you to debate an issue; that is, to present both sides of an argument and/or discuss why you agree or disagree with a particular point of view.

Many questions set by your tutors will expect you to present the evidence in favour of opposing opinions.

Such essays will require you to use phrases which indicate to the reader that you are linking or contrasting two or more ideas or pieces of research. The online content gives you some phrases which may be useful to do so.

ARGUMENT

An academic argument is a statement of a particular view or opinion, followed by the evidence to support that opinion.

 SIGNPOST

A signpost is a simple statement of what has been covered before a particular point in an essay, followed by a statement of what will come next.

In a long essay (or even in a text like this), you will need to include 'signposts' to tell your tutor/reader what has been covered and what is going to come next. These are important because they help your tutor/reader follow the arguments that you are making.

An example of a signpost might be: 'So far, this essay has looked at … However, we also need to consider … so the next section will focus on …'

The Conclusion

When you finish your essay, you will be expected to summarise clearly what you have said previously as a way of enabling the tutor to know what your view is. A conclusion is a summary, a clear statement of your view, bearing in mind the evidence you have presented. An essay without a conclusion will be incomplete, and will lose you marks.

A good conclusion will usually have one or two of these kinds of phrases:

- 'This essay set out to examine …'
- 'In summary …'
- 'The questions outlined in the introduction were … and this essay has covered those by …'

There is one comment left to make: in the social sciences (i.e. in the more discursive subjects such as business studies, politics, sociology and similar subjects which are neither clearly arts nor clearly sciences), there are rarely right and wrong answers, so students with very different conclusions can get identical grades. As we saw above, it is the quality of debate and the strength and quality of arguments that really enable a lecturer to give marks to a student. This may be different from school or your previous educational experience where getting the right or wrong answer is important.

 ━━━━━ KEY LEARNING POINT ━━━━━━━━━━━━━━━━━━━━

In degrees in Social Science subjects, there are rarely right and wrong answers. What matters more is the quality of the debate.

 ━━━━━ REFLECTION POINT ━━━━━━━━━━━━━━━━━━━━━

Take some time to think about the following questions and write down some answers.

How might the information given above change the way that you write your essays at university?
 How good were your spelling and grammar? What will you do to improve here?
 How will you ensure that your written work has a beginning, a middle and an end?

UNDERSTANDING THE AUDIENCE

A question often asked is: 'I have a tight word limit. I want to include as much information as I can to show my critical thinking skills, but how can I do so when I need to explain several theories in the first place?'

It is a fair question, and while we may not think that this has a lot to do with our audience, understanding our audience makes answering this question much easier.

━━━━ FOR YOU TO DO ━━━━

Glance through the following individuals. Which one(s) do you think most closely resemble the audience for your work?

Your parents

The intelligent man doing a professional job

Another student

The local councillor or Member of Parliament

Your best friend

A well-known professor at another university

A PhD student

A younger brother or sister

An individual who struggles with English

Your (future) husband or wife

The list above is not mutually exclusive (the intelligent man doing a professional job could also be your parent or the local councillor), but it is designed to get you to think about: (1) the level at which you write (your vocabulary or 'register'), and (2) the amount of detail you include.

You need to be writing for an individual who is intelligent and who can pick up ideas quickly if they are written clearly. This means that you do not have to give all the details of every idea or theory you are discussing, but that you should allocate more space in the essay to the areas where the potential for getting higher marks is greatest – that is, on demonstrating your critical thinking rather than simply describing theory.

━━━━ KEY LEARNING POINT ━━━━

In an essay where word limits are tight, you should allocate more space to the areas where the potential for getting higher marks is greatest - that is, on demonstrating your critical thinking rather than simply describing theory.

ACADEMIC STYLE

There is no one academic style for writing a traditional essay and many lecturers will expect you to develop your own style as you go through university. Even your lecturers will have different styles, since they will be required by their work to write journal articles based on research and theory, and each journal will have different styles.

═══════ FOR YOU TO DO ═══════

PART A

Have a brief look at three articles from different journals:

1. How similar is the kind of language used in the three journal articles? Which one(s) are easier and which are more difficult to understand?
2. Look at the way the different sources are referenced within the articles. Do all the articles use the same referencing style?
3. How similar are they to your own personal style of writing?

PART B

Think about writing a letter to your parents or family members. Would that style of writing be different from the way you would write an essay at university? If so, how? Why?

Your own style will develop, but it will need to share *some* of the characteristics from the three articles you have read – although which characteristics will depend on the kind of work your lecturers expect, and there are some notable exceptions to the rules given below in Box 7.1. For example, reflective writing will break many of the rules. You can find more information about this on the companion website at https://study.sagepub.com/morgan.

FURTHER
READING

═══════ BOX 7.1 ═══════

WHAT MAKES 'ACADEMIC STYLE' ACADEMIC?

There are some important rules to follow when it comes to writing academic work. You need to remember that you are writing for an academic audience. That means:

- You should be making an argument based on evidence obtained by research – either from primary or from secondary sources – and not based on emotion.
- Your own experience can count, but evidence from a large body of research involving hundreds or thousands of people tends to carry more weight. Use research evidence as the basis for your argument and supplement it with additional examples and anecdotes if you need to.
- Use the 'passive voice' wherever possible: instead of writing 'I did this', talk about *what was done*.
- Avoid long, complicated sentences: keep them short and focused on just one or two issues.
- Avoid using 'colloquial' language: for example, writing 'employees' is better than writing 'people'; 'in subsequent research' is better than 'after that'; and '10 out of 12 employees' is better than writing 'a lot of employees'. You need to keep it relatively formal.

(Continued)

(Continued)

- Some people advise against using the same nouns or verbs more than once in one short sentence or in immediately adjacent sentences. For example, 'A number of ideas were proposed at the meeting. One idea was to ...' might be better phrased as, 'One proposal was to ...' or 'One suggestion was to ...'.
- Try to be succinct: is there a way of cutting down on words and yet keeping the same meaning? This usually requires a reasonable vocabulary, but writing succinctly is something that is as important in academic life as it is in professional life.

When writing an essay, it is usually better to avoid definitive statements of truth, phrases such as: 'There is no research' or 'Employees never …' may well result in a comment from a lecturer arguing that there is some research into something; or instead of 'How can you say that no one will ever …?' it is better to say that: 'It appears that …' or 'it seems that …' However, when you are analysing a case study, you can repeat the facts given to you in the case study material itself, but be sure that you are interpreting such material correctly.

Developing your own voice and style is not an easy thing to do, and comes with practice and time, but it develops a lot quicker *if you do more reading*.

Expressing Your Own View

Some students struggle to write in an academic style (and there is not just one) yet want to express their own opinion. This is a really important issue, especially when critical thinking is such an important part of assessment, so how does it get done? Look at the following exercise and see if you can identify the phrases that are used to express the author's opinions, rather than those of other people.

--- FOR YOU TO DO ---

The following is a fictional passage from an essay which summarises the views of others as well as expresses the author's own views. Underline those sentences or phrases which you think are opinions of the author, and circle those phrases which you think simply summarise what others have said:

Understanding essay writing seems to be a challenging task for many students – according to much research (Watson, 2003). Research has suggested that students particularly struggle with giving their work structure and with understanding the criteria that lecturers use (Watson, 2003; Paulson, 2012). Of course, there are other areas that some students seem to struggle with as well: providing sufficient references to research is something that many academics note as an issue (e.g. Scott, 2004) and – as noted by Blade (2002) – understanding whether evidence from personal experience is better than evidence from the literature is also a difficulty for many students. As stated by Scott, 'These basic issues are key to doing well in academic work' (2004: p. 112).

However, what this debate misses is how lecturers and academics can enable students to understand how academics think. Lecturers can teach students about the criteria and show students what good work looks like, but until the student understands what is in the mind of an academic and how assessment

(Continued)

(Continued)

works, then a great deal of this teaching may be ineffective. Students need to be given examples and be given the chance to assess others' work.

Some work has already begun in this area. Work by Price (2003) has shown that assessment feedback and engaging students in peer-to-peer learning has some benefit, but of course the effectiveness of this rests on how well the students can understand what the criteria mean and how they can be recognised in academic work. What may be of some considerable interest is some research work into how academics develop those skills themselves, and studies in this area may provide some clue as to how to help students understand and recognise these skills also.

In conclusion, we can argue that we are making progress. It is not easy and there will be challenges along the way, but if we can develop students' understanding of how to demonstrate their critical thinking skills, then we will have gone some way to fulfilling our aim as facilitators of learning.

1. How easy was it for you to identify the two different sources of view: those from research and those from the author?
2. Write down some of the phrases and wording used by the author to express the author's own view. (Some ideas are given on the companion website.)
3. Rewrite this passage in your own academic style. Think about how you might change the language and sentence structure to make the passage one that reflects your own academic style.
4. Is there anything else that you can learn from the passage above about academic writing?

When you were completing this exercise, you would have listed a number of phrases which could be useful to you. Learning to express your own view in an academic style is vital if you are going to demonstrate your own opinion, and showing your own opinion is going to push you towards those higher grades. There is a list of useful phrases that you could use to express yourself on the companion website at https://study.sagepub.com/morgan.

DOWNLOAD

One of the fears that many students have is that they will be committing plagiarism, but there is a very simple rule here:

- Any statement that has a citation will have come from the literature and other people's research. Any statement that does not have a citation will be assumed to be your own thinking. If it is *not* your own thinking, then you may be committing plagiarism.

As a student, you will need to find your own style. Some lecturers might be happier with your using a less conventional academic style and, as we have said before here, the best source of information is always going to be *your tutor*.

DISSERTATIONS

If you are a postgraduate student, then you will almost certainly need to complete a dissertation, probably around 15,000–20,000 words, but many undergraduate students need to do dissertations as well. This might sound scary. You have probably never written anything of that size before, but it is easy to think of dissertations as large essays and, in some ways, that is what they are. However, they are more than that. There are three significant differences between essays and dissertations:

- Their size.
- The usual requirement for a student completing a dissertation to undertake some form of research.
- The process for completion.

Of course, dissertations are solely individual pieces of work, so we will not look at group working in connection with dissertations.

Size and Structure

If an essay is usually around 3000 words, then a dissertation could be five or six times as long. On the surface of it, the criteria for assessment are probably the same, but the expectations for depth of analysis may well be greater. However, the size makes issues of structure far more important.

In a large piece of work, a reader needs to be reminded of what they are reading and how it fits into the overall work. This means that the dissertation needs to be split into chapters, and each chapter needs to have an introduction and conclusion.

A typical *conclusion* to one chapter might read: 'This chapter has examined … It has outlined the theory regarding … and has shown that … The following chapter will extend this investigation by …'

The *introduction* to the following chapter might then read: 'The dissertation has so far discovered that … It has shown … It is now important to examine … by … Therefore, this chapter will begin with …'

In effect, then, the dissertation becomes a series of essays which *together* introduce the reader to some issues relevant to your degree programme, identify some research questions, investigate those questions and present some answers in a credible way. The dissertation effectively takes the reader on a story revolving around some research questions.

A dissertation based on primary research will usually have a structure similar to that in Box 7.2.

==== **BOX 7.2** ====

TYPICAL STRUCTURE OF A RESEARCH DISSERTATION

There is no on definitive way of structuring every dissertation, but most research-based pieces of work follow a similar structure to a research journal article. This results in a chapter structure similar to that set out below.

Chapter 1: Introduction

Introduction and overview

This chapter provides an oversight of the contents and objectives of the dissertation, establishes the reader's interest and tells the reader how the work is structured. Many supervisors recommend making this the last chapter that you write because, by then, you will have a good idea of know what each chapter has covered.

Chapter 2 (or maybe two chapters): Literature – Secondary Sources

What are you looking at and why?

This chapter provides the theoretical background to the research questions and displays your critical thinking skills. If there is a particular issue to be addressed at a particular company, then there needs to some

(Continued)

(Continued)

background to the company. This may be given in Chapter 1 or in a separate third chapter, but needs to be given before the research questions are set out, which usually happens before the research methodology is given.

With the exception of MBA projects (which are usually different in nature), the literature review will likely form nearly *half* of your dissertation. It has to be evaluative and critical (see Chapter 4), comprehensive in covering the topic, up to date, and should inform both the questions you intend to ask as part of your research and the discussion chapter, where you will be comparing the results of the research with the literature that you have found. As such, the literature review forms probably the largest part of the dissertation.

Chapter 3: Methodology

How will we investigate this?

This chapter establishes the methods used to gather the information required by the research questions. It should give information on the sample and provide some justification for gathering the information in the ways proposed. The discussion could also include some arguments about why other methods were not used. This section could also set out the statistical analyses used, but these could also be given in the results chapter.

Chapter 4: Results

What did we find?

This chapter gives the results of the investigation. It may include a commentary on the findings in a separate 'Conclusions' chapter, but usually simply gives the findings of the research questions asked earlier on in the dissertation.

Chapter 5: Conclusion and Discussion

Did we find what we expected, based on the literature? How useful are these results for other researchers?

The final chapter does three things:

1. It compares the results obtained from the study with expectations developed from the literature, and tries to give some explanation where those results differ from expectations.
2. It investigates the strengths and weaknesses of the research methodology adopted.
3. It sets out some further questions for investigation.

Bibliography

This needs to include the sources that you have included and used in writing the dissertation.

Appendices

The appendices should allow the reader to learn more about your research than you are able to write in the dissertation. The appendices should include your methodology (questionnaire, interview schedule etc), details of the sample and the responses, and more detailed statistics than was used in the main text. They might also include your research proposal.

There is no requirement for a research-based dissertation to follow this five-chapter model precisely, and you will need to discuss this with your dissertation supervisor as you start working on this large piece of work.

A Need for Research

The second aspect by which dissertations can differ from smaller essays is that there is often a need for primary research. Not all universities or programmes require students undertaking a dissertation to complete a piece of primary research, but it is a very common requirement to do so. This means that, as a student, you need to have a number of particular skills:

- **Good time management:** No one will be pushing you, so you will need to keep setting milestones in order to get this large piece of work completed on time.
- **Motivation:** To keep working on this for possibly six months or a year.
- **Good understanding of research methodologies and statistics:** The more you know before you start your work, the less time you will need to spend finding this out.
- **Access to information:** Sometimes, including organisations and companies, depending on the nature of your work, will make it difficult to arrange access to busy people in a short space of time, so the more access you have before you begin, the easier your investigation will be.
- **Clear and succinct writing style:** It is a long piece of work, so a clear style will mean that it is easy to follow the ideas and arguments. Such a style also makes a dissertation more pleasant to read.
- **Critical thinking skills:** Essential. You will need to find, read and evaluate journal sources relating to the topic you are investigating. The more descriptive your work, the lower the mark and the less interesting it will be.
- **Ability to learn independently:** Essential. You will need to find your own information, analyse it yourself and come to your own conclusions.
- **Organised:** You will need to organise your information so that you can find and comment on it easily, should the need arise. Your supervisor will also expect you to attend meetings on time, so you will need to be able to manage your diary well (see the first bullet point above).

All of the above are requirements for a student undertaking a dissertation. If you do not have these qualities and you are required to do a dissertation, then you will need to develop them fast.

The Process for Completion

The final areas where essays are slightly different from dissertations relates to the process for completion. In a typical essay, you will look at the question, develop some thoughts about relevant reading, investigate those sources, and add your notes and thinking together to develop a piece of written work which you believe answers the question well.

A dissertation works differently. Firstly, for most dissertations, there are no set questions: you develop your own questions based upon your interests, your career aspirations, and so on. The choice of topic is important: it will signal to an employer your interests; it will need to be completed within the timescale set; it will need to answer questions that you can actually get answers to. Above all, it is highly likely that you will not be able to change the topic suddenly without a full discussion with your supervisor.

Secondly, if you are doing a dissertation, you will be undertaking 'independent learning'. This means that the relationship you have with your supervisor is important here. It is a one-to-one relationship, where you do the work and receive feedback on that work. There is no teaching but there is guidance. Some suggest that the dissertation supervisor has the same role as a sports coach. They are not there to do the work for you, but to give feedback on the content, style, critical thinking, and so on, that you display in your own writing. They may not be an expert on the particular topic that you have chosen, but they can give you guidance on how and where to look for information and on the other criteria that we discussed above in relation to essays. They will also be able to give you advice on how to complete a dissertation, probably reflecting the ideas given in Box 7.3 below.

BOX 7.3

COMPLETING A DISSERTATION: DOS AND DON'TS

Do

- Start early and get organised
- Keep in touch and maintain good relations with your supervisor
- Clarify and follow agreed objectives
- Have a detailed proposal/project plan – a Gantt Chart
- Make sure you keep the tense the same throughout the dissertation; this is not always easy for a long piece of work
- Ensure you have ethics approval for your work, where needed
- Set targets/milestones and deliverables
- Back up, and then back up your backup
- Follow any dissertation guidelines given to you by your university or department
- Critically evaluate theory and research where possible/appropriate
- Link chapters to each other – develop a narrative
- Include a methodology
- Contextualise findings in relevant literature
- Keep records and reference properly
- Read the project that you have written
- Allow time for feedback – particularly at end

Don't

- Underestimate the amount of time and work needed
- Be vague about the project purpose and outcomes
- Ignore any ethics process your university will require your proposal to adhere to
- Be vague with respect to methodology
- Change the proposal or research and not tell the supervisor
- Ignore relevant key literature
- Include long, rambling chapters
- Copy straight from the book or the Internet without referencing
- Leave it to the last minute and rush the writing up
- Expect instant review and feedback from the supervisor

Thirdly, on a practical note, dissertations may be undertaken during the summer, as is very commonly the case for Master's degree programmes. If this is the case, then it is your responsibility to ensure that you find out when your supervisor will be available to meet you, when they will be away and how to contact them when they are away. In any event, arranging meetings with your supervisor should be something that is planned in advance. You cannot expect a supervisor to be available just when you want them to be, though, if they are, then that is great. The first meeting with your supervisor is usually when such practicalities are discussed.

In summary, completing a dissertation is unlike most other pieces of work that you will ever do at university. It is usually large in terms of word length, time consuming in terms of the hours of reading and research that will be needed, and challenging in terms of the motivation needed to complete it.

Students who ignore the guidance above tend either to do very poorly on their dissertation (because they have not obtained regular feedback or because they could not actually do what they were hoping to do as an investigation or for some other reason) or get caught plagiarising and cheating. There are no shortcuts to undertaking a dissertation properly, but the skills that you develop and demonstrate during the dissertation will be extremely useful in future careers.

REFLECTION POINT

Take some time to think about the following questions and write down some answers.

If you needed to do a dissertation, what would be the first thing that you would do: talk to the tutor, or start reading some relevant literature? Why?

How easy is it to develop your own style of writing?

INTEGRATION AND APPLICATION

You should now have some ideas in your mind about how to write essays and dissertations. Dissertations are very similar to essays in many respects, namely style, need for critical thinking, citations and evidence, but usually students undertake a piece of research. Completing a dissertation requires working with a supervisor, while writing essays should be an individual piece of work. However, apart than that, the mechanics tend to be similar; they are given on pages 151–2.

Step 1: Do some reading around the subject and make some notes. For the moment, we will assume that you have done some reading and have made some notes. An essay which has no signs of reading will have lots of signs of personal opinion and 'common sense', and those kinds of essays tend to do very poorly when it comes to academic assessment. Start making a note of what pieces of reading you have done and use a tool like EndNote to compile your bibliography.

Step 2: Practically, prepare yourself and your writing area. You are preparing to write a draft, so do not get too stressed about doing this.

Step 3: Consider the question carefully. Try to rewrite the question in your own words two or three times. Check key nouns and verbs in the question to make sure you understand what is being asked for in the essay.

Step 4: Draw up a rough structure of what you might cover in the essay. You will then need to confirm the order of what you cover and when, and ensure that there is some logical flow to what you are writing. Remember: introduction, middle (if a discussion, then arguments in favour, arguments against), conclusion.

Step 5: Start writing. This is often seen as the toughest part of essay writing. Many people start with the introduction, which is a good idea if you have an idea of your final structure, but if that structure might change, then starting with the introduction may not be the right thing to do, unless you have a reminder to change the introduction as well.

Step 6: Review what you have written. Ask yourself whether the structure makes sense for any argument you are presenting, whether the evidence you have is strong enough and whether your point of view comes through clearly in the conclusion. Above all, make sure that you have *not* copied anything into your work that is from another source without stating that you have done so.

Step 7: Check the formatting and bibliography. Ensure that all is as it should be. This generally takes a bit of time, so make sure you plan for it. In a long assignment, make sure that sections are numbered correctly. The most important issues are to:

- Show that you can answer the question intelligently.
- Include evidence that is sufficiently strong.
- Make sure that you include references to others' ideas and work wherever you use them.

Completing a written assessment is not an easy thing to do, but if you have followed these steps, then you should do well.

CONCLUSION

By now, you should have a better idea of how to:

- Develop your own academic style for writing essays and assignments.
- Understand what your tutor means by the questions they set.
- Evaluate how good your English grammar and spelling are.
- Understand clearly how a tutor approaches the assessment for a piece of written work.
- Express the difference between an essay receiving a pass and one receiving a high mark.

FURTHER
READING

The companion website at https://study.sagepub.com/morgan contains a significant amount of material relating to reflective writing and case studies, and gives you the chance to assess two students' examination essays and compare your marks with those of the tutor.

FINAL REFLECTIONS

Based on the content of this chapter, what do you now know about writing essays or dissertations that you did not know before?

What key learning point had the most impact? Why?

Do your answers to either of the above questions have the potential to change your attitude to studies at university? If so, why?

What will you now do differently? (Write this down and put it somewhere where you can see it regularly.)

 INTERVIEW QUESTIONS

In Chapters 5 and 6, it was suggested that there would be few interview questions regarding assessment specifically, but that interviewers might ask questions around the topic to find out other things about you (e.g. your ability to think critically or to plan an activity). The same applies to this chapter as well: if you ask

(Continued)

(Continued)

'Why would an interviewer want to know about my assignments?', then the only reasonable answer is to understand something more about your personal transferable skills, not the assignments themselves.
Think about the following questions. What might your answers be?

1. What was the most challenging piece of written work you have worked on? And why? How did you go about ensuring it was a good piece of work?
2. Tell me about your experience with writing reports. Can you briefly tell me about a report you have written?

Chapter 17 gives a lot more information on selection interviews and the online content gives some guidance on these questions.

ADDITIONAL RESOURCES

Want to learn more? Visit https://study.sagepub.com/morgan to gain access to a wide range of online resources, including interactive tests, tasks, further reading and downloads.

Website Resources

Greasely, P. (2016) *Doing Essays and Assignments* (2nd edition). London: Sage (chapter in book), see: https://uk.sagepub.com/en-gb/eur/doing-essays-and-assignments/book244296

Walliman, N. (2013) *Your Undergraduate Dissertation.* London: Sage (chapter in book), see: https://uk.sagepub.com/en-gb/eur/your-undergraduate-dissertation/book239008

Furseth, I. and Everett, E. L. (2013) *Doing Your Master's Dissertation.* London: Sage, see: https://uk.sagepub.com/en-gb/eur/doing-your-masters-dissertation/book240102

Textbook Resources

Bailey, S. (2011) *Academic Writing for International Students of Business.* Abingdon: Routledge.
Clark, I. L. (2007) *Writing the Successful Thesis and Dissertation.* Upper Saddly River, NJ: Prentice-Hall.
Cottrell, S. (2008) *The Study Skills Handbook.* Basingstoke: Palgrave (particularly chapter 8).
Courtney, M. and Du, X. (2014) *Study Skills for Chinese Students.* London: Sage (see 'chapter 5: Research and Dissertations'.
Irwin, D., Jovanovic-Krstic, V. and Watson, M. A. (2013) *So Where's your Dissertation?* Toronto: Nelson Education.
McMillan, K. and Weyers, J. (2012) *The Study Skills Book* (3rd edition). Harlow: Pearson (particularly chapters 51 and 52).
Metcalfe, M. (2006) *Reading Critically at University.* London: Sage.
Muth, M. F. (2006) *Researching and Writing: A Portable Guide.* Boston, MA: Bedford/St Martins.
Seely, J. (2005) *Oxford Guide to Effective Writing and Speaking.* New York: Oxford University Press (particularly section D, p. 247–80).
Swetnam, D. and Swetnam, R. (2009) *Writing Your Dissertation* (3rd edition). Oxford: Howtobooks.
Tissington, P., Hasel, M. and Matthiesen, J. (2009) *How to Write Successful Business and Management Essays.* London: Sage.
Whitman, A. and Demarest, K. (2000) *Communication Works*! Upper Saddle River, NJ: Prentice-Hall (particularly chapter 2).

/8/ EXAMINATIONS AT UNIVERSITY

CHAPTER STRUCTURE

Figure 8.1

When you see the 🌐 this means go to the companion website https://study.sagepub.com/morgan to do a quiz, complete a task, read further or download a template.

━━ AIMS OF THE CHAPTER ━━━━━━━━

By the end of this chapter, you should be able to:

- Describe the different forms and different meanings of examination question that are used at university.
- Identify the practical issues you need to know in relation to the examinations that you will be taking.
- Evaluate various mechanisms for improving your revision and memory.
- Avoid some of the common failings when answering university examination questions.

INTRODUCTION

In many cases, mention of the word 'examination' tends to fill most people with a sense of dread and fear, but knowing what to expect and what is expected of you will reduce that stress considerably.

Universities will differ from each other in the extent to which they use examinations for assessment, and they will also differ in how they carry out those examinations and in their format. For example, some universities will use much less formal in-class tests in the early stages of a degree, while others will use multiple choice questions in the first year of a degree. We will spend some time looking at how universities conduct examinations and the various formats being used, but we begin with a brief look at what lecturers look for in good examination answers and provide some suggestions regarding issues of preparation, including revision.

SKILLS SELF-ASSESSMENT

It is not easy to assess your ability to pass an examination successfully unless you have one to take, but you can at least see how prepared you feel and how much you know.

Look at the items below. Complete the brief questionnaire to see how much you know about your examinations at university. Give each item a score of between 1 and 5, where 1 is 'I strongly disagree' and 5 is 'I strongly agree'. Answer each item quickly. There are right and wrong answers to *some of these*, so be sure to complete the interactive test and compare your answers with those on the companion website at https://study.sagepub.com/morgan.

INTERACTIVE TEST

Number	Item	Score
1.	I am really happy to take examinations	
2.	I prefer multiple choice questions because generally I like to guess the answers	
3.	I am not very good at calculations and prefer essay questions	
4.	I revise for examinations by focusing my time or energy on two or three main topics	
5.	I am sure I know what topics will come up in my next examination	
6.	I know how long each of my examinations will last	
7.	I would never cheat in an examination	
8.	If I see others cheating in an examination, I will report it to the person in charge of the examination	
9.	Cheating in an examination is academic misconduct	
10.	Examinations are all about managing your time	
11.	Open book examinations are much easier than closed book examinations	
12.	If I write more in an examination, then I will get a higher mark	
13.	In an examination, I need to include citations and a bibliography	
14.	If there is something in my life which prevents me from doing well, I can just take the examination again	

(Continued)

(Continued)

Number	Item	Score
15.	Making a plan for any essay is vital if I am going to get a good mark	
16.	Calculation examinations are easier than essays	
17.	I know where and when all my examinations are going to take place	
18.	Examinations which last a shorter period of time are easier than longer ones	
19.	I always feel anxious before going into an examination	
20.	I always check past papers to see what topics are going to appear in the examination	

With the exception of item 9, there are no right or wrong answers to this exercise (the answer to item 9 is likely to be 'agree' or 'strongly agree', since cheating in an examination is definitely an example of academic misconduct). However, it would be interesting to see whether your view is the same as that of others in your class.

Longer responses to essay questions do not always get higher marks, but there is a stronger possibility of their doing so because you are more likely to include more content. Shorter examinations may expect you to write very succinctly, which can make them harder, and not everyone finds calculations easy. It would be a very useful exercise for you to take your answers to your personal tutor or a module lecturer and discuss them together.

 'BUT I HAVE A QUESTION ...' ═══════════════════

... Why do universities use examinations at all? In the real world, we never have to do things from memory, right? What about assignments?

Yes, assignments can be more interesting and the point about doing things from memory is true, but some tutors want to assess your ability to develop a good argument quickly – and that is also what is needed 'in the real world'. In meetings, you will rarely have time to look up information online, so knowing what you are talking about is crucial.

Some people believe that examinations are used because students cannot plagiarise or cheat in them – or it is at least more difficult. There is some truth in that, but it is never an acceptable reason for using examinations over assignments – and students do still try to cheat. As I have mentioned, it is all about being able to develop a good argument quickly and without reference to external resources.

A third and final reason why universities use examinations is to help others know that the student is able to work calmly and efficiently under pressure. For most people, timed examinations are fairly stressful situations, and while it is not fair to put excessive pressure on students, the ability to work calmly under pressure is a valuable skill.

DIFFERENT QUESTION TYPES AND EXPECTATIONS

Finding out what makes a good answer will depend on the kinds of questions being asked. In some ways, the answer has similarities to those in Chapter 6 and Chapter 7, but there are some subtle differences. There are various types of examination questions, and each will look for slightly different things, as in Table 8.1.

Table 8.1 Types of questions

Question type	Example	High marks typically given for
Multiple choice	Which of the following is *not* a county in the UK? (a) West Yorkshire (b) South Yorkshire (c) East Yorkshire (d) North Yorkshire	Demonstrating understanding and ability to apply course content to the question (Marking can sometimes be negative for wrong answers)
Calculation	If 46% of a company's turnover is profit, and the company had sales of £20,500 three years ago which have risen consistently by 5%, what was the company's profit this year?	Demonstrating the ability to apply concepts covered in the course
Essay	Discuss the advantages and disadvantages of applying Maslow's motivation theory in the workplace	Demonstrating all the requirements of a good essay identified earlier in this chapter – including good structure, relevant knowledge and critical thinking (see Chapter 4)
Case study	Bearing in mind the information given in the case study for the examination, answer the following three questions …	The ability to analyse information and develop arguments and solutions to problems as given in the case study
Practical exercise	Using the information given in the passage, use Excel to calculate the mean, range and standard deviation …	Your ability to take information and use relevant equipment

The type of question will depend on what the lecturer wishes to assess (i.e. the module's learning outcomes) and on your level of study, but you should have good notice of the type of question that will be used in any examinations you have to undertake. Box 8.1 reflects on whether examination assessment reflects the realities of working life after graduation.

BOX 8.1

DO EXAMINATIONS ASSESS THE RIGHT THINGS?

We said earlier that university is about 'learning how to think' (pages 8-9 and page 15) and, as a result, demonstrating critical thinking skills is important to being able to do well, so the question then is how examinations do this. Some suggest that examinations only really assess a student's ability to remember, but the validity of any assessment criterion can only really be determined in comparison with the needs of employers. If examinations only assess memory, then some suggest that this is not a valid method of assessment, so do they only assess memory?

Perhaps there is some truth here, but it is a long way short of the complete picture. At a basic level, examinations assess knowledge, and it is true that the reproduction of knowledge is based on what someone can remember, but there is a separation between knowing something well and knowing it because it is something that someone has revised. Take the example of a student who has thought and read a lot about

(Continued)

(Continued)

Maslow's Hierarchy of Needs: they will probably not need to revise it because they will have thought about it (and 'chewed over' the theory). The thinking they have done about the theory means that they know it well.

One other set of skills that examinations assess is related to time management, both in terms of planning for revision and in terms of being able to manage time within the examination itself. There is validity in doing so because being able to complete tasks efficiently is a key aspect of managerial functioning.

There are, however, different forms of examination which can assess other skills. In many cases, the only examinations that students take are those where they sit down, wait a moment or two in silence with just their pens or pencils and then turn over the paper once they are told to 'Begin!'. However, there are some additional formats for examinations used for some courses.

One such variation is the open book examination where students are allowed to take into the examination room any materials they wish. This sounds like an easy examination and reflects one aspect of the real world, since people have access to a wide range of resources to help them in their work and so the argument is that an open book examination best reflects life after university.

'Easy', however, is a word that does not necessarily relate to open book examinations: if a student does not understand some course content or does not have a basic knowledge of the topic, then all the resources available to them will not improve their examination performance. Tutors who offer an open book examination may also have higher expectations anyway and marks may be harder to obtain.

Writing an examination essay is only slightly different from writing an assignment essay and the criteria for assessing an essay will be very similar to those for academic work generally (see Chapter 6). Apart from the fact that an assignment essay is not done under timed conditions, an examiner will generally have fewer expectations when it comes to referencing or providing a bibliography (you need to check the detail of this with your lecturers), but you will still be expected to provide evidence for your arguments and points of view.

There is no ideal length for an examination essay (you could write the same point several times in an essay six sides long!) but a short answer will be unlikely to cover all of the content expected in the depth required for a good answer.

We will now turn to look at some of the preparation issues to consider before an examination.

PREPARING FOR AN EXAMINATION

There are a number of issues here. We will begin by looking at handling nerves (i.e. how we prepare ourselves) and then look at various aids to revision, such as using past examination papers, revision timetables, ideas for memorisation and making notes.

Nerves and Emotions

The issue of nervousness before examinations can seem slightly different to that for presentations listed above. With group presentations, it often concerns our thoughts about what others might be thinking of us and our expectations about looking at a sea of unfriendly faces (which is hardly ever the reality anyway). With examinations, the issue is often different, but we can still have reactions that we do not always expect – as shown in Box 8.2.

━━━━━ **BOX 8.2** ━━━━━

REACTIONS TO EXAMINATIONS

In his 1998 text *Learn How to Study*, Derek Rowntree identified a number of reactions that folk can have towards examinations. Have a look at those below. Which ones are closer to your own feelings?

1. I wouldn't say that I take them in my stride, but I wouldn't say that they give me sleepless nights either.
2. No, I won't go bananas. I'll just ration my time out more carefully and think positively.
3. I know I am under a lot more strain when the exams come around, but I just play a lot more squash – that's my way of working off the pressure.
4. I've started smoking again. What more can I say?
5. I get depressed when other students tell me about all the areas they've been looking into and I realise I haven't done anything about them, by how other students seem to have covered so much more of the work than I have and there's no time to catch up.
6. There's so much to remember – I can't believe my memory's good enough to cope with it all.
7. I can get so paralysed with fear that I couldn't think what to revise or get the willpower even if someone told me.
8. I'm that panicky and depressed I feel like going off and never coming back.
9. Of course I'm worried and anxious: who wouldn't be? But I need it. It's the only way I can work up enough steam to get the work done in time.

Examinations generally produce uncertainty about what will be there on the paper when we turn it over (i.e. a fear of the unknown). We can minimise this to some extent, but if your lecturers were to remove this fear completely by telling you the questions in advance, then there would be little difference between doing the examination and submitting a piece of coursework. The best that we can do sometimes is simply to spend time ensuring that we have completed the practical preparation and have done our best to ensure we can remember the content presented to us during the modules we have taken.

The answer to some of this may rest with the ideas given in the chapter on presentation skills (see Chapter 9), which mentions issues of preparation, and similar ideas apply here. In some ways it can be useful to think of an essay as an oral presentation without the voice and the PowerPoint slides. It might be useful to look at Table 8.2 which provides a checklist of items to find out before the examination.

There are some things that we can do to limit nerves and some things we can do to relax. The impact of both will be the same – we will be more relaxed – but the way we address them will be different. In addition to the practical preparation we can do before an examination, we can do some physical and emotional preparation.

Get some sleep: Some students believe that spending the whole night revising is the best way to prepare for an examination, but this is rarely true. It might be what some are used to, but the brain is not as alert after a sleepless night as it is after a good night's sleep. If you are used to spending a sleepless night revising for an examination, then you might like to try the next exercise below.

Table 8.2   Examination Preparation Checklist

Item	Do I know this? (Yes/No)
1. How long the examination will last?	
2. Will I be given advance notice of topics or questions?	
3. What books and other materials do I need to have with me?	
4. How many questions will I have to answer?	
5. Whether any questions contain options within them?	
6. Are some questions likely to be compulsory?	
7. Is the paper split into parts? Do I have to answer questions from each part? Is there a difference between the parts to the paper (i.e. a reason for the split)?	
8. Do some questions carry more marks than others?	
9. Which topics have appeared with more frequency than others?	
10. Are there any areas on which considerable stress has been put (i.e. taken up a lot of time etc.) but not been examined recently?	
11. What might the questions ask me to do (e.g. discuss, evaluate, etc.)? Do I know what these mean?	

 ━━━ FOR YOU TO DO ━━━━━━━━━━━━━━━━━━━━━━━━━━━

This is a test of your memory in some ways, but you will get to see the impact of a lack of sleep on your memory if you complete both parts of this exercise.

PART A

Try the following exercise when you are in your normal state of alertness. Below is a series of numbers. Look at them for about 30 seconds and try to remember them:

1 3 5 7 9 11 12 14 16 18 22 24 19 26 48 27

Now close the book and write down the numbers in the list in the order that they are given.

How many did you get correct?

PART B

Try the same exercise when you have had less sleep.

How long do you have to look at the numbers in order to remember them?

───

This exercise should have indicated to you that it takes a lot longer and a lot more effort to remember information when we are tired than it does when we are alert.

An issue related to this is that we do not necessarily sleep well when we are stressed or worried or when we don't eat well, and often the times when we don't eat well are those same times when we are anxious, so these two aspects can interact with each other and make life awkward for us. The best way to break this is to have a good meal before relaxing and going to bed. The worst way to deal with this is probably to try and stay up all night – in which case probably make ourselves more tired.

Using Past Examination Papers

There are two ways to use past examination papers in preparing for an examination: (1) as a way to 'question-spot'; and (2) as a way to practise the kinds of questions which might arise during the examination itself.

Let's look at 'question spotting' for a moment. Of course, if you have an examination paper where you have to answer three questions, then you might be tempted to revise four topics rather than six or eight. It is a lot less work and enables you to focus your reading.

Lecturers will be aware that some of their students may do this, and generally will not approve. In principle, it does not allow you to demonstrate all the knowledge that you should have for passing your courses, and that is something which some academics feel strongly about.

On a more academic note, question spotting does not always work. Multiple choice questions, for example, typically cover the whole syllabus; examination papers might be structured into parts so that you have to answer one question from each part (or a compulsory question and then questions from other parts, or something similar); or questions might link two topics together around a theme common to both. Equally, you might spot the wrong topics or have a question that asks about a topic you have prepared in a way that you did not expect – and that is the risk. Question spotting might sometimes work, but the risks associated with getting this wrong can mean that you waste time trying to question-spot, rather than using that time to prepare and revise thoroughly.

'QUESTION SPOTTING'

If a student attempts to 'question-spot', then they will be trying to work out what topics will appear in the examination.

This is often done by looking at patterns of topics in past papers to determine what has and has not been covered more recently.

— **KEY LEARNING POINT** —

Question spotting is potentially very risky and failing an examination could put your degree and future job in jeopardy. Some lecturers combine topics in a single examination question.

The second way to use past papers is to prepare answers. The best way to do this of course is to look at some questions from past papers and get some feedback on how well you are able to answer them. The feedback is crucial: without it, any preparation becomes merely an exercise in how well you can remember what you have revised and in being able to write an essay or answer questions under time constraints. Both of these are helpful in themselves, but the real benefit comes when you know that you can do well under timed conditions. This only really happens when you get the feedback on your work.

Note especially that if you are going to use past papers to revise from, you must make sure that the format of the paper and the syllabus of the course have not changed. If the syllabus has changed then the topics examined by the paper in previous years will be different, of course.

Developing a Revision Timetable

Before we go too far, it is useful to clarify what we mean by 'revision'.

Revision can take a number of forms and different people prefer to use different strategies and techniques to build up that memory.

Put simply, a revision timetable is a schedule of what you will revise and when. Different people work in different ways: some prefer to spend a long time on one topic and revise in a block, others prefer to vary things and spend short blocks of time on different topics. You have to work out what is best for you, but most people will need to mix topic with topic and revision with food breaks from time to time.

 REVISION

Revision is the act of building up sufficient memory of a body of knowledge in order to be able to do well in a subsequent examination.

The challenge, in many cases, is not what to revise and when, or even to build the revision timetable, but usually to keep to it. Most people who make a timetable keep to it for a few days and then lose interest.

Sticking to a timetable requires the same kind of motivation and time management that we referred to in Chapter 3. We need to find motivators and these can come in three forms:

- Incentives that we can link to specific progress in fulfilling our schedule.
- Something that helps us see and record the success we are having in our revision.
- Some mechanism by which we can be accountable.

How we implement each of these will depend on our own motivations and environment, but most of us need to do something around these three issues if we are going to use a revision timetable successfully. Not everyone uses revision timetables and they work better for some people than for others.

 ━━━ FOR YOU TO DO ━━━━━━━━━━━━━━━━━━━━━

Developing incentives for maintaining a revision timetable

Look at the ideas below in relation to increasing your motivation to keep to a revision timetable. Which ones could be the most effective incentives?

- A bar of chocolate
- Chance to play a computer game
- Chance to chat with friends on social media
- Chance to watch TV
- Buying yourself a present

- Going out with friends
- Glass of wine/pint of beer
- Day off for leisure
- Listening to iPod
- Enjoying a hobby
- Playing football
- Something else

(Continued)

(Continued)

Which mechanisms could help you see how much progress you are making in your revision?

- A diary where you tick off each day of revision
- Testing yourself against the notes you have made to see if you can recall them
- Talking to a friend about the items you have revised
- A checklist where you tick off topics that you have revised
- Writing practice essays under examination conditions for a tutor
- Studying with a friend to check your progress
- Other ideas?

Making Revision Notes

Making notes of your notes can sound like a strange idea – if they are notes in the first place, why would you want to make further notes about them? It is a reasonable question. If notes are intended to be a brief summary of larger content, then notes of notes are intended to become a summary of a summary. In effect, notes become easier to remember than larger content, but it is important also to ensure that what we remember has depth to it.

Some students choose to read through an entire module before specialising in certain areas and making notes of those specific topics. That gives them an overview of how all topics within the module link together, enabling them to demonstrate that synthesis referred to earlier.

Using Revision Guides

Various publishers produce summaries of a course syllabus (e.g. business studies). These are very popular and have some use if you are struggling to remember basic information, but the keyword here is basic. The summaries often provide sufficient information to just about pass a module in most universities, but will be unlikely to give enough information to do very well; they cannot provide a brief overall summary and provide evaluative content and detail at the same time. If they did, they would not be providing a summary, they would be repeating the main textbook.

These guides can be useful as an aid to memory, but making your own summary through your own notes is far more useful to learning: it is much easier to remember something that you have written yourself than printed information on a page.

Enhancing Your Memory

There are a variety of tools that students use to enhance their ability to remember information in preparation for examinations. Mnemonics, acronyms and acrostics can be very useful for improving your ability to remember key information, but we could also consider how we use and engage with information more broadly.

Mnemonics, acronyms and acrostics

Information in lectures is often presented in the form of lists, and these can enable students to develop mnemonics, acronyms and acrostics which help to recall information.

MNEMONICS, ACRONYMS AND ACROSTICS

Mnemonic: Any learning device or tool that improves memory – including acronyms and acrostics.

Acronym: A word made up of the initial letters of other relevant words.

Examples are: TEFL (Teaching English as a Foreign Language), AIDS (Acquired Immune Deficiency Syndrome) and BBC (British Broadcasting Corporation).

Acrostic: A sentence constructed from the first letters of words.

Example: The colours of the rainbow – Richard Of York Gave Battle In Vain (Red, Orange, Yellow, Green, Blue, Indigo, Violet).

There are also other ways of trying to remember key pieces of information. Marketing has the 4Ps (Price, Product, Place, Promotion), organisational designers have their 7Ss (Skills, Shared Values, Systems, Structures, Strategy, Staff and Style) and strategists have PESTLE (Political, Economic, Social, Technological, Legal, Environmental) to describe the factors which impact on business strategy.

One of the challenges with such lists is to remember what they actually relate to. It is great to remember PESTLE as a framework for making business decisions, but a nightmare when someone cannot remember what PESTLE actually means in practice.

Engaging with Information in Different Ways

Figure 8.2 indicates a number of ways in which we can handle information. The word 'handle' is probably the wrong word, however, because handling something implies that we are passive with it (i.e. we do nothing with it). We handle a birthday present, but if we simply handle it then we will never find out what is inside. We should really 'engage with' information, and if we follow the analogy of the birthday present, then we would enjoy unwrapping it, opening it and relishing its contents. The figure gives some ideas as to how we might engage with information.

Some of the ideas here may not have been ones that you have thought about, so let's look at each in turn.

Writing out information is better than merely reading it. If we write it out, we are doing something with it, albeit maybe simply repeating it.

Turning information into lists is partially covered above under mnemonics but can refer to any information that is taken from a formalised paragraph and transferred to a bullet list. Again, the act of 'turning information' implies some active engagement with that information.

Giving information a sequence again implies some form of action, but can make information easier to remember. Information that is in a logical order is much easier to remember than random

> Write out by hand
> Turn information into lists
> Give information a sequence
> Use headings
> Draw pictures
> Personalise
> Use shape and colour
> Repeat, sing or act out the information
> Personalising it
> Play with information
> Active listening and review

Figure 8.2 Ways of engaging with information

information that has no particular order (in the same way that an essay which has a logical sequence to its argument is much easier to read).

Using headings makes information stand out on a page. If you are a visual learner (see Chapter 2), then it will be easier to remember something which stands out than something which is just in normal text.

Drawing pictures can work for some people. Doodles are not particularly helpful to anyone unless they relate perhaps to the content you wish to remember, but diagrams which put the lecture content or your reading into pictures can be useful, especially if you are a visual learner.

Personalising information is about trying to apply the information given to you in a lecture to your own situation. This is clearly not possible in every situation, nor for every subject, but for some subjects (e.g. consumer behaviour, organisational behaviour, marketing) it is very easy to see how the theory relates to your own experience and to business practice.

Using shape and colour is a great idea and works particularly well for those who learn visually. Words can be coloured in your notes (coloured pens can do as well as a coloured font on an iPad) and that makes them stand out on the page when you are revising.

Repeating, singing or acting out information sounds like a strange idea, but does work for auditory learners (see Chapter 2) in particular. Actors often learn their lines by hearing them repeated and repetition can help us to remember information very easily.

Playing with information means that someone looks at it, imagines the information in practice, considers whether it would work in all places and at all times, and generally thinks about it in some depth. The idea of 'playing with' information implies that we can imagine ideas applying to new contexts or subjects.

Active listening and review is the process of thinking about what we hear and trying to enhance the understanding we have of what we are reading. One useful idea might be to rephrase what we hear and put it into our own words.

These are a series of ideas which might help in engaging with information. The more we engage with the information we are given and find for ourselves, the more we are likely to remember it without a huge amount of effort for revision.

MIND-MAPPING

Mind-maps can be very effective methods of organising informa-tion for both memory retention and written work more generally, especially if you are a visual learner (see Chapter 2). Mind-maps are visual representations of what you have covered.

MIND-MAP

A mind-map is a visual representation of information.

They begin with a central concept and then the ideas are repeatedly subdivided until there is little sense in doing so any more. See Figure 8.3 for an example of a mind-map for this chapter.

Mind-maps in real life can be made more complex than this, showing relationships between ideas (see also Chapter 14 on creativity and the reorganisation of information) and showing how certain ideas might be more important than others, where risks for a project might be greater (using colour, thickness of lines, arrows, etc.). At its heart, a mind-map is a graphical way of showing how information and ideas are organised. When it comes to revision, drawing a mind-map and then ticking off the top-ics as you cover them is a good way to ensure that your revision is organised.

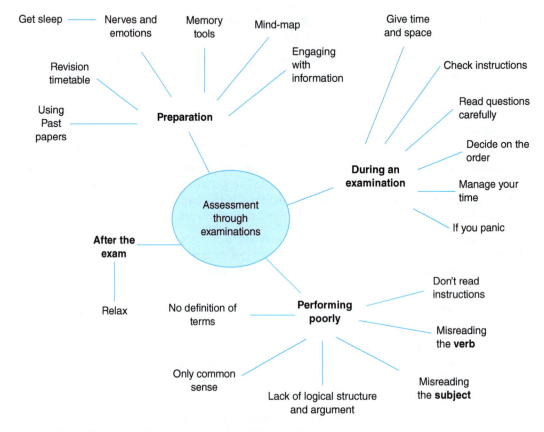

Figure 8.3 Example of a mind-map for this chapter

━━━ KEY LEARNING POINT ━━━━━━━━━━━━━━━━

Revising is one way to ensure that we can remember information before we go into an examination, but it is much better to learn the key ideas as the course progresses – by reading around such ideas and by trying to apply them to the real world.

━━━ REFLECTION POINT ━━━━━━━━━━━━━━━━━

Take some time to think about the following questions and write down some answers.

How nervous do you get before an examination? Why?

   In your preparation, do you try to spot questions which might come up? Is that a good or a bad idea, do you think?

DURING THE EXAMINATION

Of course, it is during the examination itself that performance becomes vitally important. Having taken time to relax before we go into the room, we need to recognise that there are some fairly simple actions we can take to ensure our performance is as good as it can be.

Give Yourself Time and Space

Arrive early, do *not* rush and do *not* arrive at the last minute. Of course, no one intends to do that (or very few do) but some students always seem to arrive a minute or two either before the start of the examination or after it has started. Some universities do not allow students to enter after the examination starts (it disturbs other students who have already started), so beware!

Make sure that you bring everything you need: Student ID card? Several pens? Calculator? A watch? A drink? Make sure you know what you can and cannot bring into the room, and do *not* take any unauthorised materials to your desk.

Some universities will allocate you a specific desk, so make sure that you know which room (and which desk, if appropriate) to go to.

Finally, make sure that you go to the toilet before you enter the examination room. Once you enter the room, you will probably not be allowed to leave for a particular period of time (depending on the rules for your university).

Carefully Check the Instructions on the Examination Paper

Of course, you should check that the examination paper on your desk is the one you are expecting, but do not turn over the paper until the examination starts and you are told to do so.

Once the examination begins, you should make sure that you follow the instructions. This sounds obvious, but there will be at least one student who answers five questions when they should answer three, or who answers two questions from one part of the paper when they should answer just one. So make sure you know what you are doing.

Also, make sure that you know how long the examination lasts. There may be a warning a few minutes before the end of the examination, but being told 'Please put your pens down now!' should not be a surprise to you.

Read all the Questions Carefully

If you have the chance to select which questions you answer, then take a few moments to think them through. There are some common mistakes which individuals make at this point (see Figure 8.4 below). If a question has two parts, then make sure you answer both parts fully, paying attention to parts of a question which might carry more marks than other parts.

Decide on the Order in Which You Want to Write Your Answers

If you are asked to write three answers, it is likely that your second answer will be the best. You will typically be more relaxed than you were when you started writing the first answer and have more time than you will have for the final one. Answer the most difficult question first if you can because you will need more time to plan and think through how you will answer the question, and that time can evaporate very easily towards the end of the examination.

Manage Your Time

This is very important. It sounds obvious, but if you have two hours to answer three questions, then you need to allocate time according to the marks given for each question. For example, if a paper is two hours long, all questions have the same number of marks and you need to answer three questions, then each question should take no longer than 40 minutes, but if one question is worth 60 marks and the remaining two are worth 20 marks each, then clearly the first question requires more time and thought.

This time for each question includes the time to think and plan your answer, which should take around 5 to 10 minutes per answer for an essay-based examination (and less for a pure calculation question).

Some questions may have two parts, so make sure that you are careful in the way you use the time given.

Some students write a comment such as 'Ran out of time: Sorry! Please be generous.' Unfortunately, requests like this are not going to result in 'generous' marks. Tutors can only mark what they see and read, and if it is not written down, then no marks will be given.

 'BUT I HAVE A QUESTION ...'

... What should I do if I run out of time? And how much time should I give to reading through my answers at the end?

If you really do run out of time, then the best you can do is to write down what you think is relevant in as short a way as you can. Sometimes this can be with bullet points and brief English. It is better to get something down that you do know, even if there is no detail, than just miss out relevant content entirely.

On the second question, there is less of a simple answer here, because examinations with calculations can take a lot longer to read through than essays sometimes. Again, I would give allow 10 minutes or so at the end – though it will depend on your reading speed. Check through and make sure that everything you have written makes sense.

And if You Panic?

Breathe! Take a few long, slow breaths in and a few long, slow breaths out. This can sound very clichéd, but it does work for most people. If you have a drink with you, then take a moment to have a sip. Many people can react wrongly and think 'If I slow down, I'll have even less time and I'll panic even more,' but, in reality, 5 minutes of calm thinking can produce much more than 10 minutes of thinking in a panicked state of mind.

If you feel ill during the examination, let the invigilator know. They may give you the option of getting some water or using the bathroom.

UNDERSTANDING WHY PEOPLE DO POORLY IN EXAMS

This section is intended to examine why people do poorly in examinations, and to answer the question above.

In some ways, the errors made in examination essays may be the same as those made in essays generally, for example a lack of structure, unconvincing arguments, and so on, but in an examination situation, the urgency of getting something down on paper and a lack of time to prepare can make the probability of errors increase.

Failing to Read the Instructions

Failing to take time to understand how many answers you need to write or from which parts of an examination paper has been covered above, to some extent, but writing more answers than you need to will lower your mark. You will have less time to devote to each answer and so the quality of each will be less. Your university may or may not have a policy on how to deal with this – some universities will ask tutors to mark the first answers that they see, others may accept the essay with the highest mark – but you should not expect to do better than if you had written the required number.

Similarly, if you write fewer answers than is expected, then it is highly unlikely you will increase the mark of one by a sufficient amount to compensate for the lack of an entire piece of work.

A final scenario relates to a situation where a student is expected to answer one question from part A and one from part B, but instead answers two from part B. In this situation, it is likely that the student will only have one essay answer marked, and will lose a significant number of marks overall.

Misinterpreting the Verb in the Question

The verbs (e.g. analyse, compare, discuss, contrast) in the question will tell you what you need to do: if you do not do it, you will write an answer which does not answer the question and will likely fail. No examination essay will ask you to 'Write all you know about …' So make sure that your content is relevant, avoids unnecessary content and is focussed on the question that is being asked. Answers containing largely irrelevant information are likely to fail.

Read through the verbs listed in Chapter 7 (see Table 7.1, pages 137–8) and make sure that you understand what each one means and what you would be expected to do.

> - Failing to read the instructions
> - Misinterpreting the verb in the question
> - Misreading the subject of the question
> - Lack of logical structure and argument
> - Woolly theorising and common sense responses
> - Lack of time
> - Too much time for description and too little time for critical thinking
> - Failing to define key terms

Figure 8.4 Common errors in examination essays

Misreading the Subject of the Question

We can use motivation theory here to give a simple example ('Explain the relevance of Herzberg's hygiene factors to motivational practice in the workplace') and we can imagine a situation where a student writes about 'motivator factors' instead, or a question which asks about Modules but where a student writes about Moodle (an Internet-based learning resource). Misreading the subject means that the essay is very likely to fail on the grounds that the answer is not relevant.

Lack of Logical Structure and Argument

There is no real difference here between an examination essay and one which is completed during the semester as an assignment. If an essay is good (contains sufficient critical thinking, evidence for the arguments given, covers sufficient content) then a lack of structure is unlikely to lead an answer to fail, but it could reduce the mark by 10–15%. A lack of logical argument, however, will mean that the essay is likely to fail, since the quality of reasoning is important – as the next point shows.

Woolly Theorising: Common Sense Responses

The kind of answer which ignores any reading, any lecture content and gives a simple response 'This is what I think because it is what I think' is extremely likely to fail. Not only is it likely to irritate the assessor (who will have taken time to give you the lecture content and reading related to the subject), but it also shows a significant lack of engagement on the part of the student towards the course. Universities expect you to do the reading and to present an argument for the view you have; this is what critical thinking is all about, so it is quite reasonable for this kind of answer to fail.

In social science degree courses, this is particularly an issue for subjects related to law. Business students studying law modules can struggle sometimes because they write in a way that might provide a decent argument but does not reference the points made on a case-by-case basis. In a law-based essay, common sense is always insufficient and *will* lead to a failed answer (see Table 8.3).

Table 8.3 Comparison of Minimum Expectations in Business and Law Essays

Minimum expectations for business essays	Minimum expectations for essays in law-based modules
Reasonable structure	Reasonable structure
Reference to some theory	Points made are supported by reference to law and by reference to specific cases
Reasonable argument	Coherent argument
Covers most of the relevant content	Covers most of the relevant content

Too Much Time for Description and too Little Time for Critical Thinking

As indicated in the 'But I Have a Question …' section box above, some students never seem to have enough time to really answer a question in depth. They would always need to spend too much time describing a theory before they could evaluate it and so would run out of time.

The answer to this is to make explicit the assumptions that you are making when you write your answer. For example, if you are assuming that the assessor already understands a particular theory and you feel that you do not need to explain the theory, then it is worth saying so in order to prevent a misunderstanding.

It is true that different tutors will take a slightly different approach to this, and it is a good idea to check before you go near an examination, but most will appreciate the fact that you are spending more time demonstrating your critical thinking skills than merely providing another explanation of a theory that they have read many times. After all, it is not possible to provide evidence of your critical thinking about a theory unless you have a good understanding of that theory first. Simply make explicit the fact that you are doing so within the examination essay. For example, you could probably write something like 'I will not explain Maslow's theory in detail, but will focus on evaluating his ideas' in an examination essay.

Failing to Define Key Terms

In the same way that the introduction to an assignment should clearly indicate the boundaries of the essay (i.e. what the essay will and will not cover), so, too, should the introduction to an examination essay provide the definitions that you are using of the keywords in the question.

Of course, defining a keyword incorrectly at the beginning will raise concerns in the mind of your lecturer about whether you have a sufficient understanding of what you have been taught, but it will at least give the lecturer something clear to feed back to you should you ask for that.

─────────────── KEY LEARNING POINT ───────────────

The criteria for getting a good mark in an examination essay are little different to those for getting a good mark in other forms of assessment: content, critical thinking and coherent structure are expected whatever the nature of assessment.

─────────────── REFLECTION POINT ───────────────

Take some time to think about the following questions and write down some answers.

How often do you take a few moments and write down an essay plan, or do you just start straight away and hope it makes sense to the tutor later? Which is best? Why?

Have you ever had feedback from an examination before? Why or why not? Would you ever consider getting some feedback from your lecturer?

Is there anything you know you usually forget before an examination but that you need during it? What can you do to make sure you do not forget next time?

AFTER THE EXAMINATION

Few people really enjoy examinations and most are happy once they are able to leave the room. In many cases, there is then a process of 'debrief', where students release the built-up tension by talking to each other about the questions they answered, what they included in each answer, and so on.

This is great for releasing tension and is a natural thing to do, but if you find others (and the emphasis here is on several others, rather than just one or two) saying that they included content that you did not, then it is good to remember a few things:

1. They are not marking your examination – your lecturer is!
2. Marks usually depend as much on the extent to which you demonstrated your critical thinking as on the content you included – the 'how' you wrote the answer is as important as 'what' you wrote about.
3. You may have taken an interesting approach to answering the question, an approach that may be more appreciated by the lecturer than by the other students.

If you do feel nervous and anxious about the examination, you might want to speak to a lecturer or someone who can help you think things through in a systematic and logical way. It is always good to learn and be reflective: that reflection can help us improve.

INTEGRATION AND APPLICATION

There is little anyone can do about the tensions and anxieties that people feel before taking an examination, and the pressure to perform can be immense in certain cultures and countries. The steps suggested above should help you limit that tension, so how about trying the following simple ideas?

Firstly, get to know as much information as you can about any forthcoming examinations. Knowledge reduces uncertainty, so the less you do not know, the more you should feel OK.

Secondly, try to practise some past papers and get some feedback from the lecturer. The feedback should help you feel more confident about the things you know and find out what you are not really so sure about.

Thirdly, revise in a way that works for you, so find out what works best. Think about your notes and whether you are a visual learner or learn best from what you experience or hear. If a revision timetable works to schedule your revision, then great, but do not use one simply because everyone else is.

Fourthly, try to get sufficient exercise, sleep and food. When we are stressed, our daily routine tends to stop, so make sure you do all you can to maintain a normal lifestyle.

Fifthly, during the exam, maintain a good sense of time and calm. Plan your time carefully, do not panic, and write whatever you think is helpful in giving a good answer to the question. Remember to look carefully at the verbs and nouns in the question.

Finally, relax after the examination. It is over. You may have others to come, and you will need to concentrate on those, so do not spend a lot of time worrying over your last answer or last examination paper.

CONCLUSION

You should now be able to:

- Describe the different forms and different meanings of examination question that are used at university.
- Identify the practical issues you need to know in relation to the examinations that you will be taking.
- Evaluate various mechanisms for improving your revision and memory.
- Avoid some of the common failings when answering university examination questions.

Examinations are stressful for most students, but they do not need to be. Thoughtful revision, sufficient preparation, and careful analysis and planning of the questions once you turn over the paper will all help to ensure you are able to produce answers that are as good as they can be. However, there is no substitute for learning and thinking about what you are being 'taught' as you go through your modules, rather than all at the end. People rarely have time to do sufficient reading and thinking during a stressful revision period, so it is much better to do that reading and thinking during the preceding weeks of a module.

FINAL REFLECTIONS

Based on the content of this chapter, what do you now know about undertaking an examination that you did not know before?

What key learning point had the most impact? Why?

Do your answers to either of the above questions have the potential to change your attitude to studies at university? If so, why?

What will you now do differently? (Write this down and put it somewhere where you can see it regularly.)

━━━━━━━━━━━━━━ INTERVIEW QUESTIONS ━━━━━━━━━━━━━━

In Chapter 5, it was suggested that there would be few interview questions regarding university studies specifically, but that interviewers might ask questions around the topic to find out about your ability to make decisions or think critically – or to find out more about the way you behave or react to certain situations. The same is true for issues around assessment.

Think about the following questions. What might your answers be?

1. How successful were you at planning your revision?
2. How have you used the feedback from your examinations to improve your performance?

Chapter 17 gives a lot more information on selection interviews and the online content gives some guidance on these questions.

ADDITIONAL RESOURCES

Want to learn more? Visit https://study.sagepub.com/morgan to gain access to a wide range of online resources, including interactive tests, tasks, further reading and downloads.

Website Resources

Burns, T. and Sinfield, S. (2016) *Essential Study Skills* (4th edition). London: Sage ('Chapter 29: How to understand and pass exams': https://uk.sagepub.com/en-gb/eur/essential-study-skills/book 245619#contents

(Continued)

(Continued)

Guidance from QS (University Ranking website): www.topuniversities.com/student-info/health-and-support/exam-preparation-ten-study-tips

University of Hull Library resource: libguides.hull.ac.uk/ld.php?content_id=3166177

University of Leicester website: www2.le.ac.uk/offices/ld/resources/study/revision-exam

Textbook Resources

Cottrell, S. (2012) *The Exams Skills Handbook* (2nd edition). Basingstoke: Palgrave Macmillan.
McIlroy, D. (2003) *Studying @ University.* London: Sage (particularly chapters 8 and 9).
McMillan, K. and Weyers, J. (2011) *How to Succeed in Examinations and Assessments.* Harlow: Pearson.
Turner, J. (2002) *How to Study: A Short Introduction.* London: Sage (particularly chapter 8).

PART IV
EMPLOYABILITY SKILLS

As we saw in Chapter 2, there is a significant overlap between the skills required for being successful in your studies and those required for the workplace. This is probably what you would expect, otherwise universities would not be producing employable graduates. What is also true is that is while you will have a different set of skills and abilities from others, your overall abilities in relation to critical thinking and your knowledge in a particular discipline will be roughly the same.

This part provides this link, *by focusing on the skills that you will develop during your studies but which will have significant relevance to the workplace*. University tries to prepare you for the workplace, so this link should not be a surprise, but the emphasis here will be on enabling to behave in a way that will also help you succeed in the workplace. The features employed in Parts I-III will be continued, and there will be relevant online content to provide extra information and help support your learning.

However, there is a challenge here: every workplace will be different and the skills required for performing well will be different. Working in a multinational organisation is going to be very different from working in a small startup business with six or seven other people, so the importance of the skills will vary and each context may require you to apply them in different ways. This text cannot address every possibility, but it will try to give you some guidance for some of the more important and generic aspects of these skills.

Thus, in this part, we will cover a number of interpersonal skills: oral presentation skills (Chapter 9), team-working (Chapter 10), leadership (Chapter 11) and effective communication (Chapter 12); and two areas of intrapersonal skill – cross-cultural awareness (Chapter 13) and problem solving and creativity (Chapter 14). The intention is that this will provide you with sufficient understanding of these areas to be able to apply them well.

GENERAL PRINCIPLES

Whenever we start to discuss human behaviour, there are a number of things we need to bear in mind if certain behaviour is to increase. We could think very simply through the idea of means (do you have the knowledge and ability to demonstrate a particular skill?), motive (are you motivated to do so?) and opportunity (does your course and/or university life in general provide you with the opportunities to demonstrate and develop the skills you need?). The answer to the latter is probably 'yes' – although life is usually a little more complex than that.

As shown in Chapter 2, the development of skills comes through a number of different processes (e.g. taking advantage of opportunities to gain experience, gathering information and knowledge in different ways, reflecting on our experiences, thinking through the possibilities, and so on). No skill can be demonstrated and then developed without such issues being thought through, but it is important to recognise that there is a variety of other factors which can influence behaviour.

We could think about your life and career goals (see also Chapter 3 on time management) and the skills you need to achieve them; we could think about how you get feedback on your abilities (see Chapter 2 and Chapter 5); whether you have the resources and knowledge to demonstrate and develop these skills; and, finally, we could think about the extent to which other personal factors might affect your behaviour and performance.

The chapters that follow in this part will help you to identify where your weaknesses may lie and will go some way to helping you understand what needs to change.

PRESENTATION SKILLS

CHAPTER STRUCTURE

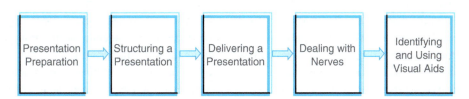

Figure 9.1

When you see the 🌐 this means go to the companion website https://study.sagepub.com/morgan to do a quiz, complete a task, read further or download a template.

═══ AIMS OF THE CHAPTER ═══

By the end of this chapter, you should be able to:

- Understand why presentations fail to achieve their objectives.
- Prepare, structure and deliver a good oral presentation.
- Choose and use visual aids relevant to the audience and goals of the presentation.
- Use appropriate strategies for dealing with nerves.

INTRODUCTION

For many people, giving a presentation in front of others can be scary, for a number of reasons. In fact, presentations can be scary for various reasons – sometimes because it is fear of the unknown: Who will be looking at me? What will they be thinking? What questions might they ask? Will they be in a bad mood?

The reality is that there are very few occasions when we probably have much legitimate justification for being nervous about a presentation. In business, the ability to give a good presentation is seen as a fundamental skill – it is impossible to lead without communicating, and presentations are a standard part of business and employment life.

 PRESENTATION

A presentation is the oral delivery of information to achieve (a) particular objective(s).

Of course, this chapter also is relevant to you as a student: because giving presentations is a key part of business life, your university studies will need to prepare you for doing them. At university, the answers to the questions above are those which are relatively easy to find. The answer to the last question may be unknown, but any assessment should be based on evidence and feedback from the tutor.

This definition seems very vague. The reality, however, is that everything you see on TV, hear on the radio or get in some other way is a presentation in some way. It may not be called a presentation, but such situations will 'present' you with some kind of information or will entertain you – or both. By definition, then, they are 'presentations'. This means that there are a large number of ways and situations in which presentations can take place. For an academic presentation at university, we can even imagine the presentation as very similar to the spoken version of an academic essay. For the purposes of this text, however, we will concentrate on those which occur in an academic setting or a typically more formal business setting, though styles and expectations can vary significantly.

We will begin this chapter by giving you the chance to reflect on your own abilities. Some students find presentations quite scary and this is a chance to examine your own thinking and behaviour. The chapter will present some issues relating to the identification of presentation goals, give some thoughts on the various skills that are involved in preparing and delivering a presentation, and then move on to consider some issues of presentation structure. The final two areas to be covered in the chapter relate to the variety and appropriate use of visual aids, as well as some suggestions on how individuals might handle their nerves.

SKILLS SELF-ASSESSMENT

Complete the brief questionnaire below to see how well you prepare and deliver oral presentations. Give each item a score between 0 and 5, where 0 is 'not at all like me' or 'I strongly agree', and 5 is 'very much like me' or 'strongly disagree'.

Item	Statement	Score
1.	I know my facts	
2.	I am confident in delivering my presentation	
3.	I give a clear introduction to my presentation	

(Continued)

(Continued)

Item	Statement	Score
4.	I maintain a logical sequence to the content of the presentation	
5.	I give a clear summary to the content I have presented as a conclusion	
6.	I ensure that the audience can hear everything that I am presenting	
7.	I use eye contact, gestures and other small behaviours to maintain audience engagement	
8.	I use varied pitch, volume, speed and tone of voice, and speed of delivery to create impact	
9.	I produce visual aids that are very clear, are relevant and help the presentation achieve its aim	
10.	I do not let nerves affect my delivery	
11.	I have the right amount of content for the length of presentation	
12.	I do not feel nervous	
13.	I ensure that any technology I wish to use will do exactly what I expect it to do	
14.	I go to look at the venue beforehand to ensure that I know what I can and cannot do	
15.	I write out brief notes to use as an aid to memory	
16.	I make sure that I have taken some time to think about my goals	
17.	I take some time to think about the audience – how they will react to what I have to say, how they may be feeling and how big the audience will be	
18.	I move around 'the stage' to try to create interest and engagement	
19.	I start my presentation with a striking comment designed to get the audience's attention	
20.	I think about the possible questions that might be asked after the presentation	

The answers to these questions are personal – they are about you, so there are no right or wrong answers – but you might want to discuss them with a classmate.

FOR YOU TO DO

Think through the questions below and discuss your answers with another student.

1. Think about the most exciting lecture you have attended and the least exciting one. What issue(s) makes the difference between the two?
2. What should the objectives of a lecture be: To entertain? To inform? To persuade? To teach? To inspire? Something else? If more than one, then which are the most and the least important?
3. Take one of your lectures from last week. If you were to give that lecture yourself, what would you change? Why?
4. How do you feel about giving presentations? Excited? Nervous? Just fine? Why?
5. What are the differences between giving a presentation to three people and talking about a hobby of yours to three friends in Starbucks or in a pub?

The answers to these questions will have started you thinking about some of the presentations that you have seen recently. Of course, giving a presentation may or may not be the same as giving a lecture, but a lecture *is* a form of presentation. Actually, the last question above might ask us to think about some of the conceptual issues we have when we think about presentations. If we could consider a conversation about a hobby with three others as a presentation, then the idea of 'doing a presentation' might be a lot less daunting than we might otherwise imagine. (Standing up is a decision we make when we think about how to do a presentation, but we do not have to be standing to do a presentation.)

'BUT I HAVE A QUESTION ...'

... Why do universities assess by presentations? They are so stressful.

It may sound surprising but your lecturers can also find giving lectures and presentations stressful sometimes. If we are teaching a group of people that we have never taught before or a new module or delivering some training, then yes, we can get stressed about it as well. If we earn our living through delivering training and education and we are delivering something important to a corporate client, then our income does depend on it.

Regardless, a presentation develops your confidence and your ability to speak and communicate, to lead and to be creative. Everyone who leads has to give some kind of presentation or speech at some time.

The amount of stress you experience will vary from person to person. However, just because you are doing a presentation does not mean you have to get stressed about it. Sometimes it seems people get stressed because almost everyone expects them to. Presentations can be stressful, but nobody ever developed an important skill by doing something that was easy.

In most modules and most universities, you will get lots of chances to practise and develop your presentation skills in front of a tutor and receive their feedback, and, often, these chances will not count towards any grade. So – as I have said before – use the feedback to get better so that when you are assessed, you will know what to do and be able to do it.

PRESENTATION PREPARATION

The way we prepare and deliver a presentation is dependent on our goals, our audience (these two will be linked) and our abilities, which will shape what we feel comfortable with and confident about doing.

The Impact of Goals on Delivery Style

There is no best way to give a presentation. There are expected and unexpected ways of giving a presentation, and there will be appropriates and inappropriate ways of doing so, but there is no best way. Figure 9.2 indicates that different goals relate to differences in delivery method and the formality of the presentation, as well as suggesting that the more formal a presentation is, the more the focus is likely to be on content and fact; but the more informal, the more the focus is likely to be on delivery style and method. Of course, this works both ways: a one-way delivery becomes – by its nature – more formal, and the more interactive delivery also becomes more informal, but the key point here is that it is the goals that drive the style of presentation.

Formality often implies a one-way delivery. Anything more than one way can become a discussion, which by nature is informal, or an argument, which many would say has more formality to it. The opposite, however, does not apply: a presentation which is informal, on the other hand, can be one way or interactive. A comedian delivering a comedy routine in a local theatre would be seen as informal, but would largely be one way.

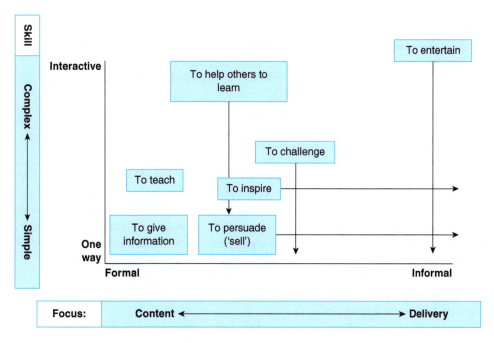

Figure 9.2 Different goals and different delivery styles

Figure 9.2 also indicates that undertaking an interactive presentation will usually require more skill, confidence and creativity. Being able to develop and use exercises well during a presentation typically takes a lot of careful planning (we look at being creative with presentations below – see pages 195–6), while a traditional one is more common.

─────── FOR YOU TO DO ───────

Look at the questions below and discuss your answers with another student.

1. Think about the following situations. How formal or informal would you expect each of the following presentations to be?

   • Presentation to the executive management board of an international company.
   • Sales presentation in a home to three individuals around a table.
   • A typical academic lecture on marketing techniques.
   • A training session for part-time workers at a chain restaurant.
   • A sermon at a local place of worship.
   • An assessed presentation by students, undertaken as part of their degree course.
   • A drama acted out as part of a presentation in class.
   • A speech at a wedding.

2. Why would you expect the above situations to be so formal or informal? How much might an audience's expectations impact on someone's style?

(Continued)

(Continued)

3. Is there anything else (other than the goals and/or audience's expectations) that drives the style of the presentation?
4. Which of the above presentation contexts (the list in question 1) would you personally find easier? More difficult?

The Impact of the Audience

A question above asks whether the expectations of the audience have an impact on the delivery style. The answer is that it depends on the goal. If you are trying to sell something or persuade your audience of something, then there is a sense in which you will need to consider their expectations. Not meeting those (and other) expectations will mean that you are likely to be unsuccessful, but if you are trying to teach or merely give information, then you have more control over your success as a presenter.

'The audience' does impact on presentations in other ways, however:

- **Their knowledge and understanding** – which should dictate what you need to say as background and what you do not.
- **Their emotions about what you are saying** – which can impact on whether they accept what you are saying or not.
- **Their emotions about how you are giving the message** – which can impact on whether they like you or not, and then on whether they accept what you are saying or not.
- **Their general state of health and alertness (e.g. tiredness?)** – which can impact on how effectively you are able to get your message across, how you deliver your presentation and how long the presentation should be.
- **How many people there are** – which can impact on the methods used to deliver the presentation.
- **Where they are sitting in relation to you as presenter** – which can impact on how formal and informal the presentation becomes (a stage or a podium *can* be a significant barrier to being informal).
- **The information is already provided for them** – which impacts on the content you deliver and whether any additional explanation is necessary.

The above points could indicate that giving a presentation is a nearly impossible task since the list of factors to be taken into account is too large to balance effectively. In some cases, this is true (e.g. where a chief executive is addressing the needs of a large and potentially diverse group of shareholders at an annual general meeting) and in those cases it is simply important to use a personal style developed over a long time, but in many situations it is possible to take account of those things in preparing for the presentation, and thinking through what the implications might be.

 KEY LEARNING POINT

Recognising the nature of your audience is a key part of preparing for a presentation, and in developing content and proposed delivery method(s).

Rehearsing

Once we have identified our goals and have thought about our presentation abilities and style, the final part of preparing for a presentation is to rehearse.

Rehearsal is seen by many presenters as vital to the delivery of a good presentation. It is through the rehearsal that presenters identify what they can and cannot remember, are able to practise and perfect their para-linguistic cues (see Chapter 12) and ensure that technically everything works the way that they intend. Rehearsal for some (especially auditory learners – see Chapter 2) will also help memory: the more you hear what it is you are going to say, the better you can remember it. For actors, rehearsal and the repetition of content helps them remember their lines in exactly the same way that repetition of words helps many individuals learn a new language.

There is little substitute for practising in the room where the presentation will take place. You can check, for example, if your PowerPoint presentation works as you intend or whether the room has the Internet links you expect, but sometimes this is not possible. More broadly, technical preparation can be as important as personal preparation, as the list in Box 9.1 shows.

=========== BOX 9.1 ===========

TECHNICAL PREPARATION FOR A PRESENTATION

Preparing yourself is vital if a presentation is to go well, but many forget the requirement to undertake a technical preparation or to look at the room beforehand. It has been known for students and senior academics alike to make a series of mistakes like the following:

- Failing to check that there is an Internet connection, having saved the presentation at an online location that is now not accessible.
- Failing to check that a remote PowerPoint controller has a battery.
- Failing to ensure that there is a power socket for a laptop close to the projector.
- Failing to check that a video inserted into PowerPoint works properly on a different computer.
- Failing to ensure that the USB stick works properly.
- Failing to ensure that the version of PowerPoint (or equivalent) is the same as compatible with that in which the presentation is saved.
- Failing to find out whether someone can hear you at the back of the room.
- Failing to take a printout of the slides with you as an aid to your memory.
- Failing to find the correct room at the right time.
- Failing to ensure that any music or sound can be easily heard.
- Failing to consider questions that you might be asked at the end of the presentation.
- Failing to look at how the room is set up (i.e. locations of chairs, etc.).

It is usually not difficult to check all these, but many people are so busy with rehearsal and preparation of delivery that these things can and do get missed.

Why not develop a presentation checklist based on the above and including any other items you might see as relevant?

Rehearsal brings confidence and personal security, and helps us deal with nerves. As was noted above, many individuals suffer from nerves at some point. (We will discuss how to deal with nerves later in the chapter.)

Making Notes

The very best presenters tend not to use notes and while some will use an autocue or some visual reminders, the ability to remember an entire presentation is reserved for a very few. As a result, making notes in preparation for a presentation becomes normal for many presenters, even lecturers (some of whom will use bullet points on the PowerPoint slides that you see in exactly the same way as people might use handwritten notes).

Notes tend to be:

- On small pieces of card or paper.
- Easy to read.
- Notes, not a script.
- Brief.

Notes are not intended to be a script, and reading from a script will generally be seen as poor practice.

Technology is making the need for card or paper irrelevant. The smartphone usually has some form of note-making app (e.g. Samsung's 'Note Everything') that can be used. One of the advantages of using a phone is that you can be sure your notes will always stay in the same order, whereas it is possible to get them mixed up when using cards. One of the downsides, of course, is that the phone may run out of power – so beware!

Over-preparation

Preparation is key to a presentation going well. As Benjamin Franklin, a founding father of the United States, said: 'By failing to prepare you are preparing to fail.' It is a very good feeling to get to a place where you feel confident because of the preparation that has been put in. However, there is a slight risk that you need to be aware of, so balance is important. The risk is that over-preparation can cause problems if something goes wrong.

 ━━━━ FOR YOU TO DO ━━━━━━━━━━━━━━━━━━━

Think about the following two scenarios which relate to occasions when a presenter might be relying too much on their preparation and their notes, rather than on their own knowledge.

Scenario 1

Imagine the situation where you have prepared everything, you are using the PowerPoint slides on the screen as your notes, and you are ready to start speaking, but then the computer crashes and you cannot advance to the next slide. You have two choices: to do the remainder of the presentation from memory *or* restart the computer.

Of course, this would never happen to you, but what would you advise the presenter to do?

Scenario 2

Picture yourself in a situation where the script you are reading is the wrong version. You are following what you have written but the slides have been changed since then, and in your group presentation other people are getting nervous because you are taking up their very limited time.

What would you do?

The other issue with too much preparation relates to the following: that in rehearsing too much, the presentation loses its spontaneity and can become less passionate or enthusiastic as a result. Delivering a presentation that has been carefully scripted and memorised word for word may lead to a fairly stale delivery, though confident delivery with extensive eye contact and good memorisation *can* go some way to impressing an audience. One way around this is as follows (and seems embarrassing, but it can work):

- Face a mirror.
- Imagine that you are having a conversation with a friend about something really interesting (or, if it is less embarrassing, ask a friend to use their phone to video you during a real conversation).
- Watch your facial expressions. What do you do during particularly interesting parts of the conversation? What do you do when you want to make a particularly important point?
- Rehearse doing those same facial expressions so that they become part of your presentation.

KEY LEARNING POINT

We can develop the skills required for doing really well in our essays, examinations and other assessed work. The preparation we put in and the way we go about presenting content are crucial to performing well.

REFLECTION POINT

Take some time to think about the following questions and write down some answers.

How much time do you put into preparing for your presentation? Do you feel it is too much, too little or about right?

In your preparation, do you put more effort into the visual aids, considering the audience, rehearsing, or other issues? Is there an optimum balance do you think?

There can be no substitute for good preparation. A presentation that has no preparation can seem unstructured, vague and allows things to go wrong, but, conversely, a presentation that has too much preparation may lack passion and emotion. One of the skills a presenter needs to master is to learn to get the balance right. You can download a useful presentation preparation checklist on the companion website for this book at https://study.sagepub.com/morgan.

DOWNLOAD

STRUCTURING A PRESENTATION

Having a clear structure to a presentation fulfils the same purpose as the structure for an essay – it should enable the audience to know exactly what you are discussing, why you are discussing it (i.e. its relevance to the overall message) and what you are going to discuss next. This is important because it will help your audience to feel comfortable and secure as they listen to you. Therefore, like an essay, a presentation should have a beginning, a middle and an end. It is worth noting that presentations (and essays) often fail during their introductions and conclusions, and while these may not be the longest parts of the presentation (usually about 10% each of the presentation time), they are almost certainly *the most important*.

The introduction should set out where the work is going and why, and stimulate the audience's attention. The introduction can often include phrases such as:

1. 'What I'd like to do this afternoon is …'
2. 'I'd like to introduce the team who have been working on this project: they are …'
3. 'The way we would like to communicate with you about this is through a series of questions on …'
4. 'Thank you for inviting me to discuss this with you this afternoon. I have a short amount of time, so …'
5. 'We shall be going through the main points which we believe were relevant and, after the presentation, we will be happy to answer any questions, OK?'

 ━━━━ FOR YOU TO DO ━━━━━━━━━━━━━━━━━

Look at the phrases above. Why might they be important in a presentation?

Think about the last presentation that you did, and the last one that you watched. Did you hear any of these (or similar) phrases?

Excluding phrase 2, are there any occasions when saying any of these could cause a problem? Which ones? Why?

Is it better to keep questions for the end or let your audience ask questions during the presentation? Does it matter who you are presenting to?

Some of the phrases above apply to team presentations, and others to individual ones, but the principles are the same: the purpose of the introduction is to enable the audience to know: (1) *what* you are going to cover; (2) *why* those issues are important; and (3) *how* you are going to cover them.

Some of the ways in which a presenter can begin their presentation are set out in Figure 9.3.

Interesting ways to begin a presentation	
• Startling Fact	• Ask rhetorical question
• Strong and relevant anecdote	• Use an illustration
• Striking example	• Use a visual aid
• Pay the audience a compliment	• Refer to a recent incident
• Challenging question	• Tell a joke

Figure 9.3 Beginning your presentation (from Whetten and Cameron, 1996)

Whichever methods are used, they should gain the interest of the audience and enable them to feel comfortable with where the presentation is going and how you intend to take them there. If you are giving a group presentation, the introduction needs to introduce the group members and preferably indicate what each will speak about.

The middle should enable the audience to understand what you are telling them and why it is important – *to them* more than to you. It should give the message(s) in ways appropriate to the goals of the presentation and should leave the audience in no doubt about what it is that you wish to say.

Finally, **the conclusion** should be a summary of what has been said in the middle. It should be a brief summary, *not a repetition* of what has been said before. It should also thank the audience for listening and invite questions.

The conclusion might contain certain phrases:

1. 'Thank you for listening. What I have tried to do is …'
2. 'As I come to the end of what I want to present, I would like to reiterate the three main points which I think are important …'
3. 'Thank you for your time and attention. We have presented … have indicated why we think … and have given you some ideas about … Now, if you have any questions, we would be very happy to try and answer them.'

Many presentations at university and elsewhere give no conclusion and finish with something similar to: 'That is the end of our presentation, thank you for listening.' For a good presentation, this is usually insufficient as a conclusion. The conclusion should summarise the main issue(s) and any ideas. The presentation should *conclude*, not suddenly *finish*. It is, however, a poor use of time to restate *everything* that has been said previously.

In summary, the introduction should 'Tell the audience what you are going to tell them,' the middle should 'Tell them' and the conclusion should 'Tell them what you have just told them.'

══════════ KEY LEARNING POINT ══════════

A presentation that has no clear structure will confuse the audience. The structure of your presentation should be based on the objectives of the presentation.

Having prepared our presentation and given it a structure that enables it to achieve its goals, we will now move on to look at delivery.

DELIVERING A PRESENTATION

The definition of a presentation we gave earlier stated that there can be a variety of contexts within which a presentation can be given. For instance:

- Sitting down around a table with two or three others to give them some information.
- Standing up with a group of 10 or more and having a conversation.
- Delivering a lecture to 60 or more and speaking for an hour (which is typical for a lecturer in many universities).
- Giving a theatrical performance.
- Delivering training, with opportunities for interaction, group exercises and competitions.

This is not an exhaustive list. In many cases, you – as a student doing an assessed presentation – will be given the context, and the expectations will be set out by the tutor in terms of any assessment criteria. However, we need to be careful about what we think we are supposed to be doing: it is very easy to make assumptions about the expectations, and we will look at these shortly when we come to think about being creative in our presentations.

When we consider communication, we think about a number of different things, typically based on what we hear and what we see. Those senses drive our thinking, our understanding and then our reactions, so getting our delivery right is, of course, vitally important if we are going to get our message across. The question is, therefore, 'How should we give a presentation?'

The answer is less straightforward. It depends on your goals and how the context of the presentation (audience, etc.) is likely to impact on the ease with which you can get your message across. However, there are some broad principles that apply. The list below applies to a team presentation:

- Delivery – Confidence, enthusiasm, rapport with the audience, audibility (can everyone hear you?).
- Delivery methods – Which were chosen? How well were they used?
- Structure – Was there a logical flow to the arguments made in the presentation?
- Content – Did the content help to fulfil the goals of the presentation? Were any arguments convincing?
- Presentation preparation and management – Was it completed in time? Were all participants prepared? Was coordination between presenters good?

A presentation without much preparation will likely fail to achieve its objectives. A presentation with poor delivery will tend to do likewise. In technical presentations and where you are communicating in a formal environment, it is often the content that is important, but you can think of delivery as the oil which makes a presentation work well. Even in a technical presentation, get the delivery wrong and people might well be talking about how poor the presentation was, but get the delivery right and folk will be discussing the content.

It is true that most people rarely remember a presentation because of what was said, but more because of how they felt afterwards. It is really interesting to watch (or listen to, if it is on radio) an audience during a political debate, for example. A good presenter will get to their feet and give a speech emphasising one strategy and course of action with passion, excitement and enthusiasm and rising to a crescendo at the end, resulting in a positive audience reaction and perhaps a standing ovation and a smile on everyone's face. Another speaker will do the same, but this time give the opposite message delivered in exactly the same way, yet the same thing happens: everyone smiles and applauds the speaker, but the message is totally the opposite. The only variable is the way that the speaker delivered their speech. To make the argument even stronger, the same message can be delivered by one speaker with passion and enthusiasm and by another speaker in a logical, factual way, yet the reaction will be very different. Human beings like being excited, so if you are trying to inspire or generate passion, then give the audience something which inspires them.

Even for presentations that do not require a great deal of passion, it is still important to give a competent performance so that you can get your message across. As noted above, the best presentations in the board room keep things simple, straightforward and clear, and the best presentations to a large number of staff at an annual meeting try to inspire and encourage.

Either way, there are some important aspects of delivery that we need to get right. We will look briefly at them below (there are 16 of them) and give some detailed information about visual aids later:

- **Audibility:** People must be able to hear us. Make sure you can get some idea of whether people can hear you before going too far into the presentation.
- **Smiles and facial expressions:** Nerves can stop us feeling relaxed, but if you are presenting in a slightly informal context, then smiling can help your audience to relax. Once you and they both

feel relaxed, you can influence reactions by showing them a frown on your face, for example. Watch to see if they follow, or nod.

- **Clarity of message:** Be sure to use emphasis appropriately to get the message across (see Chapter 12 content on 'para-linguistic communication' about adding contrast to your voice). If you are undertaking a formal presentation, then one or two simple messages might be sufficient.
- **Watch for posture:** Try not to use a podium or lectern more than you have to. They can provide a place of 'psychological comfort' but can also act as a 'psychological barrier' between you and the audience. Move purposefully, do so when you wish to generate a reaction or grab others' attention, but do not constantly move around. Be careful not to rub your hands or move from leg to leg because of nerves. During a group presentation, stay still if you are not the one speaking.
- **Tone of voice:** Vary your tone of voice when you can, but do not do so all the time or without purpose. Speaking in a monotone is going to bore your audience, but speaking with too much variation is going to confuse them as to what is important and what is not.
- **Pace and speed of speech:** The impact of pace is similar to that of movement and intonation. Pace should change when you are making important points – usually slowing down the presentation, giving your audience time to recognise that you are making an important point and time to think about what you are saying. Also, use a more natural speed for the remainder of the presentation. Do not be worried about leaving silences at particular points of the presentation for dramatic impact.
- **Obtain and keep people's interest:** There are various ways to do this, but a powerful introduction, stories, jokes, the use of certain visual aids (see the section on visual aids below), pictures, asking rhetorical questions, videos and anything that is 'out of the ordinary' or unexpected can' be powerful here.
- **Look at your audience:** A presenter who does not look at their audience is one who does not care whether the audience is there or not. The expressions on the face of members of the audience can go some significant way to giving you some clues as to whether they understand you, agree with you, are bored, interested or thinking about tonight's dinner.
- **Anticipate audience thinking:** Recognise that the audience may be thinking about what you are saying, which gives you an opportunity to build further rapport by saying something like 'Some of you might be wondering "why …?"' or 'The obvious question from what I have been saying is "How…?"' and then giving an answer.
- **Handle information well:** Keep highly detailed information away from any information displayed on the screen. Put it in a document for your audience to read later. Consider carefully when to give out any written information, though. Give it out too early and the audience may spend the whole time reading it rather than attending to you as a speaker; too late and it might be seen as irrelevant.
- **Ask rhetorical questions:** Asking questions is one of the best ways of either getting the audience to think through what you are telling them, or persuading them that you have the answer to their problems, even though these two goals seem contradictory. If you give your audience time and space to think things through, then the technique can be very persuasive. If you rush to answer the question, then it might stimulate the audience to think, but also it might frustrate them if you give the answer before they have come to their own answer.
- **Dress and appearance:** Dress smartly. This is usually the case for most presentations, and certainly for assessed presentations. Sometimes, you can get away with being just who you are and wearing casual clothes, but for assessed presentations at university, this is not usually the case.

- **Tell jokes, if you can:** But if you are not good at doing so, then do not. It is OK to use spontaneous humour as well, if you are confident about doing so.
- **Keep to time:** This is especially important for assessed presentations (or those where you are trying to get a job or sell something to someone). Your audience may be exceptionally busy and may have very limited time for you to get your message across.
- **Be Polite, Courteous and Respectful at all times:** If you appear arrogant, irritated or unhelpful, your audience will stop giving you their attention. That is why smiling is important.
- **Say 'thank you' and invite questions:** If your audience has been listening carefully, then they might need to ask for more information or for your opinion on something that you have covered. Dealing with questions that you have not prepared for sometimes feels daunting, but there is little wrong with suggesting that you will get back to someone later with the answer (although make sure you do!).

 ━━━━ FOR YOU TO DO ━━━━━━━━━━━━━━━━━━━━━━

Prepare to deliver a presentation entitled 'Why have I come to study at university?' The presentation should be 10 minutes long and can use whatever visual aids you want.

Deliver the presentation to two or more friends (you can make this a mutual activity if you want, for all of you to do).

Taking each of the 16 items listed above, obtain feedback from those watching you.

What were your personal strengths and weaknesses?

What three things would you improve for next time?

1.

2.

3.

_____

DEALING WITH NERVES

It is not difficult to imagine a situation where all the preparation and rehearsal has been done and the delivery has been 'perfected' as far as possible, only to walk towards the room for the assessed presentation and become nervous. The good news is that you are probably not alone in feeling nervous (assuming a group presentation), but the bad news is that because everyone else is nervous, they might be too stressed to be able to help each other. This is not a helpful situation, really.

If you have done all the preparation referred to above and have rehearsed and improved, then there is little extra that you can do, so it might be useful to take a break and relax where you can. Sometimes giving others some encouragement can be good: it takes the focus off yourself and you can feel content to be doing some good for the team.

Nearly everyone gets nervous at some point about giving a presentation. When we get nervous, we show it in a number of ways:

- We speak too quickly.
- We shake – especially when we are holding notes.

- We fidget around – our feet/legs, play with hair, etc.
- We look down and not at the audience.
- We forget what we are trying to say.
- We become unable to bring our own personality into our delivery.

Therefore, we need to learn to deal with those nerves. Eliminating them completely will take time and experience, but we can manage them.

Think about Why You Might be Nervous

People get nervous for various reasons, but sometimes those reasons actually do not make a lot of sense, if you stop and think about it. If you have prepared and rehearsed with others and made sure that everything can go as well as it can, then you have controlled as much as you can control and probably should think about relaxing.

Of course, telling or pushing yourself to relax is not going to do it either – it will actually add to the pressure – so do something totally unconnected with the presentation for a while. Go for a quick walk outside, do the washing up, watch a bit of TV (it is permitted, in small doses) and then go and do the presentation.

Deal with the Reasons

If you have controlled everything that you can control, then the only things which can make you nervous are the things you cannot control – and some of them are unknown. It is often the unknown that challenges us, especially if we are used to being in control of everything.

The frequently used example is that of the driving test. If you think about it, your driving instructor will have taken you through everything you need to think about and it is now up to you. But you do not know who the examiner is going to be. You may not have any idea about where they are going to ask you to go and this person has the power to determine whether you can get in a car and drive to school or university or not. The reality is simply that you are going to face something you have never faced before and whether many people have or have not, that *can* make it difficult for them to cope with it – but it does not need to.

Typically, people get nervous in presentations because they will be the centre of attention and anything that goes wrong will be 'huge' in terms of their personal self-image. When students do presentations, they are 'on the stage' and that means that everyone watching will be judging you. Furthermore, in this social-media-frenzied world, others' opinions are thought to count. But are these thoughts and beliefs really true?

═══════════════ BOX 9.2 ═══════════════

TRUE OR FALSE?

What do you really think of the statements listed below? These beliefs have the power to determine a lot of what we think about and do, but are they really true?

- 'Things that go wrong will affect the whole of our life …'
- 'People will be judging us – our self-image …'
- 'Other's opinions of us really matter hugely …'

Interestingly, none of the sentences in Box 9.2 need to be true. Some individuals make them true for themselves, but that is their choice. Generally, things that go wrong will not be huge in terms of their life impact, and it is much better to make mistakes and learn from them than to believe that we never make mistakes.

Strategies for Handling Nerves

Even the best lecturers get nervous sometimes – perhaps when facing an important client or when delivering a new course, so they are not immune to nerves. But learning how to handle and use the anxiety is really important. Consequently, some of the strategies below might be useful:

- **Give yourself some 'breathing space':** After introducing yourself, ask the audience to discuss something relevant to the topic you are going to discuss. This is not always possible but works really well for an informal presentation to a large number of people when having such a large number of people looking at you can seem daunting. Having started the discussion, you can then take a few moments to look around and relax.
- **Appear confident:** Enter the room very deliberately, looking down if you need to (although it is better to look up if you feel able to) and walking as if you are walking to someone else's dorm room.
- **It is a conversation:** Try to remember that what you are there to do is to give some information. You are the only one who knows what you are going to say and you are the only person who can say it. Imagine that you are talking to three or four people: one or two at the back, two somewhere in the middle and a couple of people in the front. Do not stare at them, but if you find a friendly face then do smile and try to get them to smile back.
- **Do not rely on memory alone:** If you are new to giving presentations, then do not just rely on memory. Established presenters can do it, but they have had a lot of practice. Unless you are used to presenting in the same way or do not really have a problem with nerves, it is best to stay relatively close to what you are used to.
- **Be yourself:** You will have seen a large number of other presentations at university by your lecturers and possibly other students. Do not try to do what others can do so much better than you can, but, over time, learn to develop your own style. This can mean trying out different styles and experimenting, but it is perhaps better to do this in practice sessions than to do it when being assessed.
- **Keep your hands still:** If you have a tendency to move around or shake your hands when nervous, then actively do something to prevent such behaviour from affecting the presentation. If you move around, then sit down when someone else is presenting and stand (if you need to) only for your part of the presentation. If you move your hands a lot, then hold your hands behind your back or hold on to the podium, or try something to make sure that your hands do not distract from the delivery.

Above all else, there is no substitute for thorough preparation. Prepare yourself, the room, the content, the visual aids and your behaviour as a presenter (which means getting feedback from others), and all should go well.

Some students do not enjoy giving presentations, while others do. In many cases, those who do not enjoy presentations are those who experience anxiety about doing them. Whichever you are, presentations will likely form a part of your course assessment somewhere, and it is better to get practice in doing them at university than to make some significant mistakes when in the workplace.

IDENTIFYING AND USING VISUAL AIDS

Probably the most common visual aid used in presentations is the PowerPoint slide, but imagine for a moment that PowerPoint (and the now somewhat obsolete overhead projector) did not exist: what would you use as a visual aid?

This kind of question forces us to be a little creative – and, as the saying goes, 'necessity is the mother of invention'. We are so used to looking at PowerPoint presentations that we could consider that anything that does not use PowerPoint is not a proper presentation. In reality, we could use practically anything as a visual aid, so we do not have to use PowerPoint. Figure 9.4 gives some ideas which might be appropriate.

Suggestions for Interaction and Visual Aids

- Video
- PowerPoint
- Demonstration
- Role-Play/Theatre
- Quizzes
- Physical examples
- Pictures
- Volunteers from the audience

- Stories
- Handouts
- Flipchart/OHP/Digital Media
- Discussions
- True/False or Multiple Choice questions

Figure 9.4 Ideas for interactions and visual aids

The list in the figure is not exhaustive and principally anything – and anyone – can be a visual aid. Generally speaking, the more unusual or creative the visual aid, the greater the impact of the presentation. As noted in various places above, the way we do our presentation depends on the goals we have, so we choose the visual aids based on our objectives and presentation style.

Once we have chosen which visual aid(s) we wish to use, the challenge then is to use them correctly. Videos need to have a brief introduction: What do you wish the audience to notice or look out for? Why are you showing the video? Demonstrations need to make sure that everyone can see what you are doing, so we need to use them carefully.

If we are attempting to entertain our audience, then the more creative visual aids might be more appropriate. Box 9.3 gives some suggestions that may be useful when trying to enhance the creativity of our presentations. The best presenters often use surprise and excitement to engage the audience (e.g. bringing on a suitcase, so the natural question of what is in the suitcase arises in the mind of the audience, and then only gradually revealing what is actually in the suitcase). Therefore, think not just about what is used as a visual aid, but also how it is used.

════ BOX 9.3 ════

CREATIVITY IN PRESENTATIONS

Creativity is often seen as something which will inspire, grab an audience's attention and make a presentation a lot more interesting than a series of PowerPoint slides. Not all presentations will require a great deal of creativity, but the more an audience is likely to lose interest (perhaps because of the time of day or the length or content of the presentation) then the more creative you may have to be.

(Continued)

(Continued)

The following principles might be helpful:

- **Variety:** If you want to keep your audience guessing about what will come next, then ensure that your presentation includes a variety of activities. Predictability is sometimes unhelpful if you want to keep your audience interested.
- **Planning:** Using activities that you or your audience are not used to will require planning. What could go wrong, and how would you manage that? Will such activities take longer than you have allowed for in your timing?
- **Relevance:** Think through whether the activities really add value to your presentation: Do they help to demonstrate your main point in a different way? What are your audience more likely to take away – their memory of the activity or the message you wanted to convey? Is that a problem?
- **Technology:** Sometimes activities using technology may be great, but what happens if it fails? For example, your tablet or laptop battery fails, or everyone logs on to the same website at the same time: Is the wireless strong enough to handle it? Do you have a backup plan?
- **Regularity:** The more frequently you use a creative activity in a presentation, the less likely an audience is to pay attention to your message, and the more attention to the activities. Infrequent use of activities is likely to be more helpful than constant use of such activities, when a presentation can seem disjointed.
- **Timing:** Do you want your audience to learn something from the activity, or are you using an activity to show them something in another way? The level of curiosity will be higher for the former, but the learning might be more powerful from the latter.
- **Ability:** Do not try to do what you cannot. Avoid telling jokes if you are not good at telling them. Magic tricks are a great way to get people interested in a particular topic, but if you have not perfected the trick, then do not try it in front of an important audience. If the ability relates to physical qualities that you do not have, then you might be able to get a volunteer from the audience to do something that you cannot.
- **Overkill:** Too many creative activities in a short space of time for a presentation whose goals do not require creative activities (e.g. presenting a technical report to a management board) can kill a presentation. You do not always need to be creative.

As mentioned above, perhaps the most commonly used tool for presentations is PowerPoint. It is ubiquitous in its availability and use, but it is not always used well and can sometimes be less helpful than intended. Box 9.4 gives some ideas that can enhance how PowerPoint is used.

===== **BOX 9.4** =====

DEATH BY POWERPOINT

'Death by PowerPoint' is the popular name for a set of criticisms arising from poor use – and, in some cases, sustained overuse – of MS PowerPoint software. It is simple to use, which is why it is very common among lecturers, but most presenters tend to use the readymade slide templates and so the software tends to get used in exactly the same way time after time.

The following can be useful in avoiding 'death by PowerPoint':

- **Think about inserting video:** The best format is '*.wmv' (Windows Media File), which will play in Windows Media Player as well as enabling a video to play directly in PowerPoint.
- **Using animations and transitions creatively:** Do not over-animate but use them for dramatic effect (which means sparingly).

(Continued)

(Continued)

- **Turn off noises:** Animations and transitions can have sounds associated with them. Rarely should these be turned on; they usually interfere with the audience's concentration.
- **Use colour carefully:** Bright colours do not usually work well and can often distract the audience. Pastel colours tend to work a lot better. Be aware that those suffering from dyslexia can sometimes struggle with 'graduated' coloured backgrounds. Finally, make sure that your audience can read all that you write on the slide; for example, red text on a grey background rarely works.
- **Keep your content succinct:** Write bullet points with as few words as you can. Avoid writing sentences wherever possible. Remember: you should be looking at your audience most of the time, not reading your PPT slides.
- **Keep it simple and short:** Do not overcomplicate your presentation or bore your audience by making your presentation unnecessarily long.
- **Check spelling throughout:** There are few things more embarrassing than a bad spelling that is highly visible during a presentation. PowerPoint may not indicate a spelling mistake where a legitimate but incorrect word is used, so make sure that you review what you have written.

Developing and using visual aids to enhance the creativity of a presentation requires as much planning as thinking through the content of what it is that you want to say during the presentation. They can make or break a presentation and there are contexts where less creativity creates a better presentation, so their use has to be thought through carefully.

KEY LEARNING POINT

Getting the preparation, structure and delivery of a presentation right is crucial to the credibility of the message.

REFLECTION POINT

Take some time to think about the following questions and write down some answers.

After giving a presentation, do you ever evaluate your own presentation skills? Or do you get someone else to evaluate your presentation?
   Have you ever given a poor presentation? Why did it go wrong?

INTEGRATION AND APPLICATION

The chapter has consistently shown that the success or otherwise of any presentation will depend on the extent to which the goals of the presentation drive the structure, content and delivery of the presentation. In both business and academic life as a student, having unclear goals is likely to lead to failure, regardless of how much preparation is undertaken.

Bearing this in mind, we can develop a step-by-step process which will help you compile and deliver a competent presentation:

Step 1: Identify the goals of the presentation. If you need to do the presentation simply because it is part of the assessment for a course, then the goal will be 'To answer the question set in a convincing manner', and this will be explained in more detail through the criteria by which the presentation is to be assessed. If you are doing a business presentation, then you need to ask, 'What am I aiming to achieve? What do I want those listening to learn that they did not know before?'

Step 2: Do your research and gather appropriate content. Sketch out what you *want* to cover to answer the question, and then identify what you *need* to cover in order to answer the goal(s) of the presentation. Less relevant or very detailed information can be given in a handout.

Step 3: Identify how best to structure and organise that content. Identify a logical flow where possible, with examples and evidence.

Step 4: Consider how best to deliver the message(s) that you have selected. Use visual aids and other activities to add value and avoid unnecessary items which might act as distractions.

Step 5: Rehearse your presentation and get feedback if possible. Think about how your audience are likely to react to what you are saying. Where necessary, edit and restructure what you have presented until you have something which matches what is expected and will achieve your goal(s).

Step 6: Develop your introduction and conclusion. There is little point in doing so in advance of this until you are happy with what you have.

Step 7: Rehearse again until you are confident with what you have put together, and then deliver …

If you struggle with nerves, then just remember that every presentation we do is likely to make the next presentation easier.

CONCLUSION

By now, you should have a better idea of how to:

- Understand why presentations fail to achieve their objectives.
- Prepare, structure and deliver a good oral presentation.
- Choose and use visual aids relevant to the audience and goals of the presentation.
- Use appropriate strategies for dealing with nerves.

Throughout this chapter, we have noted that giving presentations is not easy and there is more than one way to deliver a message successfully. As noted, identification of the goals is essential in delivering a good presentation, but even having done so there can be issues in terms of how we prepare, structure and then give the presentation. As with all skills, there is a need for feedback and motivation to ensure that we get better at it, and the more practice we have, the more confident we become – and the more feedback we receive, the better we become.

We will often learn a lot about presentations from those we watch others give, and from those we are involved with ourselves. There is no one definitive style and you may find that you are better giving some kinds of presentations than others, so over time you will need to develop your own particular style.

FINAL REFLECTIONS

Based on the content of this chapter, what do you now know that you did not know before about giving presentations?

What key learning point had the most impact? Why?

Do your answers to either of the above questions have the potential to change your ability to give a convincing presentation? Why?

What will you now do differently? (Write this down and put it somewhere where you can see it regularly.)

INTERVIEW QUESTIONS

In some interview situations, you may be required to give a brief presentation to answer a particular question. If so, the interviewer will be looking in your presentation for all the qualities described above, but even if they do not ask you to do so, they will be looking at how you communicate through the answers that you give and the way that you give them. In effect, every question you are asked will be an opportunity for you to demonstrate your communication skills.

Therefore, it is unlikely that you will be asked to talk about your presentation skills in an interview where they can be evaluated in other ways and where time is very limited. In addition, any questions which might be asked about presentations will more likely be asked in order to determine your ability to plan and deliver a piece of work – either individually or in a group. But your interviewer might want to check that you have had experience of presentations if it is relevant to the job you will be asked to do, and so might ask you some short, closed questions such as:

1. Thinking of an example of a presentation that you had to give, how did you go about preparing and giving the presentation?
2. What do you find are the most difficult issues with preparing and giving a presentation?

Chapter 17 gives a lot more information on selection interviews and the online content gives some guidance on these questions.

ADDITIONAL RESOURCES

Want to learn more? Visit https://study.sagepub.com/morgan to gain access to a wide range of online resources, including interactive tests, tasks, further reading and downloads.

Website Resources

Algonquin College website: algonquincollege.libguides.com/studyskills/presentation-skills

Encyclopaedia Britannica Digital Learning website – resources to help with preparing for and delivering presentations: http://school.eb.com/resources/pdf/BSW_Oral_Presentation.pdf

(Continued)

(Continued)

Mindtools website: www.mindtools.com/pages/article/newCS_96.htm

University of Bradford website: www.bradford.ac.uk/academic-skills/resources/study/effective-communication/present/

Textbook Resources

Duarte, N. (2012) *HBR Guide to Persuasive Presentations*. Boston, MA: Harvard Business Review Press.
Etherington, B. (2009) *Presentation Skills for Quivering Wrecks*. London: Marshall Cavendish.
Kaul, A. (2005) *The Effective Presentation*. New Delhi: Response Books.
Matthews, A. (2013) *The Successful Presenter's Handbook*. Strensall: HLS Publishing.
McIlroy, D. (2003) *Studying @ University*. London: Sage (particularly chapter 11).
McMillan, K. and Weyers, J. (2012) *The Study Skills Book* (3rd edition). Harlow: Pearson (particularly chapter 57).
Parker, D. A. (2000) *Basic Public Speaking*. Bloomington, IN: Xlibris Corporation.
Pettinger, R. and Firth, R. (2001) *Mastering Management Skills*. Basingstoke: Palgrave (particularly chapter 4).
Seely, J. (2005) *Oxford Guide to Effective Writing and Speaking*. New York: Oxford University Press (particularly section B, p. 93–130).

/10 TEAM-WORKING

CHAPTER STRUCTURE

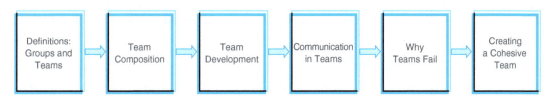

Figure 10.1

When you see the 🌐 this means go to the companion website https://study.sagepub.com/morgan to do a quiz, complete a task, read further or download a template.

━━ AIMS OF THE CHAPTER ━━

By the end of this chapter, you should be able to:

- Understand why people in groups behave as they do.
- Work more effectively with others.
- Understand how work teams are different from those at university.

INTRODUCTION

A brief look at the shelves of bookstores will show you that team-working is the subject of a large number of books. It is also true that, while you can and should use resources such as books and research articles on teams, the essence of your team-working skills is your behaviour. The way you behave with others as you work with them will have consequences for you and for them, and no textbook can change your behaviour on its own. So, the aims of this chapter are relatively modest: to give you some insights; to show you the consequences of certain actions; and to give you some resources to help you work better in teams.

The hope is that the chapter will give you some ideas and help you to understand the implications of research in this area. In the mind of many researchers, working in an effective team is emotionally different from working in a group, so we will spend a little time looking at the differences between these two. We will also examine the relationships between attitudes and behaviours, and the ways that certain attitudes can affect behaviour. The chapter will also examine some of the reasons why teams can sometimes be ineffective and will give some answers which will help to solve these issues.

There are different ways to describe the way that we 'work with others'. Universities tend to talk about 'group working' (e.g. group work assignments) while employers discuss 'team-working'. There are some important differences, and also some significant overlap in terms of human behaviour, hence the use of 'work(ing) with others', which is intended to cover that overlap. We will look at the differences and similarities shortly.

Finally, when we look at team-working in this chapter, there will be significant links between this topic and that of leadership considered in Chapter 11. The two topics are different ways of working with – or relating to – others, and each has a distinct contribution to make to the effective completion of a task. However, the role of leader is a distinct set of activities and is examined in some detail in Chapter 11.

SKILLS SELF-ASSESSMENT

Complete the brief questionnaire below to see how well you work with others. You can think of an academic university situation (e.g. assessed coursework) or your activities within a student society or working in a team in the workplace. Give each item a score between 0 and 5, where 0 is 'not at all like me' or 'strongly agree', and 5 is 'very much like me' or 'strongly disagree'.

When I begin to work with others, I am likely to …

Item	Statement	Score
1.	Really enjoy the experience	
2.	Feel anxious about whether others will accept me	
3.	Want to get started on any activity we are given straight away	
4.	Worry about whether others will do their work properly	
5.	Think about what parts of the activity are best suited to me and better for others to do	
6.	Check my understanding of what we have to do with that of other people	
7.	Have some very clear ideas about how the task should be done	
8.	Write down my thinking about what the next step is	
9.	Think about how I can show others that I can make a better contribution to the activity than others	

(Continued)

(Continued)

Item	Statement	Score
10.	Think about how the activity relates to other work I have done before	
11.	Get bored very easily	
12.	Consider how I can get others to like me	
13.	Worry about whether my English and/or accent is going to be good enough for me to help the group	
14.	Think about whether others are going to easily accept my opinions and points of view	
15.	Get excited about the potential for working with others on a project	
16.	Be really happy about starting 'a new thing'	
17.	Make a plan for who should do what	
18.	Think carefully about how I can encourage others within the group	
19.	Deal with people who don't cooperate with the group's activities	
20.	Make sure that everyone has the contact details of everyone else in the group	

Most of these questions do not have right or wrong answers, but they will all have consequences. You can complete an interactive version of this test and find answers and guidance on the questions at https://study.sagepub.com/morgan. Nearly all the answers will have consequences for how we interact with others, whether the group or team is working together for a long time (e.g. a department within an organisation) as a business function (e.g. marketing or accounting), or whether it has a specific and time-defined purpose (e.g. to complete a project within two months).

INTERACTIVE TEST

Our feelings, emotions and behaviours – and others' perceptions of our behaviours – will impact on how well we are able to work with others. If any of the answers (particularly those which start with 'Worry about …') are likely to affect your natural behaviour too much, then maybe there is a need for you to consider whether these worries are real or just built up from other experiences which may not reflect the reality of the situation you are currently in. In general, many of the things we worry about are unlikely to become reality, but the more we think about them, the more we are likely to create a self-fulfilling prophecy.

DEFINITIONS: GROUPS AND TEAMS

There are two important terms to define here – Groups and Teams – and there is no shortage of discussion in the academic literature as to what constitutes each one. In some situations, it might not matter greatly as to whether you think you are working in a group or in a team, but if other people have a different view, then their behaviour will be different.

Groups and Teams

Some (e.g. Muchinsky, 2003) have argued that groups and teams are actually nearly the same thing. Both consist of individuals working together to accomplish something. These individuals will likely have some differences in terms of their interests, personality, demographics and perhaps abilities, but there is something that brings them together. In terms of groups and teams, this is probably where the similarities between groups and teams end.

A group might be a social group (e.g. a club or a number of folk who like to meet after work). A team, on the other hand, can be quite different.

 GROUP

A group is usually defined as 'A number of people sharing something in common and meeting together in relation to their shared characteristics.'

Teams possess the same characteristics as groups, but with some notable and important additions. Katzenbach and Smith (1993) looked at teams which were performing well and those which were performing badly, and identified a number of key factors that made the difference between low- and high-performing teams:

- **Small:** You need a reasonably sized team in order to ensure you have all the knowledge and skills that you need, but a team that is too large will likely become dysfunctional. It will be difficult to coordinate diaries, to arrange meetings and then for folk to communicate at those meetings if the team is too large. A team of between five and seven is seen as ideal.
- **Complementary skills:** A team of five people undertaking a task which requires eight different types of knowledge and/or expertise is probably going to work if team members are selected carefully, but if all those five people possess exactly the same skills, then the team will not be effective. The skills and knowledge possessed by the team should complement rather than replicate those of other team members.
- **Common purpose:** The team members should be committed to the team's aims. This commitment could show itself in their willingness to make sacrifices for the team – an effort which is then repaid by others willing to give up their own ideas and activities to support each other. The purpose of the team drives the emotional effort put in by members.
- **Specific goals:** Where goals are unclear, then the level of performance required and the outcomes sought are also unclear. The outcomes sought from the team – and from any members of the team contributing particular work – need to be specific. A lack of clarity could well lead to frustration as members then feel a need to edit other members' work.
- **Common approach:** It is fine to share the goals, but the team needs to be in agreement about how it will achieve those goals. Without agreement, the team is likely to suffer from division.
- **Mutual accountability:** A team has a sense of 'togetherness', with each member supporting every other member. This has the potential to create a strong bond, which means that there is great strength in the team, but it also means that the team needs to stick together and assist each other when things do not go according to plan, and 'act as one' if the results are not good. It also means that the relationships formed within the team are maintained a long time after the team has finished what it was formed to do.

Working in a high-performing team can be an extremely rewarding experience. All those in the team understand each other, practically support each other and encourage each other as the task progresses. They put their egos aside for the good of the team.

TEAM

A team is a number of individuals working as one to achieve a particular goal to which they are all mutually committed.

Teams are typically built for particular projects where particular skills and expertise are needed (e.g. to solve a problem or develop a product). Once those activities are complete, the team will often be disbanded.

===== 'BUT I HAVE A QUESTION ...' =====

... If a team of 5 to 7 is ideal, then why do football teams have 11 players on the pitch and an even larger team in total?

Good question. If you think of the skills required, then the skills needed for each of the 11 players are often very similar, other than the goalkeeper. All the players need to be able to pass the ball accurately, to control the ball, dribble with it, and so on. There are some differences, of course – some will need to be able to take penalties and corners – but the number of players is determined more by the positions in which they need to play than the diversity of skills required by the activity.

The question which I imagine would follow is how the difficulties mentioned above can be overcome with a much larger team. The answer to that is partially about managerial style (club managers are often very directive), in which case ensuring that everyone's voice is heard becomes less important. Finding time in diaries is not an issue since everyone is usually around all the time, undertaking activities designed by the club coach or manager.

The converse of this is an environment where there is tough competition between individuals, where pride and ambition can hinder individuals' willingness to assist others in the team, where individuals have hidden purposes in what they do (the real reasons for their supporting certain actions are never really discussed) and where failure will mean that individuals blame each other.

===== REFLECTION POINT =====

Take some time to think about the following questions and write down some answers, first on your own, and then with others you might be working with.

1. Is the way that a team is formed in business any different to the way you would form a team to work on an assignment or group project? Why, or why not? What are the consequences of those differences?
2. When you are working with others on an assignment, are you working as a group or as a team? Does it make a difference?
3. According to the definition and ideas given earlier, a team working on coursework is supposed to support each other and everyone in the team is supposed to be mutually accountable for what the team does. Is this your experience when working with others on a piece of coursework? What helps or hinders this? What can be done about any hindrances?
4. It is common when working on an assignment with others to delegate responsibility for different parts of the task to certain members of the group or team, and then one final person will edit the work. Is this the best way to do a group assignment, or is there a better way?
5. Assignments where you have to work with others are often used by universities to develop your skills and abilities to work with others in preparation for employment. Do you like working with others or prefer to do your own work? Why or why not?
6. What differences and similarities are there between working on a group assignment at university and working with others on a team assignment in the workplace?

TEAM COMPOSITION

The way the team is put together is key to being a successful team. Teams can be put together in various ways – for example, according to personal knowledge, according to the importance of having certain connections outside the team, according to members' abilities and according to individuals' access to financial and other resources.

Two models are frequently discussed. In the 1920s, a system known as DISC personality profiling was developed by William M. Marston to identify the different roles that individuals play in teams. Research carried out by Meredith Belbin and his team in the 1970s and 1980s at Henley Management College resulted in what has been known as 'Team Role Theory'. We will now briefly look at both. Both models are based on an understanding of individual personality – and both have roles which are more adventurous and roles which are more conservative.

The DiSC® Model

The DiSC model of team roles was developed from a model of personality originated by Marston in 1928, while the personality questionnaire based on Marston's work was not firmly developed until the mid-1950s by Walter Clarke and then taken further to produce the Personality Profiling System in the 1970s. Marston's original work was based on four emotional reactions to individuals' environments: inducement or compliance (does the individual view their environment as favourable or unfavourable?) and dominance and submission (does the individual feel they have control over their environment?) – hence the word DISC, although the current acronym refers to issues of dominance, influence, steadiness and conscientiousness. These four words are then combined in various ways to produce eight traits, which are a mixture of the four areas (D, I, S & C, and then combinations of D & I, I & S, S & C and C & D) (from www.discprofile.com, 2009).

Respondents either choose between groupings of various words to produce their personality profile, with words indicating particular styles (e.g. dominance – direct, strong-willed and forceful; influence – sociable, talkative and lively; steadiness – gentle, accommodating and soft-hearted; and conscientiousness – private, analytical and logical), or rate themselves (1–5) on a questionnaire. This leads to the production of a report, indicating where individuals fall on the most important six dimensions of the nine identified below:

- Soft-spoken – forceful
- Daring – careful
- Patient – driven
- Sceptical – accepting
- Outgoing – private
- Tactful – frank
- Accommodating – strong-willed
- Lively – reserved
- Calm – energetic

Where people fit on these scales can be used to indicate an individual's behaviour, but while the questionnaire will have various applications, one of its uses is to examine the ways that individuals will likely interact in a team. Basic details about the four DiSC® personality types can be found online at: www.discprofile.com.

Belbin's Team Roles

Research by Belbin and others in the 1970s (Belbin, 1981) indicated that two factors were important: (1) the knowledge that a person has in order to contribute to a group – their occupational function; but, more importantly, (2) the skills and abilities that individuals bring to a task.

By analysing the performance of teams on simulations and investigating the personalities of members of the team in relation to that performance, Belbin and others argued that the combined personalities of the individuals in a team – or the combination of individual 'team roles' – could significantly enhance or detract from the ability of that team to complete particular tasks. These are not functional roles that someone asks you to perform, but rather emerge very naturally from your personality as you engage in team activities, and from your strengths and weaknesses will emerge particular functional roles and activities for you to do. Box 10.1 provides a brief summary of the nine team roles that emerged from the research. There were originally eight team roles, but further investigation gave rise to a ninth – that of 'specialist' – which emerged when the nature of the simulation was changed.

■■■ BOX 10.1 ■■■

BELBIN'S NINE TEAM ROLES

The team roles listed below arose from the research carried out by Belbin and his associates (Belbin, 1981). Look at the brief descriptions given below: these describe the respective contributions to the team and the allowable weaknesses respectively. The two-letter abbreviations are commonly used when employing this model.

Team role (and abbreviation)	Strengths	Allowable weaknesses
Coordinator (CO)	Mature, confident and identifies talent	Can be seen as manipulative, offloads own share of the work.
Implementer (IMP)	Practical, reliable and efficient. Turns ideas into actions and organises work that needs to be done	Somewhat inflexible. Slow to respond to new possibilities
Shaper (SH)	Challenging, dynamic, thrives on pressure. Has the courage and the drive to overcome obstacles	Prone to provocation, offends people's feelings
Completer-Finisher (CF)	Painstaking, conscientious, anxious. Searches out errors. Polishes and perfects	Inclined to worry unduly, reluctant to delegate
Resource Investigator (RI)	Outgoing, enthusiastic and communicative. Explores opportunities and develops contacts	Over-optimistic. Loses interest once initial enthusiasm has passed
Specialist (SP)	Single-minded, self-starting, dedicated. Provides knowledge and skills in rare supply	Contributes only on a narrow front. Dwells on technicalities
Monitor-Evaluator (ME)	Sober, strategic and discerning. Sees all options and judges accurately	Lacks drive and ability to inspire others. Can be overly critical

(Continued)

(Continued)

Team role (and abbreviation)	Strengths	Allowable weaknesses
Plant (PL)	Creative, imaginative, free thinking. Generates ideas and solves difficult problems	Ignores incidentals. Too preoccupied to communicate effectively
Team-worker (TW)	Cooperative, perceptive and diplomatic. Listens and averts friction	Indecisive in crunch situations. Avoids confrontation

Belbin suggests that we usually have primary roles – ones that are closest to our personality – and secondary roles – ones that we are very similar to and can perform if we need to.

The identification of individuals' team roles (their primary role and secondary role, reflecting what individuals would naturally do and what they could do if they needed to, respectively) emerges from an analysis of an individual's own responses to items on a personality questionnaire (Belbin Team Role Self-Perception Inventory) and observations made by trained observers watching individuals complete the simulation. The research carried out by Belbin and others suggests that the more the team reflects all the team roles, the better the team's performance on the simulation is likely to be. The team can still be kept small, since all the team roles can be found through individuals' primary and secondary roles. The task of those putting the team together is simply to ensure that all the roles identified above are represented in the team, according to the needs of the task.

Not every task will require every role, and certain team roles might be more or less important at different stages of the task. Figure 10.2 indicates at what stages certain roles might be particularly important.

There are a number of issues that some people have with this model. The questionnaire (Belbin Team Role Self-Perception Inventory) is not always seen as the easiest to complete, it is unclear why changing the simulation would allow a previously unknown role to emerge, and some claim that other internal and external contextual factors (e.g. individuals' attitudes, organisational politics or policies) can undermine the effectiveness of the team.

Stages and roles of task completion	
Task stages	**Roles seen as important**
Identifying needs	SH and CO
Finding ideas	PL and RI
Formulating plans	ME and SP
Making contacts	RI and TW
Establishing the organisation	IMP and CO
Following through	CF and IMP

Figure 10.2   Task requirements and relevant roles

The methodology and research behind the model were not fully revealed until the 1990s and some claim that research supporting the model's predictions is somewhat limited, but the model has been used extensively in business to form teams, has research support and it certainly has intuitive appeal.

KEY LEARNING POINT

Decisions taken regarding the formation of a team – who will be in the team and why – are going to have a major impact on the effectiveness of the team.

REFLECTION POINT

Take some time to think about the following questions and write down some answers.

Thinking about yourself, which of the descriptions of the team roles is closest to your own personality?
  Is there a secondary team role that you could perform?
  To what extent are the allowable weaknesses really allowable?

Finding a team with all the team roles may not be the first issue on your mind when trying to form a team for a coursework assignment. The first question is usually, 'Are my friends doing this module?', with a second being, 'Are they already in a group?'. Choosing to work with our friends, however, may not always be the best thing, as discussed in Box 10.2.

BOX 10.2

SHOULD I WORK WITH MY FRIENDS OR NOT?

When working as a university student, is it better to work on coursework with others who are your friends, or to be put in a team by your tutor? What are the consequences of either?

It is very natural – and very frequent – to find you have a group work assignment to do and suddenly decide to work with your friends. You know them reasonably well, presumably you have something in common, you might have a similar sense of humour and might live close together, but are these the best reasons to work with them?

Actually, some of these are good reasons to avoid working with friends, since they tend to ignore some of the best practice identified above. Having good relationships does not mean that you have the right skills, motivation or academic abilities to do well on a piece of coursework. What it might mean, however, is something entirely more problematic. If we take the view that everyone is equally and strongly motivated to do the project that you have been set, then the worst situation would be a group which just happens not to have the right skills. The best situation is that your friends are highly motivated, have strong bonds with each other and have all the skills needed by a particular project.

But, if we take the view that one or some members of the group are not motivated to do the task, then there is a problem. We either ignore the lack of effort from our friends and get on with the work ourselves (and keep the friendship, albeit at a reduced level of commitment), or we start to damage the friendship by criticising our friends. It is very hard to work with friends when we have different levels of motivation and commitment to a task.

So, should you work with your friends? The answer is simple: it depends. You need to ensure that you are strong enough to break a friendship, should things turn out badly.

TEAM DEVELOPMENT

Having looked at how we put teams together, it is also appropriate to look at how teams work over time. Research carried out in the 1960s by Tuckman (1965) indicated that the development of the team will occur in a number of stages, each of which can affect interaction between members of the team. The terms used in brackets are those given by Tuckman.

Stage 1: Formation (Forming)

The formation of the team does not solely mean the putting together of team members. The composition of a team based on function and skill does not guarantee that it will instantly work well. As they are put together, individuals usually have questions such as: What am I doing here? How do I relate to others in the team? How well will I perform? The 'formation stage' is designed to help members feel relaxed and comfortable working with each other, and to start undertaking the task. Much of the team leader's role at this stage is to ensure that members get to know each other, to ensure that roles and contributions are clear, and to start the task; this can be done very easily through social and informal events (e.g. meals, going out together).

Stage 2: Disagreeing (Storming)

As the task gets underway, different team members will contribute in different ways, of course. As they do so, a number of difficulties are likely to emerge. It is quite possible that team members will start to find out that other members might have strong ideas, might not appear to listen properly or respect others enough, or may not be contributing enough to the task. The natural reaction to any of these issues is to feel resentful and start to argue, hence the name 'storming' given to this stage. In some ways, the open expression of emotion could be taken as a measure of how open the relationships within the team might be, but this could be a generous way of looking at it.

   The challenge for the leader is to allow such disagreements to occur. The alternative is to close down communication, which could stop some members contributing altogether, although it is out of disagreement that creativity can emerge – but not so far as to break the team. Thus a great deal of skill and wisdom is required: knowing when to intervene to calm discussions down, and when to allow and enable free discussion, is not easy. Handling emotional conversations is discussed in the next chapter.

Stage 3: Developing Ways of Working (Norming)

In order to emerge from a time of disagreement and discussion and ensure that members do not damage group processes, both the team and the team leader will need to consider how to prevent damaging conflict, or rather, how to manage it. The process of doing so – which may be quite brief – means that rules and procedures get developed and the team acquires values or 'norms' (e.g. only one person to speak at a time) by which it operates. These processes may change a little over time and may be added to as new issues emerge.

 ━━━ REFLECTION POINT ━━━━━━━━━━━━━━━━━━━━━━

Think about a time when you were in a group where there were rules to help the group perform better.

Did you agree to them? If not, did you follow them?

(Continued)

(Continued)

Thinking back, do you think the rules were at all useful? Did they help or hinder your ability (as a team) to work better?

Would you advise others working in teams to have rules to ensure that the goal could be accomplished?

Stage 4: Performing

The fourth stage is a result of the previous three: having developed some rules on how to work, developing an understanding of the personalities and roles within the team, and feeling comfortable enough to disagree in a respectful manner, there is little to prevent motivated individuals from performing together well as a team. As a result, the task gets completed.

Stage 5: Completion and Finish (Adjourning)

As mentioned earlier, teams are often created for a particular task and usually disband after finishing that task. In a team that has developed good relationships over a period of time, this process can be emotional, so the leader needs to ensure that the ending of the team is respectful and smooth. Just as social and informal events can be used to form the team, some form of celebration and/or a more formal 'thank you for your contribution' can work well to maintain team relationships.

There has been some debate as to whether teams do go through these five stages in the order listed. In reality, teams may well disagree about different things at different times. It is usual for the group to move between the storming and performing stages several times before a task is completed. It is also common practice in many teams for rules (norms) to be made explicit early on in the team's development, during the 'forming' stage, though of course these might be renegotiated as the team progresses with its task.

=== KEY LEARNING POINT ===

It is not reasonable simply to put a team together and expect it to perform from the outset. A team needs time to form and learn how to work together, and a team leader needs to ensure that this happens.

=== REFLECTION POINT ===

Take some time to think about the following questions and write down some answers.

Consider a group or a team that you have worked with. To what extent:

1. Was the task a definite task, with a particular goal to be achieved?
2. Did your progress reflect all of the stages detailed above? Why or why not?
3. Was there much conflict and disagreement within the team? How well did the team leader handle it?
4. Did the team have rules? Did these rules get applied well?

COMMUNICATION IN TEAMS

We look at communication skills in far more detail in Chapter 12. Communication, by its very nature, takes place between two or more people, so good communication skills are vital when working with others for the good of the group/team and in order to ensure that the task is completed successfully. There are a number of issues that are important when looking at communication in groups.

PATTERNS OF COMMUNICATION IN TEAMS

Communication patterns can look at three issues: (1) the amount of communication that takes place; (2) the quality of that communication (does it help the group achieve its goal?); and (3) who is communicating with whom (and who is not communicating at all). Look at Figure 10.3.

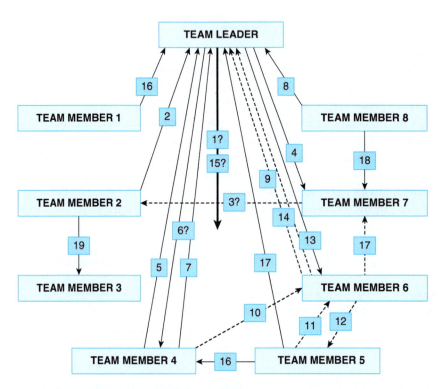

Figure 10.3   Patterns of communicating in a group

We can see that this figure is a representation of 19 different pieces of communication during what was probably the first part of a team discussion. The diagram uses various methods to indicate some detail of the contributions made.

The small numbered boxes indicate the order in which the contributions were made, and those with a question mark indicate where a question has been asked. The thickness of the arrow indicates emotion (the dotted lines indicate negative emotion or annoyance/anger; complete lines indicate positive passion). In reality, it is not easy to represent the detail of communication: even a question can be a statement of opinion; a contribution intended as a positive encouragement can be seen as negative by others; and one statement can be directed to many different selected individuals at a time. Further, the diagram indicates nothing about how long each person was speaking for. What it does indicate is that there are some team members who only speak when asked a question and others who say little.

The preceding paragraph shows that there is a variety of ways we can look at communication. Of course, we know that communication is what builds and destroys relationships and can thus act as an enabler to groups or a hindrance. Getting communication right is imperative, but it is not the only issue that affects how a group or team performs.

WHY TEAMS FAIL

In their text *Why Teams Don't Work*, Robins and Finley (1998) laid out a number of reasons why teams might fail. Some of their ideas relate to team composition in the first place, but other issues relate to factors external to the team. They noted the following issues:

Private agendas and mismatched needs: Individuals' motivations may not match those of the team more generally. This issue becomes particularly challenging when those motivations are hidden.

Confused and cluttered goals: Goals for the team either are excessively broad or appear to contradict other goals. This can often be the case for group-based coursework assessment.

Confused roles: Individuals are unclear as to what they can and are supposed to be contributing to the team, or more than one person may believe they have the same expertise when each has a different view.

Right decisions, wrong process: The team recommends decisions which may be correct but which have been taken in a way that generates a great deal of ill feeling.

Bad policies, stupid procedures: In larger bureaucratic organisations, the implementation of a good decision can be delayed by rules and processes either intended to protect the organisation in some way, or that are part of the continued history of the organisation.

Personality conflicts: People will not always agree about things, but there can be times when team members simply do not get on well. It is true to say that some individuals have personal agendas and this can influence their behaviour as part of the team.

Bad leadership: Leadership can be poor in that the leader does not provide goals, fails to communicate, contradicts their own values and has no vision for what needs to be done. This can also show itself through a lack of engagement, where certain individuals are not consulted or asked for their views.

Bleary vision: The team has an unclear idea of the vision underlying the activities being undertaken. There is no aspiration driving the team's activities.

Teams are not part of [my] thinking: There are individuals within the team who do not like to work with others for a variety of reasons. These individuals will probably be more reluctant to communicate and do the work that is needed.

Lack of feedback: The team receives no feedback on its performance and so never develops any motivation from past achievements, nor does it have any idea of how much work there is left to do.

Lack of incentives: There are few rewards either for good performance or for being a part of the team. This means that people are motivated either by the task itself or as being part of a team, but that effort may be limited when the task becomes very difficult.

Lack of trust: For a variety of reasons, members within the team do not believe what other members are saying or why they are doing certain things within the team.

Unwillingness to change: The team and its members are unable and unwilling to change what they do or how they do it when things start to go wrong.

Lack of tools and/or support: Those responsible for setting up the team provide it with insufficient resources and practical or emotional support when it is needed.

Of course, in addition to the list from Robins and Finley, we might draw from content elsewhere in this chapter and talk about:

Team roles: If there is an imbalance in the role profiles across the team (see content above on team composition), then it may be that the team will not have sufficient skills to complete a task.

A lack of ground rules: If there are no or few grounds rules, then individuals will develop and follow their own assumptions about how they should function. Teams need to have norms (see above about team development).

 ━━ FOR YOU TO DO ━━━━━━━━━━━━━━━━━━━━━━━━━━━━━

Have a look through the issues identified by Robins and Finley (1998) and answer the questions below.

1. How would you feel if you were in a team experiencing the above issues? What would go through your mind?
2. If you were leading a team experiencing these issues, how might you go about solving them?
3. Are there any other issues which affect the way that groups working on university assignments might perform?

INTERACTIVE
TEST

An interactive task and some suggestions are provided on the companion website at https://study.sagepub.com/morgan, although each individual and leader will have a different way of dealing with these issues.

CREATING A COHESIVE TEAM

Research indicates that teams perform well when there is cohesion. There are a number of ways that team leaders use to create cohesion and to create a sense of identity within a team. These methods are also sometimes used to create cohesion in much larger groups and organisations as well as an emphasis on identity and a sense of togetherness, meaning that people will be willing to commit effort even when there is no external reward to do so.

These are:

(a) **Experience of success:** A team which has never been successful will struggle to get a sense of excitement about success. Part of this is about establishing a vision for success: having that success can bring a sense of vision ('What would it be like if …') and a team that can understand success is likely to go over and above the minimum effort required to reach that success.

(b) **Challenge of a common enemy:** A team which has one enemy to fight against can focus its energy more effectively. If members of the team have different 'enemies', then it will be more difficult to create the idea that the team is trying to achieve one thing. A common enemy focuses energy outside of the team.

'BUT I HAVE A QUESTION ...'

... How can you create an enemy for something like coursework?

It's a fair question, but you're right: you can't really do that. But this doesn't mean that you can't get a team to work effectively with a sense of togetherness without a common enemy. Having a common goal is something that can create cohesion just as effectively.

(c) **High status:** A team which everyone wants to be part of because of its position in an organisational hierarchy is likely to maintain its cohesion. People will want to be members of the team because of its organisational influence, and that will motivate the team members.

Some believe that it is not just the history of the team or the way that team roles are put together that can produce success, but the gender and culture might also have a role to play (see Box 10.3 below).

BOX 10.3

GENDER AND TEAM WORKING

Bloisi et al. (2003) suggested that having females in the team can bring the team together. However, most would say that individuals are individuals and that gender does not matter. A team of gentle individuals may get on well (and might be male as equally as female), but might not complete the task.

The rationale presented by Bloisi et al. was that female composition would mean that gentleness and tact would be part of the team's ways of working. In reality, there are very prominent female leaders who demonstrate a toughness and determination that some males fail to demonstrate.

There are also many examples on popular TV shows (e.g. *The Apprentice*) where female teams become very competitive, and where females really do not cooperate well. As the work of Belbin suggested, it is really the mix of skills and abilities within the team, rather than the gender, which makes the difference.

KEY LEARNING POINT

Creating a team that is cohesive will go a long way towards fulfilling some of the characteristics that Katzenbach and Smith (1993) referred to in their work on high-performing teams.

━━━━━━━━━━━ BOX 10.4 ━━━━━━━━━━━

WORKING IN INTERCULTURAL TEAMS

Individuals might also struggle to work in intercultural teams. Where individuals differ in their cultural values and standards as to what is acceptable behaviour and what is not, individuals who experience such behaviour might find it challenging to accept cultural differences (see Chapter 13).

Of course, every individual is slightly different from every other individual anyway, but it is the extent to which behaviour (e.g. interrupting, arguing, taking control, being critical of the leader and/or others, etc.) is experienced in an intercultural team which can cause problems.

So, have a look at the behaviours below. Which would you find difficult to accept from others in your intercultural team? Which would make you feel embarrassed to be in the group?

1. An individual constantly interrupts another individual.
2. The group always meets in a pub and others in the group tend to drink a lot.
3. The group always seems to be joking and laughing around.
4. Other members of the group seem to be late to meetings.
5. Some members of the group seem to argue aggressively with each other.
6. The group has meals regularly but the food is always spicy and the leader never asks other members what they would like.
7. The leader seems to be weak – they never make a decision on their own, but always ask other people what they think.
8. Everybody seems quite selfish – the group never has any meals together.
9. The group always speaks in a language other than my own.
10. No one seems to care enough for each other: there is no friendly conversation in the group and everything is directed to the task.

The reaction that we might have may be based around our cultural values, but if those are different from others' values, then we may face a challenge in working easily with others. Chapter 13 gives a lot more information on working with people from other cultures, but if you find that you do not respect the group, then the quickest and easiest way to manage such situations is to ask your tutor for some anonymous help for all international students in the class.

INTEGRATION AND APPLICATION

This chapter has tried to present both theory and some practical ideas in relation to working in teams, but there are no real steps to working in teams. 'Team-working' is a set of skills that you will need to develop throughout your university career, and employers will be looking for cooperative and insightful team members, but more importantly team leaders.

Teams need to be composed and put together well. Moving from the 'Forming' stage of a team to being able to 'Perform' well will require the team to interact informally before it develops sub-goals, norms and processes to enable it to accomplish what it was set up to do. As we have seen, understanding how the various roles operate together and contribute at the different stages in solving the task requires that we have a clear sense of the skills and abilities of each team member – and the demands of the task.

CONCLUSION

By now, you should have a good idea of how to:

- Understand why people in groups behave as they do.
- Work more effectively with others.
- Understand how work teams are different from those at university.

It is important to work as part of teams as much as possible throughout your university career. The experience you have will depend hugely on who is in your team, how good the team leader is at balancing team, task and individual priorities, and how available the required skills are within those teams.

As noted in the introduction to this chapter, working in teams is about relationships, character, action and communication. Over time, it is also about learning and adapting. Two team situations can be very different, and leading two different groups of people can also be very different, but both sets of situations will reveal a great deal about who you are as an individual and your strengths and weaknesses to others.

FINAL REFLECTIONS

Based on the content of this chapter, what do you now know about teams that you did not know before?

What key learning point had the most impact? Why?

Do your answers to either of the above questions have the potential to change your ability to work in a team? To lead others? Why?

What will you now do differently? (Write this down and put it somewhere where you can see it regularly.)

━━━━━━━━━━ INTERVIEW QUESTIONS ━━━━━━━━━━

The areas covered in this chapter are both very broad and very important to nearly every organisation. As a result, it might well be that up to half of an interview could be devoted to these skills, so there are a large number of questions an employer might ask.

Think about the following questions. What might your answers be?

1. What do you think makes a good team-worker?
2. Tell me about a time when you needed to work with others to accomplish a difficult task. What did you do and how successful was your group?
3. Can you tell me about a time when you have had to work with others to complete a challenging task with limited resources? What did you do? What was the impact of your actions?

(Continued)

(Continued)

With nearly all the questions given above, you can answer from any experience you have had – during your course or in a student society.

Chapter 17 gives a lot more information on selection interviews and the online content gives some guidance on these questions.

ADDITIONAL RESOURCES

Want to learn more? Visit https://study.sagepub.com/morgan to gain access to a wide range of online resources, including interactive tests, tasks, further reading and downloads.

Website Resources

Belbin website: www.belbin.com/about/belbin-team-roles/

Mindtools website: www.mindtools.com/pages/main/newMN_TMM.htm

Tissington, P. and Orthodoxou, C. Study Skills for Business and Management website (particularly chapter 8 on 'Working in groups'): https://uk.sagepub.com/en-gb/eur/study-skills-for-business-and-management/book240110#contents

University of Bradford website – wide range of resources looking at working in groups: www.bradford.ac.uk/academic-skills/resources/study/effective-communication/group/

University of Reading website: www.reading.ac.uk/internal/studyadvice/StudyResources/Seminars/sta-groupwork.aspx

Textbook Resources

Gallagher, K. (2010) *Skills Development for Business and Management Students*. Oxford: Oxford University Press (particularly chapter 10).
Horn, R. (2012) *The Business Skills Handbook*. London: CIPD (particularly chapter 5).
Robbins, S. P. and Hunsaker, P. L. (2003) *Training in Interpersonal Skills*. Upper Saddle River, NJ: Pearson (particularly chapters 13 and 14).

/11 LEADING OTHERS

CHAPTER STRUCTURE

Figure 11.1

When you see the 🌐 this means go to the companion website https://study.sagepub.com/morgan to do a quiz, complete a task, read further or download a template.

━ AIMS OF THE CHAPTER ━

By the end of this chapter, you should be able to:

- Develop different styles of leadership.
- Distinguish effective leadership from ineffective leadership.
- Let who you are influence the way you lead.

INTRODUCTION

Leaders are paid more than others, have more responsibility, are often believed to have a higher profile and are generally seen as 'more successful' than others. Of course, these various qualities tend to go together – and for good reason. As we will see, leading is not easy: for some individuals, it is an exciting and rewarding activity, though for others it is seen as too risky and difficult. Individuals are different and not everyone will want to be a leader, but, in reality, leadership can come in many forms, While there are some common qualities, leadership is usually about developing a vision for yourself and others, and then setting up and monitoring processes related to the achievement of this vision. How that is done can vary significantly: given the right motivation and opportunity for development, leadership is something that anyone *can* develop.

There is a great deal that has been written about leadership. Trying to summarise this writing in a brief chapter such as this is not easy, but we will cover a number of pertinent issues. We will begin by providing a definition of leadership, looking at what good leadership is and is not in terms of values and skills. We will look at how – as leaders – we might go about handling issues of group coursework where individual(s) are not contributing as they should, examining a number of models of leadership, considering decision making in leadership (since the ability to make decisions is one type of action which is often said to differentiate between leaders and followers) before closing by looking at issues of power in leadership.

Understanding and developing leadership skills is something that can take a lifetime, but the quicker we get to begin the process and develop our understanding of what leadership actually is, the more likely it is that we will be able to demonstrate leadership when it comes to getting a leadership role after graduation. The chapter is split into four areas: understanding leadership, which will gives us a conceptual understanding of the concept and identifying the skills of leadership; and then we will examine some appropriate models of leadership from the literature and finally look at leadership and decision making.

SKILLS SELF-ASSESSMENT

Complete the brief questionnaire below to see how well you work with others. You can think of an academic university situation (e.g. assessed coursework) or your activities within a student society or working in a team in the workplace. Give each item a score between 0 and 5, where 0 is 'not at all like me' or 'strongly agree', and 5 is 'very much like me' or 'strongly disagree'.

When I begin to lead others, I am likely to …

Item	Statement	Score
1.	Really enjoy the experience	
2.	Feel anxious about whether others will accept me as their leader	
3.	Develop a sense of vision of what I want the team to achieve	
4.	Watch what other teams doing the same activity are doing, and then motivate my team to follow the same ideas	
5.	Set the standard as high as I think is needed	

(Continued)

(Continued)

Item	Statement	Score
6.	Sit back and carefully think about how I am going to lead the team	
7.	Get more information on what different team members are able to do	
8.	Ensure that I personally fulfil the my team members' needs above everything else	
9.	See what I want to do and identify things that I can delegate to others within the team	
10.	Ensure that my team does everything expected of it through identifying appropriate punishments	
11.	Tell others outside of the team that I am the team leader	
12.	Consider how I can get others to like me	
13.	Learn about leadership from books and journal articles	
14.	Make sure that I am the one people come to in order to solve the problems within the team	
15.	Learn to understand why people do and say what they do and say	
16.	Ensure that I very clearly tell my team what they need to do	
17.	Encourage the people in my team as much as I can	
18.	Think carefully about how I can encourage others within the group	
19.	Deal with people who do not cooperate with the group's activities	
20.	Make sure that everyone has the contact details of everyone in the group	

Some of these overlap with those in the equivalent questionnaire for Chapter 10, so you might wish to discuss with someone else whether they are tasks for the leader to do, or tasks for other team members to undertake.

One role for the leader, of course, is to create an environment where individuals are willing to support rather than blame each other, but this is not an easy thing to do. It is useful, finally, to develop and review the conceptions and definitions of leadership.

DEFINING AND UNDERSTANDING LEADERSHIP

Leadership is similar to some other concepts that are used in common language: it is easy to recognise when we see it but less easy to define. Someone who is a leader is seen as possessing certain qualities and abilities (see Table 11.1).

Table 11.1 List of qualities frequently cited in definitions of leadership

- Vision – developing an idea of the future that is different to the current situation
- Persuasion/influence – motivating others to create that different situation
- Direction – putting energy into achieving certain goals
- Challenging – not accepting the status quo
- Communicating – be able to listen, negotiate, persuade and communicate in a way that builds commitment from others

A great deal of leadership research is conducted with individuals who are in leadership roles. They may have been given such positions for a variety of reasons, and may be reluctant leaders at times (leadership is not easy), or they may not actually be leading at all in the way discussed above.

DEFINITIONS OF LEADERSHIP

There may be leaders who are doing the items listed in Table 11.1 with some people but not with others. They may be in leadership roles but not actually leading, which brings us to a useful definition.

 LEADER

A leader is someone who has followers.

How they do so may vary, but a leader without any followers is not leading anyone. Other definitions give particular ways in which leaders ensure that they have people following them, and mention issues of influence, vision, direction and persuasion.

 ━━━━ 'BUT I HAVE A QUESTION ...' ━━━━━━━

... Can a team have more than one leader?

If you take the definition above as being reasonably comprehensive, then you would say 'no', simply because a team that has members following two or more individuals will struggle to stay united and support each other. However, this does not mean that there will not be more than one person demonstrating leadership within the group, and people will do that in different ways, but if there is a power struggle within the group because there is more than one leader, then things may not go well.

There are slight exceptions to this – where there are sub-teams within the team generally, where the leader of the sub-team is accountable to the main team leader (in which case you might argue that there was more than one team, anyway) or where there is a deputy leader, who should share the same goals and ways of achieving those goals with the main leader anyway.

There are also some situations where the tasks of a leader are split around the team, which then operates in a democratic manner. In such situations, the whole team has shared responsibility for undertaking the tasks that a leader would undertake, with the explicit agreement of all those working in the team. Undertaking the leadership role in such a way is not easy and requires a high degree of cooperation across the team, but it can work.

For most situations, the answer is 'no'

FURTHER
READING

The question remains, however, about what to do when there is more than one person trying to lead the group and where there are distinct differences in opinion, or a desire for power. You can find additional online content on the companion website at https://study.sagepub.com/morgan, including a highly relevant section looking at 'power in teams'.

UNDERSTANDING THE QUALITIES OF GOOD LEADERSHIP

As we have already seen, a leader is 'someone who has followers', but even with a shared definition, the way that an individual's leadership is perceived and accepted will depend on our own view of what leadership is about and understanding the extent to which this reflects the behaviour of the individual in that particular role. That view can be expressed in a number of ways, as the Chinese proverbs in Box 11.1 illustrate.

============ BOX 11.1 ============

CHINESE PROVERBS

The Chinese are very adept at using imagery to convey meaning very simply and with few words. There are, of course, many Chinese proverbs, so have a look at those given below and consider these three questions:

1. How do you interpret each of the proverbs?
2. What do you think it says about leadership, if anything?
3. Do you agree with the ideas you think the proverb conveys?

   Be the first to the field and the last to the couch.

   Deep doubts, deep wisdom; small doubts, little wisdom.

   Dig the well before you are thirsty.

   Do not fear going forward slowly; fear only to stand still.

   Do not remove a fly from your friend's forehead with a hatchet.

   He who is drowned is not troubled by the rain.

   If you are patient in one moment of anger, you will escape a hundred days of sorrow.

   To know the road ahead, ask those coming back.

   Don't open a shop unless you like to smile.

   Give a man a fish and you feed him for a day. Teach a man to fish and you feed him for a lifetime.

If you discuss your ideas with others, you will start to develop your own ideas about what you consider good leadership to be.

WHAT LEADERSHIP IS ABOUT

However you might conceptualise leadership, there do tend to be some ideas that appear regularly. Leadership is about:

- Creating the correct atmosphere/culture for action to happen.
- Inspiring others to increase emotional and practical effort towards a particular goal.
- Having a vision – and communication that vision effectively – for how things can be different and having a commitment to realise that vision.
- Building effective relationships with followers to ensure that they can follow you in tough times as well as easy times.
- Communicating effectively and regularly, so that followers understand where action and effort are needed.
- Doing things differently and creating a profile/brand for the team or organisation.

FOR YOU TO DO

Are you ready to lead?

A leadership position is something that many graduates aspire to achieve, and certainly many employers want to see something special when they take on someone who has been through university – after all, they will pay more for those with leadership potential. However, it is something that carries a number of challenges for many students, bearing in mind the different ideas that come together. The questions that you need to answer over the time of your studies are these: Are you ready to lead others? What challenges do you think you will face as you do so?

Think about the following issues, which might help you to answer these questions.

1. How courageous are you? How ready are you for people not to like you, or what you do?
2. Are you a determined and persistent individual, or do you give up fairly easily when things get hard?
3. How would you deal with a situation where you have made a mistake that negatively affects other people?
4. How do you respond to criticism?
5. Think of a good leader you know well. How do you demonstrate the skills that they show in their leadership role?
6. What do you do/have you done to improve the situation around you?
7. One individual's personal value statement is 'Work hard. Be nice. Dream big.' What would yours be? How have you implemented such ideas in your situation?

These are similar to some typical interview questions designed to help organisations identify those who have had leadership roles or have leadership potential, but they are very good to consider before you get anywhere near a selection interview.

WHAT LEADERSHIP IS NOT ABOUT

Leadership does take courage and determination and an ability to implement actions leading to sustained change. Having a leadership position can be fantastic if you have the right abilities, and there are certainly rewards spread across a career for those who are good at it, but unless we are leading an organisation we ourselves own, we are likely to be there on a temporary basis. In a university team or a task team in an organisation, this will be for just the duration of the task. For more senior leadership roles, we are leading on behalf of others (shareholders, owners, etc.). From an ethical point of view, this will put limits on what we have the right to do. The implication of this is that we may be expected to act in particular ways.

Some believe that leadership is not about the following:

- **It is not about being popular at the expense of everything else:** If you go into leadership because you think that it is about being popular, you will never be able to make decisions that have negative consequences for some people but good consequences for others – or the organisation. In addition, you cannot always provide all the resources or make all the decisions that everyone wants or needs all the time, so you will disappoint some of your followers some of the time.

- **It is not about delegating *everything* to other people** so that you do not have to do any work. If you do this, you will find that people will stop taking on tasks or will leave your team/ organisation because they do not respect you.
- **It is not about gaining power** for the sake of gaining power. Those who seek leadership positions solely for the purposes of gaining power will likely be the ones who use power inappropriately – to push and bully others into doing what they want them to do. There may be times when power does need to be used strongly, but that should never be the reason for someone wanting a leadership role.
- **It is not about getting emotionally close to lots of followers:** There may be a time when followers need a little emotional support, but building strong emotional relationships with many people is difficult. And there will probably be times when you have to disappoint those with whom you have a good relationship, which can then be very difficult.
- **It is not about doing nothing:** A leader who changes nothing is probably not leading, and when there is no vision for any change, then that becomes reflected in others' emotional commitment to their roles, and individual motivation will decrease.
- **It is not about your ego:** Some people become leaders because it will give them self-esteem and status when talking to others. The best leaders usually show some humility somewhere, since it is rarely they themselves who have had the vision, developed action plans and implemented that vision – they have usually had a significant team of well-qualified others to help them do so, and since maintaining 'followership' is key for a leader, recognising that effort publicly is often important.

'BUT I HAVE A QUESTION ...'

... I want to be a leader because I want to change a small part of the world around me. So, how can I do that?

There are a range of levels at which people can consider the idea of leadership. Obviously, working on a team project at university is one way and leading a student society is another, but think about the following questions to begin with:

1. Why did you decide to study at university? Were you just following others, or was it a conscious choice with a good reason behind it? Why are you studying the subject you are studying at the university you are at?
2. Think about your life after university. How do you see your life as different from your life now? How do you think you will have benefited from a university degree?

The first question is about making decisions that are right for you, regardless of what other people do: if you are just following the decisions that other people make, then how do you know it is right for you?

The second question is about vision for your own life (and is not really intended for you to discuss how better – or worse – off you will be financially). If you do not have a vision for your own life, then it is quite possible that you might struggle to enrol others in a vision for things which are going to affect their work and their lives.

If you want to change a small part of the world around you, then it might be an idea to consider: (1) how you would like your life to be different, and (2) how you might improve the experience of other students around you and then seek to make the necessary changes. This might mean some emotional challenge somewhere, but you will almost certainly develop and demonstrate persistence. Making changes to your situation and those of others is key to demonstrating effective leadership.

Leadership is a complex skill or, in reality, a series of skills: communicating appropriately, managing relationships, decision making, handling emotions, dealing with uncertainty and complexity, influencing and persuading, demonstrating self-awareness and emotional intelligence, and developing and implementing vision. Each situation will require a slightly different approach, and research has come to the conclusion that there is no one way of leading all of the people all of the time.

THE SKILLS OF LEADERSHIP

Guirdham (2001) lists a range of qualities sought by followers in order to influence them to follow:

- Institutional knowledge: A leader ranked hierarchically would be expected to possess a great deal of institutional knowledge.
- Competence in both keeping a group well managed and using their expertise to contribute to a task.
- Status, as defined by their expertise and activities outside of the group.
- Loyalty to the group: A leader who shows their loyalty to the group will have the group's respect and then 'followership' becomes easy to expect and it is easier to influence the group.
- A leaders' motivation must be sincere and not about undertaking tasks selfishly.
- A leader must be seen to be undertaking tasks which support the group.
- A leader must communicate in a way and using language which is appropriate for the team.

Some of these qualities are about situations in which a leader finds themselves, but when a leader shows all of these characteristics, they will be able to influence their followers more easily. But if the definitions of leadership that we provided above are true, then we should see that a number of communication skills become important.

Smith (2007) cited research suggesting that leaders need to be:

- Energetic and tenacious.
- Motivated by the act of leading others.
- Honest, trustworthy.
- Able to organise.
- Intelligent and verbally fluent.
- Self-confident and interpersonally skilled.
- Commercially astute.

This is an interesting list, but some of these points are more perceptual qualities than real skills or behaviours. Whether others see you as honest and trustworthy is not always within a leader's control; there are times when an energetic leader operating with a team of people who are not energetic might find themselves struggling; and the list does not seem to be exhaustive. However, it is true that a leader without the ability to understand the importance of characteristics or apply them where necessary is likely to find life as a leader less than the motivating experience they had hoped for.

Sternberg (2007) has suggested that a simple acronym, WIC (Wisdom, Intelligence – in a practical sense – and Creativity), is sufficient, although these three words actually break down into a much wider set of skills. For example, wisdom includes personal values, tacit organisational knowledge and the ability to determine the right skills at the right time. Intelligence means the ability to deliver solutions by applying previous experience and knowledge.

KEY LEARNING POINT

Asking individuals how someone should lead (i.e. 'what to do as a leader') is unlikely to get one universal answer, but asking them what characteristics good and bad leaders 'possess' is more likely to get a more coherent response. Personal qualities are more important as a leader than prescriptive actions.

REFLECTION POINT

Take some time to think about the following questions and write down some answers.

How might the information given above change the way that you think about leadership and leading others? How confident would you feel about taking on a leadership role in one of your groups for coursework? What would make you more confident? Why?

LEADERSHIP, COURSEWORK AND 'THE POOR CONTRIBUTOR'

One of the main challenges in leading a team at university is when it comes to dealing with individuals who present challenges. They might be 'free-riding' (doing little while benefitting from the effort and work of others), not turning up to meetings, not communicating, doing poorer quality work than desired or creating problems in the group when their ideas are not listened or agreed to. Leading such a team is not easy at all – it is more challenging than when you *do* have a position of authority and *can* implement sanctions against individuals, which is why being able to lead a successful team in a coursework project for university can be such a strong indicator of leadership success, especially if those in your team were chosen for you.

Such situations demand two kinds of skills: the problem-solving skills to be able to identify the issue(s); and the communication and conflict resolution skills to be able to implement the interpersonal issues that occur.

FOR YOU TO DO

Some suggest that the mark of good leadership is to be able to solve conflicts and resolve difficulties. It is certainly true that, in the mind of some, this ability is key to leading a team. Have a look at the brief scenario given below about how a leader intended to assist a team to work on a piece of group coursework, and think about the three questions given.

'In a group-working situation at university, the group had hit a stalemate about a critical decision for our project. The views of the group were mixed although there were – broadly speaking – two distinct options. It appeared that neither side wanted to compromise their position, as they all believed that a compromise or decision to take the alternative action would seriously affect their grades.

'As a previously neutral and passive member of the group, I could see both sides of the argument. In my opinion, this made me the most qualified to take charge of the situation and lead the group to an amicable

(Continued)

(Continued)

decision. The situation then quickly escalated and it was essential at this point to bring in rational thought in order to maintain group cohesion. At this point, I entered into the discussion and calmed matters down by suggesting that the group took a break. This gave each member time to collect their thoughts and consider each others' positions. It was no surprise that, during the break, two distinct sub-groups formed, as was shown after the break in terms of seating arrangements.'

Questions:

1. Do you think that this is a good solution?
2. Is there anything that the team leader could have done differently?
3. What should the group leader do next?

Some of your modules might be developed in a way that enables the team leader (and sometimes team members) to implement penalties against those not working well, but, as a team leader, dealing with performance issues is part of the job. Often this means having a private discussion with team members, but also means dealing with things carefully, as laid out below (see also Chapter 14 on problem solving).

Step 1: Find out what the issue seems to be.

It is very tempting in a very busy world to accept what members of the team are saying without finding out more details – finding out information takes time, and leaders and team members rarely seem to have time. We can imagine a situation where a team member complains about other team members but we make the following mistakes:

- We might hear something from one team member and assume that their view is held by everyone; in reality, this might not actually be the case.
- The team members report what is happening with this person, but their judgements are merely guesswork.
- We can assume that everything is the fault of the individual who is not engaging with the task, but in reality:

  o The team might actually not be communicating in the right way for the other person to be involved sufficiently in the task.
  o The expectations might not be clear enough for the other team member to understand
  o The 'reluctant' team member might be a non-native speaker of English and cannot contribute as other members speak too quickly.
  o Relationships between some team members might already be established and the other team member is excluded from those.
  o The team members all live on campus, while the other team member lives some distance away.

Step 1 is to gather information: What is happening/not happening? How often? When is it happening/not happening? How many people are involved? Asking detailed questions with factual answers and examples is important for step 2.

Step 2: Discussion with the 'problematic team member'.

This text will cover some of the details on how to have a difficult conversation in the chapter on effective communication (see Chapter 12) while problem solving is covered elsewhere (see Chapter 14), but if a problem is to be solved then the leader needs to have a conversation with the problematic team member as quickly as possible after the discussion with others from the team. Ironically, it needs to be a discussion whose purpose is to do almost exactly the same as step 1, that is to gather information, except this time you, as the leader, will be checking information already gathered as well. It is important here to:

- Withhold judgement until you have sufficient and comprehensive information from both parties.
- Try to explore why certain things might be happening. There might be very good reasons relating to any personal or practical issues that are a problem, or a lack of:

  o Clear goals by which to define expectations.
  o Feedback from other members of the team.
  o Motivation to do the task.
  o Cooperation and engagement by other members of the team.
  o Resources to do the tasks given to them.
  o Confidence to communicate with other members of the team in another language.
  o Ability to do what they have been asked to do.

- Examine possible solutions – which may include some penalty or penalties, or may simply be ways of solving the problem. These would usually include phrases such as 'If this situation arises again …' (and such phrases could be used as advice to the 'problematic' individual, as to what action to take if they find themselves in similar situations in the future).

For example, someone might not be attending meetings because they have a part-time job, but all the other team members can only attend at that particular time. This is not an easy issue to resolve, but it does not stop the team leader consulting the member with the job about the things they will discuss before the meeting and then talking to them after the meeting to convey decisions. In other situations (e.g. domestic commitments at home), technology (Skype, etc.) can be used to enable participation in discussions, for example. Problem solving often takes some imagination and creativity, and there are usually ways around most team issues.

Step 3: Give feedback about your decision to the team and monitor what happens next. As a team leader, you have the 'legitimate authority' (see the content below on legitimate power) to implement solutions.

Leading a team when there are few sanctions or motivators available is never going to be easy: you have to rely on others' willingness to help and on the more intrinsic motivators (sense of value, excitement, passion and interest in the job, etc.), but some people are not necessarily that willing to help sometimes. This is one of the biggest challenges of leadership. Try as far as possible not to take the issue to the module leader. It is not wrong to do so but sometimes it is necessary; however, try to solve the problem on your own first. An employer at an interview will want to see that you are likely to be able to solve difficult problems without needing to get advice as soon as there is any kind of problem.

━━━━━━ FOR YOU TO DO ━━━━━━

Look at the various situations described below that relate to working in teams on pieces of university course-work.* If you were the leader for each of the six teams listed below, how would you go about handling these situations? What would your first action be? What possible reasons might the 'problematic individual(s)' give for their behaviour? And how would you address them?

(Continued)

(Continued)

1. You are concerned about Asif. He has been causing problems by criticising others in the team. Julie is quite upset because Asif told her that her spreadsheet charts were not very good and were unclear. She spent ages doing those charts.
2. Sarah, whom you don't know very well, is in your team. She seems very bored when she comes in and keeps apologising that she has forgotten to do her actions. She got very defensive when you mentioned that this is holding up the team and now seems quite distant with you. Aisha tells you Sarah has been telling other people that you bully her.
3. The team had a meeting last week and you thought everyone had agreed to do something. This week nobody seems to have done anything at all. The team seems to have forgotten what was agreed and spends most of the meeting discussing the same things as last time. This is really frustrating.
4. Ika and Roman have just had a huge bust-up in a meeting. Ika has accused Roman of not doing what he agreed to do and called him lazy. Roman called Ika a control freak and stormed out of the meeting. Each of them is refusing to come to the next meeting if the other is there.
5. Simon and John don't seem to want to work with Michelle, Keisha and Thomas. They often don't turn up to meetings and are hard to contact. Michelle and Keisha are worried because they are high-achieving students and are concerned about their grades, especially as the group mark is shared and Simon and John are supposed to do a certain part of the project.
6. The team has just found out that Robert has gone into hospital. He was supposed to complete the images for the presentation and is the only one with copies.

(Cases written by Martin Sedgley at the University of Bradford)

Step 4: Work with the team to develop norms and an agreement governing how the team works in solving problems generally. Problems should never be left unaddressed, otherwise they will just remain and eventually either the team will complete its work/coursework and adjourn, or other team members might struggle with the emotional pressure that other individual(s) bring and show extreme annoyance at some time.

 ━━ KEY LEARNING POINT ━━━━━━━━━━━━━

How *you* deal with each of the issues above is going to be based on a mixture of your own attitudes, learning from other situations and learning from others' mistakes. Leaders rarely do things right all the time, but they usually have a reason for doing what they do in the way that they do it.

MODELS OF LEADERSHIP

We will look at three models of leadership. There are similarities, and differences, in each approach.

The Ohio/Michigan Leadership Studies

In the 1950s and 1960s, two sets of studies were launched to try to investigate the qualities of effective leadership. In using factor analysis, both sets of studies concluded the same thing: that there were broadly two factors which differentiated leaders from one another, arranged around getting the task completed, termed 'Initiating Structure' and 'Production Centered Supervision' by Ohio and Michigan

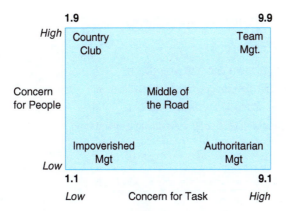

Figure 11.2 The managerial grid (Blake and Mouton, 1964)

The Managerial Grid (Blake and Mouton, 1964) Gulf Publishing Co. Houston

Universities respectively, and the maintenance of workforce relations, termed 'Consideration' and 'Employee Centered Supervision'.

Similar ideas were made very fashionable by two researchers, namely Robert Blake and Jane Mouton from the University of Texas, who were contracted by Exxon in the 1960s to conduct an organisational development programme. Their work at Exxon led to the development of the Managerial Grid. There have since been various versions of the Managerial Grid, but the same basic idea still underpins the model: that there are two dimensions that underpin leadership behaviour – the way that leaders do what they do revolves around the task and the people.

The model (Figure 11.2) bears a close resemblance to work done by McGregor (1960) at MIT in examining human motivation. His work suggested that individuals tended to fall into one of two categories: those who would work only when pushed and were punished because of their inherent laziness (Theory X); and those who would be motivated by opportunities to be creative and who were inherently self-motivated (Theory Y). These two aspects of managerial behaviour are not usually seen as different dimensions but rather two ends of one dimension.

In developing the ideas given above, the question that was being asked by the researchers was 'What leadership style is the most effective?' In the case of the Managerial Grid, the answer was a '9.9 – Team Management' approach, but that means that leaders still have to be effective at dealing with the task and with the people. What emerged reasonably quickly from these ideas related to a development of the research question to 'What variables influence the effectiveness of different leadership styles?' Research into leadership acknowledged that there was not one way to lead, but there were issues that a leader had to take into account when developing 'followership'.

Hersey and Blanchard's (1977) Situational Leadership Theory

Paul Hersey and Ken Blanchard developed their model of situational leadership as a way to help answer part of this question. Their model matched specific leadership styles against the maturity and readiness of others to be led in particular ways, but still referred to the two dimensions of 'Task Behaviour' (provision of guidance) and 'Relationship Behaviour' (provision of support) incorporated into their model, giving rise to four 'situations'. There were four leadership styles (Telling, Selling, Participating and Delegating) and four ways to describe follower-readiness (see Table 11.2).

Table 11.2 Aspects of situational leadership theory

Styles of leadership:

Telling – Provide specific instructions and supervise closely

Selling – Explain decisions and give opportunities for clarification

Participating – Sharing ideas and facilitate decision making

Delegating – Turn over responsibility for decisions and implementation

Follower-readiness:

Leader needs to direct:

R1: The follower is unable and unwilling (or insecure) to do what is needed

R2: The follower is unable but willing to do what is needed

Follower directs:

R3: The follower is able but unwilling (or insecure) to do what is needed

R4: The follower is able and willing to do what is needed

Situations and appropriate leadership style:

S1/R1: Low relationship (no supportive behaviour needed) and high task-centred (guidance on task needed) leadership style needed, i.e. *Telling*

S2/R2: High relationship (little supportive behaviour needed) and high task-centred leadership (guidance on task needed) style needed, i.e. *Selling*

S3/R3: High relationship (little supportive behaviour needed) and low task-centred leadership (guidance on task needed) style needed, i.e. *Participating*

S4/R4: Low relationship (little supportive behaviour needed) and low task-centred leadership style needed, i.e. *Delegating*

The model began to help leaders understand why no one leadership style was always going to be effective all of the time, and gave them a rationale by which to evaluate and then adopt different styles.

Robbins and Hunsaker (2003) have suggested a number of additional situational variables which affect the suitability of different leadership styles:

Follower trust: Enabling others to trust you is about establishing integrity (being honest and truthful), competence, consistency, loyalty and truthfulness. A leader cannot establish trust unless there is integrity, and particularly honesty.

Clear goals: Establishing clear goals is vital for any team leader, but teams will vary according to the extent to which they are ready to aim for certain goals. If they are too ambitious, then the teams will feel that they are being pushed too far, but make them too easy and the sense of purpose will inspire a great deal less.

Task characteristics: A structured task will probably not need a leader to intervene in the task very much, but one that is unstructured 'might require leaders to help clarify and structure the work' (Robins and Hunsaker, 2003: 146) somewhat. This builds on Fred Fielder's work (Fiedler, 1967) looking at the ways in which leaders and team members interact (or exchange) with each other (commonly referred to as Leader-Member Exchange, or 'LMX').

Rewards: A leader can engage with different members of the team by offering different kinds of rewards, according to individuals' preferences (and organisational policies). Offering the same rewards to all can be seen as fair, but may not produce the engagement from every team member that the leader might seek.

Time: Making decisions in very short timescales can be problematic for those who like to see their leaders consulting other team members more. In a situation where there is less time, decisions may not be made in a particularly consultative manner. (We will look more at this when we look at leadership decision making.)

Action-Centred Leadership

John Adair's model of action-centred leadership (Adair, 1973) is conceptually similar to those identified above, in that it still contains issues related to task and issues related to relationships. However, as a model of leadership, it has the advantage of being simple to remember.

The principal idea is that effective team leadership is demonstrated when leaders recognise and act on the interplay between paying attention to the tasks being undertaken, the well-being of the individuals within the team, and the 'togetherness' of the team itself (see Figure 11.3).

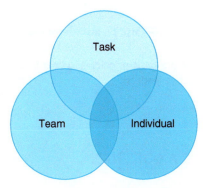

Figure 11.3 Adair's model of action-centred leadership © John Adair, 1973

The model emphasises that a leader needs to have some way to monitor and then improve each of the three areas as a team develops and progresses. The leader might have a style, but their behaviour is intended to be flexible and address the three issues on a regular basis. There is a body of literature which discusses what is known as 'Servant Leadership' – Box 11.2 provides more details on what this approach really means.

━━━━━━━ BOX 11.2 ━━━━━━━

SERVANT LEADERSHIP

The Servant Leader

In 1970, Robert Greenleaf – as a senior executive working in AT&T – published some ideas relating to the role of the leader as a servant to others in the organisation (republished in 2002). At the heart of his ideas were the following:

> The servant-leader is servant first … It begins with the natural feeling that one wants to serve, to serve first. Then conscious choice brings one to aspire to lead. That person is sharply different from one who is leader first … The leader-first and the servant-first are two extreme types.

(Continued)

(Continued)

> The best test [of effective leadership], and difficult to administer, is: Do those served grow as persons? Do they, while being served, become healthier, wiser, freer, more autonomous, more likely themselves to become servants? And, what is the effect on the least privileged in society? Will they benefit or at least not be further deprived?

This view of leadership is often at odds with the impression that is given of good leadership in western media and in professional publications, yet those ideas have received significant support from such researchers as Peter Senge, John Kotter and Ken Blanchard, among others.

Do you think the ideas of servant leadership, as briefly summarised above, could work today in a western commercial organisation? Could they work in an Asian/Chinese organisation? Finally, could they work in the public sector or an NGO (non-governmental organisation, e.g. an international charity such as the Red Cross)?

KEY LEARNING POINT

There is no one way to lead, but there are basic principles to bear in mind, and it is the appropriate use of those principles that will lead to effective leadership.

'BUT I HAVE A QUESTION ...'

... If leadership is so straightforward, then why are so few good at it?

The simple reason is that to do these things is not straightforward, and being a good leader involves a complex set of skills. What has been discussed above is a very simple way of ensuring that leaders pay attention to a number of factors, but how leaders do so with a wide number of different people is not straightforward. For example, if we try to apply the Hersey and Blanchard model to just one individual, then it is not difficult to determine how ready and able a team member might be, but if there are different team members with different skills and different ability levels, then the best we can do is to adopt different approaches towards different people at the same time.

Developing trust, integrity, being able to offer appropriate rewards, communicating appropriately, behaving consistently for how you would like to do things differently, having a vision and the other qualities identified by Robbins and Hunsaker actually make life more complex.

Look back at the possible interview questions about whether you want to and are ready to lead. It is a set of skills developed over a long time in a variety of situations.

KEY LEARNING POINT

There are different ways to conceptualise and to theorise about leadership. Leadership research will continue to grow and develop, but it is unlikely that we will develop one easily applicable theory that explains all leadership successes and failures.

REFLECTION POINT

Take some time to think about the following questions and write down some answers.

What model(s) of leadership (given above and from other reading perhaps) do you find easiest to understand? How easily could you apply any of these ideas to any leadership role you might have?

LEADERSHIP AND DECISION MAKING

One important skill for the leader to possess is that of making the right decisions at the right time in the right way. Vroom and Jago (1988) identified five key ways in which leaders make decisions, but the leader needs to know how to make different decisions appropriately and when different decision-making styles are needed. Once again, the situation determines which approach is suitable, rather than the personal preference of the leader, and the various interests of those being led is one of those factors.

The various methods are categorised into three sections.

Section I: Alone (A)

Leaders can make decisions alone based on their leadership instinct (A1) or with data that they gather (A11). This is particularly useful when decisions need to be made very quickly (i.e. there is a serious time pressure) or when the leader has faced the same decision before and has a good understanding of how others are likely to react.

Section 2: Consultative (C)

Sometimes it is important to consult others when making decisions. This can be done one individual at a time (C1) or by calling a group meeting (C11) and making a decision based on what has been said. Either would be appropriate when the decision has a significant impact on individuals and when the leader needs to work to ensure that the decision is implemented by others who agree with it.

There are reasons why C1 can be better in some situations and C11 can be better in others. C1 works well when a leader has a significant amount of time and wishes to avoid public conflict by consulting privately (i.e. there is a likelihood of conflict within the team if there was to be public consultation), but C11 works better when the group is likely to be united, when there is a shortage of time and when the decision made has an impact on certain individuals and groups.

Of course, technology and email make private and widespread consultation a lot easier. Blogs, emails and polling websites make it easy to gather views quickly from a large number of individuals in a private manner.

Section 3: Group (G)

The fifth and final method of decision making is used when there is some time available and when the decision has limited impact on the organisation, but a significant impact on the motivation or well-being of the workforce in general. Under group decision making (G11), the leader simply

> Leadership and decision making
>
> - **Authoritarian**
>
> A1 alone
> A11 with extra data
>
> - **Consultative**
>
> C1 one at a time
> C11 all together
>
> - **Group**
>
> G11 delegate

Figure 11.4   Various styles of leadership decision making (Vroom and Jago, 1988)

delegates authority to make the decision to others, though they would usually set some timescales and parameters around which any such decision would be agreeable to the organisation. The five styles are summarised in Figure 11.4.

There are other ways of influencing and making decisions, or getting others' views. Documents for consultation can be circulated and edited one person at a time and then circulated to the next person before being finally agreed (which is a form of C1, but done in a particular order of individuals). Some decisions are complex and sub-decisions may need to be done in a sequence: different parts of the decisions might be taken in different ways, though the leader would need to explain how the process is going to work in order to ensure others' commitment.

 ══ FOR YOU TO DO ════════════════════════════

Think about the parameters within which decisions are made – time available, information available, experience of the leader, possibility of conflict, impact on others – and see which of the five styles identified above might be appropriate for the following kinds of decisions:

1. Who should receive the prime car parking spaces at work.
2. Who should give permission to staff for their holidays/annual leave.
3. What colour paint should be used for offices.
4. How much funding should be allocated to IT projects from next year's budget.
5. What qualities are important for the next leader of the team.
6. Whether someone should be given travel expenses for a rail or car journey to a local town.
7. Who should interview the next assistant to the department.
8. What the strategic priorities of the team should be.
9. Who should make what kind of contribution to the team for the project.
10. Which of two long-serving employees is correct in a dispute over behaviour.

There is no answer that is correct or incorrect, but making decisions in unhelpful ways may have implications for a leader's effectiveness, moving forward. Box 11.3 looks at this issue in more detail.

====== BOX 11.3 ======

LEADING AND MAKING DECISIONS FROM A POINT OF STRENGTH: KNOWING YOURSELF

When you are leading, you have to have a good understanding of the individuals you are leading. Every decision you make, every problem-solving process (see Chapter 14) and every opportunity for communication (see Chapter 12) you take require you have some kind of understanding of those you lead directly and how they might react. You need to consider whether this is really going to change *what* you do, though it might have an impact on *how* you do what you do. It may seem strange, therefore, that there is a section here on knowing yourself.

However, those you are leading well will look to you for solutions to challenging situations, for a sense of vision and an ability to bring others together. Doing so well will mean that you will need to have a sense of vision and the self-confidence to see that vision become reality, and this means bringing your personality into how you lead. Much of the time, organisational leaders do not seem to connect with those they are leading – they seem to remain distant and somewhat aloof, maybe because it is what others have thought of them which has led to their getting promoted, so those who follow them tend to follow what they see or mimic their behaviour. They are taught to perform, but not to relate, yet it is often their values that have caught the eye of those promoting them.

What does this mean in practice? That we should not be nervous about allowing our personality to show, to let our values guide what we decide to do and not to do, and that we should be sufficiently confident to be spontaneous and to let who we are show to others. Brittain (2012) puts it like this:

- **Trust in our unique gift set:** We are unique in who we are. Allow our intuition, faith and creativity to guide us, rather than feeling as if we need to perform to a particular role model we have seen in the movies or in our employment.
- **There is no perfect decision:** We live in a world full of unpredictability, volatility, complexity and ambiguity, so a decision can often be outdated or made imperfect as quickly as it is made. The challenge is not to make perfect decisions, but in how we respond as individuals.

Allowing our own personality to show will enable others to feel relaxed about letting themselves be themselves as well. Besides, decisions made by someone with little personality and who does things in a different way to others tend to inspire (as long as they have a sensible rationale to them). This will tend to produce a group of followers who are less stressed, more confident and more agile in making decisions.

Just as there is no perfect human, so too is there no perfect leader for every individual in every situation, which leads to the question 'Why try to be what we are not?'

====== REFLECTION POINT ======

Take some time to think about the following questions and write down some answers.

What reaction do you have to this kind of viewpoint?

To what extent do you find your own behaviour driven by others' expectations of you, rather than who you are?

Are there times when you think you know what to do or say, but do not say it because you are nervous about what others will think?

How much does nervousness about 'making the *right* decision' affect your ability to make decisions?

Is there ever one right decision?

POWER IN TEAM LEADERSHIP

Some people take the view that human nature is frequently selfish and that people seek their own good rather than the good of those around them. Whether you subscribe to this kind of view or not, people do sometimes like the idea of having – or at least having access to – power, and some people will compete aggressively to get power. Sometimes, the actions that will be taken to obtain power will be nasty, dishonest and unethical. Of course, leaders have power usually by virtue of their position and responsibilities, but leadership power can come from different sources – and just because someone is not a leader does not mean that they have no power.

If you are leading a team, then your power as a leader can come from a number of sources. It is important to recognise which sources of power you have as a leader in order to ensure that what you need to happen actually does happen, because misjudging why others follow you can cause big problems.

In their important work some time ago, French and Raven (1959) identified five and then six (Raven, 1965) sources of power:

- **Reward power:** Leaders can have power by their ability to offer rewards to individuals. Rewards can be offered to individuals in return for the demonstration of particular behaviour(s). Impersonal rewards might be promotion or a salary increase, whilst personal rewards could be encouragement, a smile or some other interpersonal interaction. Reward power is simply the power to offer these.
- **Coercive power:** This is the ability to 'force' people to do what they need to do. It can be applied either in an impersonal manner (e.g. threat of dismissal) or in an emotional/personal manner (e.g. disapproval). In reality, resisting coercion by a manager might result in approval by work colleagues, and followers have the power to disrupt a leader's activities through the withdrawal of cooperation or by leaving the organisation.
- **Referent power:** Leaders can appeal to their followers on the basis of 'affiliation' or of common interests and goals – that is, their power comes from being able to serve the same interests as those of the individuals they lead.
- **Legitimate power:** If a senior leader gives someone a leadership role, then that individual will also be given (implicitly) the power to do what is needed to carry out their responsibilities and the individual has 'legitimate power'. Of course, the extent to which they can use this power is influenced by the culture in which they are working. A leader can use this power very effectively where the culture enforces respect for leaders, but much less effectively in cultures where relations between leaders and followers are close.
- **Expert power:** A leader has 'expert power' where they have specific knowledge that the team needs in order to undertake technical tasks, and the team has to trust the leader to make good decisions based on that expertise.
- **Informational power** (added 1965): A leader has informational power when they have (and can obtain) relevant information that no one else has access to. This might be because of particular relationships with individuals who hold that information or access to certain information on social media, but once this information is given away, there is no power.

As a leader, it is important to know where your power comes from, and this can change over time as well (and sometimes very quickly). For example, using only 'reward power' when really people give you their respect and follow you because of your expertise ('expert power') could mean that their respect towards you might decrease, unless you acknowledge and use your 'expert power' from time to time as well.

=========== 'BUT I HAVE A QUESTION ...' ============

... The word 'power' is one I am uncomfortable about using. How should I use my power if I am a leader?

In reality, good leaders rarely need to use their power explicitly; instead they influence others to do what needs to be done. Sometimes, this is through negotiation: 'I need you to do this, so I will provide you with this to motivate you' (the motivator could be something tangible, or merely be some respect); but, sometimes, it will be through the authority they carry as a leader: 'I'm asking you to do this because it needs to be done, and I want you to do it.'

Which strategy a leader employs to get things done will depend either on the specific individual they are talking to, or on their own philosophy of leadership more generally. Some individuals will readily do what their leader asks (simply because they are the leader), while others will need something in exchange.

Using power openly can cause problems. If, as a leader, you use your authority to get things done that others do not want to do, then you will likely face resistance. Some leaders are perfectly happy to meet that resistance (i.e. have a 'fight for power') in order to establish and increase their power, or to remove individuals from the team, but that can cause ill feeling within the team more broadly, so it is usually more effective to influence and persuade. A leader who regularly uses their power on the basis of 'I am the leader so you need to obey me' is likely to be highly ineffective in many cultures.

=========== KEY LEARNING POINT ============

A leader has followers because they have some power given to them, either by the organisation or by their followers. How they use that power is important to their effectiveness as a leader.

INTEGRATION AND APPLICATION

The challenge in leading well is that it is complex, and your behaviour and values will be unique to you. There is no one model which will explain all that you can do in terms of being a leader, just as there is no one style which can make you successful all of the time, but there are some common ideas:

Idea 1: Be assured that who you are – rather than others' views of who you are – is what is going to carry you through. People judge leaders and their decisions more harshly than they judge others, but if you know that you made the right decisions for the right reasons, then no one can really criticise you for that.

Idea 2: Engage with your followers, otherwise you are not going to lead anyone. Let your personality – your sense of humour, your interpersonal skills – help you build relationships. There is no reason why the skills that you have developed throughout your life should be any less useful when you become a leader.

Idea 3: Monitor what is really happening – you need to be able to see what is likely to happen in the future with regards to external issues outside your team, as well as what is happening inside your team.

Idea 4: Think of those you lead as a group of individuals who are as imperfect as you, but who are willing and capable. If they are not willing, then you might need to find the reasons for this, but ultimately you might want them out of the team. If they are not capable, then they should first be given training before any discussion of whether they should leave the team. If you expect them to be perfect, then you will find that they will always disappoint you, and that will frustrate you and demotivate them.

Idea 5: Be sure to have a vision of where you are going to lead people – and why. People engage with a clear statement of where they are being led. Having such a statement will enable them to feel confident about their journey, even if the journey might be a bit tough at times. Not having that vision will mean that people might enjoy the journey while it is easy, but will be more likely to dismiss the leadership when things are hard.

CONCLUSION

By now, you should have a good idea of how to:

- Develop different styles of leadership.
- Distinguish effective leadership from ineffective leadership.
- Let who you are influence the way you lead.

It is important to take as much leadership responsibility as possible throughout your university career. The experience you have will sharpen your leadership abilities in a situation (being at university) that will give you 'safe' opportunities to show an employer what you can do before you actually get into a situation where poor leadership can have 'live' risks in the workplace.

As noted in the introduction to this chapter (and that of the previous chapter), leadership is about relationships, character, action and communication. However, there is always going to be a balance between how committed a leader is to a particular vision and understanding where flexibility with that vision becomes necessary. Leading two different groups of people can also be very different, of course, but doing so without a sense of vision or by using inappropriate styles of communication is going to test all your strength and determination.

FINAL REFLECTIONS

Based on the content of this chapter, what do you now know about leading others that you did not know before?

What key learning point had the most impact? Why?

Do your answers to either of the above questions have the potential to change your ability to lead others? Why?

What will you now do differently? (Write this down and put it somewhere where you can see it regularly.)

 INTERVIEW QUESTIONS

The areas covered in this chapter are both very broad and very important to nearly every organisation. As a result, it might well be that up to half of an interview could be devoted to these skills, so there are a large number of questions an employer might ask.

(Continued)

(Continued)

Think about the following questions. What might your answers be?

1. Can you tell me about a time when you felt that you needed to take the initiative to achieve a goal? What did you do, and how successful were you in achieving your goal?
2. Tell me about a time when you needed to persuade someone to change their mind.
3. Tell me about a leader that you admire. Why do you admire them?
4. How would you describe your personal leadership approach?
5. How would you go about leading a team member who seemed not to be producing the work they needed to? Can you give an example of a time when you have had to do so?
6. What was the most pioneering activity that you have undertaken?
7. Can you describe how you have gone about setting goals for a team you have worked with?

With nearly all the questions given above, you can answer from any experience you have had – during your course or in a student society.

Chapter 17 gives a lot more information on selection interviews and the online content gives some guidance on these questions.

ADDITIONAL RESOURCES

Want to learn more? Visit https://study.sagepub.com/morgan to gain access to a wide range of online resources, including interactive tests, tasks, further reading and downloads.

Website Resources

Ken Blanchard Companies – material on leadership traits: www.kenblanchard.com/img/pub/pdf_critical_leadership_skills.pdf

Kent University website: www.kent.ac.uk/careers/sk/leadership.htm

Mindtools website – a comprehensive series of resources around leadership development: www.mindtools.com/pages/main/newMN_LDR.htm

Prospects website leadership course – designed for students at university: http://leadership.workready graduates.com/

Skillsyouneed website: www.skillsyouneed.com/leadership-skills.html

Textbook Resources

Horn, R. (2012) *The Business Skills Handbook*. London: CIPD (particularly chapter 18).

Pettinger, R. and Firth, R. (2001) *Mastering Management Skills* Basingstoke. Hampshire: Palgrave (particularly chapter 11).

Robbins, S. P. and Hunsaker, P. L. (2003) *Training in Interpersonal Skills*. Upper Saddle River, NJ: Pearson (particularly chapter 11).

Smith, M. (2011) *Fundamentals of Management* (2nd edition). Maidenhead: McGraw-Hill (particularly chapter 8).

/12 COMMUNICATING EFFECTIVELY

CHAPTER STRUCTURE

Figure 12.1

When you see the 🌐 this means go to the companion website https://study.sagepub.com/morgan to do a quiz, complete a task, read further or download a template.

━ AIMS OF THE CHAPTER ━

By the end of this chapter, you should be able to:

- Describe the communication process and how it can go wrong.
- Identify the various verbal, non-verbal and para-linguistic behaviours that can influence communication.
- Evaluate and develop your communication skills with a particular focus on communicating in difficult situations, giving feedback and active listening.

INTRODUCTION

Understanding human communication is not easy – we could have based this whole book on communication skills. We probably know some people who love to talk, but, on the other hand, there are others who seem to have nothing to say. We could say that both are good communicators if they use their skills appropriately, and in the right situations, but communicating is no more about talking than it is about being quiet all the time. So, we could ask: 'What does "use their skills appropriately" mean, and what are the "right situations"?'

There is no way to cover in one chapter everything that could be covered or that could enable you to become an expert communicator in one go. The subject is the topic of complete modules and degree programmes in themselves. The aim of this chapter is to give you an awareness of the key things to bear in mind as you communicate.

Your ability to communicate has implications for a large number of areas covered elsewhere in this text. It will affect the demonstration of your leadership skills (Chapter 11), your ability to work in teams (Chapter 12), to give presentations (Chapter 9) and to work cross-culturally (Chapter 13). Your communication skills will be vital for performing well at interviews (Chapter 17), and will and even being able to say 'no' in an appropriate way so that you can manage your time better – Chapter 3). In so many situations, the ability to communicate in a way that ensures a message is understood in the way you intend is critical to being able to perform well in nearly every job role. Yet it is the one thing that tends to cause the most problems in employment (and personal) relationships. Poor communication with others – or even an unwillingness to communicate (and an awareness of when or why not to communicate) – is important to get right, which is why it is included here.

Finally, much of the content below relates to oral communication, some of which will overlap with Chapter 9 on presentation skills, but there is some content on written communication in Chapter 7. This set of skills – getting grammar and spelling correct, ensuring your academic work is well structured, demonstrating your critical thinking – is also covered in Chapter 7 in relation to academic work. Within employment, however, there is a need to ensure that emails and letters are written in a particular way, so there will be some content covering these areas.

SKILLS SELF-ASSESSMENT

Complete the brief questionnaire below to see how well you communicate with others. Give each item a score between 0 and 5, where 0 is 'not at all like me' or 'strongly agree', and 5 is 'very much like me' or 'strongly disagree'.

When I communicate with others, I know that I ...

Item	Statement	Score
1.	Never interrupt other people in a conversation	
2.	Find myself daydreaming during most conversations because I find what others talk about is quite boring to me	
3.	Want to be the last person to say anything during a discussion	

(Continued)

(Continued)

Item	Statement	Score
4.	Think I can reduce tension during an emotional discussion or argument	
5.	Want to think of something funny to say	
6.	Never misinterpret what someone else is saying	
7.	Vary the intonation (pitch) of my voice	
8.	Smile as much as I can	
9.	Speak very slowly to ensure that I can get my message across	
10.	Am happy to be passionate about a topic if I think it is important	
11.	Speak too loudly	
12.	Use facial expressions (frowns, smiles) to emphasise the message I want to give	
13.	Judge the person who is communicating with me	
14.	Feel nervous about how others will react to what I want to say	
15.	Consider the words I use carefully to ensure that the other person does not react emotionally	
16.	Choose my language and the words that I use so that the other person will understand	
17.	Get impatient with other people if they are taking a long time to say what they want to say	
18.	Am interested in what others have to say	
19.	Do not care how others will react to what I want to say	
20.	Am happy to let others talk if they are saying what I want to say anyway	
21.	Regularly get emotional about what others say	
22.	Always understand exactly what others are trying to say	
23.	Cause problems in my relationships with them, but I do not know why	
24.	Believe that others will interpret my messages in the same way as I intend them	
25.	Enjoy myself	
26.	Struggle to understand different accents when I am talking with or listening to people from different places	
27.	Think carefully about whether I believe what someone is saying	
28.	Reflect on how well I am communicating with others	
29.	Understand when I need to be formal and business-like, rather than informal and friendly	
30.	Recognise how my own personality, perception and past experiences can affect how well I communicate	

This questionnaire is longer than that of any other chapter, indicating the complexity of what we refer to as 'communication skills'. It is also deliberately focused on oral communication, rather than written communication, simply because oral communication is more frequent in most people's lives than written communication, though some of the issues that affected your answers to these questions will also be apparent in your engagement with written communications as well. There are few right and wrong answers to this questionnaire, but for most answers the answer we give will have consequences for the quality of our relationships with others – especially those whose answers may be very different to our own.

═══════ **FOR YOU TO DO** ═══════

With others you know reasonably well, choose any five of the questions above (maybe randomly) and discuss the following:

1. Do you know others who might have different answers to you for these questions? Are they easy or difficult to work with?
2. What might the impact be of working with people whose answers to those questions are different to your own?
3. Why the questions might be important to consider in relation to communicating better with others.
4. Do you think there are better and worse answers to these questions?

THE CONTEXT OF COMMUNICATION

Very little communication takes place in isolation. Unless we are a brand-new manager taking over a local business or a new student who has just enrolled on a course, most communication will take place in the context of relationships which already exist. Figure 12.2 summarises the complexity of such a situation.

We will examine most of these processes and technical terms below, but the quality of relationships we have with others tends to be influenced by a number of factors, as outlined in Figure 12.2.

The way in which we behave through various media – our words, our facial expressions, tone of voice, and so on – will create impressions of us in the minds of others. Usually, whether we are successful in communicating what we wish to communicate will be influenced by aspects of communication that we can control: our body language (non-verbal behaviour), the way we use our voice (para-linguistic behaviours/cues), the context of and learning from the conversations we have had previously, the ways we communicate (channels, e.g. email or face-to-face) and the words that we use. These issues will all affect the way we 'code' our messages.

However, whether any message will be received and interpreted in the way that we expect will depend on whether those same issues help the recipient of the communication to 'decode' it in the same way.

The ongoing and important challenge is that where communication is not interpreted correctly (i.e. 'as intended'), it will have consequences for the beliefs and attitudes of the recipients, their emotions and then their broader behaviour, which is why many relationship issues in teams, at work and elsewhere tend

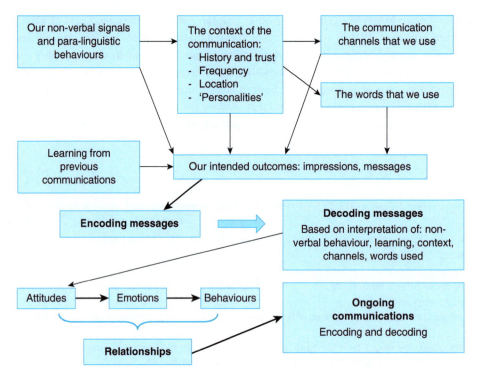

Figure 12.2   The context of communication

to arise from poor communication. Resolving where the origins of any poor communication arose can often help to do something to repair relationships, though sometimes this is not possible. The challenge is often that there are no absolutely 'correct' ways to communicate and that every individual has to work out a system (i.e. a set of tools for communicating usefully) that works for them in a variety of situations.

The model presented in Figure 12.2 indicates that: (1) the process of communication does not take place in isolation; and (2) there is a definitive process of communication that requires the 'coding' and 'decoding' (or translation) of information. Later sections of the chapter give more details of how these processes of encoding and decoding happen.

UNDERSTANDING THE PROCESS OF COMMUNICATION

Before we get into the details of how different communication skills are best demonstrated, it is important to understand the basics of how all communication processes work. The principles are relatively straight-forward to understand; of course, the challenge comes in applying them to our communications. Unless we think about them, all the processes and issues identified below happen unconsciously, but when we do think about them and change what we do as a result, then our communications become much more effective. Let's use an example to illustrate what we mean, and show how things can go wrong:

(a)   **We find/have something we want or need to communicate to others and we put it into a form of words (code) that we can send to others in some way.** This may come from anything that we have in common with other people – perhaps we are working on something with others, or share a common interest with them in some way. Regardless, the information gets coded in our minds in a way that experience tells us is usually interpreted correctly with minimum negative consequences for us. (I will have 'coded' my words here in this text in a particular way reflecting my own experiences and ideas about what works.)

The experiences we have picked up have gradually expanded from our parents to siblings to friends and then to fellow students and colleagues at work, so the way we have learned to communicate (i.e. the code that we use) as young children will change as we unconsciously learn how to communicate with our expanded 'circle of friends'.

> Example: I want to check whether someone has done the work I asked them to do, so I use the following question: *'Have you been able to finish that section of the assignment yet?'*

(b) **We give that information (in code) to others and assume that others will understand the code in the way we intend.** There will be some who understand that code well, namely those with whom we share a 'common language'. The 'language' we use can include technical language or 'jargon' or abbreviations that only those with a particular background or experiences will understand. In addition, there may be words used in a certain way that only certain people will understand correctly. Therefore, the assumption that we make about people always understanding us is rarely true.

(c) **We select a 'media channel' as a way of sending a message at a time and place we think will work.** It may be passive and is often a reaction to how a communication was passed on to us, but we have a choice as to how we respond to others' communications. It may be via a meeting, or a reply by email or a corridor conversation, but the channel that we use to communicate does have implications for the way in which that communication is received.

> Example: I send the following question as an email: *'Have you been able to finish that section of the assignment yet?'* The real intention is to find out whether someone has finished their section of the report.

It is certainly quicker and easier to send an email to many people at once, but for many individuals, most of their email communication (including the use of synchronous chat tools, such as WhatsApp, WeChat, Line, Facebook messenger, etc.) is to individuals. There are times when it is slower to send an email to an individual than it would be to speak to them on the telephone or go to see them (and clear up any communication which is unclear or ambiguous), but the choice of 'best channel to use' will depend on the urgency of the communication, the number of people involved, and the potential for and consequences of any misunderstanding. Box 12.1 explains this in more detail.

BOX 12.1

WHICH COMMUNICATION CHANNELS ARE BEST?

The answer will depend on a variety of factors. Email and other forms of one-way communication (e.g. newsletters) might be effective for communicating for a lot of people at one time, but are not always the most effective if you want to deal with a sensitive issue that is relevant to just one person and where written communication is likely to lead to misunderstanding.

(Continued)

(Continued)

Written communication is simply *content* and can be interpreted in a number of ways, assuming that the written communication is actually read of course! Someone reading an email at the end of a tiring and stressful day might interpret the email very differently from someone who can take their time, think about what it means and knows well how you usually communicate. Communicating with one individual by email may or may not be effective, but if someone does not know you well, then you will need to be very clear about your meaning, using language that most will interpret correctly.

Oral communication over the telephone adds what we call 'para-linguistic cues': small 'behaviours' (some call them 'behavioural tells') which add to the meaning of just giving the words themselves. In written text/chat communication, we have 'emojis', which perform the same function. Although we will cover them in more detail below, these tells – such as speed of speech, pitch, volume and variation in any of these – indicate how important different words and issues might be, and a telephone conversation will give you this extra information in a way that a letter or an email rarely will.

The richest and most complete form of communication is **face-to-face communication**. With this, others will be able to see your body language and facial expressions, as well as understand your tone of voice, which means that the chances of your message being interpreted correctly are increased. (This is one of the key reasons why employers use face-to-face selection interviews when selecting their staff.)

One word of caution: the interpretation of your message – even when given face-to-face – is *only as good as the decoding* used by the recipient of your communication, and this is not usually something that is within your control. The additional advantage of face-to-face communication is that you can seek the feedback mentioned above and check instantly whether the message was actually received in the way you intended.

(d) **Even if the code is understood, there can be a range of issues which distort the reception of the message.** Broadly speaking, communications experts call these 'noise' and 'perceptual filters'. The 'noise' is the external background factors which can impact on the 'hearing' of a message (e.g. the number of tasks we have to deal with, the effort required to decode a message, motivation and interest in relation to the subject content – anything which can affect whether we actually hear parts of a message), while the 'perceptual filters' are internal factors which affect our interpretation of a message (e.g. our own knowledge and previous experience about an issue, trust we have in the individual). Both affect the accuracy of any 'decoding' process that takes place, and therefore the accuracy of the interpretation of any message.

> Example: The question *'Have you been able to finish that section of the assignment yet?'* is received by someone (let's call them 'B') who believes that you do not trust them, and is interpreted as *'I don't think you've finished this part of the report* either *but I am just checking ...,'* indicating impatience.

Such distortions in communication are particularly important when communicating across cultures. Cultural expectations can really distort the way that messages are given since the encoding will usually be very different (see Chapter 13). The point is made clearer when we think of differences between direct translation and interpretation. *Direct translation* from one language to another takes the words and translates them into another language. This is helpful to some extent, but the recipient of that translation is still left to give meaning to those words. *Interpretation*, on the other hand, finishes the job, giving meaning to the words and phrases so that the recipient can understand them.

Example: The question *'Have you been able to finish that section of the assignment yet?'* is interpreted by someone with poor English as *'Have you found the resources and the ability to finish the section of the report?'* Remember: the original intention was to find out if they had finished the section of the report, not really whether they *had been able* to do so.

(e) **We rarely check that others have understood the messages that we give in the way we intend.** To check that this is so takes a lot of time, especially if we are communicating to a large number of people (e.g. by email). That is one reason why large corporate communication events tend to be largely inspirational and thin on detail – the detail will usually need to be discussed in smaller units where clarification is much more possible.

However, even in one-to-one discussions: (1) individuals rarely ask the other person to summarise what has been agreed or to rephrase any instructions given (perhaps because of a fear of seeming to be patronising or worry over whether someone will feel embarrassed because they have not interpreted something correctly); and/or (2) even when they are asked, individuals can simply repeat a phrase or statement without any understanding of what it really means. That feedback is crucial in establishing whether a message has been received in the way it was intended.

'BUT I HAVE A QUESTION ...'

... You say that communicating face-to-face is better than communicating over the telephone or via email. Does this mean that if I give more information about an issue in my e-mails, the chance that my communication will be understood will increase?

The simple answer is: not necessarily. Let's assume for the moment that this is a communication via email to several people (maybe group members working on a project). If you regularly add increasing detail to the information you give, then you will probably confuse others and it is quite likely that they will just wait for what they think is the final communication. The best thing is often to give as much detail as you think you need to in order to inform the other individual(s) about whatever the issue might be; if they have questions, then be sure to invite them to ask – though the challenge will be with those who *think* they understand, but whose understanding is actually incorrect.

KEY LEARNING POINT

Communication is a complex process which does not always produce the outcomes you intend. Checking that the understanding of your message(s) is the same as you intend with those who receive it is always important.

REFLECTION POINT

Take some time to think about the following questions and write down some answers.

Do you ever have emotional arguments with other people, or with someone you know? Why do those arguments begin?

Do you find it easier to communicate with someone you know well, or someone you do not know? What makes the difference?

Do you ever try to find out whether someone has understood your message(s) in the way you wanted them to? Has that ever led to any arguments?

COMPONENTS OF COMMUNICATION

Having examined the way that the communication process works, it is useful to examine the various behavioural 'inputs' into the communication process. These were briefly referred to earlier on as aspects of 'non-verbal behaviours' and 'para-linguistic cues'.

 NON-VERBAL BEHAVIOUR

Non-verbal behaviour is any form of behaviour which communicates a message without using speech.

 PARA-LINGUISTIC CUES

A para-linguistic cue is any type of oral behaviour which adds meaning to the words of a message.

In some ways, it would be wonderful if communication was just made up of the words we use and if everyone interpreted those words in the same way – it would make life much easier and more straightforward. In other ways, having the extra information can give us more clues as to what someone might be trying to say, as long as we interpret those clues in the way they were meant of course.

We use non-verbal behaviours and para-linguistic cues all the time, but the way we use them in combination with our words can radically change the meanings. Some individuals are better than others at recognising those meanings.

Para-linguistic Cues

There are broadly four areas where we can change our behaviour to have a particular impact. Professional speech coaches will give a great deal of advice on these so that individuals can give speeches that have an impact (some of these areas are covered briefly in Chapter 9), but they also have an impact in every day conversations:

Speed of speech: Some people will speak more slowly than others, and some may take more time to speak and contribute than others. This may be a sign of being more thoughtful or of needing a little more time to think something through, but we cannot conclude this from speed of speech alone. However, there is usually a rhythm to our speech which helps others understand when we are about to finish a sentence.

Volume of speech: In usual conversation, people do not speak loudly enough for others to hear, so a loud conversation is often taken as a sign of heightened emotion, especially if the pitch of voice is also raised (both do often occur together). It can, however, be an indication that someone is struggling to hear, so we have to be careful in interpreting behaviour.

Pitch and intonation: The more monotone our voice, the less interested someone is likely to be in what we are saying. We naturally indicate important issues within a conversation by changing our pitch. There is no better tone – higher pitch is not better than lower pitch – but the pitch we use will probably send a message to others about how calm, emotional or authoritative we are about a particular issue. Higher pitch (and volume) tends to indicate more emotion, but it is not universally the case, and some individuals communicate their negative emotion by using much lower pitch than normal. With the pitch of our voice, we can indicate scepticism, sarcasm and humour as well as a range of emotions.

Change and modulation in any of the above: When we continue to use a normal pattern of speech, then the hearer is likely to assume that the information is of 'average' importance compared with other information, but if we suddenly change any of the three aspects above, we signal to the hearer that there is some information that they need to pay careful attention to.

To demonstrate the impact of intonation, consider the example in Box 12.2.

━━━━━━ **BOX 12.2** ━━━━━━

THE IMPACT OF INTONATION

Let's take a very simple phrase: 'I want to have a cup of tea.' Which of these five phrases represents the meaning here?

(a) I have been waiting ages and I am very impatient to drink my cup of tea.
(b) You have brought me a cup of coffee but I really want a cup of tea.
(c) Thank you very much for asking: my favourite drink is a cup of tea.
(d) I asked for a cup of tea, but you have brought a flask of tea.
(e) Everyone wants to have some coffee, but I would like to have a cup of tea.

The simple (and maybe obvious) answer is that we cannot tell. Without knowing where the emphasis was – or whether there was any emphasis at all – we have no idea. So, let's add some emphasis by indicating some intonation:
I want to have a cup of tea.
If you say this out loud, then it is clear that the emphasis is on the word 'tea' in order to create a contrast with anything else, so the correct meaning appears to be (b). But if the emphasis is put anywhere else, then the meaning changes considerably. If we add volume of speech and facial expressions as well, then we can determine whether someone is simply making a comment, or whether they appear to be emotional and making a complaint.

Try taking all the alternative answers ((a) to (e) above): how would you indicate intonation and volume for each of these possibilities?

━━━━━━ **BOX 12.3** ━━━━━━

PUNCTUATION AND PARA-LANGUAGE

When we read the page of a textbook or a fictional story, we take notice of the punctuation that is there. The punctuation gives us an idea of how we should use para-language to convey the meaning of the words on the page. Consider the following:

A '?' [question mark] at the end of the sentence means that our tone of voice should go up as we ask a question.

(Continued)

(Continued)

A ',' [comma] between phrases means that there is a short pause at the end of the statement before moving on to the next statement (or 'clause').

A '.' [full stop] means that we have finished a particular statement; our intonation should go down at the end of the sentence, indicating the end of that issue. Over recent years, there has been a trend for people to raise their tone, as if they were asking a question; this is not how the 'full stop' or 'period' (US English) should be used.

A '!' [exclamation mark] usually expresses disgust, surprise, shock or a strong negative reaction of some kind. As such, the volume and tone of voice usually go up.

This should help us understand more of what someone is trying to communicate, according to their tone of voice. Consider the words below:

> The impact of punctuation is obvious to see whenever someone speaks out loud they use their into-nation to express feeling and emotion about what is being said of course that is not the entire story speed of speech and volume become important as well and none of these things can be taken sepa-rately from the non-verbal behaviour we observe from others and the words they use it is clear that the words are just a small part of the story.

Are you able to read these words aloud? Where would you put the punctuation? Would that punctuation change how you use your voice to read the sentence?

TIP: A good suggestion for seeing if a written sentence is too long is to see if you can say the sentence in one breath. If you can, then the length is probably reasonably good, but if that is not possible, then the sentence probably needs to be punctuated or broken up.

KEY LEARNING POINT

Para-language is a component of communication that can be used effectively to indicate particular empha-ses and to differentiate important issues from general 'background communication'.

Non-verbal Behaviour

If the vocal expressions – volume, pitch and speed – say something about our feelings, then other forms of non-verbal behaviour add to the interpretation of the message. The more information we get about the communication and the more consistent that information is, the more likely we are to interpret a message correctly (assuming that we do actually notice any inconsistencies). However, these signals all add together in terms of the meaning of someone's message. In particular, we can consider facial expres-sions, body gestures and posture, touch, 'proxemics' and movement.

FOR YOU TO DO

Consider the emotions displayed below.

1. As you do so, draw a 'smilie' or 'emoji' (a small face indicating the positions of the eyes, the mouth and the eyebrows) reflecting what you think someone expressing that emotion would show on their face.

(Continued)

(Continued)

Happy Sad Concerned Confused Curious Angry Laughing Excited Amazed Upset

Sceptical Uncertain Joking

2. After you have done so, compare your drawing with that of the person next to you: how similar are your drawings? (The similarity may indicate something to you of how your assumptions about interpreting others' non-verbal behaviours may be correct or incorrect. If the person you compare your drawings with comes from a culture that is not your own, those assumptions may be very incorrect.)
3. Take one of these emotions and find someone from a different culture: did they draw something very different from you?

Facial expressions

Our eyes, the way we move our eyebrows, the amount of eye contact we give and the extent to which we smile all send messages to others. The challenge is to ensure that the message is interpreted in the way we intend. There are around 250,000 different facial expressions, meaning that the brain has to work very quickly to recognise the signals being sent by others.

It is actually difficult not to smile at someone who is smiling at us – it takes some effort and focus – which is why we often interpret smiles as a positive thing. Some people do not seem to smile very much; we could interpret that as a sign of seriousness, though any interpretation needs to be checked carefully. In Chinese cultures, showing the mouth when laughing is not seen as appropriate, so most Chinese will cover their mouth when laughing at a joke between friends.

We often move our eyebrows to show curiosity or surprise (raised) and lower them to show concern or scepticism or negative emotion (frowning).

Direct eye contact is a sign of confidence in western cultures (with a lack of direct eye contact being seen as indicating a lack of self-confidence), but used to be considered a sign of a lack of respect in Confucian heritage cultures (e.g. China and Asia). Of course, these two reactions are not exclusive – it is quite possible to show deep respect to others and still have a great deal of self-confidence – but in some places the idea still continues, so we need to be careful when interpreting the behaviour of others where values are represented in ways we might not expect or understand.

We also move our eyes around in different ways. When we remember something, when we are trying to think of something or when we are trying to imagine something, we look in different directions. You may suspect that someone is not telling you the truth because they avoid direct eye contact when they are talking, which is why people often ask others to 'look them in the eyes' when saying something that may not quite be true, but we also need to be aware that they *may simply be thinking about something* or trying to remember something, rather than telling you something that is not true.

Body gestures

What we do with our head, our arms and our hands adds to others' interpretations of a message that we give. There are those who say that someone with crossed arms is adopting a defensive and potentially aggressive approach to a conversation. In reality, whether this is true this will depend on two other factors: (1) whether other non-verbal behaviours are giving out the same signals; and (2) whether this individual normally behaves in that way, even if they are relaxed. We interpret these behaviours instinctively, without thinking too much. It is quite possible for someone to sit in front of you with their arms crossed, to be smiling and to have a relaxed and friendly conversation.

Hand movements are often assumed to be very useful indicators of what is going through another individual's mind at the time they are speaking, though hand (and head) movements when someone is supposed to be jus listening can be taken as an indication that they are reacting to something, have stopped listening and are preparing to speak.

Gestures are often used alongside para-linguistic cues to add emphasis to the words that are communicated, especially in formal presentations, but a lack of any hand gestures should not be seen as a lack of emphasis. Some people deliberately hold their hands in a particular way (e.g. behind their back, or hold their hands together) in order to hide their nerves or to try to avoid distracting their listeners from the actual content (facts and figures) they are trying to deliver.

 FOR YOU TO DO ━━━━━━━━━━━━━━━━━

Examine the photographs of the gestures given below. What do you think this individual is trying to say with these gestures? Do others agree with your interpretation?

Gestures and movement

Of course, the more regularly a particular gesture is made, the more likely it will be that the message conveyed by the gesture will be emphasised. This is not a problem if the meaning of the gesture is clearly understood, but if there is some 'mistranslation' taking place, then repeating the gesture many times may lead to increased misunderstanding.

If we are perfectly content, are thinking of the same thing constantly in the same way, or have no motivation at all to change our position, then it is unlikely we will move. Humans move when there is a reason to do so, and that reason can be large and urgent (e.g. people rushing out of a building when there is an earthquake) or small and relatively insignificant (e.g. someone getting up from the sofa when they have been watching TV because they are bored with what they are watching). So when we see people moving, we would naturally assume there is a purpose behind their doing so.

The challenge comes, then, when people do not behave in ways we might expect, either because we expect someone to move or gesture in some way but they do not, or because someone moves when there is no reason for them to do so. Both scenarios create varying levels of confusion, which then gets misinterpreted.

Both the movements we demonstrate and the frequency with which we demonstrate them can be signs of self-confidence. It is assumed that occasional and purposeful movement indicates more self-confidence than erratic movement.

'BUT I HAVE A QUESTION ...'

... There is a lot to consider, but how can I possibly pay attention to all of this when I am having a conversation with a friend or with a colleague at work?

This is a good question – and the simple answer is that in most situations you cannot. if you were to think consciously about all of these things then your communication would seem odd, because you would be trying to reconcile their perception of you with their behaviour caused by your behaviour and your tone of voice, and you would be trying to second-guess and assume the impact of all the communication signals you were sending.

The value of the information above comes from three things: firstly, reflecting on conversations that you have had where the other person misinterpreted your meaning and recognising what you might have done differently; secondly, identifying just one or two areas where you could give more clarity in how you say what you have said and working on those; and thirdly, becoming better at making sure that you gather feedback from the other person and check that they have understood your message as you intended it.

Focusing on a small number of areas will make the challenge of improving your communication skills much more manageable.

BOX 12.4

MISUNDERSTANDING TOUCH

One type of gesture that some like to give is that of touch.

This is an extremely delicate issue to cover, but it is very important to do so. In some cultures, and for some individuals, touch is something that is unwanted and can cause very serious misunderstandings.

Depending on the kind of touch, it can show compassion, kindness, friendship, love and more. Of course, it is never wrong to show kindness (even if definitions of 'kindness' may vary from situation to situation) and most would say that there is nothing wrong with a hand on the shoulder for encouragement, but *the potential for touch to be misinterpreted is very large* and workplace definitions of sexual harassment often include reference to unwanted physical contact.

In some cultures, it is frowned upon for people to be overly familiar with each other in public. In some cultures (e.g. particularly Arabic cultures), it is very common to see men walking down the street holding hands and greeting each other by kissing on the cheek, but in other cultures this kind of touch could be perceived as inappropriate.

BOX 12.5

CAN YOU TELL IF SOMEONE IS LYING?

Behavioural psychologists tell us that there are a number of behavioural signs or 'tells' we can look out for when someone is not telling the truth. Most are similar to those occasions when someone is suffering from stress:

1. Having a dry mouth – and needing to drink frequently.
2. Overly frequent 'aggressive gestures' (e.g. forming the hand into a fist).
3. Blink rate – the rate is usually 20 blinks a minute, but is someone blinking faster than that?
4. Hand gestures – does anything appear to represent information being hidden?
5. Covering the mouth with the hand – information is being prevented from 'escaping'.

The key thing for all of these is that, in isolation, it is difficult to conclude that someone is not telling the truth. However, if there are many 'tells' occurring at the same time, then perhaps someone is being economical with the truth.

It appears that individuals are very likely to tell lies to those they do not know well or do not care about very much, especially if they want to make others feel better about themselves. University students are suspected of lying regularly to their parents and some believe that individuals lie to every other person they communicate with.

Can you tell if someone you know is lying?

Proxemics

Put simply, proxemics is the study of the impact that location has on communication. The simplest way of demonstrating this is to consider the legend of King Arthur, who was supposed to have reigned in southern England around AD 800. He reputedly had his close followers sit around a round table, rather than one with definite ends, in order to create a discussion among equals, rather than have a clear hierarchy.

A choice to sit at each location will have certain consequences. Certain locations will inhibit the number and kind of (supportive or negative) contributions to a discussion – for example, where direct eye contact becomes difficult or where the location seems a long way away from the leader of the discussion. In meetings and other situations, physical distance is often interpreted as reflecting emotional distance, and such an interpretation will have implications for individuals' communication with others. The location someone sits in will have an impact on:

- The number of contributions they are able to make easily without interrupting others.
- The formality or informality of the discussion.
- The sense of support or otherwise for the leader of the discussion.
- The extent to which individuals are engaged in the discussion.

FURTHER READING

Further online content on the topic of proxemics can be found on the companion website at https:// study.sagepub.com/morgan.

━━━━━ BOX 12.6 ━━━━━

SITTING IN LECTURES

Whether we like it or not, where we sit sends certain implicit messages to others. It may imply that we are not really interested in a particular discussion, or that we are intensely interested and have something we want to say.

You may or may not have a preference as to where you sit when it comes to your lectures, but if you do, and if you have freedom to choose your seat, consider that preference carefully. Many students seem to like to sit at the back of the lecture theatre for lectures, and this will send a message to your lecturers just as much as sitting at the front does.

1. Why do you sit in that/those particular location(s)?
2. Is where you sit better or worse than any other seat when it comes to encouraging you to learn during those lectures?
3. Do you change where you sit depending on the subject/lecturer?
4. How do you think your lecturer interprets where you sit?
5. What would encourage you to change where you sit?

━━━━━ KEY LEARNING POINT ━━━━━

Non-verbal communication consists of our facial expressions, body gestures and movement, and proxemics. They help us to add meaning to the other signals we receive – the words and the para-language.

━━━━━ REFLECTION POINT ━━━━━

Take some time to think about the following questions and write down some answers.

How 'expressive' are you in the way you communicate to other people? Do you use a lot of intonation, or speak in a monotone most of the time? What about your facial expressions, or gestures?

Have you ever been told that your use of non-verbal behaviour affects others' reactions to you?

Do others communicate with you in the way you communicate with them? Do those same people communicate differently with others?

OUR WORDS AND LANGUAGE

So far, we have examined the impact that our para-language, our non-verbal behaviour and proxemics can have on the ways that communication can be interpreted. What we have not yet examined, of course, is the actual language that we use. Examining language is an academic discipline in its own right – a degree in Linguistics is not uncommon across universities – and is extremely complex as an area of study.

What we will examine here are four aspects of language: the function that different forms of language can take; power and confidence issues; the ways in which the words we choose may or may not be particularly tactful or diplomatic; and, finally, the use of questions in conversation. There are other components to the study of language, for example the use of what linguistics call 'register' (we will not cover 'register' here, but, in very broad terms, it refers to the technical vocabulary level needed to understand conversations), but we will simply address the four areas highlighted above.

Language Function

When we write words as a sentence on a page, it is usually fairly clear what we are trying to do with the sentence. We might be trying to ask a question, give a suggestion or make a statement, and we use punctuation to indicate the functions that our language is trying to represent. As we saw in Box 12.3 above, punctuation is usually represented by our para-linguistic cues and so usually it is clear whether we are asking a question, giving a statement or making a suggestion.

However, there are occasions when things are much less clear. Take the phrase, 'You could always ask the marketing department for their ideas': is this a suggestion – that we *should* ask the marketing department – or an *instruction* that we are expected to/have to ask the marketing department? Alternatively, take the phrase 'The marketing department usually have some good ideas': is this a *suggestion*, an *instruction* or merely a *statement* of fact which we can ignore if we wish to? Box 12.7 examines the various functions that language can play.

■■■■■■■■■■■■■■■ BOX 12.7 ■■■■■■■■■■■■■■■

ARE QUESTIONS ALWAYS 'QUESTIONS'?

We can usually think of questions as being tools for gathering information, and in many situations this is exactly what they are used for. However, questions can be used for a variety of purposes, and not just for gathering information. The examples below show how five fairly similar questions can be used to guide another individual's behaviour and influence decision making:

(a) *'Don't you think that would be a really bad idea?'* Leading questions can be used forcefully to push someone to reconsider their actions.
(b) *'Do you think there would be any negative consequences to that idea?'* This is a similar but much more gentle way of getting someone to reconsider their actions. Such a question might be used in coaching or counselling situations.
(c) *'What do you think senior management might think of this idea?'* This could have a similar function to (b), but might (or might not, depending on who is asking it and how) include a threat - to tell senior management about this.
(d) *'Why are you persisting with this really bad idea?'* This shows more about the negative emotion of the person that is asking it, than it does in gathering any actual information. When individuals are emotional, they often need to express it in some way.
(e) *'Wouldn't that idea cause a problem with X (other issue or individual)?'* This is clearer than (b) but is a leading question and so it achieves the same purpose. Being specific might indicate a desire to learn on the part of the person who is asking, or it might indicate a desire to put some pressure on an individual - more than is represented by (b) but not as much as (a).

(Continued)

(Continued)

The way that an individual would respond to any or all of these questions would give a particular impression of their leadership 'style'.

All of these are questions but have a purpose beyond simply gathering information. The simple information-gathering form of the question would probably be something like 'Can you tell us what you wish to do and why?', but even the interpretation of this would depend on the non-verbal behaviours and intonation used to ask the question.

The answer will often relate to the context of the statement (Who said it? Under what circumstances?) and to the non-verbal and para-linguistic signals (tone of voice, volume, eyebrows, eye contact, smile, posture) given while saying it. When we are communicating orally, we take in all these signals and our learning from previous experience gives us an indication of which function the language is playing. When we are communicating by email, however, those signals are not there, and unless there is a '!' we are often left to our own devices to interpret the function that the message is giving us. We do not always get the interpretation correct, but there are occasions when we should probably check.

'BUT I HAVE A QUESTION ...'

... Why don't people just say what they mean?

One of my team members – someone who was the team leader – on a group assignment recently said to us, 'Perhaps you might like to do the introduction and perhaps you could do the analysis and the conclusion? I'll do the literature review, so let's meet next Monday, OK?' None of us actually thought she was telling us to do these things, we just thought we were going to meet next Monday to discuss whether we wanted to do those parts of the assignment, so she was pretty annoyed with us when we actually met and found that we hadn't done any work. Why don't people say what they mean?

Misunderstanding others' communication in this way is very common, so you are not the exception. As we have seen, we can be clearer about the meaning of a phrase once we get to know someone better. We get to understand how they use their para-language and their non-verbal behaviour, and this helps us interpret what they are saying.

Of course, words and phrases such as 'might', 'could', 'should', 'might have', 'could have', 'should have', 'might like to', 'could possibly', 'should probably', and so on, tend to be seen as suggestions, but may actually be intended as gentle instructions.

Why do people use what can be seen as *ambiguous* language, that is phrases and words that can be misinterpreted? There can be a variety of possible reasons: maybe they did not want to appear too bossy and alienate other group members, or maybe they did not have the self-confidence to be a directive leader, or feel that they knew the other group members well enough to know how others would react and so took a gentle approach. You cannot blame her for any of these things (all of which can seem OK), though she probably should have checked that everyone understood her 'instructions' before closing the meeting.

What is very clear from what you have asked is that our personality and self-confidence can have a major impact on the way we communicate, and particularly when we take leadership roles.

Chapter 13 covers issues of context in more detail with respect to communicating across cultures, where our interpretations of behaviour *can* be very inaccurate.

KEY LEARNING POINT

The function of a phrase can have a marked impact on whether we take any subsequent action and on the nature of any action. If there is a lack of clarity, then it helps to *check that our understanding* of the function of what others have said is the same as the person communicating with us.

Confidence, Communication and Power Behaviour

Whether we like it or not, the ways we communicate (our para-language, non-verbal behaviours, the words we use) can give others very different impressions of who we are, our thinking, our attitudes, our emotions and our self-confidence. Such impressions may or may not be correct, of course, and are always culture dependent. Nowhere are such impressions more important than when we are attending job interviews or giving important presentations, so while we need to behave as we usually would in our more normal (and relaxed) state most of the time, it does help to consider how we might help ourselves to show self-confidence in the presence of others.

There are certain behaviours that we show when we are communicating, which can give the impression of being unsure or having a low degree of confidence, and behaviours that can give the opposite impression, of course.

Table 12.1 Verbal behaviours displayed in situations of low and high confidence

Low-confidence indicators		High-confidence indicators	
Type of behaviour	**Example**	**Type of behaviour**	**Example**
Hedges and qualifiers	'Maybe ...'	Positive talk	'We can do this!'
	'You know,' 'sort of'	Give credit to others	'I'm not the real hero here, it is ...'
Irritators	'Really (good),' 'awfully (bad)'	Learning from experience and accepting responsibility	'I agree, we messed up'
Intensifiers			'So, this is how I suggest we should do this'
Tags	'... didn't you?' '... aren't you?'	Persuade others	'This is our situation: X is good, Y is OK, but Z is poor'
Hesitations	'Em', 'er', 'ah', 'uhh', 'Well, ...'	Decisive speaking	
		Tell the truth	'If you look, you will see ...'

Table 12.1 simply refers to the kinds of words we may use. Of course, our body language will also differ in situations where we have little confidence from those where we are very sure of what we are doing. Our body language – our eye contact, posture, handshake, tone of voice, volume, speed of speech, amount of erratic movement – will change as our brain struggles to find a way to communicate in what might be a stressful situation.

Using Language and Communicating Tactfully in Difficult Conversations

Communication becomes particularly stressful when we need to say something very important but do not know how to say it because of the personal consequences of doing so, or because of how the individual may react.

This is particularly difficult when we get frustrated with others. In such situations, we tend to want to express that emotion very forcefully to those who might be frustrating us. For others, they might hold things in for a while and then 'explode'. Expressing our frustration emotionally, however, is almost always not the best thing to do.

It is in these kinds of situations that we might find some 'tools' or phrases useful. We know of course that the longer a difficult situation goes on, the worse and more stressful it becomes – and so we do need to develop some tools, ideas and principles for dealing with them.

1. **Check any assumptions:** Ensure that you check any assumptions you have made before starting the conversation. Emotion can sometimes cloud an individual's judgement. This may include the *reasons for* someone's actions, especially if they are unusual and out of character, as well as the actions themselves. Be clear about the evidence you have for the behaviours you wish to change, and gather evidence from others *if* that will not harm other relationships.

2. **Reframe the purpose of the conversation:** See the conversation as a chance to solve a problem and to change someone's behaviour, rather than as a time to get really tough and make an example of someone. If you take the latter approach, it is likely that the atmosphere will be tense, the language will become aggressive and you will likely create more problems than you solve.

3. **Use passive and active voice appropriately:** Try to keep negative feedback in the 'passive voice', rather than the 'active voice'. For example, 'You did this badly' becomes 'This was done badly'. The identity of the person who performed the action will be implicit anyway, but removing the personal criticism can remove the 'sting' for someone who is lacking in confidence or who is likely to become defensive. The opposite is true for good news or positive feedback (i.e. 'You did this really well'), where personal praise is usually a good thing.

4. **Use a 'praise sandwich':** In the 'praise sandwich' remove the word 'but' from negative communication. For example, 'You did XXX really well but I wish you had done YYY much better. But I am glad to see that you also did ZZZ well' becomes 'You did XXX really well. We might have to consider further how we move forward with YYY since there seem to be some issues with that, but I am glad to see that you have made some progress with ZZZ.' The word 'but' is almost expected after you praise someone, and it means that the initial praise becomes relatively meaningless, with the only thing that the other person remembers being the negative comment. In the example here, a new sentence removes the conjunction.

5. **Watch your language:** Our input into a conversation will affect someone else's input, so being careful about our language can enable us to achieve our objectives in a way that being very direct will not. For example, (1) refer to 'we' (rather than 'you') as much as possible. Referring to 'we' indicates two people (as a team) working together on improving someone's performance (i.e. they will be supported in the future) and is likely to encourage someone to commit to personal change. (2) Similarly, there are a number of words that will likely increase the emotions of the person hearing the message: for example, 'problem to deal with' can become an 'issue to manage' or a 'challenge', or sometimes even 'an opportunity for improvement'. (3) As mentioned above, try to remove the words 'but', 'however' and (even worse) 'although' from messages about things that have gone wrong. (4) Finally, some people use phrases such as 'less well' to talk about things which went 'badly', or 'not always the best thing to do' or 'unhelpful' to talk about things which would be 'a bad idea'.

6. **Be clear about consequences:** Do not be afraid of informing someone of the consequences of their future actions. It is unfair to give someone the idea that they can continue to do things

poorly without any consequences, if those consequences might well happen: 'but of course, we don't want to see those things happen, do we?' Of course, never try to bluff: if the consequences are not there or cannot be enforced, then do not make them up.

7. **Assume good intentions:** Unless you have information to the contrary, try to assume good intentions. You can always change your view later, but it is very hard to get back to that point if you start off believing that someone had bad intentions or did not care. 'I am sure you did not expect or want XXX to happen. Anyway, it has, so now we have to address it.' Doing so will educate someone to the unintended consequences of their actions.

8. **Avoid emotion during a conversation:** Focus on the evidence throughout the conversation, rather than your reactions to it. Emotions will cloud judgement and will make the conversation far more painful and challenging than it will need to be. Language in an emotional conversation tends to become more destructive than helpful. Of course, this includes the recognition that others more senior to you may already have expressed some emotion to you (which is what human beings do, but it is not always helpful), but that does not mean that you need to express that emotion to others. After all, your main priority is to solve a performance problem, not to show how tough or angry you can be.

9. **Ensure that there are no surprises:** There is nothing worse than being told off for something when you did not know that it was wrong – though certain things (bribery, theft, etc.) will be 'known' as wrong anyway. The basic principle here is to ensure that if you need to have a difficult conversation with someone about an issue, then they would be expecting that conversation at some point.

10. **Leave the conversation on a positive note:** If you can, after having agreed some specific goals and perhaps having put some resources or safeguards in place to prevent the problem from arising again. There is nothing worse than having a conversation which is aimless and does not agree a way forward when there is clearly a problem to be addressed.

11. **Use language which allows for some doubt:** Give the other person 'a way out' without making them feel embarrassed, and, similarly, be prepared for evidence which contradicts your view – you may have got it (your judgement) wrong. If you can, talk about actions which 'might have happened' or 'seem to have' happened, or consequences which 'could have happened' rather than things which definitely did happen. It is a lot easier to recover from a conversation where you have made incorrect judgements before hearing all the evidence if you phrase things as possibilities, rather than from a conversation where you have begun with an incorrect accusation that you later need to apologise for.

12. **Listen well and do not interrupt:** Give someone space to put their own side of the story, even if the evidence you have seems to contradict it. Individuals will often feel very aggrieved if they have not had the chance to share their view. At the end of the conversation, always check that your understanding is the same as those of others involved in the discussion.

13. **Encourage self-reflection:** Give an opportunity for self-reflection early on in the conversation. Some good communicators ask others to comment on what *seems to have happened* first before telling the other person what they think. This gives the conversation a more friendly atmosphere, rather than getting very quickly into a heated argument where neither person is willing to listen to the other.

14. **Do not be afraid of silence:** Silence can give people time to think. If the conversation seems to have stopped, then reminding the other person of the last thing that was being talked about or making an observation about the other person's emotion can be useful for restarting the discussion.

15. **Do not match someone else's 'mood':** If someone is angry, then one of the worst ways of trying to solve a problem is to become as angry as they are. The same is true for a situation where someone is upset: having two people in tears does not really help anyone. Focus on the issue you are trying to solve – together.

16. **Do not focus on what you cannot change:** Be specific about the behaviour you want to change, but trying to change someone's personality is not going to work (and might be regarded as unethical by some).

17. **Consider whether you need to apologise:** Many people find this hard – and it can be very hard – but giving an apology can be very powerful at healing friendships and workplace (or personal) relationships. Often the more specific the apology, the more powerful it will be – and many people will appreciate that you have done so. There may be some who take advantage of it and exploit it to show others that you are not good at what you are supposed to be doing , and so getting some advice from others may be useful sometimes. However, be very wary of apologising for something over which you had no control – something which was not your fault. The next time the same thing happens, the other person will blame you and their trust in you will decrease.

18. **Do say 'Thank you':** Even if a conversation has been hard or has not achieved any of your objectives, the other person has still given up some of their time for you. They may well have seen the conversation as a waste of time, but it is appropriate to thank people wherever possible and for whatever you can.

FOR YOU TO DO

Think about the phrases given below, all of which seem to arise from frustration with other people in some way. The phrases may all be quite emotive to the person hearing them, so think about how you might rephrase them if you were trying to give the same message in a more neutral manner.

'You have a problem because your performance is just generally not good enough! You never get the work done on time.'

'The English in this work is rubbish. Why don't you get a dictionary? I think you need to do this again.'

'I am so tired of this! No one ever communicates properly with me and I am finding it impossible to continue like this!'

'Guys, can you arrange meetings so that I can actually attend? You know how difficult it is for me with childcare.'

'I like the fact that you email me every day, but it is getting to be too many each day. Can you please stop? Thanks.'

'Why don't you listen properly??! I have already said that same thing at least twice.'

'So, you're saying that my work is no good?' (And maybe think about how you would react to this.)

'BUT I HAVE A QUESTION ...'

... This is useful, I suppose, but why can't I just be direct and say what I think?

Of course you can - if that is your normal style of communication and you are absolutely confident of what you think, believe and know, then sure. Be direct.

(Continued)

(Continued)

But these ideas are there for those situations when you are unsure about how to handle the conversation, where information might be ambiguous or when you might be dealing with someone whose reaction might be somewhat unpredictable. There are times when less self-confident individuals might find direct communication threatening, so you need to think about whether being direct is the best way to achieve what you want to achieve.

It is also worth noting that some cultures are more used to using direct forms of communication to get their message across than others (see page 282 'High- and Low-Context Cultures'). This has serious implications for business negotiations and other forms of intercultural communication.

 KEY LEARNING POINT

The words and language we use send messages to others. These messages are supported by our non-verbal behaviour and para-linguistic cues.

Questions in Conversation

Usually, conversations are two way: they involve two or more people, both of whom contribute to the ongoing dialogue. At some point, it is quite likely, if not inevitable, that one individual or both will ask questions, to check their understanding, gather more information or open up a different topic of conversation. As we have already seen in Box 12.7 on page 258, questions can have very different purposes but generally fall into one of four types. In formal situations or interviews (disciplinary, selection or performance appraisal interviews), questions are usually asked in the order shown in Figure 12.3, representing a 'funnel', where the first open questions gather a great deal of information, the probing questions gather more detail on one particular issue, the closed question (with a 'yes' or 'no', or a numerical answer) finalises the information gathering and the reflective question checks the information in summary form.

In a more informal setting, there is no need for any such structure and the variety of questions asked can be much broader, but any conversation that consists of mainly closed or reflective questions is likely to be one without a great deal of natural 'flow'.

The funnel technique

Open question
'Tell me about ...'

Probing question
'How did you ...?'

Closed question
'When was this?'

Reflective question
'So you ...?'

Figure 12.3   The four key question types

COMBINING THE COMPONENTS: ESTABLISHING RAPPORT

In this chapter, we have covered three elements of communication: para-language, non-verbal behaviour and the language that we use. There is one other area we can note in relation to these three elements, and it concerns the concept of rapport. We say that two people have 'rapport' when they seem to understand each other and enjoy each other's company.

We often know what rapport looks like. If we allow ourselves to enter a social setting, we might expect to be able to recognise individuals who have rapport with those around them and those who do not. Those who have rapport will be smiling at the same time that others smile, will be contributing to the conversation in some way and will be seen as part of a group. If we were to

RAPPORT

Rapport is a state of being where two or more individuals feel relaxed in each other's company.

look at dating couples in the same setting, we might be able to see them making eye contact with each other, listening well and not interrupting, and maybe copying each other's gestures (picking up their drinks, putting their hands on their head, etc.) at the same time. We know that rapport has been established when that 'mirroring' of each other's behaviour occurs.

In sales environments, salespeople are trained to copy the language used by the other party, their body language and para-linguistic cues (or, in the case of telephone sales, the tone and speed of speech), until they seem to be 'matching' each other. Once that has occurred, it is believed that rapport has been established and, rather than following the behaviour of the other person, the salesperson can actually lead their behaviour – with the salesperson's body language being reflected in the behaviour of the person they are trying to sell to. In establishing rapport, the salesperson has established a bond of friendship and, by inference, of trust, leading the customer to exactly where the salesperson wants them to be.

Of course, the challenge for all non-verbal behaviour is that we make assumptions about the meanings of others' behaviour based on our own behaviour ('if they do X then they must be thinking Y, because that's what I do when I do X') but we rarely think to actually check our assumptions, and it is this lack of checking (the feedback mentioned in Part III) that can easily lead to misunderstandings in communication.

▬ KEY LEARNING POINT ▬

Getting our language right with someone who might be used to interpreting these same words and messages in different ways is not easy, so getting feedback wherever possible is important.

As noted in the introduction to this chapter, we apply these different skills in different ways in different situations. The language we use and other signals that we give will be very different when we are counselling others, giving others feedback, negotiating, seeking to influence others and interviewing others, either for jobs or just to gather information. It is the application of these skills that can create effective or ineffective communication. We will now look to see how that can be done in two contexts, namely active listening and giving feedback, both of which are essential management skills in their own right.

Further online content on the topic of active listening can be found on the companion website at https://study.sagepub.com/morgan.

FURTHER
READING

APPLYING COMMUNICATION SKILLS: ACTIVE LISTENING

The way in which we combine all these different elements of communication will vary according to the needs of any given situation. A situation is composed of two (or more) people, a series of messages, a context or goal, why there is a need for communication at all, and perhaps a history. Regardless, we will need to apply verbal communication, non-verbal and para-linguistic elements of communication and other factors together in different ways to achieve different aims: to negotiate, to listen, to persuade, to caution or discipline, to appraise, to interview or maybe to counsel others. To do so consciously takes a great deal of time and effort, but in some instances (e.g. disciplinary or appraisal interviews) it is vital to plan the conversation and be very clear about the issues which need to be raised, as well as the *ways in which* these issues will be raised. This will vary according to the individual you are talking to.

Of the four communication skills we have at our disposal (the two active ones – speaking and writing – and the two passive ones – speaking and listening), listening is one of the most frequent, one of the most important and often not very well done. In reality, listening well is anything but passive: it takes energy, time and effort if it is to be done well, which is why it is frequently not done well. Your ability to listen well will have an impact on whether others feel respect towards you, whether people continue to communicate openly with you ('I'll not bother – he never listens to a word I say anymore,' which can have significant implications on decision making in management) and the broader impression that people will have. Therefore, being good at listening is important and is one of the most valuable communication skills sought by employers.

 FOR YOU TO DO

Have a look at the following questions. When you are in a conversation with another person, how often do you ...

- Maintain eye contact with the other person?
- Ask questions to ensure that you actually understand the emotion and facts that are being conveyed?
- Wait until the other person has stopped talking before thinking about what to say next?
- Ensure that you understand what the other person has been saying before they finish their sentence?
- Interrupt the other person because they seem to be saying too much or rambling on for too long?
- Try to summarise what the other person has been saying before the end of the conversation?
- Avoid facial expressions of judgement?
- Ensure that your seating arrangement is appropriate for listening well?

In nearly all cases, the more we do these things, the better our listening skills will be. The exceptions are the fifth and sixth items, which are bad practice when it comes to listening well.

Active listening is not the same as hearing. We talk about 'listening to music', but unless we are processing the words and/or the music in some way, the actual activity we are usually undertaking relates to hearing rather than listening.

 ACTIVE LISTENING

Active listening is the active search for an accurate understanding of another's message, through the interpretation of verbal and non-verbal messages.

Hearing, therefore, is the passive reception of information by the ears, whereas active listening requires far more engagement from the individual, and far more processing of that information.

Active listening is not easy, it requires effort, and typically anything which requires effort tends not to be done particularly well.

Tiredness, distractions, accents, active disinterest and making judgements or getting emotional about what is being said can all get in the way of our taking in information, and as soon as we omit information we are likely to miss out on certain parts of that information. Active listening, though, does involve ensuring that we take in and use as much information as we can, so not making judgements and trying not to think of what to say next are important.

We have so far looked at the principles of communication, examining the process of coding and decoding, issues of perception in communication and the non-verbal, para-linguistic and verbal skills we use in communicating. We have also looked at the way we can apply these behaviours and skills to difficult situations which require active listening. If we move to or communicate with people from another culture, we add an additional layer of complexity to the process of encoding and decoding information, so we will now look at why this is not easy and what we can do to improve how we communicate.

APPLYING COMMUNICATION SKILLS: GIVING FEEDBACK

For managers, being able to give feedback to a strong performer is not difficult, but being able to do so to a poorly performing employee is much less easy. It is an essential communication skill, but one that is not always done well.

Using the definition given here, we can assume that feedback can be non-verbal as well as verbal. A raised eyebrow or a frown can be as useful in communicating a message as what an individual actually says.

FEEDBACK

Feedback is any communication to a person that gives them information on some aspect of their behaviour.

The earlier section above on using language and communicating tactfully in difficult conversations (pages 260–3) contains some ideas on how we might phrase messages in such a way as to avoid too much conflict, but there are some additional principles we need to bear in mind when giving feedback in order to improve an individual's performance – which is the main goal of giving feedback.

PRINCIPLES OF GIVING FEEDBACK

While giving feedback is an essential part of managing others' performance, it is something that many individuals do not necessarily do well, or often enough. This is particularly the case for negative feedback, where emotions can become barriers to a calm discussion aimed at improving an individual's performance. There are, however, some principles to bear in mind which can make it easier to have such difficult conversations:

1. **Be specific:** Focusing on broad generalities might possibly produce general improvement, so if you wish to see an improvement in specific areas of performance, then you need to have both a reason why the performance needs to change and some examples to support your conclusions about someone's poor performance.
2. **Keep it impersonal and descriptive:** Adding personal emotions to the feedback is what turns feedback into criticism and will likely produce a defensive reaction. Describing evidence rather than offering an evaluation of the evidence is more likely to be constructive.
3. **Ensure that the feedback is goal oriented:** The feedback conversation should be intended to help someone improve their performance, rather than the opportunity for you to express all of your anger or annoyance at someone else. Expressing anger or annoyance may help you feel

better in the short term, but will likely give rise to resentment and further problems in the long term – and it will be unlikely to improve the other person's performance.

4. **Time the delivery of feedback well:** It is helpful to give feedback as soon as possible after undesirable behaviour has occurred, but you will need to ensure that they have sufficient information before giving the feedback. Often, it is helpful to give feedback again shortly before the specific performance is likely to reoccur.

5. **Ensure the feedback is understood:** By using reflective questions and asking the recipient of the feedback to put the feedback into their own words, it is possible to ensure that they understand the message that they are being given in the way that was intended.

6. **Give feedback on controllable behaviour:** There is some value in finding out about issues that affect an individual's behaviour, but it is unlikely that someone will change their behaviour if the issues leading to it are not under their control.

7. **Tailor the message:** The way we give a message will usually be shaped by our relationship with the individual, but it is also important to bear in mind someone's emotional state when we are giving feedback. Negative feedback given when someone is upset will not change anyone's behaviour and will likely reduce the quality of their relationship with you.

 KEY LEARNING POINT

Giving feedback to others is something that many people find hard. It requires the use of strong interpersonal skills, especially if we do not have a strong relationship with an individual, but the way in which we give feedback is often more important for the outcome than the feedback we give.

 REFLECTION POINT

Take some time to think about the following questions and write down some answers.

How easy do you find it to tell someone what you really think about what they did or said?
   What was the most difficult message you have ever needed to communicate? Why was it so hard?
   How could some of the ideas above help you to convey the message(s) you want to communicate?

INTEGRATION AND APPLICATION

Learning how to communicate effectively is something that will probably take a very long time. We start at birth when our eyes are taking in all the information they can, and when our brains are trying to develop ideas about what certain facial expressions of our parents mean, and ends when we stop communicating with others. Our brains make generalisations about what individuals mean and we learn to communicate with others in a way which we think helps get our messages across. Sometimes these generalisations are correct, sometimes they are nearly correct, but sometimes they are wrong, and we need to revise what we communicate and how we do so. The challenge is that individuals may well have slightly different interpretations of the meaning of the same message because of the perceptual and contextual distortions we will cover in the next chapter.

The most effective solution is to ensure that we engage in seeking feedback from others that the message we intended to send is the same as the one received by others. Whether we are presenting some information to an audience (Chapter 9), attending a job interview, (Chapter 17) or writing a CV (Chapter 16), or whether we are listening to others, giving feedback to others, working in a team (Chapter 10) or trying to lead others (Chapter 11), the way that we try to overcome perceptual/contextual noise and then encode and send messages will have a significant impact on our ability to do well.

There is an important question which this chapter has not fully addressed and it is this: 'Should we try to adjust our "communication style" for each individual we are talking to?' The answer is simple and complex at the same time. As a leader, we do need to be consistent in how we communicate what we need to communicate: if we are inconsistent, then our followers may well become confused and their trust in us may start to erode. Our communication is likely to have a slight formality about it and may be less humorous. As a friend, however, we should probably recognise that our ability to establish rapport and relate to others is based on how well we, as friends, understand and use similar patterns of communication and language to them. We could probably joke with a friend in a way that we might struggle to joke with a boss. Finally, as a colleague in a team, we might wish to use a mixture of informal and formal language but build others' confidence in our ability to do a good job by making definitive commitments and communicating regularly about our own progress. So, to answer the question, it is often less about the personal characteristics of the individual that we are talking to, but more about their own emotional situation and how we relate to them, in order to work well with and/or enjoy the company of others.

CONCLUSION

By now, you should be able to:

- Describe the communication process and how it can go wrong.
- Identify the various verbal, non-verbal and para-linguistic behaviours that can influence communication.
- Evaluate and develop your communication skills with a particular focus on communicating in difficult situations, giving feedback and active listening.

During this chapter, we have covered a wide range of issues related to how we communicate with others. We have actually covered a lot here. We have looked at the context and process of communication and the impressions we create, the impact of using different communication channels, and the verbal, non-verbal and para-linguistic aspects of communication, including the words we use. These components of the communication process were then applied to different scenarios such as communicating tactfully, using questions appropriately and establishing rapport. Finally, the chapter closed with an examination of how we can communicate effectively through active listening, giving feedback to others and communicating effectively with those from other cultures.

FINAL REFLECTIONS

Based on the content of this chapter, what do you now know about the processes of communication that you did not know before?

What key learning point had the most impact? Why?

(Continued)

(Continued)

Do your answers to either of the above questions have the potential to change your ability to communicate effectively? Why?

What will you now do differently? (Write this down and put it somewhere where you can see it regularly.)

══════════ **INTERVIEW QUESTIONS** ══════════

Think about the following questions. What might your answers be?

1. Tell me about a time when you tried to communicate an important message, but the message was misunderstood. What went wrong and what did you do afterwards?
2. What have you learnt by watching others around you communicate with each other?
3. Which communication skills do you think are the most important? Why?
4. Imagine that you need to communicate a complex idea to an intelligent audience. How would you go about it? What issues would you need to take into account?
5. From your own experiences, can you give some examples of poor communication?
6. Describe a time when a relationship with a fellow classmate, team member or someone you had to work with went wrong. How did you resolve the issue?

Chapter 17 gives a lot more information on selection interviews and the online content gives some guidance on these questions.

ADDITIONAL RESOURCES

Want to learn more? Visit https://study.sagepub.com/morgan to gain access to a wide range of online resources, including interactive tests, tasks, further reading and downloads.

Website Resources

Mindtools website: www.mindtools.com/pages/article/newCS_99.htm

University of Kent website: www.kent.ac.uk/careers/sk/communicating.htm

University of Manchester website: www.careers.manchester.ac.uk/experience/skills/communication/

University of Salford website: www.careers.salford.ac.uk/page/communication

Textbook Resources

Gallagher, K. (2010) *Skills Development for Business and Management Students*. Oxford: Oxford University Press (particularly chapter 4).

Hasson, G. (2012) *Brilliant Communication Skills*. Upper Saddle River, NJ: Prentice-Hall.

Pettinger, R. and Firth, R. (2001) *Mastering Management Skills*. Basingstoke: Palgrave (particularly chapter 3).

Rees, W. D. and Porter, C. (2008) *Skills of Management*. London: Cengage (particularly chapter 8).

Robbins, S. P. and Hunsaker, P. L. (2003) *Training in Interpersonal Skills*. Upper Saddle River, NJ: Pearson (particularly chapters 3, 4 and 5).

Smith, M. (2011) *Fundamentals of Management* (2nd edition). Maidenhead: McGraw-Hill (particularly chapter 11).

DEVELOPING CROSS-CULTURAL AWARENESS

CHAPTER STRUCTURE

Understanding the World Around Us	→	Perception and Cross-cultural Communication	→	High- and Low-Context Cultures	→	Models of Cultural Differences	→	Towards a Deeper Understanding of International Cultures

Figure 13.1

When you see the 🌐 this means go to the companion website https://study.sagepub.com/morgan to do a quiz, complete a task, read further or download a template.

AIMS OF THE CHAPTER

By the end of this chapter, you should be able to:

- Analyse your own and others' world views.
- Overcome perceptual and other cultural barriers in order to develop a good understanding of others' communication.
- Develop your insight into other cultures.
- Become more of a global citizen, able to operate with understanding in other cultures.

INTRODUCTION

We live in a global world. We can travel pretty much anywhere nowadays, we can see strange and amazing things, we can interact with people who are vastly different to ourselves and we can enjoy some of the most wonderful places that nature can provide. Yet, very often, our interaction with this international world in which we live does not help us to understand the people who live in it or the impact that they might have on us in our home country. Whether we like it or not, international economics and global trade affect the value of a house and the amount of tax we pay, as well as the exchange rate when we go on holiday. Those same pressures affect some of the social issues we experience and which we see played out on the international news – immigration, battles and wars, education, and so on – and yet the issues affecting us in our home country – an aging population, unemployment, international diplomacy – are likely to be exactly the same as those affecting millions of others in countries we can now travel to.

Even if we do not live in another country during our lifetime, we will almost certainly interact with individuals who look and speak differently to us, who eat different food and who have different world views, values, attitudes and behaviours. Societies are becoming much more diverse as global movement and travel becomes easier, yet typically we make little effort to learn another language, to learn about others' values and to understanding how others think, behave and communicate – and that level of effort will not help us in the longer term. In reality, as human beings (or even as animals), we tend to protect ourselves from and fight against that which we do not understand; this is natural, but there is a great deal more value in developing that understanding than in being defensive.

If we are open to learning about others' values, then we can start to change perceptions. Of course, sharing a common language makes life easier, but sharing a common language does not mean that we share the same values in the same way that looking similar does not mean that we share the same outlook on life. The globalised world that we now live in requires culturally literate managers and leaders who understand what it means to recognise that others might be thinking in very different ways to them. Being able really to communicate and understand how others from diverse backgrounds might react will enable us to operate far more cross-culturally than those competing for the same jobs, something that is very much needed in this international world.

If you are an international student (and even if you are not), you should read this

If you are an international student and have come to study in a country which is not your own - or are perhaps a student in your own country but studying in a language which is not your own - then you are probably already one or two steps ahead of many of the students in your classroom. You will likely have come to the university through a foundation programme or have achieved IELTS results of 6.0 or 6.5 or above. To become so good in a second language that you can study for a degree in that language is a great achievement, so well done! You may not understand everything that is being said and may struggle sometimes with different accents, different kinds of food, or the weather, and so on, but you are doing something that the home students might not understand, but should appreciate. They might not have left their family, their familiar surroundings and their community to spend a considerable time in a city and culture which may or may not appear welcoming.

Being an international student is not easy but can be a great adventure, and if you can break out of the need to spend all your time with other students from your own culture (if there are any) to learn more about the culture, people and language in which you are studying, then the experience can be a fantastic one. Learn how the transport system works, get to visit some of the key places, make friends with local students, improve your language skills and read the study skills chapters of this book.

(Continued)

(Continued)

If you are an international student (and even if you are not), you should read this

Above all, try to break out of your own community. For example, if you are a Chinese student, try to spend some time with home students, because it is one of the best ways to learn about the culture. What is the value of an education in another country if all you do is spend time with those from your own culture, visit some tourist spots and struggle with your English? You may not feel confident in your own English language abilities (even though you have every right to be confident if the university has accepted you onto the degree programme), but you will never develop that confidence or learn about others' cultures if you never break out of your own cultural group.

Finally, do try the local food! If you are in the UK, potatoes feature in nearly every meal somehow, fish and chips can seem pretty tasteless without salt and vinegar, each person will probably order their own meal, and there are distinct 'stages' in a meal (starter or appetiser, main course and then dessert with coffee) rather than of it all coming at the same time.

This chapter will examine the ways in which perceptual processes can impact helpfully and unhelpfully on building cross-cultural awareness. We will also spend time looking at how individual cultures might differ, how communication works differently in different cultures and what individuals can do to give themselves a competitive advantage in developing an international career.

Throughout the chapter, we will mention China fairly frequently for a number of reasons. Firstly, politically China is a not always an easy country for the western student to understand, but economically the impact of China on the global economy is very significant. Trying to develop a successful international career without understanding something – or without speaking at least a couple of words in Chinese (Mandarin or Cantonese) – about China is going to be hard. Secondly, the number of Chinese students studying overseas is very large, with any coming as postgraduates to complete a Master's degree or PhD in the UK. Thirdly, it is a country that western media and governments do not always understand well and occasionally view with suspicion. Finally, Chinese culture is very different from western culture, so to assume that Chinese thinking bears any resemblance to non-Chinese cultures is to make a significant mistake. However, there is no one Chinese culture, and for every statement that could be made about Chinese culture which is broadly true, there could probably be 10 other statements to contradict it. Some generalisations are given, but the intention here is not to offend or upset anyone. All non-Chinese readers of this chapter should take the ideas given here and treat them as hypotheses to be discussed with any Chinese students studying on the same course.

We will begin with a skills assessment, looking at our awareness of other cultures, our attitudes and values, and our engagement with the international environment.

There may well be very different responses to the questions posed above. While the world has become more global in terms of trade, and while we have a much better understanding of the world than we might have done some years ago thanks to the Internet, much of the world does not seem to want to understand how to operate with what some call 'global literacy' – and that is what the remainder of this chapter is about.

SKILLS SELF-ASSESSMENT

Complete the brief questionnaire below to see how well you could do when it comes to developing a global career. Give each item a score between 0 and 5, where 0 is 'not at all like me' or 'strongly agree', and 5 is 'very much like me' or 'strongly disagree'.

Item	Statement	Score
1.	As a human being, humility is an important quality for me to possess	
2.	I enjoy travelling to other countries	
3.	I love trying international and unusual food	
4.	I find it easier to talk to someone who looks like me than someone who does not	
5.	I think most other cultures are friendly	
6.	From what I hear on the news and read online, I do not think I really want to live in another country	
7.	Learning another language is something that I will never need or want to do	
8.	I believe that if people speak the same language – grammar, vocabulary – then they can easily understand each other	
9.	I am likely to find living in another county really stressful	
10.	The national and online media have a significant influence on my attitudes towards those from other countries	
11.	I do not really believe this chapter is an important one for me; I am never going to interact with those from other cultures	
12.	I know what a passport is, and I know (in very broad terms) what I need to do, practically, to get a visa	
13.	I have a good number of friends who come from a culture which is not the same as mine	
14.	I only really see the value in communicating with others who come from the same culture as me	
15.	My values and attitudes are more important and useful than those of people from other cultures	
16.	If you do not agree with me, then I am likely to think you are a bit weird or strange	
17.	I have a passport [Answer should be either 0 or 5 for 'yes' or 'no' respectively.]	
18.	I use my passport regularly to travel to countries which are quite different from my own	
19.	I have never spoken to someone who disagrees with my view of how the world operates	
20.	If I lived in another country, I know what I would find difficult	
21.	Going on holiday is one of the best ways to find out about others' cultures	
22.	Being at university has exposed me to many people who come from cultures which are different to mine	
23.	I interact regularly with individuals who do not speak my language	
24.	I am more likely to meet up with people who are from my culture than from other cultures	
25.	I know something about the history and culture of other countries	

UNDERSTANDING THE WORLD AROUND US

Viewing the world around us can be done on so many levels at any one time. At one end of the scale, perhaps you have been on holiday or perhaps you have actually lived in another country. Maybe you are an overseas student who is trying desperately to make sense of both living in another country and simultaneously trying to adapt to a university system which can seem somewhat strange. Whatever your level of engagement, developing an understanding of how the world operates is something that we build up over our lifetime, most of the time wholly unconsciously. We call it our 'world view'.

The view we have of how the world operates comprises a range of thinking on a number of levels (see Figure 13.2). Usually, we do not think – or be asked to think – about what our world view is. We simply carry around with us a series of assumptions about how the world operates. That view will be based on our beliefs.

WORLD VIEW

Our world view is our view of how the world operates.

The best way of explaining how this works is to illustrate it with a couple of contrasting examples. This might be according to religious or philosophical belief. One interesting area of study is that of the differences between eastern/Chinese cultures (more referred to as Confucian Heritage Cultures – CHCs) and western cultures. Take, for example, a Confucian viewpoint: a typical Confucian attitude will indicate that life carries us along and it is for us to make the best of it that we can. This differs considerably from a typical western viewpoint which 'empowers' the individual to 'go out and change the world to make it a better place' in some way.

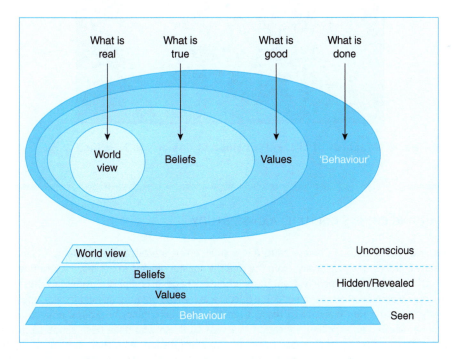

Figure 13.2 Components of a world view

CULTURE

Culture is the overarching system of rules and guidelines which determine what is and what is not acceptable.

Those beliefs often influence our view of what is good and what is bad – our values. From the view of the traditional CHC, we might suggest that modesty, respect for elders, filial piety and hard work are espoused. In a western culture, it would be very unusual to see a statement of values, since there is tolerance for a wide range of views about what is good and what is bad – often referred to as 'post-modernism' philosophy. The statement in the photograph in Image 13.1 – outside a department store in Anshan, in China's Liaoning Province – encourages adherence to a particular set of views. Cultural values play a significant role in creating a cohesive society, but are not always straightforward to understand or apply, as shown in Box 13.1.

Image 13.1 Basic standards of citizenry: values of one city in NE China

━━━━━━━━━━━━ **BOX 13.1** ━━━━━━━━━━━━

UNDERSTANDING CHINA'S CULTURE: A CASE STUDY

Trying to describe the totality of Chinese culture in a small box is a bizarre idea; actually, it is not possible. China has many cultures: *geographically*, from the wealthy coastal regions to the much less affluent interior, especially to the north west; *financially*, from those who work in government or business to those who work in the rural areas (some of whom have suddenly become extremely wealthy as land is built upon for housing); *culturally*, from the Han majority to those from the 56 ethnic minority groups; *educationally*, from those who have received an excellent education overseas to those who have been schooled in their own villages; and in terms of *family*, from those raised in a western manner with their mother and father (and occasionally a brother or sister) in an apartment, to those whose parents are migrant workers, living in a

(Continued)

(Continued)

city often hundreds of miles away, and who are raised usually by grandparents. Also, we could talk about differences in terms of local languages (often relating to the specific cities in which people were raised, e.g. 'Shanghainese' or 'Ningbonese' for those from Shanghai and Ningbo respectively) or in terms of the impact of the Chinese Communist Party on people's lives.

China is a huge country, but it has been changing a great deal, especially in terms of wealth. As indicated above, some less educated folk who lived in the countryside with a small farm and who were until recently fairly poor have suddenly found themselves millionaires as the cities have grown and land has been needed for housing. Families have sometimes been provided with up to three or four very nice western-style apartments in return for giving up the rights to their land, and with this comes access to travel and luxuries. Those who have grown up during the period of China's growth seem to have no problem displaying their wealth – watches, expensive cars, apartments – in contrast to a more Confucian viewpoint. Families which can afford to do so now often take overseas holidays during the Chinese Spring Festival holiday.

Socially, things are changing. The one-child policy – which reportedly distorted a preference for boys, based on the fact that the ancestral line of males had more influence in the family than did that of girls, and which meant that disabled children were abandoned or put up for adoption by their parents more frequently than their healthy counterparts – was halted in 2015 (Gracie, 2015), having left China with a major headache in trying to deal with an aging population. Young Chinese people now have more independence and less loyalty to the authorities than their predecessors, resulting in a law requiring Chinese students to honour their parents more (by allowing parents to sue their children) (Coonan, 2013), and anecdotally the Chinese Spring Festival TV Gala broadcast on CCTV is watched by young people less than it used to be.

Geopolitically, China is also facing some challenges. Some of its maritime neighbours are nervously watching Chinese military expansion on islands in the South China Sea, and North Korea is now explicitly seen as no longer a country China wishes to count as a friend. At the same time, China's alliances with a large number of countries have been growing. The Asian Infrastructure and Investment Bank (AIIB) has attracted a large amount of international attention. China has also been involved in the development of the BRICS (Brazil, Russia, India, China and South Africa) bank and has sought to expand its alliance with the ASEAN (Association of South Eastern Asian Nations – Singapore, Malaysia, Indonesia, Thailand, etc.) network. China is now a very well-networked country.

This is just a very small snapshot of some of the changes that China has been experiencing. Over the next few years, its leaders will need to deal with some spectacular challenges on a huge scale. It is likely that the economy will perform much less well than it has done in the past, while the expectations of its citizens in regard to personal wealth have been raised considerably. The aging population will likely cause issues for the quality of social infrastructure and healthcare, since national pensions are very small and healthcare provision is not free. The ever-increasing and constant investment in building the domestic airline and high speed rail network is a gamble that will have to pay off for the national economy; tickets for train and air travel in China are not expensive by western standards.

Finally, the current anti-corruption campaign is making working in the government a much cleaner occupation than it ever was. To a westerner, there is a perceived relationship between the 'Guanxi' culture (whereby the showing of respect to others by offering gifts is usually seen as a way to enhance a good personal relationship, and hopefully enhance the chance of sealing a business or family deal) and corruption, though the relationship is much less clear than might be expected. Government officials are no longer able to purchase excessively expensive gifts for others, nor are they able to accept them. This has included the provision of expensive management training (e.g. MBA programmes) for senior government officials at certain institutions (Zhang, 2014); time will tell whether that is a wise decision.

How well China is able to adapt to these pressures remains to be seen, but one thing is certain: China is not going to stop being a significant player in the world any time soon, and those who wish to do business in Asia will do well to learn more about the country.

REFLECTION POINT

Take some time to think about the following questions and write down some answers.

Thinking about your own country (if it is not China), what changes have been happening – socially, economically, politically?

How easy is it to identify your own country's culture?

How could any changes your country is facing impact on your own national culture?

While your own view of what is real, true and good are generally hidden, your own behaviour – what is done – is seen and is visible. Similarly, you will see the behaviour of those from other cultures. Our behaviour is the outworking of our reaction to what we see and experience, and that reaction is based on our perception.

As we have indicated, others' behaviour is a result of their reaction to events based on their own world view, just as our behaviour is a reflection of our world view. Because we do not usually talk about our 'world views' in conversations (or sometimes do not, even in conversations with those who are different!), we can arrive at an incomplete understanding of why people behave as they do, and this can cause us problems in accepting others.

KEY LEARNING POINT

Understanding another person's 'world view' is crucial for understanding how that person is behaving and what they are thinking – and why. This implies that we need to have increased conversations with those who are different to ourselves, to find out what they really think.

PERCEPTION AND CROSS-CULTURAL COMMUNICATION

The impression(s) that others have of you will determine how others communicate with you. For example, if they have the impression that you are lazy, then they might be somewhat more aggressive towards you than if that were not the case. Alternatively, if they think you are a hard worker and that you put more effort into your activities than others, then they will probably be more likely to believe you if you say you are overworked and too busy. This does not mean that we should do all we can 'to get people to like us' – going into a managerial career because we want people to 'like us' is a recipe for disaster, simply because we will always face conflicting priorities – but it does mean that we should communicate well enough for people to understand why we do what we do. Doing so in a world of uncertain perceptions is not easy, but if we understand how perception works, then we can probably minimise the impact of poor perception by controlling how and what we communicate.

 PERCEPTION

Perception is the unconscious process of attending to, interpreting and organising information so as to develop an understanding of the world around us.

The process of 'attending to' information refers in the definition to the fact that we do not pay attention to all that happens around us at any one time, but only to that which is within our perceptual 'field of vision' because it is going to have a strong and/or immediate impact on our situation, because it relates to something we are interested in, or because it will have a clear impact on others around us. We 'interpret' information according to our previous experiences and ideas about likely meanings. If we cannot easily interpret what we see, then we will likely investigate further, but if we think we have interpreted something correctly, that is much less likely – even if we are not correct in our interpretation. This becomes a particularly challenging issue when we are communicating across cultures. The final unconscious element involves 'organising' information and categorising it so as to ensure our brain can find the information next time we need it. Any mistakes in any of these three unconscious processes can lead to difficulties on our part and on the part of the recipients in the way our communication is delivered or interpreted.

There are several reasons for what we call 'perceptual errors':

1. **We form impressions and make judgements and decisions about people on very little information.** Our brain likes to take as little time as possible to reach judgements on others and, as a result, fills in any gaps in information itself from what it thinks is likely to be true.

2. **Underlying this is a need for meaning.** We try to categorise experiences/situations/people so as to achieve stability. This stability helps us to believe that our view of the world is the correct one, but, in doing so, we unconsciously introduce bias and distortion.

3. **We may attribute behaviour incorrectly.** If we believe that someone is highly capable and intelligent, we may believe that their poor behaviour on a particular occasion was due to factors outside of their control. This supports our stable world view and concurs with the 'information gaps' that our brain has already 'filled in' for us.

4. **Such processes are unconscious.** Rarely do we challenge or think about our judgements, preferring to believe that our original understanding is correct. As a result, we become reluctant to change our views. We are likely to do so only if we are challenged to support our original judgement with hard evidence, or if something significant happens that forces us to re-evaluate our original assessments.

5. **What seems similar in some aspects, is probably similar in all aspects.** Relating this to point 1 above, if there are two things that seem similar, then they probably are similar. When we are perceiving people, we can believe that two people who act in a similar way are probably demonstrating not only the same behaviours, but also the same attitudes and values. This leads to stereotyping and to incorrect approaches to communicating with two people who may display the same behaviour but for very different reasons.

6. **I find personal security with those who are like me, and what is different from me is not my preference.** This is not dissimilar to point 5: those who look like me will probably act like me, think like me and enjoy the same things that I enjoy. Of course, the reality is not usually so simple, but believing this means that the brain has to do a lot less work. In practice, what all of this means is that what I understand of the world around me and how it works is not necessarily the reality, and that means that I can get things badly wrong when I am planning how to communicate with others from different cultural backgrounds.

BOX 13.2

A FRIEND IN AN ASIAN COUNTRY

Some time ago, I had a friend who was working in an Asian country. After he had been there for some time, I asked him how it was going. His answer surprised me: 'I am finding it OK, but I am not sure if the locals like me very much.' On hearing this, I asked why he had said that. He replied, 'Because they are often spitting at me.'

We react to what we interpret of others' behaviour. People in his own country did not spit in public. In his culture, spitting was something that was seen as rude and impolite. That was his perception and he was reacting to it. In some other cultures, particularly some tribal cultures in Africa where water is scarce, spitting is seen as a sign of respect.

Some months later, I met him again and asked how things were going and whether people were still spitting at him. His response this time was much more accepting of others' behaviour: 'Oh yes, but I've learnt that the spitting was nothing to do with me – they were simply clearing their throats of phlegm.'

His perception had changed based on a lot more experience of that culture – and on many conversations he had had with local individuals much more familiar with this culture.

We interpret others' behaviour in the light of our own experiences, but when we move to another culture, *those experiences and interpretations become less relevant.*

One of the best ways to prevent inaccurate perceptions from affecting how we engage and communicate with others is to challenge ourselves and ask ourselves questions about our earlier assessments of others. This typically involves deciding to try to collect information which actually contradicts our original assessment. If we cannot find any having made an honest and definite attempt to do so, then we can be reasonably sure that our assessment is probably correct, but, of course, once we have *gathered* the information, we need to be very careful to ensure that we *interpret* the evidence accurately as well.

Of course, it is not just us that are affected by those perceptual processes – those receiving our communication are just as subject to these processes as we are, though they may not be aware of it. Some people like to discuss this with others that they communicate with on an ongoing basis, so that any misperceptions can be addressed easily. Some organisations will engage in what is known as '360° feedback', where information from others is used as part of a performance review process. This may not necessarily change *what* is done, but may change *how* it is done and *how* the individual communicates with others.

The final note here is that all the forms and components of communication covered below will generate perceptions in others. Our non-verbal behaviour, our para-language, our movement and gestures, and our appearance will all have an impact. Some of these we will be able to control, and others we might struggle to control, but it is important to recognise that the perceptions that others have of our communications will be affected by the way they interpret the ways we have communicated previously.

 ## FOR YOU TO DO

This is a perceptual activity and a private one for you to do on your own. Think of one individual that you are struggling to work with or get on with, and then ask yourself the following questions:

1. What is it that they did which originally generated your impression of them?
2. Why do you believe they did what they did?

(Continued)

(Continued)

3. What evidence do you have for that assumption (in question 2)?
4. Is there any other possible interpretation of that evidence? Could there have been anything externally which influenced them to do what they did?
5. Have they done the same thing, before or since?
6. If not, what set of factors might have led them to do what they have done? Will you change your perception? If so, what can you do to prevent it from happening to you? To others?

Whether your original perception was correct or incorrect, it may still not be possible to work with them. We do not all have the same values or attitudes and sometimes those can cause conflicts, but *if we have perceived someone incorrectly*, then at least we can start exploring those other issues with a little more objectivity.

KEY LEARNING POINT

Other people's perceptions of us will have a significant impact on how the messages we communicate are received and acted on.

REFLECTION POINT

Take some time to think about the following questions and write down some answers.

Have you ever found the behaviour of an individual from another culture to be rude and impolite?
    Did you discuss what you saw with other individuals from that culture?
    How do you know whether your interpretation of the behaviour was accurate? Or were you simply interpreting what you saw based on your own perception?

THE IMPACT OF UNDERSTANDING OTHERS' VALUES

Chapter 12 showed us that accurate communication processes require that messages encoded in one way should be interpreted or decoded in the same way, enabling both parties to understand the meaning. It also indicated that there should be a feedback loop to ensure that all parties were clear on whether the message had been understood well or not.

Communication across cultures causes problems in both these processes. Firstly, the encoding and decoding processes might work completely differently in different cultures (depending on how different the cultures are in terms of their world view). Secondly, the feedback loop might not yield the information expected for a variety of reasons, including that where some cultures might even find the need for such a feedback loop quite offensive.

Resolving these challenges sometimes requires a good degree of knowledge of how different cultures might use and interpret the communication processes. In cultures where individuals say exactly what they mean and this is clearly understood, there may not be a big challenge. However, other cultures might require a reasonable understanding of cultural values in order to interpret others' communication accurately and, in doing so, we start to talk about high-context and low-context cultures.

HIGH- AND LOW-CONTEXT CULTURES

HIGH- AND LOW-CONTEXT CULTURES

High-context cultures are those where, to communicate well, a deep understanding of the culture is needed.

Low-context cultures are those where little understanding of the culture is needed.

Since we look for meaning, one of the key difficulties with communicating cross-culturally is that we assume that items and behaviours we see as familiar may have very different meanings from our understanding. This becomes problematic when we are operating in what we call 'high-context cultures'.

Understanding the culture is sometimes vital to understanding the underlying meaning of what someone is trying to communicate. In a low-context culture, individuals will be clear and direct about what they mean, and communicating in low-context cultures is relatively straightforward.

 ── FOR YOU TO DO ──

Look at the statements below. Assume that they are given with a pleasant facial expression and little in the way of para-linguistic or non-verbal cues. Without knowing anything about the culture of the speaker, which of the three ideas below each expression do you think is being communicated by the speaker?

1. 'Thank you for your presentation. Very informative. Let me discuss your findings with my colleagues. We've no questions at this stage. Thank you again.'

   (a) 'It was a really great presentation which answered everything I think we need to know.'
   (b) 'I think your presentation told us some things, but it didn't really inspire us. It wasn't really what we are looking for.'
   (c) 'We're confident that you have given us what we are looking for, but if we agreed to everything you said right now, then we would look a bit foolish. No one ever agrees to everything right away without checking their information.'

2. 'We are concerned about the delays in this project. We were hoping that we can work with you more effectively than this, so if there is anything we can do to help you, please let us know.'

   (a) 'We want to continue to work with you to resolve these delays.'
   (b) 'We are not really satisfied with how this project is progressing. You shouldn't really ask us for any help, but we are offering it in order to maintain the relationship.'
   (c) 'We want to stop the contract and offer it to someone else who we think can do a better job.'

3. 'We like to maintain a cooperative and friendly culture here, so if you have any concerns, please let us know, OK? We're here as professionals to help each other work together in an effective manner.'

   (a) 'Please tell us about anything which concerns you: we really do want to help.'
   (b) 'We are here as professionals, so if you behave unprofessionally and complain about things, your behaviour will seen negatively.'
   (c) 'Unprofessional behaviour will be punished, so please complain to us about anything you see which you think is unprofessional. Anything seen as unfriendly is not tolerated here.'

4. 'The analysis of our own data tells us beyond any doubt that customers do not approve of the technology we are using for this product. We cannot go on like this!'

(Continued)

(Continued)

    (a) 'In order to avoid a problem, we will have to work as a team to change what we do.'
    (b) 'The person who thought this up must have been stupid. I hope he's no longer part of the organisation.'
    (c) 'I believe that the organisation's Chief Technical Engineer has the answer.'

5. 'I have always worked to make a difference to others' lives, but I don't know if this organisation wants me to spend time doing that.'

    (a) 'I am thinking of leaving this organisation.'
    (b) 'I am thinking of changing what I do'
    (c) 'I am thinking of changing this organisation.'

In reality, there are no right or wrong answers to any of the above statements, but an understanding of an individual's values and attitudes might have a significant impact on how you interpret their statements. If we take two countries – the Netherlands (which is a low-context culture) and China (which is a high-context culture) – we can see these differences very clearly. The messages given in high-context cultures can be very difficult to understand accurately. Box 13.3 provides some examples.

■ BOX 13.3 ■

EXPRESSING MESSAGES IN DIFFERENT CULTURES

Below are a number of statements indicating how individuals in high- and low-context cultures may express similar kinds of messages.

Expressing dislike about someone

Direct, low-context culture: 'I don't like them.'

Indirect, high-context culture: 'I am sure they have some significant strengths.'

Refusing hospitality

Direct, low-context culture: 'Thank you, but I really don't want any more.'

Indirect, high-context culture: 'It is very kind, but my wife needs me to be back at home.'

Offering hospitality

Direct, low-context culture: 'Can you come to the restaurant tonight?'

Indirect, high-context culture: 'My colleagues and I would be honoured if you could join us.'

Giving negative feedback

Direct, low-context culture: 'This was not done well.'

Indirect, high-context culture: 'The effort you made was very welcome. We have asked someone else to continue your wonderful beginning.'

Asking for more time to complete your work

Direct, low-context culture: 'I need some more time. Is that possible?'

Indirect, high-context culture: 'We are becoming more and more confident that we will be finished around the deadline that you gave us.'

The messages given in a high-context culture may seem contradictory to the message that is being given, but that is because there is little understanding of the values underlying the communication. If we take the examples above and assume they are given by a CHC such as China, Hong Kong or Japan, then we might recognise that:

1. Preservation of the other party's dignity is extremely important.
2. It is vital that the other person's confidence in us is not damaged.
3. The collective 'we' guides a lot of what is done: 'if you wish to work with us, then you will need to become part of the collective team'.
4. Hierarchy is really important, so that offers made by senior individuals should be received with a significant amount of respect.

These attitudes will govern the phrasing of the above messages. Other cultures will have their own attitudes, often around such issues as time, the speed at which good relationships can be built up, the extent to which hierarchy is important, how hard-headed (or, alternatively, empathetic) someone is allowed to be, how much risk is acceptable when undertaking new activities (or engaging in new relationships), and on how strongly they are expected to sacrifice personal activities and goals for the good of society.

 'BUT I HAVE A QUESTION ...'

... If this is the case, how can I be sure that I understand what anyone from another culture is really saying? And how do I know if someone comes from a high-context or a low-context culture?

These are good questions. There are various ways of getting to know a culture, though some are less beneficial than others. Visiting a place as a tourist is perhaps the most superficial action anyone can take. Apart from visiting or living in a second country, the best way to get to know another culture is by making friends and asking lots of honest questions. Learn from those friends and find out what their attitudes and values might be, and the extent to which these values affect styles of communication.

Doing those things – along with some background reading – will help you understand more about the cultures with which you are interacting.

In all of these things, the most effective approach is often a cautious one, which means not expressing yourself directly. It is not difficult to become direct subsequently, but to be direct and then to become more cautious is much more difficult.

 KEY LEARNING POINT

Communication with individuals from cultures other than our own means that messages may well be misunderstood. We need to recognise that this is the case and ensure that we gather feedback on our own communication and check the meanings of others' messages wherever possible.

MODELS OF CULTURAL DIFFERENCE

As we saw when we discussed China's multiple cultures (see Box 13.1, pages 276–7), stating that any country has one culture is likely to ignore subtle variations. Firstly, countries change: cultures and values evolve over time. Secondly, assuming that everyone in a particular culture shares the same values or behaves in the same way is likely to be inaccurate. Individuals from the same countries do differ. Research published in 2014 indicates that even the United States and Canada have distinct regional cultures (Dheer et al., 2014). However, while there is a variety of models accessible to researchers, two frameworks for identifying and explaining differences in behaviour have become accepted knowledge, and it would be inappropriate to ignore them completely.

Hofstede's Dimensions of Culture

The best known framework was developed by Geert Hofstede, a Dutch researcher, in the 1970s. Hofstede undertook research for IBM across its national subsidiaries in various countries and then produced his findings in a book called *Culture's Consequences*. Hofstede's model is one of the easiest to remember and the website that bears his name is well regarded by practitioners in the field.

Hofstede's model originally contained dimensions:

- **Masculinity v femininity:** How hard-headed and 'tough' is the national culture? Does it show much mercy, or is it intolerant of failure? How much pride is shown in the country by individuals living in that culture? Does the national culture seek harmony or show readiness to enter a conflict if pushed a little?
- **Power distance (high <> low):** How accessible to the general public are organisational and national leaders of the country? Are leaders and managers expected to be aloof and deeply respected, or is the general attitude one of friendliness? Are organisations likely to be very hierarchical, or relatively flat in terms of structure?
- **Uncertainty avoidance (high <> low):** How readily do individuals in the country accept (or even embrace) risk? Is there an entrepreneurial spirit, or do individuals prefer a cautious approach? How quickly would decisions be made if things were uncertain?
- **Individualism v collectivism:** How readily do individuals put the national interest above their own? Is there a noticeable desire to serve others, or are people generally competitive and/ or selfish? How is wealth regarded in the country – as a personal asset or as something to be shared?

A fifth dimension was added, following research into Chinese/Confucian cultures.

- **Long-term outlook v short-term outlook:** To what extent are individuals interested in closing the single deal or in a much longer term relationship? How will parties react if one party breaks the agreement in a minor way? Will countries be interested in talking to solve a problem, or will they resort to more 'para-legal' means?

The most recent edition of the book included a sixth dimension (Hofstede, 2010):

- **Indulgence v self-restraint:** To what extent does society allow individuals to freely express emotions of excitement and joy? Is there societal pressure not to express such feelings? How freely can individuals enjoy having 'fun'? Societies which are free to have more fun tend to believe that they are in control of their own destiny.

The questions given here are not exhaustive, but should give you enough information to understand the dimensions of the model.

Hofstede's original research has been criticised by some on the grounds that it committed a fatal flaw in undertaking the research in the way that it did. When we are examining what we see and trying to make deductions based on what we see, we are in serious danger of interpreting behaviour based on our own understanding (see Box 13.2 for a simple example of this), and that may well be inaccurate. Some have criticised Hofstede for carrying out research in just this way: that interpretations of culture were originally based not on reality but on perceptions and interpretations of reality by individuals who did not necessarily understand whether those interpretations were accurate, or did not take time to check. As time has moved on, the model has received a great deal of acceptance internationally and research methods for Hofstede's recent work have become somewhat more refined.

 'BUT I HAVE A QUESTION ...'

... You mentioned earlier that it is dangerous to generalise, so presumably it is really dangerous to stereotype and generalise at a national level? If so, what can we do about it?

Yes, you are correct on both issues. It is dangerous and unlikely to be wholly accurate to generalise or to say that everyone from a certain culture will be high on 'power distance', low on 'masculinity', and so on. In some ways, this addresses a fundamental issue about the application of research. Research can only model what it sees, and what research sees is always measured in terms of probabilities. It hardly ever produces absolute certainty, and the same is true for cross-cultural research: it produces a model or a series of hypotheses which need to be tested every time we meet others.

So, to answer your second question, on what we can we do about uncertainty, we need to test those hypotheses – it is as simple as that. So, we use as many opportunities as we can to find out about people, to learn what is important to them, how they deal with certain issues and how they determine what is important and what is not important. As we will see later on in the chapter, learning about others' attitudes and cultures from individuals themselves – often called 'ethnography' – is one of the most important steps to understanding another's culture.

Having said that, the models given above do give us a set of thoughts from which we might start asking questions, and in some business settings, groups of individuals in some countries are more inclined to follow a national culture than to follow their own individual values. This is going to be particularly true in more collectivist/communitarian societies, of course.

 FOR YOU TO DO

Think about your own national culture. Your own culture (world view, beliefs and values) will have an impact on how you see other cultures and how you behave towards them. Try to answer the following questions:

(Continued)

(Continued)

1. Looking at the dimensions listed above, how high or low on the dimensions given would you place your own culture?
2. How easy was it to answer question 1? How clearly defined is your own national culture?
3. Can you readily think of individuals from your country who do not fit your own national culture?
4. What would be the dangers of ignoring the cultural differences between you and someone else in (a) a group coursework situation and (b) a business meeting?
5. What could you do to get to know international students studying at your university?

==================== KEY LEARNING POINT ====================

Describing individual, group and national cultures is not easy, and unless we are dealing with individuals there will always be a degree of generalisation taking place. We can, however, begin with our own analyses of individuals we know by using the models as a framework - to be tested and proved or disproved as appropriate.

TOWARDS A DEEPER APPRECIATION OF INTERNATIONAL CULTURES

As a student, you are likely to be exposed to a large number of students from international backgrounds. In the early 1990s, there were very few international students in the UK, but as political systems around the world changed and as countries began realising the cultural and other benefits of inviting international students into their classrooms, those numbers have grown considerably.

This brings certain challenges – to nations, groups, institutions and individuals – but also opportunities to learn about the world around us, which have never before been so easy to find out. It is rare but now possible to find students studying in the UK from Papua New Guinea, as it is to travel to China to learn in a Chinese university. As mentioned in the introduction, the world has become global and to ignore others' cultures is something we do at our peril.

The questions therefore are: 'What skills and qualities do we need to develop in order to become culturally aware?' and 'What can we do practically develop such awareness?'

There are a number of answers to these questions. For the former question, Box 13.4 outlines some of the qualities leading to 'intercultural competence' identified in research, and the content below (based on Figure 13.3) identifies some relevant actions, some of which give us a fairly superficial view and others which help us understand other cultures in considerably more depth. Figure 13.3 shows some ideas.

==================== BOX 13.4 ====================

WHAT IS 'INTERCULTURAL COMPETENCE'?

Sheridan (2005) identified a number of characteristics - the 7Cs - of what was called 'intercultural competence', relating to the extent to which an individual:

(Continued)

(Continued)

- Possesses knowledge about being 'cross-cultural' (Capability).
- Considers all stakeholders – including international customers and employers – in making decisions (Care).
- Is used to engaging with diverse and international communities (Connection).
- Is humble enough to be aware of their own strengths and weaknesses in relation to cross-cultural operations (Context).
- Understands situations without making any judgements (Contrasts).
- Develops followers according to their cultural backgrounds (Consciousness).
- Has experience of living abroad (Cultural immersion).

Questions:

1. When you look at these 7Cs, to what extent do you possess these qualities?
2. How could you develop those qualities you do not possess?

Let us look at how each of these can give you some benefit when it comes to developing intercultural competence. Much of this is written from the perspective of a UK student wishing/needing to develop their intercultural competence in relation to other cultures, though exactly the same principles will apply to anyone wanting to learn about a culture which is not their own.

- **Visiting new places** can help us to understand the more obvious differences between cultures, for example the language or the history of a particular place, but we are unlikely to develop any kind of

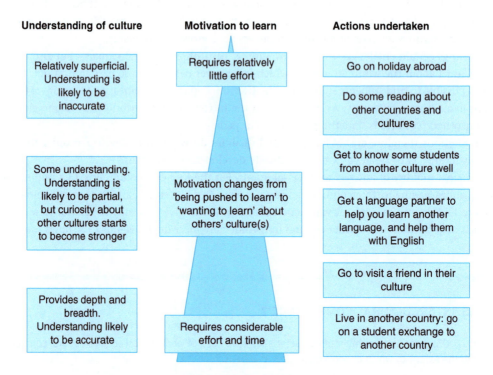

Figure 13.3   Developing an awareness of others' cultures

detailed understanding of the culture simply by seeing things which are different. In fact, the more things we see that are different without trying to understand them, the more we will be in danger of developing stereotypes based on very limited knowledge of the culture. Perceptual theory tells us that we are then more likely to find evidence to support that inaccurate understanding, rather than evidence which contradicts it. However, it is better to realise that cultures are different than stay at home and wonder why other 'strange' cultures do not understand you.

- **Doing some reading about other cultures** can be more helpful. This still has a sense of superficiality about it in some ways since you are relying on what you read (and reading comments on Facebook is not going to be helpful), but you will learn things. Reading develops your knowledge about a country and, without knowledge, your understanding will be very limited. Box 13.5 provides some basic knowledge with regards to life in China.

■■■■■■ BOX 13.5 ■■■■■■

DEVELOPING YOUR KNOWLEDGE: HOW MUCH DO YOU KNOW ABOUT ONE OF THE WORLD'S FASTEST GROWING ECONOMIES – CHINA?

The questions below are intended to prompt you to develop and deepen your knowledge of life in China. That 'knowledge' only becomes 'understanding' when you start to discuss these questions with others and identify the implications of the answers.

For non-Chinese students: Once you have tried to answer these questions yourself, through your own research, find a Chinese student to help you understand how the various issues given here are important in China.

If you are not from either the UK or China yourself, then feel free to replace the phrase 'different from the UK' with 'different from your own country'.

If you are Chinese, then be open to helping others understand your culture, and do not worry about laughing gently at their answers sometimes, but do not embarrass them too much, of course.

1. What are QQ and Weixin (pronounced 'Way-shin')?
2. Why are there so many migrant workers in China? And why do they often leave their children behind to work many hundreds of miles away?
3. How does Mandarin differ from Cantonese? Which is easier to learn?
4. Who or what are Pin-Ying, Baidu (pronounced 'buy-doo') and Guanxi (pronounced Guang-shee')?
5. The word for 'horse' and 'mother' is written *ma*, so how does a Chinese person differentiate between the two meanings when they are speaking?
6. What is the 'Spring Festival'? And the 'Qing Ming' holiday?
7. How far (in km) is Beijing from Hong Kong? How long would it take to do that journey by high-speed train? How are trains in China different from those in the UK?
8. Which are more secure: Chinese train stations or UK train stations? How far in advance do you know the platform for your train in China?
9. What is the name of the Chinese currency: the renminbi, the yuan or the 'kwai'?
10. What is Houkou (pronounced 'Who-koe')? And how does it affect the lives and welfare of Chinese people?

You might want to try and develop a similar set of questions for others to learn about life in your own country, but do not humiliate or embarrass anyone else in the process – unless they give you permission to do so!

If you have the correct answers (and you will need to talk to a Chinese person to get these; they are not provided in this book), then you will be able at least to begin a reasonably good conversation with another Chinese student.

- **Get to know some students from another culture well.** While we do need to be very aware that not everyone from one particular culture is the same, the better we can get to know other individuals and their cultures – their behaviours, their values and their beliefs, and their world view – the better we can engage in constructive relationships with others from that culture. A great deal of learning can be developed through discussion. The easiest way of doing this is to work with international students on group coursework.

 ——— 'BUT I HAVE A QUESTION ...' ———————————————

... We are a group of students from a variety of different cultures working together on coursework, which can sometimes present certain challenges. Are there ways to make this easier?

Working with those who have different values and cultures from our own can sometimes present challenges, and in some cases can even produce conflicts within the group. Of course, the solution is to identify exactly where the problem might lie. It may be that some students:

- May not seem to speak as much in the group. This does *not* mean that they do not wish to contribute to the group, only that they may not understand as much as native speakers, or that they need more time to process the information. The solution is to find out informally what the issue is, to reassure those students that their contribution is valuable, and then to give time and space to ensure that their contributions are heard and made.
- May do their work in a different way or at a different timescale to others. This may be related to their values and experience in their own culture. The solution is often to ensure that the group develops some standardised rules and values (including procedures for communicating effectively) and then to ensure that everyone understands the values and norms of the group before getting too far into the work (see page 210 on storming in Chapter 10).
- May want to stick together with other students from their own culture rather than others. If you were living in another country, you would probably want to do the same. It is a lot easier to understand and communicate with those who naturally eat the same kind of food, share your cultural values and speak your language.
- Do not want to go out drinking or take part in other social activities with group members. Certain social events might be very common in some cultures, but may be disapproved of by certain cultural values or contradict religious values. The group needs to ensure that social events can be accessible to all students; it would not take too much imagination to organise such activities.

There may be other challenges that you face. As in working with anyone with a slightly different lifestyle or background to your own, solutions usually relate to addressing concerns from *all* individuals in the group, rather than just the leader, or the loudest.

- **Get a language partner to help you learn another language, and help them learn to speak your language.** This is a great way of showing how committed you are to learning more about others' culture. In the UK, we (in general) are very lazy about learning languages, partially because we think: 'So many people around the world speak English, so why bother?'
  - The answer is very simple: It shows commitment and engagement with that culture, and more often than not, it will be a significant advantage to being able to do business in that culture.
  - Doing so with a language partner rather than in a class will enable you to ask questions which occur to you about that culture as you progress, and will also help the international student to develop their English skills in an informal situation.

- **Visit a friend in their culture.** Spending time with people you know in their own culture is probably one of the best ways to learn about that culture. Because they are a friend, you can ask them nearly anything you wish about their culture, you can see what they do, how they act and how they relate to others and the world around them. You can never buy that kind of experience from a book (even this one!).

CULTURE SHOCK

Culture shock is the emotional reaction to recognising that your experience, knowledge and understanding of a different culture are incomplete or inaccurate, but knowing that you cannot isolate yourself from that culture.

  - Some cultures would be very happy for you to ask whether you can do this, while others would not react well to such a request and would expect you to wait to be invited, so you need to take time to develop the friendship first so that you can understand which is most acceptable. You also need to be very clear on who will pay for what. Assume at the outset that you will need to pay for everything, including a gift for your host. Misunderstandings can damage friendships and it would be a big shame if you got this wrong.

- **Live in another country or go on a student exchange.** Long-term exposure to another country cannot fail to enhance your understanding of other cultures, and so a semester abroad – either on an exchange programme or, if not, as part of a study abroad programme – would be a great place to start. Your university will usually have a number of 'partner universities' where students can go and study for a semester or a year, and where their students will come to your own university. If you do go abroad, make sure you ask questions about health insurance, bank accounts (including getting access to your own money while abroad) and visa requirements; these can take some time to set up.

  - Student exchange programmes are usually free in terms of course fees, will contribute to your degree in the same way as if you were studying in your own university, and will usually give you a good 'study experience' in the other culture. Study abroad programmes will vary in these areas, but will usually require you to pay extra. You must also check whether such programmes will contribute to your degree, or whether they are going to mean that you just add a year onto your degree.
  - You also need to be prepared to experience culture shock as you immerse yourself in that second country (see Box 13.6). The best way of reducing culture shock is to get to know as many people as you can from that country and talk to them about what you might expect to experience, or go to that country on holiday, where things may still seem strange, but where you will be able to escape 'the strangeness' relatively quickly and insulate yourself against it temporarily by staying with other foreigners. (This latter strategy will *not* work if you are genuinely trying to become culturally competent, but it can serve as a short-term coping strategy.)

===== BOX 13.6 =====

LIVING IN ANOTHER COUNTRY: DEALING WITH CULTURE SHOCK

Living in another country for a period of time is the best way to develop an understanding of that country. Not only can you build on any understanding that you developed while talking to people from that country in your home situation, but also you can get to see the culture in action. It does take a certain amount of

(Continued)

(Continued)

courage and an adventurous spirit to be able to go and live overseas, but then employers will very likely appreciate seeing that same adventurous spirit in any candidate who applies for a job. If you are an international student, you may have already experienced culture shock

Culture shock arises from a realisation that some of all or your expectations are not being met. Individuals going through culture shock typically go through a number of stages, as shown in Figure 13.4.

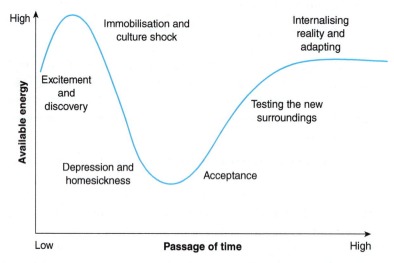

Figure 13.4 Emotional reactions to culture shock 'Kubler-Ross Transition Curve'

The graph in the figure – based on the Kubler-Ross Transition Curve – was developed to explain individuals' reactions to situations where they were being subjected to changes in their environment over which they have no control, and thus it could apply to any student coming to university for the first time (see Chapter 1) as much as to someone going to live abroad.

At its heart, the model works like this. An individual going abroad might be expected to have an initial sense of excitement regarding their new situation. Everything seems different and those differences make life interesting and exciting. Just as we might enjoy becoming like children again and learning (see the relevant content in Chapter 14 on 'Physical and Practical "Play"'), so too we now enjoy learning from our new situation by trying to make sense of it. After a time, however, we recognise that the sense of fun starts to decrease as we struggle to get basic things done. Recognising that we need help with our language skills and cannot do what we would find second nature in our own country raises some serious issues for us. We may for a while try to deny that we find certain things hard, but eventually come to accept that we need help. Having found sources of help, we learn to experiment within our new environment and test out ways of doing what we need to do. Eventually, we find ways to cope and adapt and we get used to living in the new culture. This does not mean that we never have any more issues in getting used to the culture: there may still be surprises – some exciting and some depressing – that we experience, but it does mean that we can relax and be more content.

Questions:

1. If you have always lived in one country, how would you feel about living abroad? What would be the main challenges you would face – cooking, travelling, finding friends?
2. How would you cope with these issues?

REFLECTION POINT

Take some time to think about the following questions and write down some answers.

How important do you think it is to develop your own sense of awareness of the world around you?

Do you study with (attend lectures, do group work, live in the same accommodation, etc.) people from a different cultural background? What have you done to find out about their culture?

Do you think you can use any of the ideas in this section to develop more cross-cultural awareness?

INTEGRATION AND APPLICATION

Living in a global world requires that we engage with the world around us. To do so, we need a number of personal qualities:

1. Humility – to admit that there may be other and better ways of doing things.
2. Open-mindedness – to accept that others can have a different way of doing things.
3. Acceptance – to allow others to continue doing things their way if they actually work well for them and have no impact on the organisation.
4. Understanding – of the idea that others have a point of view which may be different to yours.

In developing our cross-cultural skills and our readiness for a world that is unquestionably global, we need to possess knowledge about other cultures, but knowledge is not going to be sufficient – the ability to apply our skills to use that knowledge is crucial.

In all that we do, we need to have motive, means and opportunity. In seeking to develop cultural literacy, we can consider the following:

The motive for being global. We look at the world around us and see changes happening on a scale that limits the effectiveness of unilateral action, and we wish to position ourselves strategically (see issues related to personal branding for job applications in Chapter 16) to ensure we can take advantage of such opportunities.

The means. We can look at the ways in which our skills (or lack of them sometimes) can be enhanced so as to demonstrate to employers that we can work in a global world, and take action to do so. This can sometimes take us on journeys – including real physical journeys sometimes – during our studies which can appear scary, or alternatively as adventures.

The opportunities. There are now numerous ways in which we can take advantage of opportunities to interact with other cultures. From examining the diverse communities in which we live (including student accommodation) to spending time with individuals we know in an environment which is unfamiliar, we would be foolish not to seek to understand those with whom we interact – and will interact – on a daily basis.

CONCLUSION

You should now have a good idea of how to:

- Analyse your own and others' world views.
- Overcome perceptual and other cultural barriers in order to develop a good understanding of others' communication.

- Develop your insight into other cultures.
- Become more of a global citizen, able to operate with understanding in other cultures.

This chapter has sought to establish an awareness of what it means to interact in a global world. We have covered what we mean by a world view and discussed issues relating to our beliefs, values and behaviours. We have discussed issues of Chinese culture and practice as a way of providing examples of what it means to have a global mindset and what it means to try to understand one of the most important economies and biggest countries in the world. We have discussed how perceptual processes can present challenges in understanding others and how communication processes can become difficult, particularly in high-context cultures. The chapter has also presented a brief discussion regarding theoretical models of culture – useful for comparing cultures with each other – and provided some practical steps that individuals can take to develop an increasingly important ability, namely cross-cultural literacy.

FINAL REFLECTIONS

Based on the content of this chapter, what do you now know about being a global citizen that you did not know before?

What key learning point had the most impact? Why?

How have you engaged with other cultures?

How could you change your perceptions and attitudes regarding different cultures?

What will you now do differently? (Write this down and put it somewhere where you can see it regularly.)

 ━━━ INTERVIEW QUESTIONS ━━━━━━━━━━━━━━━━━━━━━━━━

In nearly all cases, the questions in previous chapters have only been about determining your skills and abilities in certain areas. However, being a global citizen involves knowledge as well as skill, and so some of the questions which might be asked in this area could try to find out how much you know as much as what you are able to do.
    Think about the following questions. What might your answers be?

1. What do you think are the biggest issues currently facing international organisations?
2. What difficulties would you expect to face if you were offered a role in another country?
3. Imagine a situation where you - as a departmental manager - needed quickly to resolve a conflict between two individuals of different cultural backgrounds about an issue where both held very strong and opposing views. How would you handle such a situation?

Chapter 17 gives a lot more information on selection interviews and the online content gives some guidance on these questions.

ADDITIONAL RESOURCES

Want to learn more? Visit https://study.sagepub.com/morgan to gain access to a wide range of online resources, including interactive tests, tasks, further reading and downloads.

Website Resources

Blog website from a student at Oregon State University: http://blogs.oregonstate.edu/dorrespblog/cssa-competencies/4-multicultural-awareness-knowledge-skills-and-ability/

INSEAD Knowledge website: http://knowledge.insead.edu/career/the-rise-of-multicultural-managers-2552

MindTools website – cross-cultural communication: www.mindtools.com/CommSkll/Cross-Cultural-communication.htm

MindTools website – working with diverse groups: www.mindtools.com/pages/article/cultural-intelligence.htm

Sage publication: www.sagepub.com/sites/default/files/upm-binaries/4965_Connerley_I_Proof_3_Chapter_5.pdf

Study.com website: study.com/academy/lesson/cross-cultural-communication-definition-strategies-examples.html#lesson

Textbook Resources

Smale, B. and Fowlie, J. (2009) *How to Succeed at University: An Essential Guide to Academic Skills, Personal Development & Employability.* London: Sage (particularly chapter 10).

14 PROBLEM SOLVING AND CREATIVITY

CHAPTER STRUCTURE

The Typical Problem-solving Process → Creative Problem Solving → Understanding Creativity → Techniques for Enhancing Creativity → Blockages and Barriers to Creativity

Figure 14.1

When you see the 🌐 this means go to the companion website https://study.sagepub.com/morgan to do a quiz, complete a task, read further or download a template.

━ AIMS OF THE CHAPTER ━

By the end of this chapter, you should be able to:

- Follow both rational and creative problem-solving processes.
- Describe the key components of creativity.
- Develop and enhance your creativity.
- Recognise blockages to creativity in yourself and in others.

1. INTRODUCTION

Before we go too far into this topic, let's look at two quick questions:

'How many seconds are there in one year?'

'A horse rider arrived in a town on Friday, stayed for three days and left on Friday. How can you explain this?'

We will have a quick discussion of the answers in the conclusion to this chapter.

There are a number of factors which distinguish an effective manager from an ineffective one. Two of them are the ability to make effective decisions based on good and timely information and the ability to solve problems that others cannot solve. The latter requires an ability to analyse situations from unusual perspectives; that is what this chapter is about.

There are discussions about whether individuals are naturally creative or are more comfortable following rules and solving structured problems by using solutions which have worked before. In reality, most individuals can be helped to add more creativity to their thinking. This creativity relates not just to solving problems – although that is often an area where creativity plays an important part – but also to establishing an innovative vision for an organisation, where capturing individuals' imagination can be a powerful motivator, or to giving a speech where presenting a unique view of something can enable individuals to see things in a totally different way.

This chapter will set out some of the ways that this can be done and will first look at standard models for solving problems before moving on to examine some of the issues involved with understanding creativity and applying tools to enhance our creativity, but as usual it begins with a skills assessment.

SKILLS SELF-ASSESSMENT

Complete the brief questionnaire below to see how well you are able to solve problems. Give each item a score between 0 and 5, where 0 is 'not at all like me' or 'strongly agree', and 5 is 'very much like me' or 'strongly disagree'. Some of the questions here may seem the same as others, but there are some subtle differences.

When I am faced with a challenging problem, I usually …

Item	Statement	Score
1.	Will try to seek help from others around me	
2.	Look to see whether there are any answers in the books I have	
3.	Will try and try and try to fix it	
4.	Will wait until the problem has passed	
5.	Will ask someone else to solve the problem for me	
6.	Will try to find a parallel situation which helps me to find a solution	
7	Will look to see what others do	
8.	Adopt a very structured and analytic approach to solving the problem	

(Continued)

(Continued)

Item	Statement	Score
9.	Watch how others have solved similar problems	
10.	Work on the problem for hours and hours to show how committed I am to finding a solution	
11.	Try to use my understanding of relationships between relevant concepts to build up solutions	
12.	Am sure that I can develop a solution	
13.	Am able to evaluate potential solutions recommended by others	
14.	Feel comfortable accepting untested ideas from others	
15.	Enjoy doing new things without being able to fully evaluate their impact	

Developing novel solutions to complex problems is something that many managers have to do, especially those in highly competitive markets where innovation is the main source of competitive advantage. The faster that creativity can be facilitated and used, the more impact a manager is likely to have in such organisations.

INTERACTIVE
TEST

You can find an interactive version of this test, along with answers, comments and thoughts about these questions can be found on the companion website for this book at https://study.sagepub.com/morgan.

THE TYPICAL PROBLEM-SOLVING PROCESS

The frameworks for solving a structured problem can seem relatively straightforward and typically follow a set of stages: clarifying the problem, establishing causes, developing options and making a choice. You can find a lot more about the stages of problem solving by going to the companion website at https://study.sagepub.com/morgan.

FURTHER
READING

Stage 1: Clarify the (real) objective – what do you really wish to achieve (what is the problem you really want to solve)?

In some organisations, there can be tension between what is said and what is believed, or between what is said and what the underlying issues really are. Here personality really does play a part. If you are nervous about upsetting others or want to please other people, then it is possible that any disagreements between people will not be addressed and any solution will not really help the organisation move forward. Instead, you will likely end up with a solution that maintains the present situations.

The challenge for solving any problems in this case is that the way you 'frame' the problem (i.e. the way you describe what the problem is) will have significant implications on the solutions proposed and chosen. If the real objective is not clarified at the beginning of the process, then it is unlikely that the problem will be solved, and the same is true if the problem is not identified correctly.

Stage 2: Establishing the cause(s) of the problem

In the 1950s, two British individuals, Charles Kepner and Ben Tregoe, identified a decision-making process which became a well-established framework for problem solving (Kepner and Tregoe, 2013).

This rational and scientific approach helps to identify and verify the cause of a problem by seeking to identify where, when and with whom problems are occurring, are not occurring, and any changes or differences in situation which might explain why they do and do not occur.

The K–T process (as it is called) has five steps (reflecting the first two steps, 'Problem definition' and 'Establishing the causes', of a typical process):

1. Define the problem.
2. Describe the problem.
3. Establish possible causes.
4. Test the most probable cause.
5. Verify the true cause.

Defining, describing and establishing possible causes (steps 1–3) for a relatively structured problem is quite straightforward in the K–T approach, and when it comes to gathering information, the process identifies some very useful questions to ask.

Let's take a simple example: 'We have an individual in a team who does not seem to be working particularly hard.'

(The words 'seem to be' give us permission to be flexible over how we define the issue.)

As a simple issue, we could see this as:

• A failure of the management to set up policies to penalise poor performers.
• A poor attitude on the part of the worker.
• As a lack of ability to do what is required.
• Or, as lacking a good understanding of what the worker's role is and what they should be doing.

However, to take a more structured approach to identifying the causes of the issue, we could produce a table such as Table 14.1 in order to help us to get to step 3 in the approach, that is to establish possible causes. The main advantage that the K–T approach gives is found in the headings across the top of the table: where the problem is, where we might expect the problem but where it is not occurring, what makes the difference now, and what has changed over time.

If we include some information about the example given above, then this will help to develop the table.

Table 14.1 Defining, describing and establishing possible causes for a problem

	Is	Could be but is not	Differs in the situations	Changes over time
What the problem …	You hear reports that a team member is engaged with the activity	You hear reports that other team members are completing their work	The issue seems to be with this team member	Up until three months ago, the team member worked as hard as the others
Where the problem …	This individual is located in the sales team	This individual also works in the project management team, but it has not reported any issues	The sales team is smaller and has a larger budget and task to undertake	Similar problems were reported in the data collection team a year ago, but stopped three months ago

(Continued)

Table 14.1   (Continued)

	Is	Could be but is not	Differs in the situations	Changes over time
			This individual came from an IT company whereas others rose through the organisation to join the sales team	This individual has become less and less engaged with the task
When the problem ...	This happens every time the team meets	This does not happen in any of the other activities the individual is involved with	The team is different The demands on the team have increased	The problem has become more pronounced over the past three months
Extent of the problem ...	Limited to just this individual	Could be that no other team members seem to feel engaged, but this is not the case	The individual is not behaving in the same way as the other members of the team	Gradual apparent decline in effort over the last three months

The above analysis can lead us to a very different hypothesis from the four alternatives listed. When we look at this information, we might argue that the issue is less likely to be a failure of the management to set up policies to penalise poor performers, a poor attitude on the part of the worker, a lack of their ability or a poor understanding of their role, but more likely to relate to team dynamics in some way, since that is the only differentiating factor.

The next two steps are testing and verifying the probable cause (steps 4 and 5). When we look at technical problems, this pattern works well. We find out what the issue seems to be by addressing possible solutions according to how likely it is that we think they are going to solve the problem. However, when it comes to the management of people, we need to recognise that actually implementing and testing different solutions may cause additional problems itself, so we need to gather information from the individual to see what might work on a hypothetical basis.

To test our thinking, we need to examine where the issue *is occurring* and *is not occurring*. If we are to identify an accurate potential cause, then it should clearly differentiate between these two situations. In addition, we could look at our potential causes to identify where the cause is occurring, and whether the same problems are arising as a result. Table 14.2 gives us a framework to analyse our example.

Table 14.2   Developing possible causes for a problem

Potential cause	True if ...	Likely cause?
The team does not have the correct resources	All the team are reacting the same way	No
The leader's behaviour is not appropriate to motivate the individual	There are/have been issues in this team and no other teams; there have been issues in other teams that this leader has led	Possible
The task is too difficult for the individual	The individual's behaviour has been consistent	Unlikely – the individual's engagement has decreased

The five steps above are all intended to help us to understand what the real issue is and to identify the cause correctly, which in turn helps us to generate options which will more accurately focus on the particular problem.

————— 'BUT I HAVE A QUESTION ...' —————

... What do you do if you do not know and cannot get data about where problems are or are not occurring, and so on?

Sometimes we cannot get all of the details we might like to know to follow the Kepner-Tregoe approach as fully as we might want. In such situations, we sometimes have to investigate the causes of problems as far as we can, implement a solution and see whether that solves the issue. If not, then we simply need to start again.

There are times when we simply do not know what the cause may be. Sometimes, the issues can be those of life and death. If we take something like the discovery of AIDS in the 1980s, then all that seemed to be happening was that people were getting colds and pneumonia and had a much lower immunity to certain conditions than they should have had. It was not until some investigation revealed linkages with other situations that the AIDS virus was discovered. It was then that the search for a treatment could begin.

You can read more about how the discovery of AIDS took place at: www.healio.com/infectious-disease/hiv-aids/news/print/infectious-disease-news/%7B6ce521b4-db00-4c51-830b-7d0873677e36%7D/hivaids-the-discovery-of-an-unknown-deadly-virus.

Of particular relevance was the way that researchers made these linkages - identifying where the condition was and was not - as a means to discovering what was really going on.

Stage 3: Generate the options for solving the problem

Once the main problem has been identified, the next step is to generate options which might help to solve the problem, and often this is where creativity becomes an essential part of the process. Ideas on how to use different techniques to produce creative results are presented on pages 306–317. There is also often a need for balancing the rational and the intuitive, as explained in Box 14.1.

————— BOX 14.1 —————

RATIONAL AND INTUITIVE STYLES OF PROBLEM SOLVING

In referring to our use of certain parts of the brain, psychologists sometimes tell us that some people are more 'right-brained' (they use the right side of the brain more than the left side) and others who are more 'left-brained' (they use the left side of the brain more than the right side), and that this can lead to two distinct sets of abilities.

The argument is that those using their left side more will tend to produce more standard answers to problems, while those using their right side might produce more novel and innovative answers. The reason is that the left side of the brain is where rational activity occurs: decisions will be broken down into small steps in a process so that decision making becomes a scientific activity.

In contrast, those using their right brains more frequently will be adept at solving unstructured and novel problems and will take a holistic approach - involving many different concepts - where decision making becomes a creative art. One of the key phrases here is 'more frequently': individuals are rarely *only*

(Continued)

(Continued)

right-brained or *only* left brained, and most people will operate both intuitively and rationally depending on a variety of factors.

Similarly, there is not 'one best approach': either approach may help to make most decisions and solve most problems, and while a management team will be unhappy about supporting a decision without relevant facts and figures, a good team will also understand the role of intuition. In some ways, the two approaches are seen as complements, rather than substitutes. If your style is more rational than others and you struggle to accept ideas and suggestions from those taking a different approach, then the best advice is to:

- Learn to listen for signs of intuition.
- Accept hunches from others.
- Come to terms with fears associated with intuitive styles.
- Yield to, and go along with, hunches.
- Encourage those using such styles to carry out post-decision validation.

Which best describes your preferred approach – or do you think that it depends on the nature of the decision to be made?

Do you struggle to accept the ideas of those who base their ideas more on intuition than facts and figures?

Stage 4: Make a balanced choice

Once a small number of appropriate solutions have been identified, the next step is to choose which to implement, and how, when and with which people. A decision about the choice of solution would usually be based on a number of criteria related to the problem we are trying to solve. We would usually score each solution according to those criteria. For some decisions, the criteria would need to be weighted to indicate relative importance. Making mathematical calculations then becomes relatively easy and the best decision would then be the one with the highest score.

Making and/or implementing the decision is likely going to rest with the relevant team or committee, which in turn needs to be provided with appropriate resources over a particular timescale.

Whatever is chosen, it needs to be capable of addressing the relevant problem without creating bigger problems. A large organisational change project will almost certainly create other issues (e.g. staff morale, people being made redundant or even internal sabotage) but in the longer term, the benefits have to outweigh the costs.

USE OF RATIONAL PROBLEM SOLVING

In some form or another, we are conditioned to solve problems in this kind of way. Time, effort, social convention and other constraints force us to have a logic explaining why we do what we do, and ensure that we have the facts and figures to support our point of view. Such processes are even at the very heart of academic life, where critical thinking demands that we support our case with logic and ideas based on good research and published theory.

Given the right circumstances, we can often be more creative than we are conditioned to be. The next section will examine how creative individuals construct processes to assist them in developing innovative ideas and solutions.

KEY LEARNING POINT

Following a systematic process can be helpful and useful when solving certain kinds of problems.

REFLECTION POINT

Take some time to think about the following questions and write down some answers.

How confident are you that you can solve problems that you come across in your life?

Do you think others have the same problems to overcome as you?

How often do you ask others how they have gone about solving a particular problem – that is, do you ask for advice or do you prefer to solve the problem on your own?

CREATIVE PROBLEM SOLVING

As mentioned above, we are typically 'programmed' to engage in rational, common sense decision making. However, given the right circumstances, we can often be more creative than we are conditioned to be. At Harvard Business School (see Box 14.2), the teaching is universally done through the use of reality-based business problems which are discussed in class, with the aim of enabling students and managers to see things from different perspectives.

BOX 14.2

CASE STUDIES IN CLASS

Since problem solving is an important skill for students to develop, lecturers sometimes use what is known as 'The Harvard case teaching method' (www.hbs.edu, 2016). This involves using detailed and extensive information about scenarios, often about 15–20 pages in length. Students are asked to identify what they think are the 'real issues', and then develop potential solutions. Case studies are used constantly at Harvard as a way for aspiring managers to develop their analytical, problem-solving and debating skills.

Case studies are an excellent way of developing your problem-solving skills. The issues are usually complex and the case material is often full of information which is distracting and unhelpful. This can be seen as problematic, but it reflects real life where the issues are unclear and vague, and where different people will be giving you different pieces of information.

In class, there is only very limited use of PowerPoint and class time is spent in a carefully managed discussion of the issues. At Harvard Business School, students are graded on their engagement with each other in class as well as in more formal ways. These discussions will develop individuals' self-confidence and their ability to defend a particular point of view.

By the end of the class, the board will be full of the relevant concepts and theoretical models written by the course tutor as the discussion has gone on. The world is not straightforward, and as much as we try to construct a world that is simple so we can adopt and apply solutions easily, the use of case studies goes a lot further than many teaching tools to show that believing in a simple world without ambiguity is likely to be unproductive.

UNDERSTANDING CREATIVITY

Creativity in terms of problem solving means that we can see a problem in a new way and/or we can identify new possibilities that have the potential to change something around us in some way. In order to understand how to use it, we need to understand more about what is involved in 'being creative'.

We recognise creative ideas when they make us sit back and think 'I wish I had thought of that', but understanding what creativity is can potentially be more problematic. In fact, we can examine creativity on a number of levels. We can think about the outcomes of creative processes, we can think about what people call 'the creative arts' (where representations of reality are shown in different forms – dance, poetry, artistic painting, drama), we can think about biological functioning and how hormones and our brains function, and we can think about the psychology of creativity and how mental functioning can impact on how creative we are.

 CREATIVITY

Creativity is a personal quality shown through the production of innovative ideas.

The definition of creativity, therefore, might also vary accordingly, so we might need to take a very broad view.

Amabile (1998) indicates that the ability to be creative has three components: technical knowledge, creative abilities and motivation. As we will look at below, undertaking tasks creatively can be a great deal of fun, though it does require an ability to enjoy 'fun'.

KNOWLEDGE

Knowledge and expertise come in very different forms and may be used by different people in different ways. Creative individuals use knowledge not simply by applying it to situations based on previous experience, but by identifying relationships between different concepts and ideas. The mental manipulation of those relationships enables creative individuals to develop innovative ideas that others will not have thought about. Knowledge can also apply to processes as much as to facts and ideas, so changing relationships between concepts and then understanding how those changes can lead to changes in process can radically alter the view an individual might have of any one particular problem.

There is a slight irony here in that, often, the longer someone has been in a job role, the less creative they are. We might expect that the greater someone's knowledge from their experience, the more creative they would be. In reality, the longer someone has been in a role, the more fixed their ideas become – perhaps based on thinking that they 'have seen it all before'.

CREATIVE ABILITIES

Solving a novel or unstructured problem will require the ability to see the problem in relation to ideas and knowledge gained from elsewhere, but in a way that others are unable to do. It seems that successful scientists spend a great deal more time defining a problem than those who are less successful (Mumford, 2000). However, it also seems that more creative individuals will spend time playing around with visual representations of problems to identify relevant concepts and possibilities than will those who are less creative. It is at this stage that extensive knowledge and expertise becomes essential, since it is necessary to know which concepts may be relevant and useful, and then to know how they may be reorganised.

Constructing and manipulating a visual representation of a problem requires an understanding of the relevant ideas, concepts and processes, but research indicates that developing a creative definition of a problem is more successful when the individual concentrates on processes and concepts, rather than on goals (Mumford, 2000).

Understanding how to be creative is about understanding how to build hypothetical possibilities – without restrictions – and then working out how those hypothetical possibilities can be brought into reality. Solving a problem that others cannot solve often involves seeing the problem (to conceptualise it) differently from others. Typically this means that we conceptualise the issue differently, come up with solutions that others have not developed and/or implement a solution in a way and at a time that others have not thought about.

KEY LEARNING POINT

Allowing our mind to be flexible and to play around mentally with ideas, knowledge and concepts is much more likely to lead to the development of innovative ideas and solutions to problems.

REFLECTION POINT

Take some time to think about the following questions and write down some answers.

What is going through your mind as we start to look at creativity? Do you think you are creative? Do you love being creative, but feel that you cannot for some reason?

Were you creative as a child, do you remember? Did you enjoy painting, drama, writing poetry? Did that ever stop? If so, why?

Do you ever 'see', in your mind, the ways that ideas could relate to each other? Do you ever ask yourself the question 'If this changed, what would happen?

PROCESSES AND FORMS OF CREATIVITY

As a process, creativity comes in stages and in different forms. Whetten and Cameron (2011) indicate that there are four stages in a creative problem-solving process:

- Stage 1: Preparation (which involves problem definition and gathering information)
- Stage 2: Incubation (largely unconscious, where ideas are combined in an attempt to find a solution)
- Stage 3: Illumination (a conscious 'Eureka!' moment, where an insight is recognised)
- Stage 4: Verification (where evaluation of the proposed solution is undertaken).

The development of innovative ideas can take place at any stage, but the conscious enhancement of ideas typically takes place in the preparatory stage.

As indicated above, there are different forms of creativity (Whetten and Cameron, 2011):

- Imagination – where creation is seen in terms of the creation of new and radical ideas (e.g. Google Glass).
- Improvement – taking an idea and making it better in ways that others had not thought about (e.g. development of flat screen TVs).
- Investment – taking a competitive approach to achieve results faster than others (e.g. the 'battle' between Samsung and Apple to develop similar but different products).
- Incubation – where networks of individuals are brought physically together and lively discussion of new possibilities can take place (e.g. businesses in Silicon Valley).

These forms of creativity are complements and suitable for different circumstances, depending on the magnitude of the change and the speed with which any change needs to be implemented. Each of these four forms of creativity can take various forms, reflecting different techniques for enhancing and demonstrating our creativity, but, in reality, most individuals can demonstrate at least one of them.

TECHNIQUES FOR ENHANCING CREATIVITY

Maybe you consider yourself to be creative or maybe not. However, most people are creative to some extent (as indicated above in terms of the four forms of creativity), though it is true that some need more encouragement to feel free to demonstrate that creativity and, for others, a little insight into various tools and techniques may be useful.

Brainstorming

This very frequently used word describes an activity where individuals contribute to a discussion. It can be used at any stage of a problem-solving process (including identifying the nature of a problem), but is most often used when trying to develop solutions to problems. A record is usually taken of these contributions in a way that others can see (e.g. flipchart) and a discussion can be very energetic.

There are, however, a significant number of pitfalls when undertaking what is typically called 'a brainstorming exercise':

- The discussion becomes evaluative. The golden rule of brainstorming is that there should be no critique or evaluation of anyone else's ideas. Brainstorming is solely for gathering ideas and thoughts, and should never be evaluative.
- The discussion can be uni-thematic. That is, the line of thought initiated by the first individual to speak can dictate the area of focus for the entire brainstorming exercise. If a discussion does not give space for other, and perhaps contradictory, ideas, then the discussion may lose its value and may not help solve the problem.
- Group-think may mean that no one feels able to contradict what others have said. Perhaps this is because they might be made to feel that their ideas had no value or are intimidated in some way. Having unity within a team is very important for a team to be able to function well (see page 204 on the characteristics of an effective team) but developing a sense of unity which does not allow for disagreement is not helpful.
- Not everyone has the chance to talk. If a discussion is progressing at a fast pace, then there will probably be little chance to ensure that everyone has a chance to contribute and the group may get to a decision too quickly for others to voice any disagreement. Those chairing such discussions need to be sure that everyone has the chance to say exactly what they think.

- The written record is not accurate. There may be occasions when individuals unconsciously filter out and do not record aspects of the discussion which might later prove to be really valuable. Those omissions may mean that certain pieces of information are never followed up.
- The discussion is based on assumptions. It is very tempting to believe everything that everyone says, but often (and particularly in a single fast-moving conversation) statements can be made based on subjective opinion, rather than on the more objective evidence. There are times when assumptions can be correct, but trying to develop solutions to a problem means that we need to be sure that those solutions will actually solve the problem, rather than generate a set of brand-new and more challenging problems.
- The wrong objective. It is very encouraging to have a discussion where the objective is to reach a decision – or even gather a number of ideas – but brainstorming is not about making decisions, it is about gathering ideas. There are often times when gathering ideas needs much more consideration than one meeting will allow. Extending the process over more than one meeting may mean that accurate information can be collected and people can have time and space to think about other ideas.

As a tool for bringing people together in order to generate options, brainstorming can be very effective and will engage others in the final solution.

Examining Past Experience

The great thing about some problems is that either we have solved the same issue previously, or someone else has probably experienced the same problem before and has found a way of solving it. It is extremely tempting to assume immediately that a solution tried and tested previously is going to work for you – or that what worked last time will work again. There is often a sense of 'Yes! That will work …' when we find that someone else has developed a solution for the same problem that we are examining, but we do need to exercise a little caution and perhaps ask questions such as these:

- Is our situation exactly the same as the one experienced before?
- Has anything changed in terms of the timing of our problem compared with that previously?
- Are the people involved this time likely to react in the same way?
- Are the resources we have access to the same as those we had before?

Adopting others' solutions – or adapting them to fit our own circumstances – is a common approach. It is why managers seek to learn from others, attend training courses and read appropriate books and journals. There is little wrong in learning and trying a solution that others have found works for them. Box 14.3 presents some ideas that may help you adopt a solution.

━━━━━━━━━ BOX 14.3 ━━━━━━━━━

SOURCES OF IDEAS

If a manager has a problem that is relatively common or has been faced before by others, then there are a variety of sources of information at their disposal:

(Continued)

(Continued)

- **Professional magazines:** These magazines (published by professional organisations such as the Chartered Institute of Personnel and Development (CIPD), Chartered Institute of Management (CIM), Institute for Chartered Accountancy for England and Wales (ICAEW) , etc.) will often contain stories about how particular individuals or organisations have gone about solving a particular issue.
- **Academic business magazines:** Publications such as the *Harvard Business Review* have a long history of providing articles giving expertise and case studies on how particular issues might be solved in a variety of organisations.
- **Training courses:** Short training courses are a very common source of information if an organisation is struggling to know how, for example, to motivate its people or undertake a particular process. These are often more useful for knowing how to implement a solution once a solution has been identified than for identifying potential solutions, but informal conversations at training courses can often be very insightful.
- **Conferences:** Attending a conference on a particular theme can be a very useful way of obtaining expertise from those presenting talks about how they addressed particular issues (or for giving the results of academic research into particular ideas, which can help to stimulate thinking).
- **Networking events and activities:** Discussing your problems with others can often be done easily and effectively over a cup of coffee at networking events, or at conferences or training courses. It is during informal conversations that you can learn about others' ideas and get the opportunity to take such conversations further. People are often more open to discussing real challenges in an informal setting that they would not wish to discuss in a formal one.
- **News articles:** There are occasions when innovative solutions to particular problems can be seen in the regular press. Innovative ideas will often capture the imagination and so do sometimes appear in appropriate business publications (e.g. *Wall Street Journal*, *Financial Times*, etc.).
- **Internal sources:** Individuals sometimes stay in organisations for a long time, and may have valuable 'institutional memories' of where something has not worked but a good solution was found, or where a solution did not work. Those individuals can often hold key information giving detailed context and may have a good understanding of why something arose in the first place. Minutes of meetings may also give some information, though going through a lot of detailed comments and information is not something most managers have a great deal of time to do.

 REFLECTION POINT

Take some time to think about the following questions and write down some answers.

If you were to use any of the above sources of information, which would you be most likely to use first – or not at all?

   If you did use such sources to identify potential solutions, what would be your next step in using the information?

Analogies and Metaphors

What you know of how the world operates can be used very effectively to develop analogies and representations of problems from very different angles – some refer to this as a process where we make the 'strange familiar' or the 'unfamiliar strange'. These analogies may come from nature, from other activities we undertake, from other forms of relationship, from sport, and so on, but the idea is that we take the situation we are facing and use an analogy to see the problem in a different way, without the constraints of one view of the problem. The better analogies are those where there is no close relationship between the real situation and the picture we are creating in our mind, but they are also used more effectively where we are very familiar with both situations and are clear about the elements – verbs and items (or nouns) – present in our pictorial representations of the real situation.

Let's imagine for a moment that we have a problem in our organisation. We need to increase the amount of creativity we are seeing, but we are uncertain of how we can do that, so we think about the assumptions we are making and ask ourselves a number of questions. We could assume, for example, that everyone has some creative talent that they wish to use and, therefore, the issue is releasing that talent.

Does this remind me of anything? Perhaps a pan with a lid being heated on a gas stove, where we are boiling some water to cook some vegetables, and we wish to let the steam escape to impact on the environment outside the pan.

What are the elements in what I am thinking about? There are the pan, the water, the steam, the vegetables, the lid of the pan and the heated gas.

What might those elements represent? The pan could be the individual, the boiling water could be the ability to be creative, the steam could be the explicit demonstration of that creativity, the lid could be the constraints and the heated gas under the pan could be the motivation and incentives.

Are there any elements of this analogy missing, or which need to be removed or changed in some way? There may be different kinds of vegetables in the pan. It is unclear, perhaps, what the vegetables are, so we might be able to remove them, but we must make a note that we have done so in order to track back in due course. Alternatively, we might be able to suggest that the lid of the pan could be made of glass rather than metal, implying perhaps that we develop some way to determine how much creativity is taking place and keeping an eye on it (i.e. we can see the water moving) where perhaps that has not taken place previously. In any event, the answer to this question is very likely to bring us closer to solving the problem.

Bearing in mind this analogy, *how are we representing the problem?* We would like to see how we can heat the water faster so as to allow more steam to escape from the pan more easily.

At this point, we can ask one more question about the analogy as a way of facilitating the generation of ideas, but we almost need to forget that we are using an analogy. If we wanted to heat the water so that we had more steam escaping more quickly, what could we change? Some ideas that we would naturally think of might be to:

- Add some salt so that the water heats up more quickly.
- Remove the lid to allow more steam to escape.
- Stir the water to ensure that the gas is heating all the water equally.
- Turn up the heat under the pan.
- Put less water in the pan so that the water heats up more quickly.

The final step here is to reinterpret these solutions in the real situation – to 'de-analogise' the situation, if you like – and, in doing so, we may find that the ideas do not always fit. This is fine, because an analogy is just that – it is not intended to be a 100% accurate representation of the real situation – and, in fact, in presenting representations that do not reflect reality, we may find additional ideas that we would not have otherwise identified. (The only thing that can be 100% accurate is the situation itself.) Looking at the example above, we could reinterpret the five ideas above as follows:

Add some salt so that the water heats up more quickly	Add something - training, mentoring, incentives, conferences - to the organisation or the individual to increase their creativity
Remove the lid to allow more steam to escape	Try to identify and remove any barriers to creativity
Stir the water to ensure that the gas is heating all the water equally	Create situations where individuals are mixing - or are being mixed - with other individuals to create more creativity The additional question then becomes: 'What are we using to stir the water? Would stirring the water with different items - spoon, fork, large spoon, small spoon, etc. - make this idea more or less effective?
Turn up the heat under the pan	Stimulate creativity, in different ways. Perhaps, create different or more incentives for individuals to be creative, perhaps make creativity more explicit as an organisational objective
Put less water in the pan so that the water heats up more quickly	This would work for the analogy (pan heating water), but would not work in a situation where we represent individuals with less creativity (i.e. less water) producing more creative outcomes (i.e. more steam), so the analogy falls down here, but that is OK

As in the example above, some solutions do not seem to work, but most people would argue that it is better to have more ideas than less, and we can always discard them later on when deciding which solution(s) to implement (and, of course, the example means that we could implement a series of ideas, rather than just one). However, if an analogy does not work or 'retranslate' well back into the specifics of the real-life situation, then we could always ask the question 'Is there a way of making the solution in the analogy work better?' Using the last solution proposed in the analogy above, this might mean *replacing* the water with something else which heats up faster and produces more steam than water, or, translating this back, *replacing* the individuals in the team or the organisation with more creative individuals.

Note that the verb used here, namely 'replace', is used in both the analogy *and* the real-life example. One of the great things about using an analogy to manipulate (or 'reorganise') the imaginary situation is that you can change the verbs *and* the nouns in our pictorial representations, or vice versa. Taking the example above, our thoughts might go like this:

We might decide that we can stir the water – i.e. stir up or stimulate creativity – in various ways, but could we replace the word 'stir' with something else – e.g. 'divide'? Well, we can't 'divide water', so is there a better analogy that we could use? Maybe we should use something other than a pan holding water as an analogy? Translating this back: of course, our knowledge about creativity would tell us that division rarely enhances creativity (or indeed many things), so maybe the analogy we are using is fine.

━━━━━━━━━━━ ▪ BOX 14.4 ▪ ━━━━━━━━━━━

CREATING A PAINTING: AN ANALOGY ITSELF

When we think of what some call 'the creative arts', we might think of drama or painting or writing. There are many ways to undertake those activities, but there are times when we can view the problem-solving process itself as an analogy. Let's take the example of creating a painting.

For example, we could imagine a painter sitting down with a very well-defined image in mind of what the artist would like to produce. The perceptions of light and colour are clear and the artist knows exactly where items within the image might fit in order to produce something very pleasing to the eye.

In a way, we could argue that the finished piece of work is evidence of a great deal of skill. Every detail is precise: on the face of an individual in a portrait, for example, the light reflected in their eyes appears very natural, the shadows in the room are consistent with the light source and the picture even shows the detail of the thread of the fabric in the clothing. Everything is planned and clear, and the time and effort required for most people to produce that piece of work would be considerable.

We could argue that the outcome of a creative problem-solving process should be something very natural, where there has been a great deal of thought and where the artist has produced something using their knowledge of paint and human perception. In creating the painting, we could suggest that the artist has taken time to mix their colours, to imagine the impact of the painting if items were lit in a different way or if there were different elements in the image, but the execution and creation of that imagine have been exquisite.

However, we could use the process of painting to demonstrate the creative process in a very different way. For most of us lacking such skill in producing fantastic works of art, we might start with a sheet of paper, some paint and paintbrushes, and, with a vague idea of what we want to create, we could just start and adapt the image as we go. As we paint, we are not constrained by the need for accuracy or for an accurate representation of the image we have in our mind, we simply enjoy creating something new. (In some ways this represents how I am writing this box itself.) We have fun and we are creating and then recreating an image by asking questions: 'What if I put a person or a chair in that position, rather than that one? What if that box was pink instead of blue, or dark blue instead of light blue?'

The image is probably not going to be something that you would hang in a gallery – you might need some expert to come in and help you produce and define your image – but you will have asked a large number of questions either implicitly or explicitly in creating what you have created, and you will have created something that you enjoyed creating.

In the same way, we can see that creativity often comes in the early stages of solving problems where we are defining problems and generating alternative images for ourselves, while needing those who are good at attending to detail and putting plans into place to implement the output of a more creative process. As such, we could say that producing a creative work of art is an analogy to the creative problem-solving process.

All the examples above represent a progressive series of thoughts and questions which can arise when we start to use the familiar to represent unfamiliar problems we are struggling to solve. We can see that by following the process above – thinking of an analogy, identifying the different items in the analogy and then manipulating the analogy – we can start to define problems in very different ways, and by 're-translating' the example, we can actually identify further questions which might help us further. It is the *ability and freedom to ask questions* which can start us developing some solutions we might not have thought about before. Having a *working knowledge of the issues* is vital for the re-interpretation of the analogy: without that knowledge, it is not possible to play around with mental images of relevant concepts and issues (nor would we know what is and is not relevant).

FOR YOU TO DO

Look at the problems given below. What kinds of analogies might be used to represent them?

1. The production line keeps slowing down because the operators work at different times. Is there a way of enabling the production line to move at a constant pace?
2. An individual in the workplace is acting as a bully and needs to be brought under control. How could this be done?
3. There is a political battle going on between two senior managers, both of whom have the same amount of power. How might you stop the battle?
4. The organisation needs to develop new and innovative projects which can enable the company to establish a completely new business product line, but while the workforce is happy to take risks, it seems that the workforce is not particularly creative. How might you go about ensuring those new lines are established?
5. An individual in your company is very traditional and feels more comfortable with old processes than new ones, even if the individual knows that the old ones are inefficient. How might you convince this individual to try the new ones?

There are no right and wrong analogies for any of these, but as you explore how they might be used, you might find that you change your analogies to fit the situation closer.

Reverse the Definition

Understanding how all the elements in an issue come together to form a problem can help us to expand our range of potential solutions, but by deconstructing the problem and recognising those linked but separate elements, we can often develop solutions which seem insightful and original. Key to being able to do so is the recognition of the verbs, adjectives and nouns we are using. The clearest and well-known example of this kind of a situation (where you will probably be aware of the solution adopted) was when one well-known car producer needed to increase car production greatly in order to keep up with demand in the United States in the early 1900s. Cars were made by teams of employees working together and each car took a while to build. Once one was built, the team moved around the factory to build the next one.

We can state that the problem was 'How to get the teams to work faster to meet demand by moving from one car to the next more effectively?' Immediately, some clear solutions come to mind:

1. Increase efficiency by decreasing rejection rates and increasing quality.
2. Decrease the size of factory so that the teams do not have to move too far.
3. Subcontract production to other car producers.
4. Improve the training given to the teams.
5. Improve the number of teams working in any one factory.

All of these might well have the impact of increasing car production, but of course there would be a cost to pay. Buying a new factory would incur significant financial investment, ongoing rental payments, increased numbers of employees needing training in complex skills quickly, and increasing efficiency can only be done so much: the stronger the demand for faster production, the more likely efficiency would decrease, not increase.

Examining the nouns and verbs in the way we have defined the problem above gives us:

- Teams
- Faster
- Work
- Move
- Car

The words 'meet' and 'demand' might also have some impact here, except that they refer to the outcome of the problem, not the problem itself. In the same way, it is not helpful to consider adverbs (e.g. 'more effectively') since they describe how well something might be done, and again refer to intended outcome rather than the inputs to produce such outcomes and so cannot really be changed.

Using the idea of 'reverse definition', we could ask 'How might we view the problem if we changed any of these words?' If we changed the word 'team' to 'individual', how might that impact on our perception of the problem – likewise, for 'fast' and 'to work'? 'How might limiting the "movement" of the teams in some way help us deliver our outcome? Are there parts of the "car" that we can change or remove so that we can speed up the process?'

Asking such questions might suggest to us that maybe the words 'more effectively' are better than 'faster', and perhaps we might develop proposals that refer to improving the teamwork rather than anything else. Alternatively, we might consider the nature of 'the work' itself, and enable the teams to work in a different way, or not at all.

In this real-life example, the problem was viewed as simplistically as this: 'The team built and then moved the car before starting on the next one.' Instead, the production process could be done by individuals working on small elements of the work and the car could be moved rather than the team. As a result, Henry Ford developed the world's first production line, and the car production revolution began.

Physical and Practical 'Play'

Being creative can be great fun, but requires that we are OK with having 'fun'. Enabling senior managers to play with ideas can sometimes be a challenge. Senior managers can sometimes appear to believe that they are expected to keep our sense of fun hidden, or even that it disappeared the day that they took on any managerial responsibilities. With the right encouragement or facilitation, however, most people can be encouraged to let the more child-like side of their personality emerge for others to see.

Our ability to play with ideas and allowing ourselves to see possibilities that we had not thought about before can be enhanced by aspects of physical play, especially in terms of using our hands to create new representations of reality. Two tools that get used in childhood have perhaps surprising applications in management, namely Lego® and Playdough®. Both come in different colours, and blocks of Lego come in different sizes, shapes and configurations. Each characteristic (size, shape, colour) can be used to represent different aspects of mental concepts and physical realities, so creating and recreating those realities can enable new possibilities to be established. In the same way, Playdough can be used in a very flexible way to allow individuals to create items which are not constrained by being forced into particular shapes (perhaps representing organisational rules).

Management consultants can sometimes use such tools to enable individuals to come up with ideas that they had not thought about before. In the same way that analogies and metaphors can enable certain aspects of life to represent particular elements of managerial problems, so, too, can 'physical analogies' such as Lego be used to represent particular aspects of organisational life (Image 14.1). They have the advantage that they can be used in different ways, without any processes limiting what would otherwise be seen as difficult or challenging, so that an innovative solution can be developed and further problem solving can be done subsequently to reduce any implementation difficulties.

A typical session using Lego or Playdough would begin with a warm-up exercise, to enable participants to feel comfortable about engaging in something playful. In many cases (and ignoring for the moment those situations where participants have children who might enjoy playing with such toys), it will have been quite a long time since these adults engaged in something considered playful. Some individuals will relish the experience, while others will struggle a little to relax and reveal that aspect of their behaviour which is more child-like.

Once participants are comfortable with the idea of this and engaging in some playful activity, the facilitator will usually explain how the 'toys' can be used to represent certain aspects of whatever problem or issue is being dealt with. This may require a little demonstration, but the facilitator will need to consider carefully how much they use the toys themselves to demonstrate the process: too much and the participants may limit the extent to which they allow themselves to think freely about the issue; too little and the exercise might not work because the participants may not understand how the toys could be used to represent reality.

The third stage is to give sufficient space and time for the participants to play with the toys, to discuss with each other the potential consequences and outcomes of constructing realities in various ways, and then finally – as the fourth stage – participants may have some fun looking at each other's creations (animals, structures, buildings, etc.) while someone explains how they went about creating what they have created and why.

Enabling a sense of play is an important aspect of facilitating creativity. Most people enjoy being a little child-like and having some fun, and if that enjoyment can lead to the development of innovative solutions, then the activity will have served a number of purposes.

Subdividing Problem Characteristics: Concept Mapping

This method of developing creative ideas and solutions derives from activities undertaken to define the problem. By clarifying the characteristics of the problem, the range of potential solutions can be increased considerably.

Image 14.1   Managers on a training course using Lego® to build representations of their organisation

Let's take a brief example. We wish to increase the efficiency of a manufacturing process. Without breaking down the problem, we might seek to reduce waste, change the machinery or train the employees. However, by examining each aspect of the manufacturing process, we can identify many more alternatives. At a more abstract level, we could ask individuals to find as many uses as possible for a paper clip. Suggestions might be a hook, an earring or a pendant for a necklace, but if we were to recognise explicitly the qualities of the issue at hand – that the paper clip is metal, extremely flexible, small and easy to carry – then it might remind those trying to find ideas of other items which have some of the same characteristics.

We could do this by a process known as concept mapping. Concept mapping is a way of representing knowledge which gradually develops understanding. In a group, this can be seen as a similar process to that of brainstorming, but it enables individuals to address issues and ideas in turn. Relationships between the ideas and concepts discussed are seen as 'relating to' other concepts in terms of items which:

- cause
- require, or
- contribute to

other processes and concepts. The key difference between this form of brainstorming and that of mind-mapping is in terms of the focus on relationships between different concepts. We have previously identified that one aspect of creativity relates to reorganising information and relationships between concepts and ideas. Concept mapping provides a way to do so which can be shared beyond the single individual by using others' knowledge to extend gradually the number of ideas involved in building a model of how 'things work'. Figure 14.2 provides an incomplete representation of a number of ideas relating to human performance in the workplace and the next 'For You to Do' section below asks you to consider some questions to complete the concept map.

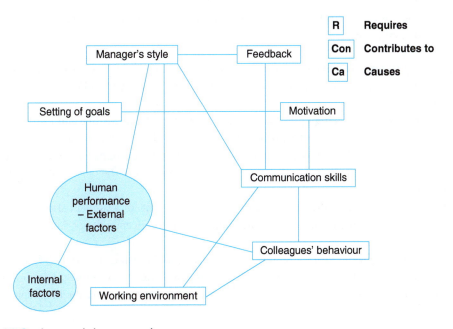

Figure 14.2 Incomplete concept map

FOR YOU TO DO

The concept map in the figure was constructed in order to help a manager improve the performance of one of their employees. It shows how some ideas relate to each other, and to understanding human performance. You need to complete the diagram and help the manager identify potential solutions, by:

1. Identifying the relationships (requires – R, causes – CA and contributes to – Con) between the ideas shown by writing 'R', 'Ca' and 'Con' respectively along the line between the two items which have some relationship.
2. Extending the diagram to include internal (e.g. personality, intelligence – others?) factors which might affect performance.
3. Rearranging the diagram to indicate which relationships are close/strong and which are distant/weak; those which are close should represent items that are physically close in the diagram.

Question 3 should help prioritise the likely solutions to the problem.

The above example shows the importance of knowledge in the creativity process. It would be nearly impossible to complete the diagram without an understanding of how the various ideas might link together.

ENHANCING OUR OWN CREATIVE ABILITIES

There may be times when we do not necessarily have a problem that we need to solve creatively and so we may be tempted to ignore our natural creative abilities, but the more we get used to using them on a day-to-day basis, the more likely we will be to recognise the abilities we have and use them when we really need to.

Whetten and Cameron (2011) provide some useful ideas that we can use to enhance our own creativity on an ongoing basis:

1. **Discussing ideas with others:** Clearly, if two or more individuals share the same knowledge, abilities and motivation to be creative, then discussing a problem with others can lead to a larger number of creative ideas.
2. **Give ourselves time:** Being busy is an enemy of creativity: to be creative and just to think without worrying about any restrictions is also important. Relaxation time can lead to daydreaming, and while in most situations daydreaming is not encouraged, doing so when thinking about problems or issues that you are facing can enhance the chance of coming up with a new solution or idea.
3. **Seek a relaxing place:** Finding a place to think is important for a similar reason: it removes us from the pressures and busy-ness of life and enables us to reconceptualise or reorganise the relevant ideas and facts.
4. **Read something new:** Reading something interesting and outside of your own area(s) of interest can build up knowledge of how different processes work, and can help in two ways: (1) it can enable the development of different metaphors and analogies around the new topics; and (2) it can stimulate interest in new topics and new ideas.

5. **Remove yourself from barriers:** Examining how creativity can be blocked can help us to recognise where those barriers might be affecting our own creativity. The implication is that, where possible, we remove ourselves from those barriers. This might include our own busy-ness for a while and from others who restrict our creativity with comments such as 'That will never work' or 'I'm not sure why you're really bothering – we've tried that before and it will never work.'

── REFLECTION POINT ──

Think about a problem you have encountered recently and struggled to solve. How might you have used any of the techniques above to develop useful ideas?

Are there any ways listed above that you can use to enhance your creativity?
   How do you feel about having fun at work?

There are many ways in which we can 'become' more creative. In reality, some of these ideas are about releasing our latent abilities, but which are rarely used for a variety of reasons. Learning to play with information and concepts, having fun and releasing ourselves to enjoy developing creative ideas are key parts of most jobs, even if we do not realise it.

── KEY LEARNING POINT ──

We can learn to apply our creativity to problem solving by using various tools and techniques. Not all tools can be used by all people, but most people can demonstrate creativity in some way, if they are given the chance.

── REFLECTION POINT ──

Take some time to think about the following questions and write down some answers.

Do you ever use any of these ideas? If not, are there any which you might consider using?
   Do you think of them as processes which can help develop your own and others' creative ideas?
   Have you ever seen anyone else using these ideas or processes?

BLOCKAGES AND BARRIERS TO CREATIVITY

When we think about our behaviour, there are always a number of issues which can influence our ability to do or feel like doing certain things. Some issues will prevent us from undertaking what we wish or need to at the quality we would like, while other issues will act as enablers, and, of course, there are times when the things which prevent us from using our abilities in certain ways may be the opposite of those things which enable us to do so. When it comes to creativity, the same principle applies: there are certain factors – some within ourselves (e.g. attitudes, abilities, etc.) and some imposed on us by others – which can help or hinder the development and demonstration of our creativeness. In reality, we may well have the ability to be far more creative than we believe – we just need to 'let it out'. The content below is intended to help us understand more about how to do that.

We can think systematically about blockages in terms of the three elements needed for creative activity to take place, which we identified at the start of the chapter, namely creative ability, motivation and knowledge.

Pressure

Pushing people to be creative in ways that they are not skilled at doing is not going to produce creative outcomes. (In fact, pushing people to demonstrate any skill that they are not able to do is not going to produce a positive outcome.) Winstanley (2005) stated that: 'The more you try to think about solving a problem, the less likely you will be to develop a solution.' The issue is particularly pertinent, however, with *requiring* people to be creative (rather than selecting people who naturally *are* creative) since giving people time and space to think is one of the ways in which creativity can be enhanced. Removing that time and space but requiring people to be more creative are typically very contradictory intentions.

Conceptual Blocks

Conceptual blocks can come in a great many forms, but they all share one outcome: that thinking becomes constrained. At one level, we could argue that someone's openness to something or someone new could be limited simply by their stereotyped impressions of that situation or individual, or their bias against a particular department's 'apparently' political agenda.

When it comes to problem solving, we have also recognised that the way we define a problem has a significant impact on our ability to generate creative solutions. We could think about a failure to ask questions, assuming that present problems are very similar to past problems, or anything that constrains us from having an open mind. Nowhere does this become more apparent than in police investigations, where having a closed mind in relation to searching for evidence or lines of enquiry can mean that homicides are not solved as quickly as they could be.

 CONCEPTUAL BLOCK

A conceptual block is any way of thinking that prevents us from being open to new possibilities.

━━━━━━━━ BOX 14.5 ━━━━━━━━

THE HUNT FOR 'THE YORKSHIRE RIPPER'

In the late 1970s and early to mid-1980s, the West Yorkshire Police were in the midst of a media frenzy and a great deal of concern from the female population living in Leeds, Bradford and the surrounding area. The area was experiencing a series of notorious murders. The murders went on until the attacker, Peter Sutcliffe, was apprehended in South Yorkshire, just as he was about to strike again.

For the police at that time, investigative methods were significantly different to more recent times. Digitised records were not available to the police, so they struggled with a huge amount of data from

(Continued)

(Continued)

thousands of interviews. DNA testing and computer facial recognition (and psychological profiling) did not exist and criminals were able to go undetected for significant periods of time.

In investigating the murders, conceptual blocks (shown in bold below) added significantly to problems surrounding the investigation. The first block was based on the fact that a number of victims were prostitutes. Rather than recognising that this might have been because they were easy targets, **the police made the assumption that any attack which was not made on a prostitute was not relevant to the case**. Similarly, any murder victim who was killed in this way was clearly a prostitute. This block meant that good descriptions of the attacker (who was quite distinctive in appearance) given by survivors of very similar attacks before the murders began were ignored.

During the investigation, the lead investigator was sent a recording of someone purporting to be the killer. The recording was very personal, indicated a strong north eastern UK accent and verbally taunted the police officer in charge. As a result, the **investigation started to hunt for someone from the north east, without questioning whether the recording actually came from the attacker**. Some years later, an individual was arrested for making and sending the recording; it did not come from Peter Sutcliffe, but from someone who had no involvement in the killings at all.

════ REFLECTION POINT ════

Take some time to think about the following questions and write down some answers.

In the problems you have to solve, do you ever constrain your own thinking, or that of other people, by making certain assumptions?

Do others do this to you?

How willing are you to challenge your own and others' conceptual blocks?

One conceptual block that does limit individuals on occasion is the belief that they are not, and cannot be, creative. Few researchers in this area would agree, suggesting that individuals do not get much opportunity to exhibit creativity or to play around with ideas. What does seem to be apparent, of course, is that people are creative in different ways, and that the different forms of creativity are equally important.

Motivation, Emotions and Behaviour

Of course, there may be any number of reasons why someone does not want to be creative. They may not feel comfortable playing and take the view that anything which is 'fun' cannot be seen as 'work', or that 'fun' is not 'part of my life'. This is perhaps a significant indictment of particular managerial styles and approaches than it is a reflection of reality, and it is a pity that some individuals and managers constrain their contributions to an organisation in this way.

There are others who may just not want to be creative and are more content with situations as they are, rather than changing anything, and are quite happy with the habits they have. This can occasionally be satisfactory in the situation where nothing in the external or internal environment is changing, but rapid changes in technology, politics and society in general mean that such situations are now very rare.

Lack of Appropriate Knowledge

Knowledge, as we have seen earlier, is required for solving problems creatively. It therefore follows that a lack of expertise in particular subject domains can significantly impact on an individual's ability to generate creative options, or to ensure that the definition of the problem is sufficiently broad to allow for a variety of views. Imagine a car mechanic trying to determine why a car will not start without having an understanding of how a car engine works.

The good news on this issue is that knowledge is not that difficult to obtain, and while there is an obvious need to ensure a good awareness of how particular knowledge might fit a particular situation, a willingness to search for knowledge is usually a good thing anyway.

 ━━━ KEY LEARNING POINT ━━━━━━━━━━━━━━━━━

Many people have blockages to creativity, but they can be overcome. Those who develop creative ideas have often worked out ways of overcoming these blockages.

 ━━━ REFLECTION POINT ━━━━━━━━━━━━━━━━━

Take some time to think about the following questions and write down some answers.

What sort(s) of things stop you from being creative? When was the last time you felt you developed a creative solution to a problem?

When was the last time you had child-like fun at university? Do you ever feel that you should not have this kind of 'fun'?

How could you go about establishing a knowledge base to help you solve problems more creatively in the future?

INTEGRATION AND APPLICATION

As we have seen, most problem solving can be broken down into a series of relevant questions.

Question 1: Is this a new problem? Problems that we have encountered before and where solutions are relatively easy to develop and identify can be said to need less creativity than those that are new, so the first question that managers need to be able to answer is whether it is a new problem or a problem that has been faced previously.

In making such a decision, any manager will need to take care to ensure that they are actually facing the same problem: the question is not always an easy one to answer.

Question 2: If this is a new problem, what can we do to solve it? If it seems to be a new problem, then the first two stages of the problem-solving process (defining the problem and generating alternatives) can become very different. A sense of fun, creativity and the use of a range of techniques can be employed to solve the issue in an innovative way.

Question 3: What can we do to ensure there are no blockages to enabling individuals' creativity? We need to be careful that we are not limiting the creativity of ourselves and others by putting up or maintaining inappropriate barriers. Make sure you keep an open mind and maintain it in others.

CONCLUSION

You should now have a good idea of how to:

- Follow both rational and creative problem-solving processes.
- Describe the key components of creativity.
- Develop and enhance your creativity.
- Recognise blockages to creativity in yourself and in others.

Becoming more creative is often as much about allowing yourself the freedom to come up with crazy, strange and weird ideas as it is about actually having the appropriate abilities in the first place. This chapter should have gone some way to helping you to engage in creative activities and creative problem solving a little more, and to see how such activities can be fun.

We still need to address the questions asked at the beginning of this chapter.

The first question, 'How many seconds are there in one year?', can be addressed in two ways. Most people will begin by calculating 60 (seconds in a minute) × 60 (minutes in an hour) × 24 (hours in a day) × 365 (days in a year). A more creative answer would be 12, assuming that each month has a 2nd. Which did you choose? Identifying the latter answer used our lateral thinking abilities by redefining the term (second) in the question.

The second question was a riddle: 'A horse rider arrived in a town on Friday, stayed for three days and left on Friday. How can you explain this?' The answer is that the horse was called 'Friday'! Did you get it right?

FINAL REFLECTIONS

Based on the content of this chapter, what do you now know about creativity and creative problem solving that you did not know before?

Think of a time when you had to be creative or solve a difficult problem. What was the situation and what did you do? Did you use any of the techniques discussed in this chapter?

Based on what you have learnt in this chapter, what would you do differently and why?

Do your answers to either of the above questions have the potential to change your ability to be creative? Why?

What will you now do differently? (Write this down and put it somewhere where you can see it regularly.)

INTERVIEW QUESTIONS

In nearly all cases, the questions in previous chapters have only been about determining your skills and abilities in certain areas. However, being a global citizen involves knowledge as well as skill, so some of the questions which might be asked in this area could try to find out how much you know as much as what you are able to do.

(Continued)

(Continued)

Think about the following questions. What might your answers be?

1. Tell me about a time when you solved a problem that others were struggling to solve.
2. How would you go about finding a new way of delivering one of our services? (Or 'a new use for one of our products?', if the company is a manufacturing company.)
3. Imagine a situation where you – as a departmental manager – needed quickly to resolve a cash flow problem. How might you go about it?

Chapter 17 gives a lot more information on selection interviews and the online content gives some guidance on these questions.

ADDITIONAL RESOURCES

Want to learn more? Visit https://study.sagepub.com/morgan to gain access to a wide range of online resources, including interactive tests, tasks, further reading and downloads.

Website Resources

Creative Education Foundation website: www.creativeeducationfoundation.org/creative-problem-solving/

Kent University and the IDEAL model of Problem-Solving: www.kent.ac.uk/careers/sk/problem-solving-skills.htm

Kent University and Lateral Thinking: www.kent.ac.uk/careers/sk/lateral.htm

TED talks on Creativity: www.ted.com/topics/creativity

Textbook Resources

Gallagher, K. (2010) *Skills Development for Business and Management Students*. Oxford: Oxford University Press (particularly chapter 11).

Isaken, S. G., Dorval, K. B. and Treffinger, D. J. (2000) *Creative Approaches to Problem Solving: A Framework for Change*. Dubuque, IA: Kendall Hunt.

Pettinger, R. and Firth, R. (2001) *Mastering Management Skills*. Basingstoke: Palgrave (particularly chapter 9).

PART V
UNDERSTANDING EMPLOYEE SELECTION

THE FIRST DAY ... OF THE REST OF YOUR LIFE

The first day of university – whether you are a postgraduate or an undergraduate student – is when your career begins. You start learning knowledge and developing your skills through the experiences you gain from your degree programme. It is too late to start doing that in your final year when you are thinking about the jobs that you could apply for. It is towards the end of your time at university that the importance of the skills you have developed becomes very clear. This part is not so much about developing skills as it is about developing awareness – an awareness of the selection processes used by employers and understanding what lies ahead of you after graduation. If a graduate job is not something you are sure you wish to commit to just yet, then this part also addresses other options for you to consider.

This final part of the book is somewhat different to Parts I–III, which were largely about university study, and Part IV, which was about the development of skills for employability (and life in general). This part is not so much designed to develop your skills, but rather to give you some information so that you can understand what an employer is looking for when setting up a selection process for either general applications to a broad selection process (e.g. graduate training scheme) or for specific vacancies within an organisation.

This part will largely focus on selection methods used at graduate level (i.e. what you need to know when applying for jobs with some responsibility) but the same principles will probably apply for voluntary internships, part-time work and work placements undertaken as part of a degree course. The main differences between these areas will be the extent to which resources are devoted to the selection process, since the status of the job will usually be linked to the resources applied to finding the 'best' candidate.

This part will begin by taking a look at how employers select their graduates (Chapter 15), and then cover a range of components of the process in the order that they would typically occur in a graduate selection process. The second chapter here examines applications, that is CVs, covering letters and application forms (Chapter 16). If successful at the application, a candidate would then expect to attend a selection interview (Chapter 17), followed by psychometric tests and an assessment centre (Chapter 18). Of course, organisations do vary and not all organisations use these processes in this order (as Chapter 15 makes clear). Finally, Chapter 19 provides some ideas for additional options after graduation, such as setting up your own business, taking a gap year and further study (MSc or PhD studies).

The chapters will focus on giving specific guidance, taking the view that you might be either applying for jobs or considering what to do after graduation. Each chapter will set out specific ideas, provide you with reflective questions and exercises to work through and include answers to questions which might occur to you; there are no skills assessments in these chapters.

It is true to say that there is a wealth of information and guidance available from AGCAS (Association of Graduate Careers Services) and from a very wide range of other organisations, including your own university. You will almost certainly be able to make an appointment at your own careers service to help you find your way through what is available.

It would be good, however, to deal with some limitations of a text like this.

WILL YOU HELP ME CHOOSE MY CAREER?

The simple answer is 'no'. What these chapters will not do – as much as you might wish them to – is to cover in detail the important issue of 'What should I do? What kind of job should I go for?' There are some principles to consider and to some extent your degree title *could* limit your options, but this is unusual. Choosing a career is as much about you and your personality and motivation as it is about the skills you have, and this needs careful discussion with someone at your careers services. The earlier you do this in your university career, the better.

Degree subjects (and your university school or department) are generally classified into groups or faculties. You might be studying business or politics or sociology. If so, then you are studying what is called a 'social science' designed to develop interpersonal (interacting with others) and intrapersonal (making yourself more effective) skills, a broad range of knowledge relevant to your subject and critical thinking skills. If you contrast these with someone studying engineering or medicine, then technical knowledge becomes the priority (most people would rather have a doctor with poor interpersonal skills but a great knowledge of medical treatment than the other way around, although both would be helpful of course). Someone studying law needs to have an excellent background in whatever area of law they practise, but someone studying a social science could move into any one of a number of career areas. In other words, a social science degree (politics, history, sociology, psychology, marketing, business, HRM, economics and other subjects) gives you the critical thinking skills you need to take you into a leadership role and your specific knowledge becomes less important. The subject you are studying at university does *not* need to limit your choice of career.

This does not mean, however, that the knowledge that you learn is not important: it is very important. In times of economic recession or when companies are selecting fewer graduates, companies do use the degree subject as a way of 'screening out' applicants that they would need to train as opposed to those who already possess the relevant knowledge.

Having noted that the degree subject is not always the main issue in choosing a career, you might need to think about what you are interested in. Your careers services will have access to a number of tools designed to help you identify the characteristics of things that you are interested in. At a basic level, this might be something as simple as 'Do you prefer logical and structured activities and hobbies or unstructured ones where you can be more creative?', and they will match those to what is known about certain career and job types. If you are unsure of what you want to do after your degree, you should strongly consider getting some advice from your careers services.

There is one thing which is vitally important and which has been stressed throughout the earlier chapters: academic success in your degree is going to be a very significant factor in your being able to get the future you want, but it is not the only factor. To an employer, a student who has a first-class degree in Philosophy but no leadership or work experience or no involvement in social activities is more likely to be overlooked for a graduate role than one who has a lesser degree (e.g. 2:1 or 2:2, more rarely a 3rd class), but leadership experience in a student society and some work experience. It is about balance, and employers are looking for competent and able individuals who are critical thinkers, analytical and able to use their communication and interpersonal skills to work well with others. This means that your working career starts on day 1 of your university studies - and your choices made during the start of your time at university *can have* a significant impact on your employability at the end of it.

In previous parts of this text, the chapters have included interview questions relating to the abilities covered in each chapter. Of course, this is not relevant to the chapters which follow but Chapter 17 does present a review of each of these questions and gives some guidance. However, each of the following chapters should enable you to develop some understanding of how to give yourself a good chance of getting through to at least an interview.

/15/ UNDERSTANDING EMPLOYEE SELECTION

CHAPTER STRUCTURE

Figure 15.1

When you see the 🌐 this means go to the companion website https://study.sagepub.com/morgan to do a quiz, complete a task, read further or download a template.

━ AIMS OF THE CHAPTER ━

By the end of this chapter, you should be able to:

- Understand how employers view the recruitment and selection processes.
- Describe how employers select and use different selection tools.
- Identify the qualities needed in different kinds of roles.
- Understand how your studies and other experiences have helped you to develop these qualities.

INTRODUCTION

Developing an understanding of the recruitment and selection process is key to understanding how employers develop a selection process and how and why they use certain tools. Human resources management (HRM) or the personnel department is usually responsible for the development and administration of the process, and while it is usually senior and middle-level managers who will be involved in its operation, the HRM or personnel literature is usually a good place to start reading more. Occupational psychologists will usually help to design the process in a scientific manner, but the process will vary in nature and in the order of certain activities according to what the organisation can invest in the process and what it sees as important.

 RECRUITMENT

Recruitment is the process of identifying a number of applicants who are willing to apply for a particular job or training programme.

 SELECTION

Selection is the process of comparing information from the applicants with the requirements as specified in the advertisement, and selecting those who meet the essential requirements to move forward in the selection process.

This chapter sets out how the processes of recruitment and selection work and will give you an idea of the experiences you could expect at different stages, if you were successful. However, it is useful to give some definitions of the two processes here, with other definitions being given here.

The process will be set out in detail below, but nothing further can happen unless there are applicants willing to apply for the job. Once they have submitted their applications, then the process of selection can begin.

These two processes can work differently depending on the situation:

- A job vacancy that is advertised because the previous job holder has left the organisation will be developed in one particular way.
- A vacancy that is advertised as a new job role may have a little more uncertainty about it, but will be broadly similar.
- A vacancy on a graduate training scheme will be developed around some core skills and values possessed by the desired candidate, making them suitable for the organisation generally, while their suitability for a specific role in the organisation will be identified during the scheme.

Each of the above will have a slightly different emphasis on how the process is conducted and what employers will be looking for. There is one additional scenario: that is, employers will recruit internally. This is carried out in a different way, but is less relevant for most graduate applications, so we will not be examining it further.

HOW AN ORGANISATION DEVELOPS A RECRUITMENT PROCESS

The recruitment process itself has a number of elements to it, some of which are more straightforward than others, but when you see a job advertisement or an invitation to apply for a graduate training scheme, the organisation will usually have undertaken some kind of job analysis and developed some way of identifying and describing what it is after.

Job Analysis

A job analysis is the process of identifying what tasks the job will involve. This is useful for you, so that you know whether you might like the job, and useful to employers, who can use it to identify the kinds of qualities they are looking for. There is a variety of ways that employers might undertake this role – interviews, question-naires, discussions, diaries of those doing similar jobs – and all have strengths and weaknesses, but employers will have taken some time looking at the job.

COMPETENCY AND CORE COMPETENCY

A competency is a quality (skill, behaviour, attitude or personality trait) which helps an individual to perform a job well.

A core competency is a quality that is an essential requirement for all employees operating in similar job roles.

An analysis of the tasks involved in doing the job itself, however, is not going to produce a rounded picture of the 'ideal' candidate. Employers also need to consider the organisation and whether a candidate is going to be a good fit to the values and culture of the organisation, so these areas need to be considered as well. At a basic level, it is fine to have someone who can do the job, but if they are going to behave unethically, then that is going to be problematic. Employers call an ability to conform to the values of an organisation 'person–organisation fit' and an ability to do the job 'person–job fit'.

If the job is a general one (i.e. for a training scheme), the requirements are less important than 'person–organisation fit', although organisations will usually have some 'core competencies' – that is, essential qualities required for most or all jobs operating at a particular level.

Developing a Person Specification

The organisation will have taken the job description and other information (e.g. organisational core competencies, organisational values) and will have developed an idea of the qualities required from the successful candidate. These are usually referred to in terms of the 'knowledge', 'skills', 'abilities' and 'other' qualities (or KSAOs) that are sought. In this context, 'other' can refer to attitudes and values, educational attainments and experience.

For graduate-level jobs, the KSAOs will usually relate to:

- Leadership and team-working skills
- Reasoning and critical thinking abilities
- Numeracy
- Interpersonal and communication skills
- Self-confidence
- IT literacy (proficient in use of Excel, Access, etc.)
- Presentation skills

- Self-awareness
- Ability to learn
- Ethical values and honesty
- Problem solving and creative abilities
- Organisational abilities
- Knowledge gained during the degree course
- Attitudes – towards others, studying, etc.

━━━━━━ FOR YOU TO DO ━━━━━━

Have a look at the list of qualities given above. How many of these have you developed during your course? How has your university course helped you to develop them?

For example, you might have developed your team-working skills during your time working on various group assignments.

(Continued)

(Continued)

Which KSAOs have you developed through:

- Student societies?
- Part-time employment?
- Family life?

(You can add to the list of KSAOs if you think you have extra qualities to offer.)

The organisation will separate the list of competencies into 'essential' qualities ('the candidate selected must possess …') and 'desirable' ('the candidate selected should also …') qualities. The lists are separated according to whether a particular skill can be trained or not, and then how important it is to the job. Although rare in graduate recruitment, an organisation might also mention 'undesirable' qualities and those qualities which would disqualify someone from working in a particular kind of organisation (e.g. fraud conviction for a position in a bank or 'fear of flying' for an airline stewardess). The qualities being sought will establish the criteria against which each candidate is assessed.

 ━━ 'BUT I HAVE A QUESTION …' ━━━━━━━━━━━━

… How do I know what skills and abilities the company is looking for?

Well, usually the company will tell you in the advertisement. Remember that what the company is looking for is evidence that you have the appropriate KSAOs for the job. Organisations will be looking for two things: firstly, job–person fit and, secondly, person–organisation fit. The first refers to your ability to do the job, while the second seeks to assess whether your personality would enable you to do well in the organisation's culture. It is fantastic if you can do the job well, but it would not be great if you have a particularly ambitious attitude while the organisation takes a much more risk-averse and cautious approach.

The issue in relation to the question is that the first one is usually spelt out quite clearly, but the second is far more implicit. There are times when you can guess what the culture of the organisation might be like (i.e. what it is like to work there) by the language used on the company website or in a company brochure, but at other times you will have to be yourself and if the company is different from you, then it is obviously not going to work out in the long term anyway.

One of the broader qualities that graduate employers look for is work experience. This could be part-time work in a student bar, but the best kind of experience is from working in a professional role for a year as part of a placement programme. Many universities actually assess your performance during a work placement in some way (e.g. behaviour in the job, reflective assignment done while on a job placement, etc.) as a way of encouraging you to obtain that work experience. In reality, there are few substitutes for obtaining relevant work experience in a professional environment, either as part of a sandwich degree or in an internship. Having such experience alongside leadership responsibilities in a student society will put you ahead of other candidates when you are applying for jobs.

Employers and their organisations usually have a number of personal characteristics (KSAOs) that they are looking for in a new employee, and it is up to candidates to apply for jobs where they think they can match the essential (and hopefully desirable) qualities sought.

REFLECTION POINT

Take some time to think about the following questions and write down some answers.

What would be your ideal job?
    What KSAOs do you think would be required for your ideal job?
    How many of these do you already possess? And how many (and which ones?) do you need to develop?

HOW AN ORGANISATION DESIGNS A SELECTION PROCESS

The selection process is a series of stages, but the first activity for an employer is to remove from the pile of applications those that do not possess sufficient evidence of the essential abilities the employer is seeking – that is, the screening process.

Screening

The process of screening refers to the process of examining the applications and deciding which candidates are the most appropriate for inviting to interview. Most vacancies for graduate trainee positions that are well advertised will likely attract several hundred applicants, and that can either be discouraging ('Why should they pick me?') or give you a sense of determination ('Someone has to get the job, so why shouldn't it be me?'). Your attitude will be important in life generally and will show itself especially when things do not go well.

The process of screening can be relatively fast and brutal: a CV can be dismissed in as little as 10 to 30 seconds – or even be electronically scanned by relevant software for keywords so that it is never actually seen by a selector. This means that your application needs to be eye-catching and relevant, and you will need to learn how to market yourself. Selectors will be looking for significant evidence relating to the requirements of the job, which is why engagement with responsibilities in student societies or part-time work or voluntary experience is so important.

SELECTION METHODS

1. A *selection interview* is a conversation designed to determine whether someone has the appropriate abilities to do the job.
2. A *psychometric test* is a test of an individual's mental abilities, developed using scientific methods to ensure consistency and accuracy.
3. An *in-basket exercise* is a timed exercise involving candidates that deals with a range of issues in different email/memo messages.
4. A *personality questionnaire* is a questionnaire designed to elicit information regarding an individual's behaviour and personality.
5. A *work sample* is an example of someone's work.
6. An *assessment centre* is a structured programme of selection exercises, designed to enable selectors to see an individual in a simulated work environment.*

* This method of selection can include a wide range of other methods carried out over a day or longer.

FOR YOU TO DO

What makes you different?

Being different and special in a way that is useful to an organisation is one of the things that you will need to do in order to get your application noticed. In marketing terms, those selling services or products usually emphasise their USP (Unique Selling Proposition, namely their unique qualities) to their customers. Bearing in mind that employers are your customers in this instance and will be looking for candidates who possess the relevant KSAOs, what are your USPs?

Think about:

1. Your skills and abilities.
2. Your knowledge.
3. Your other qualities – attitudes, values, character.

Having identified the skills required for a job, the organisation will then examine the best methods for determining whether a candidate possesses the skills required. Because employing graduates has an element of risk to it (they might have some relevant experience, but it is unproven in the commercial or 'real' world) and because organisations might be taking on a large number of trainees all at once, the investment that organisations put into the selection process is considerable.

The most common selection methods are detailed in the following chapters.

FOR YOU TO DO

Do you understand the brief definitions given above? Look at the descriptions below and match them to the selection methods defined on page 331.

A. 'I needed to indicate which of the answers (A to D) was most like me and least like me. One of the guys from the company then spent some time with me discussing my results and asking me for examples of my typical behaviour. It was quite interesting really – no one had ever done that before – but I am not sure if I was convincing in the answers I gave.'

B. 'I think this exercise was about my administrative and organisational skills, but also my communication skills. Each of the pieces of information I needed to deal with required me to do something – either add something into my diary or respond to a particular message from an employee or customer. It was tough: there wasn't really enough time and I needed to think very quickly.'

C. 'The questions were quite hard and both of the managers I was talking to looked really strict. I needed to give examples of times when I had done something particularly special or difficult. At the end, I did get the chance to ask any questions, but there didn't seem to be a great deal of time to answer the questions. I never really knew who I should look at.'

D. 'This was a large event, actually. There were around 20 people there, and we met in a hotel. During the day, we had to do some reasoning tests, we had an 'inbox exercise' to complete, I had to read a case study and do a presentation and then at the end we had an interview. Lunch was good, but I couldn't really relax, as I was sitting next to one of the guys from the organisation.'

(Continued)

(Continued)

E. 'It was a difficult thing to do and I didn't finish in the 30 minutes they gave us. I had a calculator and made some notes for the questions as I went along, which was a really useful thing to do because they were then useful for other questions. But it was tough and I don't think anyone finished. I think I guessed some of the answers, because the questions were multiple choice.'

F. 'I had to do a presentation before my interview and then they asked me questions about it. I was nervous, a bit shaky and I am not sure if I did what I was really capable of doing or had done before, but I did it.'

Not all companies will use all of these methods, and even when they do, they might use them in a different order or vary the specific methods (e.g. telephone interview v face-to-face interview) or the people involved. Some companies use psychometric tests or personality inventories/questionnaires to screen out candidates *before* they get to the interview stage. The order in which companies use the selection methods is usually determined by how important those qualities are. There is little point in engaging with a candidate to the end of the process through some expensive selection methods only to find that they do not possess one of the basic requirements of the job, see Box 15.1 below.

REFLECTION POINT

Take some time to think about the following questions and write down some answers.

Are any of the selection methods listed above ones which you have experienced before?

From the descriptions above, which methods might be the most and least stressful for you? Why?

In using these methods, employers are just trying to find out if you have the KSAOs they are looking for, so do you ever feel that you should 'put on an act' and pretend to be someone you are not? Or do you just try to be yourself? Which is better, do you think?

BOX 15.1

THE POLICE HELICOPTER CREW

The role of the police helicopter is to oversee police activity and criminal behaviour, and to assist police officers on the ground to apprehend those alleged to have committed some crime. Within the team in the helicopter there are a pilot, an observer and a rear crew member. The rear crew member's job is to ensure that the helicopter is where it needs to be and to plan where the helicopter needs to be. As such, it is quite a complex job.

The skills required for the job relate to the following:

- Accurate and timely communication skills.
- Excellent geographical/navigation skills.
- An ability to multitask and use multiple resources at the same time.
- An ability to fly in a helicopter while using navigational aids without feeling airsick.
- Good team-work skills.

(Continued)

(Continued)

- An awareness of relevant laws.
- Good strategic planning skills.

If you were to put these in order, which would you consider the most critical and therefore would look for first?

During the selection exercise for a rear crew member, one police force used more theoretical exercises (including a paper exercise where candidates needed to draw the route being taken by the helicopter on a map in order to prove their navigation skills) early on in the process. This would save costs in that only a small number of candidates making it through to the end of the process would need to be given a simulated exercise in the helicopter, rather than taking all candidates up in the sky and making a large number of expensive trips. In the end, however, one of the three finalists let slip that they had a fear of flying and was denied the job.

Bearing in mind the reasons for their decision, would you have done any differently? Why?

As noted above, the choice of selection methods is made according to the skills sought. As an obvious example, you cannot reliably examine someone's presentation skills merely by asking if they are good at presentations during an interview, or even by asking for an example of when they have given a presentation. The best way to assess someone's presentation skills is to ask them to do a presentation. This is why graduate employers often use a variety of different methods to select candidates – because they will be looking for slightly different things.

 FOR YOU TO DO

You are a manager who needs to recruit a new staff member. Look at the hypothetical job advertisement below.

Trainee Client Relationship Manager

This is an exciting opportunity to make a major contribution to the operation of a new but quickly growing advertising consultancy. BWK was established three years ago with an office of 6 staff and has now grown to 32 individuals, each of whom plays a significant role in the development of their own business within the BWK family, which now has an annual turnover of around £3m. We aim to expand to set up other offices around the UK and to have a turnover of around £18m within the next five years – and you will be making a contribution to that success.

You will be a self-starter, able to establish and work with clients, and excited about the possibility of working for BWK. It will be hard work and will be challenging – the expectations will be high – but you will be working with an excellent and growing technical and customer support team who have recently won regional awards for their expertise and assistance. Your excellent organisational skills will complement your IT skills and enable you to liaise promptly with clients and write/analyse reports regarding your progress, while your excellent interpersonal skills will help you develop client relationships with customers who will stay with BWK for the long term.

In return, BWK will provide you with a salary and appropriate transport commensurate with this exciting role, and training opportunities relevant to your own development needs. We see this as a long-term relationship with you as well, and while we are not perfect, we do take a great deal of pride in the team-work atmosphere we have at BWK.

If you think you are who we are looking for and/or want to know more, then please contact us at madeupjob@bwk.co.uk or on 0123 456 7891.

(Continued)

(Continued)

Questions for you to consider:

1. What qualities are the company looking for in the successful employee?
2. Would this job fit your abilities and qualities? Why, or why not?
3. What kind of person would do well in this organisation? Are there any qualities which might be important but which are not stated explicitly?
4. Would this organisation be one that you could work for? Why, or why not?
5. Take your list of the qualities the company is seeking and then establish whether those skills are desirable or essential.
6. Look at the list of selection methods used by organisations in Box 15.1. Which method(s) would the company be likely to use to establish whether a candidate has the necessary qualities to do the job?

'BUT I HAVE A QUESTION ...'

... Do companies really do all of this? It seems really lengthy ...

Not all companies, no – and even those that do will not do it for every vacancy. At the end of the day, an organisation has to decide whether it is worth the expense (and risk) to do so. A job role carrying a high salary will usually carry a fair degree of risk – the responsibility will be greater – so the higher the salary, the more likely it is that the organisation will invest more in the selection process.

But it is lengthy – yes. Some selection processes can last as little as 45 minutes (e.g. interviews) while others can take a day and a half (e.g. an assessment centre). Employers will want to see as much evidence of your personality and skills as possible, and that means seeing evidence of those skills in several situations. It can make people nervous, but the best advice for any selection process is to be yourself.

KEY LEARNING POINT

Selection processes for graduate-level jobs rarely involve a single selection method, but are more commonly a combination of various methods to ensure that the candidate is the best possible fit for the organisation and job role.

IMPLEMENTING THE SELECTION PROCESS

Having carried out the screening process and identified those candidates an employer is interested in, the next stages in the process are relatively straightforward. Candidates will receive an invitation to attend for whatever selection methods are used and the selectors make a decision having seen all the candidates.

Most selection for graduate-level roles involves at least two stages, typically an interview and then an assessment centre. More details on how both processes work are given in the chapters that follow.

There is very little difference between the three types of scenarios given above: for general trainee jobs, for specific jobs and for jobs which are new to the organisation. The process as described above – and as given in Figure 15.2 – is almost identical.

- Person Specification
  - Analysing the job
  - Writing the job description
  - Detailing the skills needed
- Recruitment
  - Advertising
- Screening
  - 'Topping and tailing'
- Selection
  - Using predictors to make decisions

Figure 15.2   Overview of the recruitment and selection process

CONCLUSION

You should now have a good idea of how to:

- Understand how employers view the recruitment and selection processes.
- Describe how employers select and use different selection tools.
- Identify the qualities needed in different kinds of roles.
- Understand how your studies and other experiences have helped you to develop these qualities.

The recruitment and selection processes have a degree of subjective judgement about them. However, the greater the investment in the individual who is successful, the more detailed and careful managers tend to be to ensure they get it 'right'. Organisations do need to be careful about taking on an employee who says all the right things but cannot deliver when it comes to performance.

For you as a candidate, this means that you need to be clear in your mind about what you have done previously and the impact of those actions. The first step is selling yourself to an employer; we will look at application forms and CVs in the next chapter.

FINAL REFLECTIONS

Based on the content of this chapter, what do you now know about the recruitment and selection processes that you did not know before?

What key learning point had the most impact? Why?

Do your answers to either of the above questions have the potential to change what you would do when applying for a job? Why?

ADDITIONAL RESOURCES

Want to learn more? Visit https://study.sagepub.com/morgan to gain access to a wide range of online resources, including interactive tests, tasks, further reading and downloads.

(Continued)

(Continued)

Website Resources

Changingminds.org – job analysis: http://changingminds.org/disciplines/hr/job_analysis/job_analysis.htm

Graduate Recruitment Bureau website: http://employers.grb.uk.com/selection-methods

Guidance Paper by Margaret A Richardson on recruitment and selection processes in government of Trinidad and Tobago: http://unpan1.un.org/intradoc/groups/public/documents/UN/UNPAN021814.pdf

HR Council for the Non-Profit Sector in Canada – website detailing good HR recruitment practice: http://hrcouncil.ca/hr-toolkit/right-people-recruitment.cfm

KPMG – Overview of the KPMG recruitment and selection process: www.kpmg.com/PT/en/careers/graduates/Pages/recruitmentselection.aspx

Prospects 2010 Survey – How do graduate recruiters recruit their graduates? www.hecsu.ac.uk/assets/assets/documents/Real_Prospects_2010_-_Main_Report.pdf

SA Power (Australian Power company) – Graduate Recruitment website: www.sapowernetworks.com.au/centric/corporate/careers/graduate_program/graduates_recruitment_and_selection_process.jsp

Textbook Resources

Arnold, J., Randall, R., Patterson, F. et al. (2010) *Work Psychology: Understanding Human Behaviour in the Workplace* (5th edition). Harlow: FT/Prentice-Hall (particularly chapter 4).
Davey, G. (2008) *The International Student's Survival Guide*. London: Sage (particularly chapter 10).
Rees, W. D. and Porter, C. (2008) *Skills of Management*. London: Cengage (particularly chapter 9).
Smale, B. and Fowlie, J. (2009) *How to Succeed at University: An Essential Guide to Academic Skills, Personal Development & Employability*. London: Sage (particularly chapter 9).
Smith, M. (2011) *Fundamentals of Management* (2nd edition). Maidenhead: McGraw-Hill (particularly chapter 7).

16 CVs AND APPLICATION FORMS

CHAPTER STRUCTURE

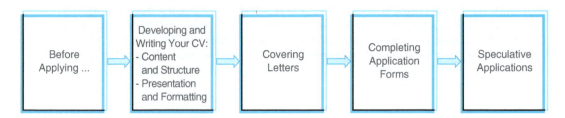

Figure 16.1

When you see the 🌐 this means go to the companion website https://study.sagepub.com/morgan to do a quiz, complete a task, read further or download a template.

AIMS OF THE CHAPTER

By the end of this chapter, you should be able to:

- Understand how employers use CVs, covering letters and application forms in the selection process.
- Identify the qualities of good applications.
- Write and compile CVs, covering letters and application forms.
- Develop speculative applications.

INTRODUCTION

The previous chapter examined the recruitment and selection process, and indicated that while there may be some common qualities that graduate employers are looking for, it is rare to find a large number of jobs which are identical in organisations which are identical. That is, most organisations will be looking for slightly different combinations of skills, education and experience. Therefore, all three of the above items (CV, covering letter and application forms) have one important characteristic in common: you *must* adapt your application – namely, these three items – to the qualities being sought in order to be successful. (It is no different to writing essays: you have to fulfil the criteria to get a good mark.)

The chapter will take some time to give advice on building up your profile, CV structure, content and presentation, and then give some advice on completing application forms in a way that helps you to stand out. However, when developing your CV, you *must* make it relevant to the job being advertised: if it is not, the application will be ignored.

THE BASICS

Completing a job application or writing a CV is something that nearly everyone who wants to work for someone else will need to do at some point in their life, and most people start by believing that this is an easy process that they can probably do using a 'CV Wizard' (a simple template) online in a very short space of time. Another thing that people believe about a CV is that it is a simple list of everything that you have ever done. Finally, there is a belief that once you have done a CV, you can use it for every job you apply for.

None of these ideas are true!

Any CV is expected to be accompanied by a covering letter. If you have never written a professional business letter before, then the first experience of doing so can be daunting.

The covering letter gives the employer a formal introduction to what is contained in the CV. More details are given below, but key to writing a successful covering letter is your ability to write succinctly and clearly in a way that makes the employer interested in you.

Application forms tend to be more structured documents, again aimed at giving employers specific information about you so that they can assess your suitability for moving forward in the selection process. They tend to be completed online.

CV (CURRICULUM VITAE)

A CV is a document aimed at convincing an employer that who you are, your qualifications, work experience and your skills makes it worthwhile for them to offer you either work experience or a chance to move forward in a formal selection process.

COVERING LETTER

A covering letter is a professional business letter which provides an employer with an introduction to an accompanying CV.

APPLICATION FORM

An application form is a document completed by a job applicant (usually completed online) aimed at gathering information about the applicant's experience, skills and abilities.

── KEY LEARNING POINT ──

Any job application *must* be matched to the criteria being sought by the organisation in order to be successful. A single application cannot simply be sent out for lots of different jobs: it must be adapted appropriately.

In this chapter, we need to be very clear on the purpose of the application: it is submitted in order to help an employer know more about your suitability for the job, and to feel confident enough to invite you to interview. In some cases, the application becomes less relevant after the interview stage. Examples will be given of how each area *might* look, but there is no one best style and your application needs to reflect who *you* are, so you will need to personalise any application that you make.

It is worth noting that between 95% and 99% of companies use online application forms, while only 18% of graduate recruiters ask for CVs (Association of Graduate Recruiters, 2014). This enables companies to compare candidates easily, and where there are a large number of applications, it enables computers to scan the applications for useful and significant words. If you submit a CV when the company needs an application from you, you are very likely not to get through the first stage, and since your application may be dismissed in less than three seconds, do follow instructions. The reason for putting the CV content first is a simple one: constructing your CV will help you to collect enough examples of the relevant activities that you have been involved in to be able to answer specific questions on the application form.

BEFORE APPLYING

It is really tempting simply to apply for every vacancy you find. You look in your careers services or a national newspaper or a profession-related magazine or on LinkedIn, find all the jobs you can and submit a CV and letter that you had prepared for a previous vacancy for those jobs. This might seem a bit of a 'lucky dip' approach, and in reality it is, so this section will explore what you – as an applicant – should do before applying. One or two of the ideas here need to be considered a long time before you start thinking about applying for jobs.

Find out about the Organisation

There was a time when employers used to give out brochures about their organisations, and some still do, but the best way of finding out about the organisation is to talk to it – or at least do some investigations on its website. Larger organisations will often attend graduate job fairs or are usually happy to respond to politely and professionally worded emails sent to the graduate recruitment department. Gently developing contacts within the organisation on LinkedIn in order to ask relevant questions can also work (Facebook might be more difficult in this regard). It might help you to decide whether you really want to work for an organisation if you find out the following:

- What is the organisation's strategy for doing what it wishes to do? (This may be challenging to find out since it is commercially sensitive, but it will show you where the opportunities might be within the organisation in a couple of years.)
- How does the organisation train and develop its staff?
- What is it like to work there – are individuals friendly, or are lower level employees not treated well?
- Are there many rules and procedures to follow, or are people fairly free to get on with their work in their own way?

At this stage in the process, you will want to find out whether you want to work for the organisation. However, at interview, companies will also want to see evidence that you know what they do, where they are located, how they work and the impact of any external factors (e.g. government regulation) on the way they do what they do.

Creating Your Personal Brand

During the academic year 2013–14, nearly half of all UK employers recruiting graduates received more than 2500 applications, and 13% of employers received more than 10,000 applications, an average of 69 applications. A year later, during 2014–15, graduate employers typically received around 75 applications per vacancy (Association of Graduate Recruiters, 2014, 2015). Financial services organisations seemed to attract around 107 applications per vacancy, while those dealing in fast-moving consumer goods received around 150 per vacancy. What is interesting is that, while the number of applications per vacancy is high, around 5% of graduate vacancies were going unfilled, so there is scope for finding a graduate job if you are prepared to look hard – and if you are able to make your application *stand out* in some way. This means that you need to think about what makes you special – and make sure that the employers get to see it, for the right reasons.

━━━━ FOR YOU TO DO ━━━━

Consider the following companies and places. What makes the brand stand out? When you think of these 18 items, what qualities or images come to mind?

1. Apple	7. Gucci	13. Vidal Sassoon
2. Mercedes-Benz	8. Tesla	14. Virgin Atlantic
3. British Airways	9. Emirates (airline)	15. Monaco
4. Iceland (country)	10. United States	16. Latin America
5. Rolex	11. Go-Pro	17. Canon
6. Sony	12. Body Shop	18. Hello Kitty

These items will usually bring some image to people's minds that makes them different from other companies or places, so when you sell yourself to employers, you need to think about what it is that makes you different.

It is highly likely that, as a forthcoming graduate, you have around three or four years of university life to talk about. If you are a mature student or a postgraduate student, then you will have longer, of course. If you have been wise, then much of that time will have been spent constructively on both your studies and a reasonable range of other interesting and useful activities that you could discuss in the future with an employer at an interview.

There are three aspects to generating a personal brand or your 'Unique Selling Proposition' (USP): (1) what you have done; (2) who you are as an individual; and (3) making sure that the world – particularly employers (your 'target market', as it were) – knows about it, and the fastest way to do that is to go online.

In part, developing a personal profile is going to help you to compile a CV and complete an application form by giving you a list of achievements from which you can select and use according to the job you are applying for, and in part you can use it to write a succinct summary to let a prospective employer know what your USP is as part of your CV.

Over time, who you are, what you have done and how you sell yourself need to give an employer the same message. For example, it makes little sense trying to persuade an employer that you wish to have an international career when you have never been abroad, do not speak a foreign language and have no international friends. Instead, if you really wanted such an international career, you would have put effort into doing things – like going on a student exchange, organising potentially adventurous trips for you and your friends to unusual places, making friends from various places to find out more about their culture, and so on. These would show an employer your curiosity, sense of adventure and willingness to put effort into something that was not going to be easy.

Your experience

It may not seem like it, but you will have done a lot, either as part of your degree or via experience at school or part-time employment. If you are a postgraduate student, then the range of your activities should be even greater. At the stage of developing a CV, it is highly unlikely that you will have any kind of interview for a graduate-level position, so the best that you can do is get prepared to apply. The best way to do that is to make a list of anything that you have done or achieved that is significant to you or which had a positive impact on others around you. The following kinds of activities might be a good place to start, but will not be exhaustive:

- Activities and learning that you undertook at school before you came to university – employability and work experience sessions?
- Any leadership responsibilities you have had in student clubs or societies.?
- Any unusual or interesting projects that you did as part of your degree. Did you go to visit any companies and write reports about them? Did you do a consultancy project of any sort?
- Anything you have done that was not part of a module or a degree course, but was connected to your university – teacher-led voluntary activity or skills development programme?
- Any leadership that you have done at work or during an internship which might have changed the way the organisation worked?
- Any high marks, university or regional awards or scholarships that you have received?
- Any dissertations or projects which show your interest and motivation in a particular area?
- Anything that you have been able to change in your role as a student representative?
- Any activities and responsibilities that you have had outside of your life at university – including at your previous school or college?

Make the list as comprehensive as you can, put dates by the activities and keep updating it regularly. As time moves on, you will probably forget many of the things that you have done and, for an employer, the more recent activities might be more useful (if you made a small change five years ago, then it would be of less relevance than a large change in the last couple of years).

This document does not need to be well formatted or include any personal details, it is solely a record of achievements and activities which will: (1) serve as a reminder of what you have done (which should be an encouraging thing to read); and (2) give you some content, which you can later use to complete an application form or CV.

If you find yourself struggling to think of activities and leadership actions that you have undertaken, then try asking tutors, friends and/or family for some ideas of what you have done.

About you

Many CVs will include a brief character statement at the top. Writing this brief statement (two to three brief sentences; no more than 50–80 words) enables you to give an employer a very rapid and focused idea of who you are – your skills, your personality and your character. The list of your achievements can help here, but if you do decide to include a character statement within your CV, then its purpose should be to entice the reader to read more about the skills and achievements that you can offer.

══════ FOR YOU TO DO ══════

When you think of well-known brands such as Zara, Apple, Canon, Louis Vuitton, there will be some images which come to mind. When you are constructing a CV or job application, you will need to consider your brand. Think about the following questions:

1. What makes you different from others around you? Think about your character, your skills, your education and your experience.
2. As an individual, would there be some kinds of organisations that you would prefer to work for, and others you would not? Why?
3. If you were leading others in an organisation, what words might describe your leadership style?

These questions (and others you can think of) should help you to identify your 'brand' – which, in turn, should help you use the right kinds of words when writing your CV and covering letter.

If you spend a little time matching your brand to the culture of the organisation (i.e. bringing together the above sections on 'find out about the organisation' and 'creating your personal brand'), then this can give you some kind of idea as to whether the organisation might be one you would like to work for.

══════ 'BUT I HAVE A QUESTION ...' ══════

... Does this mean that I should not apply for organisations that do not fit my personality?

The issue is not so much 'not apply for' as 'prioritise your effort'. If there are certain organisations that you would prefer to work for and you think you might be more suitable for, then spend more time on those applications. Write down how you meet all the criteria and then be very clear to the organisation how you – your knowledge, skills, abilities and other things (KSAOs) – meet each one of the criteria.

If your research tells you that you do not think you would really like to work for the organisation, then obviously a decision about whether you apply for the job depends on you, but think about the end of the process. If an employer you do not really want to work for offers you the only job you can get, then would you want to work for them? The answer is probably yes – if only to use it to get experience and then move on to another organisation after a while.

But even if it is no, the experience you get of completing the application and then hopefully performing well at an interview will be helpful in developing your self-confidence and giving you experience of a process – and some feedback from that process – which can be mean it is less challenging in the future. Whether you think that is worth it will be entirely up to you.

Your online profile

Your brand is not helpful if the right people do not get to see it, so an online presence is very important, but for some organisations the wrong online presence will mean you might not be offered the vacancy. Box 16.1 gives more detail.

━━━━━━━━━━ ▬▬▬▬▬▬ BOX 16.1 ▬▬▬▬▬▬ ━━━━━━━━━━

WHAT IS YOUR ONLINE PROFILE LIKE?

This might seem like a strange question, but it is an important one. To rephrase the question, 'What would someone looking at your social media profile think of you?' One of the things that employers sometimes do at some stage in the selection process is to look you up on Facebook (or other social media) and see what your profile looks like – and they can do so without you knowing.

So, ask yourself the following questions:

- Are there any photos of me which I would not like to be made public?
- Do I make any racist, sexist or provocative comments which could make me unacceptable to a company I wish to work with?
- Is there anything there in terms of web-links or photos from websites which would be classed as socially unacceptable?
- Is there anything on my social media site that I would not wish my father/mother or a younger brother or sister to see?

In particular, have you ever posted:

- Unnecessarily critical comments about others?
- Photos that indicate a lifestyle around aggression or excessive drinking?
- Items that you have shared which indicate any of the above?
- Items *that others have shared* which feature you (via tags)?

If the answer to any of these is yes, then be careful. An employer wanting to give you a good job will want to make sure that you are reliable and professional in all you do. Many employers might be reluctant to take you on if they think that you might do something which compromises the professional image of their organisation, or which might lead to your being seen as uncooperative or unhelpful.

In looking through social media such as Facebook, employers will usually get a very quick impression of what is important to you. There is nothing worse than being considered for an interview only to find out that, when an employer has looked at what you have posted, they have discounted you on the grounds of a lack of ethics or as an individual who had the potential to bring their organisation into disrepute in some way.

Conversely, many organisations use more professional websites such as LinkedIn to find employees. LinkedIn is a professional, work-based network where you can post your CV and where employers can see what you have done. In many cases, LinkedIn is useful for people who already have some work experience, but from the perspective of someone looking for a job, you can build up your network of the kinds of people and organisations for whom you might wish to work, and then send a brief, professionally worded email to let them know what you can offer.

Make sure that you engage well with LinkedIn, and keep it up to date. The contacts you have on LinkedIn can also provide you with advice and guidance on what sort of information recruiters will be looking for – and sometimes on how to structure your CV.

(Continued)

(Continued)

If you do have a LinkedIn and a Facebook (or equivalent) page, consider making sure that the two match up. There could be a potential clash in having a very professional LinkedIn page but a very different Facebook profile.

Finally, **be very careful what you post!** If you keep an eye on the news, you will almost certainly come across a story somewhere of someone who has posted something inappropriate – and has perhaps lost their job, or worse. (Imagine a situation where a father had successfully reached an out-of-court settlement of $80,000 with a school regarding age discrimination on condition they did not divulge the settlement, only for his daughter to do so that very afternoon. He lost the money (Collman, 2014)! On Twitter, there have been instances of students tweeting about previous employers only to find that the tweet has lost them an offer of a placement.

You do want to stand out from the crowd and get employers' attention – you want to do that for the right reasons!

REFLECTION POINT

Take some time to think about the following questions and write down some answers.

What makes you different and unique from the other graduates in your class? (If you are an international student and you are planning to look for a job in your home country after university, then you need to think about what makes you unique from other graduating students at home.)

Does that uniqueness come through in your CV?

If an employer were to look at your online profile – on Facebook, Twitter, Weixin – would they recognise the same uniqueness? Or would it be a more confused picture?

Do you think you need to change anything about your online profile?

Finding out about the Vacancy

Having taken some time to examine the organisation and your personal qualities, the final part of the process is to identify what the organisation is looking for in terms of KSAOs. This information can come from two sources: your analysis of the organisation (which should help to determine how well your values, ideas and behaviour might fit) and information given on the job vacancy. The information you collected earlier in the chapter, where you analysed an organisation, will apply to any vacancy within the organisation, but the knowledge and skills that it is looking for may either be spelt out or be inferred from content in the advertisement. In some industries, employers may also be expecting you to know about the industry as well.

If the information is clearly stated, then the key issue is to ensure that you address the skills required. A simple table can help, as below.

Skills/qualities sought	Evidence
• Good organisational skills	I organised the student society party …
• Proficient at using MS Word and Excel	I needed to use MS Word to write my assignments, and Excel to analyse complex data in writing my dissertation
• Demonstrable leadership ability	I lead others in two coursework groups, as well as taking significant leadership roles in a student union society

If the skills are less clear, then you may have to use your analytical skills and do some 'intelligent guess-work'. For example, for a generic training programme, the advert may say:

> We are seeking highly competent individuals to join as graduate trainees. As such, you will be expected to analyse data produced by other team members, to lead project teams and to present your findings both orally and in writing to middle management on a regular basis.

We can see that the job requires individuals who are:

- Competent – that is, have some record of success in their academic and non-academic activities.
- Analytical – able to use analytical skills.
- Able to lead.
- Experienced in project management – it is difficult to lead a project team unless you have project management skills.
- Skilled in presentations – 'orally'.
- Skilled in writing reports – 'and in writing'.

Therefore, any application needs to address at least these skills and show that the organisational values are those of the candidate. The application will need to give evidence to show how these skills have been demonstrated and developed. In themselves, all job applications require a significant level of analytical ability.

It is worth noting two further pieces of information. Firstly, the information you receive about the graduate vacancy or training scheme may or may not give an indication of salary. Average salaries for those graduating in the UK in 2015 were around £30,000 (High Fliers Research, 2015), but if salary is not given, it does not mean that it will be low. Many graduate recruiters do not reveal their graduate starting salaries for reasons of commercial confidentiality – and because different graduates working in different areas of the business with different qualifications (in different locations) may be paid differently.

Secondly, there may be a very limited time window for you to apply for the job. Most graduate employers are able to select their employees within a five-week window from application to offer (Association of Graduate Recruiters, 2015), which means that timescales are tight.

 KEY LEARNING POINT

An analysis of the organisation, of your capabilities and of the skills required for a general vacancy is the starting point for the development of any application, and is likely to take some time to complete.

DEVELOPING AND WRITING YOUR CV

If you have never written a CV before, then it can seem daunting, but if you have compiled a list of all you have done and any significant or interesting projects (see the list on page 342), then developing your CV is not going to be too difficult. The challenge comes in ensuring that your CV is targeted well towards a job vacancy. The structure and content of a CV is challenging, but getting the presentation right is also vitally important.

Note that the examples given here are *simply illustrative*: they are presented to give you an idea of what your content *could* look like and *could* include, but are meant solely to be a guide; not every employer will like the way these are presented. The section of this chapter on the presentation of your CV gives you a lot more information to consider in terms of presentation style.

CV Content and Structure

The typical CV will include the following content.

Personal contact details

These should include any university and personal email addresses and an up-to-date telephone number. Including your Skype details is also a good idea (see e.g. Table 16.1), but you do not have to give your date of birth, though many people do. Some might suggest that you should also include a photo, but there is no requirement to do so. Some people also give a LinkedIn username. This can be useful if an application is taken further to interview stage, but an employer will likely struggle to find time to look at this at the screening stage. Giving a Facebook account is not usually a good idea: not only is it a little informal, but also people often have content on there that business professionals might find inappropriate. If you are going to be away from your accommodation during university holidays then you need to give an alternative address as well, and the dates that you will be there.

Table 16.1   An example of contact details

Personal contact details

Name:	Mr Mike Smith
Email:	Mike.smith@anyoneemail.com
Telephone:	07777 777 7777
Address:	59 Madeup Street Townsville Nice Place XX12 3ZZ
Skype username:	Mrsmith98

It is worth checking your email address and, if necessary, setting up a new one. An email address which sounds silly or immature (e.g. littleredridinghood@yahoo.com or muscleman2@gmail.com) will show more of your personality than you might want. If you need to get a more professional email address, then do so. The importance of creating the right impression at this early stage cannot be understated, and while some information will be briefly scanned, the email address is one small piece of information which should not draw the wrong kind of attention.

Personal statement

This is not something that all applicants or CVs contain, but it has become more common recently. Building on the content you identified on page 342, a brief personal statement should be no longer than three lines, or maybe two to three sentences. An example is given in Figure 16.2.

Personal statement

I am a highly successful individual who is likely to obtain a **first class honours** degree in Business Studies. I have strong **leadership abilities**, enjoy **working in teams** and am able to **present well**.

Figure 16.2   Example of a personal statement

If you do use one, then be sure that you have the evidence to support what you say. Some people advise refocusing this on your career goals. At the start of your career, this may be a good thing to do, but as with many aspects of CVs, there is no one correct way to do this.

 'BUT I HAVE A QUESTION ...'

... Do I have to include a personal profile? I cannot think of anything to write.

No, there is no necessity to include a personal statement, but it can bring the qualities and strengths that you have to the attention of the selectors very easily, and give them quickly a very clear idea of what you can offer.

On the second issue – that you cannot think of anything to write – the suggestion would be that you need to consider some of what was written in Chapter 2, about knowing yourself very well. You will have certain strengths and weaknesses: the personal statement is not the place to discuss your weaknesses, but you will have knowledge, skills, motivation and experiences that you can mention here. The example given above is just an example – you could instead talk about what motivates you or particular achievements, but it *must* be kept short.

It *must* also be relevant. Including a personal statement which is not relevant will mean that your CV will be rejected very quickly: in professional terms, it is the equivalent of writing a letter and sending it to the wrong person.

Education and qualifications

When writing a CV, some students omit the necessary details here. Employers will be looking for someone who pays attention to detail, so it is important to get this correct. You need to indicate:

1. Your qualification title: BSc (Hons) Business Studies/A-Level/AS-Level/GCSEs/Gaokao/International Baccalaureate or other internationally accepted and relevant qualification.
2. The dates (month and year) when you started and then received each of your qualifications.
3. Your result – or, in the case of your degree, your anticipated result (e.g. 2:1) and three to four results from relevant modules (make sure that the results are good and from relatively recent modules).

You should always list the most recent qualifications and studies first; most people write this in a table form (Figure 16.3). If you have not yet graduated, then you will need to indicate your expected outcome.

Qualification	Dates (from/to)	Institution	Outcome (or expected outcome)
BSc (Hons) Business Studies	September 2015 – July 2018	University of Macclesfield	2:1 Hons (expected to graduate: July 2018)
A-Levels:	August 2015	General High School	
Geography			A
English			B
Biology			B
GCSEs:	August 2013	General High School	
10, including:			
Maths			A
English Literature			A
English Language			C
Biology			B

Figure 16.3   An example of results

 **'BUT I HAVE A QUESTION ...'**

... I have heard something about a 'HEAR' or 'GPA'. What are they?

Universities in the UK are trying out more ways to be fairer to students who are very skilled at what they do, but may not get the best results academically. The result of discussions on how to do this has resulted in the *Higher Education Achievement Report*, a document which provides information about academic and non-academic activities undertaken during your time at university.

It is broken down into eight sections:

1. Data about the individual – name, date of birth, etc.
2. Confirms the qualification title.
3. Confirms how the qualification fits with others (MSc is higher than a BSc, for example).
4. Qualification details – module and qualification results, mode of study, etc.
5. What the qualification is intended to help an individual to do (e.g. enter a career in ...).
6. Extra-curricular activities, awards, particular achievements and prizes.
7. Authentication of the HEAR.
8. Web-link to the relevant national university system of the institution.

The intention of the UK government is to increase the availability of the HEAR across universities (Universities UK, 2012) and to increase its use by employers. The expectation is that employers will engage with it more.

(Continued)

(Continued)

Details are available at the HEAR website: http://www.hear.ac.uk/

Some UK universities are also considering the use of Grade Point Average, a cumulative marking system used more in the United States and internationally than in Europe. Students in the United States, where a fail mark is anything less than 60, receive one of five grades: 0.0, 1.0, 2.0, 3.0 or 4.0 (or 4.33, representing an A+ grade). Graduation or passing is usually dependent on achieving 2.0 or sometimes 2.75, depending on the university.

There may be some qualifications that you took some time ago or qualifications that are not educational (e.g. Duke of Edinburgh Award scheme). These do not fit here, but should be mentioned under a section on personal achievements, or in your brief personal statement (e.g. 'I demonstrated leadership skills when I was …'). Sports certificates are not usually relevant for management roles, but might be included within your 'Hobbies and Interests' section.

International qualifications are always helpful, though sometimes an international employer will need a little help to understand their significance. Similarly, terms such as 'BSc' and 'MSc' translate to 'MS' and BS' in the US system.

Work experience

As in education and qualifications, start with the most recent work experience first, give the dates (month and year) of each period of work, the job title and two or three points (10–15 words) outlining what you did and/or your key achievements (Figure 16.4). If you have had responsibility for some aspect of management while in that role, then you need to state clearly what you were doing and what you achieved.

Work experience

Smith & Sons (Accountancy firm): Trainee Accountant (July–September 2015)

- Responsible for auditing receipts from clients
- Customer service duties: arranging appointments, responding to emails
- Communicating with managers, customers and other stakeholders to ensure smooth operation of customer service

---

Figure 16.4   An example of work experience

 'BUT I HAVE A QUESTION …'

… If I worked for just two weeks on a voluntary basis, should I include that?

The simple answer is that it depends what it adds to the impression an employer might have of you. If your longer term work experience was working in a bar serving customers (which could have led to your developing your communication skills and 'customer orientation') but the two-week experience was work shadowing a senior CEO from a major multinational, then it would make sense to include it.

(Continued)

(Continued)

On the other hand, if that two-week voluntary internship was making the coffee and photocopying reports, then it is probably less useful to mention it.

Anything you put into the CV needs either to add evidence of your credibility as a candidate to evidence of a certain skill which has already been presented, or to add evidence of a new skill. Try not to be repetitive.

Additional responsibilities and activities

This important section tells an employer what you have done outside of your studies. For example, you may have reasonable grades, but if you have been president of a student society or had some responsibility for managing the budget of an athletics club, then this is something that a prospective employer would be extremely interested in (Figure 16.5).

If you are successful in the application process and are taken on by the organisation, you will likely be leading others in some management role, so if you can demonstrate that you have already done so while at universities (when you can make mistakes that will not affect businesses and public organisations), then you will have a much better chance of getting to the interview stage than without such experience.

Key responsibilities

President, University Canoeing Society (September 2015 to November 2016)

- Leading canoeing committee: setting agendas, scheduling meetings, leading team, setting goals, delegating event duties, responsible for increasing club profile
- Liaising with student union: dealing with queries, report writing, negotiating club budget
- Communicating with society members: established members' newsletter, developing club recruitment video (through leadership team), established club competition

---

Figure 16.5   An example of key responsibilities

Whatever you have done, you need to demonstrate to an employer that you have gained relevant skills and understanding from those activities. When it comes to activities that you have undertaken as part of a group (and hopefully in a position of some leadership or responsibility), you also need to be clear about your contribution to the achievement of the team's goals. What specifically did you do which helped the team achieve its goal?

Hobbies, interests and achievements

It may not seem the most relevant part of who you are, but including these can reveal a great deal about your abilities on occasions (Figure 16.6). You might have organised a travel for a group of people during your time at university (showing organisational skills), or be good at a second language or musical instrument (showing persistence and determination), or be responsible for the finances in your student house (showing administrative and leadership skills). This section is your opportunity to indicate to an employer that you are an interesting individual who does more than just study, and tells the employer more about what motivates you and what you enjoy.

Hobbies, interests and achievements

Photography: I have been interested in photography for about five years and have had my photographs printed in two local magazines and a national newspaper. I have also organised my own exhibitions locally and have sold prints to clients.

Sailing: I have been taking sailing lessons every month for the past two years and have reached Level 3 in the National Sailing Standards Certificate.

Figure 16.6   An example of hobbies, interests and achievements

References

You will normally need to indicate two referees who can provide an employer with a reference. You should give a minimum of one academic referee – often a personal tutor or a lecturer you know well – and one other, who can be a previous employer or another academic tutor. Referees should *always* be asked before their name and contact details are given and should never be:

- A relative.
- A personal friend.
- Another student (even if they have worked with you on group projects).
- Anyone who does not know you well enough to comment on your strengths and weaknesses.

Academic tutors are very used to writing references, but if they have no formal responsibility to do so for you, then be very polite in how you ask them to do it for you. Do not give them a short time limit to do so.

When giving references, you need to give the referee's:

- Formal title (including Dr or Professor as appropriate – be sure to get it right) and name.
- Job title (Personal Tutor, Academic Lecturer, Associate Dean, etc.).
- Place of work.
- Postal and email addresses, and telephone numbers.

Some applicants choose not to give references and that is acceptable (particularly if you have no space left on the page), but if you decide not to give any names, then you do need to indicate that you are willing to do so, should the need arise, by saying 'References available on request.'

Skills-Based Structure

The above structure is a traditional way of developing your CV, but it is not the only way. Some people like to use a skills-based structure, as follows:

1. Personal and contact details.
2. Education and qualifications.
3. Brief list of work and social activities completed.
4. Details of how each of a number of relevant skills have been developed and demonstrated (see the example in Figure 16.7).
5. References.

> **Skill 1: Communication skills – Developed through:**
>
> - Social activities as president of the university abseiling club
> - Academic modules requiring me to undertake presentations as part of a group
> - Internship with PWC, where I needed to undertake presentations on management issues
>
> **Skill 2: Team-working skills:**
>
> - Group activities (e.g. marketing assignment) undertaken as part of my university studies

Figure 16.7 An example of skills content

This structure is a good way to indicate clearly to an employer the skills you have and how you have developed them. Some applicants find it easier to write according to chronology (i.e. in the order that they have developed the experience) and some employers find it easier to see how someone has progressed in their studies and experience if the CV is done according to the detail presented above. For those applying for jobs and having had more life experience, a CV that is done chronologically will more clearly show any gaps in either employment or studies – employers are often very interested in such gaps.

Put simply, there is no one way of structuring a CV, nor should you ask an employer what their preferences are, of course – an employer will expect you to make up your own mind.

─────── **KEY LEARNING POINT** ───────

There is no one ideal CV structure, but employers will look to see if they have sufficient information on which to base a decision to select or reject.

CV PRESENTATION AND FORMATTING

Getting the presentation of a CV correct is very important, but we can talk about two areas here: spelling and grammar; and visual appearance. The former clearly have some right or wrong practices, but when it comes to visual presentation, there is no right and wrong, only personal preferences. Chapter 7 covered issues of spelling and grammar, and included a short exercise to work through; we will not repeat it here, but we can look at issues of visual presentation. One piece of advice, however, is to try to develop your own style rather than use a 'CV Wizard' available online. These tend to produce very standard applications that do not always stand out as much as you need to. It is similar to producing a wonderful garden with lots of roses, only to find that everyone else has done exactly the same. Box 16.2 highlights a common error when submitting a CV.

─────── **BOX 16.2** ───────

A COMMON SPELLING ERROR IN CVs

How do you spell CV properly? People simply write 'C V' at the top of their submission, but it is also common to write out the words in full. Getting that very first heading wrong can mean your CV never gets looked at.

(Continued)

(Continued)

The correct spelling is 'Curriculum Vitae', but it is not uncommon for employers to see variations on the first word, such as:

'Curiculum Vitae'

'Curirculum Vita' or

'Curriclum Viate'

or some other variation. Of course, this is not the only kind of spelling mistake that can occur. The most disastrous spelling mistake would be getting your email address (or that of your referees) wrong, and this happens from time to time as well. Other mistakes in section headings, like 'personel details' or 'work experience', can be surprisingly common. Employers' names should always be spelt correctly, of course.

Getting your spelling (and in a covering letter or application form where you are writing in full sentences – your grammar) correct is important for a variety of reasons, not least because poor spelling or grammar implies a lack of attention to detail, especially in a situation where you are trying to make a good impression.

When it comes to the presentation of your application, you are looking to ensure that the recipient can easily see what you want them to see (which presumably is what is required for the job). This might mean a little variety in how you present certain information and how you colour, format and present your CV. What it does not mean, however, is that you need to use expensive paper or fancy and elegant fonts, and that you do not need to have a CV 10 pages long.

Length

Your CV should not be longer than two sides. Some recommend developing a CV that is one side long, but that is going to be a challenge if you have sufficient information to match all the required skills for the role. There is no word count, but write succinctly. CVs which are two sides long are fine.

Using bold text

Bold text – or *italics* or <u>underlining</u> – is a great way of ensuring that certain words in your CV stand out, but use bold formatting sparingly. A sentence that has every other word in bold will obviously not have the desired effect.

Using bullet points

These are used a great deal in CVs and can be useful for ensuring that the recipient knows that they are getting outline notes, rather than complete sentences (e.g. 'I spent three years working as a hotel receptionist during my time at university' can become 'Three years' experience as hotel receptionist during my studies'). General advice is not to have absolutely everything in bullet points – the danger is that it becomes a little repetitive and unappealing to the eye.

Colour

Using colour in your CV is usually not necessary. For many graduate positions, it is highly likely that your CV will be photocopied in black and white, and circulated to a variety of people, so colour in your CV becomes fairly irrelevant. However, a controlled and purposeful use of shading can be quite useful, either for headings or to highlight occasional and important words. If you do use shading, ensure that it is dark enough to be photocopied, but not too dark so as to obscure any writing.

'Clutter'

It is not easy to define what is meant here, but a balance is needed between something which looks 'very busy' (lots of information, untidily crammed into a small space, where it is not easy to distinguish relevant words from less relevant ones) and something which looks so neat and tidy that it looks very sparse, as if you have hardly anything to say about yourself. A CV which has so much information that it needs to use a font smaller than Calibri size 11 (font and size) is probably going to be too cluttered; the suggestion would be to reduce the information on the page.

Indent your text where necessary. A CV should look inviting to read.

The best way to see if your CV looks cluttered is to hold it at arm's length and see whether it appears 'neat but not empty' to you.

Care and attention to detail

The following need to be **avoided**:

- Careless spelling mistakes (watch out for using the wrong words: a spell-checker will *not* identify these for you!). Make sure that you spell headings, the names of previous employers and referees correctly.
- Sentences, paragraphs or tables which go over the page break.
- Informality and being too chatty: keep the CV succinct and focused.
- Text that uses different fonts, or fonts of different sizes. Be consistent throughout.
- *Any* dishonesty: if you are dishonest, you will almost certainly be found out, and if that happens then you will either be fired (if the truth comes out after the job offer has been made) or you will not progress. Be aware that employers and HR professionals do talk to each other, even if they are from different organisations, so lying on one application may mean you do not get considered for others as well.

=========== KEY LEARNING POINT ===========

What you do include is usually as important as what you do not include. Before submitting your CV and covering letter, you need to check through carefully to ensure that everything is as you want it to be. Try to get someone else who can give you some good advice to go through it as well.

Use of 'power words'

Those who provide careers guidance often talk about 'power words'. These are words that can significantly enhance the significance of what you have done. Table 16.2 gives some examples of the kinds of words which create more of an impact than they otherwise would.

Table 16.2   Power words for use in a CV or covering letter

• Advised	• Discovered	• Performed
• Analysed	• Distributed	• Planned
• Arranged	• Edited	• Prepared
• Assembled	• Evaluated	• Prescribed
• Assisted	• Examined	• Presented
• Audited	• Expanded	• Processed
• Calculated	• Identified	• Produced
• Charted	• Implemented	• Promoted
• Collected	• Improved	• Provided
• Completed	• Increased	• Recorded
• Conducted	• Installed	• Referred
• Consolidated	• Instituted	• Represented
• Consulted	• Instructed	• Researched
• Coordinated	• Interpreted	• Reviewed
• Corresponded	• Interviewed	• Served
• Counselled	• Invented	• Sold
• Created	• Lectured	• Solved
• Delivered	• Maintained	• Studied
• Designed	• Managed	• Supervised
• Determined	• Negotiated	• Supplied
• Developed	• Networked	• Trained
• Devised	• Observed	• Translated
• Diagnosed	• Obtained	• Wrote
• Directed	• Operated	
	• Ordered	
	• Organised	

 KEY LEARNING POINT

Your CV is an advertisement for yourself. There is no perfect or universally ideal way of writing a CV, but a poorly written one will be very memorable.

COVERING LETTERS

A covering letter introduces you to a prospective employer. If the CV is the bones of who you are and what you have done, then the covering letter provides the linkages and the muscle. The CV should be written in note style (it does not need to be in full sentences), but the letter is a piece of business writing, written in good English and formatted in a particular way.

However, in the same way that a CV should not reflect literally everything you have done, so too the covering letter should summarise why you are suitable for the job. It must not be a list of everything that you have done and should supplement rather than repeat the information in the CV, but each of the main paragraphs should relate to a different aspect of your suitability.

Understanding Business Writing

Before we go into detail on writing a covering letter specifically, it would be helpful to address some aspects of writing a formal business letter. Business letters tend to be laid out in a fairly standard format.

FOR YOU TO DO

Have a look at a formal business letter that you have received. It might be from your bank, from a university or from another organisation that you have contact with.

1. Look at the formatting. On the letter, where is your address? Where is the address of the sending organisation? Where on the page is the date?
2. Look at the kind of language used. If a friend was writing this to you, how would their language and words differ from those in the letter in front of you?
3. How does the letter end?

Noticing the layout and the language used in the letter will help significantly in ensuring that your own covering letter meets a minimum professional standard. A possible layout is given in Figure 16.8.

| | Your address and postcode |
| | Your email address(es) |

Recipient's address and postcode

Date

Dear Sir/Madam,

Re: Job Application for Vacancy Ref: XXX

I am writing to express my interest and to submit an application for the role of … I enclose my CV, which gives details of my degree, my work experience and my involvement in university clubs and societies. I would like to use this opportunity to explain why I think I am suitable for this role.

{Paragraph explaining your education and why it is relevant. What relevant knowledge and skills have you developed during your degree?}

{One or two paragraphs explaining how your experiences have contributed to who you are and the skills you have.}

{Paragraph explaining your education and why it is relevant. What relevant knowledge and skills have you developed during your degree?}

{Brief paragraph explaining your motivation for a particular career.}

Thank you for taking the time to read my application: I hope you will find that I have the skills and abilities to be able to take the application further, but please do not hesitate to contact me if you should need any additional information.

I look forward to being able to discuss my application with you in the near future.

Yours faithfully,
{Signature}
{Print your name}

Figure 16.8   An example of a covering letter

If you can find out the name of the individual who might be dealing with graduate applications, then that could be useful, but applications to a graduate training scheme may go to departmental managers. Try to find a name if you can (it will make the application seem a lot more personal), but be cautious about using a name if you are unsure.

Always refer back to the CV as much as you can, using phrases such as 'As shown in my CV …' or 'The CV also indicates that …' Do not forget that the purpose of the covering letter is to direct the prospective employer to the important parts of your CV, but the covering letter should *not* repeat the CV.

Have a strong, positive ending, including information on how and when you will follow up, and inform about availability for interviews if applicable.

Writing in a Business Style

In the earlier chapters, we covered how to write in an academic style. Writing in a business style is somewhat different. Some tips are as follows:

1. Keep your sentences short and focused on evidence for the skills that employers are looking for.
2. Be unemotional and keep your letter factual: words like 'amazing', 'wonderful', 'really' and 'fantastic' are not appropriate.
3. Be specific about your contribution to any team activities.
4. Be polite but try not to overdo things. Phrases such as 'Your amazing magnificence …' are a little excessive.
5. Do not tell employers everything, but give them enough about your KSAOs (your knowledge, skills, abilities and other qualities) to make them interested; they can always follow up with questions at an interview.
6. Remember that your reader will have lots of such letters to read, so make yours stand out.

Business letters usually end 'Yours sincerely' or 'Yours faithfully' (notice small 's' and small 'f'). They both have a very specific use:

'Yours faithfully' is used when you are writing to someone *you do not know*, in which case you will have started the letter with 'Dear Sir/Madam,'.

'Yours sincerely' is used when you are writing to someone *you do know*, in which case you will have started the letter with 'Dear Mr XXX,'.

COMPLETING ONLINE APPLICATION FORMS

The principles which govern good CV writing also apply to completing an application form well: both require you to demonstrate to an employer that you have the skills to do the job they are recruiting for. However, an application form has more in common with a selection interview than it does with a CV. The use of an application form (whether online or in a paper version) gives the employer the opportunity to ask those questions that they want to ask.

Understanding the Application Form

In one sense, application forms are fairly straightforward and standardised. All application forms will ask for your contact details, your educational qualifications and your work experience, and will ask you to give the names of referees who can testify to what you have done and how well you have done it. However, this is probably where the similarities between application forms from different employers will stop.

Most graduate application forms will give you an opportunity to talk about how you have developed and demonstrated specific skills that the employer is seeking. If you have undertaken little extra-curricular activity during your time as a student, then you might struggle with some of the questions which appear on application forms.

Most also give you a tight word limit (often 200–300 words) in which to give your answers.

FOR YOU TO DO

Look at the following questions. How would you respond?

1. Give an example of a time when you had to make a difficult decision without complete information. How did you go about it and what was the result?
2. Discuss an occasion when you contributed to the learning and development of others. How did your input change their behaviour?
3. Describe a time when you had to inspire and motivate others. How did you go about it, and what impact did you have?
4. How have you used your creativity to solve a difficult problem? Briefly outline the situation and indicate how successful you were.
5. Outline a situation in which you had to prioritise conflicting demands on your time. How did you go about deciding on your priorities?
6. Describe a situation in which you realised that you had made a serious mistake in your work. What action did you take after you had realised you had made the mistake? Why did you take such action?

Each of the questions given above is designed to assess your previous experience in demonstrating the skills employers are looking for. Looking at each question in turn, it is not difficult to see the skills that they are seeking:

1. Decision making.
2. Management of others' learning.
3. Inspiration and leadership.
4. Creativity.
5. Time management.
6. Ability to deal with a mistake.

At one level, these are obvious, but each of the questions will have been designed to assess your competence in other ways as well:

- Q1 is also about how you respond to uncertainty. In management, many decisions need to be made quickly, with incomplete information. How confident you might be in doing so could be a key success factor when it comes to being successful in your job.

- Q2 could also be about how you give feedback to others. 'Contributing to others' learning' is often more about one-to-one management than it is about standing up and giving a training seminar. If you have done this in a student society or at work, then you have a story to tell.

- Q3 is about leadership, but the question asks 'How did you go about it?', so there is a less obvious 'planning' aspect to this. The question also asks about the impact of what you did, so your answer should also indicate that you know how to evaluate the impact of actions, whether those are your own actions or those of others who might be working for you.

- Q4 is perhaps more obvious, but the more difficult the problem, the more excited an employer is going to be when they read that you were able to solve it successfully. What is important, however, is that you have actually tried to solve difficult problems, rather than given them to someone else to solve.

- Q5 is probably not difficult for many students to write about. You have probably had two assignments due at the same time, or job hunting and assignments taking place together, but the more unusual and challenging the situations you give, the more impressive will be the fact that you have had success.

- Q6 is somewhat different, because this question has no apparent right or wrong answer. The question is about your values, rather than your skills. When specific employers are looking at the responses to a question like this, they will determine whether someone's actions would be desirable or undesirable for their own organisation. The 'correctness' of an answer depends on the culture and values of the organisation, but it is clear that an employer will expect you to be honest.

 ━━ FOR YOU TO DO ━━━━━━━━━━━━━━━━━━━━━━━━━━

Look at the three answers given below for the first question above, repeated here:

Give an example of a time when you had to make a difficult decision in without complete information. How did you go about it and what was the result? (200 words max.)

(a) 'I needed to decide how to complete a coursework assignment but the criteria were not clearly described in the course documents. I was able to talk to other classmates and find out about their ideas and that helped me get the assignment completed. In the end, I got a mark of 65%.' (52 words)

(b) 'I was on the committee of the canoeing club and we were holding a social event to attract new members. As part of that social event, we wanted to ensure that we had good catering for the event and we had two possibilities but neither could commit to supplying food and drink without knowing whether they could really supply what was needed (which was based on how many people would be coming), which we could not confirm at the time. The price of one supplier was cheaper than the other only if there were more than 65 people at the event. I made the decision to choose that supplier based on numbers who had attended a similar event at the same time last year. We finally had 120 students turn up for the event and we made a profit by choosing the cheaper supplier.' (144 words)

(c) 'I was working as part of a group and we had to interview three local firms as part of our coursework. The intention was that we interviewed individuals in these firms to find out about their strategy and whether there were any difficulties in their trying to achieve their strategy, but the course materials didn't give much guidance so we decided to find just anyone who was working in those companies. We interviewed six people and so our strategy was quite successful.' (82 words)

(Continued)

(Continued)

Questions:

1. What do you think makes a strong and a weak answer?
2. What weaknesses do these answers show about their other qualities? Is there anything that was mentioned which did not give a good impression of any of the candidates?
3. Does length make a difference to the strength of the answer?
4. Which do you think is the stronger and weaker answers? *Why?*
5. Bearing in mind your thinking about weak and strong answers, try to provide your own strong answers to the remaining five questions above (question 2 – 'Discuss an occasion when you contributed to the learning and development of others. How did your input change their behaviour?' – to question 6).

In all the questions above (and probably others that you will find in application forms), there are some commonalities. They all expect you to give an example ('of a time when you …'), to communicate succinctly and clearly, and to evaluate the outcome of your actions.

Employers are also looking to see your breadth of experience. If you have part-time work experience and have taken a leadership role in a student society or led a coursework team, then you will probably have enough experience to answer the questions well, but make sure as far as possible that *your answer to each question uses an example of a different situation.* (One situation which involves all the challenges and difficulties asked for is either likely to be stressful or has been managed very badly by yourself and/or others in your team.)

Always talk about what *you* did: Chapters 10 and 12 talk about using 'we' in your communication, but when you are applying for a job, using 'we' makes it somewhat unclear as to what your own contribution was.

Completing an application form is not easy, so take time to practise your answer. Online application forms will usually ask you to enter text into webpages, but will usually enable you to prepare an answer offline. Such forms may give you an option to download and save your form, and might be scanned by a computer for keywords, but you *must* keep a copy of what you send – employers will almost certainly want to know more once you get to an interview.

It is also worth noting that if the process is facilitated online, then you will not be able to apply after the closing date, so you will need to get your application in *on time*.

=== **KEY LEARNING POINT** ===

Targeting your application is more difficult with a CV than with an application form, but completing an application form for a graduate job can take a great deal of time and skill.

SPECULATIVE APPLICATIONS

The above sections work well when you are applying for a specific vacancy, or a specific training programme. Some people will select particular companies that they wish to work for on the basis of accurate and good information they have about what it is like to work there (e.g. 'employer of the year' awards etc.), and will write to them asking whether they would have any vacancies in the near future.

There is a significant difference between the principles outlined above and those identified here. In the traditional process, an application will need to be focused on the criteria required to be able to do the job well. However, a speculative application would (by definition) approach a particular individual asking for consideration in relation to any forthcoming vacancies.

The Internet has considerably impacted on the need for speculative applications. There is a great deal of information publicly available that was not available previously. Websites such as LinkedIn and Monster.co.uk enable individuals to upload their CV and vacancies are posted on organisation websites, so if you have a particular company in mind, you *must* check its website before making a speculative application – if you do not, then you might give the impression that you cannot be bothered to do so.

A speculative application needs to be approached with caution. A CV needs to be no longer than two pages, so you need to consider carefully what goes into the CV and what you leave out, but, without having a particular role in mind, it can sometimes be difficult to know what to include and what to leave out. Including skills that are not relevant for any vacancy a company might have – or leaving out ones that are – can mean that your application does not get the attention you might want it to receive.

The letter that would accompany a speculative CV also needs to be worded very carefully. If you wish to make a speculative application, then you need to ensure that the impression you create is neither of someone who is desperate, nor of someone who can do any job that might exist in that organisation. Box 16.3 gives more information.

BOX 16.3

PHRASES TO USE IN SPECULATIVE APPLICATION LETTERS

Getting the phrasing right in a speculative application is important for the impression you want to create. Again, many of the 'power words' given earlier can assist in this, but here are some additional phrases and their meanings which might prove useful:

'I am {intending to work in/seeking} a marketing role.'

'After some careful thought, I have decided that I {would prefer/am extremely keen} to work in a {multi-national/small/public} organisation like your own because ...'

'I would like to work for {name of organisation} because ...'

'I believe that my skills, knowledge and experience are suitable for this kind of a role because ...'

'My education {indicate your degree} has given me ...'

'I am a confident and innovative individual who ...'

'I understand that you may not be able to give me a reply, but would be grateful if you could keep my application for any forthcoming vacancies.'

One perceived advantage of speculative applications is that you can apparently send the same – or very similar – applications to many different organisations with relatively little effort. In effect it is like direct marketing of yourself to the 'customer', but just as a great deal of direct mail is put into the bin, it can take a fair amount of luck to catch the right organisation at the right time.

However, there are some ideas which can help increase your chances of success:

1. Look in the financial and business news for companies and industries which are expanding and which are exploring new markets, especially if you have knowledge or skills (languages) in those new markets.
2. Look in the personnel magazines for vacancies related to graduate recruitment. If new graduate recruitment staff are being taken on in an organisation, it might mean that they are expecting to recruit more graduates.
3. Consider carefully whether to apply to organisations that are making lots of people redundant or to ones that are merging: organisations which merge often do so to save costs, though such mergers might give some interesting opportunities. You might decide, however, that organisations which are going through such changes provide less certainty than those which are more stable.
4. Think about applying to smaller companies, especially those which have only recently begun. Such businesses often need expertise quickly, but because they are not well known, many graduates would not know about them. They rarely have significant resources to devote to graduate recruitment, so might well welcome speculative applications. They can be great places to work as their small size and hopefully rapid growth can give you early responsibility and breadth of experience very quickly.

Speculative applications rarely succeed, but if they are targeted and constructed carefully (which means finding out about the organisation, understanding the culture and then reflecting those same values in your application), then they can sometimes be successful.

======= KEY LEARNING POINT =======

A well-targeted speculative application will usually take as much work and time to complete as a more typical application.

INTEGRATION AND APPLICATION

Covering letters, CVs and job applications all require you to know about yourself and your experience, so one of the first steps to take in making a job application is to find out about yourself.

Step 1: Make a list of all the significant activities you have done and what you have achieved through them.

Step 2: Next to each one, identify the skills that you have developed and demonstrated through those activities. Each activity will probably have more than one skill.

You now have a list of your skills, and evidence for each of them.

Step 3: Review and discover what skills are needed for each vacancy that you are applying for and select those events/activities that are relevant.

This should now give you a focused list of activities, ready for emphasising on an application form, and for mentioning in your CV.

Step 4 (for the CV/covering letter)**:** Prepare a standard structure and format for your CV and covering letter so that you can 'slot' the information into that structure, using appropriate 'power words' (as long as they are truthful).

Step 4 (for the application form): Review the questions and draft your answers carefully in a document. This gives you time to edit, use appropriate power words and ensure that, as far as possible, each question deals with a different situation you have faced.

Step 5: Check your spelling, check relevance and reread your application carefully.

Step 6: Give your application to someone else who can give you some expert advice – maybe a careers guidance counsellor. You could give it to a friend who works in a managerial role, but they will need to reflect carefully on what the recruiter is looking for, rather than on their own judgement.

Step 7: If you are happy with your application, make sure you submit it *before* the closing date! A late application will not usually be considered, unless there is a shortage of applicants.

The Link with Your Studies

The skills needed to complete a good job application are similar to those needed to do well in your studies. A CV will require you to write succinctly; application forms will require you to provide a relevant and direct answer to any question; both will need you to present evidence for the points that you raise; both will need you to demonstrate your analytical skills; and the work you need to do to find out about the organisation is little different to what you might need to do for an academic assignment.

There are some limits to this parallel, of course: you should never include paragraphs of text in your CV; you should not be citing research; and while your letter should have some sort of structure, it should not start with the same sort of introduction or end with the same sort of conclusion as a traditional academic essay. However, it is useful to recognise that the skills you use for your academic work are going to be useful in other contexts as well.

CONCLUSION

By the end of this chapter, you should have a good idea of how to:

- Understand how employers view the recruitment and selection processes.
- Describe how employers select and use different selection tools.
- Identify the qualities needed in different kinds of roles.
- Write and compile CVs, covering letters and application forms.
- Develop speculative applications.

Submitting good applications takes a great deal of time and effort. You will need to analyse the vacancy (if there is one), determine the skills being sought and then provide evidence to the recruiters that you have exactly those skills. Further, you also need to suggest to them that you have the knowledge and education that will help their organisation to progress and achieve its goals.

This evidence needs to address sufficiently all the essential requirements and some of the desirable ones as well.

FINAL REFLECTIONS

Based on the content of this chapter, what do you now know about CVs, covering letters and application forms that you did not know before?
What key learning point had the most impact? Why?

Do your answers to either of the above questions have the potential to change your ability to write a convincing application and CV? Why?

What will you now do differently? (Write this down and put it somewhere where you can see it regularly.)

ADDITIONAL RESOURCES

Want to learn more? Visit https://study.sagepub.com/morgan to gain access to a wide range of online resources, including interactive tests, tasks, further reading and downloads.

Website Resources

Much of the guidance here is provided by university careers services.

Kent University: www.kent.ac.uk/careers/cv.htm

Leicester University: www2.le.ac.uk/offices/careers-new/information-for-students/apps/cv

Liverpool Hope University (includes a Prezi presentation by a careers adviser): www.hope.ac.uk/gateway/careers/careerdevelopment/applicationsinterviewsandselection/writingacv/

Prospects website: www.prospects.ac.uk/careers-advice/cvs-and-cover-letters

Purdue University: https://owl.english.purdue.edu/owl/resource/641/01/

University of Birmingham: intranet.birmingham.ac.uk/as/employability/careers/apply/cv/index.aspx

University of Nottingham: www.nottingham.ac.uk/shared/shared_careers/pdf/app-Writing_a_CV.pdf

University of Sheffield: www.sheffield.ac.uk/careers/students/gettingajob/cvs

University of Sheffield – Social Media and Your Career: www.shef.ac.uk/careers/students/gettingajob/media

University of Strathclyde: www.strath.ac.uk/careers/apply/yourcv/writingeffectivecvs/

Textbook Resources

Bailey, S. (2011) *Academic Writing for International Students of Business*. Abingdon: Routledge (particularly part 4.2).
McIlroy, D. (2003) *Studying @ University*. London: Sage (particularly chapter 10).
Price-Machado, D. (1998) *Skills for Success*. New York: Cambridge University Press (particularly chapter 4).
Turner, J. (2002) *How to Study: A Short Introduction*. London: Sage (particularly chapter 11).

17 SELECTION INTERVIEWS

CHAPTER STRUCTURE

Figure 17.1

When you see the 🌐 this means go to the companion website https://study.sagepub.com/morgan to do a quiz, complete a task, read further or download a template.

━ AIMS OF THE CHAPTER ━

By the end of this chapter, you should be able to:

- Identify potential questions you might be asked in advance of an interview.
- Understand some basic dos and don'ts.
- Identify questions to ask the potential employer.
- Evaluate the impact of your non-verbal behaviour as well as the content of the answers that you give.

INTRODUCTION

Undergoing a selection interview is often seen as one of the most nerve-wracking and challenging experiences that an individual is likely to face. In the perception of many, the stress of the experience is not dissimilar to taking your driving test or giving a professional presentation for the first time, but the reality is that it does not need to be. This chapter aims to dispel some of the myths surrounding the selection interview, and to present some ideas about how employers assess individuals' responses. The chapter will examine how employers construct selection interviews, what goes through their minds when undertaking interviews and how they develop a structure and questions. It will also examine how employers make judgements after a selection interview and will give you the chance to be in the interviewer's shoes and evaluate different answers.

One of the assumptions, though, in being invited for a selection interview is that any decision making is one way: that if the organisation decides you are the individual for the role (or for a general training scheme), you will accept it. While reading this chapter it is important to recognise that the interview is probably one of the few chances you will have to find out about the organisation before you commit to working for it, if you are given the chance to do so.

The principal communication skills required for doing 'well' at an interview are likely to be similar as those used in a good conversation. Establishing a sense of rapport, smiling and speaking clearly are generally important, but being skilled at engaging in conversation is not going to be sufficient for performing 'well' at a selection interview.

The chapter will begin by looking at what 'performing *well*' means in practice and will establish what the selectors' objectives are. It will then look at the various stages of a selection interview and give some views from those who are used to conducting selection interviews, and who have seen the mistakes that candidates have made. The chapter will move on to examine some issues that you might like to think about when considering whether it is a job role that you want, and will give some advice for when things do not really go the way you had hoped.

PERFORMING WELL: THE EMPLOYERS' OBJECTIVES

It might seem strange to put the two sides of the interview – the candidate and the employer – together at the start of this chapter, but it is important to define clearly what we mean by 'performing well' and the only way we can do that is by considering what the employer is seeking to gain from the encounter. (In this way, it is no different to considering how to write a good essay by defining what a lecturer is seeking.)

An employer will likely be seeking to answer one or more of the following questions:

1. Is this candidate likely to be able to perform well in the role?
2. Is this candidate likely to be able to perform at an acceptable level within the organisation?
3. Is this candidate likely to fit into the culture of the organisation?

The first question will certainly apply where there is a specific job on offer, whereas both the other questions address the two requisite qualities for performing well in an organisation: namely, person–job fit and person–organisation fit. The second question might be more important for a selection interview where successful individuals will the join a general training scheme of some kind.

SELECTION INTERVIEW

A selection interview is a conversation with the purpose of deciding whether a candidate has the ability and sufficient experience to perform well in a job role.

If the objective is to identify whether a candidate is likely to be able to perform well in the role, then, as we saw in Chapter 14, the questions asked will be designed around the job role. A skilled interviewer will want to ask questions based on the job role that they have in mind, will do so in a structured and systematic manner, and will always be seeking information to enable them to answer one of these two questions. They will, therefore, reject candidates who fail to give sufficient information, who give information that fails to answer the question asked or who give an answer that would be considered inappropriate or 'incorrect' in some way.

The time given to any first stage interview is limited. A final-year undergraduate will need to convince an employer within 30 or 45 minutes that they are worth taking to the next stage. If the interviewer is seeking convincing evidence that the candidate possesses five qualities (usually it is more) and allows the candidate to ask questions as well, then they would have five minutes or less to gather evidence about each quality; if it is seven or eight qualities, then the time drops to about two or three minutes. This means that candidates need to give sufficient answers that are succinct and convincing.

In order to gather the convincing evidence that they are seeking, employers will be trying to gather specific examples of when the candidate has done particular activities or demonstrated particular skills relevant to the job role.

KEY LEARNING POINT

In a selection interview, employers have limited time to seek examples and gather convincing evidence of the skills and attitudes they require for the job role.

PREPARING FOR A JOB INTERVIEW

It is possible to consider a job interview in the same way as we might think of an academic examination: we do not know exactly what the questions are going to be but we do know how long it will last and we should know where and when it will take place. We might also have a reasonable idea of what the employer (or in the latter case, examiner) might be looking for, but the unpredictability in both situations comes from uncertainty regarding the questions.

Review Your Application

Therefore, the preparation for both situations is very similar. For an examination, we do revision, usually over a long period of time. We could think of a selection interview as an examination where the topic is 'yourself', so the revision you need to do is to go back over your application and remind yourself of what you have described and the experiences you have had. More broadly, however, it would be a good idea to go back over all that you have done during your time at university which might be relevant, so you can recall events and situations in the interview.

Review the Job Specification

When interviewers are preparing to conduct a selection interview, they will have a look at the KSAOs (Knowledge, Skills, Attitudes and Other factors) listed in the person specification. Time will be limited in a first-stage selection interview, so, first of all, employers will want to concentrate on identifying evidence for those skills deemed essential, and, secondly, those deemed desirable if there is time left. As a candidate, it makes perfect sense to do the same.

Sometimes, those qualities will be very clearly stated, but where the application is for a graduate training scheme, the qualities will probably be far more general and might relate more to your suitability for the organisation than for a specific job role. The advert for such a scheme might be very clear, but the values, motives and attitudes that the employers are seeking may or may not be explicitly listed in any advertising.

──────── FOR YOU TO DO ────────

Read through the information given below – a fictional example of an advertisement for a graduate training scheme – and then try to answer the questions which follow.

'RED International seeks to grow steadily over the next five years and is seeking well-qualified and able graduates to join its team. The organisation – with its headquarters in Zurich – is developing its strategy for international expansion. Growth is expected to be slow and steady but opportunities for increasing personal responsibility and promotion will be significant.

'Zurich is a beautiful city and the organisation has offices in a number of locations throughout Europe, but it is now time to extend our success into the UK. RED is setting up offices in three locations – Edinburgh, London and Birmingham – and managers in these locations have been working to develop a graduate training programme which will see individuals moving around the UK.

'The training programme consists of a variety of appointments according to each individual's skills, but a central core developed around projects covering the areas of Marketing, Budgeting and Accounting, Information Analysis and Leadership. For successful applicants, the programme will last two years.

'Those applying should expect to achieve the very best in their studies, evidence of competent leadership and should expect to work hard during their programme.'

Questions:

1. How risk averse do you think the company is?
2. What do you think the company's attitude to innovation might be?
3. Do you think the company is more task oriented or people oriented?
4. How do you think the answers to these questions might affect the questions you could be asked at an interview?
5. How might your perception of the culture affect the way you might answer questions?

The answers to the five questions given above should tell you something about whether the company is one you would want to work for and what it might be looking for in terms of the personalities of those it selects. Selection is always a two-way process, and the better the fit between your personality and that of the organisation, the more likely you will be to stay.

Dress Appropriately

Identifying what is meant by 'appropriate' is hard, but the best advice is always to adopt a more conservative and formal perspective than a relaxed one. In most cases, something smart in dark or pastel colours will be expected.

Whatever you wear, your dress should be comfortable. The interview should not be the first time you have worn the clothes: you need to concentrate on answering the questions, rather than trying to deal with any pain or unease caused by ill-fitting shoes or trousers which are too tight. If you are not sure what to wear, then ask a friend or a careers adviser what impression a certain combination of clothes will create. There is nothing wrong in wearing something that makes an impression and gives an indication of an extravert and confident individual – if that is what you are *and* if you are sure it fits with the culture of the organisation (e.g. through a previous internship). However, most organisations will expect interviewees to wear something quite conservative.

Consider the Questions You Might be Asked

There is less science than you might expect in developing good interview questions. While occupational psychologists are correct in trying to ensure that the questions asked have maximum predictive validity (i.e. they predict behaviour on the job), in many cases managers use their intelligence and a bit of common sense.

However, it is also true that managers are trained to ask good questions, and 'good' questions are not designed to trick candidates, but to separate those who have the potential to do the job from those who do not. Examples of different types of good questions are given on pages 377–79, but, as you look through them, try to imagine why some of the qualities sought are important and then consider a question you might be asked to see if you have each particular quality.

Be aware that they almost certainly will not ask you 'Are you good at handling people?' (to which the answer would probably be 'Yes, I am very good at handling people'), but more likely to seek an example: 'Can you give an example of when you think you handled a difficult person very well?'

Finally, once you have identified some potential questions, develop some good answers for them; see pages 380–83 for what constitutes a good answer. There is nothing worse than sitting in an interview and thinking 'Yes, I came up with this question when I was preparing, but I have no idea now how to answer it!' Remember that some questions might appear regularly, but each job will be a little different, so the questions you prepare for each interview might need to be different.

Role-play the Interview with a 'Critical Friend'

If you have done your preparation and identified some potential questions, then there can be nothing better than to go through these questions with someone. Often your careers services will be able to give some time to do this if you give them sufficient notice. The advantages of using your careers services are: (1) they usually have professional experience in some way and can find some good additional questions to ask (or can rephrase the questions you have developed); and (2) they can be objective when it comes to giving you feedback.

If possible, role-play the whole interview from when you enter the room to when the interview comes to a conclusion. It is not just the answers that you give that will make the difference. it is how you give them and the broader impression you create while answering them. Feedback on all of these aspects will help you improve your interview performance.

KEY LEARNING POINT

Preparation is going to be very important to your performance at interview and to reducing your nervousness in the interview room.

Find out as Much Information as You Can about the Interview

Often, the first indication that you have been successful in your job application is an email or a letter inviting you for a job interview. The letter will state where and when the interview will take place and it may tell you how long the interview will be and sometimes who will be interviewing you. If there is information that you would like to know which is not given in the invitation, then contact the relevant graduate recruitment department or individual who is arranging the interviews – either by phone or by email.

Contacting a professional organisation by phone and speaking to someone is something that some individuals would find challenging. If you have never done this before, then there can appear to be something 'special' about individuals who are working in a particular business, but such individuals are just human beings and there really is nothing to be worried about, even if English is not your first language. In addition, you will be speaking to managers from the organisation in the near future anyway, so it may help to get some practice over the phone.

REFLECTION POINT

Take some time to think about the following questions and write down some answers, first on your own and then with others that you might be working with.

How much time do you think you will need to spend preparing for a selection interview?

Would you feel nervous before a selection interview? What could you do to help you to reduce your nerves?

You need to look professional for the interview. What would you wear? Do you have smart business-like clothes?

AT THE INTERVIEW

The Interview Process

Interviews are always seen as occasions when we feel nervous. We can feel that someone is judging us and that there is nothing we can do about it. In some ways, this is true – we are being assessed – but the assessment is about whether we can do the job, rather than whether we are a 'good human being'. Our value as an individual is not determined by whether we can get through a job interview or not, it is about far more than that, but the more we can give convincing answers to show we can do the job, the better our chances of getting the job. Therefore, the less nervous we are, the better our answers should be.

Our nervousness can be reduced when we:

- Believe that the interview is really just a conversation to find out if we can do the job.
- Believe that the interviewers are interested in us and want to find out more about us, because there is something in our application that has caught their eye.
- Have prepared as much as we can – both practically (travel arrangements, etc.) and in terms of the questions we might be asked.
- Eat well and get a good night's sleep the day before the interview.
- Understand that the worst that can happen is that we do not get the job – and whether you believe it or not, there are much worse things that can happen to us in life.
- Know roughly what is going to happen during the interview.

It is this last point that the next section is designed to deal with.

Interview Structure

An interview is usually composed of four sections: in a 45-minute interview, the structure and length of each section will be similar to those described in Box 17.1.

━━━━━━━━━━ BOX 17.1 ━━━━━━━━━━

THE STRUCTURE OF A TYPICAL JOB INTERVIEW

Typical Graduate Selection Interview Structure (Timings are based on a 45 min graduate interview)

1. **Welcome and introduction** (1-2 min): You will be given the name of the interviewer. If it is a panel interview, the chair of the interview panel will introduce each member on the panel and usually for a graduate-level job, there would be no more than two people interviewing you. The interviewer would also outline the structure of the interview, give an indication of the length of the interview and check that you are ready to start the interview.
2. **Questions to you** (25-35 min): These questions will relate to the qualities being sought by the successful candidate. You will be asked to respond to questions about your skills, attitudes, experiences and/or motivation in order to determine your suitability for the job. As mentioned elsewhere in this chapter, the answers you give and the way that you give them will determine whether you move through to the next part of the selection process.
3. **Your questions** (approximately 5 min): You will be invited to ask the interviewer(s) any questions you might have about working at the organisation. You will need to ask some questions, or have engaged with the interviewers beforehand, to find out the information you wish to know.
4. **Thank you and summary of next steps** (1-2 min): Unless you have already asked, the interviewer(s) will outline what will happen next and indicate how quickly you might expect to hear whether you have been successful or not. The interviewers will thank you for attending and will usually shake your hand as you leave.

Every interview may be slightly different, but knowing what to expect is important if you have never been to a job interview before.

Entrance and First Impression

The idea that many interviewers make very quick assessments of a candidate's suitability for the job has some truth to it. Research seems to indicate that the first 30 seconds is key, but good interviewers (i.e. those who gather accurate information and make a judgement about the relevance, breadth and significance of that information after the interview) will withhold judgement until after the interview.

Regardless, a 'weak' entrance will not be seen as a good start and you may find yourself with an uphill battle to convince an interviewer afterwards. It is also important, however, not to enter in a way which is overly enthusiastic, so it is important to get the balance right. This means the following:

- **Shake hands:** Firmly, but do not crush their fingers! You do need to create an impression of 'friendly professionalism' so try shaking hands with a friend and get their feedback. Hold your hand firmly but not stiffly. Make sure that your hands are clean and dry.
- **Smile:** You need to smile as you enter. If you do not naturally smile, this may take some practice, but you should avoid having a smile which is so big and sustained as to appear artificial. If this is not easy for you, then perhaps try taking some 'selfies' and get some feedback from friends in order to develop a smile which others like.
- **Eye contact:** Look at the interviewers in the room. You may have only one or two interviewers, but as you enter the room make sure that you make eye contact. Imagine that this is a business meeting and you are trying to sell something to the people in the room: you want to be friendly and confident, even if that is not quite how you feel.
- **Move purposefully:** When you move from the door to the chair, do so in a way that demonstrates confidence (i.e. be deliberate). Walk towards the chair and the interviewer(s) in a calm but confident manner. Practise this with a friend if you feel you need to. Avoid having too much with you: coats and bags can make your entrance rather less smooth than desired.

As was stated above (see the 'Dress Appropriately' section), you must pay attention to your appearance. You want to demonstrate to an employer what they might expect from you if you were to go to a business meeting.

DEALING WITH INTERVIEW QUESTIONS

Being able to give 'good answers' to the questions you are going to be asked is what is going to help you get further in the selection process. There are some very common interview questions that you should prepare for, regardless of the nature of the job. (Further, more complex questions relating to each previous chapter in this text are given on pages 377–79.)

═══════ FOR YOU TO DO ═══════

Have a look at the questions listed below. What would your answers be?

1. Why did you choose this university and your degree course?
2. Why do you want this job?
3. Why do you want to work in finance, marketing, HR, etc.?

(Continued)

(Continued)

4. What are your strengths and weaknesses?
5. What was your biggest achievement?
6. What makes you suitable for this graduate training scheme?
7. What can you bring to this role?

During a selection interview, the interviewer(s) will be following a strict structure or 'interview schedule', asking each candidate the same questions in the same order in the same way. The aim is to ensure that the validity of the interview (i.e. whether it collects accurate and truthful information) is high.

The questions asked above should not be difficult to answer: if they are, then you might struggle with some of the others, but there is no need to panic. Think carefully about your answers before you give them.

Question Types

Questions asked at interviews can take a number of different forms, but regardless of the type of question, the interviewers' objective is simply to gather enough information to help them identify whether they think that you can do the job and/or fit the organisation.

Open questions

Open questions invite you to tell the interviewer as much information about a particular subject (often yourself) as you wish to: for example, 'Tell me something about yourself.' These are usually asked at the start of the interview and are designed to help you relax: talking about yourself is something most people should have little problem doing. It is true, however, that employers might expect you to give an answer which is relevant in some way to the job, or to give information that you consider important in your answer first. Open questions will usually be followed by probing questions.

 OPEN QUESTION

A question designed to begin a conversation where the questioner has little or no information about the respondent.

Probing questions

These are designed to get more detail about a relevant aspect of the information that you have given. For example, if you talked about 'leading others' in your first answer, then you might expect to be asked something like, 'So what was the most difficult part of your leadership role there?' On occasions, interviewers may ask probing questions to find out if you are really telling the truth. Answers which are vague or unclear in some way are often seen as indicators of something that may not be completely true or may be exaggerated in some way.

Closed questions

Closed questions are designed to check the information that you have given and make sure that the interviewers have accurately interpreted what you have said: for example, 'And was he satisfied with that action?' One of the issues that interviewers often face is a lack of time. If you have seven or eight qualities that you are seeking and 45 minutes or an hour to conduct the interview, then your time for each quality (which usually relates to one question) will be very short and the use of closed questions will be limited.

Leading questions

The advice given to most interviewers is not to use leading questions, since a candidate can be led to answer a particular question in a certain way. If you are asked a leading question and you want the job, then you will likely give the answer that is closest to what you think the interviewer is looking for. Interviewers' facial expressions and tone of voice can also have the same effect when reacting to an answer or asking a follow-up probing question, even if the question is not designed to lead a candidate.

However, leading questions can be useful in terms of seeing whether a candidate holds a particular view strongly and is able to develop their own ideas independently of others, or is likely to be easily led towards a particular answer. For example, 'Don't you think that it is important to protect an organisation from employees who are likely to make significant mistakes?' The leading answer to this is 'Of course it is,' but rarely are situations so black and white, so the interviewer may be expecting you to debate the question a little more.

It may also be that the answer you give is not important, but the evidence you give for your answer and the passion with which you defend your point of view are always going to be important.

Hypothetical questions

Hypothetical questions broadly ask 'What would you do if ...?', so you need to consider carefully how you might react in various situations faced by managers at work (Table 17.1). In technical terms, interviewing using this kind of question is termed 'situational interviewing'.

Table 17.1   Examples of hypothetical questions

1. What would you do if two of the employees in your business started fighting in the office?
2. If you were the manager of a footballer who had suddenly become uncharacteristically aggressive towards another player on the pitch, what would you say to them?
3. If your part of the business was suddenly losing money after a period of sustained profit, what action would you take?
4. How would you handle a well-liked member of staff whom you knew was lying to others on a regular basis about important issues?
5. If one of your managers made a mistake which cost the organisation up to 5% of its revenue, what would you do?

Consider the troublesome employee, a rebellious union, an emotional customer or employee, a bad decision made by a junior member of staff, and so on. How would you react? What would you do? How would you manage your own and others' behaviour?

The best type of answer to this is to refer to an occasion when you actually have faced these situations, and that is why gaining leadership experience before you graduate cannot be underestimated in terms of its importance. If you are unable to think about a real situation when you have faced these kinds of issues, then consider quickly how you might handle them. The truth is that there are rarely purely right or wrong answers – every action might be right in some organisation – but there are answers which would fit with the culture of the organisation and others which would not: that is, there are answers which are 'better' and answers which are 'worse'. The situations described in these kinds of questions may be rare, but they often make the difference between a successful and an unsuccessful manager. Not having an opinion is not going to be an option.

Behavioural questions

In some ways, these are very similar to hypothetical questions, but they ask about a time when you have actually done something. Their main purpose is to find out what you have actually done, and they do so based on the idea that the best predictor of your behaviour in a future situation is your behaviour in a previous one. The technical term is 'behavioural interviewing'.

Behavioural questions tend to request examples of what you have done, how you have done it, and so on. Some examples are given in Table 17.2.

Table 17.2 Examples of behavioural questions

1.	Tell us about a time when you needed to manage conflicting priorities. What did you do and how successful were you?
2.	Give an example of when you have had to give negative feedback to someone you believed was creating problems for others.
3.	Provide an example of an occasion when you have had to persuade somebody to change a view that they had previously held strongly.
4.	Can you describe a situation when you have had to analyse uncertain information quickly in order to make an important decision?
5.	Have you had any experience of working in a team? What role did you play? What was your contribution?

The questions given above all ask for an example. Again, if you cannot think of any examples, then you will struggle with the interview. However, there are hidden subtleties in these questions. The first is about breadth and the second is about significance.

Breadth refers to the number of situations you have experienced, so if you have only had one leadership position for a very short time, any questions you are asked about leadership are going to refer to the same situation. Employers will look for as much breadth as possible in the scenarios you describe.

Significance refers to the importance of the situations, and usually the risks involved in getting something wrong. For example, leading a student club of 50 people is seen as more significant than leading a team of 4 working on a small piece of group coursework.

If you can provide answers demonstrating significance and breadth of experience, then you are more likely to be rated highly by the interviewers.

For both hypothetical and behavioural questions, interviewers will usually have a scoring system with which they score each answer, according to whether certain issues are covered.

Sample Interview Questions

Throughout the previous chapters, this text has presented some typical questions that you might be asked at the selection interview, with the aim of encouraging you to consider succeeding at the selection process as one of the key the goals of your university career. Remember that interviewers are looking for evidence that you can do the job well, that you want to do the job and that you could fit into the organisation.

════════ FOR YOU TO DO ════════

The questions below are repeated from those given in the preceding chapters: the chapter headings are given to help you find the answers. The first few questions come from the study skills chapters of the text, so there is mention of 'university' much more than might often be the case.

There are two things to do here:

1. If you have not already done so, have a look at the interview questions from the previous chapters of the text which are collated below. Prepare some answers and, with a friend, review whether they would seem to give the interviewers the evidence that they need.
2. You can find an interactive version of these questions along with helpful guidance on answering them on the companion website for this book at https://study.sagepub.com/morgan. Does that guidance make sense? How might it confirm (or change) the relevance and nature of the answers you give?

INTERACTIVE
QUESTIONS

Chapter 1

1. Why did you choose the university, and the course you have been studying?
2. How successful have you been at achieving the goals you set out to achieve by studying at university?

Chapter 2

1. How have you changed or tried to develop yourself while at university?
2. What were the most useful and least useful parts of your studies at university?

Chapter 3

1. Can you give an example of a time when you have had to balance conflicting priorities? How did you do so? How successful were you?
2. How have you gone about establishing goals and objectives?

Chapter 4

1. Imagine that you are in control of a government department. The employees in that department want you to achieve one thing, the public want you to achieve something else, and you personally believe that the right thing to do is one that neither group has thought about. What would you do?
2. What do you think are the most challenging problems facing society today?

Chapter 5

1. Thinking about your learning at university, which parts of your course (lectures, tutorials, presentations, assignments, etc.) taught you the most?
2. How easy did you find it to adjust to studies at university after school or college?

Chapter 6

1. What was the most stressful experience you have had?
2. Can you give an example of a time when you have used feedback to improve your performance?

Chapter 7

1. What was the most challenging piece of written work you have worked on? And why? How did you go about ensuring it was a good piece of work?
2. Tell me about your experience with writing reports. Can you briefly tell me about a report you have written?

(Continued)

(Continued)

Chapter 8

1. How successful have you been at planning your revision?
2. How have you used the feedback from your examinations to improve your performance?

Chapter 9

1. Thinking of an example of a presentation that you have had to give, how did you go about preparing and giving the presentation?
2. What do you find are the most difficult issues with preparing and giving a presentation?

Chapter 10

1. What do you think makes a good team-worker?
2. Tell me about a time when you needed to work with others to accomplish a difficult task. What did you do and how successful was your group?
3. Can you tell me about a time when you have had to work with others to complete a challenging task with limited resources? What did you do? What was the impact of your actions?
4. Can you tell me about a time when you felt that you needed to take the initiative to achieve a goal? What did you do, and how successful were you in achieving your goal?
5. Tell me about a time when you needed to persuade someone to change their mind.
6. Tell me about a leader that you admire. Why do you admire them?
7. How would you describe your personal leadership approach?

Chapter 11

1. Can you tell me about a time when you felt that you needed to take the initiative to achieve a goal. What did you do, and how successful were you in achieving your goal?
2. Tell me about a time when you needed to persuade someone to change their mind.
3. Tell me about a leader that you admire. Why do you admire them?
4. How would you describe your personal leadership approach?
5. How would you go about leading a team member who seemed not to be producing the work they needed to? Can you give an example of a time when you have had to do so?
6. What was the most pioneering activity that you have undertaken?
7. Can you describe how you have gone about setting goals for a team you have worked with?

Chapter 12

1. Tell me about a time when you tried to communicate an important message, but the message was misunderstood. What went wrong and what did you do afterwards?
2. What have you learnt by watching others around you communicate with each other?
3. Which communication skills do you think are the most important? Why?
4. Imagine that you needed to communicate a complex idea to an intelligent audience. How would you go about it? What issues would you need to take into account?
5. From your own experiences, can you give some examples of poor communication?
6. Tell me about a time when a relationship with a fellow classmate, team member or someone you had to work with at work went wrong. How did you resolve the issue?

Chapter 13

1. What do you think are the biggest issues currently facing international organisations?
2. What difficulties would you expect to face if you were offered a role in another country?

(Continued)

(Continued)

3. Imagine a situation where you – as a departmental manager – needed quickly to resolve a conflict between two individuals of different cultural backgrounds about an issue where both held very strong and opposing views. How would you handle such a situation?

Chapter 14

1. Tell me about a time when you have solved a problem that others were struggling to solve.
2. How would you go about finding a new way of delivering one of our services? (Or 'a new use for one of our products?', if the company is a manufacturing company.)
3. Imagine a situation where you – as a departmental manager – needed quickly to resolve a cash flow problem. How might you go about it?

If you struggled to answer the questions in the above exercise then you might need to think very carefully about what examples you can give for what you have done. You may need to revisit the suggestions for how these questions might be answered given in the interactive test on the companion website at https://study.sagepub.com/morgan.

INTERACTIVE
TEST

════════════════ **KEY LEARNING POINT** ════════════════

The clearer the answers to your interview questions, the more likely it will be that you will be successful in moving further through the selection process.

════════════════ **REFLECTION POINT** ════════════════

Take some time to think about the following questions and write down some answers, first on your own and then with others that you might be working with.

Which of these interview questions would you find difficult to answer? Which would be the easiest? Why?

Are there any questions – relating to your abilities – that you would not like to be asked? If you did get asked them, how would you reply?

════════════════ **'BUT I HAVE A QUESTION ...'** ════════════════

... I've heard that many employers will ask about my strengths and weaknesses, so how should I answer that?

It is a good question, and yes they do – and it is expected that you will have a very good answer ready. They ask for a couple of reasons. Firstly, they like to know what you know about the job. A personal 'strength' is only a strength if you are good at a particular skill *and* the situation is likely to require it. If the situation does not require it, then being particularly good at that skill does not make it a strength (e.g. being a fantastic presenter when the job does not require any presentation skills), and the same is true for a personal 'weakness'. The best

(Continued)

(Continued)

advice here is to do your preparation and a good analysis of how your skills and abilities match up with those required for the post.

The second reason an employer will ask is genuinely to find out about your abilities, and to gather evidence to help them understand whether you should be taken any further in the selection process. Your skills will have various qualities but some skills – often those which are clearly evident from observable behaviour – are easier to train than others. So, in addition to the advice given in the paragraph above, think about weaknesses that you could be trained in quite easily, and wherever you talk about your strengths, you *must* give evidence to support your comments.

In answering this question, try to respond in a way which is confident, but not arrogant. You might have all the right strengths, but many employers would prefer to have someone that they can mentor and develop a little, rather than someone who thinks they have nothing to learn and that they will be CEO in two years' time. Give some examples of where you have demonstrated your strengths, but importantly some examples of when you have developed yourself in areas where you were previously weak. It is OK to have a weakness, but knowing that you have a personal weakness and apparently doing nothing about it is not going to get you the job.

The final comment here is that how you demonstrate your skills in one setting may not relate exactly to how you might demonstrate your skills in another. The situation and context will change how you go about working with others or doing a presentation, for example, so be aware of this in how you prepare your answer to this question – one single bad presentation does not mean that you will always be bad at giving presentations.

So:

- Consider your relevant strengths and weaknesses carefully, based on the job you are applying for.
- Discuss examples of when you have used your strengths.
- Identify weaknesses that you can develop, and give examples of when you have developed those skills.
- Answer honestly, but in a manner which shows some humility. Even if you are graduating with an MBA, you will still have something to learn.

Giving Good Answers

Understanding the kinds of questions that will be asked at a selection interview is important, but so too is the ability to give a good answer.

 'BUT I HAVE A QUESTION …'

… What do you mean by a 'good answer?

This is an important question, so let's look at it from the perspective of an interviewer. Each candidate will be asked the same questions, but the answers may vary significantly. So let's examine two hypothetical situations where an interviewer asks the question 'Tell us about a time when you have had to persuade someone to change their strongly held view' and evaluate the two answers below.

Candidate A replies, 'I needed to persuade all my group mates to work harder on a piece of group coursework. We were getting closer to the deadline and I felt that people weren't working hard enough to get the work finished.'

Candidate B replies, 'I needed to persuade the Dean to allow my student society to use an academic facility that had not been available for students to use before, and to give us a budget for refreshments. Once I presented the case, he let us use the room and agreed to sponsor the event.'

(Continued)

(Continued)

Answer B is the *stronger* answer, even though there are lots of important details missing from both answers, which would usually be expected. Persuading the Dean to provide a venue and some sponsorship takes more effort than persuading some classmates to complete their coursework faster. In addition, answer B talks about specifics – a venue and finance – whereas answer A is quite general.

Finally, answer A gives an answer which shows as much about the respondent as it does about those the respondent was trying to influence. Answer A seems to be quite judgemental and critical, and actually shows that the respondent was not very successful at either planning the completion of the coursework or motivating other group members earlier on.

Understanding the information that is missing in the above two answers requires thinking through an approach that careers advisers typically refer to as the 'STAR framework' (Situation, Task, Action, Result). A good interviewer will be seeking answers to behavioural questions that conform to this model.

Let's illustrate this with the question 'Tell us about a time when you have had to persuade someone to change their strongly held view' and use answer B. The model is based around the need for information regarding: the Situation; the Task that needed to be done; the Action taken; the Result or impact of that action.

A GOOD ANSWER

A good answer is one which provides convincing evidence to an interviewer that you have the capability and potential to do what is needed in the job.

Situation

Briefly describe the situation you were facing. Be as complete as you can, but remember that they can ask follow-up questions if they need to, so give the most important information.

In using the example above, the candidate might have responded:

It was the end of the semester and we – the Student Management Society – had just been told that the venue we were hoping to use for catering was not going to be available since it had been booked by another group the week before. The only other venue was out of bounds for undergraduate students – it was the MBA facility – and the costs of hiring that privately (as a non-MBA organisation) were too high for us to bear. So, I needed not only to persuade the Dean of the Business School to give us permission to use it, but also to ask for his help in paying some of the fees.

This part of the answer gives us the context for the action that was taken. It indicates how easy or difficult the task was, and thus gives the interviewers an indication of the candidate's abilities.

For this particular answer, it also shows a number of other things:

- The candidate uses the word 'we', implying someone who is usually a good team-worker. In outlining the actions taken, *the candidate will need to talk about what they did as an individual*, but 'we' usually shows a predisposition to work well with others.
- It might imply some creativity and an ability to think creatively when resources were not readily available, but it can only imply that here. We do not know whether the problem solving that was done was the candidate's, or whether the solution was developed by others in the team.
- Use of 'not only … but also' adds to the impression that this was not going to be an easy thing to do.

The task that needed to be done

There is overlap here with the situation, but you need to let the interviewer(s) know why the task was significant, why it was difficult and what would have happened if you had not taken any action. Consider the following response:

> We needed to have the party since it was the highlight of the undergraduate year at our university. We could have cancelled it, but that would have meant that the main social reason for people joining the society would have been ignored, which would have decreased the motivation for students to join next year. So as president of the society, I needed to find an alternative venue, and for that I needed to persuade the Dean.

The answer given above provides a succinct and relatively comprehensive view of what was happening, but it also shows:

- An ability to analyse information and reflect on the consequences of various alternatives, including doing nothing, an option often implicitly ignored.
- An understanding of human motivation and behaviour.
- An acceptance of responsibility for the position this candidate has in the society.

The action taken

Having outlined the need for action and the situation being faced by this candidate, the next step is to outline what action the candidate took. It is vital that the information in this part of the answer is accurate and relates to the behaviour of the candidate and no one else:

> I made an appointment with the Dean, having thought through and developed a case which I thought was persuasive. I wanted him to sponsor the event, so I recognised that he would want to receive something in return, so I decided I would ask him to present some of the society prizes and would ask him to give a brief speech. As an undergraduate society, I was aware that he might be more reluctant to sponsor us than the postgraduate students (who pay a great deal more for their studies) but I wanted us to draw as many students to the event as possible – which would be done by getting the Dean to make a presentation at the event – and by showing him that we were a dedicated and credible group of students.

> I met with the Dean who asked me how we had found ourselves in this situation and what we planned to do about it. When I asked for his help and the benefits that this would give our society and the school more generally, he listened carefully and then asked for some suggestions as to how we could limit the impact on the MBA students. We had a discussion about those, and the meeting ended after about 35 minutes.

The answer above details the specific actions that the candidate took and gives full details on the candidate's planning and preparation. It shows:

- Insightful awareness of the situation faced by the other party in this event.
- Careful consideration of the thinking, planning and preparation which went into the discussion with other individuals involved.

- Creativity in developing incentives for someone who might be difficult to persuade – and the recognition that incentives were necessary.

In demonstrating these issues, the candidate is giving a strong enough answer to the question as to give the interviewer(s) sufficient evidence for them to conclude that the candidate is a highly competent and credible individual.

The result of the action

The final part of the answer to a behavioural question should succinctly indicate the result of the actions taken: were the intended objectives achieved? If the answer did not previously give or imply the intended objectives, then there was something missing, but those can be given here. In our example, the candidate might say:

> As a result of my discussions with the Dean, we were able to use the MBA venue and we were given a little budget to order some refreshments from the school canteen.

This part of the answer does not need to give lots of information, though if the intended objectives were not achieved, then you need to give some analysis of what else might have been done, or what should have been done differently. Interviewers can be forgiving when objectives were not achieved, but would be less forgiving if there was no information given of why that was the case.

FOR YOU TO DO

Thinking about the same question (i.e. 'Tell us about a time when you have had to persuade someone to change their strongly held view'), how would you use the STAR framework to construct your own convincing answer?

Overall

The STAR framework should be used when answering behavioural questions, but in answering any questions:

- Keep answers as comprehensive but as brief as possible. If you read aloud the answers above in order, then it would take around two and a half minutes, excluding any time given for thinking about the answer initially.
- Watch your speed of speech: when we are nervous, we might typically speak more quickly than usual.
- Imagine the issues you might face in doing the job, and prepare examples of how you have demonstrated, or might demonstrate, your skills in handling those issues well.
- Focus on *your* contribution and activities – the interviewer is after evidence of *your* skills. If you refer to 'we' all the time, then your own contribution will be blurred.
- Be honest: even if you do get through the interview and get the job, you will need to demonstrate your skills anyway.

'BUT I HAVE A QUESTION ...'

... What do you do if you cannot think of an answer to a question they asked, or if you do not understand a question?

This happens fairly frequently in graduate interviews, so the first thing to say is, 'Don't panic!' Of course, it is easy to say that, but it is perfectly OK to:

- Ask for a little time to help develop an answer, as long as the silence in the interview does not last for an uncomfortably long period of time.
- Ask the interviewer to repeat the question; they will probably not rephrase it, but they can repeat it.

If they are asking about a situation you have never faced, or where you are not sure how you would deal with it, then the best thing is to be honest and say so. That will probably not help you get further in the selection process, but it might be that the quality they are asking about it is not an 'essential' criterion, or that all the candidates might struggle to answer it. It is not appropriate to make up an answer since that will come through in a number of ways and will mean that the interviewer(s) will not trust any of your other answers either.

Above all, be sure to give a relevant answer the question. There is nothing worse than giving what you think is a really great answer only for the interviewers to conclude that they have insufficient information to make a decision. Have a look at the next 'For You to Do' section below.

FOR YOU TO DO

Look at the two answers below to the question: 'Can you give us an example of a time when you have had to work with others, and tell us how you worked together?'

Answer A: 'I had to work with others in a student society. We had a party to organise and after we had decided how we wanted to separate the tasks, my role was to obtain funding from sponsors, and there was one other person doing the same thing. I went about identifying potential sponsors but I kept the team and the other person informed of what I was doing. We met every week and I needed to give an update on my progress.'

Answer B: 'I had to work with others as part of a coursework assignment. It was a case study for a module on strategic management. I was leading a group of five people and I had to decide what we were going to do and how. I did the part of the work that related to gathering the literature, which was actually quite hard because the library is not really well equipped and does not have enough books.'

Which of the two answers do you think is more *relevant*?

The strength of an answer is measured by the extent that it helps the interviewer believe or otherwise that you have the potential to fulfil the requirements of a role in a way that matches the expectations of the organisation.

———— 'BUT I HAVE A QUESTION ...' ————

... How should I answer questions – should I be passionate or should I keep my emotions out of my answers?

This is not an easy question to answer, but the best answer is to be passionate about those things that you are passionate about, and to be calm when that is appropriate. The best advice is not to be too extreme in the way you answer the questions. Use hand gestures purposefully and to emphasise what you say, but the key is usually moderation.

Showing no passion or conviction during the interview will probably mean that your interviewers are not going to be passionate about your answers, or you as a candidate. At a basic level, a lack of passion or emotion will be interpreted as a lack of interest in the job – and that will disqualify you very quickly.

———— KEY LEARNING POINT ————

Remember that the objective of the interviewer is to gather sufficient evidence to be able to say with some confidence that: 'Yes, we think this person can do a good job for us.'

QUESTIONS YOU MIGHT WANT TO ASK AT THE END OF AN INTERVIEW

At the end of an interview, you will be invited to ask the interviewer(s) questions. These could be questions about the organisation or about the job role. Selection is always a two-way process and the best candidates might have more than one job offer, so this is an opportunity to determine what working in the organisation is going to be like. Not having any questions is going to indicate a lack of interest in the vacancy (or vacancies) and asking inappropriate questions is also going to send the wrong signals. You should never ask about salary (or any other terms and conditions) until you have a job offer.

The best questions are those which reveal that you have thought carefully about what it will mean to work in this role. Consider the following:

- What kind of training might I receive?
- What assistance is available for me in terms of finding accommodation?
- What is it like to work for this organisation?
- Would I be working with a team or largely independently?
- How formal are relationships between junior and senior management?
- How resistant are people to change in your organisation?
- How would my performance in the job be evaluated?
- ... and any other issues that might affect whether you would enjoy working there.

When thinking about the questions you ask, you need to be honest in asking what you want to know. There are some questions which appear 'clever', but which could count against you, for example:

'What is the company's view on "dress-down Fridays"?' or 'What are the company's plans for increasing annual turnover?' These would not be relevant for your decision about whether you take the job or not, and would just be seen as a potential sign of arrogance or 'being clever for the sake of being clever'. Such questions should be avoided. ('Dress-down Fridays' are those days when an organisation's formal dress code would be relaxed, but not every office has a dress code.)

What you do need to know is whether you might enjoy working there, so any questions that would honestly help you make this decision are to be encouraged. However, it is not wise to ask any questions that are already on the company website (e.g. 'How many employees do you have?', 'How many offices do you have and where are they?'). This will show a lack of preparation and/or a lack of real interest in the company.

You probably need to have two or three questions ready and they should not be closed questions giving you a 'yes' or 'no' answer. Remember that the interview is a conversation with a purpose, and a conversation which has just yes or no answers is not going to last very long.

KEY LEARNING POINT

The interviewer needs to get as much information from you as possible to determine whether you are suitable for the job. Giving full and complete answers to their questions is essential to enabling the interviewer to make that decision.

REFLECTION POINT

Take some time to think about the following questions and write down some answers, first on your own, and then with others that you might be working with.

In a nervous situation, it is our emotion which usually takes over rather than rational thought. How could you become so used to using the STAR framework that it becomes instinctive?

How good is your memory about the activities you have done? Is there anything you can do to improve the range of examples you could give?

GENERAL BEHAVIOUR AT INTERVIEWS

If you have never had an interview before, or have never worked in a professional office before, then you might have questions about what is appropriate and what is not. Understanding professional values in terms of day-to-day behaviour is something that you will have to do when it comes to working in a professional environment if you are to work well with others. Those values can vary significantly from organisation to organisation, but they are not always written down; the only times that individuals pick them up is when they or someone else acts in a way which contravenes them. For the graduate selection interview, however, there are some basic expectations which are less hidden (Table 17.3).

Table 17.3 Some common interview dos and don'ts

Do	Don't
Dress smartly, and make sure that you look in the mirror before going to the interview	Have a cigarette or drink alcohol immediately before an interview
Go to the bathroom before the interview starts	Be late or leave yourself with too little time to get to the interview
Use formal language	Be too friendly or overly familiar with the interviewers
Maintain eye contact with the interviewer(s) as much as possible	Blame others for mistakes or errors – it creates a negative impression
Use facial expressions, hand gestures and tone of voice appropriately (i.e. only when you want to emphasise something). Using them all the time will be seen as a little odd	Use humour to denigrate others (even if you think it is funny)
Respond appropriately to non-verbal signals from the interviewer(s) indicating that they have heard enough of an answer to a question	Use slang or jargon
Sit upright and lean forward when answering questions	Slouch in the chair, look disinterested or excessively fiddle with your hands or hair
Prepare some questions to ask at the end of the interview	Use the interviewers' time to answer questions they have not asked or show them evidence of something they have not wanted to see
Always turn your phone off	Finish the interview by asking when you will start the job
	Don't panic! If you cannot think of an example to discuss, then be honest

'BUT I HAVE A QUESTION ...'

... I have heard that some people have telephone or Skype interviews: if I have an interview like this, should anything I do change at all?

Yes, this is an increasing trend. The Association of Graduate Recruiters has reported that 'The proportion of AGR members that use video interviews has nearly doubled from 10.7% in 2012-2013 to 21.2% in 2013-2014' (AGR, 2014: 30).

To answer your question, the simple answer is 'not really', but do make sure that your technology works well and that your interviewers have contingency plans (e.g. a landline telephone number) in case the Internet or the phone does not work. It may sound strange, but your intonation will give an impression of your facial expression – so smiling while you are talking works as well for a telephone interview as it would for a face-to-face interview. If you have a Skype interview (or equivalent on 'Gotomeeting.com' or 'zoom'), then you need to dress appropriately as well.

If you are an international student applying for a job back in your home country, then you need to make sure that you are aware of the difference in time zones – and particularly changes with BST (British Summer Time).

Other than ensuring that the technology works and that you are well prepared, nothing else should really be different. You should think about the questions that you may be asked, use the same tone of voice and give the answers in the same way.

━━━━━━━ BOX 17.2 ━━━━━━━

AFTER THE INTERVIEW

What you do after the interview will depend to some extent on the nature of the interview, and on what you have been told about the individuals who will have been interviewing you. If you have their names and email addresses (e.g. you might be applying for a specific vacancy), then a very brief email thanking those individuals and saying that you are 'looking forward to hearing from them soon' would be very appropriate. Such situations will probably be able to let you know whether you are being taken forward to the next stage of the selection process (if there is one) fairly quickly. Feedback on such interviews might be quite helpful.

Where you are applying for a graduate training scheme, however, you will not have that information, and an email to a generic graduate admissions email address is likely to have very little impact. (Such email addresses will probably be handling several thousand emails.) It may be some time before you hear of the outcome, unless you are given an indication during the interview, which can happen on very rare occasions, since, theoretically, all the first-round interviews will need to be completed first. It is also true to say that the feedback given from a generic graduate training scheme first-round interview is likely to be very brief, if it is available at all. The number of interviews being carried out makes the provision of detailed feedback challenging for employers, but there is no reason why you should not ask for it.

It is very tempting to reflect on your performance immediately after the interview – and in some ways, it is a good idea to think about the questions and whether you made a good impression and gave answers which were sufficiently detailed. Ultimately, you will not have any definitive information until you are told about the outcome, but some initial thoughts could be useful.

INTEGRATION AND APPLICATION

There are a number of steps involved in performing well at a selection interviews:

Step 1: Prepare well. Think about the job that you have applied for, identify potential questions you might be asked and role-play the interview with a critical friend. You also need to review your application carefully to remember what you have done in order to identify examples that you can draw on when answering questions.

Step 2: Behave professionally. Watch what you say, how you say it and how you behave generally. It is important that this starts from the moment you enter the building until the time you leave it. Be professional and mature.

Step 3: Answer the question well. The answer needs to be:

- Relevant.
- Complete. If it is a behavioural question (asking for an example), use the STAR framework.
- Delivered in a calm and professional manner (criticising others is not a good idea).

Step 4: Have some questions to ask. Make sure you prepare some questions which would affect your decision to accept a job, if you were offered it. The questions should not ask for information that is already available on the website.

Step 5: Review and evaluate. Think about whether you did or said anything that might have been interpreted in a way which might prevent you moving further in the selection process.

CONCLUSION

Throughout this chapter, we have reviewed what employers are looking for from a good answer and have identified the kinds of questions that may be asked.

You should now have a good idea of:

- Identifying potential questions you might be asked in advance of an interview.
- Understanding some basic dos and don'ts.
- Identifying questions to ask the potential employer.
- Evaluating the impact of your non-verbal behaviour as well as the content of the answers that you give.

FINAL REFLECTIONS

Based on the content of this chapter, what do you now know about performing well at selection interviews that you did not know before?

What key learning point had the most impact? Why?

Do your answers to either of the above questions have the potential to change your ability to perform well at selection interviews? Why?

What will you now do differently? (Write this down and put it somewhere where you can see it regularly.)

ADDITIONAL RESOURCES

Want to learn more? Visit https://study.sagepub.com/morgan to gain access to a wide range of online resources, including interactive tests, tasks, further reading and downloads.

Website Resources

Prospects website: www.prospects.ac.uk/careers-advice/interview-tips

American Psychological Society – on what to say and not to say at internship interviews: www.apa.org/gradpsych/2010/01/missteps.aspx

Businessballs.com – background information on selection interviews and tips for interviewees: www.businessballs.com/interviews.htm

Changingminds.org – information on different forms of interview: http://changingminds.org/disciplines/hr/selection/interview.htm

Graduate Recruitment Bureau: www.grb.uk.com/graduate-interview-techniques

LSE Careers website – for those interested in management consultancy jobs: http://blogs.lse.ac.uk/careers/2015/11/03/understanding-case-study-interviews/

Newcastle University: www.ncl.ac.uk/careers/interviews/

Targetjobs website: https://targetjobs.co.uk/careers-advice/interview-techniques

(Continued)

(Continued)

The Guardian newspaper – advice for interviewees seeking jobs: https://jobs.theguardian.com/careers/interview-advice/

University of Kent – Top 10 questions asked at graduate selection interviews: www.kent.ac.uk/careers/interviews/commonquestions.htm

University of Liverpool: www.liverpool.ac.uk/careers/applications-and-interviews/interviews/

Textbook Resources

Price-Machado, D. (1998) *Skills for Success*. New York: Cambridge University Press (particularly chapter 5).

Smale, B. and Fowlie, J. (2009) *How to Succeed at University: An Essential Guide to Academic Skills, Personal Development & Employability*. London: Sage (particularly chapter 11).

/18| PSYCHOMETRIC TESTS AND ASSESSMENT CENTRES

CHAPTER STRUCTURE

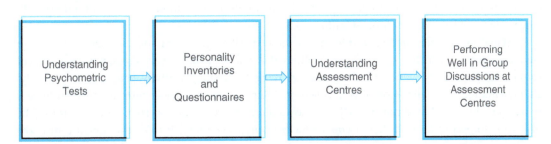

Figure 18.1

When you see the 🌐 this means go to the companion website https://study.sagepub.com/morgan to do a quiz, complete a task, read further or download a template.

▬ AIMS OF THE CHAPTER ▬

By the end of this chapter, you should be able to:

- Know what to expect if asked to take a psychometric test or attend an assessment centre.
- Feel prepared for being asked to take a psychometric test and attend an assessment centre.
- Understand why some employers use such instruments to select graduate employees.
- Feel relatively relaxed if asked to attend such a selection process.

INTRODUCTION

Assessment centres and psychometric tests are used very widely by graduate recruiters to select their candidates for jobs, and are the two most commonly used selection tools. The Association of Graduate Recruiters (2014) reports that 67% of graduate employers were using psychometric tests for graduate selection, while nearly 84% were using assessment centres or a 'selection event'.

The word 'psychometric' can generate a sense of confusion, but understanding what it means can simplify things somewhat. Psychometric tests will very likely form part of any graduate selection process, though how they are used and the specifics of what are used may vary. All methods of selection are referred to as tools and used by selectors to determine whether someone can do the job well and to find the best individual(s).

'Psychometric' is derived from 'psyche', which means 'the mind', and 'metric', which colloquially means 'to measure'. In other words, a psychometric test is one which 'measures the mind' in some way. It is a little more complex than this, but as an outcome this is what a psychometric test does. This first half of the chapter will give some information about how these tests are developed and how they are used.

The second half of the chapter will look at assessment centres. An assessment centre is an 'event', not necessarily a place. The chapter will say more about what it is and how it is used, but it is said to provide a detailed analysis of the abilities and behaviour of an individual on tasks related to the role that they will be doing.

Both assessment centres and psychometric tests are developed in conjunction with occupational psychologists, individuals with sufficient understanding of psychological models of behaviour and research statistics as to be able to develop scientific methods to help HR professionals find those individuals that will help lead their organisations forward.

As stated in the introduction to this part of the text, all the exercises and selection tools used in graduate selection will test for the same abilities that you will have been developing as a student throughout your course: critical thinking, team-working, leadership, creativity, communication, analysis, presentation skills, and so on. If you have been doing well in your degree programme, then there is no reason why you should not do well in an assessment centre – and that should be reassuring. The final issue to bear in mind is that, if you are lucky enough to be invited to an assessment centre, the employer may be able to select all of those attending or none of you. Employers will have a finite number of vacancies and could take everyone from one assessment centre and none from another; they will not fill vacancies with those they think are unsuitable.

UNDERSTANDING PSYCHOMETRIC TESTS

General Introduction

As indicated above, there can be some anxiety or uncertainty regarding what employee selection experts call 'psychometric tests'. There are actually many kinds of 'tests', all developed under similar statistical processes and all with similar characteristics, but each will have a different theoretical foundation based upon other research and academic models of personality, ability and behaviour. Tests are nearly always multiple choice and are increasingly being used as tools at the beginning of the selection process to screen out those who do not meet essential criteria relating to reasoning, or whose

 PSYCHOMETRIC TEST

A psychometric test is a valid and reliable selection tool measuring personal psychological abilities.

personality does not fit the culture of the organisation, but they are also used for developmental purposes, at 'development centres' (the equivalent of assessment centres – see below – but for staff development).

There are two broad categories of psychometric test:

1. Those tests dealing with intellectual abilities.
2. Those dealing with personality.

The key distinction between these two areas is a simple one: *the intellectual ability* of an individual is measured by their ability to correctly answer questions in a short period of time. This implies that there are right and wrong answers, and that there is a time limit. Put simply, the more correct answers an individual identifies, the higher their score will be and the more likely they will be to progress to the next stage of the selection process. Such tests were originally termed 'intelligence tests' but research into identifying what intelligence is varied in its conclusions. What psychologists can say is that the ability to understand ('to reason') with various kinds of information (numerical, written) is related to job performance in most managerial/graduate-level jobs and correlates strongly with subsequent on-the-job performance – hence the use of verbal reasoning and numerical reasoning tests. Of the graduate employers using psychometric tests in 2014, 75% and 77%, respectively, used tests designed to determine candidates' numerical and verbal reasoning skills (AGR, 2014).

Measuring the personality of an individual is more complex: a personality questionnaire has no right and wrong answers; there is no universal 'right personality' or 'wrong personality' in the same way that there are right or wrong answers, but a certain combination of responses will make an individual more or less suitable for working in a particular environment. Usually personality questionnaires are longer and ask respondents to choose particular responses based on how likely they would be to demonstrate certain behaviours.

Personality questionnaires can examine a wide range of topics – we have already come across ideas and models looking at learning styles (Chapter 2) and team roles (Chapter 10). Personality research could cover a wide range of themes and a subsequent wide range of personality questionnaires. Some dating organisations use a form of personality inventory to match individuals together for relationships, while other questionnaires have been developed to determine susceptibility to stress-based disease (based on research linking heart disease and personality). However, for the purposes of this chapter, we will examine the use of personality questionnaires as they relate to performance on the job.

NUMERICAL AND VERBAL REASONING

Numerical reasoning is the ability to understand, interpret and use numbers accurately.

Verbal reasoning is the ability to understand, interpret and use written information accurately.

PERSONALITY

'Personality' is an individual's predisposition to act and behave in a particular manner across a broad range of situations.

PERSONALITY QUESTIONNAIRE

A personality questionnaire is a valid and reliable tool which measures an individual's predisposition to act and behave in particular ways.

Understanding 'Psychometric': Reliability, Validity and Standardisation

Any form of measurement has to be undertaken 'scientifically'. There is no purpose in measuring the length of a piece of wood if the tool you are using is not used correctly or if the tool itself has some problems, but the challenge is this: 'How do we know whether something is producing the right results and is being used correctly when it comes to measuring mental/psychological qualities?'

The answer is to use three broad measures:

- **Reliability or consistency:** The same tool measuring the same quality gives the same results every time. On occasions, tests can have items with similar meanings spread throughout the test to measure and ensure that consistency.
- **Validity:** The tool produces results which accurately measure the same personal quality as other tests measuring that same quality. For tests supposedly measuring a quality that is relevant to job performance, the test will not include items that do not relate to on-the-job performance. One form of validity for ability tests refers to whether the test discriminates between individuals who do have the abilities being tested for and those who do not.
- **Standardisation:** The tool is used in the same way on all occasions to produce comparable results.

In reality, these three qualities need to be present in any selection method used to give the outcome of the selection process some accuracy. If these three qualities are not found to be present in the research and development of the test, then the test is not seen as a credible one, and employers will not be allowed to use it. Every test publisher needs to show the results of their research and publish scores (or 'norms') so that employers can interpret the test scores for similar individuals (in terms of educational or occupational level, age and gender) correctly.

The implications of this are as follows:

1. When you take a psychometric test, the individual giving the test (or the computer screen, if you are taking the test online) will give you a standard set of instructions, delivered in as nearly an identical manner as on other occasions.
2. The circumstances under which you take the test will be the same as for other individuals taking the same test, as far as possible.
3. The way that your score will be interpreted will vary slightly among different types of individuals, but your score will be interpreted in the same way as those from the same group as you.

As indicated above, any psychometric test is intended to be a scientific instrument used properly for the purposes of personnel selection. This also means that the individuals running the test (or giving you authorised access if it is done online) need to have been trained on a course which is professionally accredited. In the United States, that accreditation is given by the American Psychological Association, and in the UK the British Psychological Society provides the same certification.

Psychometric Tests: What to Expect

Administration

While some organisations use paper and pencil tests which require you to undertake a psychometric test at a particular location, the majority of employers will require you to take them online. Physical paper and pencil tests enable an employer to be sure that you really are who you say you are, but online tests are being increasingly used by employers because of their flexibility in terms of timing and low cost. If you have ever been asked to take a written test (especially a multiple choice test), then you might have some idea of what to expect when you get there.

For each person doing the test, there will be a small desk with a computer-readable multiple choice answer sheet, a pencil and an eraser. If the test that you are doing is a numerical reasoning test, then you will almost certainly find a blank sheet of paper and a basic calculator.

To ensure standardisation, your test administrator will read out some instructions from a sheet (see Box 18.1 for a typical excerpt), and, during that time, will pass out the question booklet with strict instructions not to open it until you are asked to do so. (This may well remind you of attending a university examination.) For ability tests, there will usually be a small number of examples for you to look at or to do; this is to ensure that you understand the mechanics of taking the test, and although you might disagree with the answers to those examples that the administrator might give you, they will *not* be permitted to tell you why something is right or wrong. If they see that you get a wrong answer to one of the examples, they will ask you to review that example question. Personality questionnaires will usually have a couple of example questions to look at.

============ **BOX 18.1** ============

INSTRUCTIONS TYPICALLY GIVEN AT THE START OF AN ABILITY TEST

The following is a brief excerpt from the verbal instructions given by a test administrator:

'You will not be able to leave the room once the test has started so please collect glasses or take a reading break now if you need to. [Pause]

The session will be conducted under test conditions so there will be no talking, and, to avoid distractions, can you please turn off all mobile phones now?

Please remember:

- Work quickly and accurately.
- Listen carefully to the instructions which I shall read to you from a card.
- There will be some practice questions: these are not timed or scored.

Are there any questions? [Pause]'

Once any examples have been completed, the administrator will continue reading some instructions, will tell you how long the test will last (usually about 20–45 minutes) and will use a stopwatch to start and stop the test. If you are taking a test online, then the administration will be done online, but will take an equivalent form.

You will need to work quickly, but there must be a balance between speed and accuracy of course. Certain tests are very popular with employers because they originate from a good supplier and/or have been shown to have high psychometric qualities. So, if you are invited to take a test by a number of employers, you might find that you take the same test a number of times – in which case you should be able to complete more answers each time as you get used to reusing information for different questions – but this does not guarantee that you will be more successful in the test of course.

… Can I learn how to do better on the tests? Is there somewhere I can practise?

This is a good question. Your university careers services will almost certainly be able to arrange some prac-tice sessions for you and many employers will be able to send you something from a test provider in advance, giving you an idea of what exactly to expect in terms of the questions.

But the issue of how to do better is more complex. Psychometric tests are designed to measure your ability and so the questions are kept highly confidential: if your ability in X was marked as 6/10 one week and in the next week you did the same test and got 8/10, then you could argue that the test was not really measuring your ability in X, but rather your ability to do the test. In other words, test providers do not allow organisations using their tests to give you a chance to practise first.

There are some example questions below which give you an idea of the kinds of questions to expect in an ability test.

Personality questionnaires are also timed, since employers want you to give your immediate response rather than to think about your answer too much. There may be questions about how you react in certain situations, and while the answer you might give in a selection interview to the same question might be 'It depends …' and then go on to discuss what the answer actually depends on, you will need to give a slightly more definitive response in a personality questionnaire.

This can appear unfair, but, in reality, the test will have been constructed to take account of the fact that certain issues can influence our behaviour, so you may well be asked a similar question a number of times to take account of these influences. In addition, an organisation that uses personality question-naires properly will always do a debriefing interview with you afterwards, to gather examples of your behaviour in certain circumstances and to ensure the validity of the questionnaire.

The questions

The questions in a psychometric test will be in multiple choice format, but will vary in nature according to the nature of the test. For tests of your mental ability, you will be asked to select one correct answer from four or (less commonly) five possible responses. The exact nature of the item and of the required response will vary according to the mental ability being looked for. Questions in a numerical reasoning test will typically be 'select one from the following', while questions from a verbal reasoning test will ask you to read a brief passage of text and then use your understanding of that passage to select one response, indicating whether you think a particular interpretation of the text is:

- Definitely True, given the information in the passage
- Probably True, given the information in the passage
- Probably False, given the information in the passage
- Definitely False, given the information in the passage, or
- You cannot tell from the information given.

(Or some variation of the above.)

Verbal Reasoning Test Examples

The following examples are typical of the questions which could be used in verbal reasoning tests. Read the passage and then answer the questions which follow.

——————— FOR YOU TO DO ———————

Have a look at the passages below and answer each of the questions according to the instructions given.

Passage 1

Many organisations find it is beneficial to employ students over the summer. Permanent staff often wish to take their own holidays over this period. Furthermore, it is not uncommon for companies to experience peak workloads in the summer and so require extra staff. Summer employment often attracts students who may return as well qualified recruits when they have finished their education. Ensuring that students learn as much as possible about the organisation encourages their interest in working on a permanent basis. Organisations pay students on a fixed rate without the usual entitlement to holiday pay or sick leave.

Please read the following statements and then respond to each according to whether you think they are:

- True – the statement follows logically from the information in the passage.
- False – the statement contradicts information given in the passage.
- Cannot Tell – you cannot answer whether the statement is true or false without further information.

1. It is possible that permanent staff who are on holiday can have their work carried out by students.
2. Students in summer employment are given the same paid holiday benefit as permanent staff.
3. Students are subject to the organisation's standard disciplinary and grievance procedures.
4. Some companies have more work to do in summer when students are available for vacation work.

Passage 2

Cancer is a condition which affects many people every year, for reasons that are still unclear. Cancer seems to affect individuals from all sorts of backgrounds, regardless of country, occupation, income, ethnicity or several other factors. There does seem to be a susceptibility to cancer for people who are older but even this is not universal, and just as folk who have had heart attacks can be as young as 35, cancer does not only affect older individuals. Many younger children across the world suffer from leukaemia, and this makes the need to find a cure for this form of cancer very urgent. The UK government, Cancer Research UK and the World Health Organization are amongst many bodies and organisations which are working to do so.

Please read the following statements and then respond to each according to whether you think they are:

- True – the statement follows logically from the information in the passage.
- False – the statement does not follow logically from the information in the passage.
- Cannot Tell – you cannot answer whether the statement is true or false without further information.

1. The causes of cancer are still uncertain.
2. Cancer seems to affect people from some races differently to people from other races.

(Continued)

(Continued)

3. People who have heart attacks are less likely to have cancer.
4. Finding a cure for leukaemia is more urgent than finding a cure for other kinds of cancer.
5. There are several organisations which are working together to find a cure for cancer.
6. Many people die from cancer every year.

Passage 3

This is a test of your ability to recognise the conclusions being drawn from a passage of text. Please read the passage below and then, based on the information given in the passage, indicate whether you believe that the conclusion is:

- Strong – this is a strong conclusion and is one of the main arguments being made in the passage.
- Weak – this is a relevant issue but is not an important argument according to the passage.
- False – this conclusion contradicts information contained in the passage.
- Cannot Tell – the conclusion does not come from information given in the passage.

Schoolchildren are often seen being collected by their parents after school. The process usually starts half an hour before the school closes, when a large number of parents arrive in their cars and park by the side of the road. It is unlikely that schools will ever ban parents arriving by car, but the large numbers of parents doing so in order to collect their children is actually increasing the level of danger around the school for a number of reasons. When cars are parked so closely together, it is difficult to see around them to be sure that it is safe to cross the road. Of course, any child who sees their mother or father smiling at them will want to run across the road to greet them, and maybe won't see any oncoming cars. A third issue is that the school buses which collect the children are often unable to see a child crossing immediately in front of them. Consultation with parents has developed ideas around school classes finishing at different times, having permits for parking outside the school or even creating different parking zones for different groups of children. The safety of children is always paramount, and so the issue needs to be taken extremely seriously.

1. All children should be taken on the school buses.
2. Roads leading up to schools should have strict speed limits.
3. Parents who wish to collect a child from school should not bring a car.
4. It would be better if parents arrived and parked their cars at different times.
5. Parents should not smile at their children when collecting them from school.
6. Cars and buses should be parked in different places.
7. The location of car parking at schools is something which should be monitored very closely.

The answers to all three sets of questions are given at the end of this chapter.

The above items are similar to those commonly found in verbal reasoning tests, though there are different forms of test which look for slightly different abilities. However, all will be seeking information regarding your ability to understand, interpret and draw conclusions from the information given. If you are entering a management role, then your ability to do so is extremely important.

Numerical Reasoning Test Examples

The ideas behind numerical reasoning are very similar – how well can you interpret and use data given to you in numerical form? Again, the ability to do so in a management role is extremely important.

It is also important to recognise, however, that this is not about being good at mathematics – being able to do calculus and trigonometry will not help here. Numerical reasoning is about understanding mathematical ideas and concepts and being able to apply the numbers to those concepts (in the ways that economists and accountants are typically able to do well).

═══════════ **FOR YOU TO DO** ═══════════

Have a look at the three sets of information below and answer the questions which follow. For each question, there are four possible answers. Please select what you believe to be the correct answer.

In preparation, you should have some rough paper and a basic (non-scientific) calculator. These tests would usually be undertaken under timed conditions, so you might wish to time yourself.

Set 1

Please look carefully at the information below and use it appropriately to answer the questions which follow.

Flying times **(in hours):**

	Beijing	**Shanghai**	**Dubai**
Shanghai	1.5		
Dubai	6.5	6	
New York	15	14	7

Time differences **(in hours):**

	Going from:			
Going to:	**Beijing**	**Shanghai**	**Dubai**	**New York**
Beijing		0	+5	+11
Shanghai	0	0	+5	+11
Dubai	−5	−5		+6
New York	−11	−11	−6	

Aircraft times from airport gate to runway at the different airports are usually:

- Beijing: 15 minutes
- Shanghai: 5 minutes
- New York: 30 minutes
- Dubai: 25 minutes

Questions

1. If my flight to Shanghai leaves the gate at Dubai Airport at 6 a.m., what time would I expect to arrive at my gate at Shanghai Airport?

    (a) 12.30 p.m.   (b) 12.30 a.m.   (c) 7.30 a.m.   (d) 12 p.m.

(Continued)

(Continued)

2. By what percentage is the flying time from Dubai to Shanghai longer than the flight from Dubai to New York?

    (a) 1.6%   (b) 85%   (c) 12%   (d) 16%

3. If I am flying from New York to Beijing, I can expect a headwind to add 20% onto my flying time. So, what is my total time from leaving the gate in New York to arriving at my gate in Beijing?

    (a) 15 h 40 min   (b) 12 h 30 min   (c) 18 h 45 min   (d) 16 h 15 min

4. I need to fly from Beijing to New York via a connecting flight in Dubai which will leave two hours later. My flight will leave Beijing at 4.30 p.m. Assuming no delays and no need to queue for immigration or collect baggage in Dubai, what time can I expect to arrive at the gate in New York?

    (a) 9.35 a.m. the next day   (b) 9 p.m. the same day
    (c) 10.35 p.m. the same day   (d) 6.35 p.m. the next day

Set 2

Annual data

	Salary (£)	Expenses	Investment fund rate (% per year)*
Martin	22,500	13,850	5.5%
Paul	32,800	17,650	2.3%
Sarah	29,765	12,780	4.8%
Bill	18,920	8,790	3.9%

* This is the rate of return on investments made. Calculated on a yearly basis, not a monthly one. Interest paid on the anniversary of the investment.

Questions

1. If we measure the ratio of expenses to salary as the percentage of salary spent on expenses, whose spending is the least efficient?

    (a) Martin   (b) Sarah   (c) Paul   (d) Bill

2. Martin's investments are in an investment fund where the rate will not change for five years. If Martin saves all that he does not spend in an investment fund, how much is he likely to see in that fund in three years' time?

    (a) £8650.34   (b) £9627.66   (c) £27,377.25   (d) £10,157

3. If Martin saves all that he does not spend in an investment fund, but the other friends only invest 60% of what they do not spend in similar funds, what is the situation regarding the four friends' investments?

    (a) Martin has more in his investment fund than Paul.
    (b) Paul has more invested than Sarah.
    (c) As a percentage of his income, Bill has more invested than Paul.
    (d) Martin has less in his investment fund than Bill.

4. During her second year of work, Sarah falls sick and is unable to receive a salary for half a year. However, during her first year, she was able to invest 85% of her net income (income minus expenses) into her investment fund. Assuming a 3% increase in salary and a reduction to save only 35% of her net income but no other changes, what would her investment (as a percentage of her total income over that period) be?

    (a) 32%   (b) 49.7%   (c) 37%   (d) 69%

(Continued)

(Continued)

How did you find these? How long did they take you to do?
  It is often true that the information you write down can be used a number of times.
  Answers are given at the end of this chapter.

It is important to note that the tests used for graduate selection are not the same as those that might be used for lower level administrative positions. Individuals being recruited for management roles generally need to have higher levels of critical thinking/verbal reasoning than those in more administrative roles, and if employers gave graduates the same tests that they used for lower level jobs, then the tests would not distinguish between different levels of ability. After an applicant has taken a test, the employer will then use standardised results tables (called 'norm tables') to ensure that they are comparing individuals with a reasonable peer group – other graduates, in the case of graduate selection. If you are able to achieve a certain position in comparison with other graduates, then you will have passed, but the particular position required by different employers will vary, so passing the test with one employer does not mean that a candidate will pass with all employers. The questions in a numerical test are usually graded, with the easier questions appearing early on and more challenging questions appearing towards the end of the test. An increasing number of tests are now online, as indicated in Box 18.2.

=== BOX 18.2 ===

ONLINE AND PAPER-BASED TESTS

It was mentioned earlier that some psychometric tests can be taken online. Some consultancies make their tests available online so that applicants do not have to travel to a certain location in order to take the tests. The challenge is always how the organisations know whether the person taking the test is the same as the one whose application they have.

Organisations use a number of means to find out - including questions at interview, should the applicant get that far - but the test would be the same as a paper and pencil test and done under the same conditions, with an automatic timer. The additional advantage for the organisation is that the test feedback is instant and decisions can be made very quickly.

For the applicants, sitting at home and taking a psychometric test means that they can be more relaxed. The instructions to applicants would be the same, but being in familiar surroundings without the need to travel elsewhere can seem far less exhausting.

Feedback to the candidates will likely come in the form of either a letter inviting them for interview and further assessment, or a 'Thank you, but we will not be taking your application any further.' The latter seems very impersonal, especially if the test is online and is used in such a way that a candidate has never actually met the organisation or anyone from it. However, testing is intended to be an objective measure of someone's suitability for the role(s) being advertised.

Personality Inventories and Questionnaires

For personality tests, the formats vary considerably. You might be asked to select the answer that is 'most typical' and one that is 'least typical' from a group of four alternatives, or 'strongly agree/disagree' to every item in what is called a 'Likert scale format', or distribute a particular number of 'points' across a range of statements according to how you consider yourself to behave 'typically'.

In contrast to an ability test, a personality questionnaire is not a timed exercise to see how many answers you get right and wrong. Instead, the organisation will be trying to find out how you are likely to behave and what you are likely to do in certain situations. The implication is that there are no right or wrong answers. The temptation, however, is to believe that there are, and to give answers that are what you think the organisation will expect. In reality, there are methods within the scoring of the questionnaire to determine whether you are answering in what is termed a 'socially desirable' way, and if you 'trigger' something which indicates that you are not answering honestly, then your results will not be seen as very useful.

It is reasonable to say, though, that unless you are particularly unsure of yourself or have something to hide, there is every reason for you to answer honestly, without needing to consider your responses. If you get the job and the organisation finds out that your answers are not really accurate, then it would have every right to reconsider its offer to you. Alternatively, you could argue whether you really want to be in an organisation where your personality really does not fit so well.

The questions in a personality questionnaire will vary according to the personality inventory being used. Box 18.3 provides some sample questions. Some will ask you to rate how 'similar to you' a particular item is on a 1–4 or 1–5 Likert scale, but many will ask you to identify 'least typical' and 'most typical' responses from a group of four possible behaviours. There are different statistical approaches used in each questionnaire and the exact format will depend on the approach taken to develop the questionnaire and the underlying theory.

 LIKERT SCALE

A Likert scale is a rating scale (usually from 1 to 5) which asks you to respond (with strongly agree, agree, neutral, disagree, strongly disagree) according to your view of the statement given.

See Chapter 4, page 71 (Skills Self-Assessment questionnaire), for an example of a questionnaire which uses a Likert scale.

===== BOX 18.3 =====

EXAMPLES OF QUESTIONS FROM THE EYSENCK PERSONALITY INVENTORY (EYSENCK AND EYSENCK, 1975)

In the questions below, each pair has to add up to 5, so the possible combinations across (a) and (b) could be (a) 5 and (b) 0, or (a) 4 and (b) 1 or finally (a) 3 and (b) 2, where the higher number means 'I would prefer to do this' and the lower number means 'I would prefer to do this less'. This forced choice format pushes individuals away from being able to take a middle approach and giving 2.5 to each alternative. This particular questionnaire also asks individuals to reply according to how they 'would prefer' to behave. The distinction is important, since individuals may be pushed into behaving at work in ways that do not naturally fit. For example, I might quite like to undertake activities spontaneously, but in my work I would need to use a diary to plan and prepare for activities to come, and therefore not act according to my natural preferences.

I prefer:	
1a	Making decisions after consulting others
1b	Making decisions without consulting others
2a	Being called imaginative or intuitive
2b	Being called factual and accurate
3a	Making decisions about people in organisations based on available data and systematic analysis of situations

(Continued)

(Continued)

3b	Making decisions about people in organisations based on empathy, feelings and an understanding of their needs and value
4a	Allowing commitments to occur if others want to make them
4b	Pushing for definite commitments to ensure that they are made

When answering the questions, it is very likely that a number of questions will appear very similar. There is very straightforward reason for this, which relates to the issue of reliability: the test makers build this into questionnaires deliberately in order to check which behaviours are likely to prevail regardless of situations and which are less likely to, and to ensure that there is some measure of consistency (i.e. reliability) in how respondents answer the questions given. Of course, try not to remember how you answered before – the key to personality questionnaires is that they are about you and your behaviour, so you need to answer quickly and honestly.

Once all the questions are answered, the selectors then need to go through what this might say about you. Personality inventories are not infallible and there are times when applicants misunderstand questions, so post-questionnaire interviews are essential for ensuring that the answers are accurate. During such an interview, be sure to give examples to back up what you are saying. If an organisation does not hold such an interview with you, then it is not using the personality questionnaire correctly.

Finally, personality questionnaires can never be used to replace ability tests. The questionnaires can give an indication as to someone's temperament and likelihood of demonstrating certain behaviours, but cannot say anything about whether someone can think through certain problems and issues.

═══ KEY LEARNING POINT ═══

Ability tests and personality questionnaires are scientifically developed tools to help organisations understand the cognitive/intellectual abilities and personalities of applicants for key jobs.

UNDERSTANDING ASSESSMENT CENTRES

Good science and research underpins a great deal of good selection practice. In the 1940s, British Military Intelligence began using a form of assessment called the 'assessment centre' to select staff, and these methods are now used much more widely in industry. The basic principle is this: if you can observe how someone might work in enough real-life simulations, then you might be able to predict how they might perform in a real role in business. The 'assessment centre' is where that observation takes place, and whilst nearly all are private, some are very public – as Box 18.4 explains.

ASSESSMENT CENTRE

An assessment centre is a process used for managerial level selection, whereby applicants for senior role(s) are observed undertaking exercises relevant to the role(s) for which they are applying.

━━━━━━━━━ BOX 18.4 ━━━━━━━━━

THE BEST KNOWN ASSESSMENT CENTRE

Arguably the best known assessment centre is probably the TV show *The Apprentice*, shown regularly on UK and US television over a long period of time.

Candidates are recruited and screened before the TV show presents us with the 12 individuals who have been successful in getting to the final round of selection. During the show, they are placed together in a house and, each week the show is broadcast, the teams of candidates have to work together to compete with another team as they undertake a task – for example, making money by organising an event and selling tickets, or producing a calendar to sell on behalf of a charity, or setting up a small business of some kind with donated resources. After the task has been completed within the time limit, the two teams are given the outcome: the successful team is given a treat, while the less successful team is invited to account for its actions with the team leader, and one of the team will need to leave the selection process.

Although there is a significant element of entertainment built into the way the show is run and filmed, it does share many of the standard characteristics of an assessment centre. For example, applicants (or contestants):

- Have usually been applying for a real job.
- Have to undertake a number of tough group-based exercises.
- Are observed undertaking those exercises.
- Are given accommodation.
- Are 'interviewed' after each exercise to account for their actions.
- Have to both cooperate and compete in order to be offered the job.

It is clear that what the viewing public see is only a small part of the story and that there are other things going on behind the scenes. It is also artificial in that few organisations would ever really involve the direct line manager in such an intense way (or that the line manager would ever really share their opinions so directly – and often aggressively – in a real selection situation) and the show is intended to have some entertainment value, but it does give a basic idea of how an assessment centre works.

What Are Assessment Centres?

An assessment centre is usually the last stage in a managerial or graduate-level selection process. As described above, an assessment centre is a series of activities designed to determine whether an applicant for a graduate-level role has the required skills and abilities to do the role for which they have applied. It is often residential, requiring at least one night away in a hotel or corporate training centre. For the employer, it is very resource intensive, for reasons that will be outlined below, so it is only used for positions where the expense is justified and where the cost of hiring someone inappropriate could be significant – that is, usually for managerial appointments and above.

Preparing for an Assessment Centre

Being invited to an assessment centre usually indicates that you have already demonstrated to a potential employer during an interview that you have some personal qualities which would help you to do a good job and which would enable you to fit into the organisation. The feedback and notes from that previous interview would probably be in the hands of those organising the assessment centre, but you will need to focus carefully on what you are being asked to do.

If you are invited to attend an assessment centre there are a number of things you need to undertake, some of them quickly:

1. **Reply to the invitation, indicating whether you accept it.** If you have had a recent interview, keep an eye on the email address you have given to the organisation. You will probably be a well-organised individual but check your diary first: the dates of the assessment centre might just clash with a family wedding, another interview or another assessment centre (in which case, you need to ask your careers services to assist in negotiating with the organisation).

2. **Make the practical arrangements.** Accommodation will usually be arranged by the organisation but you will need to arrange your own transport. Your costs will usually be paid by the organisation, but do not take this as an opportunity to travel first class or by air when the cost of a standard-class train ticket would be reasonable. If you are unsure, then ask; organisations will usually indicate in their invitation what they would accept as reasonable.

3. **Learn about others' experiences of that organisation's assessment centre, if possible.** Knowing roughly what to expect will reduce your anxiety about it. Sometimes, your careers services will have some information from someone who attended an assessment centre from that organisation recently, or there may be some information on the Internet, so it is worth doing a search.

4. **Make sure that you have a copy of your application to this organisation.** It is highly likely that you will be given another interview (or maybe more than one) as part of the assessment centre and you need to have your application with you.

5. **Find out as much as you can about the organisation.** This was covered in Chapter 15, but at this much later stage you will be expected to know things in a lot more detail. You will be expected to know where the company operates (and perhaps where you might like or need to be based), what it will be like to work there, why you want to work with that organisation and not a different one, how your skills match what it is seeking and how much investment it puts in to developing its people. You might wish to find out about the organisation's strategy, what its strengths and weaknesses are, and how it might change what it does to overcome any increased success from its competitors.

6. **Ensure that you have the correct clothing available to you.** For male applicants, this will mean at least two ironed shirts, a decent tie, a clean suit and smart shoes (and maybe some shoe polish). For female applicants, it will mean a business suit, comfortable shoes (you will need to wear them for a lengthy period of time, so do not wear any shoes that may be uncomfortable) and two blouses. If you need to pack smart clothes into a suitcase for travelling, then use a suit cover which you carry separately (usually available from any tailor or shop that sells suits) or fold and pack them carefully: there are ways of packing clothes to keep them flat during long journeys. Check what you have available to you in advance: you do not really want to find that, with two days to do at the assessment centre, your suit is dirty in some way.

The above should help you in preparing for an assessment centre, both practically and in terms of thinking things through, but there is little substitute for knowing what you will be doing there. What is certain is that you will be doing a number of exercises, you will be observed at every opportunity and you will be assessed – and accepted or rejected for the role(s) – according to the qualities you show.

What to Expect at an Assessment Centre

A good assessment centre is designed around the skills and qualities that an employer will be seeking, thus every assessment centre will be different. However, it is reasonable to say that there are some features in common:

- It will usually last between one and two days.
- There will probably be a formal dinner with all the candidates and all the observers.
- It will be tiring, so relax, be yourself and enjoy it as much as you are able.
- You will almost certainly have a formal interview at some stage (there may be other informal discussions over lunch, so note that an interview is a 'conversation with a purpose' and does not need to happen in an office).
- There will likely be at least 15 other candidates there, and quite possibly up to 30.
- You will very likely need to deliver a presentation.
- You will need to do verbal and numerical reasoning tests.
- The observers will be looking for a variety of skills (negotiation, critical analysis, persuasion, giving others feedback, developing strong arguments, planning, giving information, personal organisation, etc.) during the assessment centre exercises, but will *need to see you lead others successfully* in at least one exercise and work constructively with others throughout the assessment centre.
- All exercises will have strict time limits, which need to be monitored carefully.
- The observers will have regular meetings during the assessment centre to identify gaps in information (where they do not have sufficient information about you from what they are seeing), to corroborate information that they do have from what they have seen, and to reallocate groups so that all candidates get the chance to work with as many of the other candidates as possible.

If there are four candidates working together on a team exercise, then there will likely be two observers, each watching two different candidates and taking notes about what they do, what they say and how they do it. The structure of a typical assessment centre is outlined in Box 18.5.

═══════════ **BOX 18.5** ═══════════

TYPICAL STRUCTURE OF AN ASSESSMENT CENTRE

Day 1

Candidates arrive early to mid-afternoon, register and settle into the hotel

4 p.m. Introduction by HR manager

4.30 p.m. Group allocation and introduction for Exercise 1

4.45–5.30 p.m. Ice-breaker and Exercise 1

6 p.m. Formal dinner with selectors and other candidates

7.15 p.m. Exercise 2

8 p.m. Company presentation

9 p.m. Informal drinks in the hotel bar

Day 2

7–8 a.m. Breakfast

8.15–9 a.m. Debrief interview ('What did you think of the exercises last night?')

(Continued)

(Continued)

9.15 a.m. Verbal and numerical reasoning tests

10 a.m. Coffee break

10.20–12 a.m. Exercise 3 (including presentation)

12.10 p.m. Formal interview

1 p.m. Lunch

2–2.45 p.m. Exercise 4: 'In-basket exercise'

3 p.m. Informal discussion with selectors about the organisation

3.30 p.m. Tea break

3.45 p.m. Debrief interview from Exercise 4 ('Why did you do what you did?')

4.30–4.45 p.m. Brief assessment centre debrief interview ('Any comments on what we have done here?')

5.15 p.m. Thank you and final announcements

5.30 p.m. Candidates depart; observers meet to discuss their notes

---

The details of exactly what an assessment centre will involve will vary according to the skills being sought, but you may be asked to undertake some of the following.

- **Negotiation exercise:** You need to negotiate resources in competition with other candidates, based on information given to you. How will you form your argument? How will you use your communication skills to ensure that you get what you need? What will you be willing to compromise on? Would you take the role of chairing/leading the discussion?
- **Business case study:** You are part of a team facing an important business decision. Will you lead the exercise? How will you analyse the information? What do you think are the important issues? How can you help the team arrive at the decision which is right for the organisation?
- **Role:** You are given a role to play as part of a team discussion and an objective for that role to achieve. How will you go about achieving that objective? What are the strong arguments? The weak ones? Will you lead the discussion?
- **Information gaps:** Everyone in the team has different and complementary pieces of information, and all the information is needed to achieve the objective. You will need to give your information. Will you lead the activity? How will you structure the team's information gathering activity: according to the team member or according to the nature of the information – or both? How will you organise the information that team members give?
- **'In-basket exercise':** You need to catch a flight in 30 minutes, but you have some urgent emails and memos to deal with before you go. Some of these will relate to your diary appointments, some will relate to communications with the public or your employees, or senior managers, and some will require immediate action while actions for others are not urgent, but your ability to pay attention to detail is very important. How will you respond to each email? What is urgent, and what is less urgent? Can you ensure that there are no diary clashes? If you are being asked to do two things at the same time, how will you decide which to do? How will you respond to 'ceremonial' requests as opposed to day-to-day management activities and meetings? How would you change your language to deal with people in different levels of management?
- **Practical/physical exercise:** You are given some instructions, some resources and asked to build or make an object. How will you work with others to plan and develop some designs? How would you use the resources appropriately? How will you evaluate your success? How do you lead?

- **Individual presentation:** You are given some information which you need to analyse quickly and present a summary to other members of a team. How will you structure, develop and deliver your presentation to ensure that the key points from the information come through? What parts of the information will you need to focus on? What is less important? How will you conclude your presentation? How will you explain any complicated ideas?
- **Ice-breaker discussion:** This is a brief activity to enable folk to learn about and then succinctly present each other, according to some questions given to you. How will you present the information? Will you be a little humorous or serious? What will you say, and what will you leave out?

In thinking these through, you might wish to have some ideas in mind about how you will go about performing and behaving in those assessment centre exercises you need to do. Each exercise will examine a number of important skills and each skill will be assessed at least twice for each individual in different exercises.

 'BUT I HAVE A QUESTION ...'

... What do employers look for during these various exercises?

Well, each exercise will look for a number of skills, but the skills commonly sought in an assessment centre will be:

- Analysis and problem solving
- Critical thinking
- Interpersonal skills
- Communication (listening, speaking clearly)
- Personal drive
- Leadership potential
- Team-working (organising, time keeping, making sure others have their say).

The individual who does well in these situations and who demonstrates these skills consistently and successfully will likely be offered a job role. It is true that focusing on so many of these skills at once is difficult, unless they become part of naturally occurring behaviour. That is why university gives you so many opportunities to work in teams and lead others.

PERFORMING WELL IN GROUP DISCUSSIONS AT AN ASSESSMENT CENTRE

Part IV of this text dealt with employability skills and three areas from that part are relevant here, most notably team-working, leadership and communication skills. However, a team such as those described in earlier chapters will need to work together over a relatively long period of time. At an assessment centre, you do not have time to get to know each other properly, or have conflicts or develop any rules. You will get a short period of time to undertake the exercise, so the emphasis is on how you can best help your team to do that. Some basic rules are given below:

1. **You need to contribute somehow:** If you do not contribute, then the observers will have nothing to take away as evidence of your skill, and you will not be successful.

2. **Are you the person making notes?** This is not a great role to have in a situation like this. It is helpful to your team to be able to complete the exercise by making a written record of the points raised, but it is also very difficult to listen, contribute and make notes at the same time. It is quite possible that the person taking notes will not make a great contribution to the exercise.

3. **Are you the team leader?** Within an assessment centre exercise, leaders are not appointed by anyone, they emerge naturally. If you are leading the exercise, then consider the roles that individuals are going to play in the exercise – including someone to manage the time! – and ensure that all are aware of the goal of the exercise before starting the exercise itself. Finally, you will need to think about how the team intends to plan what it needs to do. All of these can be done quickly, which is important because you will not have a lot of time.

4. **Eye contact:** Any individual who does not look at the others who are speaking or who avoids eye contact will not be successful in the assessment centre. Avoiding eye contact means that you will not be able to perceive others' interpersonal skills and you may miss important nuances in what people say.

5. **Competition v cooperation:** Although you may be in competition to some extent with others that you see at the assessment centre, it is worth recognising that employers may be able to select all of you or none of you. In light of this, it is much better to cooperate and work with those in your team, rather than trying to compete. Employers will be looking for this far more than they will be looking for competitive behaviours.

6. **Tone of voice:** If you have something to say, say it clearly and ensure that your voice gets heard. This does not mean, of course, getting upset, emotional or shouting, but it does mean ensuring that anything you say gets heard. It is better to keep your voice calm and unemotional – a low pitch is better than a high-pitched voice.

7. **Persistence:** You should not be afraid of pushing for an idea if you think it is a good one, but you need to be able to do so in a way which discourages others from making contributions or in a way which is going to alienate others. There may come a point when you decide that the good of the team is more important than achieving the task successfully, but that is a risky judgement in the face of a short exercise.

8. **Listening skills:** Listening is usually an underrated skill. It is very tempting to want to interrupt and make your point clearly, especially when the pace of the conversation is very fast, but doing so will be seen as evidence of very poor communication skills. Do not interrupt, let others finish and then say what you wish to say. If you think that the pace of the conversation is too fast, you can slow it down yourself when you get to speak.

9. **Using questions for team building:** It is a good idea to use questions to get people to see your point of view, but they can also be useful for checking information that has already been given and for checking for agreement from others. If asked calmly, questions can be a useful way of persuading people of your point of view.

10. **Acknowledging and encouraging (quieter) others:** It is very easy to consider that you are in a selection situation and it is your performance that is being watched, but it is also important to recognise that part of your performance (especially in a leadership role, although this applies to everyone in the team) will be encouraging and acknowledging the views from quieter team members. It is not something that is done particularly well, but it is something that observers will notice.

11. **Balance between listening and talking:** Be mindful that the one talking all the time may not be the best candidate for the job. You do need to make some contribution, but dominating others without listening properly to what is being said is not the best way to demonstrate your team-working, leadership or communication skills.

12. **Seating and body posture:** Depending on the layout of the room or table, you may find that you have your back to others in the team. Whether you are leading the team or not, make sure that everyone can easily see everyone else. This might mean physically moving your chair, or turning around a little.

 KEY LEARNING POINT

While there are many things to bear in mind when attending an assessment centre, the main point of an assessment centre is to see whether you have the right kinds of skills that the organisation is looking for. So be as natural as you can and practise what you can in order to develop your skills.

INTEGRATION AND APPLICATION

Passing an interview, then psychometric tests and then an assessment centre is not something that anyone else can do for you – you will have to do this yourself. Your careers services can help you with some of these areas and can give you opportunities to practise, but the demonstration of your skills is something that will be up to you, bearing in mind the activities you have done at university, the earlier content of this text, any part-time work or responsibilities in student societies and your engagement with the careers services.

In nearly all selection processes, it is fear of the unknown that can make life hard, so the current chapter has sought to provide some idea of what you might expect from ability tests, personality questionnaires and assessment centres. There are some basic principles to think through:

1. **Prepare:** Find out information, try some exercises and tests, and get some experience in the kinds of activities you will be asked to do.

2. **Act:** Demonstrate the skills and abilities (behavioural and cognitive/intellectual) that have been tested and developed throughout your time at university.

3. **Review:** Consider how well you did in the exercises and the tests. You can normally get some feedback on the exercises and a little feedback on the tests, so use that feedback to improve, whether you were successful or not.

You should always be able to receive feedback on your performance in any part of the selection process, but the feedback that could come from an assessment centre has the potential to be much more detailed than that which could come from a single interview.

CONCLUSION

You should now:

- Know what to expect if asked to take a psychometric test or attend an assessment centre.
- Feel prepared for being asked to take a psychometric test and attend an assessment centre.

- Understand why some employers use such instruments to select graduate employees.
- Feel relatively relaxed if asked to attend such a selection process.

Having an understanding of what the tests and assessment centres are and what they look for does not guarantee that you will do well, but it will probably help to reduce nerves and make life slightly more relaxed. One of the things that individuals who have been invited to a number of assessment centres find is that they have a better idea of how they work and this, in turn, helps them to prepare better – which really been the purpose of this chapter. In terms of tests, they also find that there are times when different employers will use the same reasoning tests (because they look for similar qualities), so the ability to remember what information to record and what calculations to do means that individuals are more likely to finish the tests the more they do them, but this does not guarantee that they (or you) will get more answers correct, of course.

FINAL REFLECTIONS

Based on the content of this chapter, what do you now know about psychometric tests and assessment centres that you did not know before?

What key learning point had the most impact? Why?

Do your answers to either of the above questions have the potential to change your ability to perform well when taking a psychometric test/personality questionnaire or attending an assessment centre? Why?

What will you now do differently? (Write this down and put it somewhere where you can see it regularly.)

ADDITIONAL RESOURCES

Want to learn more? Visit https://study.sagepub.com/morgan to gain access to a wide range of online resources, including interactive tests, tasks, further reading and downloads.

Website Resources – Assessment Centers

Bangor University – leaflet including a large number of additional websites: www.bangor.ac.uk/careers/services/documents/AssessmentCentres11-12ENG.pdf

Changingminds.org: http://changingminds.org/disciplines/hr/selection/assessment_center.htm

Jobsite.co.uk – Hot to impress at selection centres: www.jobsite.co.uk/hobsons_articles/select_centre.html

Prospects website: www.prospects.ac.uk/careers-advice/interview-tips/assessment-centres

University of Aberdeen: www.abdn.ac.uk/careers/resources/topics/18/

University of Birmingham: https://intranet.birmingham.ac.uk/as/employability/careers/apply/assessment-centres/index.aspx

University of Liverpool: www.liverpool.ac.uk/careers/applications-and-interviews/assessment-centres/

University of Sheffield: www.shef.ac.uk/careers/students/gettingajob/assessment

Website Resources – Psychometric Tests

Careerplayer.com: www.careerplayer.com/psychometrics

Changingminds.org: http://changingminds.org/disciplines/hr/selection/psychometric.htm

Manchester Metropolitan University: www.mmu.ac.uk/careers/students-and-graduates/resources/guides/aptitude-personality-practice-tests.pdf

Newcastle University: www.ncl.ac.uk/careers/interviews/tests/#preparation

Practice Aptitude Tests.com – giving you the opportunity to practice reasoning tests you might be given at an Assessment Centre: www.practiceaptitudetests.com/psychometric-tests/

Prospects website – SHL practice psychometric tests: www.prospects.ac.uk/careers-advice/interview-tips/psychometric-tests/preparing-for-shl-practice-tests

University of Liverpool: www.liverpool.ac.uk/careers/applications-and-interviews/psychometric-tests/

University of Sheffield: www.shef.ac.uk/careers/students/gettingajob/psychometric

Answers to Verbal Reasoning Questions

Passage 1

1. It is possible that permanent staff who are on holiday can have their work carried out by students. *True*
2. Students in summer employment are given the same paid holiday benefit as permanent staff. *False*
3. Students are su]ard disciplinary and grievance procedures. *Cannot Tell*
4. Companies have more work to do in summer when students are available for vacation work. *True*

Passage 2

1. The causes of cancer are still uncertain. *True*
2. Cancer seems to affect people from some races differently to people from other races. *False*
3. People who have heart attacks are less likely to have cancer. *Cannot Tell*
4. Finding a cure for leukaemia is more urgent than finding a cure for other kinds of cancer. *Cannot Tell* (It is urgent, but no information is given about whether it is more urgent than other kinds of cancer.)
5. There are several organisations which are working together to find a cure for cancer. *Cannot Tell* (They may be working, but no information is given about them working together.)
6. Many people die from cancer every year. *Cannot Tell*

Passage 3

1. All children should be taken on the school buses. *Cannot Tell*
2. Roads leading up to schools should have strict speed limits. *Cannot Tell*
3. Parents who wish to collect a child from school should not bring a car. *False*
4. It would be better if parents arrived and parked their cars at different times. *Strong*
5. Parents should not smile at their children when collecting them from school. *Weak*
6. Cars and buses should be parked in different places. *Weak*
7. The location of car parking at schools is something which should be monitored very closely. *Strong*

Answers to Numerical Reasoning Questions

Set 1

1. If my flight to Shanghai leaves the gate at Dubai Airport at 6 a.m., what time would I expect to arrive at my gate in Shanghai Airport?
   (a) **12.30 p.m.**   (b) 12.30 a.m.   (c) 7.30 a.m.   (d) 12 p.m.

2. By what percentage is the flying time from Dubai to Shanghai longer than the flight from Dubai to New York?
   (a) 1.6%   (b) 85%   (c) 12%   (d) **16%**

(Continued)

(Continued)

3. If I am flying from New York to Beijing, I can expect a headwind to add 20% onto my flying time. So, what is my total time from leaving the gate in New York to arriving at my gate in Beijing?

   (a) 15 h 40 min   (b) 12 h 30 min   (c) **18 h 45 min**   (d) 16 h 15 min

4. I need to fly from Beijing to New York via a connecting flight in Dubai which will leave two hours later. My flight will leave Beijing at 4.30 p.m. Assuming no delays and no need to queue for immigration or collect baggage in Dubai, what time can I expect to arrive at the gate in New York?

   (a) 9.35 a.m. the next day   (b) 9 p.m. the same day
   (c) **10.35 p.m. the same day**   (d) 6.35 p.m. the next day

Set 2

1. If we measure the ratio of expenses to salary as the percentage of salary spent on expenses, whose spending is the least efficient?
   (a) Martin   (b) **Sarah**   (c) Paul   (d) Bill

(Sarah's is 57%, higher than Martin's at 38%, Bill's at 53.5% and Paul's at 46%.)

2. Martin's investments are in an investment fund where the rate will not change for five years. If Martin saves all that he does not spend into an investment fund, how much is he likely to see in that fund after three years of growth?

   (a) £8650.34   (b) £9627.66   (c) £27,377.25   (d) **£10,157**

(£8650 is just unspent income, £9627.66 is after two years, £27,377 is just 3 × £8650, and £10,157 is £9627.66 × 1.055, and so is the amount after three years of growth.)

3. If Martin saves all that he does not spend into an investment fund, but the other friends only invest 60% of what they do not spend into similar funds, what is the situation regarding the four friends' investments after the first anniversary?

   (a) Martin has more in his investment fund than Paul.
   (b) Paul has more invested than Sarah.
   (c) **As a percentage of his income, Bill has more invested than Paul.**
   (d) Martin has less in his investment fund than Bill.

(The order and amounts are: Martin has £9125, Paul £9299, Sarah £10,680 and Bill £6315. As a percentage of his salary, Bill has 33% in his fund, whereas Paul has 28%.)

4. During her second year of work, Sarah falls sick and is unable to receive a salary for half a year. However, during her first year, she was able to invest 85% of her net income (income minus expenses) into her investment fund. Assuming a 3% increase in salary and a reduction to save only 35% of her net income but no other changes, what would her investment (as a percentage of her total income over that period) be?

   (a) 32%   (b) 49.7%   (c) **37%**   (d) 69%

(First year: Sarah saves £16,985, invests £14,437 and has a fund of £15,130. In her second year, she saves just £2548, invests £891.98 (35%) and adds that to the £15,130, giving £16,021. The interest on the combined amounts gives her £16,791. Her salary for the second year is £30,657, half of which is £15,328. So the total salary for the two years is £45,093. As a percentage of her salary, £16,791 represents 37%.)

/19/ ALTERNATIVE OPTIONS AFTER GRADUATION

CHAPTER STRUCTURE

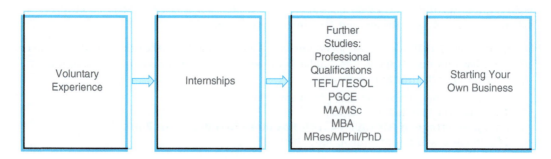

Figure 19.1

When you see the 🌐 this means go to the companion website https://study.sagepub.com/morgan to do a quiz, complete a task, read further or download a template.

━━ AIMS OF THE CHAPTER ━━━━━

By the end of this chapter, you should be able to:

- Recognise that graduate employment is not the only option after undergraduate studies.
- Understand your own capacity to take up additional options.
- Evaluate which option(s) are applicable to your own situation.
- Develop practical strategies for taking up alternative options.

INTRODUCTION

It is generally thought that a university education is intended to prepare you for a career, usually a career with a blue-chip multinational organisation. The idea is that, after you graduate, you will find a management or graduate trainee position where you can earn a good salary and start to develop your career towards the top of whatever organisation you start working for. There used to be the view that graduating meant you were almost guaranteed a career.

Neither is necessarily the case. Graduates from university have a range of options, and even if those options include employment, organisations can be very different. Public sector employers – including universities and local authorities – are often the biggest employers in many UK towns, while voluntary organisations can offer very rewarding opportunities for those with a strong social view. But there are other alternatives as well – including volunteering and internships – which can be low-risk options for those unsure about what they want to do.

We do need to be clear about what we mean by 'job' and 'career'. A career is usually seen as long term, maybe 20 years or more. We talk about people having 'a career in …' and follow with something relating to a particular business role (e.g. HRM), or 'a career with …' a particular company. Both uses of the word refer to something different from a 'job', which is usually seen as short term, something which can be changed relatively easily and something which is primarily used to pay for living expenses on a day-to-day basis. Many people aspire to develop their career, and most will have a series of jobs before 'settling' on one career and moving forward in that role or company.

This chapter outlines some basic thoughts regarding these options, giving some benefits and risks to each option. The one outcome that nobody wants (and that this text has been intending to prevent) is to be unemployed with no daytime activities; this has been shown to harm mental health. Assuming that you do not wish to be unemployed and that you do not have a graduate trainee contract, this chapter may give you some ideas moving forward. It will look at voluntary work, setting up your own business, postgraduate study (Master's, PGCE and PhD) and teaching English as a foreign language. The structure of this chapter is somewhat different to those of other chapters; the aim is to give you information rather than to facilitate your learning and development. We begin by looking at voluntary work experience and examine the kinds of opportunities available, the personal qualities needed and additional issues to consider before starting a career.

VOLUNTARY EXPERIENCE

Voluntary experience is by its very nature 'voluntary' (i.e. it is typically unpaid) and is undertaken by individuals who want or need to gain some kind of experience before entering the workforce.

Such experience can take a variety of diverse forms:

- Working on a farm or in a factory.
- Undertaking charity work, either in your own country or overseas (e.g. nature conservation, building a school, providing healthcare).
- Work shadowing a company manager.
- Teaching English. (Note that you should be trained and qualified if you are doing this for a professional organisation.)
- Leading or taking part in an expedition (e.g. Operation Raleigh or Duke of Edinburgh's Award scheme).

'VOLUNTARY EXPERIENCE'

Voluntary experience is work undertaken without contract or obligation on either party, which is unpaid and undertaken to gain experience.

There are no formal obligations or accountabilities when it comes to voluntary work experience, so it is entirely up to you as to how you structure, plan and thus benefit (or otherwise) from any such experience.

The aims of such a form of experience are usually to obtain some practical work experience that you did not get during your degree, and to add to that experience in a real world setting. You probably will not get a decent level of experience (you will not usually be asked to handle any large budgets, for example) that requires a more formal arrangement and additional accountability, but you might have the chance to develop some skills relevant to the roles you wish to fulfil. Companies familiar with providing voluntary experience may need you to sign some type of statement that, whatever you do in front of others as a representative of the company providing the experience, limits their liability (e.g. if you break something while visiting a customer). Box 19.1 discusses how to obtain voluntary work experience.

BOX 19.1

HOW TO OBTAIN VOLUNTARY WORK EXPERIENCE

Because there is less formality to voluntary arrangements, you will not see companies going through a formalised recruitment process. It is possible that some organisations might advertise that they provide voluntary experience in some instances, but by far the easiest way to obtain such experience is simply to write and ask.

Find some organisations which are either in the kind of business you wish to work in during the years ahead or local and large enough to provide you with something interesting to do, find out the name of the local manager, and then politely write and ask.

Explain what kinds of activities/experiences you are looking for and/or the kinds of skills you want to develop, and why. Also, ask whether there might be anything you can do to help them out.

It takes some initiative and a little bit of courage if you have never done it before, but if you approach the right person and explain what you are looking for, then there will often be something interesting you can help with.

Personal Attributes Required/Developed

The nature of the skills you develop and the personal qualities you need to make the experience work for you will vary from person to person, and from experience to experience. To begin with, you might need a little tenacity to try to get the experience you are seeking and some creativity to find the right kinds of opportunities, but it is really important to think through what skills you wish to develop.

Having had some voluntary experience, you will probably be able to persuade an interviewer that you are proactive (if you went out and asked for the experience, rather than waited for someone else to suggest it), you are determined (if you asked a number of individuals for the experience) and you are able to work independently (if your experience required you to do so) and/or as part of a team (if your experience required you to do so). If the work experience was very structured with definite start and stop times each day, then that might mean you had to be disciplined, and if you had to communicate with others, then that is something to be noted.

If you have chosen to work with a particular organisation or with people working in a particular role, then exposure to that organisation and that role and the decisions individuals have to take will help you understand what it is like to work in such an organisation, which will prepare you for interview.

Issues to Consider

Why are you seeking this experience?

If you are seeking voluntary experience with a work organisation, you should think about why you are undertaking this experience with this individual organisation. Wanting to develop your skills is fine, but there is nothing worse than turning up to an office one day with nothing to do, so be clear about your reasons for taking up the experience and the kind of work you want to do.

Is there any kind of reimbursement?

Seeking money from an employer for voluntary experience you have sought from it would likely be seen as inappropriate: if you have agreed to undertake voluntary experience, then voluntary it should be. However, some employers might wish to *offer* some small benefits, as a thank you. Regardless, the correct thing to do is to wait until anything is offered, rather than seek it before you begin the work.

How long will this experience last?

It is always useful to set a definite length to the time you will be 'working with' an organisation, though the importance of this will depend slightly on the nature of the experience you seek. If you are working with a voluntary organisation, a charity or an employer on a voluntary basis, then they will almost certainly expect you to tell them how long the experience will last, so they can make some formal plans. If you are working on a voluntary basis with a very small business or in a rural setting then it might be less important, but the main issue here is to ask them: (1) whether they need to know, and (2) how much notice they would like to have of your intention to leave.

How structured will this experience be?

By its nature, the structure of any voluntary experience that you are seeking may well be up to you to negotiate with those who are making such experience available to you. You are the one seeking the experience, you know what you want to get out of it, and you should have an idea of how structured the experience should be, so this should be up to you. The less clear it is, the less it will impress someone who might be able to offer you that experience (and the less likely they might be to offer you that experience, of course).

Think about doing a project on …, or attending meetings about …, or being involved with a team which is working on … Have some ideas as to what you want to do – ideas based on what you wish to get from the experience.

How Can I Use this Experience to Begin My Career?

There are two main ways in which you can use voluntary experience. Taking the initiative to obtain voluntary experience (particularly in a work setting) can impress a manager, so if you have been professional in how you set it up and used the experience well, then the manager might be inclined to offer you a post when a suitable vacancy arises. If the manger is very impressed, then they may be able to create a post for you, and although this is fantastic, it is not common and should not be expected.

More commonly, individuals use such experience carefully to develop their skills and give themselves something to talk about when it comes to a subsequent interview. Working overseas on a charity project to build a school or do some teaching can provide a large number of opportunities to develop team-work and practical skills, to show some commitment to others at your own expense (which usually impresses others, if the cause is humanitarian!) and to broaden your experience to include working in a culture usually very different from your own. All of these qualities and motivations are usually seen *very positively* when vacancies arise.

 REFLECTION POINT

Take some time to think about the following questions and write down some answers, first on your own, and then with others that you might be working with.

What sort of voluntary experience would work for you?
  What would a 'poor' period of voluntary experience be like for you?
  Is this an option that you would enjoy?

INTERNSHIPS

An internship is very similar to voluntary work experience but has a number of important differences. It is halfway between a job and voluntary work experience. For example, an internship is usually an opportunity offered by a company. A vacancy is created by the organisation, an individual – often a student or a recent graduate – will apply and they will then work with the organisation for a defined length of time. The individual will not usually get paid, but there will be some recompense in the form of a bursary or a minimum payment to cover some expenses.

 'INTERNSHIP'

An internship is a structured piece of work experience, usually organised by the employer, but carries no formal salary and has a defined length.

An internship can often be better than an unstructured period of voluntary work experience, since structured work defined by an employer may lead to definite tasks to be done and the development of specific skills. Employers do use them as a way to determine whether individuals should be offered jobs in the future, but internships are usually very popular with those seeking jobs, or with those about to graduate.

Other than the above, the same considerations that apply to voluntary experience (goals, length, structure and using the opportunity to find a job) also apply to internships.

FURTHER STUDIES

Taking postgraduate qualifications after you have graduated from an undergraduate degree is not as common in the UK as it is overseas. In India, anyone graduating from a reasonable university and hoping for a career in management will almost certainly expect or want to do an MBA. If you are from

China, then doing a postgraduate qualification is simply another 'automatic' step on the road to a good career – it is expected that students will do a postgraduate qualification, but it is not so common for students from the UK.

There are broadly four kinds of further study that can be undertaken in the UK and, in different ways, most will give you an additional advantage over those who graduate, leave university behind and start looking for a career. They are as follows:

- Professional business qualifications (ACCA, CIPD, etc.).
- Qualification in Teaching English as a Foreign Language (CertTEFL).
- Teaching qualification for school teaching (PGCE).
- Academic postgraduate qualifications (MSc/MA, MBA, PhD).

Of course, there are other postgraduate professional qualifications in a variety of occupations and you will usually be able to find information about those from your university careers services or online, but the ones described below are those most frequently taken by graduates in social science subjects (including management).

If you are already a postgraduate student and have completed both an undergraduate and a post-graduate qualification in the UK, you might wish to be careful about choosing to take another – there are time limits on how many years you can spend studying in the UK.

Professional Business Qualifications

These cover qualifications particularly in Human Resource Management (through the UK Chartered Institute of Personnel and Development, or CIPD), Marketing (through the Chartered Institute of Marketing), Accountancy (through Certified Public Accountancy qualifications, CPA; Association of Chartered and Certified Accountants, ACCA; Institute for Chartered Accountants for England and Wales, ICAEW; Chartered Institute of Management Accountants, CIMA; and others), Psychology (British Psychological Society, BPsS) or other professional disciplines.

These qualifications are often a requirement for technical roles, and seeking to obtain such qualifications can assist you in getting closer to interview. The effort and time that you take to get them is usually recognised by managers as a sign of commitment to the career you wish to take, and of expertise in the relevant field.

It is also worth checking with your university whether you could obtain exemptions from professional certification on the basis of your previous studies. This would mean that you do not need to take exams for certain subjects again. However, obtaining the *full qualifications* does require, in some cases, that you are undertaking a professional role and there are some professional associations which cannot grant you the full qualification until you have completed two years in a professional setting and a relevant role.

Qualification in Teaching English as a Foreign or Second Language

The TESOL/TEFL qualification is a very popular option for graduates who wish to get some international experience, who wish to travel and who wish to start a teaching career but who do not wish to teach in a school.

There are some places where it is quite possible to get a job as an English teacher without any qualifications. Being good at English is a very important skill in many places and can create international mobility for those good at English as much as those who are native English speakers and who wish to travel themselves. There are also a large number of 'temporary language schools' which are set up in the UK during the summer (when teenagers from across Europe take summer holidays and when their parents wish to send them to the UK to learn English) or summer language camps overseas, where teaching qualifications are seen as less important. Some take the view that qualifications are not that useful and the ability to speak and read in English is more important.

However, have a look at the following five questions and imagine that you are being asked these in a language class:

1. There are two sounds for 'th' (one 'hard' and one 'soft'), so how can I write these on a board in a way that non-native English speakers can understand?
2. What is the present simple tense and when do I use it?
3. When should I say 'I have done' instead of 'I did'?
4. I know that I should say 'I can't do' rather than 'I can't done', but why?
5. Why is 'taller' correct English grammar and 'more tall' incorrect?

All of the questions above are based on simple English grammar rules, but most English native speakers will not be aware of why they use the language that they do. Taking a recognised qualification will not only teach you how to teach – which is vitally important – but also teach you the English grammar that you will need to know.

Options for taking such qualifications are extremely varied, just like the length and costs of the course. You should take a course which:

*   Is recognised and certified by the British Council and by accreditation organisations such as Pitman.
*   Gives you actual teaching experience with students in a real classroom.
*   Gives you accurate and useful feedback on your teaching.
*   Requires you to write assignments about your teaching and the students you are teaching.
*   Teaches you to be creative in your teaching techniques, yet sensitive to those you are teaching (especially if teaching from countries with a more conservative culture).

If taking one of these courses full time, then you will probably have a very good experience over four very full weeks. If you do well and graduate with a CertTEFL or equivalent recognised qualification, then you will probably have little trouble finding a job – either in the UK or elsewhere.

Finding a suitable employer

As mentioned above, language schools vary considerably in their nature and in what they offer. Some will emphasise one-to-one tuition, others will conduct programmes for corporate clients, and some will run during just the summer; however, some language schools will do all of these.

Once qualified, you will need to consider carefully what sort of work you wish to undertake, and where. Whatever you do, you need to ensure that the employer is one that meets your needs and offers a professional service to their students.

If you are hoping to work abroad, you will need to ensure that you can meet the visa regulations for the country you are visiting. China, for example, recently tightened up the requirements for a visa to take employment by teaching English by insisting on much more experience than had previously been the case.

Qualification in Teaching – Postgraduate Certificate in Education

The PGCE qualification is designed for a very specific purpose: to enable you to begin a career in teaching. By its very nature, the qualification is designed to teach you how to teach. You will need to spend a considerable time in the classroom during the programme, to be supervised during that experience and to attend taught classes.

If you are considering a career in teaching, the main issue for you is to think about the age group you wish to teach. The teaching techniques used for very young children (4–7 years old), where you will be expected to teach a broad selection of subjects at a basic level, are significantly different to those for teenagers a specific subject so they can pass their exams at 16 and/or 18. Programmes designed for teaching in a secondary (11–18 years old) school will typically include some content around the subjects, but it is usually expected that you will have graduated in that subject to begin with.

You will also need to consider the kind of school you wish to work in. Fee-paying schools tend to have a vastly different culture (class size, organisational resourcing) and student background (social background, international mix) from those in the state sector, but are of course more difficult to get jobs with. If you spend a number of years in one sector, it is often more difficult to change sector.

The nature of the PGCE programmes offered by universities in the UK is regulated by the Teaching Qualifications Authority (TQA) and does change from time to time. Funding and loans for such programmes are not usually difficult to obtain, but you are best advised to speak to your careers services to obtain the most up-to-date information about the nature of the courses available and funding.

Taught Master's (MSc and MA) Qualifications

These are typically one-year programmes (in the UK at least) and fall into two types – Type I and Type II:

Type I qualifications are postgraduate degrees which have a specialist focus (e.g. MSc Marketing) and which usually require a first degree or experience in a relevant discipline. For example, you might do an undergraduate degree in management and then choose to specialise and advance your knowledge in a particular field (e.g. marketing).

Type II qualifications are designed as an introduction to a discipline when applicants have studied in a different area. For example, you might have studied for a BA (Hons) in English but then changed academic focus and taken a postgraduate qualification in Management (e.g. MSc Management Studies).

Both forms of postgraduate qualification are seen as potential routes to PhD studies, should you be seeking that. They will nearly always have a large dissertation towards the end of the programme (often taken in the summer and contributing to around a third of the programme), and will provide you with research training in order to undertake the dissertation. You will need to apply research techniques, both qualitative and quantitative, and statistical analysis in order to identify your conclusions (see Chapter 7).

Such qualifications will typically be taken by individuals shortly after graduation and applicants will usually be applying for such programmes in semester 1 of their final year to meet deadlines in early December, although many institutions do accept applications much later in the academic year. The admissions requirements to such programmes usually consist of qualifications related to English language (typically IELTS between 6.0/6.5 and 7.0, perhaps with some requirement that no component score should be less than 6.0) and an upper second-class honours (2:1) degree. You will usually need two references from academics who know you (US institutions typically need three) and also need to submit a personal statement.

Where you cannot meet the language requirements, any offer may require you to take a pre-sessional language course. These usually vary in length but take place during the summer so that when the academic year begins in September, your level of English should be sufficient to enable you to cope with the English language demands of the programme.

 'BUT I HAVE A QUESTION ...'

... What should I write in my personal statement? I have never seen one before.

This is understandable. Admissions tutors sometimes see personal statements which start by telling them how wonderful their institutions are - that is not what is required here. You may want to say that, but the personal statement - and the entire application, including the academic references - is intended to show the institution you are applying to that you are: (1) capable of passing the programme, (2) motivated to do so (usually according to some career goal), and (3) careful about how you select your course(s).

So, that means ensuring that the institution receiving your application understands your academic strengths and weaknesses - in terms of your critical thinking abilities as much as your grades - understands how the programme in question will benefit you in terms of your career goals, believes that you would work well with others on the programme (so, what kinds of activities have you undertaken in your degree: group projects, case studies, examinations, individual assignments?) and has some confidence that you will make a personal contribution (in terms of adding to the life of the university) to the institution.

The personal statement is usually one of three kinds of documents the institution will need to see, but it will usually ask academic referees to comment on your personal and academic strengths and weaknesses in terms of critical thinking, oral and written English, insight, creativity and innovation, ability, willingness to work with others, and so on. There are times when it might ask the referees to rank your performance against others in the class.

BOX 19.2

SHOULD STUDENTS APPLY THROUGH AN AGENT?

Many international students wish to use agents to manage their application - and many will cost around £1000. For some people, this is a lot of money, so the question is always whether they are worth it. The answer, sadly, is not definitive.

Students use agents for a variety of reasons, but one of the most common relates to their knowledge of technical governmental processes relating to immigration. An agent will work with the prospective student

(Continued)

(Continued)

to ensure that all the documentation is exactly as it should be so that everything is ready when the visa application is submitted. Another reason – and one that agents use to sell their services – is that agents may previously have been successful in getting students into the top postgraduate courses around the world, especially in the UK and the United States.

Agents also come in two types, some of whom are employed directly by an institution (or a small number of institutions). Those institutions give an incentive to agents to recruit students and often provide them with information and training on their courses and admissions processes. The second type are funded directly by the applicants, rather than by the institution, and provide wider advice and services (e.g. immigration/visa advice) than do those who promote certain institutions. However, this type of agent will likely not be so familiar with the institutions, the courses they offer, the living environment, the social opportunities and the general quality of the programmes as the first type. Neither type can give a guarantee of an offer and it can be risky to spend such a great deal with little guarantee. However, for a busy student completing their final year of undergraduate studies, using an agent to deal with the complex documentation for visas can be the best way forward.

Institutions and their recruitment and admissions offices can sometimes take very different views towards educational agents. Some agencies seem to appear and then disappear overnight, others have been known to fake reference letters for poor-quality students so as to ensure they get admitted. (Universities do talk to each other and some faked letters are very easy to spot.)

For you as a potential applicant, the question should always be: 'To what extent do I believe that they will tell me the truth about the institution and work in my interests to help get me admitted?' That is the only way to determine whether the service they offer is value for money.

Master of Business Administration Programmes

MBA programmes are seen – in the eyes of some – as *the* career-enhancing qualification in management. The idea is that if you want to move into middle or senior management, you need an MBA – and the more you spend to go on a better ranked (according to the *Financial Times* or *Wall Street Journal*) MBA programme, the better. They are qualifications designed to help individuals enhance their practical understanding of management and their ability to manage individuals and organisations, where those individuals have previously graduated in a non-management subject.

Good MBA programmes will carry the AMBA (Association of MBA studies) accreditation and will not usually accept students with less than three years' professional experience, although there are a very large number of institutions offering 'MBA' programmes of less quality. Alongside UK governmental institutions, AMBA requires institutions to manage their admissions processes carefully and indicates to institutions what such programmes should cover.

They are offered in a wide variety of formats: online or distance learning, part-time (evenings and weekends), full-time, international (across different locations, e.g. New York, London and Shanghai), executive (often part-time, but taking students who are already in senior management) and specialist (e.g. MBA in Healthcare Management). UK-based full-time programmes are usually a year in length, while part-time programmes tend to be more flexible and between three and four years.

Good MBA programmes are often seen by those wishing to join them in the same way that a branded bag might be seen by a consumer. An MBA from Harvard or from London Business Schools is often taken as a badge of having participated in a vastly superior educational experience, and the costs of taking an MBA at such institutions reflect this. Whichever programme you select, you need to ensure that it will give you an opportunity to:

- Build your international network of contacts in middle/senior management roles.
- Go beyond the theoretical aspects of management education and give you a chance to apply what you are learning to the real world.
- Stretch yourself – your skills, knowledge and experience.
- Progress into a worthwhile career.

MBA programmes are typically intense, very hard work and costly, but those who take them will usually see them as an investment which will yield rewards in the longer term. If or when you decide to take an MBA, you should probably discuss this with those closest to you. Your life will change considerably while you are doing it, particularly in terms of the time you have available for others, and perhaps the amount of stress you experience.

 'BUT I HAVE A QUESTION ...'

... How do I find the money for an MBA, if courses are so expensive?

If you are serious about taking an MBA, it is important to see it as an investment, rather than as a piece of paper. Here are some ideas:

- **Scholarships:** Some business schools will offer scholarships for students from certain countries or regions, or to those who are suffering financial hardship, but these will be very specifically targeted when it comes to MBA programmes. (MBA programmes are often a significant source of income for business schools, so it does not make a lot of sense for money to be given out without a very good reason.)
- **Career loans:** Banks may sometimes be willing to give loans to individuals to enhance their careers (just as student loans are made to UK undergraduates). These are sometimes long term and sometimes the interest rates can be higher than for other purposes, but they are available for some candidates in some places.
- **Government loans:** The UK government has now made available loans for postgraduate study. It might be worth comparing the details with payment arrangements made for loans from banks. The requirements state that this is only available to those ordinarily living in England. (https://www.gov.uk/funding-for-post graduate-study). For those living in Scotland and the EU, similar loans are available from the Student Awards Agency Scotland (http://www.saas.gov.uk/forms_and_guides/postgraduate.htm).
- **Employers:** It is not to be taken for granted, but some employers might be willing to consider part-funding a talented individual through an MBA under certain conditions. Other employers may have a leadership development programme which includes an MBA.
- **Others:** Family, friends and others who might be able to contribute to support you financially.

If you decide to do a full-time programme, you will need to find income to provide for daily living expenses in addition to the course fees. These may be more or less expensive, depending on the cost of living of where you decide to study.

 KEY LEARNING POINT

Postgraduate studies can be a useful way of enhancing your knowledge and skills, either by specialising in a particular area or by obtaining management qualifications and abilities which build on the academic skills from a non-management area.

REFLECTION POINT

Take some time to think about the following questions and write down some answers, first on your own, and then with others that you might be working with.

What would a taught postgraduate course give you, above your current qualifications?
  Would a taught postgraduate course be useful to you? Why?

Postgraduate Research Qualifications

Postgraduate research qualifications such as a Master's in Research, Master of Philosophy, Doctor of Philosophy (MRes, MPhil, PhD) are designed to enable you to start a career in a research role, either as an academic or as a professional consultant (or sometimes as an expert in a very specific business role). They are very different to any other form of postgraduate qualification, and if you are used to studying in a large class and discussing how to complete particular assignments, then you need to be aware that the experience of studying for them will be hugely different.

There is no requirement for you to have done a Master's qualification before taking such a qualification – you can start a PhD straight from your undergraduate studies – but the completion of a dissertation at postgraduate level can significantly help your chances of being successfully admitted and then completing your qualification. In order to apply for a PhD place, you will usually be required to submit a research proposal outlining what topic(s) you wish to study and identifying the relevant literature in that particular area. It is on the basis of your awareness of the existing literature, your ability to analyse and evaluate this literature and your identification of issues that have not yet been investigated that you will receive an offer of a place.

What is it like to undertake an MRes, MPhil, PhD?

The qualification, lasting between three and six years, requires you to undertake a piece of research, but is completed in stages (see Figure 19.2).

Students apply for and register as MPhil, or in some cases MRes. Transferring to PhD status is dependent upon their identifying and developing research questions that have not previously been asked. A doctorate qualification is only ever awarded on the basis that the thesis adds to the broader literature on a particular subject.

If successful in their application, the student will be allocated a supervisor before beginning the programme. The supervisor will be the student's mentor and guide through the research process, but from an analysis of the literature through to writing up the findings of the research, the work has to be that of the student themselves. The supervisor will also work with a PhD student to produce research in their own area and will usually publish joint papers in journals and conferences over the duration of the student's programme. This may be formally expected of the student during the programme (particularly if they enter an academic career after completion of the PhD) but is a good idea anyway: publication of work in a reputable journal usually confirms that the work is of a very good standard when it comes to the oral examination at the end of the programme.

In order to complete their programme (and not all do), PhD students are required to produce a thesis which describes what they have researched and how, why they have done so (usually relating to the

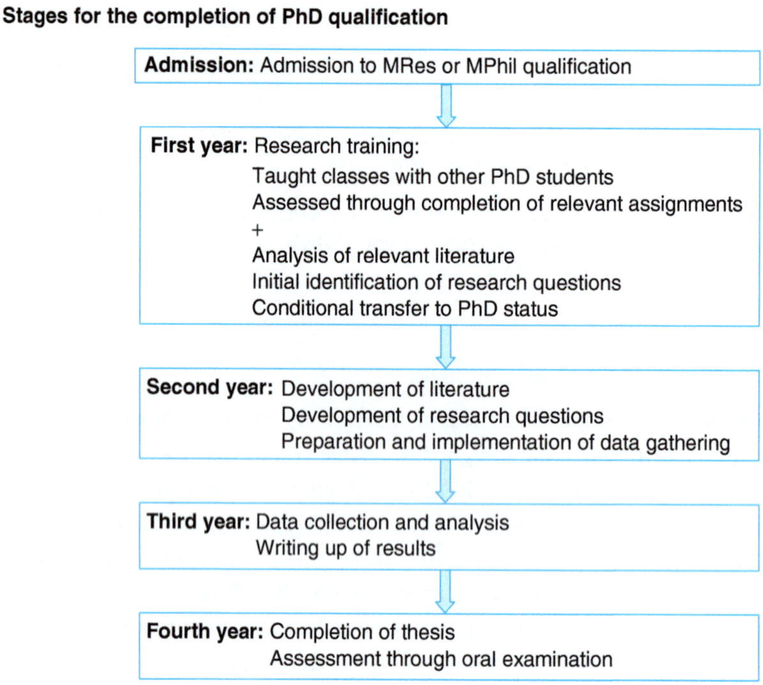

Stages for the completion of PhD qualification

Admission: Admission to MRes or MPhil qualification

First year: Research training:
　　　　　　Taught classes with other PhD students
　　　　　　Assessed through completion of relevant assignments
　　　　　　+
　　　　　　Analysis of relevant literature
　　　　　　Initial identification of research questions
　　　　　　Conditional transfer to PhD status

Second year: Development of literature
　　　　　　　Development of research questions
　　　　　　　Preparation and implementation of data gathering

Third year: Data collection and analysis
　　　　　　Writing up of results

Fourth year: Completion of thesis
　　　　　　　Assessment through oral examination

Figure 19.2　Structure of a typical PhD programme

fact that it is important and no one else has yet answered these questions, and explaining why the research and statistical techniques they have used were appropriate), what they have found, what else could be investigated, and how their research relates to the current body of knowledge. In terms of structure, it is not dissimilar to the way that an undergraduate dissertation might be compiled, though the arguments would need to be much stronger.

Completing a PhD can be a lonely process. You will be working on a research project that no one else is working on, but a good supervisor and a reasonable number of other students going through a similar experience can make the experience an interesting one. You will usually get a desk in an office, have access to resources and individuals that you might have struggled to get access to as an undergraduate, and get resources to attend research conferences with others researching in broadly the same area. You might be given some teaching to do, and some relevant training to undertake that teaching. This would be a minor aspect of your work, but would help you when it comes to applying for academic jobs after you complete the PhD. You will also have a fairly large amount of independence and freedom. Most supervisors will expect you to be disciplined and get on with your work, but how and when you do so is largely going to be up to you.

Finally, obtaining funding to do a PhD is usually very easy, if you have the right qualifications and your application (and references) is a good one. Most institutions have funding available to support PhD studentships, either from research grants that academic faculty have received (in which case, you would become an employee, a Research Assistant, who is undertaking research more closely aligned with your supervisor's interests rather than your own, but producing a thesis alongside the research work you are doing), or from scholarships (called studentships) offered by the university itself as a way of increasing its own research output – and, in some cases, producing future employees.

STARTING YOUR OWN BUSINESS

For some people, this is one of the more challenging – some would say 'scary' – options. For others, it is the ultimate idea of freedom and reward. A small business can be a replication of what someone else does elsewhere, or it can be related to something that you are interested in or have links to, or it can lead to the establishment of a company which produces something that you or others have needed, but which does not currently exist. It might also be one of the following:

- A franchise operation, where you invest in setting up a branch of an established brand (e.g. a McDonald's Restaurant) and run the operation in an area where that brand does not currently exist.
- Offering your own personal resources (practical resources, skills, contacts, etc.) to others who might need those resources (e.g. Airbnb, Uber, wedding planners, photographers, lawyers).
- Developing a physical or digital innovative product (e.g. Facebook, smartphone apps) where you have noticed a need that you and others have and developed a way of meeting this need.
- A network which individuals pay to join in order to get certain benefits and enjoy those experiences together (e.g. World Ventures and DreamTrips).
- An online distribution channel for customers to obtain products without needing to pay for warehousing and storage (e.g. companies on Facebook or eBay).

Some new ventures offer products and services to businesses and others offer such items directly to consumers. The kind of product or service you decide to offer will be based on the expertise and resources that you have access to and the viability of getting such resources to the marketplace so that others can access them easily.

═══════════ FOR YOU TO DO ═══════════

Look at the statements below and try to identify those which are closest to your own personality, desires and ambitions, and those which are furthest away. They are fairly obvious in their implications, but try to answer them honestly.

Give each item a score between 1 and 5, where 1 is 'strongly disagree' and 5 is 'strongly agree'.

1. I really enjoy seeing the outcomes of my actions.
2. I tend to prefer to be in control of my own situation.
3. I do not like someone else telling me what to do.
4. I intend to have a mentor, someone who can help me when I am not sure what to do.
5. I am comfortable when I know what I am doing
6. My friends would describe me as 'conservative', as someone who does not really enjoy taking risks.
7. I really love working on something pioneering.
8. When I start an activity, I put all my effort and everything I have into that project.
9. It is more important for me to earn a lot of money as quickly as I can than to see my achievements in other ways.
10. I respond well to a challenge.
11. I am excited by being the first to do something.
12. I am extremely persistent and determined in what I do.

(Continued)

(Continued)

13. I do not care if others tell me that I will not succeed.
14. Life is all about passion, rather than being rational.
15. I have an idea for a business which I know others will really love.
16. I love the idea of others coming to me for a service.
17. I know that others will put as much effort into helping me with my innovation as I do.
18. I think that setting up and running a small business is easy.
19. When I have had ideas for activities in the past, I have been able to motivate others to follow me.
20. I do not wait for permission to do what I want to do: I just think we should get on and do it.
21. I have done an undergraduate business degree so I am pretty sure I know what running a business is about.

If you answered 4 or 5 to most of the questions above, then you might have some of the personal qualities needed to set up and run a small business, but there are a couple of questions above where the better answer is 1 or 2, and others where a little comment might be helpful. As you read below, think of the issues involved in setting up two kinds of business.

The first is a small online business selling clothes made by someone else and distributing them to the public. The second is a production business, making an innovative product, largely for distribution to other businesses. The challenges and issues will be vastly different for each one, so it is not easy to generalise about the issues that will be faced, but the following may give some guidance.

I really enjoy seeing the outcomes of my actions: Great. This is one of the things that will motivate you, although do not expect the outcomes to appear quickly. Sometimes they take time, motivation and a great investment of personal energy, though they can be straightforward.

I tend to prefer to be in control of my own situation: OK, although there are generally very few occasions in life when we are totally in control. If you set up your own business, there will be other stakeholders, all of whom will have a role in helping you to run your business. It is helpful to perceive them as 'helping'. Some might take the view that they are 'interfering', which can lead to very negative perceptions and relationships.

I do not like someone else telling me what to do: OK, although ensure that you are interpreting someone's communication accurately. If someone is offering a suggestion but you interpret it as an instruction, then the legitimate help being offered may be incorrectly seen as interference.

I intend to have a mentor – someone who can help me when I am not sure what to do: For most businesses and individuals, this can be really important, even if you are fairly sure that what you are doing is correct. Even very established organisations have a 'non-executive Board of Directors' whose role it is to advise the business and help it to grow.

I am comfortable when I know what I am doing: This is true for nearly everyone – there are very few people who feel comfortable when they have no idea what they are doing, but setting up a new business can seem like this at the start! Many entrepreneurs simply do what they think is common sense at the very beginning, which is fine and might help a business grow initially, but life is rarely as simple as common sense would lead us to believe.

My friends would describe me as 'conservative', as someone who does not really enjoy taking risks: If this is true for you, then it does not actually mean that you could not be an entrepreneur. Risks come in various forms and sizes, and the questions are: 'How much risk are you comfortable with?' and 'How much risk is required for this particular project?' If the answers to these questions do not match, then maybe you might need to think about one of the other options, but some kinds of business have very little risk.

I really love working on something pioneering: Without doubt, the best and longest lasting businesses tend to be those that develop a new and sustainable idea or innovation, and seeing such ideas become reality can be fantastic. Most businesses will not become the 'Apple' or 'Virgin' of their day, but this does not mean that there is no space for something new – and it does not mean that your business idea cannot become as significant as those organisations in the future. Working on something different and new can be extremely energising and can make the idea of 'getting into work' something quite significant.

When I start an activity, I put all my effort and everything I have into that project: This is important, especially if you are seeking to produce and market a physical product, rather than act as a distributor. Setting up a successful small business will require all your effort and work – firstly to 'sell' your idea to others who can help you with finance, and then later in terms of physically setting up an office, developing a small team who are as passionate about your service as you are, identifying your suppliers, ensuring that costs and income are on target, and so on.

It is more important for me to earn a lot of money as quickly as I can, than to see my achievements in other ways: If you answered this question, then you need to consider carefully the kind of business you might want to set up. Many production businesses might take a couple of years to break even financially before you start to see any significant income, although some kinds of services might bring in some income very quickly.

I respond well to a challenge: This is very good to hear, because in setting up most businesses, there will be a series of important challenges. (Some people might call them 'problems' but seeing them instead as a challenge to be overcome is far more useful.) Having the ingenuity, determination and creativity to overcome those challenges is going to be very important.

I am excited by being the first to do something: This is not dissimilar to the item above about 'working on something pioneering'. Many people can take a business idea they see working and either copy it in a different location or make it work more effectively, but developing a new idea entirely brings a new set of challenges and overcoming those challenges so that your product or idea becomes the first to do a particular thing can put it very firmly in the minds of your potential customers.

I am extremely persistent and determined in what I do: Good – in most situations, you will need to be. You can set up a business relatively easily – even a digital business – but making it work, sourcing enough supplies (and/or equipment) at the right price and then ensuring that your customers purchase your service or product are going to take effort and use all your persuasive skills.

I do not care if others tell me that I will not succeed: That sense of rebellion can be very useful sometimes, but there is a question of balance in the way we use others' views. Just because they might disagree with you does not mean that they are wrong, of course, and wisdom from others who have been in your situation and failed can be more valuable than anything else. The temptation is sometimes to react defensively if you get discouraging views from others, but sometimes they may have a view which just helps nudge your business into a new area where there is more potential. Of course, reacting passionately to such a view and deciding to push ahead faster can sometimes give you the motivation you need.

Life is all about passion, rather than being rational: If you want to run a successful business, you will have to have a sense of passion. It will be difficult to overcome seemingly impossible hurdles without it, but passion without some rational thought will produce a scenario where you go to a business financier or the bank manager with lots of excitement but no business plan. You will need to learn how to channel your energy into your passion, and ensure that the same sense of vision has a rational foundation.

I have an idea for a business which I know others will really love: Great! But how do you know? If you or others are going to invest a significant amount in your business, you will need to have done some comprehensive research into your idea. Think about the following questions:

- Who will use your service or buy your product?
- What do they really think of it?
- What kind of price would they be willing to pay?
- How often will they need it?
- What other products or services will they buy instead if yours is not available?
- How will you persuade them to buy your product or service?
- What would make them recommend it to others?
- How quickly will they be willing and able to pay?

Of course, you should believe strongly in your own business idea, but this does not mean that others will as well, and so some good solid market research is vital in persuading others – and yourself – that your business idea is worth investing in. It will require a detailed business plan, developing convincing answers to a lot of important questions and a great deal of thinking about the information that you gather. Running a successful business is *usually* a lot more challenging than simply having an idea and putting it into practice.

I love the idea of others coming to me for a service: This is encouraging, but you will need to make it happen – it rarely happens on its own. The question, therefore, is how much hard work are you willing to invest in your business idea? The other issue here is that it can be nice to have customers coming to purchase a service from you because it adds to your own personal sense of value, but how will you react when they come back to complain? (This is almost inevitable at some time during the life of the business.)

I know that others will put as much effort into helping me with my innovation as I do: If you have a good team of workers around you, then they will – and that will be wonderful. Starting a business may require the voluntary assistance of friends or family at the outset, but when you start to consider new employees and perhaps developing a small team, then their allegiance to you may be much more questionable. At best, they will do what they do because they love their role or organisation, or because they appreciate your commitment to them and respond accordingly, but you will find that if you do not pay them what they think they are worth (assuming that they are accurate in that calculation, of course), then you may find them leaving. Motivating a small team is much easier than leading a department or organisation, but you still need to ensure that you have a good relationship with them while maintaining sufficient 'distance' to be able to give honest negative feedback if you need to.

I think that setting up and running a small business is easy: It can be remarkably easy, for some kinds of businesses. If you do not need to find any investment and can find a cheap supplier for goods or services that people want, and can get those goods or services out to customers cheaply and easily, then it can be remarkably easy. But if you can do that, then others might be able to as well. The implication of this is that setting up a small business easily means you will probably have a large number of competitors all doing the same thing as you. The challenge is to do something differently from others, and that is much less easy.

At the other end of the scale, setting up a production business for an innovative product for which you have just produced a prototype that you will sell to business clients is much harder. The amount of investment needed is larger, you will probably need a team of workers to produce your innovation, the physical space to do so and people around you who can persuade others firstly to invest in the business and secondly to buy your products – and neither of these is at all easy.

When I have had ideas for activities in the past, I have been able to motivate others to follow me: That is good and is a good sign when you have to lead your business. If those 'others' were your friends, you will need to recognise that leading friends is a lot easier than leading talented people who may have very different views and ideas to your own. You may not always get your own way, and sometimes you should not, but it is the well-being of the business that counts more than your own ego.

I do not wait for permission to do what I want to do: I just think we should get on and do it: This shows initiative and some of that slightly 'rebellious spirit' mentioned above, both of which can be effective in getting a business idea off the ground. However, there are times when we need official permission to do what we want to do – this may be a building fire inspection or some kind of licence to set up the kind of business we wish to undertake – but we cannot start a business without official approvals if we need them.

And, finally, …

I have done an undergraduate business degree and so I am pretty sure I know what running a business is about: If you have a business degree, then you probably have more knowledge about running a business than if you studied a different subject, but it will not guarantee that you do well. Managing a business and making decisions about resources, people, strategy and stakeholders is not a science, and the ability to lead others so that you can overcome challenges in unpredictable situations is going to require all your personal determination and take you beyond your business degree. Of course, your degree should have helped you to develop some of the insight, determination and leadership skills that you will need to do what you wish to do, but it is the personal qualities that you possess as much as the knowledge that you have which will enable your business to be a success.

The above analysis has given an indication of some of the issues that we might need to bear in mind if we want to run our own business. For those who make it successfully, the rewards can be great, but many folk who do make it 'successfully' have often spent time developing businesses which have previously failed.

There are some issues noted above which need expanding on a little and which may or may not help you to decide whether this kind of option is right for you. Watching others set up their businesses can be inspirational, and if you do have an idea for a product or a service that you think would work, then you might like to speak to those lecturers who you trust to give good advice and who know something about setting up a small business in order to evaluate your idea.

Issues to Consider

Finance

It is true that the larger the risk, the larger the return. Most – if not all – new businesses will require finance of some kind, either a large amount to make a new product or simply a small amount to allow for some publicity about your product or service. Putting a video on YouTube or its equivalent will likely cost hardly anything, but can – if done well – get your product out to your potential customers very effectively.

Banks, private investors (otherwise known as 'Business Angels', who will invest significant sums in return for some level of ownership), individuals and, of course, yourself may all be useful sources of funding, but they will want to be reasonably sure that they will not lose their investment.

People

Depending on the nature of the business, you will likely have to recruit, select, manage (i.e. use appropriately according to their skills and expertise, give feedback, develop and train, and possibly promote or dismiss or reassign) and lead (inspire, motivate) your team in a way that helps your business grow. For many people, this means the development of additional skills and knowledge, and perhaps seeking some personal development via a mentor or another established entrepreneur.

Legal

There is little doubt that at some stage – potentially including the very early establishment of the business – you will likely need some legal advice. This could include everything from protecting your customers against any accidents arising from your work (termed 'public liability insurance' in the UK) to defects in products that you produce *and/or* source from elsewhere (for which you *do* have responsibility as far as the customer is concerned) and the arrangements for closing down the business if you are working with others in a legal partnership. Legal issues will also affect your advertising, the recruitment, health and safety and dismissal of your employees, and – of course – your liabilities for managing finances and taxation.

Market

If your idea does not have a market which can cover the costs of delivering or producing that idea, then it will not work as a business idea. It might be nice for you to do and might be interesting, but it will not be viable as a way of making money. This is why the issues above relating to the information you gather are so important.

One issue to be aware of is who the product or service is intended for. The individual paying for the product or service may not be the one who actually ends up using it. The classic example is the market for children's toys, where the parents pay but the decision to buy is based on whether the child will enjoy the product. In such instances, any market research should not be about the purchaser alone, but the end user.

Of course, making money may not be the aim of your idea. You may have developed it to help solve a problem for others in situations less fortunate than many, where the resources for developing and implementing the idea or product might be borne by a non-governmental organisation or a charity. In this case, the market will be the NGO or charities who pay for the product based on the promise that it will alleviate some need very effectively.

The plan

While planning the growth of a new business in an unpredictable situation is a precarious idea, it will be difficult if not impossible to get external funding for the business and to evaluate the performance of your business without a comprehensive business plan – based on the comprehensive market research you have done. Creating a realistic plan is not easy, especially if you are excited and passionate about an idea that you think you could make and sell tomorrow, if only you did not have to take time to produce a business plan! However, it is vital and important to develop this idea if you want to establish a growing business. You will need to think about *how the market and your products will grow and change* (is it likely to be affected by demographics; is there space to take the business online; is there scope for diversifying and adding to what you think the business could offer?), *when and how your financing will come* (how long will it take you to break even; how will you ensure that you have adequate cash flow; how will you cover any periods of time when you have no money coming in; what accounting ratios will be most important to you, and why; what funding will you need as a cushion against any unexpected expenses?) and *how your workforce might need to grow and change* (how will you cover against sickness; how big will your leadership team need to be; how will you access expertise if you need it on a temporary basis?). All of these decisions – and others – will need to form part of your organisational strategy and business plan.

Conclusion

In the digital age, setting up a small business on eBay and publicising it on Facebook (or Taobao and Weixin in China, or Line in Korea) is not difficult. If you act as a distributor, then all that is needed is for you to find a way to obtain the goods at a decent price and then get them to the final customer. If you get the publicity and the pricing right, and have a reliable system for distribution, then making a little money can be very straightforward. If you decide to operate a franchise, then you need the financial resources to make the investment and then nearly everything else is done for you. If you wish to offer your resources to others, then you simply need a way of giving your clients and customers access to those resources – and that is what makes a business work.

=========== KEY LEARNING POINT ===========

Running your own business can be very easy, but can be very difficult. A great deal will depend on the nature of the business you wish to run and the ease with which you can get our goods and/or services to those who might wish to use them - in a cost-effective way.

CONCLUSION

By now, you should be able to:

- Recognise that graduate employment is not the only option after undergraduate studies.
- Understand your own capacity to take up additional options.
- Evaluate which option(s) are applicable to your own situation.
- Develop practical strategies for taking up alternative options.

This chapter has outlined a number of options for you to consider outside of what some see as the usual process of getting a job with a graduate employer, so if you do not have an offer with a major organisation, do *not* worry. Instead, you might like to think about some of these ideas or others.

The important thing is to make sure that you *do* something. Organising formal events, holding social activities or getting involved in social groups or local charities are all seen positively by employers as activities which demonstrate your skills. Even activities such as organising a holiday for friends or family will require you to use a range of skills. So, whatever you decide to do with your time, make sure that you do it well, that you enjoy it and that you give yourself the best chance for a great future.

That has been the entire intention of this book. Good luck!

FINAL REFLECTIONS

Based on the content of this chapter, what do you now know about additional options for you that you did not know before?

Which key learning point had the most impact? Why?

Do your answers to either of the above questions have the potential to change your ability to perform well at selection interviews? Why?

What will you now do? (Write this down and put it somewhere where you will can it regularly.)

ADDITIONAL RESOURCES

Want to learn more? Visit https://study.sagepub.com/morgan to gain access to a wide range of online resources, including interactive tests, tasks, further reading and downloads.

Website Resources

About Careers – Information about gap year programmes (US website): http://jobsearch.about.com/od/college-job-search/a/gap-year-programs.htm

Gapyear.com – website providing information on gap year jobs: www.gapyear.com/jobs

Kent University – alternative ideas after graduation: www.kent.ac.uk/careers/alternatives.htm

Newcastle University – advice on further study: www.ncl.ac.uk/careers/study/

Newcastle University – 'Is a gap year before employment a good idea?' www.ncl.ac.uk/careers/planning/timeout/

Prospects website – ideas around work experience and internships, both in the UK and abroad: www.prospects.ac.uk/jobs-and-work-experience/work-experience-and-internships

Prospects website – 'What can you do with your degree in …?' www.prospects.ac.uk/careers-advice/what-can-i-do-with-my-degree

SAP.com Gap Year Programme (others are available): www.sap.com/careers/students-and-graduates/gap-year-program.html#

Target Postgrad – information on further study: https://targetpostgrad.com/advice/choosing-postgraduate/why-do-postgraduate-study

University of Aberdeen – further study: www.abdn.ac.uk/careers/further-study-funding/index.php

20 CONCLUSION: SKILLS AND EMPLOYABILITY

When you see the 🌐 this means go to the companion website https://study.sagepub.com/morgan to do a quiz, complete a task, read further or download a template.

INTRODUCTION

We began this book with a welcome message in Chapter 1: 'Welcome to the rest of your life!' You are now several years on from when you first read that chapter, or perhaps you are reading this chapter now in order to get some kind of perspective on some of the issues you will be facing in the future. Whichever it is, this chapter is intended to be quite different from other chapters in its content, style and structure.

This chapter is something of a conclusion. As we have seen when we were talking about writing essays (see Chapter 7), a conclusion is really intended to bring the previous material together in a brief summary. This conclusion will do something slightly different.

The previous chapters of this book have given you some ideas on how you could extend your abilities, try out new things, develop your skills, and so on. As I was planning this chapter, I was wondering what we could do in it, because I wanted to include some real experiences from others so that you could benefit from what others have learnt.

The people who contributed to this chapter have come from a variety of backgrounds: public sector/ private sector, recently graduated or graduated many years ago, working in the UK or working in a variety of countries, working in a startup and in major corporations, studying for PhD or MBA programmes, and so on.

They were asked two questions, one broad question about the lessons they had learnt from their life and career so far, and a second question which asked them to give their thoughts on the particular skills that we have covered in the preceding chapters. I did ask for a couple of sentences, but some of them have generously given much more than that. They have all given their permission to use this material and I have tried not to edit their thoughts in order to let you benefit completely from what they have sent me.

A QUICK REVIEW

Figure 20.1 indicates how the parts and chapters of the book link together. In reality, some of the chapters (e.g. presentation skills, critical thinking) could have been put into the chapters on learning how to study, employability skills or assessment (or even selection methods), so decisions have been made on the basis of where the content may be most appropriate, but this does not mean that they are *only* appropriate in those parts.

The process of personal development and learning should be continuous and should continue throughout the rest of your life. You will make mistakes – some big, some small, some painful – but learning from those mistakes and being humble enough to recognise when you are making them is important, which is why skill development is seen as a theme running through this text. This applies to skills most relevant to university life when you are doing essays and examinations, but also to employability skills, such as those covered in Part IV, and need to be demonstrated when going through employee selection processes, outlined in Part V.

Figure 20.1 provides a graphical illustration of how each chapter might relate to your time at university and then beyond graduation, with the timeline at the bottom of the figure.

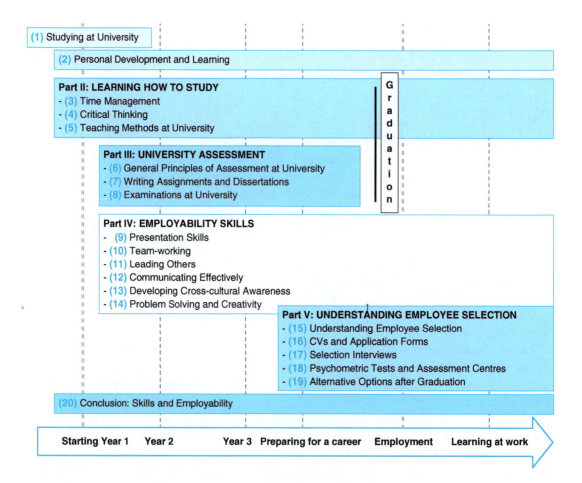

Figure 20.1   An illustration of how the chapters relate to your time as a student and beyond

It is helpful to get some perspectives from others on how the development of your skills, your values and your world view needs to continue throughout the rest of your life – and this is what the next section is intended to do.

WHO RESPONDED?

There is a reasonable variety of individuals who gave their thoughts. I do not wish to give their names here, but I would like briefly to share something about their background. One has been working in a marketing role for a year in a brand-new startup business in Malaysia, having studied for a UK degree. Another works for a manufacturing organisation in the UK, a third is a UK-educated corporate lawyer and mother of two, working in Singapore. A fourth one has a senior role in the China office of one of the big four accounting firms, having had an undergraduate education in Singapore, UK and then the United States, and studied their Master's degree in New York. Another respondent completed their undergraduate studies in China before moving on to do a Master's in the UK, then worked for some time as a PA for a Business School Dean before doing an MBA in the United States. Another was an Indian student who studied for both their undergraduate and postgraduate degrees in the UK before beginning their career as an accountant relatively recently. Another respondent graduated in the UK and began their career in operations management in the UK before moving to a senior role in a large multinational communications company. Two further respondents both work in higher education, one as a Business School Dean in the United States, having worked previously in business education in China, and another who rose quite quickly to a senior management role at a UK university, before deciding that enjoying their role was more important than salary, and took a significant reduction in status and salary to become a careers adviser. So, the diversity of individuals willing to offer advice has been encouraging.

Making Sense of Their Views

With that diversity, however, comes contradiction. These are individuals who have various levels of experience, but even with that experience they offered advice as different individuals – with different attitudes, personalities, world views (see Chapter 12) and learning. Perhaps if we were to add a 'key learning point' here, it would be that there is no one definitive way to lead or manage others, or work in a team, or communicate with others, or become globally aware, etc. Instead, each person needs to find what works for them.

Each action and decision will have consequences, however, and you will need to consider those in the decisions you make and the way that you implement and communicate them. Hopefully, these consequences will be ones you can live with and which will not affect the motivated and able staff you will have around you – but even if they are not, then it is a mistake you will need to learn from and not make again.

CONTRIBUTIONS FROM OTHERS

It is time to let those working in 'the real world' speak. The comments below are largely unedited and I prefer not to give too much comment – even though that is very tempting. Some key highlights from their comments are given above each person's contributions.

FOR YOU TO DO

1. As you read the comments below from professionals with several years of experience, think about how they might help you to do what you want to do better than you might have done it before.
2. As you read the comments below, underline, circle or make note of anything which seems to be a recurring theme for you, or which is interesting. Some ideas are repeated regularly, others may be suggested just once or twice, but you need to think about what is being said here.
3. If you have been in employment previously, then think about whether you agree with what has been written here.
4. If you disagree, then think about why you disagree.
5. Is there anything you might need to change in your behaviour now?

In each case, a little background information is given so that you can contextualise the comments made. These descriptions are those given by the individuals themselves but the names given here are fictional.

A. **John graduated two years ago and has been working in a small but successful startup organisation based in Kuala Lumpur, Malaysia.**

Highlights: Think about your goals; build character; cross-cultural communication is important.

Little things matter – in life there're many times we feel that we're just doing 'small things' and we always want to achieve 'BIG thing'. What I learned is that the pursuit of excellence in doing even the little things is how you achieve, how you achieve your 'BIG thing'. Never underestimate how doing little things well can build your character. Transparency and openness is one very crucial practice that allows better communication and understanding. Sometimes it might be a simple sentence but different people of different personalities, cultural backgrounds will interpret it very different. It is good to always explain the reasons for anything you speak in a discussion.

B. **Mark has had several years' experience working in an organisation in the engineering industry in the UK. His work often takes him overseas to source materials and items for use in manufacturing.**

Highlights: Care about others; relationships count, so solve problems rather than threaten.

A couple of things I've learned working in the private sector in 'modern' times: (1) If you want people to care [about] what you know, they need to know that you care. Even in 'hard-nosed' business, people matter, and you'll get more from your team if they know you care about them personally. (2) Business doesn't have to work on a linear scale, so that the more one party 'wins', the more the other party has to 'lose'. People can paint themselves into a corner whereby they have to fight their way out. Often, there is a solution that avoids one person having to win at the other's expense. For example, under pressure to recover costs for weekend work, etc. 'required' to support above-contracted-capacity demand, I was coming into conflict with the customer's purchasing team, who weren't set up to support claims. Under pressure to get something, you start making subtle references to threats (to hold shipments, refuse to support future spikes, etc.) which never go well. I learned that by: (a) working with Operations to plan further ahead, (b) finding a dedicated team at the customer who could handle such claims, when made in advance, and (c) communicating clearly and logically the basis for the claim, I was able to recover the costs without damaging relationships.

C. **Sarah worked as a corporate lawyer in private practice for seven and a half years and has been a compliance officer in a financial institution for almost four years.**

Highlights: Pace yourself; be consistent; respect others.

Three lessons I have learnt over the years. (1) Pace yourself. Your career is a marathon not a sprint. Burn out is a very real thing. I learnt that, where possible and necessary, do not be afraid to ask for a time extension or turn down a time-sensitive project if you are working at full capacity. (2) You are only as good as your last piece of work. People do not always remember the good you have done but they will definitely remember when you screw up, so be consistent and do your best each time. (3) Respect and be nice to everyone. From your boss to the tea lady who looks after the pantry. Spend a few minutes when you can to get to know the administrative staff and the secretaries better. This will set you apart from the majority of your peers. I cannot count the number of times that my boss's secretary saved me by putting my work at the top of his review pile and squeezing me into his appointment schedule ahead of others when I needed to see him. I think that the attribute that stands out for me is communication skills. I'm in a role where I tell people what they can and cannot do under the law. It is not a job that will make me popular in the company any time soon. My colleagues are, however, less resistant when it comes to following the rules if I let them know that I am not out to make life difficult for them but to help them succeed. I am still telling them what they can and cannot do but how I communicate it to them makes all the difference.

D. **Philippa is a Wall Street investment banker turned knowledge management practitioner in a professional services firm. She has spent more than half her life schooling, working and living away from her Singapore home in the US, UK and China. She counts her husband and three children as her greatest blessings in life.**

Highlights: Prioritise your life carefully; be good at cross-cultural management; lead with humility.

Prioritise what is important to you in life. As much of a cliché as it is, money isn't really the most important thing in our lives, so don't have your head buried in your work, never lifting it up to appreciate everything else around you. Invest in your family, your friends and yourself. Find a hobby, spend time with your spouse and children, seek fulfilment on things that truly matter. No one will ever say on their death beds that they wished they had spent more time at work, but rather, wish they had spent more time with the people they love. Make your life count.

Being truly cross-culturally aware requires us to clear our minds of any pre-conceived notions of what we THINK we know of others' cultures and norms. When in doubt, ask. You will probably find most people happy to share about their cultures and work norms which may be vastly differently from what you thought it was. A good one is to stop referring to time periods as Winter or Summer since this means something different to an American than to an Australian!

A real leader needs to set aside her title, rank and pride and truly lead by example with humility and kindness. Listen and provide counsel with sincerity and honesty. Most of all, recognise each team member as an individual with many facets to their lives which involve more than just work.

E. **Lisa is a Chinese MBA student at a good graduate college in Boston, MA. Previously, she had worked for a Business School Dean in China, and had completed a Master's degree in the UK. She writes about leadership.**

Highlights: Don't be too aggressive in leadership.

Leadership is nothing to do with power. All power is transient, and the more you use power directly the more likely to lose it. But the problem is while those of us who know the truth of leadership such as quietly confident, working hard, and staying focused on our strategy, the aggressive ones around us often perceive us as being weak. And, even if we will win through our wisdom, the aggressive ones can make our life miserable in the meantime.

F. **Lorraine trained as a professional accountant, having done both her BSc and MSc in the UK. She has been working for about four to five years.**

Highlights: Prepare for the unpredictable.

Having been an organised and methodical person, my biggest lesson has been that life is never constant. No matter how much you plan, something unpredictable may happen. It is therefore imperative that one must not fear change but positively embrace it. We should empower ourselves and have some courage to face the unknown.

On time management: Often whilst working in an organisation, one becomes too focused on following standard routine procedures. Being proactive rather than reactive means that we can challenge systems and processes and improve them rather than wait for the mistake to happen. This is an important aspect of time management.

G. **Peter is a Finance Manager in the telecommunications and travel industry.**

Highlights: Incentivise your employees properly; get a sense of perspective about work; stand out and communicate well.

'You get what you measure' – think carefully about how you measure people's performance and incentivise them. You get what you measure – even if it is not what you really wanted! 'We are not saving lives.' For the vast majority of people (not my doctor!) try and keep things in perspective. No matter how important and critical you think a task is – it is just work. Relax!

Out of the topics in this book: Leadership and communication stand out. Anyone at any level can provide leadership – it is not about your job position. Don't wait to be led. Decide to lead! The most successful leaders I have seen are a mix of intelligent, apparently boundless energy, clear long-term vision, demanding of very high standards, empower people to do their job, great story tellers. Although, ideally, a good leader is also a great communicator. It is not totally necessary – as you can employee people who are great communicators as a part of your team!

H. **Winnie rose rapidly in her organisation to become a senior manager in the public sector, before deciding that salary was not the most important thing in life.**

Highlights: Be organised; be creative.

The biggest lesson I have learnt in life is to be organised. Don't put off stuff you don't feel like doing until the last moment. Take the time to get things right in advance. When you have to do tasks that don't interest you, set yourself a time limit and give yourself a reward. With other tasks that can be a time suck, e.g. emails, set a time limit on those too and stick to it. Don't wander from one site to another losing time and productivity! Be aware of what you are doing and why you are doing it.

On creativity: Many people struggle with creativity but it doesn't have to mean you're James Dyson or an award-winning artist. Be creative in how you approach tasks – do things differently to appreciate the impact that might have on how you solve a problem. Listen to other people and observe how they approach things. Ask yourself why you are doing something rather than just doing because you can or feel you ought to.

I. **Jeffrey is a Business School Dean in the United States.**

Highlights: Be persistent and innovative; lead with people in mind.

While superior intelligence and a college education (particularly a Master degree or more) is certainly an advantage and can help accelerate and lever success in business, the most important qualities in my view are relentless persistence and an eye toward innovation that centers on creating a unique competitive advantage. Think of any modern business icon – whether it be Steve Jobs, Warren Buffett, or Bill Gates – all of them have these qualities in spades.

Leadership at the top of an organisation is essential for achieving extended success. The best leaders are able to create positive organisational cultures resulting in lower employee turnover, higher productivity and more innovation, and more loyal customers – all resulting in more successful brands and organisations.

J. **Janice is President and CEO of an international private higher education provider.**

Highlights: Be purposeful, but flexible.

For about a decade now, I've been influenced by the philosophy of Viktor Frankl and more recently by the positive psychology movement. Success for me is about having purpose and pursuing it through helping others to achieve their goals. It's really about how one reacts to circumstance; however adverse, a positive, constructive reaction will always feel right and produce results. Critical in all of this is to 'have a plan' and to execute that plan, since time management is critical.

K. **William is a Strategic Advisor in the gaming industry.**

Highlights: Be patient with yourself; skills of team-working, communication and time management are most important.

Individuals need to be hardworking and patient with themselves, learn from their colleagues, don't jump from one job to another in a short period of time.

On the skills needed for employment: In every job, team-working, communication and time management are ultimately the most important elements. Without these basic skills, one is hard to progress to a higher position in an organisation.

L. **Blake is a digital content QA tester.**

Highlights: A range of skills are important, but there may not be one best way of demonstrating each.

Daily life and work are often well defined and highly repetitive and shouldn't need much thought, spending time on what's important requires perspective and understanding.

Plan not to do everything, you need to be realistic, everyone has their strengths and limits, you have to prioritise what you can do then delegate or say no.

Simplify your life and organise your surroundings, you'll find it time well spent and feel better for it.

Time management is all about making decisions and planning to do the right things at the right time.

Creativity often goes hand-in-hand with innovation as they are required to improve or better ourselves and everything that goes on around us.

Team-working is an essential part of the complex world we live in. No single person can be expected to do everything. We can work together to achieve things more rapidly or by combining our skills and knowledge improve the world around us.

Leadership is the driving or guiding force from the people in our lives that give us meaning and direction.

Cross-cultural awareness is more important than ever as we can travel and connect with virtually anyone anywhere in the world. The way of life of others may differ from our own and we need to recognise, respect and understand how to live with those differences.

Communication skills are important to help us understand one another and allow us to work together. The style and frequency of our written and verbal communication as well as our body language all influence how others view and judge us. Tailoring your communication to fit the audience and the moment can literally open up a world of opportunities.

M. **Philip is a forensic engineer.**

Highlights: Be focused and determined.

Don't let others dictate your life; if someone tells you that you are unable to do something, take a deep breath, find your inner strength and go out and prove them wrong.

Who wills can. Persistence, persistence, persistence. Remember to enjoy the ride (i.e. enjoy what you do!).

Communication is king! Without it your ideas won't fly!

N. **Jackson is Company Secretary of a listed company in Singapore.**

Highlights: Be persistent; be humble.

When there is a will, there is surely a way. Do not give up but continuously strive for improvement with the eventual aim of succeeding. It is important that one never looks down on oneself as every one of us has talents to contribute. However, be humble.

On time management: Be organised. List down a list of priorities and tasks to be done for the day at the start of each working day.

On communication skills: Follow up in writing (by email) after a meeting or an important conversation to ensure that one has listened well to what was conversed or agreed earlier

 REFLECTION POINT

Take some time to think about the following questions and write down some answers.

How did you react to the ideas given above? Were there any which struck you as unexpected or unusual?

(Continued)

(Continued)

Make a list of the key themes which came through to you as you read. Which ideas and themes do you think are going to be most important? Rank them in order of importance.

Talk to your personal tutor or a careers adviser about your ranking. Do they agree with you?

CONCLUDING COMMENTS

Some of the 14 comments here are more specific and detailed than others, and some include a reason for saying what they have said, but all are from individuals who believe that they have something to contribute to help you understand what will face you in the world of work.

And that is where I hope this book will take you next, after graduation. Assuming that you have done well in your degree studies and assuming that you know what will happen after your graduation, then the chapters on personal development and learning employability skills will help you as you build on your experiences at university, while those on assessment and teaching styles and life at university are now less relevant to you. Keep it, use it and may it help you as you develop your career.

REFERENCES

Adair, J. (1973) *Action-Centered Leadership*. New York: McGraw-Hill.

Amabile, T. M. (1998) 'How to kill creativity', *Harvard Business Review*, September–October, pp.77–87.

Anderson, L. W. (ed.), Krathwohl, D. R. (ed.), Airasian, P. W., Cruikshank, K. A., Mayer, R. E., Pintrich, P. R., Raths, J. and Wittrock, M. C. (2001) *A Taxonomy for Learning, Teaching, and Assessing: A Revision of Bloom's Taxonomy of Educational Objectives*. New York: Longman.

Angeli, E., Wagner, J., Lawrick, E., Moore, K., Anderson, M., Soderlund, L., and Brizee, A. (2016) *General Format*. Retrieved from: http://owl.english.purdue.edu/owl/resource/560/01/. Accessed 15 July, 2016.

Association of Graduate Recruiters (2014) 'The AGR Graduate Recruitment Survey 2014: Summer Review'. Available online at: www.agr.org.uk/CoreCode/Admin/ContentManagement/MediaHub/Assets/FileDownload.ashx?fid=125071andpid=11533andloc=en-GBandfd=False. Accessed 14 April 2016.

Association of Graduate Recruiters (AGR) (2015) 'The AGR Graduate Recruitment Survey 2015: Winter Review'. Available online at: https://www.abdn.ac.uk/careers/documents/AGR_Winter_Survey_2015_Results.pdf. Accessed 11 April 2016.

Belbin, R. M. (1981) *Management Teams: Why They Succeed or Fail*. London: Heinemann.

Blake, R. and Mouton, J. (1964) *The Managerial Grid: Key Orientations for Achieving Production through People*. Houston, TX: Gulf.

Bloisi, W., Cook, C. W. and Hunsaker, P. L. (2003) *Management and Organisational Behaviour*. Maidenhead: McGraw-Hill.

Bloom, B. S., Engelhart, M. D., Furst, E. J., Hill, W. H. and Krathwohl, D. R. (1956) 'Taxonomy of educational objectives: the classification of educational goals', in *Handbook 1: The Cognitive Domain*. New York: David McKay.

Brittain, B. (2012) 'Leadership perfected: leading from the whole you', *Ivey Business Journal*, September–October. Reprint 9B12TE02.

Britton, B. K. and Tesser, A. (1991) 'Effects of time management practices of college grades', *Journal of Educational Psychology*, 83, 405–10.

Collman, A. (2014) 'Ex-headmaster who won $80,000 age discrimination settlement against his school LOSES entire payout after his daughter posted "SUCK IT" message on Facebook', *Daily Mail*, 27 February. Available online at: www.dailymail.co.uk/news/article-2569226/Daughters-SUCK-IT-Facebook-boast-costs-ex-headmaster-80000-discrimination-settlement-against-prep-school.html#ixzz47hO7ve00. Accessed 11 October 2016.

Confederation of British Industry/Universities UK (2009) 'Preparing Graduates for the World of Work'. Available online at: http://highereducation.cbi.org.uk/uploaded/HRE_091_Future%20Fit%20AW.pdf. Accessed 12 February 2011.

Coonan, C. (2013) 'China law forces adult children to visit and care for their elderly parents'. Available online at: www.independent.co.uk/news/world/asia/china-law-forces-adult-children-to-visit-and-care-for-their-elderly-parents-8681677.html. Accessed 30 November 2015.

Covey, S. R. (1989) *The Seven Habits of Highly Effective People*. New York: Simon & Schuster.

Dheer, R., Lenatowicz, T. and Peterson, M. F. (2014) 'Cultural regions of Canada and United States: implications for international management research', *International Journal of Cross-cultural Management*, 14, 343–84.

Eysenck, H. J. and Eysenck, S. B. G. (1975) *Manual of the Eysenck Personality Questionnaire*. London: Hodder & Stoughton.

Fiedler, F. E. (1967) *A Theory of Leadership Effectiveness*. New York: McGraw-Hill.

Fleming, N. and Baume, D. (2006) 'Learning styles again: VARKing up the right tree!', *Educational Developments*, 7(4), 4–7.

Fleming, N. D. and Mills, C. (1992) 'Not another inventory, rather a catalyst for reflection', *To Improve the Academy*, 11, 137–155.

French, J. P. and Raven, B. (1959) 'The bases of social power', in D. Cartwright (ed.), *Studies in Social Power*. Ann-Arbor, MI: Institute for Social Research. pp. 150–67.

Gallagher, K. (2010) *Skills Development for Business and Management Students*. Oxford: Oxford University Press.

George, D., Dixon, S., Stansal, E., Gelb, S. L. and Pheri, T. (2008) 'Time diary and questionnaire assessment of factors associated with academic and personal success among university undergraduates', *Journal of American College Health*, 56, 706–15.

Gibbs, G. and Simpson, C. (2004) 'Conditions under which assessment supports students' learning', *Learning and Teaching in Higher Education*, 1, 2004–5, 3–31.

Gracie, C. (2015) 'China to end one child policy and allow two', BBC News. Available online at: www.bbc.com/news/world-asia-34665539. Accessed 30 November 2015.

Greenleaf, R. K. (2002) 'Essentials of servant-leadership', in L. C. Spears and M. Lawrence (eds), *Focus on Leadership: Servant-Leadership for the Twenty-first Century*. New York: Wiley. pp. 19–26.

Guirdham, M. (2001) *Interactive Behaviour at Work* (3rd edition). Harlow: Pearson Education.

Hersey, P. and Blanchard, K. H. (1977) *Management of Organizational Behavior – Utilizing Human Resources* (3rd edition). Englewood Cliffs, NJ: Prentice Hall.

High Fliers Research (2015) 'The Graduate Market in 2015'. Available online at: www.highfliers.co.uk/download/2015/graduate_market/GMReport15.pdf. Accessed 4 May 2016.

Hofstede, G. (2010) *Culture's Consequences: Software of the Mind* (3rd edition). New York: McGraw-Hill.

Honey, P. and Mumford, A. (1992) *The Manual of Learning Styles* (3rd edition). Maidenhead: Peter Honey.

Information Age (2012) 'Open University to launch new online learning platform'. Available at: www.information-age.com/it-management/skills-training-and-leadership/2137308/open-university-to-launch-new-online-learning-platform. Accessed 10 April 2014.

Katzenbach, J. R. and Smith, D. K. (1993) 'The discipline of teams', *Harvard Business Review*, 71, March–April, 111–46.

Kepner, C. H. and Tregoe, B. B. (2013) *The New Rational Manager*. Princeton, NJ: Princeton Research Press.

Kolb, D. A. (1984) *Experiential Learning: Experience as the Source of Learning and Development*. Englewood Cliffs, NJ: Prentice Hall.

Kubler-Ross, E. (1969) *On Death and Dying*. USA: Scribner.

Luft, J. and Ingham, H. (1955) 'The Johari Window: a graphic model of awareness in interpersonal relations', University of California Western Training Lab.

Marshall, L. and Rowland, F. (1998) *A Guide to Learning Independently*. Buckingham: Open University Press.

Marton, F. and Säljö, R. (1976) 'On qualitative differences in learning: I – Outcome and process', *British Journal of Educational Psychology*, 46, 4–11.

Maslow, A. H. (1943) 'A theory of human motivation', *Psychological Review*, 50 (4), 370–96.

McGregor, D. (1960) *The Human Side of Enterprise*. New York: McGraw-Hill.

Muchinsky, P. (2003) *Psychology Applied to Work* (7th edition). Pacific Grove, CA: Brooks-Cole.

Mullen, J. (1997) 'Graduates deficient in soft skills', *People Management*, 6 November, p. 18.

Mumford, M. D. (2000) 'Managing creative people: strategies and tactics for innovation', *Human Resource Management Review*, 20(3), 313–51.

Nielsen, J. A., Zielinski, B. A., Ferguson, M. A., Lainhart, J. E. and Anderson, J. S. (2013) 'An evaluation of the left-brain vs. right-brain hypothesis with resting state functional connectivity magnetic resonance imaging', *PLoS ONE*, 8(8): e71275. Available online at: http://journals.plos.org/plosone/article?id=10.1371/journal.pone.0071275. Accessed 18 April 2016.

Novotney, A. (2013) 'No such thing as "right-brained" or "left-brained", new research finds', *Monitor on Psychology*, American Psychological Association. Available online at: www.apa.org/monitor/2013/11/right-brained.aspx. Accessed 18 April 2016.

Orsmond, P., Merry, S., and Reiling, K. (2002) 'The use of exemplars and formative feedback when using student derived marking criteria in peer and self-assessment', *Assessment and Evaluation in Higher Education*, 27(4), 309–23.

Payne, E. and Whittaker, L. (2006) *Developing Essential Study Skills* (2nd edition). Harlow: FT/Prentice Hall.

Prospects (2011) 'What do graduates do?', Prospects. Available online at: ww2.prospects.ac.uk/cms/ShowPage/ Home_page/What_do_graduates_do__2008/What_do_employers_want_/p!ebfpppd. Accessed 1 March 2011.

Quality Assurance Agency (2007) Benchmark statement for 'General Business and Management.' Available online at: http://www.qaa.ac.uk/academicinfrastructure/benchmark/statements/GeneralBusinessManagement.pdf. Accessed 10 April 2011.

Rabin, L., Fogel, J. and Nutter-Upham, K. E. (2011) 'Academic procrastination in college students: the role of self-reported executive function', *Journal of Clinical and Experimental Neuropsychology*, 33, 344–57.

Raven, B. H. (1965) 'Social influence and power', in I. D. Steiner and M. Fishbein (eds), *Current Studies in Social Psychology*. New York: Holt, Rinehart & Winston. pp. 371–82.

Robbins, S. P. and Hunsaker, P. L. (2003) *Training in Interpersonal Skills*. Upper Saddle River, NJ: Pearson Education.

Robins, H. and Finley, M. (1998) *Why Teams Don't Work*. London: Orion.

Robinson, W. L. (1974) 'Conscious competency: the mark of a competent instructor', *The Personnel Journal (Baltimore)*, 53, 538–9.

Rowntree, D. (1998) *Learn How to Study* (4th edition). Exeter: Warner Books.

Sheridan, E. (2005) 'Intercultural leadership competencies for US leaders in the era of globalization', PhD Dissertation. University of Phoenix Online. Available at: http://www.dialogin.com/fileadmin/Files/User_ uploads/executive_summary_delphi_study_results_sheridan_june_2005.pdf. Accessed 15 July 2016.

Smith, M. (2007) *The Fundamentals of Management*. Maidenhead: McGraw-Hill.

Sternberg, R. J. (2007) 'A systems model of leadership: WICS', *American Psychologist*, 62(1), 32–4.

Tuckman, B. W. (1965) 'Developmental sequence in small groups', *Psychological Bulletin*, 63(6), 384–99.

Universities UK (2012) 'Bringing it all together: introducing the HEAR', Higher Education Achievement Report. Available online at: www.hear.ac.uk/tools/bringing-it-all-together. Accessed 10 January 2016.

Vroom, V. and Jago, A. G. (1988) *The New Leadership: Managing Participation in Organizations*. Englewood Cliffs, NJ: Prentice Hall.

Whetten, D. A. and Cameron, K. (1996) *Developing Management Skills for Europe*. Harlow: FT/Prentice Hall.

Whetten, D. A. and Cameron, K. S. (2011) *Developing Management Skills* (8th edition). Upper Saddle River, NJ: Prentice Hall.

Winstanley, D. (2005) *Personal Effectiveness*. London: Chartered Institute of Personnel and Development (CIPD).

www.discprofile.com (2007–2009) 'Everything DiSC® Application Library: Research Report'. Available online at: www.discprofile.com/DiscProfile/media/PDFs-Other/Research%20Reports%20and%20White%20Papers/ EDApplicationResearchReport.pdf. Accessed 11 April 2016.

www.hbs.edu (2016) 'The HBS case method', Harvard Business School. Available online at: www.hbs.edu/ mba/academic-experience/Pages/the-hbs-case-method.aspx. Accessed 5 May 2016.

Zhang, L. (2014) 'Xi's war on corruption spreads to China's executive MBAs', *Financial Times*. Available online at: http://www.ft.com/cms/s/2/7804742c-34aa-11e4-b81c-00144feabdc0.html#axzz47h6Or6jU. Accessed 4 May 2016.

INDEX

4Ps of marketing 166
7Cs of international competence 287–8
7Ss of organisational designers 166
'360° feedback' 280

ability, presentations 196
academic misconduct 123–31
academic staff 9
  personal tutors 13
academic style 145–8
academic success 21–3
acceptance, personal quality 293
achievable goals 39
acronyms 165, 166
acrostics 165, 166
action-centred leadership model 233
active listening 167, 266–7
active reading 105–6, 167
activists, learner types 96, 107–8
Adair, J. 233
agents 422–3
AIDS (acquired immune deficiency syndrome) 301
Amabile, T.M. 304
AMBA (Association of MBA studies) 423
American Psychological Association (APA) 97, 129, 394
analogies 308–11
analysis, Bloom's taxonomy 85–6
analytical skills 22
andragogy 95–6
animations, presentations 196
anonymous marking 120
apologies 262
apostrophes 142
appendices 150
application
  active reading 106
  Bloom's taxonomy 84–5, 98
application forms
  basics 339–40
  links with studies 364
  online 340, 358
    creativity 360
    decision making 359
    error handling 360
    feedback, providing 360
    leadership 360
    time management 360
  understanding forms 358–61
  see also covering letters; CVs; job applications
The Apprentice (TV show) 76–7, 404
Arena, the 29
argument(s)
  definition 143
  strong and weak 73–7

ASEAN (Association of South East and Asian Nations) 277
Asian Infrastructure and Investment Bank (AIIB) 277
assessment 115
  academic misconduct 123–31
  bibliographies 128–9
  citations 126–7
  content and argument 121–2
  different methods of 122–3
  feedback 109
  formative 119
  formatting references 129
  general nature of 119–20
  integration and application 131–2
  minds of lecturers 120–1
  plagiarism 123–6, 130, 131
  qualities lecturers look for 121–3
  quotations 127–8
  skills self-assessment 118–19
  summative 119
assessment centres 331, 392, 403–4, 410–11
  exercises 407–8
  features 406
  group discussions 408–10
  integration and application 410
  preparation for 404–5
  purpose of 404
  structure 406–7
Association of Graduate Recruiters 387, 392
assumptions
  brainstorming sessions 307
  communication skill 261
attendance 100
attitude 329
audience expectations
  essays 145
  presentations 184, 190, 191
authoritarian leadership style 235, 236
autocues 186

barriers, creativity 317, 317–20
in-basket exercises 331, 407
behaviour
  assessing 71–3
  attributing incorrectly 279
behavioural questions 376
  see also STAR framework
Belbin's Team Roles 206, 207–9
  Belbin Team Role Self-Perception Inventory 208
  primary roles 208
  secondary roles 208
beliefs 275
belonging needs 83, 87
bibliographies 106, 128–9
  research dissertations 150

Blackboard™ 110
Blake, R. and Mouton, J. 231
Blindspot, the 30
blockages, creativity 317–20
Bloisi et al. 215
Bloom's taxonomy 81, 82
    analysis 85–6
    application 84–5
    evaluation 87–9
    knowledge 82–3
    synthesis 86–7
    understanding/comprehension 83–4
body language 260
body posture 410
books, citing from 129
brain functions 97
brainstorming 306–7
breadth, interview questions 376
breathing space, nerves 194
BRICS 277
British Psychological Society 394
Brittain, B. 237
business acumen 23, 25
Business Angels 431
business case studies 407
business letters 356–8
business, starting a 427–31, 433
    business plans 432–3
    finance 431
    legal advice and issues 432
    market 432
    personal qualities required for 427–31
    staffing 432

calculations 159
can-do approach 25
careers 415
careers service 13, 370
case studies, exam questions 159
CBI (Confederation of British Industry) 25
CertTEFL qualification 420
challenging
    leadership skill 221
change
    leadership and 225
    unwillingness to 214
chapters in books, citing from 129
Chartered Institute of Management (CIM) 308
Chartered Institute of Personnel and
        Development (CIPD) 308
China
    ageing population 277
    case study in culture 276–7
    high-context culture 283
    knowledge about 289
    one-child policy 277
    western understanding of 273
Chinese culture 104
    giving and losing face 31
    interpretations of 273
    school classrooms 104
    smiling 253
Chinese proverbs 223
Chinese Spring Festival 277

citations 126–7
    essay writing 140
clarity, presentations 191
Clark, D. 45
Clarke, W. 206
closed questions 264, 374–5
clothing see dress and appearance
coded information 246, 247, 281
coercive power 238
cognitive skills 23, 24
colloquial language 146
colour
    exam revision 167
    presentations 197
commitment 25
common enemy 215
common language 247
communication IT skills 23, 24
communication patterns 212–13
communication skills 22, 25, 243, 329, 439, 442
    active listening 266–7
    assessment centres 408
    channels of communication 247–8
    coded information 246, 247, 281
    components of
        body gestures 253–4
        facial expressions 253
        gestures and movements 254–5
        lying (untruths) 256
        non-verbal behaviours 250, 252, 259
        para-linguistic cues 248, 250–1, 251–2, 259
        proxemics 256
        sitting in lectures 257
        touch 255
    context 245–6
    decoded information 246, 248, 281
    feedback 267–8
    integration and application 269–70
    leadership 221, 223–4
    rapport 265
    skills self-assessment 243–5
    understanding the process 247–9
    words and language 257–8
        confidence, communication and power
                behaviour 260
        language function 258–60
        questions in conversation 264
        tact 260–3
    see also conversations; language
competence 226
    definition of competency 329
    four stages model 37
    intercultural 287–91
Completer-Finisher (CF), Belbin team role 207
compliance, DiSC profiling 206
comprehension, Bloom's taxonomy 83–4
concept mapping 314–16
conceptual blocks 318–19
conferences 308
confidence
    communication skill 260
    handling nerves 194
    high-confidence indicators 260
    low-confidence indicators 260

Confucian heritage cultures (CHCs) 104, 275, 276
conscientiousness, DiSC profiling 206
conscious competence 37
conscious incompetence 37
consequences of actions 261–2
consultative leadership style 235, 236
content, essay writing 140
conversation, handling nerves 194
conversations
  apologies 263
  avoiding emotion 262
  interruptions 262
  positive notes 262
  questions in 264
  reframing 261
  saying thank you 263
  self-reflection 262
cooperation 409
Coordinator (CO), Belbin team role 207
copying 131
core competency 329
core skills 27
coursework feedback 109
covering letters 356
  business style 358
  business writing 356–8
  purpose of 339
  see also application forms; CVs; job applications
Covey, S. 15–16, 38
  Time Management Matrix 59–61
creativity 297, 329, 441
  abilities 304–5
    enhancing our own 316–17
  blockages and barriers 317–18, 320
    conceptual blocks 318–19
    lacking appropriate knowledge 320
    motivation, emotions and behaviour 319
    pressure 318
  definition 304
  knowledge and 304
  online application forms 360
  presentations 195–6
  problem solving 303
  processes and forms of 305–6
  sources of ideas 307–8
  techniques for enhancing
    analogies 308–11
    brainstorming 306–7
    concept mapping 314–16
    examining past experience 307
    physical and practical play 313–14
    reverse definition 311–12
  understanding 304 see also problem solving
credibility 77
credible evidence 77–9
credits 10, 55
crises 60
critical thinking 22, 23, 24, 42, 69, 329
  assessment centres 408
  credible evidence 77–9
  demonstrating 73–7
  dissertations 151
  essays 136, 141

critical thinking cont.
  evaluating the quality of evidence 79–80
  integration and application 90–1
  skills self-assessment 70–3
  theoretical frameworks 81–9
  understanding and defining 69
  see also Bloom's taxonomy; Maslow's Hierarchy of Needs
cross-cultural awareness 272–3, 439, 442
  appreciation of international cultures
    intercultural competence 287–91
    international students 287
  culture shock 291–2
  expressing messages 283, 284
  high- and low-context cultures 282–4
  integration and application 293
  models of cultural difference 285
    Chinese/Confucian cultures 285
    Hofstede's dimensions of culture 285–6
  others' values 272, 280, 281
  perception and communication 278–80, 281
  research 286
  skills self-assessment 273–4
  students working together 290
  world view 275–8
culture
  Chinese 104, 253, 273 31
  Chinese case study 276–7
  communicating across 248
  company 330
  definition 276
  interaction and 104
  intercultural teams 216
  student 15
  university 13
  see also cross-cultural awareness
culture shock 291–2
Culture's Consequences (Hofstede) 285
customer awareness 25
CVs
  basics 339–40
  character statement 343
  developing and writing 346–7
    additional responsibilities and activities 351
    education and qualifications 348–50
    hobbies, interests and achievements 351–2
    personal contact details 347
    personal statements 348, 350
    references 352
    skills-based structure 352–3
    voluntary work 350–1
    work experience 350–1
  experience, previous 342
  links with studies 364
  presentation and formatting 353–4
    bold text 354
    bullet points 354
    clutter 355
    colour 354–5
    detail, care and attention to 355
    length 354
    power words 355–6
  speculative 362

CVs *cont.*
  spelling errors 353–4, 355
  see also application forms; covering letters; job
    applications

debating societies 90
decision-making skills 23
  leadership styles 235
  online application forms 359
decisions
  perfect 237
  team failures 213
decoded information 246, 248, 281
deductive learning 99
deep learning approach 98
degrees 10
delegation, leadership and 222, 225
demonstrations 195
diagrams 167
diaries 62–4
direct translation 248–9
direction, leadership skill 221
DiSC personality profiling model 206
discussions, creativity enhancement 316
dishonesty 355
dissertations 148–9, 153
  dos and don'ts 152
  primary research 151
  process for completion 151–3
  size 149
  structure 149–50
dominance, DiSC profiling 206
dress and appearance
  assessment centres 405
  interviews 370
  presentations 191

ego, leadership and 225
email addresses 347
emojis 248
emotional relationships, leadership and 225
employability skills 24–6, 44, 177
  general principles 177–8
  university preparation for 15–16
employee selection 328, 336
  degree subjects 324
  leadership experience 324
  recruitment process 329
    desirable qualities 330
    essential qualities 330
    job analysis 329
    person specification 336
    undesirable qualities 330
  selection process, designing
    investment of organisations 332
    screening 331–5, 336
    selection methods 331
    USPs of candidates 332
  selection process, implementing 335–6
  skills required from 24–6
  work experience 330
  see also interviews
employers
  assessing online profiles of applicants 344–5
  employability skills 24–6

employers *cont.*
  graduate recruitment 341
  graduate salaries 346
  incentivisation of employees 440
  public sector 415
  as university stakeholders 8
  see also interviews; organisations
EndNote software 106, 129, 130
English language 12, 141
entrepreneurial personality 25
escape activities 60
esteem needs 83
essay writing 22
essays 136–7, 153, 159
  academic style 145–8
  conclusion 144
  definition 136
  introduction 142–3
  mechanics of writing 137–9
  middle section 143–4
  minds of tutors 140
  personal views, expressing 147–8
  qualities tutors look for 139–42
  structure 138–9, 142, 153
  understanding the audience 145
esteem needs 83
et al. citations 127
ethical values 329
evaluation
  active reading 106
  Bloom's taxonomy 87–9, 98
evidence 75, 76
  credible 77–9
  essay writing 146
  evaluating the quality of 79–80
examinations 157
  debriefing 174
  integration and application 174
  mind mapping 167–8
  open book 160
  performance during
    allowing time and space 169
    checking instructions 169
    managing time 170
    order of answers 169–70
    panicking 170
    reading questions carefully 169
  poor performance
    failing to define key terms 173
    failing to read instructions 171
    lack of structure and argument 172
    misinterpreting verbs 171
    misreading subject questions 172
    overemphasis of descriptions 172–3
    underdevelopment of critical thinking
      172–3
  preparation
    engaging with information 166–7
    memory enhancement 165–6
    nerves and emotions 160–3
    past papers 163–4
    revision guides 165
    revision notes 165
    revision timetable 164–5
  question types 158–60
  reactions to 161

examinations *cont.*
  skills self-assessment 157–8
  sleep 161–3
  time management 160
examples, essay writing 140
experience 33
experiential learning 33–7
expert power 238
external examiners 120
Exxon 231
eye contact 253
  assessment centre exercises 409
  interviews 373
Eysenck Personality Inventory (EPI) 402–3

Facade, the 29–30
face, giving and losing 31
face-to-face communication 248
Facebook 344, 345
facial expressions, presentations 190–1
feedback 35, 36, 108–10
  answers to past papers 163
  communication skills 267–8
  definition 109, 110, 267
  interviews 388
  online application forms 360
  principles of giving 267–8
  teams, lacking 214
female teams 215
Fielder, F. 232
Fleming, N.D. and Baume, D. 97
Fleming, N.D. and Mills, C. 97
flexibility 25
focus 56–7
followers 226
  follower-readiness 231–2
  trust of 232
formal presentations 182–4
formative assessment of learning 119
Four Stages of Learning a New Skill model 37
franchises 427
Franklin, B. 186
free-riders 227
French, J.P. and Raven, B. 238
further studies 418–19
  Master's degrees 421–2
  MBA (Master of Business Administration) 423–5
  PGCE (Postgraduate Certificate in Education) 420
  postgraduate research qualifications 425–6
  professional business qualifications 419
  TESOL/TEFL qualification 420

Gallagher, K. 34
George et al. 52
gestures 253–4
  movement and 254–5
globalisation 272, 293
goals 56
  confused and cluttered 213
  established by leaders 232
  good 38–40
  little things, importance of 438
  presentation skills 182–3, 198
  prioritisation of 57–8

goals *cont.*
  SMART goal setting 38–40
  of teams 204
good answers 380–3
good goals 38–40
good intentions 262
gossip 78
government
  requirements for universities 14
  as university stakeholder 8
Grade Point Average (GPA) 350
grades 109
  assessment 122
  essays 140–1
  examination questions 159
grammar, essay writing 141
Greenleaf, R.K. 233–4
ground rules, team failures 214
group assignments 90
group leadership style 235, 236
group presentations 188
group-think 306
group working 22
groups
  definition 203–5
'Guanxi' culture 277
Guirdham, M. 226

habits 38
hand gestures 254
hands, keeping still during presentations 194
Harvard Business Review 308
Harvard Business School 303
Harvard case teaching method 303
Harvard style of referencing 127, 128
headings 167
hearing 266
Herzberg, F. 87, 88–9
hierarchy 284
Hierarchy of Needs, Maslow's 82, 83, 83–4, 84–5, 85–6, 86–7, 88–9
high-context cultures 282–4
high-performing teams 204
Higher Education Achievement Report (HEAR) 349–50
Hofstede, G. 285–6
holidays 60–1
honesty 329, 383
  psychometric tests 402
Honey and Mumford learning styles 96
humility 293
hypothetical questions 375–6

ice-breaker discussions 408
ideas, sources of 307–8
IELTS (International English Language Testing System) 12
illumination, problem-solving process 305
imagination, form of creativity 306
Implementer (IMP), Belbin team role 207
importance, dimension of 59, 61
improvement, form of creativity 306
incentives
  revision timetables 164–5
  teams, lacking in 214

incubation
  form of creativity 306
  problem-solving process 305
independent learning 151
individualism v collectivism dimension 285
inducement, DiSC profiling 206
induction 11
inductive learning 99
indulgence v self-restraint dimension 286
influence
  DiSC profiling 206
  leadership skill 221
  on others 23
informal presentations 182–4
information
  access to 151
  active listening 167, 266–7
  attending to 279
  brainstorming sessions 307
  citing sources 124
  coded 246, 247, 281
  decoded 246, 248, 281
  engaging with 166–7
  interpreting 279
  Johari Window 29–31
  objective 32–7
  presentations 191
  sources of 77–8, 79
  subjective 28–9
Information Age (journal) 111
information gaps 407
informational power 238
Institute of Chartered Accountancy for England and
    Wales (ICAEW) 308
institutional knowledge 226
intelligence 226
interaction 103, 104
intercultural competence 287–91
  friendships 291
  language partners 290–1
  reading about other cultures 289
  student exchange 291
  visiting new places 288–9
intercultural teams 216
interest, maintaining during presentations 191
internal sources 308
International Office 13
international students 11–12, 272–3, 287
  applications through agents 422–3
internships 418
interpersonal skills 329
  assessment centres 408
interpretation 249
interruptions 60
interviews 331, 367, 389
  employers' objectives 367–8
  feedback 388
  general behaviour 386–7
    dos and don'ts 387
  integration and application 388
  preparation 371
    anticipating questions 370
    dressing appropriately 370
    gathering information prior to 371
    reviewing the job specification 369

interviews cont.
    reviewing your application 368
    role-play 370
  process 371–2
    entrance and first impression 373
    structure 372
  questions
    behavioural 376
    closed 374–5
    common 373–4
    full and complete answers 386
    good answers 380–3
    hypothetical 375–6
    interviewee 385–6
    leading 375
    open 374
    passionate and emotional responses 385
    probing 374
    repeat 384
    sample 376–9
    strengths and weaknesses 379–80
  Skype 387
  telephone 387
intonation 251, 252
  assessment centre exercises 409
intuitive style of problem solving 301–2
investment, form of creativity 306
investors, private 431
IT skills 22, 23, 24, 25, 329

job applicants
  assessing the vacancy 345–6
job applications 339
  analysing the organisation 340–1
  developing contacts 340
  integration and application 363–4
  links with studies 364
  lucky dip approach 340
  online profiles 344–5
  personal brand, creating a 341–2, 343
  speculative 361–3
    financial and business news 363
    merging organisations 363
    personnel magazines 363
    phraseology 362
    small organisations 363
  vacancies 341
  see also application forms; covering letters; CVs
job descriptions 329, 336, 369
  student 53–6
job-person fit 330
jobs 415
Johari Window 29–31
jokes, presentations 192
journal articles, citing from 129
judgements 279
  challenging 279

K-T process 299–301
Katzenbach, J.R. and Smith, D.K. 204
Kepner, C. and Tregoe, B. 298–9
knowledge 304, 329
  Bloom's taxonomy 82–3, 98
  creativity and 304, 320
  institutional 226

Kolb's Experiential Learning Cycle 33–7
KSAOs (knowledge, skills, abilities and other qualities) 329–30, 331, 332, 343, 345, 369
Kubler–Ross Transition Curve 292

language
    allowing for doubt 262
    ambiguous 259
    careful use of 261
    colloquial 146
    common 247
    emotional 262
    English 12, 141
    function 258–60
    rapport 265
    university 13
    see also conversations
language schools 420
latent abilities 317
Leader-Member Exchange (LMX) 232
leadership 23, 220
    aggression in 440
    assessment centres 408, 409
    challenges of 224
    conflict resolution skills 227–30
    coursework projects 227–30
    decision-making methods
        authoritarian (A) 235, 236
        consultative (C) 235, 236
        group (G) 235–6
    definitions 221–2
    delegation of tasks 222, 225
    good, qualities of 222–3
    integration and application 239–40
    managing teams 210
    models
        action-centred leadership 233
        Hersey and Blanchard's situational leadership theory 231–3, 234
        Managerial Grid 231
        Ohio/Michigan leadership studies 230–1
    multiple leaders 222
    online application forms 360
    personality and 237
    poor 213
    power and 237–8
    problem-solving skills 227–30
    servant 233–4
    skills 226–7, 329
    skills self-assessment 220
    what it is 223
    what it isn't 224–6
leading questions 375
Learn How to Study (Rowntree) 161
learning
    ability 329
    adult 95–8
    applying styles of 106–8
    deep approach 98
    formative assessment of 119
    Honey and Mumford learning styles 96
    independently 151
    opportunities at university 99
        feedback 108–10
        independent reading 99, 104–6

learning cont.
    lectures 99, 100–3
    MOOCs (Massive Open Online Courses) 111–12
    seminars 99, 103–4
    teaching and learning tools 99–100
    tutorials 99, 103
    virtual learning environment 110–11
    strategic approach 98
    summative assessment of 119
    surface approach 98
    VA(R)K learning styles 97
learning outcomes 119
lectures 99, 100–3
    definition 94
    sitting position 257
left-brained individuals 97, 301–2
legitimate power 238
Lego® 86, 313, 314
Likert scale 401, 402
linguistics see language
LinkedIn 344, 345
listening, active 167, 266–7
listening skills 23, 24, 25
    assessment centre exercises 409
lists 166
literacy 25
loans
    career 424
    government 424
long-term outlook v short-term outlook dimension 285
low-context cultures 282–4
low-performing teams 204
loyalty 226

magazines
    academic business 308
    professional 308
management
    arguments, strong and weak 75
    managerial life 61
    MBAs 423–5
    skills required for 24
Managerial Grid 231
marking process 120
marks see grades
Marston, W.M. 206
Marton, F. and Säljö, R. 97
masculinity v femininity dimension 285
Mask, the 29–30
Maslow's Hierarchy of Needs 82, 83, 83–4, 84–5, 85–6, 86–7, 88–9
Master's (MSc and MA) degrees 421–2
    applying through agents 422–3
    personal statements 422
MBAs (Masters of Business Administration) 423–5
McGregor, D. 231
measurable goals 39
media channels 247
memory
    enhancing 165–6
    examinations 158, 159, 162, 164, 165–6, 167–8
    mind-mapping 167–8
    presentations 185, 194
    reproducing knowledge 81, 83

memory enhancement 165–6
metaphors 308–11
mianzi 31
Michigan leadership study 230–1
mind mapping 167–8
mind maps 86
minutes, of meetings 308
mnemonics 165, 166
Monitor-Evaluator (ME), Belbin team role 208
MOOCs (Massive Open Online Courses) 9, 111–12
Moodle™ 110
motivation 151
  revision timetables 164
  sincerity of 226
  theory of 83, 83–4, 84–5, 85–6, 86–7, 88–9
MPhils (Master of Philosophy) 425
MRes (Master of Research) 425
multiple choice questions 159, 163

negotiating skills 24
negotiation exercises 407
nerves
  examinations 160–3
  interviews 371–2
  presentations 192–4
    dealing with 193
    signs 192–3
    strategies for handling 194
    thinking about 193
Netherlands 283
networking 308
news articles 308
Nielsen et al. 97
noise
  decoding messages 248
  presentations 197
non-verbal behaviours 250, 252, 259
  rapport 265
norm tables 401
note taking
  assessment centres 409
notes
  lectures 101, 102–3
  presentations 186
  seminars 104
numeracy skills 23, 24, 25
numerical reasoning tests 393, 395, 398–401

objective information 32–7
Ohio leadership study 230–1
one-to-one discussions 249
online courses
  MOOCs (Massive Open Online Courses) 9, 111–12
  Open University 111–12
open book examinations 160
open-mindedness 293
open questions 264, 374
Open University (OU) 110
  online courses 111–12
oral communication 23, 24, 25, 248
organisational skills 151, 329
organisations
  brochures about 340

organisations *cont.*
  operations of 340
  see also employers
others' values 272, 280, 281
overkill, presentations 196

pace of speech 191
para-linguistic cues 248, 250–1, 251–2, 259
  rapport 265
parents
  as university stakeholders 8
partner universities 291
passion, presentations 190
passive voice 146
PDPs
  personal development plans 27, 41
  professional development plans 27
pedagogy 95
perception 278–80, 281
perceptual errors 279, 280
perceptual filters 248
perceptual theory 289
persistence 409
person–job fit 329
person-organisation fit 329, 330, 367
personal development and learning 9, 19, 44
  academic success, skills needed for 21–3
  employability skills 24–6
  good goals 38–40
  information
    Johari Window 29–31
    objective 32–7
    subjective 28–9
  integration and application 40
  Kolb's Experiential Learning Cycle 33–7
  personal skills, development of 27
  skills self-assessment 19–21
personal development plans (PDPs) 27, 41
personal statements 422
personal tutors 13
personal views 147–8
personalising information 167
personality
  conflicts 213
  inventories 402–3
  leadership and 237
  psychometric tests 393
  questionnaires 331, 395, 396, 402, 403
personality profiling 206, 207–9
  primary roles 208
  secondary roles 208
persuasion
  leadership skill 221
  skills 24
PESTLE 166
PGCE (Postgraduate Certificate in Education) 420
PHDs (Doctors of Philosophy) 425–6
physiological needs 83, 84, 86, 87, 88
pitch (voice) 251
placement programmes 330
plagiarism 123–6, 130, 131
planning 35
  learning about 38
  over-planning 62

planning *cont.*
  presentations 196
  time management 61, 62
  see also PDPs
Plant (PL), Belbin team role 208
play 313–14
Playdough® 313, 314
playing with information 167
PLoS One 97
policies, team failures 213
political debates 190
popularity, leadership and 224
portability, presentations 190
post-modernism 276
postgraduate studies/qualifications 418–19
  Master's (MSc and MA) degrees 421–2
  MBAs (Masters of Business Administration) 423–5
  research qualifications 425–6
posture, presentations 191
power
  leadership and 225, 238–9
  sources of 238
power distance culture 104
power distance dimension 285
PowerPoint 195, 196
  death by 196–7
practical exercises 159
practice makes perfect 36–7
pragmatists, learner types 96, 107
praise sandwich 261
preparation, problem-solving process 305
presentation skills 22, 24, 43, 180, 329
  assessment centres 408
  creativity 195–6
  delivering presentations 189–92
  integration and application 197–8
  nerves 192–4
  preparation 184, 194
    audience expectations 184
    delivery styles 182–3, 184
    goals 182–3, 198
    importance of 187
    notes 186
    over-preparation 186–7
    rehearsals 185, 187
    technical 185
  skills self-assessment 180–2
  step-by-step process 198
  stress 182
  structuring presentations 187–9
    conclusion 189
    introduction 188
    middle section 188
  technical presentations 185, 190
presentations 190
  definition 180
prioritisation 57–8
private agendas 213
private investors 431
proactive attitude 23
probing questions 264, 374
problem solving 297, 329
  assessment centres 408
  case studies 303

problem solving *cont.*
  coping 23, 24
  creative 303
  integration and application 320
  intuitive style 301–2
  process
    balanced choices 302
    clarify the objective 298
    establishing the cause(s) 298–301
    generating options for solving 301–2
  rational style 301–2, 302–3
  skills 25
  skills self-assessment 297–8
  visual representations of problems 304–5
  see also creativity
professional business qualifications 419
professional development plans (PDPs) 27
proxemics 256
psychometric tests 331, 333, 392, 392–3, 410–11
  administration 394–5
  integration and application 410
  intellectual ability 393, 395, 403
  numerical reasoning 393, 395, 398–401
  online 401
  paper-based 401
  personality inventories 402–3
  personality questionnaires 393, 395, 396, 402, 403
  practising for 396
  questions 396
  reliability 394
  standardisation 394, 395
  validity 394
  verbal reasoning 393, 397–8
punctuation 251–2, 258
purposeful movement, interviews 373

qualifications
  CertTEFL 420
  PGCE (Postgraduate Certificate in Education) 420
  postgraduate 418–19
  professional business 419
  TESOL/TEFL 419–20
Quality Assurance Agency 8, 24
quantitative skills 22, 24
quantitative subjects 121
question spotting 163
questions 258–9
  interview 370
  inviting after presentations 192
  team building 409
  types of 264, 374–6
quotations 127–8

rational style of problem solving 301–2, 302–3
reading
  essay writing, research for 153
  independent 99, 104–6
    active reading 105–6
  lecture preparation 102
  new subjects 316
  seminar preparation 104
  skills 22

realistic goals 39
reasoning skills 329, 393
record keeping
    bibliographies 106
    brainstorming sessions 307
    student time management 55
recruitment *see* employee selection
references 422
referent power 238
reflection 33–4
reflective questions 264, 268
reflectors, learner types 96, 107
regularity, presentations 196
rehearsals 185, 187
relaxation places, creativity enhancement 316
relaxation time, creativity enhancement 316
relevance
    essay writing 140
    presentations 196
repetition, exam revision 167
report writing 22
research
    cross-cultural awareness 286
    dissertations 149–50
    learning opportunity 99
    postgraduate qualifications 425–6
    primary 151
research and library skills 22, 23, 24
Resource Investigator (RI), Belbin team role 207
resourcefulness 22
reverse definition 311–12
revision
    definition 164
    guides 165
    notes 165
    progress 165
    timetables 164–5
reward power 238
rewards 232
rhetorical questions, presentations 191
right-brained individuals 97, 301–2
Robbins, H. and Finley, M. 213–14
Robbins, S.P. and Hunsaker, P.L. 232
roles
    confused 213
    team imbalances 214
Rowntree, D. 161
rumour 78

safety needs 83, 84, 86, 87, 88
salaries, graduate 346
scheduling 61
scholarships 424
seating plans, assessment centres 410
selection interviews *see* interviews
self-actualisation needs 83
self-awareness 22, 329
self-confidence 329
self-image 193
self-management 23, 24, 25
self-reflection 23, 24, 262
seminars 99, 103–4
sequences of information 166–7
servant leadership 233–4

shaking hands, interviews 373
Shaper (SH), Belbin team role 207
Sheridan, E. 287–8
significance, interview questions 376
signposts 144
silence 262
simplicity, presentations 197
situational interviewing 375
situational leadership theory 231–3, 234
skills
    academic success, requirements for 21–3
    Four Stages of Learning a New Skill model 37
    gaps 28
    information 28–37
skills self-assessment
    communication skills 243–5
    critical thinking 70–3
    cross-cultural awareness 273–4
    examinations 157–8
    leadership 220–1
    personal development and learning 19–21
    presentation skills 180–2
    problem solving 297–8
    studying at university 6–7
    teaching methods at university 95
    team-working skills 202–3
    time management 50–1
    understanding assessment at university 118–19
    written assessments 135–6
Skype interviews 387
sleep 161–3
SMART goal setting 38–40
smiling
    communication skill 253
    interviews 373
    presentations 190–1, 192
Smith, M. 226
social media, online profiles 344–5
sources of information 77–8, 79
speaking
    in lectures 102
    in seminars 103, 104
Specialist (SP), Belbin team role 207
specific events 34
specific goals 39
speech
    pace of 191
    speed of 191, 250, 383
    volume of 250
spelling
    essay writing 141, 141–2
    presentations 197
spitting, culture of 280
stability 279
stakeholders 8
STAR framework
    action taken 382–3
    result of action 383
    situation 381
    summary 383
    task 382
status, leadership skill 226
steadiness, DiSC profiling 206
stereotyping 279

Sternberg, R.J. 226
strategic learning approach 98
strengths and weaknesses 29–30, 32, 40
    interview questions 379–80
structure
    dissertations 149–50
    essays 138–9, 142, 153
    presentations 187–9
student culture 15
student experience 12
student representative committees 12
student support services 12
students
    international 11–12, 272–3, 287
    job description 53–6
    voice at university 14
Students Union (SU) 8
study skills 22–3, 26, 44
subjective information 28–9
submission, DiSC profiling 206
success, team-working 215
succinct content, presentations 197
succinct writing 147, 151
summative assessment of learning 119
supervisors, dissertations 151–2
support, team failures 214
surface learning approach 98
Sutcliffe, P. 318–19
synthesis, Bloom's taxonomy 86–7
synthesized reading 106

tasks
    characteristics of 232
    delegation of 222, 225
teaching, definition 94
teaching English as a foreign or second language
    419–20
teaching methods 94–5
    adult learning 95–8
    applying learning styles 106–8
    feedback 108–10
    integration and application 112–13
    learning opportunities 99–106, 108–12
    MOOCs (Massive Open Online Courses) 111–12
    virtual learning environment 110–11
Teaching Qualifications Authority (TQA) 420
team presentations 188, 190
Team Role Theory 206, 207–9
Team-Worker (TW), Belbin team role 208
team-working skills 23, 24, 25, 43, 202
    assessment centres 408
    behaviour 202, 203
    definitions of groups and teams 203–5
    integration and application 216
    skills self-assessment 202–3
teams 217
    cohesive 214–16
    common approach 204
    common purpose 204
    communication in 212
    complimentary skills 204
    composition 206
        Belbin's Team Roles 207–9
        DiSC personality profiling model 206

teams cont.
    working with friends 209
    definition 203–5, 204
    development of
        adjourning 211
        forming 210
        norming 210, 211
        performing 211
        storming 210, 211
    disruptive individuals 213
    failure of 213–14
    female 215
    intercultural 216
    mutual accountability 204
    patterns of communication in
        212–13
    size of 205
    small 204
    specific goals 204
    sub-teams 222
technical presentations 185, 190
technology, presentations 196
telephone interviews 387
temporary language schools 420
TESOL/TEFL qualification 419–20
textbooks 105
theorising 35
theorists, learner types 96, 107
thinking, assessing 70
    see also critical thinking
time-based goals 40
time management 22, 38, 42, 50, 151, 440
    additional techniques 65–6
    creativity enhancement 316
    examinations 160
    focus 56–7
    good, definition of 52–3
    importance of 52
    integration and application 65
    matrix 59–61
    online application forms 360
    presentations 192
    prioritisation 57–8
    skills self-assessment 50–1
    student job description 53–6
    using a diary 62–4
timing, presentations 196
tone of voice, presentations 191
tools, team failures 214
training courses 308
triangulation 78
trust, team failures 214
Tuckman, B. 210
tutorials 99, 103
Twitter 345

uncertainty avoidance dimension 285
unconscious competence 37
unconscious incompetence 37
understanding
    active reading 106
    Bloom's taxonomy 83–4
    personal quality 293
uniqueness, personality 237

university(ies)
  attendance 100
  culture 13
  differences between 14, 15, 16
  employability preparation 15–16
  experience, the 8–9
  language 13
  non-academic side of 11–13
  processes 14
  purpose of 8–9
  skills self-assessment 95
  studying at 6
    practical student support 12–13
    principles 9
    skills self-assessment 6–7
  teaching methods *see* teaching methods
  see also examinations; written assessments
Unknown, the 30
unscheduled interruptions 60
urgency, dimension of 59, 61
USP (unique selling proposition) 332, 341, 343

values, of others 272, 280, 281
variety, presentations 196
VA(R)K learning styles 97
verbal reasoning tests 393, 397–8
verification, problem-solving process 305
videos 195, 196
virtual learning environment (VLE) 100, 110–11
vision
  bleary 213
  changing the world 225
  leadership skill 221, 223–4

visual aids 195–7
voice, active and passive 261
volume of speech 250
voluntary work experience 350–1, 415–16
  duration of 417
  personal attributes 416–17
  reasons for seeking 417
  reimbursement 417
  structure 417
  uses of 417–18
Vroom, V. and Jago, A.G. 235

weaknesses *see* strengths and weaknesses
Whetten, D.A. and Cameron, K.S. 305, 316–17
Why Teams Don't Work (Robbins and Finley) 213–14
WIC (wisdom, intelligence and creativity) 226
Winstanley, D. 318
wisdom 226
work samples 331
working, independence of others 22
world view 275–8
writing skills 42
written assessments 135
  dissertations 148–53
  essays 136–44
    academic style 145–8
    understanding the audience 145
  integration and application 153–4
  skills assessment 135–6
written communication 248
  skills 23, 24, 25

Yorkshire Ripper 318–19